C000184929

An Encyclopaedia of North-East England

An Encyclopaedia of North-East England

RICHARD LOMAS

First published in Great Britain in 2009 by
Birlinn Ltd
West Newington House
10 Newington Road
Edinburgh
EH9 1QS

www.birlinn.co.uk

ISBN 13: 978 1 84158 804 9

British Library Cataloguing-in-Publication Data
A catalogue record for this book is available on request from the British Library

Typeset in Adobe Arno by
Koinonia, Manchester
Printed and bound in Sweden by
Scanbook

For Joan

Preface

That the North East of England is a very distinctive region of the United Kingdom can be readily recognised by crossing its borders into Yorkshire, Cumbria or Scotland, where the obvious differences of speech immediately hint at differences of history, tradition and culture. It is this distinctive quality that justifies an encyclopaedia to stand alongside those, already published, of Ireland, London, Scotland and Wales. The North East of this work is the ancient counties of Durham and Northumberland, that is, the land between the River Tees and the River Tweed and between the North Sea and the eastern watershed of the Pennine and Cheviot Hills. There are, however, two exceptions: Berwick upon Tweed, which although of Scottish origin has been part of the region since the fourteenth century; and Middlesbrough, which was founded from and by the North East to serve North-East purposes.

Since the eighteenth century, much has been written about the North East, ranging from the detailed products of academic research to popular pamphlets. This encyclopaedia is the first attempt at a comprehensive compendium covering all aspects and over an extended period. The people included (none of whom is living) fall into three categories: 'natives' who stayed and achieved; 'natives' who migrated to achieve; and 'foreigners' who came in to achieve. Places range from the obvious large towns and cities to villages with particular importance or significance. With both people and places, selection has been unavoidable, with the attendant risk of disappointment and disapproval. The choice of major events, institutions and industries has proved less difficult and therefore I hope will be less contentious.

Wherever possible, I have tried to relate the specifically regional to a wider national or international context. Within entries, a term capitalised in the form St Cuthbert draws attention to the fact that there is an entry on the subject.

The format is alphabetical, since any alternative would be too complex. This said, I feel it might be helpful to delineate the significant phases of the region's evolution. The first has to be the Roman. The building of Hadrian's Wall has given the region one of the world's most famous monuments. At the time, however, it had the effect of creating two frontier zones, one Roman, the other British. The end of the Roman era was followed by the invasion and settlement of English peoples, who created the Kingdom of Northumbria, which extended from the Humber to the Forth beyond Edinburgh and flourished from *c.*600 until *c.*900. The region, the core of this kingdom, was the scene of a 'golden age' of art and religion of European importance. With the gradual division of Britain into two kingdoms, England and Scotland, in the tenth century and the fixing of the frontier between them in the 1090s by the second Norman king of England, the region again became a frontier zone, although this time all of it on one side of the divide. The long Anglo-Scottish war, sometimes hot, sometimes 'cold', between 1296 and 1603 gave the region many of its enduring monuments and characteristics. Most notable was the Palatinate of Durham, which covered a substantial part of the region and in which, uniquely, immediate rulership was vested in the Bishop of Durham, not the Crown. Most recently, the North East was one of the world's largest and most dynamic industrial complexes, renowned for coal, lead, chemicals, iron and steel, shipbuilding and engineering. Although this 'industrial age' has largely passed, as have earlier eras, their legacy is a wealth of remains, now increasingly valuable assets in one of the vital sectors of the twenty-first-century economy: tourism. Through this legacy, the North East is experiencing a 'second coming'.

Richard Lomas, June 2009

Acknowledgements

The entire text of this encyclopaedia is of my own composition. It is based in part upon research undertaken for my published (and yet to be published) books and papers but also, and substantially, upon the work of many scholars and writers whose writings I have read over the course of the last forty years. Although the constraints of space have prohibited the inclusion of a bibliography, I should like to take this opportunity of expressing my unstinted thanks to them for the knowledge and insights I have gained from reading their work. In preparing the book for publication, I have received help, advice, encouragement and information from the following, to all of whom I unreservedly render grateful thanks: Alcan PLC, Richard Allon, Ian Armstrong, Barbour Ltd, Geoffrey Berriman, Lucy Bird, Doreen and Forster Blacklock, Ann Brown, Barbara Brown, Lee Byers, Jane Carroll, Joan Copeland, Jim Craigie, Richard Cross, Howard Croston, Philip Deakin, Easington District Council, Kay Easson, Kirstin Farquhar, Fenwick Ltd, Finchale Training College, Ian and Shirley Forster, Forum Books (Corbridge), Lynne Gatland, Gosforth Park Racecourse, the late Denis and Joan Gowans, Jean Grant, Karen Hall, Harrison and Harrison Ltd, Joanna Hashagen, Martin Hatfield, David Hawkins, Mary Herbert, Irene Hindmarsh, Myrtle Hindmarsh, Lord Howick, KOSB Museum (Berwick), Clare Lomas, Joan Lomas, Kathryn Lomas, Norman McCord, Adrian McGlynn, John McGuiness, Morag Mackie, Mary and Stuart Manley, MetroCentre, Milfield Aerodrome, Morpeth Library, Northern Sinfonia, John Partridge, Tom Pattison, Euan Pringle, Colin Raistrick, RNF Museum (Alnwick), Robinson Library (Newcastle University), Ross Family, Lorna Rozner, Bill Scott, Mark Scrimshaw, Steve Scrimshaw, 'Seven Stories', Team Valley Trading Estate, Frank Thompson, Weardale District Council, Mara Helen Woods, Maureen Wreford Brown, Robert Young.

I particularly wish to thank Mairi Sutherland of Birlinn for her patience, courtesy and genuine interest in seeing this project through to completion, and Susan Milligan for her accurate and perceptive copy-editing. My most special thanks, however, are reserved for my daughter, Clare, without whose technical help and infinite patience the book might well not have been published, and above all to my wife, Joan, whose practical help, constant encouragement and perceptive and constructive criticism have made this encyclopaedia better than it would otherwise have been. Whatever faults or errors it has are, of course, entirely mine and mine alone.

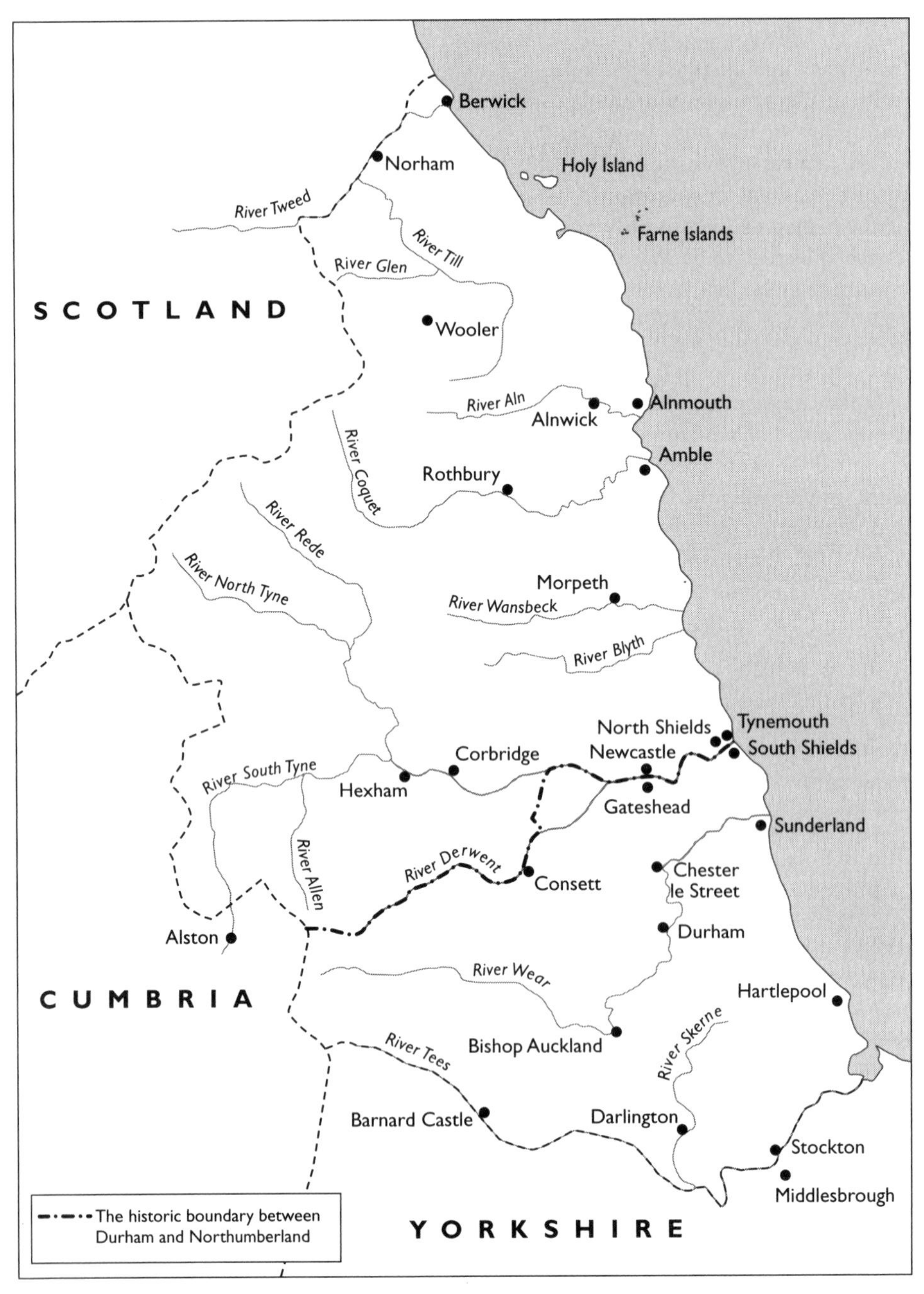

Map of North-East England

ACCA (?–740)

Acca was a major figure in the religious and cultural life of early Northumbria. When and where he was born is not known, but he was almost certainly of noble parentage, since he was sent for education to the school of the Bishop of York. In early manhood he attached himself to St Wilfrid, accompanying him on his various journeys, including that to Rome. When Wilfrid was restored to the bishopric of Hexham in 705, he appointed Acca as abbot of his monastery there, and when Wilfrid died in 709, Acca succeeded him as bishop, holding the office until 732.

During those years, he completed Wilfrid's work at Hexham, enhancing the Church of St Andrew and the other churches Wilfrid had built by acquiring relics of saints for them, adorning them with the costliest materials available, and raising the worship by securing the services of a precentor from Canterbury to train the Hexham clergy in the Gregorian chant. In the end, he achieved Wilfrid's ambition of making Hexham a leading and impressive centre of religious life and an important place of pilgrimage. Acca was equally concerned with the intellectual side of church life. He built up an extensive library, which was of considerable service to Bede, whom he encouraged in many ways and to whom Bede dedicated several of his books. He also was responsible for persuading Eddi to write his biography of Wilfrid, still a valuable source of information about this period of Northumbrian history.

As bishop of Hexham, Acca was responsible for the spiritual and ecclesiastical aspects of life between the Coquet and the Tees. He was therefore a prominent member of the Northumbrian state and it was probably a political matter that led to his removal from office in 732 and exile from the kingdom. The nature of the dispute is unclear, as is what he did in exile. It is likely that he fled to the kingdom of the Picts, taking with him the relics of St Andrew, which Wilfrid had brought from Rome. They were rehoused at Kilrymont, hence its change of name to St Andrews. His exile was not permanent, since he is known to have returned to Hexham shortly before his death in 740. He was buried outside the church, with elaborately carved crosses at the head and foot of his grave, the remains of which now stand in Hexham Abbey.

ACKLINGTON

In the Middle Ages, Acklington was a large township of nearly 3,000 acres (1,200 ha), almost 800 (320 ha) of which were enclosed as a park. In 1248, its agricultural community comprised thirty-three tenant farmers, rising to forty-seven by 1309 but contracting to thirty-five by the late fifteenth century. In the post-medieval centuries it continued as a farming community.

In World War II, however, it acquired a much wider importance. In 1936, with the growing awareness that war was increasingly likely, the government decided to revive and upgrade the small World War I airfield. Opened in 1938, it was initially used as an Armament Training Camp, but on the outbreak of war in September 1939, it was handed over to Fighter Command to be part of its 13 Group. Throughout the war it was a frontline fighter station, home to a succession of twenty squadrons with the primary role of defending Tyneside and its vital industries. Originally of grass, its runways were relaid in asphalt and a perimeter road built in 1944 by 5022 Air Construction Squadron, based in Jesmond. After the end of the war in 1945, Acklington continued as an operational RAF station until 1972, although it was only a frontline fighter station between 1957 and 1960. Its last role, between 1968 and 1972, was as a helicopter base.

On closure, its buildings were taken over by the Home Office for use as a prison. Most of the site has been subject to opencast mining and so the archaeology of what was an important World War II base is now lost forever.

ADAMS, GLADSTONE (1880–1966)

Gladstone Adams was the son of a Newcastle metal merchant who trained as an engineer at Rutherford College and subsequently ran a photographic business in Whitley Bay and then Monkseaton. He is sometimes said to have been the inventor of the car windscreen wiper. Although he did invent a wiper, which could be operated by hand or foot and also automatically by the car's engine, whether he was the first to do so is open to doubt. His invention was the result of his driving back from London (where he saw Newcastle United defeated 3–1 by Wolverhampton Wanderers) in a blinding snowstorm, which obliged him to lower his windscreen in order to see where he was going. However, although he got a patent in 1911, it was never published, and hand-operated wipers are known to have been in use in France in 1907. Perhaps it would be safer to conclude that the windscreen wiper, the utility of which was obvious, was invented by several people in different places at about the same time.

ADAMSEZ®

For much of the twentieth century sanitary ware under the brand name Adamsez was manufactured on Tyneside and marketed worldwide. In 1880, twin brothers named Adams took over the firm of W.C. Gibson, founded in Scotswood in 1840 to make tiles and bricks, and began the manufacture of sanitary ware, using fireclay from a nearby colliery. To this they added art pottery in 1904, which they marketed under the name Adamesk. But the man responsible for making Adamsez sanitary ware an internationally known product was Allan Adams, the son of Moses Adams (one of the twins), who joined the firm in 1912 and became a director in 1921. The firm lasted until 1975, when it went into receivership. After two years in American ownership, it was acquired by Anderson Ceramics, which moved production to the TEAM VALLEY TRADING ESTATE.

AETHELFRITH (see NORTHUMBRIA, KINGDOM AND EARLDOM OF)

AIDAN, SAINT (?–651)

St Aidan was one of the most formative influences in the history of Northumbria, yet we know very little about him. And what we do know comes entirely from the writings of BEDE and is therefore influenced by Bede's view of the world. When Aidan was born is not known, but *c.*600 is a reasonable guess. Nor is his place of birth known. What is certain is that, as a monk of Iona, he was Irish.

His move to Northumbria was the consequence of the decision by KING OSWALD to invite Ionan monks to his kingdom as missionaries to convert Northumbria to Christianity. Aidan was not the first to arrive, but his predecessor returned to Iona after a brief attempt, having found the task beyond him. If Bede reported correctly, Aidan virtually volunteered to be the replacement by arguing that his predecessor had been talking over the heads of his English listeners.

Late in 635, Aidan arrived in Northumbria, where he was to spend the remaining sixteen years of his life. Oswald gave him the island of Lindisfarne (see HOLY ISLAND), on which he set up a monastery and to which he brought a number of monks from Iona. From Lindisfarne, Aidan and his monks went out to the communities of

Northumbria to explain, almost certainly in the simplest terms, the Christian message, and to conduct baptisms. Since their language was Gaelic and that of their listeners was Old English, it must be assumed that, initially at least, they had to rely on interpreters.

Aidan was evidently a skilled missionary, with the ability to convey his message simply and persuasively. Bede emphasises that his personal life was austere without being exaggeratedly ascetic, a man for whom the trappings of wealth and status had no appeal. Paradoxically, this may in part explain his influence. Certainly he had the devotion of Oswald and later of OSWINE, who was briefly the King of Deira. His relationship with Oswald's brother and successor, OSWIU, was more distant, and, according to Bede, it was the murder of Oswine at Oswiu's instigation in 651 that hastened Aidan's own death twelve days later. Even though his leadership of the Ionan mission in Northumbria lasted for only fifteen years, he left a permanent legacy and laid the foundations of what has been called the 'Golden Age of Northumbria'.

AILRED (or AELRED) OF RIEVAULX, SAINT (1110–1167)

Ailred was one of the outstanding characters of the middle decades of the twelfth century and one who personified the transition from the pre-Conquest English world of Northumbria to the Anglo-Norman world. He was born in 1110, the son of Eilaf, the last hereditary priest of HEXHAM. Ailred was, therefore, as his name indicates, purely Northumbrian. He was well educated at Hexham and at Durham, becoming proficient in Latin. Not long after 1124, he moved to the court of the King of Scots, David I, whose son, Henry, and stepson, Waltheof, became his close friends. In the early 1130s, when he was in his early twenties, Ailred was appointed Steward of David's household.

But in 1134, at the age of twenty-four, he was diverted into a different life. In that year David sent him to York on a mission to Archbishop Thurstan. According to his biographer, Walter Daniel, as he returned home, he stopped at the Cistercian monastery of Rievaulx, newly founded by Walter Espec, Lord of Helmsley and Wark on Tweed. It is said that he was so attracted by the austere life he saw there that he immediately joined the community. What truth there is in this account is impossible to tell, but an alternative explanation seems more likely, namely, that David I encouraged one of his leading young men to become part of what was clearly a major international movement. At that date the Cistercian order of monks was rapidly becoming hugely popular and influential throughout Europe, both for its spiritual dynamism and for its ability to colonise the large tracts of wasteland that still existed almost everywhere. Consequently, Ailred's admission to Rievaulx, for which he was well qualified by his education, may well have had a political as well as a religious aspect.

Whatever the truth, Ailred committed himself wholeheartedly to the Cistercian way of life, with its rigorous demands of austerity, discipline and obedience. In 1142, eight years after joining the community, he was sent to Rome on important business and on his return was made novice master. A year later, he was appointed Abbot of Revesby in Lincolnshire, a newly founded 'daughter' house of Rievaulx. He was there for four years, but returned to Rievaulx in 1147 to become abbot. He was to remain in post until his death twenty years later. As abbot, his life was arduous, involving the spiritual leadership of his community and the management of its estate. In addition, as the rules of the Cistercian Order required, he made inspection visits to Rievaulx's four distant daughter houses: Wardon in Bedfordshire, Revesby in Lincolnshire, and Dundrennan and Melrose in Scotland; he also journeyed to Citeaux in Burgundy to attend the General Chapter of the Order. Not surprisingly, in the last ten years of his life he became increasingly incapacitated by a painful disease.

But his life was not all administration: between 1142 and 1166, he found time to write twelve tracts on various subjects. Three were biographical: a life of St Ninian in the late 1150s; the lives of the Anglo-Saxon saints of Hexham; and in 1162 a life of King Edward the Confessor, which he wrote for Laurence, Abbot of Westminster (a Durham man to whom he was related) on the occasion of the translation of the royal remains to a new resting place in the abbey. His most renowned writings, however, were theological: *Speculum Caritatis* (*The Mirror of Christian Virtue*) and *De Spirituali Amicitia* (*On Spiritual Friendship*). The former was written at the request (perhaps more accurately on the order) of Bernard, Abbot of Clairvaux (St Bernard), the dominant personality of both the Cistercian Order and the entire western church.

Although Ailred was never formally canonised, the erroneous belief that he was declared a saint in 1191 by Pope Celestine III indicates the high regard and affection in which he was held in the north of England.

AKENSIDE, MARK (1721–1770)

Born the son of a butcher on Butcher Bank (now Akenside Hill) in Newcastle, Mark Akenside trained as a doctor in Edinburgh and abroad and became sufficiently eminent and respected to be appointed in 1761 Queen's Physician, that is, to Charlotte Sophia of Mecklenburg-Strelitz, the wife of George III. Touchy about the fact that one of his legs was shorter than the other, a fact that some cruelly claimed was not unconnected with his father's trade, he was pilloried by Tobias Smollett in his novel *Peregrine Pickle*. Akenside was also a poet, best known for a long poem called *The Pleasures of the Imagination*, published in 1744. While it has some good verses and is full of classical erudition, it is a work far too high in noble sentiment to appeal to modern taste, despite Dr Johnson's favourable opinion of the quality of its blank verse.

ALCAN

Alcan, one of the world's leading producers of bauxite and aluminium, was founded in 1900 and has its headquarters in Montreal. It has operations in sixty-one countries, employs 65,000 people and has an annual turnover of $20.3 billion. In the UK, it has seventeen locations, a consequence of its merger with the British Aluminium Co. in 1982, which in turn led in 1986 to the change of name to British Alcan Aluminium Co. Two of its UK operations are in the North East. The larger is the giant aluminium smelter at Lynemouth on the Northumberland coast, which opened in 1972 and is now a major primary producer of aluminium. Its source of energy is the nearby Lynemouth Power Station, which it wholly owns.

ALDER, JAMES (1920–2007)

James Alder, one of Britain's outstanding wildlife artists, was born and lived much of his life in Newcastle. His talent, which was evident at a very early stage, was developed through evening classes at King's College. After a short period on the staff of the *Newcastle Evening Chronicle*, he worked as a freelance commercial artist, until he was appointed senior sculptor of birds and flowers by the Royal Worcester Porcelain Co., a post he held for many years. His reputation as a wildlife artist secured him two major commissions from the royal family, which resulted in *The Birds and Flowers of the Castle of Mey* (1992) for Queen Elizabeth the Queen Mother and *The Birds of Balmoral* (1997) for Queen Elizabeth II. His standing was recognised by the award in 2002 of an honorary DCL by the University of Northumbria.

ALDWINE (?–1087)

Aldwine was the man whose actions set in motion a train of events that led to the building of the present Durham Cathedral. About him we know nothing, except that in the early 1070s he was the Prior of the Abbey of Winchcombe in the Cotswolds and that he was moved by reading Bede's *Ecclesiastical History* to leave his house and seek out the place where Bede had lived. In this venture, he had two companions. One was another monk, Aelfwig, from the neighbouring Abbey of Evesham. The other was more unusual. He was Reinfrid, a Norman who had been a soldier in the army that brutally crushed native resistance in Yorkshire in 1069 and 1070, in the course of which he had seen the ruins of Whitby Abbey, the experience that may explain his decision to quit the military life and become a monk. Although he chose Evesham, his real desire was to return to Whitby. The three men set off for the north in 1073 or 1074. Arriving at Durham, they secured permission from the bishop, Walcher, to occupy the ruins of the monastery at Jarrow, where they re-roofed the church. Almost immediately, their actions attracted a trickle of like-minded enthusiasts. The expanded number enabled Aldwine to restart, between 1076 and 1078, monastic life at Jarrow's sister house, Monkwearmouth. Thus, by 1083, there were small but thriving monastic communities at these ancient sites. When in that year, the new Bishop of Durham, William of St Calais, decided to convert his cathedral chapter into a Benedictine monastery, he had, thanks to Aldwine's dedication and initiative, a ready-made body of monks to bring to Durham. Ten years later, he and his new monastic commumity began the cathedral that still dominates the Durham skyline. Aldwine, however, did not live to see this event.

ALLHUSEN, CHRISTIAN AUGUSTUS HENRY (1806–1890)

The son of a German merchant in Kiel, Christian Allhusen came to the North East, albeit indirectly, as the result of the Napoleonic Wars. When the French army invaded Schleswig-Holstein, the family house was confiscated and his two elder brothers migrated to England. It was in 1825, long after the end of the war, that Christian decided to follow them. However, their partnership broke up when the brothers decided to go their separate ways, one to London, the other to America. In the next fifteen years, Allhusen, in partnership with another German immigrant, Henry Bolckow, became a very wealthy man, through his shrewd involvement in the grain trade and marine insurance. However, in 1840, the partnership was dissolved and Allhusen cast around for a new business opportunity.

This he found in the chemical trade, through his purchase of a moribund firm founded in 1820 by Charles Attwood on the Saltmeadows, the riverside land in Gateshead that belonged to the corporation of Newcastle. In the following years, Allhusen built up his business (which in 1871 he registered as a limited company under the name of the Newcastle Chemical Works Ltd) until it was the largest chemical works in the world. Allhusen's success was not based upon his own scientific or technical knowledge, which was scant, or on inventions made at his works, but on his ability as a businessman. He was alive to developments in chemistry and chemical engineering and he was willing to adopt new processes in order to ensure continued commercial success. Characteristically, he was involved in many other businesses, including railways, banking, land, and marine insurance. He was a director of the Newcastle and Gateshead Water Co. and a major shareholder in the Durham District Bank. When the latter failed in 1857, he managed to extricate himself from the debacle and used his skill to prevent the closure of the Derwent Iron Works, which came back to life as the Consett Iron Co. (see CONSETT). When he died, he left a fortune of £1,125,000. In 1891, the chemical firm he had founded was absorbed into the United Alkali Co., a conglomerate formed by a major rationalisation of the industry.

ALNMOUTH

Alnmouth, which, as its name indicates, stands at the mouth of the River Aln, was until recent times called 'Alemouth' and before the Norman Conquest may have been 'Twyford' (Two Fords). That it had a pre-Conquest existence is proved by the presence of a church or chapel and a carved cross, fragments of which survive, but its size and importance are not clear. In the twelfth century, however, its development was given impetus by the de Vesci family, lords of ALNWICK, who reconstituted it as a borough, intending it to become the port of Alnwick. And it did prosper, partly because of the growth of population and partly because it was one of the few harbours on an otherwise inhospitable coast. But its growth was not sustained: during the Anglo-Scottish war it suffered from being too close to the Border and in the later fourteenth century from the general decline in the population through repeated plague epidemics.

Economic growth eventally occurred in the eighteenth century, thanks to expanding population and the increased use of the port to export grain, which was made feasible by the construction in the 1750s of TURNPIKE ROADS across Northumberland. That from HEXHAM is often described as the 'Corn Road', although there is no evidence of the use of this name at the time. In the nineteenth century, however, this development was gradually stifled by the advent of the railway, which was a quicker form of transport, and by the silting of the harbour following the great storm at Christmas 1806, which altered the course of the Aln.

The change in the course of the Aln also had a non-economic effect: it isolated the church on an island between the town and the old course of the river. This church, which was a chapel of the parish of Lesbury, had been built in the twelfth century and was dedicated to St Waleric. The name was the local spelling of an obscure French saint, St Valery, who died in 622. He had no connection with the North East, and the only explanation for his attachment to Alnmouth is that it was from the town of St Valery at the mouth of the Somme that William the Conqueror embarked on his invasion of England.

Alnmouth remains an attractive town, but Nikolaus Pevsner is right in saying that it has 'the aura of departed greatness', a feeling enhanced by the forlorn site of St Waleric's chapel and the buildings constructed as corn warehouses that are now converted to other uses.

ALNWICK

Virtually nothing is known of Alnwick before the Norman Conquest. Since its name means 'the farm by the Aln', it is fair to assume that it was a rural settlement, and it is possible that it was a member of a large estate, the centre of which was at Lesbury. The Borough of Alnwick followed the creation of Alnwick Barony by Henry I, the largest of the twenty baronies established in Northumberland between 1095 and 1135. Those responsible for bringing the borough into existence were the first three owners of the barony: Ivo de Vesci (Vassy in Normandy), his son-in-law, Eustace Fitz John (killed 1157), and Eustace's son, William de Vesci I (d.1183).

Almost certainly the first building was the castle, consequent upon the decision of Ivo de Vesci to locate the 'capital' of his barony at Alnwick, on the steep ground overlooking the haughs of the southern bank of the River Aln. Probably at the same time a chapel was built where St Michael's Church now stands. Between these two buildings a street was formed, now called Bailiffgate. Possibly this was the site of the pre-Conquest village; but it may have been laid out by the early Norman owners as the marketplace of a 'new town'. At this stage, the castle would have been an earthen construction, comprising a high mound (motte) surrounded by a moat and surmounted by a wooden tower (keep), on either side of which were enclosures (baileys) formed by ditches and earth ramparts topped by wooden walls. Later in the century, a stone shell keep replaced its wooden predecessor, which involved lowering the motte, as is still clearly evident. Probably the bailey walls were rebuilt in stone about the same time.

The decision to create (or resite) the borough on land immediately south of the newly reconstructed castle was almost certainly taken some time after 1157 by William de Vesci I. It took the form of a triangular marketplace at the junction of three roads that came to be called Narrowgate, Bondgate and Clayport. At right angles to these roads and the marketplace, building plots (burgages) were laid out which were to be let at low, fixed rents. The purpose was to attract settlers who would engage in manufacture and commerce for the benefit of the castle and the surrounding district. In other words, it was an attempt to stimulate economic development, not unlike a modern trading estate. The physical form of this borough is still evident, although in the intervening centuries, many of the burgage plots have become merged or divided and part of the marketplace has been built over. William de Vesci may also have been responsible for Walkergate, physically separate from the rest of the borough, but constitutionally part of it. Physical separation and a riverside location were essential since the walkers' (fullers) trade was noxious and required access to running water.

A little earlier, in 1147, William de Vesci's father, Eustace Fitz John, had been instrumental in founding Alnwick Abbey on the north side of the Aln, the gatehouse of which is still extant. It was given to the then popular order of Premonstratensian canons, whose headquarters were in France at Prémontré (Latin, Premonstratensia). Among the privileges granted to the abbey was the right to have its own borough, which today is represented by Canongate, running from St Michael's Church down to the river. In this respect Alnwick is akin to early Edinburgh, where the burgh of Edinburgh occupied the upper two-thirds of the Royal Mile below the castle, while the lower third, Canongate, was a separate burgh belonging to the Augustinian canons of Holyrood. Eustace gave the canons of Alnwick several churches, including Lesbury, of which parish Alnwick was a member. The church at Alnwick did not become a parish church until after the Reformation; during the Middle Ages it was a chapel of ease, subordinate to the parish church at Lesbury.

The basic layout of Alnwick was in being before 1200. The first important addition was its friary. The friars normally based themselves inside towns, but, untypically, Alnwick's friary was located in the country about two miles north-west of the borough in Hulne Park. It was founded in 1240 by a returning crusader, Ralph Fresburn, in conjunction with the then Lord of Alnwick, William de Vesci II, who provided the land. It had the distinction of being the first house in England of the Carmelite Friars, an order inspired by the lifestyle of the hermit communities on Mount Carmel. The very substantial remains, within a fifteenth-century wall and including a defensive tower built in 1486, are in the middle of Hulne Park and so not readily accessible.

Two major developments occurred in the fourteenth century. The more important was that the barony of Alnwick changed hands, following the death in 1297 without legitimate male heirs of William de Vesci III. It came into the possession of the Bishop of Durham, Anthony Bek, who in 1309 sold it to Henry, Lord Percy I (see PERCY FAMILY), with whose family Alnwick has been associated ever since. It was this man and his successors who improved the defensive capability of the castle by adding towers to the walls at their most vulnerable points and barbicans to command the gates to the two baileys.

The fifteenth century also saw important changes. The most obvious was the walling of the borough. The necessary royal licence was granted in 1433, but it was several decades before the project was complete. Although virtually all of it has disappeared, the roads circling the centre of the town identify its line. The one remaining part is the gate tower at Bondgate. Commonly called the Hotspur Gate, this is an anachronistic name in that Hotspur died nearly fifty years before the gate was built.

Today Alnwick, with a population of around 8,000, is a market and residential town. Physically, it is still dominated by the castle, which unlike so many others is not a ruin but the family home of the Duke and Duchess of Northumberland. That it is so is the consequence of the division of the Percy estate in 1750, by which the Percys lost their Yorkshire, Cumberland (Cumbria) and Sussex lands. At that date the castle, while still largely intact, was in a rundown and partly ruinous condition, due to long neglect, the Percys having made their homes at Petworth House in Sussex and Syon House near London. It was the loss of Petworth that drove the 1st Duke and Duchess to restore Alnwick as their country seat. This was done to the plans of several architects, notably James Paine and Robert Adam. What we see today is, however, not the 1st Duke's work, but that commissioned by his grandson, the 4th Duke, in the 1850s. The architect was a North-East man, ANTHONY SALVIN, but the interior design was the work of two Italians, Luigi Canina and his assistant and successor, Giovanni Montiroli. An Italian painter, Alessandro Mantovani, and sculptor, Giuseppe Nucci, also made major contributions. Much of the woodcarving, however, was by local craftsmen, thanks to the Duke's decision to bring a noted carver, Antonio Bulletti, from Florence to create a school of carving in Alnwick.

As well as its castle, much used by film-makers, Alnwick also has three other internationally known enterprises. The oldest is House of Hardy (before 1988, Hardy Bros Ltd), founded in 1872 by two local men, William and John James Hardy. Although the firm, which became a subsidiary of a larger company in 1967, has developed successful businesses in outdoor clothing and high-technology tubing, it became and remains famous for its game fishing tackle. In this field it is still a world leader and exports to over twenty countries. It continues to maintain a prestigious retail outlet in Pall Mall, London, and has an American subsidiary based in Colorado. Its fame is illustrated by the story that in 1922, King George V, on being reminded that it was Hardy's birthday, sent greetings to Alnwick. The person to whom he should have sent them was the poet and novelist, Thomas Hardy.

The other enterprises are of much more recent origin. Barter Books was founded in 1991 by Stuart and Mary Manley and is run from Alnwick's redundant railway station. Based upon the notion of book exchange as well as purchase, it has a stock of over 350,000 secondhand and antiquarian books and is the second-largest secondhand bookshop in Britain. And, because of the advent of the internet, its trade is worldwide.

The most recent venture is the Alnwick Garden, an immense project developed by Jane, 12th Duchess of Northumberland, in a redundant garden at the rear of the castle. The designers are Belgian and some of the money was raised in America, emphasising the hopes that its attraction will be international. Although opened officially only in 2002 and still developing towards full maturity, the signs are that it is proving a huge attraction.

ALNWICK, BATTLE OF, 1093

Fought in November 1093, the Battle of Alnwick was the first of two occasions when a king of Scots was killed while invading Northumberland, the other being in 1513 at the BATTLE OF FLODDEN. The king in question was Malcolm III, known as Canmore (Gaelic, Big Head), who had ruled Scotland since his overthrow of Macbeth and his stepson, Lulach, in 1057 and 1058. Throughout his long reign his ambition, inherited from his predecessors, was to extend his kingdom southwards to at least the Tyne and if possible the Tees.

His ambition was thwarted by the second Norman king of England, William II, who in 1092 without warning seized control of Cumbria, expelling its ruler, whose allegiance was to Malcolm. William built a castle at Carlisle, brought farmers from the south to colonise the Eden valley, and installed two Norman barons with responsibility for ensuring that the regime change was permanent. The following summer, Malcolm visited William at Gloucester. He got no satisfaction from William on this and others matters of grievance but was told to submit them to the judgement of a court of English barons. This was a deliberate slight, which led Malcolm to return home in fury and frustration.

His reaction was to launch raids into Northumbria, the fifth time he had done so. This time his aggression proved fatal. On 13 November, he was ambushed and killed, together with his heir, Edward, near Alnwick by local forces commanded by the Earl of Northumberland, Robert de Mowbray. Three days later his wife, Margaret, having learnt of the disaster, died in Edinburgh, probably of cancer. Although the kings of Scots did not abandon their claim to Northumbria until 1237, from this time there was no serious doubt that the Tweed was to be the boundary between the two kingdoms.

About a hundred years after the battle, Eustace de Vesci, Lord of Alnwick, built a small hospice dedicated to St Leonard on the spot where Malcolm is said to have died. It was suppressed during the Reformation and its remains were not discovered until 1845. They lie next to the road running north out of Alnwick by the Lion Bridge over the Aln and are a sad reminder of an important event in the history of England and Scotland.

ALNWICK RUM

Alnwick Rum, first produced by Alnwick Brewery during World War I, is blended from several aged rums, principally from Guyana and Jamaica, according to a secret recipe, created by John Linsley. In 1978, the brewery was taken over and ceased trading in 1986, by which date rum was no longer being produced. Production was restarted by Ian Linsley, the son of John Linsley, following his discovery of his father's recipe, which had been lost for twenty years.

ALNWICK, SKIRMISH AT, 1174

Although seemingly a minor event, the skirmish at Alnwick in 1174 was one of the most humiliating reverses suffered by the Scottish kings in their attempts between 1136 and 1237 to acquire the EARLDOM OF NORTHUMBRIA. An opportunity to do so arose in 1173, when Henry II's eldest son and designated heir, also named Henry, rebelled against his father. The King of Scots, William I (known as William the Lion), offered his support to both parties, his price being the Earldom of Northumbria. The father declined, but the son accepted. William therefore crossed the Border in force in the summer of 1173, but quickly retreated back to Scotland on the approach of an English army. Undeterred, he mounted a second incursion the following summer. His itinerary, which looks like a tour of the earldom, took him from Wark on Tweed, to Carlisle (where he left part of his army), to Prudhoe, and then to Alnwick, which he planned to besiege with a force of about 500 men. There he was surprised and captured when his horse was killed, trapping him beneath its body.

Humiliation followed: he was taken to Falaise in Normandy and brought into Henry II's presence with his legs tied beneath his horse; and as the price of his liberty he was required to hand back TYNEDALE, to surrender his castles at BERWICK, Roxburgh, Jedburgh, Stirling and Edinburgh, and to perform homage and fealty to Henry for his kingdom. Far from enlarging Scotland, he had lost land and had been forced to subordinate it to England.

ALSTON

On the east side of the South Tyne, Alston is geographically within the North East and was a member of the REGALITY OF TYNEDALE. But it became part of Cumberland (now the northern part of Cumbria) when that county came into existence in the course of the twelfth century. The reason was the determination of the kings of England to retain direct control of Alston's valuable lead/silver mines. That it should be in Northumberland is still well advertised by its parish church, which is in the Diocese of Newcastle, not that of Carlisle like the rest of Cumbria.

AMBLE

Amble, at the mouth of the River Coquet, was essentially the port of Warkworth, two miles upstream, a distance shortened in 1765, when the river changed course. Like other Northumberland coastal settlements, its medieval economy was based upon fishing and salt panning. Impetus to further development came in the nineteenth century as the result of the expansion of coal mining. In 1837, an act of parliament created the Warkworth Harbour Commission, but it took twelve years to complete the construction of modern port facilities. The coal exported came from the collieries that were sunk in the vicinity at Togston, Radcliffe, Hauxley and Shilbottle. To this activity, shipbuilding was added after 1870, albeit on a small scale. This still continues, but the coal trade ended in 1969, leaving the remnants of the wooden staithe. Fishing also continues, bolstered by the creation of a new fish dock in 1988. But the rising 'industry' is now leisure, particularly with the development of the Braid Marina.

ANDREW'S HEALTH SALTS

Andrew's Health Salts, which are effervescent when added to water, were so called because they were first made on premises close to the Church of St Andrew in Gallowgate, NEWCASTLE. They were devised in 1894 by two men, Scott and Turner, who decided that, given the right promotion, they would become a popular patent medicine. Sold in 4 oz and 8 oz tins, they gained widespread popularity and so to protect their product, Scott and Turner registered Andrew's as a trademark in 1909. Although many benefits were claimed for the salts, they are essentially a laxative. They are still available, now made by Sterling Health.

ANDY CAPP (see SMYTH, REGINALD)

ANGEL OF THE NORTH

The Angel of the North, erected in 1999, immediately became a symbolic figure akin to the Statue of Christ above Rio de Janeiro or the Statue of Liberty in New York. Unlike PENSHAW MONUMENT, it does not celebrate a particular person or event, and therefore it can mean different things to different people. And they are legion, since it is so sited as to be seen by over 90,000 vehicles every day as they travel the A1, as well as by passengers in trains on the East Coast Main Line. When it was first announced, there were many doubters, who felt that the money (£2,000,000) could have been more usefully spent and petitioned against it. Once in place, however, it converted most of the sceptics. It is a triumph of art over utility.

Its existence owes everything to the vision of the Gateshead Council, who decided to embark upon the project in 1990. The winning design, announced in 1994, was that submitted by Anthony Gormley. His vision was realised by the combined efforts of Hartlepool Steel Fabricators, Ove Arup & Partners (consulting engineers), the Geomatics Department of Newcastle University, and the Cumbrian firm of Thomas Armstrong (Construction) Ltd. Their triumph was the greater given the adverse condition of the site, which stood above old mine workings. Once these had been infilled, eight piles, each 0.75 of a metre in diameter, were created. These piles, which required 150 tons of steel-reinforced concrete, were rooted on solid rock 20 metres below the surface of the ground. Resting on top of the piles is a slab of concrete 13 metres by 8 metres and 1.5 metres thick and on this is a plinth 5.3 metres high, in which there are 52 steel bolts, each 3 metres long, to which the statue is fixed.

The Angel is made of special weather-resistant steel containing copper. The thickness of its skin and ribs is 6 millimetres and 50 millimetres respectively. It is 20 metres (65 feet) in height and its wingspan is 54 metres (175 feet). Its body weighs 100 tonnes and its wings 50 tonnes, and it is designed to withstand winds of over 100 miles per hour. It is truly a magnificent work of art, brought into existence by magnificent engineering.

ANGUS, GEORGE (1821–1890)

George Angus, who was born in Gateshead, was apprenticed at the age of fifteen to his grandfather's leather business. After he had taken control in the 1860s, he expanded it to become the leading manufacturer of driving belts, hosepipes and other industrial goods made in leather and India rubber. By the time of his death, there were branches throughout Britain and in the USA. In the years before World War I, the use of leather was discontinued in favour of canvas, which was more durable.

After George Angus's death, the business was pushed to greater heights by his two sons but particularly by his grandson, **Edmund Angus** (1889–1983). In 1936 he established a new division making oil seals, first at Walker and then at Wallsend, where it became Europe's largest oil seal factory. Expansion necessitated moving to a new site at Cramlington in the 1960s (see New Towns of the Twentieth Century), by which time Angus was the world's largest manufacturer of fire hoses, employing 3,700 people. In 1968 the firm merged with Dunlop UK to form the Dunlop Angus Industrial Group.

AREAS OF OUTSTANDING NATURAL BEAUTY

AONBs are designated areas the purpose of which is to preserve and enhance features, man-made as well as natural, adjudged by international criteria to be of outstanding beauty, and to facilitate their exploration, enjoyment and understanding by visitors. Responsibility for achieving these aims, which are embodied in agreed five-year plans, is shared by the whole range of public bodies and relevant voluntary organisations, working in co-operation with farmers and other businesses within the area and assisted by a small full-time staff. There are forty such areas in England and Wales, covering 16 percent of the land area.

There are two AONBs in the North East. The earlier and smaller, designated in 1958, is the **Northumberland Coast AONB**, which extends in a narrow belt from the mouth of the Tweed to Amble at the mouth of the Coquet. The natural features include fine sand beaches backed by sand dunes and outcrops of the Whin Sill. Also within the Area are two National Nature Reserves, Holy Island and the Farne Islands and twelve Sites of Special Scientific Interest. The other area, designated in 1988, is the **North Pennines AONB**. It is much larger, covering over 700 square miles (1,800 km^2), and is the second largest of those in England and Wales. It encompasses the main upland parts of three adjacent counties: Northumberland, Durham and Cumbria. It lies within a boundary which runs close to, but does not include, Haltwhistle, Haydon Bridge, Hexham, Consett, Stanhope, Middleton in Teesdale, Bowes, Kirby Stephen, Brough and Brampton. It contains over a quarter of the country's peat-forming blanket bog, now increasingly recognised for its ability to store carbon.

ARMSTRONG, TOMMY (1848–1919)

Tommy Armstrong, a small, bow-legged man, was one of the outstanding and most prolific working-class ballad writers of the nineteenth century, many of whose songs have, unfortunately, been lost. The most famous of those to survive are 'Wor Nanny's a Maisor' and 'Dorham Jail', the latter being based on his experience of a stretch in prison in Durham following a conviction for stealing a pair of stockings from the Co-operative Store at West Stanley.

ARMSTRONG, SIR WILLIAM, LORD ARMSTRONG OF CRAGSIDE (1810–1900)

William George Armstrong was one of the most dynamic and successful inventors and industrialists in the North East in the nineteenth century. He was the son of William Armstrong, a Cumbrian who migrated to Newcastle and became a successful corn merchant, and who was also involved in civic politics, serving as mayor for the year 1850. But his great passion was mathematics. During his life he amassed a huge library, many items of which he bequeathed to the Literary and Philosophical Society of Newcastle upon Tyne. Given his son's interests and talents, it is hard not to think that Armstrong senior's interests were not a formative influence.

However, he did not allow his son, the future Lord Armstrong, to pursue his natural bent towards science and engineering. Instead, after educating him at Bishop Auckland Grammar School, he apprenticed him to a firm of solicitors headed by one of his friends, Armorer Donkin. Fortunately, this did not prove to be an unhappy situation, since Donkin allowed Armstrong enough free time to indulge his engineering interests, and Armstrong did enough to qualify as a solicitor. These interests concerned hydraulics and electricity and led to the publication of a number of papers in scientific journals, for which he was elected FRS in 1846 at the early age of thirty-six.

The years 1845–47 were the watershed of Armstrong's life. During that time he gave up his legal practice and resigned as secretary of the Whittle Dean Water Co., founded in 1845, in order to set up two engineering companies: the Newcastle Cranage Co. to manufacture the hydraulic crane that he had invented, had successfully demonstrated on Newcastle Quayside and had patented in 1845; and W.G. Armstrong & Co., an engineering firm for which a 5½ acre (2.2 ha) site was acquired at Elswick, then a village upriver of Newcastle. This was made possible by the financial backing of four wealthy Novocastrians: Armorer Donkin, George Cruddas, Addison Potter (his uncle) and Richard Lambert, all of whom he knew through their involvement in the Whittle Dean project. The risk involved, clearly recognised at the time, was justified by success based on the steady improvement in the design of the cranes and application of the hydraulic principle to other industrial purposes.

The Crimean War (1853–56), however, led him to move into the field for which he became internationally famous: armaments. In 1855, he produced a 3-pounder field gun that was novel in all its aspects: a rifled barrel comprising a steel core encased in wrought iron cylinders; breech loading; a bullet-shaped fused round; and arrangements for controlling the recoil. Moreover, the gun was over eight times lighter and could fire further and with greater accuracy than those then in use. It was so revolutionary that eleven patents resulted from his work. Four years later, he produced a 12-pounder gun on the same principles. Not only were Armstrong's guns far better than those in current use, they were shown to be superior to those invented by his rival, Joseph Whitworth, who went to great lengths to dent his reputation. Armstrong's success led in 1859 to a complex arrangement with the government. He was appointed engineer at Woolwich Arsenal, with three years' back pay and a knighthood, in return for which he made over his patents to the nation. But, as the Arsenal could not produce enough guns, he set up the Elswick Ordnance Co., in which he had no financial interest, to be run by his associates, George Cruddas, Richard Lambert and George Rendel, on the understanding that the government would put its business exclusively to them while they agreed not to sell to any foreign power. Between 1859 and 1863, this arrangement worked well, Elswick Ordnance supplying over 3,000 guns to the British Army, worth over £1 million.

But Armstrong reckoned without the hidebound conservatism of the British Army, which decided in the face of all the evidence to return to the traditional muzzle-loaded, smooth-bore gun, a decision it maintained for fifteen years. Armstrong's response was to merge his engineering and ordnance firms to form Sir W.G. Armstrong & Co., to secure release from the 'Britain Only' market, and so to sell to foreign governments guns of steadily improving design. Only in 1878 did the British government face up to the fact that its artillery was far inferior to that of other nations. What finally convinced it was the 6-inch gun Armstrong produced using even more advanced technology than he had employed in his earlier models.

Meanwhile, Armstrong had diversified still further. In 1867 he entered into an arrangement with the shipbuilding firm of Charles Mitchell at Low Walker, whereby warships would be built by Mitchells and armed by Armstrongs (see SHIPBUILDING INDUSTRY). Their first venture was HMS *Staunch*, completed in the following year. This agreement continued until 1882, when the two firms merged to be Sir W.G. Armstrong, Mitchell & Co. Ltd, and a shipyard was created at Elswick. This development became feasible thanks to the dredging of the river as far as Elswick by the Tyne Improvement Commission, set up for this purpose in 1850, and the opening in 1876 of the Swing Bridge between GATESHEAD and Newcastle as a replacement for the low-level stone bridge of 1781. Armstrong's initial enthusism was for cruisers, warships for commerce protection that were heavily armed (10-inch and 6-inch guns) but lightly armoured (only 3,000 tons) and therefore fast (nearly 20 knots). But Armstrongs also built battleships, starting with HMS *Victoria* in 1884. He also built for eleven foreign navies, most notably Japan. By the time of his death, he had built eight warships for the Imperial Japanese Navy, including two battleships, *Yashima* and *Hatsuse*. The quality of Armstrong's ships was dramatically demonstrated in 1905, when they helped to annihilate the Russian fleet in the Battle of Tsushima. Armstrong's success was due in great part to the head of his shipbuilding department, Sir William White, who previously had been Chief Constructor at the Admiralty. Armstrongs were also pioneers in a new type of vessel, the oil tanker. The design, patented in 1885 by one of the firm's directors, Henry Swann, used the hull itself as the container, partitioned by longitudinal and transverse bulkheads to provide stability. In that year the firm launched the *Gluckauf*, built for a German shipowner, Heinrich Riedemann of Bremen. By the time of his death, Armstrong's firm had built a further fifty tankers.

The Armstrong–Mitchell amalgamation was the prelude to a greater expansion. In 1885 Armstrongs opened a factory at Pozzuoli, near Naples in Italy, to manufacture armaments for the Italian government. More importantly, in 1897 they acquired the Manchester firm of Sir Joseph Whitworth & Co. following Whitworth's death in 1887. Although Whitworth's guns proved inferior to Armstrong's and the company was much smaller, the acquisition was a sensible move since the Whitworth plant at Openshaw was modern and manufactured high-quality machine tools and armour plate. But there was a more urgent reason, namely the emergence of a powerful rival in the armaments field. This was the Sheffield steelmaking firm of Vickers, who in 1897 acquired the Naval Construction and Armaments Co. of Barrow-in-Furness and the machine gun firm, Maxim-Nordenfelt, whose product was superior to that of the Gatling gun, which Armstrong had been manufacturing under licence since 1870.

By this time, Armstrong was largely retired from the routine management of the business. In 1863, he had bought a tract of barren moorland near ROTHBURY, on the side of the Debdon Burn. Eventually he was to own 1,700 acres (688 ha), which he transformed by planting seven million trees and constructing five lakes. His original house, Cragside, was small, but he replaced it between 1870 and 1885 with a mansion designed by Norman Shaw. This house was lighted and its equipment driven by the world's first hydro-electric power generator. It was here that Armstrong spent an increasing amount of time, although not in idle retirement. At Cragside he continued to research into electricity and in 1897, at the age of eighty-seven, he published an important treatise, *Electric Movement in Air and Water*, the last in a long series of learned works on engineering problems. His academic standing was recognised by Durham University and Trinity College, Dublin in their award of honorary degrees. His overall contribution to his country was recognised in his elevation to the peerage as Baron Armstrong in the honours list to mark Queen Victoria's Golden Jubilee in 1887.

Armstrong was a benefactor on a grand scale, especially to Newcastle. He landscaped Jesmond Dene, over which he built a bridge in 1876–78, and gifted it to the city by two grants in 1878 and 1884; and he made generous contributions to institutions such as the Royal Victoria Infirmary, the Literary and Philosophical Society, the Hospital for Sick Children, the Hancock Museum and the College of Physical Science, which in 1904 changed its name to Armstrong College. Further afield, he bought from the Crewe Trustees (see NATHANIEL, LORD CREWE) the medieval castle at BAMBURGH, which he restored, setting part of it aside as a convalescent home. He also renewed his connection with the water company, acting as its chairman between 1853 and 1864, during which time it became the Newcastle and Gateshead Water Co.

He died in the last week of 1900. In the previous half century, he had built up one of the world's largest and most important engineering, shipbuilding and armaments firms. In doing so, he had transformed Elswick from a village into an industrial suburb with a works covering 250 acres (100 ha) and employing around 20,000 people. It was fitting that in 1906 a statue of him was erected overlooking Barras Bridge, but arguably his best memorials are Jesmond Dene, Cragside and Bamburgh Castle.

ART GALLERIES

Most of the region's numerous art galleries are private enterprises with a commercial purpose. The following are the most important public galleries.

Baltic Centre for Contemporary Art, Gateshead: The Baltic Centre for Contemporary Art resulted from the rebuilding between 1994 and 2002 of the Baltic Flour Mill, then the most prominent building on the Gateshead Quayside before the erection of THE SAGE GATESHEAD. The mill was built by Joseph Rank & Co. between the 1930s and the early 1950s. Although the mill ceased production in the mid-1970s and the building remained largely unused thereafter, it was so striking a piece of architecture that its demolition would have been an act of vandalism. Its conversion to its new use was, however, a massive undertaking, costing £46 million and involving the replacement of everything but its north and south walls. It is not strictly an art gallery in that it has no permanent collection, but serves to exhibit the work of contemporary artists. Its facilities include four galleries, performance space, artists' studios, a cinema and lecture space, and an archive for the study of contemporary art.

Hartlepool Art Gallery: Hartlepool Art Gallery opened in 1996 in the former Christ Church, built in 1854 as the first church in the new town of West Hartlepool (see NEW TOWNS OF THE NINETEENTH CENTURY). Previously the art collection had been housed in the Gray Art Gallery and Museum, opened in 1920 in a large house built in 1862 by the town's leading shipbuilder, WILLIAM GRAY.

Hatton Gallery, Newcastle University: The Hatton Gallery was founded in 1925 and named after Richard George Hatton (1865–1926), who joined the staff of the Art School of the College of Physical Science in 1890 and rose to become Professor of Art in Armstrong College in 1917. Although an accomplished artist, his reputation rested more on the encouragement he gave to students of all ages and on the books he wrote: *Perspective for Art Students* (1902), *Figure Drawing* (1905) and *Principles of Decoration* (1925). The gallery's permanent collection began with a small number of nineteenth-century works, but since its inception it has been considerably expanded by the bequests of Richard Hatton himself, by the Charlton, Bosenquet, Hall and Uhlman families, and by the Contemporary Arts Society. The gallery has also pursued a purchasing policy, and in this its potential was considerably enhanced by the generosity of DAME CATHERINE COOKSON. The gallery also holds temporary exhibitions and is very active in art education.

Laing Art Gallery, Newcastle: Unlike most major cities, Newcastle failed to avail itself of the powers afforded by the Museums Act of 1846 and the Museums and Public Libraries Acts of 1850 and 1855, which allowed (but did not oblige) local authorities to levy a rate for the purpose of creating a municipal art gallery. Newcastle's gallery came late and was the result of private generosity. Its benefactor was a Scotsman, Alexander Laing, who migrated to Newcastle from Forfar in 1846 and made a fortune in the beer and wine trades. In 1900 he offered the city the sum of £20,000 to cover the cost of constructing a gallery on a site in Higham Place. The eventual cost of the building, which opened in 1904, was £30,000, and the original exhibits did not belong to the gallery but were secured on loan by its enterprising curator, Bernard Stephenson. Since then, the gallery has built up an impressive collection of over 1,000 oil paintings, 4,000 watercolours (one of the finest outside London), 5,000 prints and 7,000 pieces of decorative art. The acquisition policy has focused on post-1750 British art and on the work of regional artists and depictions of local scenes. A new wing was opened in 1996, which has enabled the gallery to have a Children's Gallery and a permanent exhibition of 'Art on Tyneside'. Like similar galleries, it holds temporary exhibitions and is engaged in educational activity.

Northumbria University Art Gallery: Opened in 1977, Northumbria University Art Gallery was the brainchild of Professor Tom Bromley, Dean of the School of Art and Design at the then Newcastle Polytechnic, now Northumbria University. A gallery became possible as the result of the building of a new library, which freed enough space to house the pictures. In 2004, an extension, the Baring Wing, was added. Bromley's original intention was that the gallery would mount exhibitions of the work of artists who came to lecture or give courses within the School, and in doing so would act as a link between the Polytechnic and the wider Tyneside community. Since then, it has developed gradually and organically and is now no longer an adjunct of the School of Art and Design but a free-standing part of the University, directly under the aegis of the Vice-Chancellor's office. Over the same years, the commercial aspect has become increasingly important and has enabled the gallery to be self-financing. Alongside its role in mounting exhibitions, it has built up a collection of works by the artists with national and international reputations who have exhibited at, and sold through, the gallery. It has also given encouragement to artists of the region, notably through the annual Cravens Art Prize, formerly called The People, with the theme of The Human Zoo.

Shipley Art Gallery, Gateshead: Shipley Art Gallery, which was built between

1914 and 1917 and opened in the latter year, was the result of a bequest by a Newcastle solicitor, Joseph Ainsley Davidson Shipley (1822–1909). He left part of his fortune to pay for the building, and also his very extensive art collection. His intention was that the gallery should be in Newcastle, but the city council declined to accept the gift, hence the move to Gateshead. Shipley's collection of paintings was of uneven quality, and so only 504, of the various European schools from the sixteenth to the nineteenth centuries, were retained for exhibition, the rest being sold to help finance the project.

Other towns have smaller galleries. At **South Shields**, the gallery is housed with the museum. Its collection comprises paintings, by mainly local artists, of scenes of the town and the river mouth.

ASHINGTON 'PITMAN PAINTERS'

The title of Ashington 'Pitman Painters' is misleading in that, although the members of the group came mainly from the mining town of Ashington, where the group met, it was not exclusively a miners' club. Its genesis was the establishment of the office of the Workers' Educational Association (WEA) in the region immediately after the end of World War I with the aim of offering educational opportunities to people whose formal education had been narrow and had ended at an early age. Classes in Ashington began in 1923, but it was not until ten years later that two men, one a miner, the other a dental mechanic, asked for a course on art. This was ageed to, and an Art Appreciation course, attended by thirteen men, was started in the autumn of 1934. The tutor employed was Robert Lyon, a lecturer at Armstrong College, the forerunner of Newcastle University. His approach, naturally, was academic: formal instruction in how to study and understand a picture. This, however, was beyond the experience of his students. The problem was solved by discussion, out of which came the decision to engage in the practice of painting, not as an end in itself, but as the means of leading the members of the class to an understanding of how the artist works and thence to a better appreciation of the art of others. Progress was achieved not only by Robert Lyon's instruction, but also by the members criticising each other's work, done during the week between the Monday meetings. Because of the poverty of the students, all manner of surfaces were used and much of the paint was that used in home decoration.

The original course was eighteen sessions, but such was its success that it was extended for a further three years. The group's progress was sufficient to merit an exhibition of members' work being held at the Hatton Gallery (see ART GALLERIES) in Newcastle in 1936. By that time the members were gaining confidence and beginning to base their work on their personal experiences of life and work in Ashington. A second exhibition was held at the Laing Art Gallery (see ART GALLERIES) in Newcastle in 1941, the year before Robert Lyon left what had become King's College to take up the prestigious post of Principal of the Edinburgh College of Art. Following his departure, the group became autonomous: it drew up its own constitution, and resolved to build up a permanent collection of members' work. The aim was no longer art appreciation but the practice of art. The group's activities and achievements might have remained relatively obscure but for the interest of the art historian, William Feaver, whose enthusiasm led to much wider knowledge and to exhibitions between 1970 and 1980 throughout Britain and in Germany and China, where it proved hugely popular. By the early 1980s, however, the group had dwindled to two members, Jack Harrison, a late recruit, and Oliver Kilbourn, a founder member and generally acknowledged to be its best artist. Consequently, the group formally disbanded in 1983. The collection of its work, however, did not remain long in storage: in 1990 it was transferred to the new mining museum at Woodhorn Colliery, where many items are on permanent display.

The Ashington Group was the product of the extremely limited educational opportunities available to most people before World War I and the hardship of life in the mining communities of the North East in the inter-war years. As both situations were gradually remedied in the years after 1945, the group lost its *raison d'être.*

ASTELL, MARY (1668–1731)

Mary Astell was born in Newcastle in 1666, the daughter of Peter Astell, a member of the Hostmen, the merchant organisation that controlled the Tyneside coal trade. She was a girl of exceptional intelligence, whose subsequent life may owe a great deal to her father's early death in 1678, when she was twelve. In the absence of a father, in her adolescent years she had the benefit of an intellectual and academic education at the hands of her uncle, Ralph Astell, the curate of Newcastle parish church (now cathedral), who had access to his church's library of religious and philosophical texts.

Her independence and education help to explain her extraordinary decision in 1689, when she came into a legacy of £100, to move to London and attempt to earn a living by her pen. In fact it was not London but Chelsea where she settled and where she was to spend the rest of her life. At that date, Chelsea was a village where the Royal Hospital had been recently completed, but more importantly, it was the residence of a number of wealthy unmarried women, whose lives Astell was to influence and who in return helped to support her financially. The most important were Lady Elizabeth Hastings and Lady Catherine Jones. However, notwithstanding their generosity and the income from her publications, her material resources were always meagre. With the exception of her sympathetic and supportive publisher, Richard Wilkin, all her friends were female.

She burst upon the scene in 1694 as an author with a tract entitled *A Serious Proposal to Ladies for the Advancement of their True and Greatest Interest. By a Lover of her Sex.* In this work she advocated the creation of a college for women to serve two purposes. One was to provide a refuge for women who did not wish to marry but who feared the penury and insecurity of spinsterhood. The institution was to be run in strict conformity with the teaching of the Church of England, and although at first sight rather monastic, it was to impose no vows or irrevocable commitment. The second purpose was to provide women with a serious and intellectual education. Behind this was Astell's unwavering conviction that the female mind was equal to that of the male and that women were as capable as men of deep interest in and mastery of intellectual matters. Three years later, in 1697, she enlarged her arguments in a second edition. The ideas she put forward aroused considerable interest, and there was a serious proposal to raise £10,000 to found a college on Astellian lines. It came to nothing, partly due to male antagonism. One of the most influential churchmen of the day, Gilbert Burnet, Bishop of Salisbury, was so concerned that he went personally to see Mary Astell to rail against it, claiming that it would be tantamount to reviving monastic orders. It was also fiercely attacked and ridiculed in three issues of the fashionable periodical *The Tatler*.

It is clear that Mary Astell, in her belief that men and women had equal mental abilities and capacities, was a feminist. In contrast, what she did not advocate was women's social liberation. In publications in 1700 and 1706, although she made it clear that she considered the married state to be inimical to women's true interest, paradoxically (to our way of thinking) this did not lead her to advocate changes to the rules and conditions of marriage. Rather, her view was that if a woman wished to avoid the disadvantages and drawbacks of marriage, she must stay single.

This conviction stemmed from her belief that all forms of human authority derived from God. Because in her view the authority of a husband over his wife was divinely ordained, it followed that a woman who married must submit to that authority, for good or ill. The same divine sanction lay behind the authority of the Church of England. In 1705 she argued this in a book entitled *The Christian Religion, as Professed by a daughter of the Church of England,* and she was not afraid to oppose the more pragmatic arguments of such eminent thinkers as John Locke. Not surprisingly, the High Church party employed her to write in support of legislation against Occasional Conformity, the practice of Dissenters attending their parish churches on just enough occasions to avoid the legal and social disabilities imposed on those not adhering to the established church. And in politics, again not surprisingly, she was an ardent supporter of the Stuart monarchy, with its belief in the doctrine of the Divine Right of Kings with its absolutist implications; so much so, that after the accession of George I in 1714, government agents watched her, suspecting her to be an active Jacobite.

Mary Astell ceased to be a public figure after 1710 and lived on in the comfortable circle of ladies in Chelsea until her death in 1731, shortly after a mastectomy. Until the end, she was urging her opinions through correspondence with friends in the elegant and forceful Augustan prose that she had employed in her public writings. Throughout her adult life she was totally committed to the cause of her sex. Perhaps her epitaph should be her rhetorical question, 'If all men are born free, how is it that all women are born slaves?'

ATTWOOD, CHARLES (1791–1875)

Charles Attwood was the son of a Shropshire iron and steel manufacturer, who in 1810 obtained a share in a small glassworks in GATESHEAD. Three years later, he bought out his partners and patented an improved method of manufacture of window glass of greater transparency. Unfortunately, he became embroiled in a protracted legal case that denied him the financial rewards he deserved.

At the end of the 1820s he was diverted from business into politics, becoming heavily involved in the agitation that led to the reform of parliament in 1832. In this he was associated with his more famous brother, Thomas Attwood, one of the national leaders of the reform agitation and in the 1840s prominent in the Chartist movement. Charles Attwood was one of the founders and then treasurer of the Northern Political Union, formed in NEWCASTLE in 1830, and gained huge popularity in the region through his powerful oratory. In 1832 he stood as a Radical for Newcastle at the election that followed the passing of the Reform Act. It is evident from his manifesto that he saw the act not as a conclusion, but as a prelude to further reform, advocating elections every three years (instead of seven) and the abolition of tithes and the Corn Laws. However, he failed to be elected, coming third to Sir Matthew White Ridley and JOHN HODGSON. Thereafter, his interest in politics faded, athough he spoke vehemently against the Crimean War in 1854 and in support of the

Poles in their attempt to liberate themselves from Russian rule in 1863.

Success came to him late in life. In 1846, with the backing of Barings Bank, he founded the Weardale Iron and Coal Co. at Tow Law, then a tiny hamlet. His selection of this site was determined by the proximity of the necessary raw materials. He secured the lease of the right to mine iron ore in the parishes of Stanhope and Wolsingham; limestone was available from quarries in upper Weardale; and he obtained coal from collieries he sank at Tow Law (Black Prince Colliery) and at West Thornley, both within a few hundred yards of his five blast furnaces. He also secured control of two other collieries, Hedley Hill and Hedley Hill over the Hill. In less than twenty years, Tow Law grew from a settlement of thirty people to a small town of around 5,000, about 10 per cent of whom were Irish, driven out by great famine in the late 1840s. Fifteen years later, in 1862, he started a steel works at Tudhoe, using a Bessemer converter. Here, too, he had his own colliery, at Tudhoe Grange. Some of the iron for the steel furnaces came from Tow Law, but he also had iron ore coming from the Cleveland Hills, where he had secured the lease of mineral rights on 5,000 acres (2,000 ha) near Guisborough.

Tow Law bore a strong similarity to CONSETT fifteen miles to the north. Both were the result of deliberate decisions to locate at the point where the iron ore and limestone resources of Weardale met the western edge of the Durham coalfield. Consett, however, was to continue as a major producer of iron and then steel until the late twentieth century. In contrast, Tow Law lost its iron and steel role in 1882 and became a coalmining town. One reason for this may be that Charles Attwood and his wife had no children and therefore he had no successor. After his death, Barings continued to run the business until they found a suitable buyer.

AUCKLAND CASTLE

Auckland Castle is the residence of the bishops of Durham, the sole survivor of their once numerous similar properties. Its name, however, is a misnomer: throughout its long existence it has never been a castle; the terms 'manor house' or 'palace' are more appropriate. Its certain history began during the pontificate of BISHOP HUGH OF LE PUISET, who had a banqueting hall and necessary domestic offices built *c.*1190. Their likely use was as an impressive base on the edge of his great hunting reserve, WEARDALE FOREST. At the end of the thirteenth century, Bishop Anthony Bek made it fit for permanent residence by building appropriately sumptuous apartments at right angles to the hall and also a chapel parallel to it. The last major changes before the Reformation were made by Thomas Ruthall, bishop from 1509 until 1523, who increased the accommodation by building what are now called the Long Dining Room and the King Charles Room.

The years of the Civil Wars and the Commonwealth (1640 to 1660) were disastrous for the castle. With the abolition of bishops, it became superfluous and in consequence in 1647 it was acquired by a leading Parliamentarian, SIR ARTHUR HESILRIGE. His intention was to turn it into a manor house, and he began by demolishing Bek's chapel. However, the project was incomplete when the monarchy, and with it bishops, was restored in 1660. It fell to the incoming bishop, JOHN COSIN, to restore it as an episcopal residence. His most radical act was to convert Puiset's banqueting hall into a chapel. In doing so, he had to reverse the focal point of the building: as a banqueting hall, the dais with its high table had stood at the west end, close to the kitchens; as a chapel, however, the altar had to be at the east end. The chapel's present appearance is almost entirely the work of Cosin, to which his sumptuous tomb and the lavish display of his coat of arms bear ample witness.

For the rest of the castle, most of what is now visible is the work of the eighteenth-century bishops, particularly Richard Trevor (1752–71) and Shute Barrington (1792–1826). Trevor added the apartments that the bishop now occupies to the south side of Ruthall's range and also remodelled the Great Dining Room, while Barrington employed the architect James Wyatt to restyle the entrance hall, the anteroom and the throne room. As a result of the latter's work, the impression is of a Gothic building. Beneath the visible eighteenth-century surfaces, however, lies the basic medieval structure.

The castle lies between the centre of BISHOP AUCKLAND and a huge park, enclosed by a stone wall in the mid-fourteenth century. It is over 800 acres (320 ha) in extent and runs along the south bank of the Wear 1½ miles (2.4 km) towards Durham. Its present appearance owes much to the landscaping carried out by JEREMIAH DIXON for Bishop Richard Trevor (1752–71). It was in this park that the English army assembled in October 1346 before the BATTLE OF NEVILLE'S CROSS.

AUDEN, WYSTAN HUGH (1907–1973)

W. H. Auden is widely regarded as one of the best poets writing in English in the twentieth century. Although he was not born in the region, and did not live or work here, he spent his holidays as a schoolboy and a university student in the North Pennines. The landscape of the old LEAD MINING districts in the uplands where Northumberland, Durham and Cumbria meet deeply affected him at the time and held an abiding attraction and affection for him throughout his life. Their importance to him is perhaps summed up in lines he wrote in 1940: 'In Rookhope I was first aware / Of Self and Not Self, Death and Dread'. Allusions to these bleak hills and the old mining communities occur in many of his poems, and when he went to the USA during the World War II he took with him a map of the area.

AVISON, CHARLES (1710–1770)

Charles Avison is arguably the best musician produced by the North East. He was born in NEWCASTLE in 1710, the son of Richard Avison the town *wait* (minstrel). Presumably he received his early musical training from his father, but he must have been considerably precocious for he is known to have received support from Ralph Jenison, the MP for Northumberland, and from John Blathwayt, who had been the Director of the Royal Academy of Music. It is also thought that he studied in London with the Italian composer, Francesco Geminiani (1687–1762), a notion given support by Avison's high opinion of Geminiani and the similarities between the music written by the two men.

However long he may have stayed in London, he was back in Newcastle by 1735, when he was appointed as organist at St John's Church. His tenure lasted for only one year, for in 1736 he became organist at St Nicholas's, the parish church of Newcastle, the post he filled for the rest of his life. In addition to the demands of his office, he taught harpsicord, violin and flute and was assiduous in organising subscription concerts in Newcastle and Durham, the latter in collaboration with the Durham composer, John Garth. In 1750, with Garth he also founded the Marcello Society to promote the works of another Italian, Benedetto Marcello, for whom Avison had the highest regard.

Meanwhile, he was also writing music. In all, he composed fifty-two *concerti grossi* for strings and twenty-four trios. Until recently, the early eighteenth century was seen simply as the period of Handel, but in recent years the quality of Avison's music and that of other English provincial composers has gained increased recognition. But Avison was more than a teacher, concert organiser and composer, he was also the author of a notable book that ran to three editions: *Essay on Musical Expression*. It had three parts, the first discussing the effect of music on the emotions. The second offered a critique of a number of composers and their styles, while the last was concerned with the performance of musical works, particularly *concerti grossi*. The book was published in 1752 and it brought Avison some notoriety in that in his estimation Geminiani and Marcello were superior to Handel as composers. This brought down on Avison's head harsh criticism by William Hayes, Professor of Music at Oxford. Avison, however, was not abashed and he retained his views in the second and third editions.

Avison chose to make his living in his native town, and this was a deliberate decision. In the course of his career he declined offers of prestigious posts in London, York, Dublin and Edinburgh. Had he accepted, particularly if he had opted for a London base, it is likely that his name would have been more widely known.

BACKHOUSE FAMILY

For three generations, the Backhouses of DARLINGTON were important bankers in the region and had considerable bearing on the industrial development of South Durham and North Yorkshire. The dynasty was founded by James Backhouse, who migrated from Westmorland to Darlington in the 1750s to start a flax dressing and linen making business. In 1774, as was not uncommon in the eighteenth century, he founded a parallel banking business, J. and J. Backhouse, in partnership with his son, Jonathan (1747–1826). This proved so successful that by the time James Backhouse died in 1798 the linen business was discontinued in order to concentrate on the financial side. The name of the business was also changed to Jonathan Backhouse and Co.

Apart from innate business acumen allied to ambition, the Backhouses had the advantage of being Quakers and so part of the national nexus of Quaker entrepreneurs, who intermarried and supported each other's business ventures. Jonathan Backhouse I married Ann Pease, a daughter of the Darlington Quaker, Edward Pease, the driving force behind the Stockton and Darlington Railway and its extension to Middlesbrough (see PEASE FAMILY; NEW TOWNS OF THE NINETEENTH CENTURY; RAILWAYS). In turn, his son, Jonathan Backhouse II (1779–1842) married in 1811 Hannah Chapman, the co-heiress of the wealthy Quaker banker of Norwich, Joseph Gurney. The triangular linkage was completed in 1826 when Joseph Pease married Emma Gurney. It was the financial link with the Gurneys that made it possible for the Backhouse Bank to support Pease's industrial ventures in the 1820s and 1830s. In addition, the Backhouse Bank extended its business range by opening branches elsewhere in the region: by 1830 they were established in Durham, Sunderland, Stockton, South Shields and Newcastle.

Jonathan Backhouse II retired from the business in 1833 in order to devote his remaining years to the work of the Society of Friends. The bank continued to operate as an independent concern until 1896, when it merged with the Norwich bank of Gurney and the London bank of Barclay to become Barclay's Bank Ltd. The later generations of Backhouses were also noted for their interest and expertise in botany and horticulture.

BAGPIPES

The widely held belief that bagpipes are an exclusively Scottish phenomenon is erroneous: historically, bagpipes have been played for centuries throughout Europe and beyond. Moreover, there has been and still is a considerable variety of bagpipe, although all of them have three common elements: a bag in which air is stored; a chanter with holes and a reed by which the player determines the notes; and one or more drones to provide harmony. Bagpipes also fall into two broad categories: those where the air is mouth-blown into the bag; and those where it is forced in by means of bellows operated by the players's elbow. All pipes currently played achieved their present form in the nineteenth century.

The pipes associated with Scotland, the Highland pipes, are the largest and loudest of those in use in the British Isles and are essentially for use out of doors. There are a number of Highland pipe bands in the region, for example at Houghton le Spring, Morpeth and Newcastle. But there are also Northumbrian pipes, which are smaller and bellows-blown. Two sorts are currently in use, although there is evidence that in the past there was a pipe that was mouth-blown and not unlike the Highland pipe. The more common is the Northumbrian Small Pipe, which is not fully effective out of doors, but is excellent indoors and in association with fiddles. There is also the Northumbrian Half-long Pipe, which is also bellows-blown, but is larger and produces a louder sound and so is suitable for outdoor occasions, such as marches.

There is clear evidence that Northumbrian pipes have been made and played continuously since the early eighteenth century, and the dukes and duchesses of Northumberland have always had their personal pipers. Perhaps the most famous bagpipe makers were Robert Reid (1784–1837) and his son, James (1813–74), but their modern counterparts are continuing a vigorous tradition. The arrival of alternative forms of popular music led to a decline in piping in the late nineteenth century. That it did not completely fade away is in part due to the foundation of the Northumbrian Pipers' Society in 1928 and to the lifelong devotion of William Cocks of Ryton, who not only played and made pipes, but collected historic examples. When he died in 1971, he bequeathed his collection to the Society of Antiquaries of Newcastle upon Tyne (see LITERARY AND PHILOSOPHICAL SOCIETY OF NEWCASTLE UPON TYNE). In 1987 the collection was moved from the Society's headquarters in the Black Gate of Newcastle Castle to a Bagpipe Museum in the medieval chantry at MORPETH, which is helping to bring knowledge of Northumbrian pipes to a wider audience and is part of the revival of appreciation of their music.

BAINBRIDGE, EMERSON MUSCHAMP (1817–1892)

Emerson Muschamp Bainbridge was born at Eastgate in Weardale, the youngest child of a farmer, Cuthbert Bainbridge, and his wife, Mary Muschamp, whose ancestry stretched back to the de Muschamps, a Norman family who were granted the Barony of Wooler at the beginning of the twelfth century. In 1830, when he was thirteen, he secured a five-year apprenticeship with a NEWCASTLE draper. After serving his time, he went to London to gain further experience. On his return to Newcastle in 1837, his former master took him on as a partner in a shop that he had opened in the newly built Market Street. In 1855, Bainbridge became sole owner.

Bainbridge was an innovative businessman. He was the first shop owner to departmentalise his store (in 1849) and he introduced the principle of fixed-price labelling, with the promise that he would make up the difference if the same goods could be purchased more cheaply elsewhere. He also pioneered ready-made clothing. As an employer, his policies were governed by his strong Methodist faith, with the consequence that all his employees were (and are) partners in the firm.

Bainbridges remained an independent firm until 1952, when it was absorbed into the John Lewis Partnership. It remained in Market Street until 1975, when it moved into new premises in the Eldon Square development. However, it retained the name 'Bainbridges' until 2001, when, alas, it was changed to 'John Lewis'.

BALLIOL AND BRUCE FAMILIES

Two families, originally from France, that supplied kings to Scotland in the late thirteenth and early fourteenth centuries had their roots in the North East. The earlier of the two, the **Balliol** family, came from Bailleul en Vimeu in Picardy. In or shortly after 1095, King William II (1087–1100) granted two major estates to Guy Balliol: one centred on Gainford (later BARNARD CASTLE) on the north bank of the River Tees, then part of the WAPENTAKE OF SADBERGE, which was in Northumberland until 1189; the other on BYWELL in the Tyne valley. The grants were a consequence of William's abolition of the EARLDOM OF

NORTHUMBRIA following the rebellion of Earl Robert de Mowbray, which gave him the opportunity of implanting loyal men in strategically important locations. The **Bruces** were Normans, from Brix, a village close to Cherbourg at the northern tip of the Cotentin Peninsula. The first member of the family in Britain was Robert Bruce I, to whom King Henry I (1100–35) granted, in or very shortly after 1100, an extensive estate in the Cleveland district of North Yorkshire on the south side of the River Tees and also lands in Hartness, the district around HARTLEPOOL on the opposite, north side of the Tees. Like Gainford, Hartness too was part of the Wapentake of Sadberge.

Both families also acquired substantial estates in Scotland. The Bruce estate, comprising the whole of Annandale and extending to around 200,000 acres (90,000 ha) north of the Solway Firth, was granted to Robert Bruce I by King David I of Scotland (1124–53). The cross-border aspect of the Bruce estate presented no problems until after the death of Henry I in 1135, when his nephew, Stephen, Count of Blois, seized the English throne and in doing so usurped the right of Henry's daughter, Matilda. This provoked civil war, which gave David I of Scotland the chance to secure the Earldom of Northumbria, to which he had a strong claim through his mother. King Stephen, faced with war on two fronts, conceded David's claim at a meeting at DURHAM and as a result the overlordship of the Hartness lands was transferred from the English king to the Scottish monarch. Robert Bruce I now faced a conflict of loyalties and in consequence of his decision to side with Stephen when David invaded northern England in 1138, his Scottish estates, including Hartness, were confiscated by the Scottish king. Their loss was of very short duration, but in returning them, David did so not to Robert Bruce I, but to his second son, Robert Bruce II. When Robert Bruce I died in 1142, his Yorkshire estates were inherited by his eldest son, Adam, while Annandale and Hartness remained with Adam's younger brother, Robert Bruce II. Henceforth, there were two Bruce families, one English, the other Anglo-Scottish. It was the latter that was to produce a King of Scots. The Balliol connection with Scotland was less complex and came later, the consequence of the marriage in 1233 of John Balliol I, the fifth generation from Guy Balliol, and Dervorguila, the sole heir of Alan, Lord of Galloway.

These cross-border estates, however, were not the immediate cause of the involvement of the two families in the constitutional crisis that overtook Scotland with the extinction of its royal family as the result of the deaths of King Alexander III in 1286 and his only direct heir, his infant granddaughter, Margaret, the daughter of King Eric II of Norway, in 1290. The resolution of the succession question, which was known as the 'Great Cause', fell to King Edward I of England (1272–1307), who claimed the privilege as feudal overlord of Scotland. Although there were several interested parties, in reality only two had serious claims: John Balliol II (who was about forty years of age), son of John Balliol I and Dervorguila of Galloway, and Robert Bruce V (who was over seventy), great-grandson of Robert Bruce II. The claims of both men rested on their descent from Henry, Earl of Huntingdon, the youngest brother of King Malcolm IV (1154–65) and King William I (1165–1214), who died in 1219 leaving three daughters, Margaret, Isabel and Ada. The matter should have been easily settled: the crown passing to the descendant of Margaret, the eldest. What rendered it uncertain was that Robert Bruce V was the *son* of the *second* daughter, Isabel, whereas John Balliol II was only the *grandson* of the *eldest* daughter and, moreover, his claim had come to him through his *mother*. There was genuine uncertainty as to whether inheritance through the female line either invalidated or weakened a claim. In the end, Edward I decided that the influence of primogeniture should be paramount. As a result, John Balliol II became John, King of Scots in 1292.

His reign lasted only four years. Faced with John's unwillingness to be the compliant ruler he required, Edward I invaded Scotland in 1296 and forcibly stripped him of his office. By doing so, the English king began a war that was to last 307 years. But Edward not only deprived Balliol of his kingdom, he also took away his English estates, including Gainford and BYWELL. After a period of imprisonment in England, Balliol was allowed to retire to his ancestral property in Picardy, where he died in 1314. His removal opened the way for the Bruce family, who had never accepted their defeat in 1292. This time, the issue was settled by force, not negotiation. But it was not Robert Bruce V (who died in 1295), nor his son, Robert Bruce VI (who died in 1304), who launched the bid, but his grandson, Robert Bruce VII, who had himself inaugurated as King of Scots at Scone in 1306. It took until 1328 and many years of warfare before an English government finally recognised him as King Robert I. By that date, the Bruces had long been deprived of Hartness, this time permanently.

BALTIC CENTRE FOR CONTEMPORARY ART (see under ART GALLERIES)

BAMBURGH

Now a small village, Bamburgh was for many centuries a place of considerable importance, which it owed to the 150-foot (46 m) outcrop of the WHIN SILL that separates it from the seashore. The defensive potential of this rock is self-evident, so it is not surprising that it was occupied from at least the late Iron Age. It was the first place in the mid-sixth century that the incoming English invaders, led by Ida (see NORTHUMBRIA, KINGDOM AND EARLDOM OF), seized and fortified. This was not simply because of the security it could provide, but also perhaps because it was the chief place, or one of the chief places, belonging to the British rulers they dispossessed. Ida and his successors created the KINGDOM OF NORTHUMBRIA and made Bamburgh their 'capital'. It was also the centre of Bamburghshire, probably their largest estate and close to HOLY ISLAND, where they established their leading churchmen as bishops of Lindisfarne (see HOLY ISLAND).

Bamburgh remained an important royal centre throughout the history of the Kingdom of Northumbria, although the centre of gravity of the kingdom moved south to York. When the kingdom came to an end, it passed to its successor, the Earldom of Northumbria, and when this was extinguished by William II in 1095, it became Crown property. It was William's successors who were largely responsible for creating the present castle, notably its great late twelfth-century keep. It seems likely that they also intended that Bamburgh should develop as a town with what is now the village green as its marketplace. But Bamburgh's growth was stunted, partly by the rise of NEWCASTLE and BERWICK, but also as a result of the economic stagnation caused by the Scottish wars. Artillery and the Union of the Crowns made Border castles redundant (see BORDER TOWERS), and consequently in 1610, the lordship and castle of Bamburgh were granted by James I to Claudius Forster, son of SIR JOHN FORSTER, the Warden of the Middle March for much of Elizabeth I's reign. In 1704 the castle was acquired by the Bishop of Durham, NATHANIEL, LORD CREWE. In the last decade of the nineteenth century, it was bought by Lord Armstrong (Sir William Armstrong), who restored it to its present appearance.

BANNER OF ST CUTHBERT

In the course of the twelfth century, church banners came to be involved in war, the hope being that the saints they represented would exert influence to ensure victory in battle. Given St Cuthbert's reputation, it is not surprising that his banner became an important 'weapon'. The earliest known occasion was in 1097, when a Northumbrian army invaded Scotland and put Malcolm III's son Edgar on the throne. Thereafter, it is not mentioned until the early years of the Anglo-Scottish war, when it went on campaign five times between 1296 and 1341.

In 1346, however, at the Battle of Neville's Cross, which took place on St Cuthbert's doorstep, the monks of Durham Cathedral Priory sent his corporax cloth (used to cover his chalice) on the end of a spear. The English victory, which the monks would claim for their saint, resulted in a new banner of considerable complexity. As described in the last decade of the sixteenth century, it consisted of a flag of red velvet 15 feet (4.6 m) by 3 feet (90 cm), at the centre of which was a pouch of white velvet eighteen inches square surmounted by a red cross containing the sacred corporax cloth. The flag hung from a silver pole attached to a staff embossed with silver. Two silver bells were attached to the pole and three more to the lower edge of the banner. Thus the banner was not only highly visible, it could be heard as well. This banner was sent into battle against the Scots on at least seven occasions between 1356 and 1523, on each of which it was in the charge of one of the monks.

After the Reformation, it came to be seen as a relic of the old religion. There are two versions of its destruction. One was that it was defaced when the Cathedral Priory was closed in 1539; the other, a more dramatic version, was that the wife of Dean Whittingham (1563–79), said erroneously to have been a daughter of the Swiss reformer, John Calvin, threw it on her fire as a piece of superstitious rubbish. Nevertheless, for about five centuries it carried the trust, hopes and belief of those defending the Border. And, it seems, with justification, since it was never on the losing side.

BARBOUR WATERPROOF CLOTHING

The Barbour Company, which has been established in South Shields since 1894, was founded by John Barbour (1849–1918), the younger son of the tenant of Bogue Farm in Galloway. In 1870, at the age of twenty-one, he left the farm to start up as a travelling draper with a base in Newcastle. The following year, he married Margaret Haining, who was to be the driving force of their business ambition and whose portrait, painted in 1864 by Robert Herdman, hangs in the National Gallery of Scotland with the title *Evening Thoughts*. It was Margaret who was behind Barbour's decision to set up a business to make and sell oilskins, initially at their shop 5 Market Place, South Shields. Their success was rapid. Not only were their products popular with seafarers, their original target, they were bought in increasing quantities by people who worked on or were involved with the land. By 1908 they were sufficiently well known throughout Britain to warrant the production of their first catalogue. This ran to sixteen pages; in contrast, the 1926 edition covered 120 pages, and 120,000 copies were printed, 20,000 for overseas customers. During World War II, Barbours developed, with the help of Captain George Phillips RN, what became the standard waterproof suit for submariners, consisting of a jacket with a hood and an elasticated waist, and separate trousers.

The firm currently employs over 300 people and sells in twenty-nine countries through a network of local offices and retail outlets. The success of the Barbour product has been based on quality and on its unique repair and maintenance service.

BARNARD CASTLE

The history of Barnard Castle began in 1095, when William II created an estate in Teesdale composed of two large blocks of land: one centred on Gainford, the other stretching westwards from the present town to the head of Teesdale. Separating them were the townships of Winston, Cleatlam, Staindrop and Westwick. Shortly after 1095 William granted this estate to Guy de Balliol, whose family came from Bailleul en Vimeu in Picardy (see BALLIOL AND BRUCE FAMILIES). This grant was possible because in 1095 William suppressed the Earldom of Northumbria, to which the land belonged. Although Guy de Balliol possessed the estate for thirty years until his death in 1125, little is known about his activities, except that he built a castle. What is significant is that he located it not at Gainford, the ancient centre of the estate situated on flat ground close to the River Tees, but seven miles upstream at a far more defensible spot on top of a vertical rock eighty feet above the river. Another advantage of this site was that it overlooked the east–west road running along the river valley and its conjunction with the Roman road running north–south between Binchester and Bowes that crossed the Tees by the nearby ford. Guy's castle was of the primitive motte and bailey type, constructed of earth and wood, and may have covered no more than what became the Inner Bailey of the castle in its final form.

The real creator of Barnard Castle was not Guy but his nephew and successor, Bernard de Balliol I, who inherited the estate in 1125 and retained possession until his death in 1155. It is from this man that the town gets its name. Bernard appears to have been responsible for three major developments. One was the enlargement of the castle to comprise four wards (Inner, Town, Middle and Outer) and its reconstruction in stone. Although in the later twelfth cenury and during the thirteenth century further work was done, the form of the castle we see today is basically that devised by Bernard de Balliol I. Attached to the castle within the Outer Ward was a demesne farm and a chapel dedicated to St Margaret.

Bernard's second development was the borough. Its whereabouts are not certain, but the most recent research suggests that it was located along what is now Galgate, the northward continuation of the Roman road. It was not until the Balliols bought the township of Westwick from the Bishop of Durham in 1189 that the town acquired its present shape. This acquisition gave the necessary room for expansion: a new marketplace was created at right angles to Galgate and parallel to the castle wall; at its eastern end another extension, Newgate, was laid out at right angles to it; at their junction a new church, St Mary's, was built; and a new demesne farm was set up between Newgate and the Tees. In addition, the Bank and Thorngate ran down to another ford across the river. The purpose of the borough was to encourage economic development and to provide essential services for the occupants of the castle. To this end, the inhabitants were granted burgages, long narrow building plots that ran back from the streets at right angles, which they held on beneficial terms: low fixed rents and heritable tenure.

St Mary's was a not parish church but a chapel of ease within the extensive parish of Gainford. Guy de Balliol had granted the patronage of Gainford parish to the great Benedictine Abbey of St Mary, York, whose abbot consequently controlled the appointment of the vicar of the parish and the chaplain of Barnard Castle. Barnard Castle church was not granted parochial status until 1865. In the thirteenth century, two more ecclesiastical institutions were added, both characteristic of medieval boroughs: one was the Hospital of St John in Newgate, built to provide shelter for thirteen impoverished women; the other was the Augustinian Friary in Thorngate. Both were founded during the time of John de Balliol, who died in 1269 and who initiated the founding of Balliol College, Oxford (see OXFORD UNIVERSITY COLLEGES).

The overlordship of the Balliol family continued until 1296, when Edward I deposed John de Balliol, King of Scots. In 1307, after a period in the hands of the Crown, it was granted to Guy de Beauchamp, Earl of Warwick. In the mid-fifteenth century, the Beauchamp line ended with an heiress, Anne de Beauchamp, who married Richard Neville, Earl of Warwick, better known as 'Warwick the Kingmaker' (see NEVILLE FAMILY). As the main Beauchamp interests lay elsewhere, the only major development during their time was the building of a bridge across the Tees immediately below the castle, which in turn produced a new street, Bridgegate, connecting the bridge to the bottom of the Bank.

Neville possession was short-lived. Rebelling against Edward IV, the king he had helped to make, Warwick was killed at the Battle of Barnet in 1471. Shortly afterwards, his widow, Anne, married Edward IV's brother, Richard, Duke of Gloucester, the royal lieutenant in the north of England. During his possession before he usurped the throne as Richard III following his brother's premature death in 1483, Richard left his mark on Barnard Castle, quite literally in some places in the form of his emblem, the boar. He was responsible for alterations to the castle and, probably, the enlargement of the church. He also secured a licence to found a chantry chapel, probably in Newgate. All this suggests that had the political situation not changed, he would have made a considerable impact on the town. After his death in 1485, the lordship of Barnard Castle was retained by the Crown.

In the following century, the castle saw its only serious military action. This was between 2 and 13 December 1569, when Sir George Bowes of Streatlam (see BOWES FAMILY) defended it against the rebel army led by the earls of Northumberland and Westmorland (see RISING OF THE NORTHERN EARLS). Bowes's garrison, although numbering several hundred men, was faced with a besieging force of around 5,000. As a result, they were soon forced to abandon the Outer, Town and Middle wards of the castle and retire to the small Inner Ward. There panic set in, many defenders deserting by jumping off the walls, in some cases to their death or serious injury. With his garrison rapidly depleting, Bowes had no option but to sue for terms. Because of his soldierly defence, he was allowed to march away with the residue of the garrison and their weapons. His rearguard action was important as it bought time for the Queen's army, commanded by the Earl of Sussex, to gather and march north. A few days later, the rebel earls dismissed their followers and fled to Scotland.

The Reformation years also meant ecclesiastical changes. Following the closure of St Mary's Abbey, York, the patronage of Gainford church and thus Barnard Castle chapel was acquired by Trinity College, Cambridge, which still has it. The Augustinian Friary was also closed, but St John's Hospital survived, although control passed to the Lord Chancellor.

Finally, the fourteenth-century bridge was rebuilt in 1596.

The seventeenth century saw two major changes. One was ownership: between 1626 and 1636, Charles I sold the castle and the borough, together with Raby and Long Newton, to Sir Henry Vane (see VANE FAMILY). The other change was physical. By that date, the castle was redundant and so Vane dismantled large parts of it, using the stone to repair Raby Castle, his main residence. This in turn led to the building of houses between the Market Place and the castle walls, so giving the street its present appearance. The eighteenth century also brought changes: the Butter Cross was built in 1774; farming was modernised by the enclosure of the town fields in 1783 and the town moors in 1795 and 1799; and industry became prominent, with the growth of the woollen and leather industries.

Industrial growth continued in the first half of the nineteenth century with the development of carpet making, which led to what has been called a 'new industrial town', with factories and attendant slum dwellings in Thorngate and along Bridgegate. By 1831 the population of Barnard Castle had reached 4,430, only 500 below that of the 1991 census. At the other end of town, the railway arrived, after twenty years' delay thanks to the opposition of the Duke of Cleveland between 1856 and 1862, linking Barnard Castle with DARLINGTON, Cumbria and Lancashire via Stainmore, BISHOP AUCKLAND and Middleton. This delay may well have been detrimental to the town's ability to maintain industrial expansion. Improved transport, however, did help to develop the tourist trade, first stimulated by Sir Walter Scott's poem *Rokeby*, published in 1813, by the painting of the surrounding countryside by J.M.W. Turner and Thomas Girtin, and then by Charles Dickens, whose brief stay while researching Yorkshire schools for his novel *Nicholas Nickleby* also produced his short story 'Mr. Humphrey's Clock'. Barnard Castle also gained two cultural institutions: the BOWES MUSEUM, built between 1869 and 1892, and its immediate neighbour, the Northern Counties' School, also begun in 1869, for boys from Northumberland, DURHAM and the North Riding of Yorkshire, which was renamed Barnard Castle School in 1924.

The lack of significant population growth after 1831 is indicative of the failure of the town to build upon its early industrial start. In fact, the woollen and carpet industries did not outlast the nineteenth century, although some of the factories were used for other purposes for much of the twentieth century. Since then, the only major industrial development was the Glaxo factory, opened in 1944, which eventually employed 1,500 people. The failure of industrial development allowed Barnard Castle to revert to its earlier role as a small historic market town. The historic aspect has been preserved since 1952, when Lord Barnard handed over the castle to the predecessor of English Heritage, who have consolidated the remains and excavated some of the site. The former industrial area in Thorngate and Bridgegate is undergoing a renaissance, with two Victorian factories converted into apartments and new housing built, although it still retains renovated and modernised examples of eighteenth-century weavers' houses.

From the middle of the eighteenth century until the later twentieth century, Barnard Castle had a significant military role. This started in 1758 with the formation of the Durham Militia, under the terms of the 1757 Militia Act. The battalion, 400 strong and drawn from all parts of the county, had its headquarters at Barnard Castle since its colonel was Henry Vane, Earl of Darlington. And there they remained, because the colonelcy remained with the head of the Vane family until 1860. When, in 1853, the Durham Militia was expanded to three battalions, two infantry and one artillery, Barnard Castle became the headquarters of the South Durham Militia. As a result of the army reforms instituted by Edward Cardwell after 1871, this unit became the 4th (Extra Reserve) Battalion of the Durham Light Infantry (see REGIMENTS). From 1864, the militia had barracks built at the western end of the Museum Park, which continued in use until after World War I. During World War II Barnard Castle's military role was greatly expanded. In 1940, six camps were built around the town: Barford, Humbleton, Stainton, Streatlam, Woodside north of the river, and Deerbolt south of the river. They became the centre of a battle school for infantry and a training area for the Royal Armoured Corps. Barnard Castle's role as a military training centre lasted until well after 1945. Vestiges of this period in the town's history survive beside its northern approaches, while Deerbolt Camp is now the site of a prison for young offenders.

BARTHOLOMEW OF FARNE, SAINT (?–1193)

Bartholomew was never formally canonised but acquired the status of saint by reputation. He was born, when is not known, at Whitby and his secular name prior to his entry into the monastic life appears to have been Tostig. His early years were adventurous, including a time spent in Norway, where he became a priest. He continued to function as a priest for some time after he returned to England, but increasingly became drawn to the monastic life and in consequence secured admission to the Benedictine priory attached to DURHAM CATHEDRAL. The conventional monastic routine failed to give him complete spiritual satisfaction, however, and he found the idea of an eremitic existence more and more appealing. He was granted permission to occupy the Inner Farne, where ST CUTHBERT had spent many of his later years. Bartholomew's sojourn was much longer: he was a hermit on the Inner Farne, with one very short break, for forty-two years from 1151 until his death there in 1193. An eremitic life being then considered evidence of sanctity, Bartholomew's elevation in the popular estimation to the status of saint is not surprising.

BARTRAM, SIR ROBERT APPLEBY (1835–1925)

Robert Bartram was born at Hylton, SUNDERLAND, the son of a shipwright, George Bartram, who ran a shipbuilding business with his partner, John Lister. After a private education, he served an apprenticeship in his father's yard, becoming his father's sole partner in 1854. The Bartram business remained small, continuing to build wooden ships until George died in 1871, by which time most Sunderland yards were building in iron. At this point, Bartram went into partnership with a George Haswell, who had been trained in building in iron, and set up as Bartram and Haswell at South Dock. When Haswell retired in 1889, Bartram's sons, George and William, came into the business, which was renamed Bartram and Sons (see SHIPBUILDING INDUSTRY).

Bartram had other business interests, notably the chairmanship of a local steelmaker, Samuel Tyzack & Co. Outwith business, his strongest interest was in education. He served for many years on the Hylton and Sunderland School Boards, and following the death in 1910 of his son, George, he donated over £1,000 to assist in the education of shipyard apprentices. In 1921 he gifted £12,500 to Sunderland Borough to advance the work of its technical college. In 1964 the firm he created was taken over by another Sunderland firm, Austin, Pickersgill, and the yard was closed in 1978.

BASTLES

Bastles are a noted feature of the Border zone, particularly in Northumberland, where 230 have been identified. They were built between the middle of the sixteenth and seventeenth centuries and they were the answer to the insecurity of the Border region. Their distribution can be plotted with fair accuracy: they are largely confined to the upland dales of the Rede, the Tyne and the Allen, with smaller numbers in Weardale, Cumberland (Cumbria) and the Scottish Border zone. Their construction appears to be linked to an act of parliament of 1555 requiring the inhabitants of a zone twenty miles south of the Border to make their homes defensible. The mileage was not arbitrary but the perceived maximum distance a small raiding party could cover in a twenty-four-hour incursion. Although a response to the depredations of Border Reivers, they continued to be built in the early seventeenth century after the accession of James VI of Scotland to the throne of England, which should have ended hostilities. In this, they testify to ingrained habits and to a lack of confidence in the permanence of peace.

Bastles were two storeys high and typically were 35 feet (10.7 m) in length and 25 feet (7.6 m) in width. Their walls, up to 4 feet (1.2 m) thick, were constructed of stone, roughly shaped and usually without mortar bonding. Roofs were of slate, resting on A-frames of oak. Entrance to the ground floor was by means of a narrow door in one of the short sides and to the first floor by means of a door in one of the long sides, reached by a retractable ladder, later replaced by a stone stair side-on to the wall. The ground floor had very small apertures for ventilation, but the upper floor had larger windows. The flooring between the two storeys was in some cases of stone flags resting on oak beams; in others the flags rested on a stone barrel vault. Doors were stout, with strong drawbars. The whole was clearly designed to withstand assault by fire and force.

The purpose of the ground floor was to house animals, almost certainly the high-value cattle and horses. The upper storey, which had a fireplace, was the living quarters of the family. It may have been partitioned and there may have been a sleeping loft in the angle of the roof. The concept was a neat adaption of the traditional farmhouse, which had human and animal accommodation side by side under a single roof, the two parts separated by a cross-passage created by wooden screens. Bastles were simply farmhouses built and occupied by tenant farmers and small freeholders.

Confusingly, the term *pele* is sometimes applied to them. In fact, *peles* appear to have been predecessors of bastles, being made of wood and thatched with turf. Unfortunately, none of these earlier structures has survived. This is not so with bastles, the ruins of which can still be seen across the old Border zone. Many others, however, have survived intact and are in use as outhouses or are incorporated into later extensions.

BEAUREPAIRE / BEARPARK

Bearpark is a corruption of Beaurepaire: there was a park, but no evidence of bears. Located on the western outskirts of Durham, at over 1,500 acres (600 ha) the park was one of the largest in medieval England. It was created in the thirteenth century at a time when all landowners with sufficient land appear to have been similarly motivated. Parks served several purposes, including that of 'status symbol'. Beaurepaire, which means 'beautiful retreat', belonged to the Cathedral Priory of Durham and was created out of three major land acquisitions. The first was the village of 'Crukton', granted to the priory by the lord of Witton Gilbert, Gilbert de la Lay, some time before 1213, which the monks depopulated in order to create a farm. To this, two bishops of Durham, Nicholas de Farnham (1241–48) and Robert Stichill (1260–74), added large tracts of moorland on either side of the River Browney. In 1267 the latter also granted the monks licence to enclose the park with a wall, parts of which still survive.

It was in this park that Prior Bertram Middleton decided in 1258 to build a manor house as his retirement home. The result was an extensive complex of domestic quarters, chapel and service buildings, as the partial excavation in the 1980s revealed. Subsequently, the manor house became the principal out-of-town residence of the priors and it was there that they presided over the *ludi* (Latin *ludus*, game), which were occasions, each lasting about two weeks, when groups of monks were invited to reside away from Durham under a relaxed rule. In effect, Beaurepaire became the place where Durham monks took their holidays. The park also had considerable economic value, particularly as a source of building timber and fuel and for grazing cattle, sheep and horses. What the park was not used for, as was the case with parks belonging to lay landlords, was hunting, a pastime in which the Durham monks appear not to have indulged.

When the Cathedral Priory was dissolved and the new regime of dean and chapter was instituted in 1541, Beaurepaire was assigned to the dean's estate. Over the next two centuries it was gradually broken up into discrete farms, many of which are still in being.

It was into this rural situation that industry intruded in the second half of the nineteenth century. First came the railway, built in the 1850s to bring iron ore from the newly discovered Cleveland field to CONSETT. This transport facility made feasible the colliery that was sunk in the early 1870s opposite the ruins of the priory manor, and an attendant village built by the Bearpark Coal and Coke Company, a Middlesbrough concern (see NEW TOWNS OF THE NINETEENTH CENTURY), with the aim of producing coke for the Teesside iron and steel plants. They were very successful; Bearpark coke, especially that produced from the coal of the Busty and Victoria seams, was regarded as the world's finest. Of equal quality were the bricks made from the seggar clay. Until the mid-1920s, Bearpark Colliery regularly mined over 300,000 tons of coal annually. However, like all collieries, its life was no more than about 100 years, and it was closed in April 1984, the day the year-long miners' strike began.

Beaurepaire/Bearpark has one more claim to fame: it was the scene of the BATTLE OF NEVILLE'S CROSS, one of the most important battles of the long Anglo-Scottish war.

BEDE, THE VENERABLE (672/3–735)

Bede, the correct spelling of whose name is Baeda, was and is one of the most important and outstanding men to have been born in Northumbria. As far as we know, he never lived outside the region and only once journeyed south of the Tees, to visit York. However, it should be stressed that what we know of his life is what he chose to tell us in his writings. He was born in 672 or 673 in what is now Tyne and Wear and at the age of seven was given to the monastery of Monkwearmouth, which had been founded the year after his birth by BENEDICT BISCOP. He went through clerical orders in the normal sequence, and was ordained priest at the age of thirty. He spent his entire life, except for his visit to York and another to Lindisfarne (see HOLY ISLAND), in the monastery at Wearmouth or at its sister house at JARROW, founded in the early 680s.

These two monastic houses were physically separate (by 6 miles) but institutionally united. At which one Bede lived most of his life is not clear. Although he entered Monkwearmouth, he has come to be particularly associated with Jarrow, but this is largely because it was from there that his bones were removed in 1022 to the cathedral at DURHAM. Initially, they were buried with ST CUTHBERT, but in 1370 they were transferred to their own tomb in the Galilee Chapel, where they still lie. The lid of the tomb chest bears the legend, carved on the order of BISHOP JOHN COSIN, *HAEC SUNT IN FOSSA, BEDAE VENERABILIS OSSA* ('Here in this grave are the bones of Bede the Venerable'). If the record is correct, it would seem that he began his monastic life at Monkwearmouth but at some stage moved to Jarrow. We are also not told which sector of society he came from. Most of the leaders of the early church in Northumbria are known to have come from noble families; Bede's reticence and the fact that he never held high office, either in or beyond his monastery, may indicate an origin further down the social scale.

What is not in doubt is the quality of his work, for which he was famed in his own lifetime and thereafter. Bede was a true academic, devoting his whole life to the three scholastic imperatives: teaching, research and publication. Academics today still recognise with approval his concern to consult as many sources as possible and his pains in checking his facts. In the course of about thirty years he wrote twenty-nine books. That fifteen of them were works of exegesis of books of the Bible across its entire spectrum from Genesis to Revelation, shows where his main interest lay. Added to his biblical commentaries, he also wrote five hagiographies, a book of homilies and at least sixteen hymns. He also entered the field of science. His concerns were establishing the correct method of calculating the date of Easter and dating the Six Ages of the World. To this end, he wrote two books on the subject: *De Temporibus* (*On Times*) in 703 and *De Temporum Ratione* (*On the Computation of Times*) in 725, as well as expounding his views in letters to three monks, one of whom, Plegwin, was in the monastery at HEXHAM. For Bede, both these matters were of great religious importance.

His writings were copied and found their way to most parts of Western Europe, and remained important to the world of scholarship throughout the medieval centuries. For us, however, the one that really matters is the last one he wrote, *The Ecclesiastical History of the English People.* This book is important because it is the main, and for many matters the only, source of information we have about the years following the end of Roman control until his own time. In reading it, therefore, it is important to recognise that, for all Bede's adherence to the canons of scholarship, he wrote with an ideological purpose. For all his cautious concern for accuracy, we should remember that his writing is littered with miracle stories, which most people today would discount and dismiss.

Bede's purpose was to reveal what he saw as God's purpose, which was to use His chosen people, the English, to bring the peoples of the island of Britain to Christianity. What is not entirely clear is how precisely Bede defined the English. In places he seems to suggest the Angles, thus excluding the Saxons, but at times he seems to be implying something even narrower, the Northumbrians or even the Bernicians. Bede was, in modern terms, something of a nationalist. For him, God's main agents were the royal house of Bernicia. In pursuing this line, Bede had to square the circle by giving an honourable role to the pagan

Bernician king, Aethelfrith (see NORTHUMBRIA, KINGDOM AND EARLDOM OF). Here, the Old Testament came to his aid: he cast Aethelfrith in the role of Saul, the precursor of the great king, OSWALD, the David of his story. Even here, Bede was in some difficulty, since Oswald introduced the Irish form of Christianity, whereas Bede was a passionate and totally committed advocate of the Roman style. But all came right in 664, when Oswald's successor, OSWIU, decided at the Synod of Whitby that Roman ways should replace Irish forms.

In modern eyes Bede may appear bigoted. He hated and despised paganism, but he was able to excuse it on the grounds that, until the arrival of missionaries with the Christian message, its adherents knew no better. What he hated more, therefore, were the British Christians, who he knew had rejected the Roman mission under St Augustine: to him, they were perverse in refusing to abandon their erroneous ways. He also disliked Irish ways, since they were at variance with Roman practices, and were only approved of in the likes of AIDAN because he was not aware of the 'true faith'. This helps to explain why Bede was so obsessed with the question of how to date Easter, an obsession that actually seems rather odd, given that the Roman style had been adopted in Northumbria several years before he was born.

These reservations are necessary if the true value of Bede's history is to be properly perceived and appreciated. Bede was a polymath and a man of surpassing intellect, whose history was a tremendous work of scholarship, without which the so-called Dark Ages would have been almost totally black.

BEDLINGTON

Bedlington's early history is distinctive. Between 900 and 915 it was acquired for the Congregation of St Cuthbert (see CUTHBERT, SAINT), then residing at CHESTER LE STREET, by its leader, Bishop Cuthheard. The purchase included not only Bedlington but also its associated townships: Choppington, Netherton, Sleekburn (later East and West Sleekburn) and Cambois. The whole was known as Bedlingtonshire and it became part of the PALATINATE OF DURHAM and was formally made part of County Durham in 1512. At the Reformation, however, the lands belonging to the Bishop of Durham were taken by the Crown, which retained them until the middle of the seventeenth century, when they were sold to a member of the Fenwick family. Bedlingtonshire continued as an anomaly until 1844, when, together with NORTH DURHAM, it was transferred by act of parliament to Northumberland.

Bedlington was one of the region's leading pioneers in iron manufacture. In 1736 the Bebside Slitting Mill was founded and some years later the Bedlington Iron Works was started on the opposite side of the River Blyth, to make iron using local raw materials. The two enterprises came into the same ownership in 1782. The ironworks enjoyed its greatest period of prosperity in the first half of the nineteenth century, when it was managed and, after 1850, owned by Michael Longridge. It was Longridge who persuaded GEORGE STEPHENSON that the wrought iron rails, which he patented in 1820, were superior to those made of cast iron. Longridge went on to supply Stephenson with boilerplates, axles and wheels, as well as rails, and in 1837 began to build locomotives. In fact, the first train to leave King's Cross station in London was hauled by an engine supplied by the Bedlington Iron Co., which also supplied the first locomotives to run in Holland and Russia. Longridge retired and sold the company in 1853, at which date he was employing about 2,000 men. Over the following fourteen years it had three other owners, including John Dixon. But in 1867 it was closed, basically because after 1850 the iron industry rapidly shifted to Teesside, following the opening of the Cleveland ore field.

Bedlington is now more widely known for the Bedlington Terrier, although in the nineteenth century it was also known as the Rothbury Terrier. Of curious appearance, more akin to a lamb than a dog, and at between fifteen and seventeen inches high, it is very tall for a terrier. Its height, which was the consequence of the inclusion of the Whippet in its breeding, gave it speed, which made it ideal for hunting rabbits. It is because of this that it is said to have been popular with poachers and to have acquired the nickname 'Gypsy Dog'.

BEILBY, WILLIAM (1740–1819), RALPH (1743–1817) and MARY (1749–1797)

William, Ralph and Mary Beilby were the children of William Beilby, senior, who was born in Scarborough but in 1733 moved to Durham City, where he married Mary Bainbridge. By trade, Beilby was a silversmith and jeweller, and by all accounts a good one. But he was not a good businessman, and as a result of the failure of his business the family moved to Gateshead in 1759.

That their fortunes recovered was largely due to the business acumen of Ralph Beilby. After education at the grammar school in Durham, he trained in Birmingham as a silversmith and jeweller, but then added copper engraving and seal cutting to his range of skills. He soon had a thriving business at Amen Corner by St Nicholas Church, Newcastle (now the Anglican cathedral). It was there that in 1767 he took as an apprentice the fourteen-year-old Thomas Bewick. Ten years later the two men became partners, and produced a number of works, most notably *A General History of Quadrupeds*, Beilby supplying the text, while Bewick engraved the illustrations. A quarrel between the two men led to the dissolution of the partnership in 1798. Shortly afterwards, Beilby set up in business with another partner, making watch glasses and clock parts. Ralph Beilby retired in 1807 and died ten years later.

Ralph Beilby was a skilled craftsman with a good head for business, but the genius of the family was his older brother, William. Born in Durham City, he too was educated at the ancient grammar school before family impoverishment led to his being sent in 1755 to Bilston near Birmingham to learn the craft of enamelling. Upon his return north in 1760, he developed a process for enamelling lead crystal wine glasses, goblets and bowls. This involved mixing a metal flux with the pigments and firing the painted vessels at an exact temperature. To achieve this, he worked in conjunction with the furnace makers at glassworks in Closegate in Newcastle to design a furnace that prevented fumes getting to the enamel. As a result, his enamel paintings, especially heraldic arms, were brilliant in colour and completely bonded to the glass. Equally important was William Beilby's talent as an artist: his designs were accurate and his execution of the highest standard. Some, but not all, of his pieces were signed, and many bore his hallmark, a butterfly. His artwork was done at the workshop of his brother Ralph at Amen Corner, but the firing of the painted articles was carried out at the glassworks of John Williams & Co.

All Beilby's output was produced between 1761 and 1779, in which year he moved to London. Why he did so is hard to fathom. One factor may have been the death of his mother, Mary Beilby, who seems to have been the strength of the family; but there were also commercial problems for the glass industry because of high taxation.

Whatever the reason, the subsequent history of William Beilby is not entirely clear. He is known to have settled in Battersea, working as a schoolmaster. In 1785, he married an Ellen Purton of Putney, the niece of a wealthy man named Falconer. Three years later, Falconer went to live on an estate he had purchased in Scotland, taking William and Ellen with him. When Falconer died in 1798 leaving his wealth to his niece, William and Ellen left Scotland and settled in Hull. It was there, at 4 English Street, that William Beilby died on 8 October 1819. He is buried in the old cemetery of Holy Trinity Church.

Little is known about Mary Beilby, but it is important to note that William, to whom she was very close, taught her to paint in enamel on glass. Although none of the Beilby pieces bears her signature, it seems likely that a few are wholly or partly by her. She seems to have hoped to marry Thomas Bewick, but their ages and circumstances prevented this, and a few years later she suffered a stroke. When William abandoned the glass painting business, she accompanied him to London and lived with him in Battersea and then in Scotland until her death in 1797.

The work of William Beilby, although small in quantity, is both art and craft of the highest quality and deservedly has an international admiration.

BELL, GERTRUDE (1868–1926)

Gertrude Bell was one of the most influential people involved in the shaping of the political geography and structure of the Middle East in the years immediately after the end of World War I. The daughter of Hugh Bell and the granddaughter of Sir Isaac Lowthian Bell, one of the most influential figures in the region's iron and steel industry, she was born at Washington Hall in 1868. She grew up to be a highly intelligent, if snobbish and intellectually arrogant, woman, who at the age of twenty and after only two years' study, achieved a First in Modern History at Oxford, although the regulations then in force did not permit her as a woman to take the degree. Her interest in the Middle East, then part of the Turkish Ottoman Empire, began in 1892. In that year, she accepted an invitation from a relative of her stepmother to visit Baghdad. There she fell in love with Henry Cadogan, a penniless aristocrat, who was First Secretary at the Embassy. Because of his lack of means, Gertrude's father forbade the marriage. Shortly afterwards, Cadogan died and Gertrude threw herself into a life of travel.

In the course of the next twenty years she travelled widely, increasingly in the Arab lands of the Ottoman Empire, teaching herself Persian and Arabic and acquiring expert knowledge of, and doing seminal research in, the archaeology of the region. She published a number of important works, notably *The Churches and Monasteries of Tur Abdin*, based on the survey she made between 1911 and 1913, and *The Palace and Mosque of Ukhaidir* (1914). Her diaries and letters contain a wealth of information about the region and its people, acquired through careful and acute observation and close interrogation. This became of considerable military value in World War I, when the Ottoman Empire became an ally of Germany. In 1916, she joined the Arab Bureau, an adjunct to the army's intelligence branch at General Headquarters in Cairo. Among her significant contributions was to advise her friend T.E. Lawrence prior to his epic exploits in helping to defeat the Turks, in particular urging him to ally with Ibn Saud and to seize the port of Aqaba. After the expulsion of the Turks from Baghdad in 1917, she was appointed Oriental Secretary in the civil administration of what was then called Mesopotamia and through her office she was able to exercise considerable influence.

In the immediate post-war years, her political importance was at its height. She demonstrated her mastery of the issues in her 1920 White Paper, *Review of the Civil Administration of Mesopotamia*. Following the conference held at San Remo at which the League of Nations gave Britain a mandate to govern the area, the Mesopotamia Conference, held in Cairo in 1921, created the new state of Iraq. Bell's influence was considerable. She was very largely responsible for defining Iraq's boundaries with Kuwait, Saudi Arabia and Turkey. The result was an artificial state containing an ethnic and religious mix full of inherent tension: although the majority of Iraqis were Shias, there was a substantial Sunni minority; and there was a significant Kurdish population that was denied union with fellow Kurds in Turkey. Convinced that democracy would not suit the Arabs, she favoured a monarchy 'advised' by a British High Commission, a view that became British policy. As regards the person of the monarch, Bell secured the selection of her choice, Faisal ibn Hussein (who claimed descent from the Prophet) despite his being a Sunni.

She was to regret her work: as with Lawrence, depression followed success. After the new constitution came into operation in 1924, her influence waned: Faisal proved to be a poor choice, and once on the throne, he gradually marginalised her. Nor was she happy with what she regarded as excessive British control.

However, with her political influence on the wane she returned increasingly to her original interest, archaeology. It was in this field that she made a truly worthwhile contribution, not only to the state she had helped to create, but also beyond it to the wider world. This was the National Museum in Baghdad, opened in 1926, of which she was the fundraiser, driving force and Director, and for which she is still favourably remembered. If she is one of those on whom blame for the present travails of the region can be laid, she deserves praise for her efforts to rescue and conserve the remains of the 'cradle of civilisation'.

Bell died of an overdose just before her fifty-eighth birthday, although whether this was suicide or accident is uncertain. Her library of around 2,000 books and thousands of photographs she took at archaeological sites in the Middle East, and also her letters to her family, were given to Armstrong College by her sister, Lady Richmond, and are housed in the Robinson Library of Newcastle University.

BELL, SIR ISAAC LOWTHIAN, Bt (1816–1904)

Lowthian Bell, one of the giants of the North East's iron and steel industries, was the son of a Cumberland (Cumbria) man, Thomas Bell, who moved to NEWCASTLE in 1808 to join the alkali and iron makers, Losh & Co., which later became the Walker Iron Works of Losh, Wilson and Bell. Thomas Bell gave his son a first-class scientific education: after his school years at Dr Bruce's famous academy in Newcastle, he was sent to study in Germany, Denmark, Edinburgh University and the Sorbonne in Paris. When he joined his father's firm in 1835 he was fully prepared for a career in a science-based industry.

Bell's career as an industrialist really began in the mid-1840s: in 1844, in conjunction with his two brothers, Thomas and John, he started an iron smelting business, known as Bell Bros, at Wylam; and in the following year, after the death of his father, he took over the management of Losh, Wilson and Bell at Walker. In the 1850s, however, with the discovery of the extent of the iron ore field in the Cleveland Hills, the iron industry shifted south to Teesside. Bell obtained leases of the right to extract ore on the Normanby and Skelton estates and promoted a railway to bring the ore to the south bank of the Tees, whence it was taken across the river to the ironworks at Port Clarence on the north bank. Like the other major players in the industry, he recognised the benefits of horizontal integration and as a result he acquired limestone quarries in Weardale and coal mines at Browney, Brancepeth and Tursdale, which by 1890 were producing nearly 600,000 tons of coking coal per annum. Some of these developments were made in conjunction with RALPH WARD JACKSON, the founder of West Hartlepool (see NEW TOWNS OF THE NINETEENTH CENTURY). In the mid-1860s Bell sold his railway lines to the North Eastern Railway, of which he was made a director, a position that enabled him to keep his transport costs to a minimum. Like all other iron makers, Bell Bros went over to steel in the 1880s. At the end of the following decade, during a period of mergers in the industry, Bell Bros merged with one of the region's other great steelmakers, Dorman, Long (see DORMAN, SIR ARTHUR JOHN, BT).

By accident, Bell Bros were also blessed with another industrial asset, salt. In 1874, a bore sunk near their Port Clarence ironworks to a depth of 1,127 feet (344 m) revealed the existence of a salt bed 80 feet (24 m) thick. Exploitation of this asset did not begin until early in the next decade, but by 1883 Bell Bros were producing over 300 tons of salt per week. The delay was caused by the need to master the French technique of liquifying the salt by pumping hot water down to the bed and then pumping up the resulting brine.

Lowthian Bell was never a mere businessman. As a result of his extensive early education, he was deeply interested in the science and technology of iron and steel making and how experiments could lead to more economical methods of production. He furthered his knowledge by making numerous trips abroad, especially to America, to study the methods used in other countries. He also wrote six scholarly papers for the *Journal of the Iron and Steel Institute*, and he published two major studies: *Chemical Phenomena of Iron Smelting* (1872) and *The Principles of the Manufacture of Iron and Steel* (1884). Bell was recognised as the foremost British authority on the science and technology of iron and steel making, and his opinions were always sought and generally accepted. His eminence in the theoretical aspects of his industry was recognised by his election as a Fellow of the Royal Society in 1875 and by the award of honorary doctorates by the universities of Durham, Edinburgh, Dublin and Leeds. He also played a major part in the public life of the region, being twice Mayor of Newcastle, Deputy Lieutenant of Durham from 1875 until 1880, and an MP for the Hartlepools. He was a staunch Liberal and a supporter of Gladstone, who proposed him as FRS and awarded him a baronetcy in 1885.

BELL, RICHARD (c.1410–c.1495)

Richard Bell, who was very much the churchman on the make, was born in or around 1410, almost certainly in Durham. In 1426 or 1427, when he would have been sixteen or seventeen years of age (the normal age for monastic recruits), he was admitted as a novice to the Cathedral Priory of Durham. Of above average scholastic ability, in 1431 he was sent to Durham College, Oxford (see OXFORD UNIVERSITY COLLEGES), where he spent the next ten years on the course for the MA. Between 1441 and 1443, he appears to have been 'loaned' to the small monastery of Holy Trinity in York, to act as its prior. In the latter year, however, he returned to Durham, where in the following seven years he filled a number of minor administrative posts. He then returned to Oxford to take his BTh and also to act as warden. Back in

Durham in 1453, he rapidly rose to become Sub-Prior, the second in command of the establishment. Consequently, when Prior William Ebchester decided to retire in 1456, Bell was in line for the top job. But in a hard-fought election the majority of his fellow monks favoured John Burnaby. As the defeated candidate, his fate was to be exiled to FINCHALE as Prior of the cathedral's largest cell. His banishment lasted seven years. Then, in 1464, Burnaby died suddenly and this time Bell's claim could not be denied and he was elected prior.

Bell remained in office for twelve years, during which time he began the reconstruction of the central tower of the cathedral: what we see today is essentially his work, although he did not live to see it completed. His priorate was not brought to an end by either death or retirement. Instead, in 1478 he was made Bishop of Carlisle. It seems clear that he had long held the ambition of becoming a bishop and his success probably owed much to his having curried favour with Richard, Duke of Gloucester (the future Richard III), then the dominant power in the north. Achieving his ambition did not satisfy Bell, who also sought to remain Prior of Durham, possibly because he was well aware that the bishop's income in Carlisle was less than that of the Priory of Durham. He did not succeed: the monks of Durham asserted their independence and elected a new prior. Bell remained at Carlisle until 1495, when he resigned, possibly because of failing health. When he died is not known, but he was buried in his cathedral, where his grave still carries a splendid brass, which is more than he would have achieved had he remained in Durham.

BELSAY

The Belsay site, now in the care of English Heritage, comprises two buildings of major historical and architectural importance linked by a unique garden. From before 1270 until 1962 it belonged to the Middleton family, except for several decades after 1317, when it was confiscated following the conviction and execution of SIR GILBERT DE MIDDLETON.

The central feature of the earlier building, Belsay Castle, is a BORDER TOWER, arguably the finest surviving example in the entire ANGLO-SCOTTISH BORDER region. The date of its construction is not known, but some time in the last quarter of the fourteenth century is most likely. We now know that it was not built as a free-standing tower but as an addition to an earlier building, almost certainly a thirteenth-century hall-house. The tower was a proud statement of the family's wealth and importance but with the practical purpose of giving greater protection against Scottish attacks. It has been suggested that there were other buildings, which would have made the castle a far more complex and impressive structure. Further excavation will be required to confirm this hypothesis. The need for defensive measures against Scottish incursions was eliminated by the accession of James VI of Scotland to the English throne in 1603. And so in 1614 Thomas Middleton added a two-storey wing in Jacobean style, to which a further addition was made about a hundred years later by Sir John Middleton (1678–1717).

The castle continued as the home of the Middletons until Christmas Day 1817, when Sir Charles Monck (1779–1867) moved the family into the newly completed Belsay Hall. Monck had been born Charles Middleton, but had changed his name to comply with the will of his maternal grandfather, Sir Arthur Monck, which made the change a condition of inheriting Monck's Lincolnshire estate. Monck's decision to build the Hall was the outcome of wealth and a fascination with classical architecture. The design of the Hall was entirely his and was the product of his study of classical architecture made while on an extended honeymoon between 1804 and 1806, which he and his wife spent travelling through Germany, the Austrian Empire and Greece. The result reveals a clear intention that the Hall should be reminiscent of a Greek temple and in this he is thought to have been particularly influenced by the so-called Temple of Theseus in Athens. The Hall took ten years to build, between 1807 and 1817, and is in a severely restrained Doric style.

Between the Hall and the Castle, and intentionally linking the two, is a remarkable garden, which progesses from a formal layout immediately next to the Hall, through a seemingly natural woodland to a wild 'romantic' climax created out of the quarries formed by the excavation of stone to build the Hall. To complete the uninterrupted complex of Hall-Garden-Castle required the removal of the original village of Belsay, which bordered a road running between the Castle and the garden that was a continuation of the drive leading to the Hall. Sir Charles Monck replaced it with the present village alongside what was then the Ponteland Turnpike, now the A696 from Newcastle to Otterburn.

BENEDICT BISCOP (628–690)

Arguably more than any other individual, Benedict Biscop was responsible for providing the means for the religious and artistic achievements of the 'Golden Age of Northumbria', although he did so by chance rather than long-planned intent. He was born in 628, when the KINGDOM OF NORTHUMBRIA was still pagan. Like so many of the religious leaders who drove the conversion to Christianity in the next two generations, he was the son of a nobleman, and as such he served in the household of KING OSWIU. Had he pursued a conventional career, he would doubtless have become a warrior and in later life a landowner. But in 653, at the age of twenty-five, he abandoned the normal ways of his kind and set out on a journey to Rome. We can only assume that he found the secular career for which he had been prepared of declining appeal and that he was increasingly drawn to the spiritual and intellectual life opened up by the new religion. It was a bold decision, since the journey to Rome was long and dangerous. However, at Canterbury, he fell in with a fellow Northumbrian, WILFRID, and they decided to journey together for greater security. At Lyon, however, they parted company, Biscop continuing to Rome alone, possibly the first Englishman to set foot in that city.

Our knowledge of him during the next eleven years is almost nil, except for one fact of major importance: between 665 and 667, he became a monk at the famous island monastery of Lerins opposite Cannes. He then returned to Rome, where he was recruited by Pope Vitalian to act as an interpreter to accompany the Greek, Theodore of Tarsus, Vitalian's appointee as the new Archbishop of Canterbury. His sojourn there lasted from 669 until 671, when he decided to return to Rome for the fourth time. On his return to England, he went to the court of the West Saxon king, Cenwalh, with whom he was on very friendly terms. Had Cenwalh not died shortly after, it is likely that Biscop would have ended his days in the south. It was his friend's death that caused him to return to Northumbria.

There he secured the patronage of its king, ECGFRITH, who in 674 provided him with sufficient land on the north bank of the Wear to support a monastery at Monkwearmouth and seven years later, in 681, gave him more land on the south bank of the Tyne to enable him to found a twin monastery at JARROW. Both houses were built in stone by masons were imported from Gaul, where Roman building methods had survived. This was a revolutionary move: the Anglo-Saxons constructed all their buildings in wood and were ignorant of masonry techniques. Not only did the Gaulish masons build, they also transmitted their skills to English craftsmen. In addition, glaziers were brought over to glaze the monastic windows and taught their skills, which were also unknown to the English.

In the seven years between the two foundations, he made yet another visit to Rome, accompanied by CEOLFRITH, whom he was to place in charge of the Jarrow project. This time his purpose was more focused: to acquire for his monastery the books, pictures and vessels needed for worship and study. The result was that Jarrow/Monkwearmouth was equipped with one of the finest libraries north of the Alps and the means whereby English craftsmen could learn Mediterranean styles of calligraphy and painting. These books and artistic exemplars made possible such achievements as the *CODEX AMIATINUS* and the writings of BEDE. He also persuaded John the Archchanter (Precentor) of St Peter's in Rome to come to Monkwearmouth to teach the Gregorian chant. Nor was he satisfied with what he had acquired, for between 681 and 686 he made a sixth journey to Rome in order to acquire yet more books.

Biscop died in 690 at the age of sixty-two. He was devoted to the monastic life and to the ways and styles of the Roman church. He was not, however, a missionary or a noted teacher and perhaps because of this he never achieved sainthood, yet his contribution to the Christianisation of England was far greater than many who have been beatified. And he gave to Northumbria the means of becoming the most advanced cultural and artistic centre in Europe.

BERNICIA, KINGDOM OF (see NORTHUMBRIA, KINGDOM AND EARLDOM OF)

BE-RO

Be-Ro flour and baking powder (tartaric acid plus sodium bicarbonate) were products of a wholesale grocery firm located in NEWCASTLE founded in the 1880s by Thomas Bell. Originally these products were marketed under the label 'Bell's Royal', but in the early twentieth century the unauthorised use of the word 'Royal' in commercial products became illegal. Thomas Bell's solution was to relabel his products using the first two letters of Bell's Royal, hence Be-Ro.

After World War I, the firm pioneered self-raising flour; hitherto cooks had added baking powder to plain flour, at their discretion. To promote this new product the firm mounted a series of exhibitions where scones, cakes and pastries baked with it were sold at low prices. On the same occasions they also distributed free copies of a recipe book. This was the start of the famous Be-Ro cookery book. The first edition, published in 1923, ran to nineteen pages and had a picture on the cover of a local woman, baking. Very soon, the *Be-Ro Recipe Book* became an indispensable kitchen item. The book has gone through forty editions and is now eighty-six pages long. With sales exceeding thirty-eight million, it is one of the world's best-selling cookery books.

The firm was acquired in 1958 by Rank Hovis, which in 1961 became Rank Hovis McDougall.

BERWICK UPON TWEED

Berwick is unique: beginning life as a rural community (its name means barley farm) in the English KINGDOM OF NORTHUMBRIA, it became a Scottish town, which was then annexed by England. The whereabouts of the Anglo-Saxon settlement are uncertain, but the area known as Bondington, with its implication of a farming settlement, is a strong possibility. And it was as a farming settlement that it became part of the Kingdom of Scotland around the year 1000. The Royal Burgh of Berwick and its castle were, as was the case in many other places, additions to a pre-existing village. The founder was the King of Scots, David I (1124–53), who in the course of his reign Normanised much of his kingdom. Among other moves, this involved creating 'shires', local administrative units, modelled on those in England, at the centre of which he built a castle to which he attached a burgh, the function of which was to stimulate economic activity. In charge of each shire, with the castle as his centre of operations, was a royal officer, the sheriff. Contemporary with Berwick were similar developments at Roxburgh, Peebles and Selkirk.

This situation continued until the end of the thirteenth century, and during this time Berwick grew and prospered greatly: by 1290 it had become the chief port of Scotland and probably its largest town, its importance indicated by its description as 'the second Alexandria'. At this date, it was probably a larger town than Newcastle.

All this came to an end on 30 March 1296, when it was captured and sacked by the English army of Edward I. This was the opening act of a war between England and Scotland that was not finally ended until 1603, 307 years later, when James VI, the King of Scots, became also King of England. Contemporary reports say that the capture of Berwick was accompanied by a massacre of its citizens, although the extent of the atrocity cannot be verified. Edward I's victory was made easy by Berwick's lack of serious defences, probably no more than a ditch and a wooden palisade. This was partially remedied in the following decades by the construction of a wall of stone by the English, which was later heightened by the Scots. With the building of the wall, medieval Berwick achieved its final medieval form.

But ownership of it was far from resolved. The English held town and castle until 1318, during which time English settlers were imported to turn it into an English town. This phase ended on 28 March 1318, when Berwick fell to the army of Robert I (Bruce). Both town and castle remained in Scottish hands until the summer of 1333, when, following the defeat of a Scottish army at Halidon Hill, just north of the town, they surrendered to the army of Edward III. Thereafter, it changed hands on five further occasions. Four of these were very brief interludes in 1355, 1378, 1384 and 1405. The fifth occasion was much longer, lasting twenty-one years. It began in 1461, when Queen Margaret, wife of Henry VI, voluntarily surrendered Berwick to the Scots, as the price of Scottish help in her attempt to regain the throne for her inept husband and their son. Her move failed; Henry VI was captured and deposed by his rival, Edward IV. It remained in Scottish hands until 1482, when Richard, Duke of Gloucester (Edward IV's brother and later Richard III) recovered it. Since then Berwick has remained in English hands, although, until 1603, continued English possession was the major stumbling block to a final and permanent peace treaty between the two kingdoms.

It was in the last phase of the war that Berwick was transformed more radically than at any other time since the building of the castle and the foundation of the burgh. This was the building of the ramparts, still the town's most noted feature, between the last year of the reign of Mary I and the first twelve years of that of her half-sister, Elizabeth I. The decision to modernise Berwick's defences was stimulated by the loss in January 1558 of Calais, the counterpart to

Berwick in France. What made it urgent, however, was the knowledge that Berwick's medieval walls could not withstand serious bombardment by siege cannon. The building of the ramparts was not, however, the first occasion on which improvements to the town's defences had been made or planned. In the early 1520s, two bulwarks or artillery strong points had been built: the Windmill Bulwark outside the east wall, and the Bulwark by the Sands at the entrance to the river mouth. Then in 1539–40 another artillery strong point, known as the Lord's Mount, was built at the north-eastern corner of the medieval town walls. Both of these developments by Henry VIII's government were little more than gestures. In the 1550s, however, a completely radical solution was undertaken: the construction of an up-to-date citadel, strong enough to withstand artillery bombardment, across the medieval wall near its south-eastern corner. A start was made on this project, but it was not completed. Instead, late in the reign of Mary I, a new scheme was devised by the most experienced English military engineer of his day, Sir Richard Lee, who had been responsible for fortifying Portsmouth in the 1540s.

The plan was for a much smaller town within the perimeter of the medieval walls. It was to be surrounded by ramparts comprising 20 feet (6 m) of earth faced with stone and fronted by a ditch 20 feet deep. The ramparts were to be reinforced at strategic points by six bastions shaped like arrowheads, from which artillery could cover the face of the ramparts as well as fire on any frontal assault. The concept, derived from Italian examples, was to be state-of-the-art. In 1564, during the course of construction, the government called in an Italian expert, Giovanni Portinari, who recommended an alternative solution, namely a rampart with bastions across the peninsula between the river and the sea. Although Lee successfully resisted this, he was not allowed to realise his original plan. When building work ceased in 1570, the new ramparts with five bastions facing north and east were complete to defend the vulnerable landward sides of the town, but along the river frontage the medieval wall was retained. Moreover, the intention to heighten the ramparts with an upper level of impacted earth, which was part of the original plan, was not carried out.

Consequently, the new defences had a half-baked quality. The basic reason was cost. Was the expenditure worth it? Probably not: neither English nor Scots military men who inspected the new defences thought that they were capable of withstanding a concerted assault. But perhaps the most significant fact about the Elizabethan ramparts is that they enclosed an area no more than two-thirds of that of the medieval walls. They are a testimony to the extent to which Berwick suffered by its position on the 'wrong' side of a front line.

Berwick's new defences were built at a time when the religious allegiance of both England and Scotland was being determined. One consequence of this was the brief sojourn in the town of John Knox, the great prophet of the first phase of the Scottish Reformation. In 1549 Knox was released from the French galleys on the intervention of the English government, who gave him a licence to preach in Berwick. He remained in the town for almost two years, until he moved to Newcastle at the end of 1550.

Although the middle decades of the seventeenth century were a time of civil war throughout the British Isles, Berwick got off lightly. What survives from this era are two pieces of peaceful architecture. One is what is now called the Old Bridge. By 1603, the existing wooden bridge was in a parlous state, a fact tartly commented upon by James VI as he crossed the Tweed on his way to London. The problem became acute five years later, when the bridge was seriously damaged. The driving force behind the new structure, which was to be of stone, was George Home, Earl of Dunbar, the man appointed by James to enforce law along the Border. Building began in 1611, but Home died in the same year and so the work dragged on until 1626. The bridge, which was designed by a Berwick man, James Burrell, is 388 yards (355 m) long and has fifteen arches, the highest (the second arch from Berwick) being 45 feet (14 m) above water level to allow the passage of masted vessels. The sixth arch from Berwick was also significant in that it marked the boundary between Berwick, which was then in Northumberland, and Tweedmouth, which until 1844 was in Durham. The other building of this period is the present parish church of Holy Trinity, one of very few to be built during the Interregnum between 1649 and 1660. The man responsible was COLONEL GEORGE FENWICK.

In 1657, the year George Fenwick died, Berwick Corporation became the owner of Tweedmouth and Spital on the south side of the Tweed. Tweedmouth was a village in NORTH DURHAM, that part of what is now Northumberland belonging to the Bishop of Durham, and was in the parish of HOLY ISLAND. Spital was originally that part of Tweedmouth granted to a small leper hospital founded in the thirteenth century, which disappeared before the Reformation. In the sixteenth century, Tweedmouth and Spital had come into the ownership of the Howard family, which acquired a considerable amount of property in the county. In 1657 James Howard, Earl of Suffolk, sold the land to the Corporation of Berwick for £570. By this transaction, Tweedmouth became owned by, but not part of, Berwick.

The eighteenth century also saw the construction of two notable buildings. The earlier was the Ravensdown Barracks, the first purpose-built barracks in Britain. Building began in 1717, urgency being given by the JACOBITE UPRISING two years earlier, and was completed in 1725. The impetus came from the Duke of Marlborough, then Master General of the Ordnance. The design was basically that of Nicholas Hawksmoor, the architect of the duke's palace at Blenheim, although changes were made in the course of construction by Captain Thomas Phillips, the resident engineer, and the master mason, Andrew Jelfe. The barracks as completed in 1725 had two ranges of buildings; the third range, that facing the entrance, was added in 1739–41. The barracks was the depot of the King's Own Scottish Borderers (see REGIMENTS) from 1881 until 1964, when their removal to Glencorse in Edinburgh brought to an end Berwick's long history as a military town. The eighteenth century's other gift to Berwick was the town hall, built between 1750 and 1761 to replace its sixteenth-century predecessor. Although plans were obtained from a London architect, those finally adopted were drawn by a local man, Joseph Dodds.

This middle period of the eighteenth century saw the quickening of Berwick's economy. The early sign was the expansion of the salmon trade supplying the London market. This was made possible by the development of a distinctive vessel, the Berwick Smack. With a very large area of sail and a crew of ten, it was designed to get the fish to London in quick time. Built in Berwick, they were increased in size to become passenger ships as well, and for several decades they were the fastest means of transport between Berwick and Edinburgh, and London.

Eventually these vessels were superseded by the railway. What is now the East Coast Main Line between London and Edinburgh was formally completed by the opening of the Royal Border Bridge by Queen Victoria on 29 August 1850, although trains had been crossing the Tweed since 1848 by means of a temporary wooden structure. The bridge, designed by ROBERT STEPHENSON, is 2,160 yards long (1,975 m) and has twenty-eight arches. Within a very short distance of its northern end is Berwick Station, built in the 1840s by the North British Railway Company as part of its line from Edinburgh to Berwick. As passengers can still see from the fragmentary and not particularly well-preserved remains at the side of the line, it was built on the site of Berwick Castle. The virtual obliteration of the castle symbolises the end of the medieval and the start of the modern world. Transport by sea, however, did not entirely die out. The building of the new pier between 1810 and 1821 and the opening of the Tweed Dock at Tweedmouth in 1872 ensured that Berwick could function as a modern port. These developments were facilitated by the creation of an enlarged Berwick as the result of the Municipal Corporations Act of 1835, which joined Tweedmouth and Spital to Berwick and by the setting up of the Harbour Commission.

As before and subsequently, transport facilities enabled the economy to grow. A range of industries were founded and flourished for shorter or longer periods. But they were on a small scale. Berwick did not become an industrial giant like its rival, Newcastle upon Tyne, and it had no hope of regaining the parity it had once enjoyed with Edinburgh.

BEWICK, THOMAS (1753–1828)

Thomas Bewick is probably the most widely known and greatly appreciated artist to be born in the North East. He was the son of John Bewick, who, in addition to having a small farm at Cherryburn near Elringham, leased a landsale colliery at Mickley. In his youth, Bewick showed great interest in nature and drawing, and after attending schools at Mickley and then Ovingham, he was apprenticed in 1767 at the age of fourteen to RALPH BEILBY. Early in his apprenticeship he was introduced by the mathematician Charles Hutton to engraving on wood, the medium he employed for his illustrations for Hutton's book, *A Treatise on Mensuration*, published in Newcastle in 1768 by Thomas Saint. Bewick's ability was such that, at the end of his apprenticeship, he was awarded seven guineas from the Society for the Encouragement of Arts and Manufactures for some illustrations he had done for children's books.

Following the end of his apprenticeship, Bewick, like many of today's university graduates, took 'time off'. After working at home for a short time, he went on a long walking tour of the Lake District and Scotland. He also went to London, but finding the capital uncongenial, his stay was brief. Back on Tyneside in 1777, he rejoined his old master as a partner. It was some years later that Bewick proposed to Beilby that they collaborate on a book on animals, Beilby writing the text and Bewick doing the illustrations. The result was *A General History of Quadrupeds*, published in 1790 by Solomon Hodgson, a Newcastle bookseller and editor of the *Newcastle Chronicle*. Bewick not only produced 200 engravings of the animals described in the text, but also introduced 103 vignettes of Northumbrian scenes as tailpieces.

The work was a success and prompted the partners to embark on a similar venture devoted to British birds. In 1797 the first volume, *History of British Birds (Land Birds)*, was published. This, however, brought to a head the rift between the two men that ended their partnership. The issue was Bewick's claim to part-authorship of the book as well as being its illustrator, which Beilby rejected, insisting that he was the sole author. But behind this there may have been a more general tension between the two men, stretching back to Bewick's apprenticeship days. Where the fault lay is not entirely clear, but probably at least part of the blame should be attributed to Bewick, who is known to have been a difficult character on occasions. Consequently, on publication of the book in 1797, the partnership was formally dissolved: Beilby abandoned the engraving business to Bewick and concentrated on clock making.

Bewick, now with a free hand, brought out in 1799 an enlarged and corrected edition of *Land Birds*, while preparing Volume II, *History and Description of Water Birds*, which was published in 1804. Bewick did not rest content with his success: before his death eight editions of *Quadrupeds*, eight of *Land Birds* and six of *Water Birds* had appeared in print, each enlarged in scope and with more illustrations. Moreover, he contemplated a *History of British Fishes*, but was forced by declining health to abandon the project. He did, however, produce an illustrated edition of *Aesop's Fables* in 1818, his last major work.

Bewick died in 1828 at Gateshead, where he had moved shortly after 1800, and was buried at Ovingham, the parish church of his youth.

BILLINGHAM

The history of Billingham has two very distinct phases. From very early in the medieval period, it was important in both religious and secular senses. The oldest parts of the fabric of the parish church of St Cuthbert, which have been dated to around the year 700, suggest that it was very similar to the church at ESCOMB, and declare its status as an ecclesiastical centre at an early date. Its continuing importance is confirmed by its western tower, added in the late tenth century. Billingham was equally important as the administrative centre of a large estate or 'shire'. In the post-Conquest centuries, Billinghamshire, which was co-extensive with Billingham parish, comprised Wolviston, Cowpen Bewley and Newton Bewley, although the latter was not created until c.1300, and the three discrete farms of Bellasis Manor, Bewley Manor and Saltholme Manor.

The Community of St Cuthbert (see CUTHBERT, SAINT) acquired Billingham in the second quarter of the ninth century. It was seized from them and given to a Scandinavian owner during the disturbed conditions of the early tenth century but restored to them by William the Conqueror, probably during his stay in Durham in 1072. Thereafter, Billingham remained one of the most valuable possessions of DURHAM CATHEDRAL Priory and its post-Reformation successor, the Dean and Chapter.

If in the first phase of its history Billingham's importance was agricultural and ecclesiastical, in the second phase, to which there were two stages, it was industrial. The earlier, nineteenth-century, stage centred on a new settlement by the Tees on the fringe of the township: Port Clarence, founded in 1828 by Christopher Tennant and named after the Duke of Clarence, who became William IV in 1830. Initially Port Clarence was a coal port, but in 1853 SIR ISAAC LOWTHIAN BELL founded an ironworks there and after 1874 began the extraction of salt. It was salt that led to the second, twentieth-century, stage.

This began began towards the end of World War I, when the Ministry of Munitions bought a 266-acre (108 ha) farm on which they planned to build a plant to manufacture ammonium nitrate. This purchase also had a bonus in that beneath the farm was a thick bed of anhydrate, from which ammonium sulphate, the basic ingredient of fertiliser, could be derived. With the end of the war, the Ministry abandoned this project and sold the site to Sir Alfred Mond, the chairman of Brunner, Mond & Co. The next stage was precipitated by the amalgamation in Germany in 1925 of its eight major chemical firms into Interesse Gemeinschaft Farbenindustrie (IG Farben). This created the largest company in Europe and the fourth largest in the world. A British response was necessary and it was provided the following year by Sir Alfred and the head of Nobel Industries Ltd, Sir Harry McGowan, who with government approval, negotiated the merger of their firms and British Dyestuffs Ltd and United Alkali to form Imperial Chemical Industries (ICI). The creation of ICI made Billingham a major centre of research and manufacture of national importance and international standing. Industrial expansion resulted in Billingham becoming a sizeable town. In the inter-war period, this expansion was led by ICI, which built houses for its workers; but after 1945, private builders and the local authority became involved. In the 1950s, the local authority completed the development by building a town centre.

Port Clarence can be regarded as one of the NEW TOWNS OF THE NINETEENTH CENTURY and Billingham as one of the NEW TOWNS OF THE TWENTIETH CENTURY. Except for the parish church, almost all its buildings are modern. One stands out: the Forum, built between 1965 and 1967, was described by Sir Nikolaus Pevsner as 'the grandfather of leisure centres' in that for the first time such a centre included an almost complete range of leisure facilities. The Forum, together with the town centre, has become the main venue for the Billingham Folklore Festival, started in 1964, which attracts performers from all over the world and has an international reputation.

BISHOP AUCKLAND

The town of Bishop Auckland was the last place to be founded in 'Auckland', a district whose name derives from the Celtic words Allt Clud, which was also the original name of Dumbarton Rock, the 'capital' of the Kingdom of Strathclyde, which endured as a separate British state until it was absorbed into the Kingdom of Scotland in the tenth century. In contrast to the Scottish river, which retained its Celtic form Clyde, here, under Scandinavian influence, the river was renamed Gaunless. 'Auckland', as it became, was an extensive estate and/or administrative district to which the incoming English settlers in the seventh century applied the term 'shire'. That they retained its Celtic name strongly suggests that what they found was a long-established administrative and economic entity. We cannot be certain of the extent of 'Aucklandshire'. BOLDON BOOK says it comprised North Auckland, West Auckland, Escomb and Newton Cap, but the medieval parish of Auckland may indicate an earlier, much larger, district that included, in addition to those places bearing the name Auckland, Bedburn, Binchester, Byers Green, Coundon, East Thickley, Eldon, Escomb, Etherley, Evenwood, Hamsterley, Hunwick, Lynesack, Middlestone, Middridge, Newton Cap, Shildon, Westerton, Windlestone and Witton le Wear. We are also ignorant of where the centre of this estate lay, perhaps the most likely place being South Church, the centre of the medieval parish. Although the present church is largely a thirteenth-century building, fragments of an eighth-century cross found there may be an indication that when the pagan English converted to Christianity they simply gave the pre-existing administrative district an additional ecclesiastical role.

Concrete evidence of the Auckland district becomes available only in the later twelfth century. This reveals the existence of two large rural settlements, North Auckland and West Auckland; and in addition, the existence of the parish church (with perhaps a village) at South Church. These three places clearly formed the core of 'Aucklandshire'. To them BISHOP HUGH OF LE PUISET added an episcopal manor house, which became known as AUCKLAND CASTLE, and its attendant park, as part of his extensive re-organisation development of the episcopal estate.

The final element was the borough of Auckland. When precisely this was founded is not known, but it was some time in the hundred years after Hugh of le Puiset's death in 1195. The first recorded reference to it, in 1305, shows it to have been well established by that date. Its purpose, like all medieval boroughs, was to provide services for its founder, in this case the bishops of Durham and their adjacent residence, and to generate income. The borough took the form of a marketplace attached to the pre-existing rural township of North Auckland. The latter occupied the street known as Bondgate, that is, the street along which the bondmen, the tenant farmers who formed the core of every North-East township in the Middle Ages, had their farmsteads. The topography is still very apparent: the square marketplace, which formed the Borough of Auckland, with Bondgate running at right angles from its south-east corner. When the borough needed to expand, it did so along a new street, appropriately called Newgate, running at right angles from the north-west corner of the Market Place. The present town of Bishop Auckland therefore combines three earlier elements: the township of North Auckland, the Borough of Auckland, and Auckland Castle with its park.

Because of its great size, the medieval parish of Auckland yielded a very considerable income. For this reason, in 1292 Bishop Anthony Bek converted its parish church, South Church, into a college comprising a dean and nine canons. His purpose was not to provide parishioners with better service, but, since the canons were not required to be resident, to create the means of paying some of his clerical administrators. In 1428 Bishop Thomas Langley revised the arrangement, increasing the complement of canons to eleven. This college was dissolved in 1547 but it was not until the 1840s that the parish was broken up into smaller parochial units. Also because of its size, the medieval parish came to have five chapels of ease, subordinate to the parish church, but providing more readily accessible places of worship: Witton le Wear, where the important family of Eure had its castle; ESCOMB ; Hamsterley; St Helen, near West Auckland; and St Anne in the borough, its location in the middle of the Market Place suggesting that it was added after the borough had been laid out.

Bishop Auckland did not grow much before recent times: the first census in 1801 reveals a population of only 1,961. Nevertheless, with its weekly market and three fairs every year at Ascension, Corpus Christi and the Thursday before 10 October, it served as the market centre for the nearby farming townships and for upper Weardale, becoming noted for the sale of corn and cattle; it was also a place of residence for episcopal servants. Its role was given emphasis in 1604, when a grammar school, that is, one teaching Latin, was founded by Anne Swyfte.

This situation was transformed in the course of the nineteenth century, principally through the expansion of the coalfield around the town after the construction of the Stockton–Darlington railway. By 1851 twenty-five collieries were working within the area of the old parish and virtually all the old villages had expanded by the addition of a community of miners. The census of that year shows the population of Bishop Auckland to have risen to over 5,000. Mining was not the only growth sector. Bishop Auckland became the centre of a railway network, with direct links to BARNARD CASTLE, DARLINGTON, DURHAM, Ferryhill, and Crook and upper Weardale. Within the town, iron and engineering works were founded, and close by were the ironworks at Witton Park and the railway works at Shildon. There was in addition a product that became a household name throughout Britain: Lingford's Baking Powder, made by the firm founded in Durham Road in 1861 by Joseph Lingford. By 1914 Bishop Auckland was a small but thriving town with a population of over 15,000 and was also the economic and social focus of a wide neighbourhood.

The rest of the twentieth century was not kind to Bishop Auckland and its satellite communities. The collapse of the coal trade in the inter-war years turned South-West Durham into one of the worst 'depressed areas' in Britain. For many who stayed it was a time of poverty, misery and uncertainty. The alternative, for which many opted, was emigration. Between 1921 and 1931, the town's population fell from 15,602 to 14,160, a 10 per cent decline. A similar picture emerges from the figures relating to the enlarged Bishop Auckland Urban District set up in 1937 by the addition of Binchester, Coundon, Escomb, St Helens, Toronto, West Auckland and Witton Park. At the end of World War I, the population of this area totalled almost 44,500; twenty years later, on the eve of World War II, it had dropped by more than 20 per cent to under 35,500.

Although World War II brought about a revival of coal mining, it was a short-lived reprieve: the falling demand for coal from the late 1950s and the exhaustion and/or uneconomic nature of the pits around the town led to the demise of the industry. With the closure in 1968 of the last pit in the vicinity, Brusselton, the mining population around Bishop Auckland had fallen from over 17,000 early in the century to nil. In addition, the railway links to the outside world were all but obliterated and with them went several engineering works. To compensate, trading estates were created, notably that on the site of St Helens Colliery. These efforts to replace old industries with new, while not without success, did not halt population decline: by 2001, the population of the 1937 Urban District had fallen to 30,000, a contraction of 15 per cent.

One bright spot for much of the twentieth century was the success of the town's football team, which because of its population base could not become a professional side. Founded in 1886 by the Bishop Auckland Cricket Club, it was a founder member of the Northern League in 1889 and remained a member for ninety-nine years, until 1988. It was without doubt the most successful club in that league, winning the championship thirteen times. Added to this was its success in the FA Amateur Cup, which was competed for until 1974. 'Bishops' were finalists on eighteen occasions, on ten of which they were the winners. In 1955, 1956 and 1957 they accomplished a hat-trick of victories, the only club to do so. Among the many outstanding players, some of whom were English amateur internationals, while some became successful professionals, the most renowned was Bob Hardisty (1921–86), whose status as a local hero was confirmed by having a road named after him.

BLAKISTON, JOHN (1603–1649)

John Blakiston was the third son of Marmaduke Blakiston (1565–1639), a prominent canon of DURHAM CATHEDRAL and a leading advocate of High Church doctrines and practices, from which his son was to recoil. Nothing is known of his education, but as was common with younger sons of the gentry, he was apprenticed to trade, in his case a NEWCASTLE mercer. His success in business was sufficient for him to marry in 1626, to be chosen as one of the town's Chamberlains in 1632 and to be elected as one of the town's two MPs in 1640.

During the 1640s he was a very active opponent of Charles I, politically but not militarily: between 1641 and 1644, he was in London and known to have served on 102 committees set up by parliament to reform church and state. From 1645, following its capture by parliamentary forces, Blakiston was made Mayor of Newcastle, and thereafter divided his time between there and London. He fully supported the trial of Charles I, attending all but one of the court sessions, and at the end he signed the king's death warrant. He died later in 1649, and by so doing he avoided the fate of those fellow signatories still alive when Charles I's son returned from exile in 1660 to become Charles II.

BLANCHLAND ABBEY

Blanchland Abbey was the last monastic house to be founded in the region. It was the work of Walter de Bolbec III, the lord of the Barony of Styford, one of the twenty baronies created in Northumberland by Henry I. It was not strictly an abbey but a canonry, since its occupants were Premonstratensian Canons, an order founded by Norbert of Xanten in 1120 at Prémontré (Latin, Premonstratensia) in France. The members of this order differed from monks in that their rule permitted them to live outside their house and serve as parish priests. Blanchland was poorly endowed, and because of this and its proximity to the Border, it was never wealthy.

After the closure of the monasteries by Henry VIII, the site and the lands passed into lay hands, and eventually into those of NATHANIEL, LORD CREWE, the Bishop of Durham, and thence to those of the charitable trust he set up. It was they who constructed the present village on the foundations of the outer court of the monastery, with the hotel, the Lord Crewe Arms, being a reuse of a wing of the claustral buildings.

BLAYDON RACES

There are four aspects to the Blaydon Races: the races themselves; the song and its creator; the painting; and the 'revival'. The races had an interrupted and not very distinguished history, although they did come to an end in spectacular fashion. They first took place in connection with the Blaydon Hoppings in the early nineteenth century, but were ended by the building of Blaydon station on the ground where they were held. However, they were revived in 1861 on Blaydon Island in a more organised fashion, under the auspices of the Braes of Derwent Hunt and its enthusiastic supporters and Masters, the Cowen family of nearby Stella Hall. But they were again interrupted for some years after 1870 because of a failure to meet a Jockey Club rule that the total prize money should exceed £100. They finally came to an end on Whit Monday 1916, when an angry crowd destroyed the facilities, including the weighing room, after the favourite in the first race, the appropriately named Anxious Moments, which had won by six lengths, was disqualified.

The song was first heard on Thursday, 5 June 1862, that is, four days before the races on Whit Monday. It contents are entirely fictitious, except for the last verse, which must have been added later, since it tells of the heavy rain on the day and the delay in starting the racing as the result of horses not arriving on time. All the characters, however, were real people known to the audience: Jacky Broon was John Brown, the Blaydon town crier; Coffy Johnny was John Oliver, a blacksmith who was 6 feet 6 inches (2.1 m) tall and who always insisted on 'supping my coffee' before starting a job; and Dr Charles Gibb (1824–1916), the well-known Newcastle physician. The bus that took the unfortunate characters to catastrophe along the Scotswood Road was Parker's Bus that ran twice daily from the Cloth Market in Newcastle to Blaydon via the suspension bridge at Scotswood.

The song was composed by George (Geordie) Ridley, who was born on 10 February 1835 in Gateshead and began work at the age of eight at Oakwell Colliery, shortly after moving to the Goose Pit. After ten years in mining, he took a job as a wagon rider with the local iron makers, Hawks, Crawshay & Co. In 1857, however, he suffered a near-fatal accident that left him a cripple. To earn his living he made use of his good voice and talent as a mimic in the music halls then flourishing in public houses. He first performed 'The Blaydon Races' at the music hall run by John Balmbra at the Wheatsheaf Inn in the Cloth Market. The occasion was a fund-raising concert for the famous Tyneside rower, HARRY CLASPER, whose rowing days were over and who was in need of a house. The song was not an instant hit, and it was not until the twentieth century that it began to take on the role of Tyneside's 'national anthem'. Ridley composed several other songs, one of which, 'Cushy Butterfield', is still sung. Its first performance, however, landed him in trouble with those related to the principal characters, all of whom were readily identifiable. Geordie Ridley died at the age of twenty-nine on 9 September 1864 at Grahamsley Street, Gateshead. He is buried in St Edmund's graveyard.

The third element of the story is the painting of the Blaydon Races by William C. Irving, painted in 1903 and very evidently inspired by the more famous *Derby Day* by Frith. It hung for many years in the County Hotel in Neville Street, Newcastle, but has now found a permanent and most appropriate home in the Shipley Art Gallery in GATESHEAD (see ART GALLERIES).

The Blaydon Races have come back to life, albeit in a different form. Since 1980, a road race that attracts athletes of international standing has been run annually on 9 June from Newcastle to Blaydon, a distance of 5.7 miles (9 km).

BLYTH

The town of Blyth began as a small community, Blyth Snook, in the township of Newsham on the south side of the Blyth estuary. Like other similar places along the Northumberland coast, it made a living from the interrelated activities of fishing, salt making and coal mining. All were on a relatively small scale until, following the acquisition by the Ridley family (which intermarried with the White family of Newcastle), of Newsham, Plessey, Shotton and Blagdon, the new owners began to promote industrial activity. Major development, however, did not take place until the second half of the nineteenth century.

This took two main forms. One was enlargement of the port by the North Eastern Railway Co., which in 1874 bought the Blyth Harbour and Docks Co. The purpose of the expansion was to facilitate increased coal exports, particularly from the pits of the dynamic Ashington Coal Co. By 1914 Blyth was responsible for about half of Northumberland's coal exports. This trade continued to grow, until by 1961 Blyth was Europe's largest coal port, exporting nearly 7,000,000 tons.

The second major development was shipbuilding (see SHIPBUILDING INDUSTRY). The Blyth Shipbuilding and Dry Docks Co. (after 1926 the Shipbuilding and Dry Docks Co.) began operations in 1883 and by 1914 had six berths, which built a variety of ships, especially tramps and COLLIERS. Although Blyth never could hope to match the capacities of the Tyne and Wear yards, it was nevertheless responsible for two naval 'firsts'. In 1914 the Admiralty bought a tramp named *Ryton* that was still on the stocks, which was then converted into what was arguably the world's first aircraft carrier and renamed HMS *Ark Royal*. In fact, it was a seaplane carrier, capable of handling eight planes, which were lifted on and off by crane. Blyth repeated this achievement in World War II, converting the captured German cargo liner, *Hannover*, into HMS *Audacity*, the Royal Navy's first escort carrier. In both wars, Blyth also built smaller warships for anti-submarine and convoy escort duties, including in World War II five 'River' class and seven 'Castle' class frigates.

These two 'traditional' industries went into steep decline in the last third of the twentieth century, the shipyard closing in 1967 (having been closed temporarily between 1930 and 1937) and coal exports falling away as the neighbouring pits were closed. Nevertheless, the port survived and was modernised, acquiring a roll-on-roll-off facility and becoming a centre for offshore technology. Blyth also became an electric power generation centre, with coal-fired power stations built in 1958 and 1962, and more recently in 2002 the base for Britain's first offshore 'wind farm'.

Economic expansion meant population growth, which in turn resulted in developments in local government. In 1894 Blyth and Cowpen became Blyth Urban District, which was expanded in 1912 by the addition of Horton and Bebside. Ten years later, in 1922, Blyth was granted borough status. The most recent development took place in the radical reorganisation of the British local government structure implemented in 1974. This restructuring merged the borough with Seaton Valley UDC and small parts of Whitley Bay and SEATON SLUICE to form the Wansbeck Valley District.

'BOBBY SHAFTO'

The song 'Bobby Shafto', known throughout Britain, has its roots in real North-East characters. In 1652 Mark Shafto, a wealthy and influential member of the Merchant Adventurers and Hostman Company in NEWCASTLE, who served as Recorder of Newcastle and one of its MPs, bought the Whitworth estate in County Durham. As was normal, it took two or three generations for the newcomers to be fully accepted as members of county society. The family's 'arrival' was signalled by the selection of Mark's grandson (also Mark) as High Sheriff of Durham in 1709 and the election of his sons, Robert and John (successively), as MPs for Durham City between 1711 and 1741. The Bobby Shafto of the song was Robert Shafto, John Shafto's son, who also was an MP for Durham City between 1760 and 1768. He died in 1797.

The lady in the song was a Miss Bellasyse, the daughter of Sir Henry Bellasyse, whose father, Sir William Bellasyse of Ludworth and Owton, bought the Brancepeth estate in 1701 from Ralph Cole, another prominent Newcastle Hostman. Henry Bellasyse died in 1769 and as his daughter was his only child, she inherited an estate of 4,600 acres (1,900 ha) worth £2,134 a year. As a marriage prospect, she was well worth considering. Whether Bobby Shafto did consider her and whether there was, to use the term of the time, an 'understanding' between them is not clear. The song suggests that there might have been, although it could have been wishful thinking on the lady's part. In the end, Bobby Shafto married another heiress, Ann Duncombe of Duncombe Park, near Helmsley, North Yorkshire. The portrait of Bobby Shafto known to have been hanging at Whitworth Hall in the nineteenth century shows Bobby Shafto to have been a very suitable object of a lady's hopes: young, handsome and, as the song says, with blond hair.

What the fate of Miss Bellasyse was is not known, except that in 1774 she sold her inheritance to a relative, Henry Bellasyse, 5th Viscount and 3rd Earl Fauconberg.

BOLCKOW, HENRY WILLIAM FERDINAND (1806–1879)

If any individual can be said to have created Middlesbrough (see NEW TOWNS OF THE NINETEENTH CENTURY) it is Henry Bolckow. His achievement was all the more remarkable for his being a foreigner, the son of a country landowner in the Duchy of Mecklenburg in north Germany. In 1821, at the age of seventeen, he entered the office of a commercial firm in the Baltic port of Rostock, which also employed CHRISTIAN ALLHUSEN. Six years later, in 1827, he came to NEWCASTLE to join a corn merchant's business run by Christian Allhusen's brother. In the following twelve years, he enjoyed great success, amassing a fortune of £50,000. Tiring of the corn trade, he was looking for a new business opportunity when he met John Vaughan, the manager of the Tyneside ironworks of Losh, Wilson and Bell at Walker. The partnership they formed was well balanced, Vaughan supplying the knowledge of iron making, Bolckow contributing commercial expertise and acumen.

The site they chose in 1841 for their venture was not on Tyneside, but, thanks to the influence of Joseph Pease (see PEASE FAMILY), the Middlesbrough Estate, which Pease and his partners were developing on the south bank of the Tees. On the 6 acres (2.4 ha) Pease sold them they created a works for the production of wrought iron, obtaining much of the necessary pig iron from Scotland (see IRON AND STEEL INDUSTRY). Four years later they took the obvious next step by creating their own pig iron works. The chosen location was Witton Park near BISHOP AUCKLAND, for what appeared to be good reasons, namely the presence in the locality of all three essential ingredients, coal, iron ore and limestone. This turned out to be a mistake, but not one that they could have foreseen. The local iron ore was limited in quantity and low in quality and five years later, in 1850, Vaughan and a companion discovered what came to be known as the Main Seam, a seam of higher-quality ore 16 feet (5 m) thick at Eston, in the Cleveland Hills less than 5 miles (8 km) south of Middlesbrough. The partners reacted rapidly to this discovery: within two years they had secured leases for mining ore, and built blast furnaces at Eston and Middlesbrough and a railway linking Eston with Middlesbrough. By 1855 the firm of Bolckow and Vaughan was supplying the iron piping for the water system being installed in London.

In 1864, on Vaughan's retirement, Bolckow had complete control, but the following year he decided to take advantage of the recent legislation and make Bolckow and Vaughan a limited liability company. In 1871, he took another major decision, to manufacture steel. To this end, he bought the bankrupt firm of Lancashire Steel of Gorton near Manchester, in order to bring its machinery and its expertise to Middlesbrough. By the time he died in 1878, Bolckow and Vaughan Ltd was one of the giants of the Teesside iron and steel industry. They employed 15,000 men, and they owned fourteen collieries in County Durham with an annual output of two million tons, 4,000 acres (1,600 ha) of farmland, and haematite iron ore mines near Bilbao in Spain. Annually, they produced 1,500,000 tons of iron ore, 500,000 tons of pig iron and 250,000 tons of steel. After Bolckow's death, the firm maintained its position and by 1900 it was one of the big three Teesside producers, the others being Dorman, Long & Co. and South Durham Steel. In 1929, during the great recession, Bolckow and Vaughan 'disappeared' in a merger with Dorman, Long.

Bolckow's achievements as an industrialist alone are great enough to merit attention, but his reputation is further enhanced by the part he played in the development of Middlesbrough as a town. His status within the community was such that he was the town's first mayor and also its first MP, when it was granted a member of parliament by the Second Reform Act of 1867. Moreover, he was President of the Middlesbrough Chamber of Commerce, Chairman of the Middlesbrough Stock Exchange and a member of the Tees Conservancy Board. His benefactions to the town included the gift of a park at a time when municipal parks were fashionable and reckoned to be an important contribution to public health, and the financing of schools for 900 children, recognising that English education was of poorer quality than that on the continent and that improvement was necessary, if the country was to maintain its industrial prowess.

BOLDON BOOK

Boldon Book is widely quoted as 'the Domesday Book of Northumberland and Durham', one reason being that when first published in 1816, it was as an addendum to an edition of Domesday Book. The belief is incorrect. The Domesday Survey, even though it was probably masterminded by the Bishop of Durham, WILLIAM OF ST CALAIS, did not extend north of the Tees, for two connected reasons. One was that the region had only very recently been brought under the control of the new Norman regime and at the time of the survey (1085), effective Norman power was confined to the garrisons of the recently built castles at Durham and on the north bank of the Tyne. Had the commissioners collecting the desired information ventured north of the Tees, they would have faced considerable difficulty and danger. Secondly, no land had been distributed to Norman settlers, and since one of the aims of the survey was to determine how the pattern of landholding had changed since 1066, the exercise would have been pointless.

Boldon Book is in fact the record of a survey of the episcopal estate commissioned in March 1183 or March 1184 by the bishop, HUGH OF LE PUISET. Its scope was precise and limited. Far from covering the entire region, it was confined to places belonging to the bishop and from which he drew income. Excluded were: Northumberland, except NORTH DURHAM and Bedlingtonshire; those parts of southern Durham known as the WAPENTAKE OF SADBERGE, which were not acquired by the bishop until the end of the decade; and places in Durham possessed by the bishop's feudal tenants, who owed military service, and by the Cathedral Priory.

The earliest copy of the survey contains references to 140 settlements, 124 in Durham and 16 in Northumberland. In each case rents, services and any other obligations owed by the bishop's non-feudal tenants were recorded. Where the farming population held their land directly from the bishop the record was very detailed. But where an entire township, hamlet or farm was held of the bishop by an individual, only what he or she owed to the bishop was noted; the record for such places does not include information about the inhabitants and their holdings and obligations.

The book's title, which was in use from at least the early fourteenth century, derives from the record of the township of Boldon, which describes in precise detail the rents in money, kind and services owed by the twenty-two main tenant farmers, known as *villeins*. Entries relating to nineteen more places, all in the eastern wards of EASINGTON and STOCKTON, record that the obligations of the *villeins* were 'as those of Boldon'. In other words, the phrase was simply a shorthand identification of identical tenemental and tenurial arrangements. Other townships had internal structures and arrangements that differed significantly from those in this group.

Boldon Book is the earliest detailed evidence we have of the structure and functioning of North-East society. However, it needs to be used with caution, for two reasons. One is that there are four surviving manuscript copies of the survey, the earliest dating from as late as *c.*1320. Three have the same layout, while the fourth is set out along quite different lines, indicating that at an early date two master copies were made. On top of this, detailed analysis has revealed that some entries are not original but are subsequent updatings. Nevertheless, the survey does provide a wealth of information about North-East society in the last quarter of the twelfth century and the updated entries provide clues as to the direction of change within that society.

Boldon Book was not unique: three later medieval bishops, Lewis de Beaumont (1318–33), Thomas de Hatfield (1345–81) and Thomas Langley (1406–37), commissioned similar surveys.

BONOMI, IGNATIUS (1787–1870)

Ignatius Bonomi was a contemporary of JOHN DOBSON, but is generally considered to have been his inferior as an architect. He was the son and pupil of Joseph Bonomi (1739–1808), an Italian architect who came to England in 1767 and finally settled in London in 1784, where he became sufficiently fashionable to earn a mention by Jane Austen in *Sense and Sensibility*. Ignatius settled in Durham after his father's death. He was already acquainted with the area, having worked with his father at Lambton Castle (see LAMBTON, JOHN GEORGE, 1st EARL OF DURHAM); but the crucial factor was his appointment in 1813 as Bridge Surveyor for County Durham.

Like Dobson, his commissions were largely, but not entirely, in the region. Also like Dobson, his practice benefited from the rising demand for church building and restoration: between 1826 and 1850 he designed eighteen Anglican and Roman Catholic churches and repaired, extended or altered twenty more. His commissions for domestic dwellings and public buildings were larger, numbering sixty-two, exactly half of which were in the North East. His most notable buildings in the region were Eggleston Hall, Burn Hall near Durham, and Windleston Hall; he also was responsible for the repair of Wynyard Hall after the fire of 1841, although to the designs of the original architect, Benjamin Wyatt.

In his capacity as County Surveyor, Bonomi built bridges at Haughton le Skerne, Wolsingham, CHESTER LE STREET and Shincliffe; and in 1825 he also built the railway bridge over the Skerne for the Stockton and Darlington Railway.

Bonomi retired in 1850, and left Durham and settled at Wimbledon in 1856.

BORDER, THE ANGLO-SCOTTISH

For many centuries, the Border between England and Scotland has begun about 4 miles (6.5 km) north of Berwick Pier at Marshall Meadow and swung round to meet the Tweed about 4 miles (6.5 km) upstream from its mouth. It has then followed the course of the Tweed for about 15 miles (24 km) until the confluence with the Redden Burn. From there it has ascended to the height of the Cheviot, whence it has followed the watershed as far as the Cumbrian border. Long use, however, cannot disguise the fact that it is not a natural border but the product of military action confirmed by diplomatic agreement. This was so because the two countries it separates are themselves the product of the same processes.

England and Scotland were formed gradually in the tenth century by the kings of Wessex (roughly England south of the Thames and the Bristol Channel) and Alba (roughly Scotland north of the Antonine Wall between the Forth and the Clyde), the one advancing north, the other pushing south. It might have happened that one of these two kings would have defeated the other and so united the whole island of Britain under his rule. That this did not happen was not inevitable. What did happen was that from the early eleventh century the kings of Scots were not strong enough permanently to extract more land from their neighbour and that, although the kings of England had far more resources at their disposal, they were never sufficiently committed to a policy of conquering a kingdom with considerable powers of resistance.

In fact, after 1000, it was the kings of Scots who were the more aggressive, with a clear policy of extending their boundary south to the Tees. And between 1136 and 1157 they largely succeeded. In order to concentrate on his struggle to retain his throne, the usurper king, Stephen (1135–54), conceded to David I of Scots the EARLDOM OF NORTHUMBRIA, comprising the counties of Northumberland, Cumberland and Westmorland (Cumbria). David also tried but failed to get his Chancellor, William Cumin, elected as Bishop of Durham and thereby to secure control of the PALATINATE. This situation was reversed by Stephen's successor, Henry II, who forced David's successor, his young grandson, Malcom IV, to restore the Earldom to him. Malcolm died in 1165, to be succeeded by his younger brother, William. He was king until 1214, and throughout his long reign his main ambition was to recover what his brother had given away. And his son and successor, Alexander II, remained committed to the same ambition, until 1237. In that year, however, he finally accepted that having the Tees as his southern boundary was unrealisable. By the Treaty of York, mediated by the papal legate, he conceded that the Tweed–Cheviot watershed line should be the boundary between his kingdom and that of Henry III.

This, of course, meant that BERWICK UPON TWEED was in Scotland. It was as a result of the long war between England and Scotland that began in 1296 that this town and its immediate hinterland became by dint of conquest part of Northumberland and so of England. Should Scotland again become a fully independent state, it is possible that there would be a move to reverse this situation.

BORDER REIVERS

The word *reiver* means thief or rustler. It was applied to the men of the ANGLO-SCOTTISH BORDER region who practised the lifting of cattle and sheep against their cross-border neighbours, and sometimes against their own countrymen. It was a business in which there were no long-term winners, since raid invariably resulted in counter-raid. Nor were all raids successful: there were many instances where the raiders were pursued and some if not all of the booty was recovered. Reiving was not the only nefarious activity practised by the borderers: they also indulged in *black mail,* which today we would call a protection racket, and also kidnapping for ransom. Almost inevitably, deaths occurred during the execution of these purposes, which in turn triggered the *deadly feud,* in which the eye-for-an-eye rule was followed. These were the activities of a society lacking other sources of wealth and living in a land difficult to patrol and control. Thanks to the so-called Border Ballads, however, these vicious criminals became romanticised, very much as have the gunslingers of the Wild West and the

American mafia of more recent times.

The geographical scope of this thuggery was fairly circumscribed. In Northumberland, it was basically confined to the upland districts of Tynedale, Redesdale and Allendale, which were populated by kinship groups that in the Scottish Highlands were called 'clans', but here were known as 'surnames'. The most common names in Northumberland were Charlton, Robson, Dodds and Milburn in Tynedale; and Hall, Read, Potts, Hedley, Dunn and Fletcher in Redesdale. The government's agents, the Wardens of the Marches (see MARCHES OF ENGLAND TOWARDS SCOTLAND) and their deputies, could hope to do little more than contain the problem and were generally able to deal only with the head of each 'surname'. The difficulty we have in arriving at a balanced picture of this society is that most of the recorded evidence is of the second half of the sixteenth century, when it is clear that, for various reasons, the Scottish borderers were more aggressive than their English counterparts.

When James VI of Scotland became King of England in 1603, he declared that the Border no longer existed and that the counties along it should be known henceforth as the Middle Shires of Britain, a notion that has never caught on. He also made clear that he was not prepared to tolerate the criminality of the region. To deal with the problem, he appointed a trusted henchman, George Home, whom he made Earl of Dunbar. Dunbar bore down heavily on the malefactors, and was ever ready to commit to the noose those who were contumacious in their wickedness. Although at the time of his death in 1611 the problem was not completely solved, the new regime's intention was abundantly clear. But it took the passage of time and the emergence of post-Union generations for a truly pacific society to take shape.

BORDER TOWERS

One of the notable features of the Northumberland landscape is the border tower, built by the gentry as defensible residences during the fourteenth and fifteenth centuries. Hitherto, the gentry had lived in what are called hall-houses, two-storey buildings, in many cases built wholly or partly of wood. The residential parts were on the first floor. At the centre was a large hall, used for eating and dealing with public business. At one end of the hall, separated from it by a permanent screen, was the private apartment of the owner, known as the solar; and at the other, likewise separated by a screen, were the kitchen and food storage and preparation rooms. The ground floor, which was usually a basement, was used for storage purposes. An excellent, albeit ruined, example of this type of gentry house has survived at Aydon.

Although within a walled enclosure, these residences were not designed to withstand attack by determined military forces and so they were vulnerable when the Anglo-Scottish war began in the 1290s. The solution was the tower. Typically, a tower was about 50 feet by 35 feet (15m by 10.7 m) and 40 or 50 feet (12–15 m) high. Made of stone, its walls were 7 feet (2.3 m) thick at the base, tapering to 6 feet (1.8 m) further up and topped with a battlement and a gabled roof of stone slates. Most towers had three storeys. The ground floor was a vaulted basement, used for storage. The main living quarters, reached by a spiral stair in the thickness of the wall, were on the first floor and included a hall and solar. Above them was a second floor providing further accommodation. To complete the defences, the tower was within a walled enclosure known as a *barmkin*. These towers were not designed to withstand sustained attack, but they were capable of defending the owner and his household from raiding parties.

At one time, it was thought that once a tower was built, the hall-house was abandoned, but the excavations at Edlingham show that this was not so and that the hall-house was retained, perhaps for normal living, with the tower reserved for occupation in more threatening times. Most of these towers were built between 1350 and 1450. Few details have survived concerning their construction, largely because they were built without Crown licences. This is surprising, since the Crown had always jealously guarded its right to control castle building by means of 'licences to crenellate'. It is thought that the Crown's relaxed attitude arose from knowledge that the towers were not formidable fortresses, and thankfulness that the Border gentry were prepared to shoulder the burden of their own defence. The Crown was, of course, well aware of what was happening, as is made clear by the detailed survey of Border defences commissioned by Henry V as part of his preparation for invading France in 1415. This reveals the existence of eighty-seven towers, and it is known that the final number rose to around 120 in the course of the fifteenth century.

With the accession of James VI of Scotland to the English throne in 1603, the war ended and the tower became redundant. In some places, new houses were built in Jacobean style adjacent to the tower, notably at Chipchase. Some towers have continued in occupation, although modified in subsequent centuries, but many were abandoned and allowed to fall into decay and now stand as forlorn ruins.

BOWES FAMILY

The Bowes family was one of the most prominent gentry families in Durham from the early fourteenth until the nineteenth century. The progenitor may have been William, a relative of Alan, Count of Brittany, to whom William the Conqueror gave the massive lordship of Richmond in North Yorkshire. The family made its first appearance in the county in the early years of the fourteenth century in the person of Adam del Bowes, who was appointed Sheriff and Escheator of Durham by Bishop Richard de Kellaw (1311–16) in October 1312. He presumably had legal training, since he is known to have had a successful legal career, rising to become a judge. He also established himself as a County Durham landowner by his marriage to Alice, the daughter and sole heir of John Trayne, the lord of Streatlam and Stainton, County Durham, in the hands of whose family they had been for over a hundred years. To these he added other properties in the south of the county and the hamlet of Newton by Durham (later Newton Hall). He died in the late 1340s, possibly during the Black Death of 1349.

The family's landholding was substantially increased by Adam's grandson, Sir William de Bowes I (d.1399), who married another heiress, Matilda, daughter of Robert de Dalden. By this marriage he acquired a considerable estate in the north-east of the county, comprising Dalden (now Dawdon) and the manor of Humbleton Hill, which included much of what are now the southern parts of SUNDERLAND.

There are traditions that two members of the Bowes family found chivalric fame and material fortune through involvement in the French wars, as did many members of the English landed class during the fourteenth and early fifteenth centuries. Sir William de Bowes I is said to have fought and been knighted at the Battle of Poitiers in 1356; and his eldest son, Sir Robert, to have taken part in the siege of Rouen in 1419 and been killed in 1421 in a battle at Baugé. It is doubtful if there is much truth in either story. However, Sir Robert's son, Sir William de Bowes II, may have taken part in the English victory in 1424 at Verneuil, where his conduct earned him a knighthood in the field, and he spent seventeen years in France serving in the household of John, Duke of Bedford, a younger brother of Henry V (d.1422), who was charged with prosecuting the war in France during the minority of his nephew, the young Henry VI. It is entirely credible that his fees, together with the spoils of war, made Bowes a rich man, able to afford to rebuild the family manor house at Streatlam as a castle.

The French war was effectively over by the time of William de Bowes II's death in 1458. Thereafter, the military and administrative activities of the men of the Bowes family were in the service of the Crown, mainly in connection with the Border, and in that of the bishops of Durham. His son, Sir William Bowes III (d.1466), was Sheriff of Northumberland and Warden of the Middle March. Sir Ralph Bowes I (d.1512), his grandson, was Warden of the Middle March, Sheriff and Escheator of Durham for twenty years between 1482 and 1502. He also enlarged the family's estate by his marriage to Marjory, the heiress of Richard Conyers of South Cowton in the North Riding of Yorkshire. One of his sons, Sir Robert Bowes II (d.1555), played a crucial, if ambiguous, role in the PILGRIMAGE OF GRACE, the revolt in the winter of 1536–37 against Henry VIII's religious changes. Thereafter, he became heavily engaged in Border matters, culminating in his appointment as Warden of the East and Middle Marches (see MARCHES OF ENGLAND TOWARDS SCOTLAND) in 1550. In this role, he compiled for his superior, Henry Grey, 3rd Marquis of Dorset, Warden General of the Marches, *A Book of the State of the Frontiers and Marches betwixt England and Scotland*, a detailed account of the condition of the Border country, and *The Forme and Order of a Day of Truce*, a detailed explanation of how the cross-border Wardens' courts functioned. These works provide us with some of the best evidence we have of Border conditions in the sixteenth century. His younger brother, Richard (d.1558), too was an active Borderer, although he is more remembered for his wife's desertion to live with the Scottish reformer, JOHN KNOX.

Richard's son, Sir George Bowes (1527–80), continued the tradition, serving as Marshal of Berwick. His most notable service, however, was rendered during the RISING OF THE NORTHERN EARLS in 1569. Although a staunch Protestant, he had escorted Mary, Queen of Scots to Bolton Castle when she fled to England in 1568 with such courtesy that she always remembered him with affection. The following year, however, he did much to contain and then suppress the revolt that aimed to put her on the throne of England. As Streatlam was not far from Brancepeth, the centre of the revolt, he was able to keep watch on the rebels and report their movements to the authorities. He also gathered together twenty-eight loyal gentry, with whom he garrisoned the royal fortress of BARNARD CASTLE. There he endured an eleven-day siege, negotiating an honourable surrender only when desertions rendered his situation untenable. On joining the royal army as it advanced from the south, he was appointed Provost Marshal, with responsibility for hunting down and hanging the large numbers of rebels that the queen insisted should be executed. Streatlam Castle was badly damaged, but Bowes got scant compensation from Queen Elizabeth, who was parsimonious in rewarding loyalty.

His younger brother, Robert (1535–97), was also very much involved in northern affairs. As Sheriff of Durham in 1569, he helped Sir George to contain and suppress the rebellion. Subsequently he was stationed at BERWICK, except for the years 1577 to

1583, when he was Ambassador to Scotland. His letters to London are a very detailed source of information on the working of Scottish politics as well as of Anglo-Scottish relations. Like his brother, he too found that to be of service to Elizabeth I was to be out of pocket.

The accession of James VI of Scotland to the English throne in 1603 brought an end to the Border problem, and with it the long involvement of the Bowes family. The family managed to survive the civil wars of the mid-seventeenth century without suffering any great disaster, and at the end of the century another marriage brought another enhancement of fortune. In 1693, Sir William Bowes IV (1653–1706), the great-grandson of Sir George Bowes, the defender of Barnard Castle, married Elizabeth, the sole heir of Sir Francis Blakiston of Gibside. Through this marriage, Sir William's successors came into possession on Sir Francis's death in 1713 of the manors of Gibside and Marley. Although these comprised perfectly adequate farmland from which respectable rents could be expected, their real value lay in the coal lying beneath them. And the timing of the acquisition was also opportune, in that in the late seventeenth century the coal seams under land close to the Tyne were becoming exhausted, necessitating the exploitation of those under land further from the river.

It was George Bowes, Sir William's autocratic and hot-tempered younger son, who succeeded his brother in 1721, who fully exploited this new-found asset as a member of what was called the Grand Alliance, a cartel of major coal owners formed in 1726 to control output and thereby the price of coal. With his enhanced income he was able to transform Gibside. The old house, built by the Blakistons between 1603 and 1620, was left unaltered, but the grounds were landscaped, creating the Long Walk, beyond the northern end of which he built the Column to Liberty, 123 feet (37.5 m) high and surmounted by a 12½ foot (3.8 m) statue of Liberty holding the Staff of Maintenance and a Cap of Liberty, which proclaimed Bowes's commitment to the Whig Party. Bowes also built the Octagon Pond, the Lily Pond, the Banqueting House, the Bath House, the Ice House, the Stables and the Walled Garden. In the last year of his life, he began the Chapel at the southern end of the Long Walk, which was completed by his daughter between 1760 and 1768, but not furnished and consecrated until 1816. One building for which he was not reponsible was the Green House (now known as the Orangery). This was built between 1772 and 1775 by his daughter, Mary Eleanor, who had a serious and scholarly interest in botany, to house her botanical collection. However, this does not invalidate the claim that Gibside as enjoyed today was his creation.

George Bowes married twice. His first wife died ten weeks after their marriage and he remained unmarried for the next twenty years. His second wife, Mary Gilbert, brought yet more property to the Bowes family, an estate at St Paul's Walden Bury in Hertfordshire. When George Bowes died in 1760, his second marriage had produced only one child, a daughter, Mary Eleanor, who was only eleven years old. She grew to be a highly intelligent and well-educated woman, who was befriended by ELIZABETH MONTAGU and admitted to the latter's 'blue stocking' circle. Unfortunately, her intelligence did not extend to a shrewd assessment of men. This was to prove her undoing, since, with an estate then said to be worth £600,000, she was one of the most sought-after heiresses in Britain. Because of this her father had laid down in his will that whoever married her must change his name to Bowes. The man she chose, much against her mother's advice, was John Lyon, 9th Earl of Strathmore and Kinghorn, a handsome and amiable man, but her intellectual inferior, who forced her to discontinue her association with Elizabeth Montagu. They were married on her eighteenth birthday in 1767 and he secured the necessary act of parliament to become John Bowes. Although their estate centred on Glamis Castle in Angus, the Lyons had virtually become a Durham family as the result of the 8th Earl (d.1753) settling in the county following his marriage to Jane, the daughter and heir of James Nicholson of West Rainton.

The marriage of the new earl and countess was short-lived. He contracted tuberculosis, and in 1776 he died at sea while travelling to Portugal in the hope of a cure. Although the couple had not been personally very compatible, the marriage was successful in dynastic terms in that it produced five children, including three sons. Of these, George, the second son, died young; but the eldest, John, became 10th Earl of Strathmore.

The early death of the 9th Earl, however, led to two crises. The first was the precipitate remarriage of his countess. Her choice was Andrew Stoney, an impecunious army lieutenant on half-pay, who had already run through the fortune and caused the death of his first wife, Hannah Newton of Colepike Hall, near Lanchester. Despite knowing this, Mary Eleanor married him in 1777. True to character, Stoney, who also took the name Bowes, immediately began to abuse his wife and dissipate her fortune, although he was unable to get control of her property. The crisis came in 1785, when Mary Eleanor escaped from his clutches and set in motion divorce proceedings. His response was to attempt to abduct her, which landed him in prison. The divorce was finally granted in 1789, and he remained in prison until her death in 1800. She had learned the hard way and did not marry again.

The second crisis came later and involved the new earl. In the 1790s as a young man he entered into an affair with Susan, the daughter of Lord Delaval, the creator of SEATON SLUICE. Unfortunately she was already married to the Earl of Tyrconnell. After her early death in 1800, he still did not marry but in 1809 took as his mistress one of his housemaids, Mary Milner, by whom he had a son, John, the founder of BOWES MUSEUM. Although he married her the day before he died, it was not enough to secure his son's legitimacy. The issue turned on whether Strathmore was domiciled in Scotland or England: if the former, all would have been well; but the decision was in favour of the latter, which meant that John was illegitimate and so unable to inherit the Scottish title and estates, which passed to his uncle, Thomas Lyon, who became 11th Earl of Strathmore. However, John as plain Mr Bowes did inherit the Durham and Yorkshire properties. The Bowes and Lyon inheritances remained separate during the lifetimes of John and Josephine Bowes, but since they had no children, when John died in 1885 all his property passed to the 13th Earl of Strathmore, the grandson of the 11th Earl. It was his granddaughter, Elizabeth, the daughter of Claude, 14th Earl of Strathmore, who was to become Queen Elizabeth, wife of King George VI.

Although the family bore the name Bowes-Lyon, in the first half of the twentieth century it severed its links with Durham and resumed an exclusively Scottish identity. The Streatlam estate was sold between 1922 and 1927, and the castle was partially destroyed to expose the medieval core, which the Territorial Army blew up in 1959 during a field exercise. A similar fate seemed likely for Gibside. The Jacobean house continued in use until after World War I, when it was stripped of its furniture and fittings. After World War II the roof and floors were removed as a tax avoidance measure, which hastened the decay of the fabric. And similar decay by neglect meant the gradual deterioration of all the other elements of George Bowes's creation.

Gibside was rescued in the second half of the twentieth century. In 1974 the executors of the 16th Earl of Strathmore gave the Long Walk and the Chapel to the National Trust. Since then, the Trust has bought several hundred acres of land around the grounds to ensure that there were no inappropriate encroachments, and it has stabilised the shell of Gibside House, restored the Banqueting House and the Stables and plans to restore the Orangery in the future.

BOWES MUSEUM

At first sight the Bowes Museum is incongruous, although spectacular, looking as it does like the *hôtel de ville* of a prosperous French town transplanted to Teesdale. Yet it is among the best of those museums in Britain started as private collections and it bears comparison with the Wallace Collection in London and the Burrell Collection in Glasgow. It was the creation of an equally incongruous couple, John and Josephine Bowes. He was the illegitimate son of the 10th Earl of Strathmore, who because of his legal disability was not allowed to inherit the title and the Glamis estate when his father died in 1820. However, he did acquire the Durham properties, which included the rural estates at Streatlam and Gibside. The latter, with its huge reserves of coal, made Bowes an immensely rich man. But his wealth was not sufficient to counteract the stain of his birth, and in 1847 at the age of forty-six he moved to Paris.

Here, too, despite more relaxed French attitudes, he never felt fully accepted in the topmost stratum of Parisian society. This may in part explain his marriage in 1852 to the woman who had been his mistress for four years. She was Josephine Coffin-Chevallier, the daughter of a clockmaker, who was an actress at the Théâtre de Variétés (of which Bowes was part-owner) and as such bound to be considered morally dubious. He not only married her, but he bought her a title, Countess of Montalbo, from the Republic of San Marino, and the chateau at Louveciennes, which had belonged to Louis XV's mistress, Madame du Barry.

It was about ten years later that the museum project was born. Although commonly attributed to him, it is now clear that the impulse to collect and then to place the collection in a museum constructed specially for the purpose was primarily Josephine's. As a young man John Bowes had bought pictures, as was expected of a man of wealth and taste, and eventually these were transferred from Streatlam Castle to the museum. But the vast bulk of what was acquired between 1860 and Josephine's death in 1874 can be attributed to her. And it is clear that she bought with the aim of creating a balanced collection of paintings representing all genres and all the major European schools, in particular the Spanish school (Bowes Museum has the largest collection of Spanish paintings in Britain outside London), and ceramics from all the main European porcelain factories. Her taste was excellent, perhaps because she herself was an accomplished artist. However, probably the museum's best-known exhibit, which was not bought by her and which does not fit into her scheme, is the silver swan. This is an automaton made in London in the 1770s, which Bowes bought in Paris in 1872 for £200. The one aspect that cannot be satisfactorily explained is the decision to site the museum in rural Teesdale, which would seem more appropriate for a country house. Yet it is clear that the building was always intended to be a museum and never intended as a house to be lived in.

John Bowes's principal contribution was the building, designed by a French architect, Jules Pellechet, but using local stone from nearby Dunhouse Quarry. It was begun in 1869, but was nowhere near complete when Josephine died in 1874. Nevertheless, Bowes pressed on with what he acknowledged as his wife's project, even to the extent of ensuring that it was continued to completion after his own death in 1885. When it was finally opened in 1892, not only did the building look foreign, its contents too were almost entirely foreign. This foreignness is still evident, although subsequent curators have done much to acquire British and local objects to give the permanent collection a better balance. The museum, which is now owned by a trust, mounts several major temporary exhibitions every year.

John Bowes was also a highly successful owner and breeder of racehorses. Between 1832 and 1853 he won the Derby four times: in 1832 with Mundig, in 1843 with Cotherstone, in 1852 with Daniel O'Rourke and in 1853 with West Australian, which also had the distinction of being the first horse to win the Triple Crown of 2,000 Guineas, Derby and St Leger. As well as the prize money, Bowes is known to have won between £20,000 and £30,000 in bets on each occasion.

BOWMAN, SIR JAMES, Bt (1898–1978)

James Bowman, who had probably the most comprehensive career in the coal industry, was born in Great Corby, near Carlisle. His family moved to Ashington and it was there that in 1913 he started work at the colliery. At the outbreak of World War I in the following year, despite his youth, he joined the Royal Marines. After demobilisation, he returned to work at Ashington and became heavily involved in Lodge affairs. His reputation was that of a political moderate and a conciliator, and it was these qualities combined with his intelligence and ability that led to his election in 1935 as General Secretary of the Northumberland Miners' Association. The following year he joined the executive committee of the Miners' Federation of Great Britain (MFGB), becoming its Vice-President three years later, a post he continued to hold after 1945, when the MFGB became the National Union of Mineworkers (NUM). From 1939, until his retirement from the office in 1949, he was one of the triumvirate that dominated the union's affairs, the others being its President, WILL LAWTHER and the General Secretary, Arthur Horner.

The reason he relinquished his union role was his acceptance of the offer of the post of Chairman of the Northern Division of the National Coal Board (NCB). This remarkable change of sides, which he accomplished successfully, was in part because the coal industry was now in public ownership, but equally it had much to do with his reputation and standing as a person. Progress in this new career was meteoric: in 1955 he became Deputy Chairman, and in the following year, Chairman of the NCB, after the death of Sir Hubert Houldsworth. He continued in this post until ill health forced his retirement in 1961. It was during his years as Chairman that the contraction of the industry in the face of other forms of energy began and he had to close 124 pits and reduce the number of men employed in the industry from 710,000 to 583,000.

Bowman was knighted in 1957 and made baronet in 1961 on the occasion of his leaving office.

BOY SCOUTS

The worldwide organisation of Boy Scouts was founded in the early years of the twentieth century, and from the outset the annual camp under canvas was one of its central activities. The first such camp was held between 22 August and 4 September 1908 at Humshaugh, in the North Tyne valley. A camp had been held the previous year on Brownsea Island, but not all those who attended were sworn Scouts. Consequently, the Humshaugh Camp is regarded as being the first.

BRADLEY, EDWARD alias CUTHBERT BEDE (1827–1889)

Edward Bradley, the son of a surgeon, was born at Kidderminster in 1827. In 1846 he matriculated at Durham University, and obtained a degree in 1848 and a Licentiate in Theology in 1849. In 1850, like most Durham graduates of his day, he was ordained. For the next twenty-one years he served as a curate in a number of parishes, until in 1871 he became Rector of Stretton, near Oakham. He served there for twelve years until 1883, when he obtained a richer living at Lenton, near Grantham, Lincolnshire.

Thus far, his story is entirely conventional and unremarkable. What makes him interesting from the North-East perspective is the three books he wrote charting the adventures of a character he called Mr Verdant Green, a gullible innocent from rural Warwickshire, from his entry to Oxford University through to his graduation and marriage. These he published between 1853 and 1857 under the pen name of Cuthbert Bede. However, despite being a Durham graduate and assuming a Durham alias, Bradley chose to set his stories in Oxford. They are concerned not with the academic business of the university, but with the various extra-curricular activities and escapades with which a less than worldly-wise young man might become involved. The details are surprisingly accurate, although there is no evidence that Bradley was ever at Oxford, unless he was resident there in the eighteen months after leaving Durham, a period for which there is no evidence of his whereabouts. It is likely, therefore, that he combined his personal experience of Durham student life, with (perhaps) some first-hand observation of what happened at Oxford and details gleaned from the available fiction about Oxford.

His books were a commercial success. Printed in paperback, they sold for a shilling each on railway station bookstalls, which had been started in 1848 by W.H. Smith. By 1870, 100,000 copies had been sold. The Verdant Green series was the mid-nineteenth-century equivalent of the novels sold today at railway stations, airports and motorway service stations. The books are also part of a long tradition of Oxford tales, the most recent versions being the Inspector Morse books by Colin Dexter. Although Oxford was the fictional setting, perhaps necessary to ensure commercial viability, Bradley must have drawn heavily on his Durham experience.

BRAINE, JOHN GERARD (1922–1986)

John Braine was born and grew up in Bradford and trained as a librarian in Leeds, subsequently working for local authorities from 1940 until 1957. Among these was the Northumberland County Library Sevice, for which he worked from 1954 until 1956 at Newbiggin by the Sea. It was there that he wrote the novel that made him famous, *Room at the Top*. Although written while in Northumberland, the novel drew on Braine's knowledge of the West Riding of his youth. It is regarded as one of the most significant novels of the early post-war years, with its concern to explore the struggle of a young working-class man to overcome his social disadvantages in his search for success. The novel, and the film based on it, were huge successes, critically and commercially, and enabled Braine to become a full-time author.

BRAND, JOHN (1744–1806)

John Brand, the first serious historian of NEWCASTLE, was born in Washington in 1744. As his mother died in childbirth and his father remarried, Brand's upbringing was entrusted to his maternal uncle, Anthony Wheatley, a Newcastle shoemaker. In one respect this was fortunate: his uncle sent him to the Royal Grammar School, then under Hugh Moises, arguably its most distinguished headmaster. Brand's ability was such that Moises persuaded a number of wealthy men to put up the money to enable him to go to Oxford (Lincoln College), where he graduated with a BA in 1775. This led to a clerical career, which began with a curacy at St Andrew's, Newcastle in 1773, progressed to the perpetual curacy of Cramlington in the following year, and culminated in 1784 with his presentation of two associated livings in the City of London. For these he had to thank his patron, the Duke of Northumberland, who in 1786 appointed him as one of his domestic chaplains.

His move to London coincided with his election to the post of resident secretary of the Society of Antiquaries, of which he had been a Fellow since 1777. From now until his death in 1806, his church livings gave him the financial security that allowed him to pursue his abiding and passionate interest in the past. Brand published several important pieces of research, but the most valuable was *The History and Antiquities of the Town and County of Newcastle upon Tyne*, which appeared in two volumes in 1789 and which is still consulted by historians.

BRANNIGAN, OWEN (1908–1973)

Owen Brannigan, who was one of the finest British bass-baritones of the twentieth century, was born at Annitsford, Northumberland. Initially a carpenter, he trained as a singer at the Guildhall School of Music in London, winning their gold medal in 1942. This was the prelude to a highly successful career spanning the next three decades, which was launched with his debut with Sadler's Wells opera company in Newcastle in 1943. Thereafter, he sang most of the leading operatic roles for his voice at Glyndeborne, Sadler's Wells and Covent Garden, as well as performing on radio and television. In the North East, however, he will always be remembered for his live performances and recordings of the traditional songs of Northumbria. He died of pneumonia in 1973.

BRENT-DYER, ELINOR (1894–1969)

Elinor Brent-Dyer was a prolific writer of 'school stories'. She is especially remembered for her *Chalet School* series, which tell of the adventures of the pupils of a fictitious girls' school in Switzerland. Although not classed as great literature, these books have a continuing popularity, despite their dated tone, as is clearly indicated by their continuing availability in both book and audio form. She was born in South Shields and worked as a teacher there until 1933, when she moved with her parents to Hereford.

BREWIS, HENRY (**see SMYTHE, REGINALD**)

BRIDGES AND VIADUCTS

The North East has eight rivers that rise in the western hills and flow westwards to the North Sea: Tweed, Aln, Coquet, Wansbeck, Blyth, Tyne, Wear and Tees. As so many of the main land routes run in a north–south direction, these rivers are serious obstacles to the movement of people and goods. All of them can be forded at certain points, while ferries have operated from the Middle Ages, for example at Norham (Tweed), Warden (Tyne), Stockton and Billingham (Tees) down to those across the Tyne in modern times. Nevertheless, bridges were always the better solution to the problem than fords and ferries. In addition to the main rivers are seven tributaries classified as rivers, all of them wide enough in parts to be an obstacle: Till/Breamish, Derwent, Allen, Browney, Deerness, Gaunless and Skerne.

Recent detailed studies of the Tees and the Wear have established the existence of forty-nine bridges and eighty-three bridges respectively. To these can be added seventy-five for the Northumberland rivers, including thirty on the Tyne, and sixty-nine on the seven tributaries.

The earliest known bridges are those built by the Roman army (five certain and another five probable) as part of the ROMAN ROAD system. But it was in the medieval centuries between 1110 and 1600 that bridge building became widespread, with thirty-eight known examples, at least one across every river. Little or nothing is known about their construction. Almost certainly the earliest is Framwellgate Bridge across the Wear at Durham, constructed by BISHOP RANNULF FLAMBARD in the second decade of the twelfth century. This was one of the earliest stone bridges to be built in England since the Roman period, and it is unlikely that any of the region's medieval bridges pre-dates it. The latest was probably the wooden bridge across the Wear below the Watergate in Durham in 1574. That over the Tees at BARNARD CASTLE bears the date 1569, but this may mark the repair of major damage to the fourteenth-century bridge during the rebellion of that year. Most were of stone, although that at Berwick, known to have existed as early as the reign of Malcolm IV (1153–65), was of wood and had to be replaced three times before it was reconstructed in stone in the seventeenth century. Nor is much known about who commissioned them and paid for them. In the case of those in towns, whose economic activity would certainly benefit from improved means of communication, the urban authorities would be involved, even to the extent of being allowed to levy *pontage*, charges for use to help defray the cost of maintenance. Another driving force was the bishops of Durham, who had the power and the wealth to see bridge construction through to completion, as at Durham, but who also had the authority to proclaim an indulgence (remission of sins) for those contributing to the support of a particular bridge, a reminder that throughout the medieval centuries contributing to the construction and repair of a bridge was a religious act. This was almost certainly in the mind of the Newcastle merchant John Cook, who in 1379 bequeathed the sum of 20 marks (£13.34) to the bridge over the Coquet at Warkworth. Indeed, several bridges had chapels, either at their ends or in the middle. The known examples of this phenomenon were Newcastle and Framwellgate and Elvet in Durham. Bridges also formed part of the defensive arrangements of towns, hence the towered gateways originally on the bridges at Warkworth (which uniquely still stands), Newcastle and Framwellgate in Durham.

The complete list of pre-Reformation bridges is: Berwick (Tweed); Alnwick, Lesbury (Aln); Warkworth, Felton, Rothbury (Coquet); Sheepwash, Morpeth (Wansbeck); Hartford (Blyth); Newcastle, Prudhoe, Corbridge, Hexham, Haydon (Tyne); Chester le Street, Framwellgate, Elvet and Watergate in Durham, Shincliffe, Croxdale, Bishop Auckland, Witton le Wear, Wolsingham, Frosterley, Stanhope (Wear); Egglescliffe, Eggleston, Middleton St George, Hurworth, Piercebridge, Barnard Castle (Tees). In addition, seven bridges were built over tributary rivers: Twizel (Till), Linnels (Devils Water), Shotley (Derwent), Brancepeth, Aldin Grange

(Browney), South Church Deanery (Gaunless) and Darlington (Skerne). Berwick, Sheepwash, Newcastle, Shotley, Watergate and Shincliffe have disappeared completely, although all but Sheepwash have later replacements. All the survivors have been seriously damaged on more than one occasion and all have been widened, so that what we see today is not exactly what was first built. That over the Till at Twizel, believed to have been built in the fifteenth century, has a span of 90 feet (27.5 m) and is thought to have been the longest single span bridge in England prior to the CAUSEY ARCH.

Few new bridges were built in the 150 years after 1600. The only two known for certain are the Old Bridge at Berwick (still in use) built in stone between 1611 and 1626 at the instigation of James VI and I to replace the wooded structure; and the 1674 bridge at Corbridge, the only one on the Tyne to survive the great flood of 16 November 1771.

Between the mid-eighteenth century and World War I, a large number of bridges were constructed, in most cases from scratch, but in a few cases as replacements for earlier bridges. This was the consequence of two interacting factors: increase in demand for better transport arising from the growth of population and the expansion of industry; and the ability of civil and mechanical engineering to provide solutions to the obstacles hindering the satisfaction of that demand. Until 1830 bridges were built to carry road transport, but thereafter the growth of the railway system led to a new type of bridge (see RAILWAYS).

The earliest of the bridges of this period was the Sunderland Iron Bridge over the Wear, the destruction of which has been a great loss to the region's heritage. The need for a bridge was mooted in 1788, but it was not until 1792 that the requisite parliamentary act was obtained. The driving force behind the project was Rowland Burdon of Castle Eden, MP (1757–1838), who eventually put up three-quarters of the total cost of £40,000. The decision to build in iron resulted from calculations showing iron to be much cheaper than stone and more durable than wood. Who designed the bridge is not entirely clear. Although Burdon secured a patent that made him officially the designer, it is almost certain that the design decisions were those of several men, notably Thomas Wilson, the Sunderland teacher appointed as director of operations, and foundry experts at the Rotherham firm of Walkers, which made the iron parts. The masonry abutments of the bridge took two years to complete, but the iron superstructure, which weighed less than 1,000 tons, was assembled within a few weeks in the autumn of 1795. The bridge was opened in August 1796.

In 1805 horizontal bracing was added to counter the damaging effects of uneven thermal expansion. Then in the late 1850s, ROBERT STEPHENSON undertook a major reconstruction, whereby the bridge lost its humped deck and, according to Nikolaus Pevsner, its 'superb elegance'. In 1929 the bridge was replaced by the present Wearmouth Bridge, designed by Mott, Hay and Anderson, who also were responsible for the Tyne Bridge, opened the previous year.

Iron was also the material used in constructing the four interesting examples of the suspension bridge built in the early years of this phase. The first, known as the Winch Bridge, crossed the Tees at Middleton in Teesdale, and was the earliest suspension bridge in Europe. Built around 1741, it was a footbridge, 70 feet (21 m) long but only 2 feet (60 cm) wide. It was replaced by the present bridge in the early nineteenth century. More famous is the Union Bridge over the Tweed at Loan End, built by Captain Samuel Brown, RN in 1820. It was the first suspension bridge in Europe to carry vehicular traffic (as it still does) and its hangers were made of wrought iron chains, patented by Brown in 1817. The original chains were replaced in 1870 and wire ropes were added in 1902. Nevertheless, the utility of Brown's invention is underlined by the third suspension bridge, that over the Tees at Whorlton, designed by JOHN AND BENJAMIN GREEN, which has the distinction of being the only suspension bridge in Europe whose deck is still supported by its original chains. The Greens were also responsible for Scotswood Bridge, known as the Chain Bridge, over the Tyne, opened in 1831, but replaced in the 1960s.

The later nineteenth century saw the construction of three bridges of even greater ingenuity. The earliest was the Swing Bridge over the Tyne, built to replace the nine-arch Georgian bridge opened in 1781, which itself was a replacement of the mid-thirteenth-century bridge with its houses and shops destroyed by the great flood on the night of 16 November 1771. The 1781 bridge, designed by Robert Mylne, although elegant was a conventional low-level bridge that prevented all but the smallest vessels passing under it. As its name implies, the Swing Bridge has a movable section that pivots on an 'island', created midstream, to swing parallel to the river so as to allow ocean-going ships to move upriver of Newcastle through gaps on either side, each 95 feet (29 m) wide. This section is 282 feet (86 m) long and 48 feet (14.6 m) wide and weighs 1,450 tons. It was designed to line up with the piers of the High Level Bridge (see below) by John Ure of the Tyne Improvement Commission, which was also responsible for the 'island' on which it rests. Its superstructure and the steam-driven hydraulic machinery (replaced by electric pumps in 1959) that moves it were built by the firm of Sir W.G. Armstrong, whose Elswick works stood to benefit from it. The bridge was built between 1868 and 1876, during which period a temporary bridge was in use. Two years later another smaller but equally ingenious bridge by WILLIAM ARMSTRONG was opened in Newcastle. This was the Armstrong Bridge spanning Jesmond Dene between Jesmond and Heaton, which was pedestrianised in 1960. It is 552 feet (168 m) long and its deck is 65 feet (20 m) above the Ouseburn. It is made entirely of iron, except for the abutments and the footings on which its wrought iron columns stand, which are of stone.

The third notable bridge is the Transporter Bridge over the Tees between Port Clarence and Middlesbrough. The idea was first mooted by a Hartlepool engineer, Charles Smith, but considerations of cost delayed construction until 1907. The bridge, which was designed by the Cleveland Bridge and Engineering Co. of Darlington and built by Sir William Arrol & Co. of Glasgow, was opened in 1911. It consists of four steel towers on either bank, which support a cantilevered gantry. From the underside of this is suspended a platform carrying passengers and vehicles, which is moved back and forth across the river (at that point 565 feet (172 m) wide) by electric motors. The platform rides 150 feet (46 m) below the gantry on which it travels about 9 feet (3 m) above the water at high tide. Sixteen similar bridges were built elsewhere between 1893 and 1916, but only six survive.

Other notable road bridges of this period are: Tweed: Norham (1838 and 1887), Coldstream (1766); Aln: Alnwick Lion Bridge (1773), Denwick (1766), Canongate (1821); Coquet: Weldon (*c.*1760); Wansbeck: Lowford (1836); Tyne: Newcastle (1779), Redheugh (1871 and 1901), Newburn (1893), Armstrong Bridge and Byker Bridge (over the Ouseburn, 1878), Bywell (1838), Hexham (1770, 1781 and 1783), Bellingham (1834), Falstone (1843), Haydon (1776),

Warden (1826 and 1903), Ridley (1792), Bardon Mill (1883), Featherstone (1778), Eals (1773); Derwent: Shotley (*c.*1790); Wear: Sunderland Iron bridge (1796), Durham Prebends (1778), Witton le Wear (1788); Tees: Stockton (1887), Yarm (1799), Blackwell (1832), Winston (1763), Middleton in Teesdale (1800).

Twenty-four new bridges were built for the railway. Arguably the most impressive is the High Level Bridge over the Tyne between Gateshead and Newcastle (1849–50), which also has a road deck running below that for rail. It is 1,400 feet (427 m) long, with six main spans of 125 feet (38 m), and 40 feet (12 m) wide. Its lower deck is 120 feet (37 m) above the river at low water. The masonry pillars of local stone rest on timber piles driven into the riverbed by James Nasmyth's recently devised steam hammer. The iron parts, many of Redesdale iron, were fabricated by the firm of Hawks, Crawshay of Gateshead. The High Level Bridge, without which the Main East Coast Railway Line would not have been continuous, was one of the great engineering triumphs of Robert Stephenson, ably assisted by THOMAS HARRISON. Its rail deck was opened in August 1849 and the road deck in February 1850. The bridge was strengthened between 1919 and 1922, and in 2008 was reopened after a major overhaul. A similar bridge, the Queen Alexandra Bridge, was built across the Wear at Sunderland in 1909. Two other rail bridges, also in Newcastle and Sunderland, were of major importance. The earlier was that over the Wear at Sunderland (1879). This linked the rail systems on the two sides of the river, hitherto unconnected, and also allowed the construction of a central station for the town. The other was the King Edward Bridge over the Tyne between Gateshead and Newcastle (1906), which relieved the pressure on the High Level Bridge and allowed trains to run continuously through Central Station – until that time trains had to leave the station by the line on which they entered, which involved transferring locomotives from one end to the other.

Among the impressive consequences of the railway were the twenty-six viaducts. The earliest is the Victoria Viaduct of four arches, built between 1836 and 1838 to carry the Durham Junction Railway over the Wear near Penshaw. Virtually contemporary with it, but more spectacular, is the Ouseburn Viaduct built between 1837 and 1839 to carry the Newcastle and North Shields Railway over the deep Ouseburn valley. Designed by JOHN GREEN, it is 918 feet (280 m) long, has nine arches and is 108 feet (33 m) above the burn. The four outer arches are of stone, but the five inner arches are of iron resting on masonry pillars. These iron arches replaced (in 1867) the original arches made of laminated wood. The viaduct was widened in 1887. The longest viaduct by far is the Egglescliffe Viaduct (1849) of forty-three arches over the Tees and to and over Yarm, while the best known and most photographed are the Royal Border Bridge (1850) and the Durham Viaduct (1857), both on the East Coast Main Line. Six viaducts have been demolished, while that built by the Border Counties Railway north of Falstone (1862) in North Tynedale is now under KIELDER WATER. Another nine viaducts are no longer in use and include four that continue to enhance the landscape and make a dramatic visual impact: Newton Cap (1857, converted to road use in 1993); Hownes Gill near Consett (1858); Lambley in South Tynedale (1852); and Edlingham (1885).

The contraction of the rail network has led to the discontinued use of many rail bridges and in some cases demolition. This is particularly the case where the primary use of the railway concerned was moving coal. In contrast, there has been a continuous increase in the amount of vehicular traffic, which has led to the building of new roads and therefore bridges, in many cases to bypass towns and villages. The earliest and most novel bridge of the modern era is Newport Bridge (1925) over the Tees at Middlesbrough, which consisted of a steel roadway that could be raised vertically between twin towers on either side of the river to a height of 120 feet (37 m) to allow the passage of large ships. More famous and more frequently photographed is the Tyne Bridge (1928). Contrary to popular belief, this was not the model for the Sydney Harbour Bridge. Rather it was the other way round, but the Tyne Bridge, being the smaller, was opened in 1928, four years before the larger Australian version. The designer of both bridges was Ralph Freeman of Mott, Hay and Anderson, who was influenced by New York's Hell Gate Bridge, and the contract for both went to the Middlesbrough firm of Dorman, Long. The Cornish granite pylons at either end of the bridge were designed by the Newcastle architect Robert Burns Dick. The bridge, which with its associated road works cost £1,200,000, spans the Tyne gorge by means of a single steel arch 531 feet (162 m) long, with a road deck 84 feet (26 m) above the river at high water, sufficient to allow the passage of large ships up and down river. The other outstanding bridge of recent times is the third Redheugh (1983), which is far more elegant than its two predecessors. In contrast, the Scotswood Bridge (1964) has been plagued with engineering weaknesses and compared with its elegant predecessor, the Chain Bridge of 1831, has no visual appeal.

Recently, Northumbria has acquired five footbridges, three outstanding in terms of elegance and engineering invention. The earlier, Kingsgate Bridge, over the Wear in Durham (1962), was designed by Ove Arup and made of concrete. It consists of two triangular structures resting on pivots on either side of the river, which allowed it to be swung outwards to meet and be joined high above water. The other is the Gateshead Millennium Bridge over the Tyne (2001), linking the redevelopment projects along the quaysides on either side of the river. The design competition, launched in 1996, was won by the architects Wilkinson Eyre, with the world's first tilting bridge. The foot and cycle ways and the arch from which they are suspended are of steel and were fabricated lower down the Tyne and brought upriver by a giant Dutch floating crane, which lowered the arch into preconstructed concrete pivots. The arch is tilted hydraulically (the process takes under five minutes) through an angle of 40° to give a 150-foot (46 m) clearance above the water, allowing ships to pass underneath. The third, open in 2009, is the Infinity Bridge over the Tees at Stockton. The others are the Pennyferry Bridge at Durham and the Tees Millennium Bridge between Stockton and Middlesbrough. Otherwise, the major bridge works of the late twentieth century relate to the building of motorways and bypasses. A1 and A1(M): Tweed (Berwick), Coquet (Felton), Tyne (Blaydon), Wear (Chester le Street), Tees (Barton); A69: Tyne (Hexham, Haltwhistle); A19: Tees (Middlesbrough/Stockton Flyover), Wear (Sunderland). The one new railway bridge to be built is the Queen Elizabeth II Bridge (1980) over the Tyne to carry the Metro system between Gateshead and Newcastle.

BRINKBURN PRIORY

Brinkburn was one of the two houses of Augustinian canons (also known from the colour of their habit as the Black Canons) founded within the region, the other being Hexham. Like the more widely used Rule of St Benedict, the rule devised by St

Augustine of Hippo Regius (now Annaba in Algeria), imposed poverty, chastity and obedience; but it was not so rigorous and it did permit work outside the cloister, which enabled canons to act as parish priests. This made it attractive to the early twelfth-century reformers convinced that celibate canons would make far better parish priests than ordinary clergy, who were reluctant to give up their wives.

Brinkburn was founded by William de Bertram I, to whom the Barony of Mitford was granted by Henry I, on wasteland in the valley of the Coquet, five miles east of ROTHBURY. The date is uncertain, but it was probably between 1130 and 1135. The initial complement of canons came from the priory at Pentney in Norfolk. Brinkburn's early development was slow and it was not until 1188 that it was sufficiently endowed to become independent of its mother-house. It was at that time that the church was begun, its architecture, a mixture of Romanesque and Early English Gothic, indicating a construction period of around forty years between c. 1190 and c. 1220.

Brinkburn was never a rich house. Apart from the grants of land by the early members of the Bertram family, the canons acquired in 150 separate transactions by gift, purchase or mortgage foreclosure properties in thirty places in Northumberland. Included were two parish churches, Felton, gifted at the outset, and Longhorsley, acquired in 1387. In the end, its annual income of only £85 meant that it was among the first batch of monasteries to be closed under the act of 1536.

The church was restored and re-roofed in 1858–59 and reglazed between 1861 and 1864 by the Cadogan family, which had made its fortune in Barbados and which acquired the estate in 1792. The buildings were placed in the care of the Ministry of Public Buildings and Works, the forerunner of the present guardians, English Heritage, in 1965. Nothing of the associated monastic buildings remains, except part of the refectory, which was incorporated into a house that was developed on the site between the sixteenth and nineteenth centuries.

BROCKETT, JOHN TROTTER (1788–1842)

John Trotter Brockett was the first person to make a concerted attempt to collect and publish all the words in use in the speech of the region. He can therefore be regarded as the initiator of the study of the region's dialect. He was born at Witton Gilbert, but in his youth he moved with his family to Gateshead. After education in NEWCASTLE, he trained as a lawyer and subsequently practised in the city. Like many educated men of his day, he was interested in the past, particularly in numismatics and philology, which inevitably led to his membership of the LITERARY AND PHILOSOPHICAL SOCIETY OF NEWCASTLE UPON TYNE and the Society of Antiquaries. Although he published works on coinage, and contributed articles to *Archaeologia Aeliana*, the work for which he is remembered is his *Glossary of North Country Words in Use*, the first edition of which was published in 1825, not by him, however, but by JOHN GEORGE LAMBTON, the future Earl of Durham. A revised edition appeared in 1829. The final version, however, enlarged and in two volumes, was completed by a relative and published in 1846, five years after Brockett's death. Although the work is defective by the present standards of scholarship, it is still widely consulted as a valuable source of information about the dialects of the North East.

BROUGH, EDWARD (1846–1933) and JOSEPH WILLIAM (1871–1958)

Nothing is known of the origins of Edward Brough, except that he was born in America and that he had arrived on Tyneside by

1866, when he joined a firm of provisions importers, Edward Hume & Co. Ten years later he went into partnership with a man called Frazer to set up a firm to import eggs and butter. Then, in 1888, he set up his own wholesale provisions business with his eldest son, Joseph William. The latter, however, started his own retail business in 1894, and in 1900 Edward sold his wholesale concern to help his son with what was a rapidly growing enterprise.

The younger Brough's business ambition was to challenge the Co-operative Societies, which had come to dominate the retail food trade in working-class areas. This involved the use of travellers to take weekly orders from housewives, which were then made up in a warehouse in NEWCASTLE and delivered to the home by carrier. In order to secure orders, prices had to be low: Brough therefore worked on the basis of 12 per cent gross profit and 5 per cent net profit. This in turn required the turnover to be large. This was ensured from 1901 by the acquisition of a network of shops, which in effect were small local versions of the Newcastle warehouse. Each bore the slogan *Wholesale Cash Store*, emphasising Brough's policies of low prices and no credit.

The enterprise was sold in 1919 to the Meadow Dairy Co. for £216,000, although Broughs continued to trade under that name and according to the founder's policy until after World War II.

BROWN, LANCELOT (1716–1783)

Known as 'Capability' Brown on account of his habit of saying that land had the 'capability' of improvement, he was born at Kirkharle (Northumberland) in 1716, ostensibly the fifth child of William Brown, but possibly the illegitimate son of the lord of the manor, Sir William Loraine (1659–1743) and a servant girl. Whether this was true or not, it was Loraine who gave Brown an education at the school at Cambo and took him on to his gardening staff, where he learned the basics of horticulture. In 1740, however, at the age of twenty-three, he moved south supported by a reference from Lady Loraine and obtained a post on the gardening staff of Lord Cobham at Stowe in Buckinghamshire. This move led to a profound change in Brown's thinking. At that time, the grounds at Stowe were being transformed by Charles Bridgman and William Kent, who wished to abandon the rigid and geometrical formality of contemporary gardens dominated by parterres, fountains and elaborate topiary. Instead, they favoured a more 'natural' style, reshaping the landscape around a house so that it looked as though it was not man-made. Brown remained at Stowe until after the deaths of Kent and Lord Cobham, in 1748 and 1750 respectively. By then he had formulated his own ideas and philosophy and had married and started a family. In 1751 he moved to Hammersmith and started his own business as a landscape gardener and consultant.

In the course of the next thirty years Brown was to transform the grounds of over a hundred stately homes, including ALNWICK in his native county. But more than that, he altered the way their owners thought about the landscape in which their homes were located. His landscapes may have looked natural, but they were as contrived as those they replaced. Lakes were created by damming streams, small hills were made out of flat land while existing hills were levelled, and trees were planted to form shelter belts and pleasing features. Everywhere Brown skilfully assessed the potential of the ground and produced an imaginative and appropriate design. Moreover, he devised a means of transplanting mature trees, so that his patrons would get an early idea of how the long-term results of his work would appear. Brown owed his success not solely to his flair as a designer: he also had the immense advantage of being able to develop an easy and amicable relationship with the wide variety of aristocrats for whom he worked. And his success was all the more remarkable in that he was a lifelong sufferer from asthma, at that time a considerable handicap for a gardener.

Brown's career culminated in 1764 when, on the urging of many members of the nobility, George III appointed him Surveyor of His Majesty's Gardens, with responsibility for Hampton Court, St James's Park and Richmond Park. While he made major changes at Richmond, he did little to alter what must have seemed the old-fashioned style at Hampton Court. Three years after his royal appointment, Brown himself joined the ranks of the landowning class, when he purchased Fenstanton Manor in Huntingdonshire.

Brown died of a heart attack on 6 February 1783 at the age of sixty-seven. His legacy has endured to this day, despite the changes in fashion in garden design. If there is one valid criticism that can be made of what he did it is that he adhered too rigidly to his principles, in particular in destroying parterres where their retention would have complemented, not detracted from, his work. Nor was he without critics in his own day, one of whom was the poet William Cowper: 'Improvement too, the idol of the age, / Is fed with many a victim. Lo! He comes – / The omnipotent magician, Brown, appears ... / He speaks. The lake in front becomes a lawn, / Woods vanish, hills subside, and valleys rise, / And streams, as if created for his use, / Pursue the track of his directing wand ....'

BROWNE, SIR BENJAMIN CHAPMAN (1839–1917)

Benjamin Browne, who was born at Uley in Gloucestershire, the son of the Colonel of the 9th Lancers, became a major figure in the Tyneside shipbuilding industry in the last decades of the nineteenth century. As befitted a son of socially elite parents, he was sent to Westminster School and then to King's College, London. In 1856 he took a five-year apprenticeship at SIR WILLIAM ARMSTRONG's works at Elswick to qualify as an engineer. Following this, he practised as a civil engineer, including working for the Tyne Commission. In 1870, however, with the financial help of his mother, the NEWCASTLE banker THOMAS HODGKIN, and a local industrialist, John Straker, he bought the engineering firm of R. and W. Hawthorn, which had its works at Forth Banks and St Peters in Newcastle, the latter specialising in marine engines. In 1886 Browne negotiated the merger of Hawthorns and the shipbuilding company of ANDREW LESLIE, who retired in that year. Browne became chairman of the new company and remained in that post for thirty years until his retirement in 1916. During those years, Browne and his shipyard manager, HERBERT ROWELL, made Hawthorn, Leslie one of the leading makers of marine engines and steam turbines and the principal supplier to the Admiralty of engines for destroyers.

Browne, a Conservative in politics, was for several years a member of Newcastle Town Council and served as mayor from 1885 until 1887. He also had an interest in NESCO (Newcastle upon Tyne Electric Supply Co.) and was involved in setting up the Newcastle College of Physical Science, the forerunner of Newcastle University.

BROWNING, ELIZABETH BARRETT (1806–1861)

Elizabeth Barrett, herself a poet and the wife of another poet, Robert Browning, was born at Coxhoe Hall, Durham (demolished in 1956, exactly 150 years after her birth) and baptised in Kelloe church. Her father, Edward Barrett, was not of the North East, but her mother, Mary, was the daughter of a Newcastle merchant, John Graham-Clarke, who at various times owned Kenton Lodge and Fenham Hall, as well as a house in Pilgrim Street in the town. Three years after Elizabeth's birth, the Brownings gave up the lease of Coxhoe Hall and moved elsewhere. As far as is known, Elizabeth Barrett Browning never visited the North East after her departure in 1809.

BRUCE, ROBERT, KING OF SCOTS (**see BALLIOL AND BRUCE FAMILIES**)

BRYMER, JACK (1915–2003)

Jack Brymer, who was one of the best-known, most accomplished and most influential clarinet players of the twentieth century, was born at South Shields. His rise to prominence was, however, largely accidental. Although he learned to play the clarinet to professional standard by the time he was eleven years old, he attended South Shields Grammar School and then trained as a teacher at Goldsmiths' College in London. Thereafter, he taught at a school in Croydon before and after World War II, playing in amateur orchestras in his leisure time. His reputation, however, was sufficient for him to be brought to the attention of Sir Thomas Beecham, who immediately took him into the Royal Philharmonic Orchestra. Subsequently, he moved to the BBC Symphony Orchestra and then the London Symphony Orchestra, from which he retired in 1972. But Brymer was not simply an orchestral player. He was highly respected soloist, who played and recorded all the major works for clarinet and, in addition, a presenter of programmes on the BBC. And as well as the classical repertoire, he enjoyed playing lighter music and traditional jazz.

BUDDLE, JOHN (1773–1843)

John Buddle was a man of immense standing and reputation in mining circles in the early decades of the nineteenth century, so much so that he was called 'King of the Coal Trade'. In considerable part his status stemmed from his position as the agent of the 3RD MARQUESS OF LONDONDERRY'S coal empire, a post he held from 1819 until his death in 1843. The two men formed a formidable partnership. Final decisions on major matters always rested with Londonderry, who was inclined to be impetuous and did not always act in accordance with Buddle's wishes or advice, but Buddle, who was a hard-headed realist, had day-to-day control and provided the expert knowledge of the workings – technical, financial, commercial and political – of the coal trade. Above all, he was Londonderry's right-hand man in his great enterprise of building a new coal exporting port, Seaham Harbour (SEE NEW TOWNS OF THE NINETEENTH CENTURY). Arguably, Londonderry would not have achieved what he did without Buddle's expertise and sound judgement.

Buddle achieved this eminent position to a considerable extent through the grounding he received. He was born at Kyo to a self-educated man who was both a miner and a schoolmaster and whose mathematical ability and mastery of the whole range of mining matters led to his appointment as viewer at Wallsend Colliery. Buddle senior educated his son thoroughly and then trained him to be his assistant. The measure of his success was that upon his death in 1806, Buddle was immediately appointed to his father's post.

Buddle was concerned to improve all aspects of mining. He was among those who, following the disaster at Felling Colliery in 1812, set up the Sunderland Society for the Prevention of Accidents in Mines, which led to the invention of three workable solutions (see COLLIERY DISASTERS). Two years later, in a paper he delivered to the Natural History Society of Northumberland, Durham and Newcastle upon Tyne, he argued the importance of preserving mining records, and this led to the society's becoming an office of deposit for such material. His interest in mining also extended to its scientific aspects, particularly the geology, which resulted in his publishing towards the end of his life *A Synopsis of the Newcastle Coalfield.* But it was as Londonderry's agent that he had the scope for effecting practical improvements, the motive force being to increase operational efficiency and thereby profitability of the mines under his control. In his time he made notable improvements in the ventilation of mine workings and the transport of coal, both above and below ground, and he devised ways of extracting the pillars of coal that hitherto had been left unmined as roof supports.

As well as being Londonderry's agent, Buddle had a business life of his own. He acted as viewer to some coal owners and as a paid consultant to others; he was a shareholder in several collieries and shipping ventures; for several decades he acted as secretary to the Tyne Coal Owners' Association; and as a witness before parliamentary inquiries into the coal trade he more than held his own. The measure of his success is that he is reputed to have left £150,000 in his will, a fortune whose size may have been owed in part to the fact that he never married. Buddle was the most outstanding of a small group of men who were, in effect, the 'aristocracy' of the coal trade. Without their expertise, aristocrats such as Londonderry who owned the collieries would have been unable to exploit them, a fact that both parties recognised.

BUNTING, BASIL CHEESMAN (1900–1985)

Basil Bunting is now recognised as one of the best English poets of the twentieth century, although this recognition was late in coming and his reputation was not fully made until after his retirement in 1965. He was the son of a Derbyshire man, Thomas Bunting, who settled in Scotswood as a doctor and married a local woman, Annie Cheesman. Bunting's father sent him to two Quaker schools, Ackworth, near Pontefract, and Leighton Park, Reading, and it was proabably the Quaker influence that led him to be a conscientious objector in 1918, even to the extent of refusing employment, since this might release another man to fight. Twenty-two years later, however, he went to considerable lengths to be accepted into the armed forces, despite his defective eyesight. Initially he served in the ranks, but in 1943 he secured a commission and a place in Intelligence as the result of his command of Persian, which he had taught himself in order to read the poet Firdausi in the original. By the end of the war he had reached the rank of Squadron Leader.

Between the wars, he led a rather unsettled life and had a variety of jobs, both in Britain and abroad, but after 1945 his employment was much steadier. Until 1952, when he was expelled, he was *The Times*'s correspondent in Tehran; thereafter he returned to his roots and, until his retirement in 1965, he worked as a sub-editor on the *Newcastle Journal* and then the *Evening Chronicle.*

Bunting's output was not large, although he was writing and publishing his poetry from 1925. His reputation was finally established by his long poem, *Briggflatts,* published in 1965. Although the name of the title is that of a Quaker village in Cumbria, a place where he found solace, the poem is an autobiography in which Bunting recounts his life's journey, emphasising the influence of and his attachment to Newcastle and Northumberland, and to the language of its people.

BURT, THOMAS (1837–1922)

Thomas Burt had two overlapping careers of equal importance, as a trade union leader and as the first genuine working-class MP. He was born at Murton Row (now Preston Grange) in North Tyneside. His father was a miner who, like most men in that trade at that date, moved frequently under the yearly bond system. Consequently, Burt's early years were spent at several pit villages in Durham and Northumberland, where he secured two years' schooling. Notwithstanding this meagre education, he became an erudite man through his own reading, although the deepest and most abiding influences on him were, as with so many North-East miners at this date, the tenets of Primitive Methodism. In 1847, at the age of ten, he started work as a trapper at Haswell Colliery in County Durham. In the following three years, he worked at Sherburn House, South Hetton and Murton collieries in Durham, and then at New Hartley, Cramlington, Seaton Delaval and finally Choppington in Northumberland.

In the early 1860s came the first of the two great changes in his life. In 1863 the Northumberland Miners' Association was founded, and two years later Burt was elected as its General Secretary in succession to William Crawford. He was to remain in that post for forty-eight years, until 1913. His views on the relationship between his union and the coal owners who employed its members never fundamentally changed and were expressed clearly, positively and eloquently. He believed that co-operation between employer and employee was natural and in the interest of both parties and so he opposed the use of strikes, except as a last resort when employers acted unjustly or were unreasonably obdurate. To sustain this non-confrontational approach, he sought to create and develop the machinery of conciliation and arbitration. Underlying these views was a belief that wages could not be arbitrary but must relate to the sale price of coal, rising and falling with it. He also favoured minimum government intrusion into the relations between the two sides of industry, particularly in the matter of wages, although he did approve of legislation to improve working and living conditions.

In all of these ideas he was in tune with the thinking of his day, at least at the outset. By the beginning of the twentieth century, however, Burt's ideas were beginning to fall out of favour. In 1889, a national miners' organisation, the Miners' Federation of Great Britain (MFGB), was formed, with ideas markedly different to those held by Burt. Led by a militant Yorkshireman, Ben Pickard, the Federation advocated a minimum wage, payable irrespective of the conditions of trade. It also favoured aggressive strikes and a legally imposed eight-hour day. Burt opposed both policies and attitudes, in the case of the eight-hour day because in Northumberland his Association had already achieved a seven-hour day for face workers. Across the whole front of industrial relations, however, Burt was increasingly fighting a rearguard action, and in 1907 he failed to prevent the Northumberland Miners' Association voting to join the MFGB. Although Burt continued to occupy the post of General Secretary until 1913, after 1890 his other interests and then declining health led to his deputy, William Straker, undertaking the routine work of the Association.

The interest that most distracted Burt from his union work was his role as an MP. In 1874 he was elected as Liberal member for Morpeth, the first genuinely working-class man to enter parliament. This was made possible by three coinciding factors. One was the enlargement of the Morpeth constituency following the parliamentary reform act of 1867 to include the mining villages of BEDLINGTON, Choppington, Bebside, Newsham and Cowpen, and the port of BLYTH. If miners could qualify for the franchise under the terms of the act in this enlarged constituency, they would form the majority of the voters. This was achieved after much legal argument. The final factor was the willingness of the Northumberland Miners' Association to pay Burt a yearly salary of £500.

Burt's political position was notable for his advocacy of three things. He favoured legislative action to bring about the amelioration of working-class living conditions; he was hostile to a forward foreign policy, opposing the South African War and supporting the International Arbitration League; and he supported the Irish Land Act of 1881 (giving Irish tenant farmers the 'Three Fs': fixity of tenure, fair rents and freedom to sell) and the moves to give Ireland Home Rule. He also supported, reluctantly, the Irish Coercion Act, passed in the days following the murder of Lord Frederick Cavendish in Phoenix Park, Dublin in 1882. In almost everything he was close to Gladstone, too much so in the minds of some, although in fairness his political attitudes mirrored those he held as a trade unionist. As a committed Liberal, Burt strongly disliked the emerging Labour Party, on three grounds. He was fundamentally opposed to the idea of an avowedly class-based political party; he disliked the emphasis Socialists placed upon workers' rights to the exclusion of their responsibilities; and on his home ground he saw no useful purpose in the nationalisation of coal mines, although he did favour state ownership of railways.

Burt was essentially a backbencher and one whose views were presented lucidly and with cogent argument that gained the respect if not the agreement of all sides. His only time in government was as Parliamentary Secretary to the Board of Trade between 1892 and 1895, when his chief was A.J. Mundella, the strong advocate of industrial arbitration who had done much to set up appropriate machinery in the lace trade in Nottingham. A measure of Burt's general standing in the political world was his elevation to the Privy Council in 1905. By that time his career was coming to an end and in 1915 he announced that he would stand down at the next election. This came in 1918, and it was a sign of how far Burt was a man of the past that Morpeth was won by the Labour candidate, John Cairns.

Burt's memorial still stands in Northumberland Road, Newcastle. It is the Burt Memorial Hall, built in the early 1890s as the new headquarters of the Northumberland Miners' Association. Its front is crowned with a statue of a miner based upon RALPH HEDLEY's picture of 1888 entitled *Going Home*. Burt Hall is now part of Northumbria University.

BURY, RICHARD DE (1281–1345)

Richard de Bury was the son of a Leicestershire knight, Sir Richard D'Aungerville, but he is usually known by the place where he studied, Bury St Edmunds, in Suffolk. He was educated by his uncle, the parish rector, then at the abbey school at Bury and finally at Oxford, where he enjoyed a reputation for theology and philosophy and where he probably acquired his lifelong passion for books. His reputation led Edward II to appoint him as tutor to his eldest son, the future Edward III. He was also employed in various offices of state and on several important diplomatic missions, including two to the papal court at Avignon, where he impressed Pope John XXII. All the while, as was usual, he was granted a number of lucrative ecclesiastical benefices that did not require personal residence.

The ecclesiastical aspect of his career culminated in his elevation to the bishopric of Durham in 1333, although against the wishes of the monks, who elected their own Sub-prior, ROBERT GRAYSTANES. Their wishes, however, were overridden by the combined weight of the Crown and the Papacy, both of them determined that Bury should go to Durham. For the next few years Bury, heavily employed in the service of the state, can have spent little time in the diocese. In 1337 and by now over fifty, he was released from public life to spend his remaining years in Durham.

Richard de Bury's career was very conventional: university training followed by service in government and the royal household, rewarded by ecclesiastical preferment. What made him exceptional was his overwhelming passion for books, and throughout his life he spent a great deal of time and money collecting books and manuscripts. He was said by a contemporary to have had more books than all the rest of the episcopal bench and he admitted that it would be easier to bribe him with a book than with money. Although bitten by the collecting bug, there was another purpose behind this constant accumulation: to found a college at Oxford University and to donate his books to its library. Alas, he realised neither ambition. It was his successor, Thomas de Hatfield, who founded Durham College, Oxford (see OXFORD UNIVERSITY COLLEGES) and, upon Bury's death, his library was dispersed. Today a few are in the British Library and a few in the Bodleian Library, but none is at Durham.

Bury's legacy is not his collection, but the one book he wrote himself, *Philobiblon* (*Book Lover*). In it he expounded, and excused, his love of books, and championed their importance and their need to be treasured. He explained how he collected them and laid down rules for the running of the library he hoped to found at Oxford; and he also included a great deal of information about the contemporary state of European scholarship. The book has enjoyed an international reputation. It was printed in Germany as early as 1473 and it has been translated into most European languages.

It is a testimony to Bury's international reputation as a bibliophile that in the early part of the twentieth century the Grolier Club of New York paid for the present cover of his tomb (which had been discovered a few years earlier) at the south end of the Chapel of the Nine Altars in DURHAM CATHEDRAL.

BUTLER, JOSEPHINE (1828–1906)

Josephine Butler was one of the most notable nineteenth-century social reformers. She was born at Milfield in Glendale, the fourth daughter of the well-known agricultural reformer, JOHN GREY of Dilston. Her father imbued her with strong religious and ethical beliefs and gave her a very sound education, initially at home and then at a boarding school in Newcastle. At the age of twenty-four she married George Butler, whose career as a clergyman and schoolmaster took him successively to Cheltenham, Liverpool and finally to Winchester. From the outset of her marriage, she had a strong commitment to the cause of women's welfare, a matter in which she had the full support of her husband.

Initially concerned to promote the idea of higher education for women, while living in Liverpool she launched the cause for which she became famous, the abolition of legalised prostitution. This had resulted from three acts of parliament passed between 1864 and 1869, by which prostitutes in eighteen port and garrison towns were placed under the control and supervision of the police, thus giving the trade legal status while leaving its practitioners open to abuse and cruelty. Supporters of this system, which was common on the continent, now wished to see it extended throughout the country. It was this that prompted the campaign for the repeal of the acts that made it possible. The upshot was the formation in 1869 of the Ladies' National Association for Repeal, with Josephine Butler as its secretary. It took seventeen years of action and publicity before the acts were repealed in 1886. By itself, Josephine Butler's eloquence, which was considerable, would probably not have been enough. What made the difference was the active support of a rising young MP, James Stansfield, who in 1871 had become a member of Gladstone's first ministry as President of the Poor Law Board. From 1874, however, he devoted his ability and parliamentary expertise to the Association's cause, passing up the chance to join Gladstone's second ministry in 1880. Josephine Butler also campaigned in Europe against the 'white slave trade' in young girls, ultimately with success in France, Holland, Italy, Norway and Switzerland.

After George Butler died in 1890, Josephine retired to Wooler to live with one of her sons. She died there in 1906 and was buried at Kirknewton. Josephine Butler was one of the foremost campaigners for women's rights and did much to promote the principle of a common standard of sexual morality for men and women. In 2006, a hundred years after her death, Durham University named its newest college Josephine Butler College.

BYERLEY TURK

Recent DNA research in Ireland has proved that the ancestry of all thoroughbred horses in the world is traceable to twenty-eight Arab and Turkish animals imported into England in the late seventeenth and early eighteenth centuries. Three were stallions: Godolphin Arabian (1724–1753), Darley Arabian (1700–1730) and Byerley Turk (1678–1703). The Byerley Turk was so called because it belonged to Robert Byerley (1660–1714), whose family had been settled at Middridge Grange, Durham since the sixteenth century.

It was once thought that Byerley acquired the horse while serving with the forces of the Emperor Leopold I that destroyed the Turkish army besieging Vienna in 1683. But it now seems that Byerley had no involvement in this event and that he was in England during the 1680s. He was MP for County Durham in 1685 and 1687 and in the former year was commissioned to raise a troop of horse to augment James II's army that crushed the rebellion of James, Duke of Monmouth. Rather than by Byerley, the horse was captured at the siege of Buda in 1686 by Edward Vaudrey, who sold it to Byerley on his return to England. It was then that Byerley was dismissed from the army as part of James II's purge of non-Catholic officers. He was reinstated, however, by William III and between 1689 and 1691 he and his horse served in Ireland, including the Battle of the Boyne.

In 1692, Byerley retired from the army and also moved to Goldsborough Hall, near Knaresborough, which he inherited from his mother. It was between that year and its death in 1703 that the Byerley Turk served as a stallion, thereby making his contribution to the evolution of the thoroughbred. It was buried it at Goldsborough and a tree planted over the grave.

BYKER WALL

The Byker Wall, built in the early 1970s, is one of the most unusual and imaginative buildings erected in Britain since 1945. It was the work of a London-born architect, Ralph Erskine (1914–2005), who spent most of his working life in Sweden. The Wall is the outstanding feature of the comprehensive redevelopment, begun in 1969, of the rundown NEWCASTLE suburb of Byker. This was distinguished, in contrast to so much other redevelopment of the same period, by the sympathetic consideration given by Erskine's team to the views and wishes of the 2,400 people who were to be rehoused. This was quite deliberate and sprang from Erskine's belief in 'community architecture'. Erskine also, unlike architects of many other contemporary developments, was concerned that what he built should conform to the existing landscape and should make use of various materials with differing textures and colours.

The 'Wall' in fact is a curved block of flats facing up the Tyne. Its back has few windows, which helps to protect it from the incessant noise of the traffic on the Byker bypass and from the northerly winds. Below it, on steeply sloping ground, the rest of the development comprises houses in short terraces, the preferred style of the residents, in carefully landscaped settings.

BYWELL

Although only a small village, Bywell has four buildings of historic and architectural importance. Most intriguing are its two churches, St Andrew and St Peter, situated literally within a stone's throw of each other. Both are of pre-Conquest origin and both have enough fabric evidence to suggest very early foundation. Unfortunately, there is no certain explanation of this arrangement. The best clue may lie in the two baronies created in the years after 1095, between which the township was divided: the earlier was the Barony of Bywell, created for Guy de Balliol (d. c.1125), whose properties constituted the parish of St Peter's; the other was the Barony of Styford, granted to Walter de Bolbec (d. c.1142), whose properties constituted the parish of St Andrew's. The fact that the two churches had long been in existence suggests that the two baronies themselves may have been ancient estates that had acquired new owners but were not themselves new. There is, therefore, the chance that at an early date there was a single estate/administrative unit, 'Bywellshire', which had been divided and granted to different owners, each of whom wanted his own church.

The next building in time is Bywell Castle, now a substantial ruin, built in the first half of the fifteenth century by the Nevilles, Earls of Westmorland, who had come into possession of the barony in 1376. The castle is essentially a smaller version of DUNSTANBURGH CASTLE as originally conceived, in that it is basically a substantial gatehouse guarding the entrance to a walled enclosure. Bywell Castle was newly built when it was the refuge of the pusillanimous Henry VI during the BATTLE OF HEXHAM and from which he fled only to be captured some days later.

The ownership of Bywell passed in 1616 to Sir John Fenwick of Wallington, whose descendant, William Fenwick, commissioned James Paine the Elder (1725–89) to design the present Bywell Hall. Paine was also responsible for three other major country houses in the region: Belford Hall, Gosforth Park and Axwell Park. The Bywell estate was bought in 1820 by T.W. Beaumont, whose descendant was created Viscount Allendale in 1906.

CADOGAN, PETER WILLIAM (1921–2007)

Peter Cadogan, who was one of the most inveterate agitators of the second half of the twentieth century, was born in Newcastle. His education was bisected by World War II, in which he served in the RAF in the Air-Sea Rescue Service. Prior to that he had attended Tynemouth School and after demobilisation went to King's College, Newcastle (now Newcastle University), where he took a degree in History. His subsequent career in education was also in two parts: until 1965 he was a schoolmaster in Kettering and Cambridge; then from 1981 until 1986 he was in adult education as a WEA lecturer and at Birkbeck College, London.

But between 1965 and 1981 he was fully engaged in promoting a variety of 'causes'. Most notable was the work of the Committee of 100, a breakaway from the Campaign for Nuclear Disarmament, which he led in 1963. Its most sensational achievement was the exposure of the fourteen Centres of Regional Government, from which Britain was to be run in the event of a nuclear catastrophe, the existence of which was supposed to be a state secret. Other matters that engaged his strident attention were the American involvement in Vietnam and the Russian invasion of Afghanistan, to both of which he was opposed. On the other hand, he championed the independence of Biafra, the breakaway province of Nigeria, and strove to find ways of ending the sectarian conflict in Northern Ireland. For brief periods, he was successively a member of the Communist Party, the Labour Party and the Socialist Workers League, from all of which he was expelled: he was never a good 'party man'.

Although his campaigning was carried out with total commitment and considerable vigour, he achieved no significant success in any of the causes he championed.

CANALS

Except in the North East, canals were built in all regions of Britain in the eighteenth and early nineteenth centuries to meet the need for improved means of transport, especially of bulky goods. The absence of canals in the North East is therefore surprising, given its rapidly expanding coal industry. Nor can difficulties with the terrain have been a reason, considering that canals were constructed through the Pennines.

In fact, on the Tyne and the Wear ten canal building schemes were initiated, with the aim of improving navigation, and there were also schemes for linking the Tyne with the Tweed via Morpeth, the Tyne with the Wear via the Team Valley, and the Tyne with the Solway. Several of these schemes secured the necessary parliamentary approval and the initial survey work for them was carried out. Those in favour included the corporations of Sunderland and Durham, the Dean and Chapter of Durham, and some landowners. Opposed, however, was the Newcastle Corporation, since it saw all of them as threats to its monopoly of navigation on the Tyne.

Some of these schemes were obviated by lack of funds; others failed because work could not be completed within the time laid down in the parliamentary act. In the end, the problems associated with the movement of coal were solved by WAGONWAYS and then by RAILWAYS. By 1840 the canal as a means of transport was obsolescent.

Despite this, in 1883 and 1910 serious consideration was given to the idea of constructing a canal 147 feet (45 m) wide and 36 feet (11 m) deep, that is, of similar dimensions to the Suez and Panama canals, linking the North Sea and the Irish Sea, so that ships could come across the Atlantic direct to Northumbrian ports. The cost, however, proved to be prohibitive.

CANDLISH, JOHN (1816–1874)

John Candlish rose from humble origins and without connection to be a major figure in the Wearside glass bottle trade. He was born at Bellingham in Northumberland, where his family, originally from the Scottish Borders, were small farmers. In the early 1820s, however, his father took the family to Ayres Quay in SUNDERLAND, to take work at the glass bottle works where his brother was manager. Candlish was educated at local schools until the age of thirteen, when he was apprenticed to a draper. In 1836, after completing his time, he and a partner started their own drapery business, but within a year this had failed. For the next sixteen years Candlish had several jobs, including secretary of the Sunderland Gas Co.

Candlish's rise to prominence as a glass bottle maker began in 1853, when he and a partner, Thomas Greenwell, bought the Londonderry Bottle Works at Seaham. This venture was so successful that in 1860 they were able to acquire the Diamond Hall Works at Sunderland. By the time of his death in 1874, Candlish's firm was the largest manufacturer of black bottles (used for wine and beer) in the UK.

Candlish was also active in politics as a Liberal, on the Radical wing of the party. He was elected to the Sunderland Town Council in 1848 and served as mayor in 1858 and 1861. He was also Liberal MP for Sunderland from 1866 until 1874. He first stood in 1865, when he came last in a three-cornered contest, but was victorious in a by-election the following year and retained the seat in the general election of 1868.

CARHAM, BATTLE OF, 1016 or 1018

Carham is one of those battles that merit the title 'decisive' in that it determined the boundary of England and Scotland. It is therefore unfortunate that we have so little concrete information about it. Even its date is uncertain: although recorded as 1018, there are good reasons for thinking that it took place two years before, in 1016. The result, however, is clear enough: an army led by the Earl of Northumbria (see NORTHUMBRIA, KINGDOM AND EARLDOM OF), was decisively defeated by the combined forces of Malcolm II, King of Alba (modern Scotland between the Firth of Forth and the Moray Firth) and his ally, the King of Strathclyde (modern south-west Scotland and modern Cumbria).

The root of the conflict was the ambition of the kings of Alba to extend their kingdom southwards. Forty-five years earlier they had achieved some success, when the English king, Edgar (959–75), ceded 'Lothian' to Malcolm's father, Kenneth II. This agreement possibly did no more than legitimise a conquest that had already occurred. The area concerned is also uncertain, but it was probably the land between the Forth and the Lammermuir Hills. But what he had given away was part of the Kingdom of Northumbria, which had never belonged to the Scottish kings of Alba, whose kingdom had always lain north of the Forth. In doing so, he transferred the area from one culture and language to another: the Kingdom of Alba was Scottish and spoke Gaelic; Northumbria was English in both tradition and language.

But the ambition of the Scottish kings of Alba was much greater: to extend their kingdom south to the Tees. In 1006, ten or twelve years before his victory at Carham, Malcolm II had made a bold bid to realise this ambition, but he was utterly defeated by the Earl of Northumbria outside Durham. By 1016, Malcolm's power was sufficiently recovered for him to make another attempt, this time with some success. With his victory at Carham he brought his effective power down to the Tweed. His successors were to make several attempts to get to the Tyne or the Tees, but without success, until in 1237 Alexander II finally renounced the Scottish claim to the North East.

The Battle of Carham determined that the most northerly part of the English Kingdom of Northumbria should become part of the new kingdom of Scotland. Ironically, in the end English Northumbria 'conquered' Scotland in that the true Scots north of the Forth eventually abandoned their own language, Gaelic, for English.

CARMICHAEL, JOHN WILSON (1799–1868)

John Wilson Carmichael was one of the finest British seascape artists of the nineteenth century. The son of a Newcastle shipwright, he showed precocious ability as a draughtsman at an early age. Nevertheless, after some years at sea, he was apprenticed to a Tyneside shipbuilder and it was these experiences and the training he received in the shipyard that were the foundation for the accuracy he displayed in his portrayal of the sea and ships. He was also fortunate in that the owner of the shipyard, Joseph Farrington, himself an amateur artist, encouraged Carmichael to develop his artistic ability as well as mastering his craft.

Upon the completion of his apprenticeship, he decided to try to make a living in the field of art, rather than shipbuilding. From 1826 until 1846 he continued to live in NEWCASTLE, earning money by teaching pupils as well as by exhibiting and selling his paintings. Although the sea was his favourite subject, at this stage he could not afford to be exclusive. Among his many non-maritime accomplishments were detailed paintings of the construction of the Newcastle and Carlisle Railway, published in a single volume in 1839. In the same year he not only exhibited in Newcastle and Carlisle, but also in London galleries and, more importantly, at the Royal Academy.

It was his growing success as a painter that persuaded him in 1846 to leave Newcastle for London. This was a wise move, for in the succeeding years he enjoyed considerable success in finding a large number of wealthy and influential patrons, and it was in these years that he came to be recognised as an outstanding painter of maritime scenes. His reputation was such that the *Illustrated London News* commissioned him as a war artist to record the activities of the Baltic fleet during the Crimean War (1854–56). Also the artists' materials manufacturer, Windsor and Newton, commissioned him to write two books on the subject, *Marine Painting in Watercolours* (1859) and *Marine Painting in Oils* (1863). By the latter date, however, his health was deteriorating and he retired to Scarborough, although he is known to have continued to paint until shortly before his death in 1868.

CATTO, THOMAS SIVEWRIGHT, 1st LORD CATTO OF CAIRNCATTO (1879–1959)

Lord Catto was Governor of the Bank of England from 1944 until 1949 in succession to Montagu Norman. He therefore had the delicate task of overseeing the nationalisation of the Bank by the Labour Government of 1945–51. It is a testimony to Catto's skill that he succeeded in securing arrangements that preserved the Bank's operating independence.

He was born in Newcastle, the son of a Scottish shipwright who moved from Peterhead to Tyneside to find more secure work. Tragically, his father died a year later and his mother moved back to Peterhead. Having attended Peterhead Academy, Catto won a scholarship to a school in Newcastle and returned to the place of his birth. He left school at the age of fifteen to become a clerk with the Gordon Shipping Co., with whom he stayed three years. Thereafter, his long and varied commercial and financial career took him to the Middle and Far East and to the USA. In 1928 he became the managing director of the merchant bank Morgan Grenfell, and in 1940 a director of the Bank of England. He resigned the following year to become a financial adviser to the Treasury and a close colleague of the influential economist John Maynard Keynes, the two being known as 'Catto and Doggo'. His huge experience in commerce and finance in Britain and in other parts of the world made him a suitable choice to succeed Montagu Norman at the Bank. He was created Baron Catto in 1936 and his retirement was spent in Aberdeenshire, from where his family had originated.

CAUSEY ARCH AND EMBANKMENT

The Causey Arch and Embankment were built as part of the Tanfield Wagonway begun in 1724 by the mining cartel known as the 'Grand Allies' (see GREAT NORTHERN COALFIELD and WAGONWAYS) to transport coal from the expanding coalfield in the moors south of the Tyne northwards to the river at Dunston. For their time, both were immense pieces of civil engineering and both were necessary in order to span the deep and precipitous ravine of the Causey Burn. The Embankment was constructed first and carried the main line; the Arch was built shortly afterwards to replace a collapsed wooden bridge to carry a branch line to pits near Beckley.

The Arch, however, is the more famous. It was built in 1727 by a local mason, Ralph Wood, who, according to tradition, became so worried that it would collapse that before it was finished he committed suicide by throwing himself off the top of it. It is a single arch, 105 feet (32 m) long and 85 feet (26 m) high, and was then the largest single-span arch in the country and arguably the world's first railway bridge. This last statement is open to qualification in that, although the arch carried a double track, one for up traffic, the other for down traffic, the rails were made of wood and the chaldrons that ran on them were not moved by locomotives. Despite the cost and effort required to build it, its working life was short. Between 1727 and 1733, up to 930 chaldrons a day crossed it carrying approximately 2,000 tons of coal. But after 1733 several of the pits it served closed and in 1740 an explosion destroyed the Tanfield Pit. By 1770 new wagonways had taken most of its traffic and it was disused after about 1786. It was restored between 1975 and 1981 by Durham County Council.

The Embankment is a short distance downstream from the Arch and in many respects is an even more impressive construction. The burn was culverted and above it was built an embankment of earth and stone, much of it obtained from cuttings dug for the wagonway. It rises to 100 feet (30 m) above the burn and is 300 feet (90 m) wide at the base and continued to carry the Tanfield Wagonway until its closure in 1965. It was widened in the 1930s, but at a lower level, to allow for the improvement of the road between Stanley and Marley Hill.

CEDD, SAINT (?–664) and CHAD, SAINT (?–673)

These men, whose correct names were **Cedda** and **Ceadda**, were brothers whose careers followed very similar paths. Their dates of birth and parentage are not known, although it is fairly safe to assume that they came from the upper stratum of Northumbrian society. Both became missionaries and played pioneering roles in the conversion of the English peoples from paganism to Christianity. They were among the first generation of Northumbrians to adopt Christianity, which they learned from ST AIDAN at Lindisfarne (see HOLY ISLAND).

Cedd was the elder and came to prominence in 653, when he was sent on missionary work by King Oswiu briefly to Mercia and then with the status of bishop for a longer time to the small Kingdom of Essex, at, it is said, the request of its king, Sigbert II. He returned to Northumbria in the following year to found a monastery at Lastingham near Whitby, the endowment for which was provided by the king. The man behind this move was a third brother, Caelin, who was a royal chaplain. Cedd died at Lastingham, probably of the plague, in 664.

Chad's career is better known and seemingly more distinguished. Like Cedd, he was trained at Lindisfarne, but also at the Irish monastery of Melfont. In 664 he succeeded Cedd as Abbot of Lastingham, but in the following year he was appointed Bishop of Lindisfarne. His pontificate lasted four years, until 669, when he was removed by Theodore of Tarsus, the Greek prelate who had recently arrived in England, appointed by Pope Vitalian as Archbishop of Canterbury, with a brief to bring order and regularity to the rapidly expanding church in the English kingdoms. His decision to depose Chad was determined by irregularities in Chad's consecration as bishop. Almost immediately, however, Chad was reconsecrated as bishop, but for the Kingdom of Mercia, where he worked for the last four years of his life. Chad made a deep impression on Mercian society, living a life of exemplary austerity and conducting all his missionary journeys on foot, until ordered in old age by Archbishop Theodore, because of his advanced years, to use a horse on his longer tours. He made his base at Lichfield, where the Church of England cathedral is still dedicated to him, as is the cathedral in Birmingham, the seat of the Roman Catholic archbishop.

There is no reason to doubt the complete sincerity of either brother and that they went on their missionary journeys with fervent commitment. At the same time, it needs to be remembered that religion, particularly its ecclesiastical aspect, was an important aspect of public life. In sending men like Cedd and Chad into other kingdoms with a commission to introduce/impose a new ideology, Oswiu was in a non-violent way asserting an overlordship over their rulers. The two brothers were not merely churchmen but members of the ruling class of Northumbria assisting their king in the advancement of his political power, just as Pope Vitalian in sending Theodore of Tarsus to England was asserting his authority over the evolving churches in England.

CENTRE FOR LIFE

The Centre for Life in Newcastle, opened in 2000, was one of fourteen Millennium Landmark Projects. It is a striking building, designed by Terry Farrell (a graduate of Newcastle University) and costing £70 million. It brought to fruition the vision developed in the 1990s of a miscellaneous group of people working in the North East, including academics, local hospital trusts, members of the business community and those with responsibility for promoting the region's development. The Centre's purposes are broadly threefold. One is educational, in the widest sense: to promote interest in, and better understanding of, science, particularly those aspects concerned with human life, and to inspire the young towards a scientific education. To achieve these ends, the Centre has a schools programme, holds exhibitions and demonstrations, mounts an annual lecture and debating series, and manages the Newcastle Science Festival. These activities are very evident and on the surface. Less visible is the 100,000 square feet (9,000 m^2) of laboratory facilities for world-class university-based research in the related fields of stem cells, genetics and regenerative medicine. The Centre is a designated Centre of Excellence for Life Sciences, and houses the Life Biocentre, the Institute of Human Genetics, the Newcastle Fertility Centre, the North East Cell Institute, and the Policy, Ethics and Life Science Research Institute. The third purpose is to assist in the process of translating scientific discovery into profitable economic activity. Here, too, the Centre provides facilities for firms working at the forefront of the biotechnical industry. The Centre has an international reputation and is a major factor in making the region a leader in the field of life sciences.

CEOLFRITH (642–716)

Perhaps more than any other man, Ceolfrith was responsible for the conditions that made it possible for BEDE to live the life and produce the work he did. Like almost all the early converts to a religious life in seventh-century Northumbria, Ceolfrith was the son of noble parents. He was born in 642, probably in what was Deira, now Yorkshire, and entered the monastery at Gilling in 659 when he was seventeen. After the momentous decision at Whitby in 664 to impose Roman forms and practices, Ceolfrith moved to the monastery at Ripon founded by their leading advocate, WILFRID. A few years later, however, he was 'head-hunted' by BENEDICT BISCOP to help him create a new monastic community at Monkwearmouth. Ceolfrith could not settle and returned to Ripon, and it took considerable persuasion on Biscop's part to get him back. Perhaps it was for this reason that Biscop took Ceolfrith with him when he went to Rome in 678.

In 682, not long after their return, KING ECGFRITH gave Biscop more land on the south bank of the Tyne for another monastic house. The task of building and developing this new monastery at JARROW, which from the outset was intended to be the other half of the Monkwearmouth venture, was entrusted to Ceolfrith. It is not surprising that when Biscop neared death in 688 he nominated Ceolfrith his successor as abbot of the combined monastery, the post he retained for the rest of his life.

Ceolfrith not only enabled Bede to produce his great works of scholarship, but his fame as a spiritual leader allowed him significantly to influence the development of Christianity in northern Britain. His advocacy persuaded Adomnan, Abbot of Iona (who visited him) and Nechtan, King of the Picts (with whom he corresponded) that their churches were in error and that they should adopt Roman practices. With their conversion, the churches throughout Britain and Ireland were in harmony and communion with Rome.

In June 716, knowing that he had not long to live, Ceolfrith set out for Rome with the bible we know as the *CODEX AMIATINUS*, which he intended to present to Pope Gregory II. However, he got only as far as Langres in France, where he died on 25 September.

CEREBOS and BISTO

Cerebos, the name which became synonymous with table salt, was invented in 1894 by a Newcastle chemist, George Weddell. To that date, salt had been sold in blocks that had to be crushed into granular form before use. What Weddell did was to reduce his salt to a fine grain and then add small quantities of magnesium carbonate and calcium phosphate. These kept the salt in a free-running condition and also, he claimed, gave it tooth- and bone-strengthening properties. At first Weddell obtained salt at Haverton Hill, which he brought to Newcastle for processing and packaging, but in 1903 the success of his venture led him to expand his operation by buying the Hartlepool Salt and Brine Co. and in 1906 moving the business to Greatham. There, in 1913, he built a plant to operate the vacuum evaporation process, a superior means of evaporating brine that resulted in a finer-grained product. He also added another product, Bisto gravy salt (which eventually also became granules) to his company. This product, devised by two men named Roberts and Patterson, rapidly became popular, particularly after 1919 with the introduction of the 'Bisto Kids' as a marketing device.

In 1968, the firm was aquired by the expanding company, Rank, Hovis, MacDougall, which moved production of both products to Middlewich in Cheshire in 1970. The Greatham factory, however, continued to manufacture food products marketed under the names J.A. Sharwood and Brand; and from 1973 to also make Atora suet.

CHAD, SAINT (see **CEDD, SAINT**)

CHANDLER, BRIAN JAMES (1938–1996)

Brian Chandler, or 'Chas' Chandler as he was known professionally, was born in Heaton, Newcastle, and was a founder member and bass guitarist of the pop group The Animals ,which was formed in the city in 1962 and quickly achieved international fame. After the group split up, he moved from performance to management. In 1966 he went to the USA, where he became the manager of the American guitarist Jimi Hendrix, whom he brought to Europe. It was this tour that launched Hendrix towards international stardom. In 1969 Chandler became the manager of the British group Slade, a role he performed for twelve years. During this period he bought and ran his own recording studio and marketed its products under the label Barn Records. His last major involvement was with the development of the Newcastle Arena, opened in 1995, with a seating capacity of 10,000, for sporting and entertainment events. Chandler died of a heart condition the following year.

CHAPLIN, SIDNEY (1916–1986)

Sid Chaplin, who was to become the exemplar for a number of working-class writers who wrote about working-class life, was born at Shildon, where his father, Isaac (Ike), was a colliery electrician. After attending village schools, in 1931 he became an apprentice blacksmith at the Dean and Chapter Colliery, Ferryhill. In his spare time he advanced his education through the Workers' Educational Association (WEA) classes held at the SPENNYMOOR SETTLEMENT and in 1939 he won a scholarship to Fircroft Working Men's College, Birmingham. Unfortunately, the outbreak of World War II cut short his time there and he returned to Durham to work in the pits.

Despite this setback, he published in 1946 a volume of short stories, *The Leaping Lad*. This became something of an inspiration for younger writers such as JOHN BRAINE, Alan Sillitoe, David Storey and Stan Barstow. It also took him out of pit work and into journalism, working for the NCB's house magazine, *Coal*. From 1953 until 1957 he was working in London, but in the latter year, he moved back north to live in Jesmond, Newcastle. In the early 1960s he published his two most substantial novels, *The Day of the Sardine* (1961) and *The Watchers and the Watched* (1962), in both of which the leading character is a man coping with a changing working-class environment. Another of his works, *The Thin Seam*, which is considerably autobiographical, along with other stories formed the basis of the musical by Alan Plater and Alex Glasgow, *Close the Coalhouse Door* (1966).

In his later years Sid Chaplin was recognised nationally with an OBE (1977) and locally by the conferral of an honorary MA by the University of Newcastle upon Tyne.

CHAPMAN, WILLIAM (1749–1852)

William Chapman was an engineer with diverse interests. He was born in Whitby, the son of a Quaker sea captain, and initially he followed his father's trade. In 1778, however, he and his brother John leased Wallsend Colliery, where they installed the first Boulton and Watt steam pump in the North East. Their venture into coal mining ended in bankruptcy in 1782. The following year, Chapman went to Ireland, where he acted as an agent for Boulton and Watt and also engaged in various civil engineering projects, notably the Kildare Canal.

Returning to Britain in 1794, he settled in NEWCASTLE, from where he developed a civil engineering practice, designing several drainage schemes in Yorkshire and the Humber Dock at Hull (in partnership with John Rennie), and surveying a route for the proposed Tyne–Solway canal. In 1806 he again ventured into the coal industry, leasing Kenton and Coxlodge Colliery, with another brother. It was in the years following that he devised an improved method of loading COLLIERS by means of a mechanism that allowed wagons to be lowered into their holds for emptying. This resulted in less breakage of the coals than running them down a shoot. Since his second venture into mining took place at the time when colliery owners were backing the development of the locomotive as a more efficient and cost-effective means of haulage than horses on their wagonways, it is not surprising that he turned his mind to solving this problem. In 1813 and 1814 he had built two locomotives to a design that involved their attachment to a chain running between the rails. Although this mechanism proved to be a dead end in the evolution of the locomotive, one part of his second engine had an important future. This was the bogie wheel, which he realised was necessary if locomotives of any length were to be able to negotiate curves. However, there is evidence that suggests that in 1815 Chapman abandoned the chain mechanism and designed a successful six-wheel engine that was given the name *Steam Elephant*. It appears to have been commissioned by JOHN BUDDLE for the Wallsend Colliery and to have been constructed from parts made by the GATESHEAD firm of Hawks (see HAWKS, GEORGE). Chapman also had an interest in a rope-making business at Willington Quay, where he improved the design of rope-making machinery, and he continued to be involved in canal and drainage schemes and also the construction of Seaham Harbour (see NEW TOWNS OF THE NINETEENTH CENTURY).

CHARLTON, JOHN (1849–1917)

John Charlton, who became one of the most popular artists in the late nineteenth century, was born at Bamburgh. His natural talent was considerable but his training was not at all straightforward. After early instruction from his father and at the school run by the Lord Crewe Trustees in Bamburgh Castle (see NATHANIEL, LORD CREWE), he worked in the Newcastle bookshop of Robert Robinson, who introduced him to the work of THOMAS BEWICK, and then in the office of the industrialist SIR ISAAC LOWTHIAN BELL, who in recognition of his ability, allowed him one day off each week to develop his talent and also encouraged him to attend evening classes at the Newcastle School of Arts, run by WILLIAM BELL SCOTT.

By 1874 Charlton was sufficiently established for him to move to London, where he found ready work in producing illustrations for *The Graphic*. What sealed his reputation was the large picture he exhibited in 1883, *The British Artillery Entering the Enemy Lines at Tel-El-Kebir*. This established him as a leading military artist and thereafter he produced a number of works illustrating contemporary colonial conflicts as well as those from the country's earlier wars. His career culminated in a commission from Queen Victoria to paint a picture of her Golden Jubilee procession, which so pleased her that in 1897 she commissioned him to produce a like work on the occasion of her Diamond Jubilee. Both pictures are in the Royal Collection.

Charlton's life ended in tragedy in that his two sons were killed within one week in June 1916 and this may have hastened his death, which occurred in the following November.

CHEMICAL INDUSTRY

For many centuries the North East had a chemical industry in the form of salt extraction from sea water, either by evaporation or boiling. Saltpans are recorded from the mid-twelfth century at BLYTH, Horton, Cowpen, Bebside and Hartley, and also around the mouth of the Tyne, where the driving force was largely monastic. This was also the case near the mouth of the Tees, where, for example, in 1495 eight of DURHAM CATHEDRAL Priory's twenty-four tenants in Cowpen Bewley engaged in salt making and gave the monks nearly 850 pounds of salt by way of rent. Medieval records also make clear the close relationship between salt making and fishing, salt being the necessary preservative for the long-distance fish trade.

Food preservation, together with domestic requirements, continued to be the basic uses of salt, extraction of which grew rapidly in the seventeenth century. By the end of that century, 170 pans were in existence on Tyneside, capable of producing 25,000 tons of salt a year. Tyneside vied with Merseyside as the country's major salt producer and it supplied a considerable percentage of the London market. Despite the poor quality of its product, Tyneside had two advantages. One was cheap coal: the London market refused to buy small coal and consequently colliery owners were glad to sell what came to be called 'pan coal' at low prices to salt boilers. The second advantage was cheap sea transport from the Tyne to the Thames. These advantages remained throughout the first half of the eighteenth century, but then ebbed away as fuel and transport costs came down in the Mersey area. By 1790 the Tyne's annual export of salt was only 1,000 tons, only a tenth of the amount in the early years of the century.

Coinciding with the loss of the London market was the rise in industrial demand within the region for alkali and soda crystals. The answer to the problem was the process for making alkali and soda crystals from salt, invented by Nicholas Leblanc in 1791, knowledge of which was brought to Tyneside by William Losh in 1796. The following year, in partnership with Archibald Cochrane, 9th Earl of Dundonald, he set up a works at Walker, where they were able to acquire brine from a spring in the King Pit. In 1809 they were joined by Thomas Bell and Thomas Wilson and from 1823 concentrated exclusively on the Leblanc process. Forty years later, there were twenty-four chemical firms on Tyneside (nineteen registered under the Alkali Act of 1863), most notably those owned by CHRISTIAN ALLHUSEN and JAMES STEVENSON. Tyneside was jointly with Merseyside Britain's leading producer of these two chemicals, employing around half of those employed in the industry and producing 32 per cent of the nation's alkali and 70 per cent of its soda. In addition to the industry on Tyneside, there were chemical works at BLYTH, Seaham Harbour and at Urlay Nook on the Tees, opened in 1833 by Robert Wilson of Yarm to produce chemical fertiliser.

The Tyneside alkali industry was at its height in the early 1880s, when it processed nearly 200,000 tons of salt a year, 42 per cent of the country's consumption. By 1914, however, it was moribund. By that date, of its twenty-four firms, only Tennants (Hebburn) and Allhusens (GATESHEAD) remained in existence, and they too lasted no longer than the early 1930s. The demise of the industry was in part the result of its refusal to abandon the Leblanc process in favour of the more advanced process invented by the Belgian chemist Ernest Solvay (1838–1922) in the 1870s. This refusal was not due simply to inertia but to the way that the Leblanc process had been steadily adapted to produce a wide range of other chemicals, including hydrochloric acid, sulphuric acid, sulphur and manganese. Equally influential, however, was that countries to which its products were exported raised high tariffs against British goods and began to develop their own industry on the basis of lower wages. Another contributory factor may have been the growing number of regulations imposed on the chemical industry by a series of Factory Acts, which smaller firms found difficult to implement. Despite amalgamation in 1891 of the larger firms to form the United Alkali Co., the position of the chemical industry on Tyneside was weak.

But perhaps the killer blow was the discovery of the huge salt bed 100 feet thick under the Tees estuary, part of the salt field beneath much of northern and midland England, the North Sea and northern Europe. Laid down in the Permian Period around 280 million years ago, it lies around 1,000 feet (300 m) below ground level. Its existence was discovered at Cargo Fleet on the south side of the Tees in 1863 by the iron firm of Bolckow and Vaughan (see BOLCKOW, HENRY WILLIAM FERDINAND) while boring for water, and on the north side at Port Clarence by another iron company, Bell Bros, in 1874 (see BELL, SIR ISAAC LOWTHIAN). But access by the normal mining method was not commercially viable, and consequently extraction was delayed until the development in France of an alternative method. This involved pumping boiling water down to dissolve the solid salt, and pumping up the resulting brine, which was then evaporated in large vats. This method was first operated by Bell Bros in 1882, and by 1885 there were eight major salt extraction works along the banks of the Tees. Of the four on the Durham side, three involved Tyneside men, CHRISTIAN ALLHUSEN, JAMES STEVENSON and Christopher Tennant, who recognised that the future lay on the Tees, not the Tyne. Nevertheless, the heyday of the Tees salt industry was brief, lasting from the late 1880s until World War I. Between 1888 and 1914 annual output was normally above 200,000 tons and in 1894 as high as 318,000 tons, with between 75 and 80 per cent being produced on the Durham side of the river. The loss of export markets during the war and changes in home demand, however, led to a rapid decline in output, which by the mid-1920s had fallen to below 100,000 tons.

World War I had exposed serious deficiencies in the British chemical industry, particularly in the supply of raw materials for the production of explosives, which was worsened by the difficulty in wartime circumstances of importing Chilean nitrate. One consequence was that in 1918 the government set up a plant at BILLINGHAM to produce ammonium nitrate artificially by the German Haber-Bosch process, acquired as the war ended by a piece of impudent industrial espionage. However, before it became operational the government handed it over to the firm of Brunner Mond, who developed it as a subsidiary, Synthetic Ammonia and Nitrates Ltd.

The sale of the Billingham enterprise did not signal the end of government interest in the chemical industry, merely the retreat from direct involvement in manufacture. The formation in 1925 of the German chemical giant IG Farben led the following year to the merger, with government approval, of the four major British chemical firms, Brunner Mond, Nobel Industries, British Dyestuffs Corporation and United Alkali, to form Imperial Chemical Industries Ltd. The clear intention was that Britain should have a chemical firm of comparable size to IG Faben of Germany and Dupont of America.

The ICI complex at Billingham developed rapidly before World War II, manufacturing ammonia, anhydrate, Portland cement, Nitro-Chalk and other fertilisers, sulphuric acid, methanol and petrol through the hydrogenation of coal and creosote. During the war, Billingham became (with Stanlow in Cheshire) the main producer of iso-octane and victane, the constituents of the aviation fuel vital to the RAF. Also highly important for the RAF was the production of perspex, the alternative to glass required for aeroplanes. Although the most prominent, it was not the only chemical company that set up in the region in the inter-war period. Because of rapid advances in chemistry and chemical engineering, other firms – British Titan Products (Billingham), Steetley Magnetite Co. (Hartlepool), Stockton Chemical Works, Darlington Chemical and Insulating Co. and British Oxygen – developed and prospered, and the region also attracted petroleum firms, such as Shell and Phillips.

In the post-war decades, major developments in the chemical industry have taken place south of the river on the 2,000-acre (800 ha) Wilton Castle estate bought by ICI in 1943 where eventually over 10,000 people were employed. Expansion continued on the Durham side of the river and has evolved eastwards into Seal Sands, a reclamation area extending to 1,700 acres (690 ha).

The chemical industry is dynamic in that it is perpetually faced with new products arising from the work of research scientists, with the result that elements that were hitherto important have been scaled down. One dramatic consequence of this occurred in 1993, when ICI was split into two separate companies: ICI, which concentrated on bulk products, and the Zeneca Group (now AstroZeneca), which dealt with pharmaceutical and biological products. Since then, sectors of the company have been sold to other firms, and in 2007 ICI was acquired by its Dutch rival, AbzoNobel. Despite this, the north bank of the Tees remains an important centre of the chemical industry.

CHESTER LE STREET

Now a small town, Chester le Street has had a very varied and interesting history, as is suggested by its name. Chester is an English corruption of the Latin *castra*, meaning camp or fort; the *le* element is French meaning on or by the; and *street* is the English word indicating a metalled road.

In its first incarnation, Chester le Street was a Roman cavalry fort, Concagium, built by the Roman army on the raised ground above the flood plain of the River Wear and its tributary, the Cong Burn. When the fort was built is not certain, but a reference to it in the year 175 and the discovery there of coins of mid-first-century emperors points to the early phase of the Roman occupation. Its purpose, however, is clear enough: to be one of the military stations guarding and controlling the road from the Tees to Pons Aelius, the bridge across the Tyne between what are now Gateshead and Newcastle. It is unlikely to have been in continuous occupation throughout the Roman era, but it was reoccupied in the fourth century by a new type of frontier defence unit at a time when the Roman Empire was coming under increased pressure from enemies beyond its borders. It is likely that this unit continued to garrison the fort until the Roman government withdrew from Britain in 410. It is also safe to assume that at Chester le Street, as at other forts, a civilian settlement (*vicus*) would have grown up outside the gates of the fort, presumably on its southern and western sides, the eastern and northern sides being liable to flood. The size of this community is at present not known.

Also not known is what happened after 410. The first substantial event of which we have knowledge is the arrival of the Community of St Cuthbert (see CUTHBERT, SAINT) 473 years later in 883. By that date the Community had acquired large tracts of what became County Durham and it is likely that Chester le Street was the administrative centre of an extensive estate. The Community chose to build their church, to be the Bishop of Lindisfarne's cathedral and the 'home' of St Cuthbert, on the site of the Principia, the headquarters building at the centre of the Roman fort, substantial remains of which may have been extant. For the next 112 years, Chester le Street was the seat of nine successive bishops of Lindisfarne, whose ecclesiastical authority extended from the Tweed to the Tees.

This second incarnation ended in 995, when the Community of St Cuthbert removed briefly to Ripon before settling permanently at Durham, seven miles south of Chester le Street. This move, which was concerted between the bishop, Aldhune, and the other power in the region, the Earl of Northumbria, almost certainly stemmed from the need to relocate the Community to a more defensible site. Around one hundred years later, the first Norman bishops, WILLIAM OF ST CALAIS and RANNULF FLAMBARD, reorganised their cathedral and the administration of what was to become County Durham. Chester le Street was prominent in the new arrangements. Its secular role was as the centre of one of the four wards or administrative districts into which County Durham was divided. Chester Ward covered those parts of the county north and west of the River Wear and north of its tributary, the Deerness. Within its boundaries were nearly one hundred identifiable townships, hamlets and manorial farms.

Chester le Street was also important ecclesiastically, its parish being one of the largest in England. Within its boundaries were twenty-three townships and farms, and also two chapelries centred on Tanfield and Lamesley, which catered for another thirteen settlements. Since the rector of the parish was entitled to fees for his services and to tithes from its inhabitants, his income was potentially enormous. This led the Bishop of Durham, Anthony Bek (1283–1311), to impose in 1286 a new parochial establishment: instead of the single rector, there was to be a college of clergy, comprising a dean and seven canons, each with a prebend or entitlement to a specified portion of the parish revenue, and four resident vicars. Bek's purpose was not to provide better spiritual provision for the parishioners. Rather, since the seven canons were not required to be resident, it was his intention to appoint seven of his administrators, all of whom were in holy orders, who would thereby be paid at no cost to himself. This arrangement continued until the Reformation, when such colleges were suppressed, along with monasteries and friaries. In place of the college, a single stipendiary curate served the entire parish until the nineteenth century, when it was split up into parochial units of more appropriate size.

The wealth of the medieval parish is reflected in its magnificent church, one of the few in the North East to have a spire. In appearance the building looks to be essentially a thirteenth-century structure. But a recent archaeological survey has revealed hints that the chancel may be a remodelling of the church that Bishop Aethelwine of Durham is known to have built *c.*1056, while the three eastern bays of the nave were formed out of the cathedral church built in the tenth century when Chester le Street was the diocesan centre.

The church has two curious features. On the inside, along the north wall of the nave, are fourteen effigies resting on what purport to be tombs of members of the Lumley family. In fact, all but two brought from DURHAM CATHEDRAL were fabricated and installed in the 1590s by John, 6th Lord Lumley (see LUMLEY FAMILY AND CASTLE). The other, attached to the outside of the north-west corner of the church, is a rare example of an anchorage, that is, the dwelling of an anchorite or hermit. Originally it comprised two rooms, one above the other, built in the late fourteenth century and reputedly occupied by at least six hermits between *c.*1383 and 1547. After the Reformation, two further rooms were added and the building became an almshouse for widows. It now houses a small museum.

In the modern period of its history, Chester le Street has continued to be a commercial and administrative centre for the surrounding district. But the character of that district changed radically in the nineteenth century with the sinking of numerous pits and the building of associated villages. This meant a considerable growth of population, which in turn led to Chester le Street continuing its role as a modern local government centre, first as an Urban District in 1894, and from 1974 until their abolition in 2009 one of the seventeen Districts into which DURHAM COUNTY was divided. Since 1885, it has also been a parliamentary constituency.

CHEVIOT SHEEP

The Cheviot sheep, which was one of the two breeds of sheep that were to play a leading role in the transformation of the Scottish Highlands, was one of the many products of the late eighteenth-century enthusiasm for cross-breeding animals to enhance particular qualities. Exactly how the result was achieved in this case is not clear, but it seems likely that it was the product of crossing by a number of north Northumberland farmers of the native ewes with Leicester tups brought from the Midlands. The outcome was a white-faced, polled sheep with improved conformation, greater weight and strength and, above all, a short close fleece of fine wool. Its rival was the Blackface, developed in North Yorkshire and Westmorland (Cumbria) at the same period, which was horned and had longer but coarser fleece.

The years between 1790 and 1870 saw the great clearances of small farmers from the Scottish Highlands and their replacement by sheep and it was the Cheviot breed that most of the new farmers adopted. It is estimated that by 1870 about half the sheep in Scotland were Cheviots and it seemed possible that other breeds might be largely eliminated, particularly in upland areas. This did not happen. In fact, it was the Blackface that came increasingly to replace the Cheviot. One reason was that the Blackface proved the hardier and therefore more suited to the highest hills. Also, the Cheviot's initial advantage in terms of wool quality disappeared as even finer wool began to be imported from Australia. And, as regards meat, the Blackface matured more quickly and answered the developing preference for smaller, leaner joints. By the mid-twentieth century, there were five times as many Blackfaces as there were Cheviots, although by that date both breeds had been modified by crossing with other types.

CHILLINGHAM WILD CATTLE

The Chillingham Wild Cattle, which are white in colour, are a unique breed that inhabit about 350 acres (140 ha) within Chillingham Park, which covers around 1,500 acres (600 ha). They are smaller in size than domesticated cattle and have a number of different characteristics. For example, they mature more slowly, do not breed before four years of age and have a longer gestation period; and it is common for the cows, as well as the bulls, to fight each other.

How the herd came into being is not known, but it is believed that they were present when Chillingham Park was enclosed in the 1250s. Nor is it entirely certain that they remained totally uninfluenced by other cattle during the medieval centuries, since it is not until the late seventeenth century that they appear in the records. Since then, however, care has been taken to preserve them in isolation and they have attracted the interest of such diverse men as the artist Sir Edwin Landseer and the scientist Charles Darwin. They are not subject to any veterinary attention. Indeed, they kill any member of the herd on which they detect any 'foreign' scent.

As regards the size of the herd, its greatest number was eighty-two, recorded in 1913; the lowest was thirteen in 1947, following the severe winter when twenty-one died when the park was snowbound for sixty days with drifts up to forty feet in depth. The perennial threat to them is, of course, foot and mouth disease, which came within a mile of the park during the 2001 outbreak. To increase the herd's chances of surviving an outbreak, in 1972 two heifers and a bull were moved to a secret location in Scotland to start a reserve herd. The other problem is management and its costs. Since 1982 the park has been owned by the SIR JAMES KNOTT Trust, which handed over the management to the Chillingham Wild Cattle Association, founded as a registered charity in 1939 by the 8th Earl of Tankerville, whose family had owned Chillingham since the early eighteenth century.

CLANNY, WILLIAM REID (1777–1850)

William Clanny was an Ulsterman, born in Bangor, County Down in 1777. After training as a doctor in Edinburgh and serving with the Royal Navy, he set up practice, initially in DURHAM CITY, but then in Bishopwearmouth in 1805. Clanny was not only a doctor, but a scientist with an inexhaustible interest in experimentation. This led him to join the Society for the Prevention of Accidents in Coal Mines, formed in Sunderland in 1813 as a direct consequence of the horrendous loss of life in the Felling Colliery explosion (see COLLIERY DISASTERS) the previous year. He rapidly devised a lamp, a description of which he had published in the *Journal of the Royal Society*, in which the flame was insulated by glass in such a way that it could burn safely in the presence of firedamp (see COLLIERY DISASTERS). However, although some miners considered Clanny's lamp to be superior to the more famous invention of Sir Humphrey Davy, in the end the Davy Lamp became standard. Clanny continued to practise as a doctor in Bishopwearmouth until shortly before his death in 1850.

CLARK, GEORGE (1843–1901)

George Clark was the son of a SUNDERLAND iron maker, whose father, also George, set up a general engineering business in 1845. Clark senior had the distinction of building the first iron ship on the Wear and in 1856 founding the second Sunderland marine engine works (the first was started by John Dickinson at Palmer's Hill four years earlier). Clark junior was therefore able to serve his apprenticeship in his father's business, although wisely his father sent him to serve time at the famous yard of Penn of

Greenwich. He returned to Sunderland in 1864 and soon after took charge of the business. In 1872, following his father's death, he acquired a larger site at Southwick, with a 700-foot (200 m) river frontage. There he built a marine engine works, which by the 1880s had become the largest on the Wear. He was a member of the Wear Engine Builders' Association, the Institution of Naval Architects, and the North East Institution of Engineers and Shipbuilders. He was active in local politics as a Liberal, becoming a member of Sunderland Town Council and Durham County Council.

CLASPER, HENRY (1812–1870)

Harry Clasper, who was born at Dunston, was one of the most outstanding oarsmen in the history of rowing, who flourished at a time when the sport was hugely popular as a spectacle, attracting bankside crowds of over 50,000. His prowess was not only in the boat, but also as a designer of boats. More than any other man he was responsible for developing the racing craft used today.

In his early days Clasper earned his living at Jarrow and Hetton Collieries, at Brown's Shipyard at SOUTH SHIELDS and at the Hawks, Crawshay Ironworks in GATESHEAD. Rowing was his passion but perforce a leisure pursuit. To enable him to devote more time to it, in the late 1830s he became the landlord of the Skiff Inn at Derwenthaugh. His early rowing successes were with his three brothers and a brother-in-law at regattas on the Tyne and the Wear. These fired his ambition to challenge the best crew from the Thames, stroked by Robert Coombes, who were regarded as world champions. The challenge was accepted and on 16 July 1842 a match took place between the Clasper brothers and the Thames crew, the course being from the Tyne Bridge to Lemington. The Claspers were defeated, but Harry recognised that the underlying reason was not the quality of their oarsmanship but the inferior quality of their boat. To rectify this, he designed and built a boat of revolutionary design: it had no keel; in cross-section it resembled a half gun barrel; and it had outriggers to permit greater leverage. Although outriggers were not entirely his invention, Clasper improved their design and construction. The boat was named, appropriately, *The Five Brothers*. It proved its worth in London by winning at the Royal Thames Regatta in 1844, but in the rematch on the Tyne with the Coombes crew the Claspers were again defeated. The following year, however, the Claspers had their revenge, beating the London crew at the Royal Thames Regatta. But there was to be no rematch: in 1845 and 1847 two of the Clasper brothers died and Harry had to rebuild and develop his crew with replacements.

Between 1845 and 1860 Harry Clasper, either rowing by himself as a sculler or stroking a pair or four, was the most successful oarsman in regattas from Loch Lomond to the Thames and on all the rowing rivers in the north of England. This was still the time when rowing was not in the strictest terms an amateur sport. Regattas offered prize money and there were wagered matches between individuals and crews, the Oxford and Cambridge boat race being a relic of this time. In the course of his rowing career Harry Clasper's winnings exceeded £2,500, of which about two-thirds was won in four-oared competitions, and the rest in pairs and sculling races.

Harry Clasper died in July 1870, aged fifty-eight years. His funeral brought out huge crowds, who saw his coffin brought to Corporation Quay, transferred to a steam launch to be taken upriver to Derwenthaugh, and from there carried to Whickham for burial in St Mary's churchyard. Over his grave a lifesize statue of him was erected, a testimony to his fame and reputation in his lifetime.

In the following generation, two more Tyne oarsmen became world champions. The first was Robert (Bob) Chambers from Walker (1831–68), who won the world sculling championship in 1859, defeating a Londoner over a 3-mile course on the Tyne between the High Level and Scotswood bridges, and in 1863, when his opponent was an Australian. Slightly younger was James Renforth (1842–71) of Gateshead, who also won the world sculling championship, in 1868. Two years later he took a four to Canada to win a challenge worth £1,000. The following year he returned with another crew for a return match, but tragically died during the race. Like Clasper, he was commemorated in stone: a statue of him dying in the arms of Henry Kelley, a member of his crew and the man he had defeated in 1868, stands outside the Shipley Art Gallery in Gateshead (see ART GALLERIES).

CLAYTON, JOHN (1792–1890)

John Clayton was of a family that had been settled in NEWCASTLE since the late seventeenth century and had made successful careers in commerce and law and consequently in the government of the town. John was the third son of Nathaniel Clayton (1754–1832), a successful lawyer, who became Town Clerk in 1785 and held the post until his retirement thiry-seven years later in 1822. Although he had a substantial town house in Fenkle Street, like many successful townsmen, Nathaniel Clayton gentrified himself by buying a country estate, in his case at Chesters, near Chollerford. John Clayton succeeded him in both roles: as Town Clerk upon his father's retirement and at Chesters when his father died. His appointment as Town Clerk may smack of corruption, but the fact was that John Clayton was highly intelligent, well educated in Classics, and well trained as a lawyer, and he had been well schooled by his father in the roles the Town Clerk had to perform. More significantly, he fully justified his selection. He gave a masterful defence of the old Newcastle Corporation before the Municipal Reform Commission that enquired into all such corporations in preparation for the Municipal Reform Act of 1835. His responses to their investigative questions was so successful that the old corporation escaped castigation for the way it had carried out its functions and Clayton was reappointed as Town Clerk to the new corporation, a post he retained until 1867. Far more importantly for posterity, he ensured that the plans of the property developer RICHARD GRAINGER and the architects he engaged were realised to give Newcastle one of the world's finest city centres. Had not Clayton used the power and influence his role of Town Clerk gave him, and put his legal acumen at Grainger's service, it is doubtful whether Newcastle would now boast the architectural grandeur of what it now calls 'Grainger Town'.

If Clayton deserves to be remembered as a creator of a new and future heritage, he should equally be remembered for his salvation and preservation of the past. This he did by preserving and excavating HADRIAN'S WALL. Although archaeological techniques of his day were crude by modern standards, Clayton made a huge contribution to developing understanding of one of the world's major monuments. Apart from devoting every Monday to archaeology, he acquired numerous properties on which the Wall was sited and in so doing prevented its destruction by farmers and others who saw it as no more than a convenient source of building stone. Thanks to his effort, expenditure and commitment, the forts at Chesters, Carrawburgh, Housesteads and Carvoran were saved from further destruction, as were long stretches of the central sections of the Wall and their turrets and milecastles. The finds from his many excavations can still be seen in the museum next to his house at Chesters, and the twenty-one excavation reports he wrote between 1843 and 1886 can still be read in *Archaeologia Aeliana*, the publication of the Newcastle Society of Antiquaries (see LITERARY AND PHILOSOPHICAL SOCIETY OF NEWCASTLE UPON TYNE), which his father had helped to found and of which he was a lifelong member. Clayton worked on the Wall until a few years before his death, which occurred in 1890, when he was ninety-eight.

CLENNELL, LUKE (1781–1840)

Luke Clennell's story is of a highly talented artist whose career was cut short by severe health problems. He was born at Ulgham, the son of a farmer. His natural talent as a draughtsman was such that Lord Morpeth became his patron and secured an apprenticeship for him with THOMAS BEWICK, which ran from 1797 until 1804. This was the time that Bewick was preparing his second volume of *British Birds* and Clennell was responsible for a number of the tailpiece vignettes that were introduced at chapter ends. He also got commissions from John Wallis of London, who persuaded him to move to the capital, where his talent as a painter was recognised and encouraged by the American artist Benjamin West. He produced sixty-eight illustrations for Sir Walter Scott's *Border Antiquities*. In 1814 he was commissioned to paint a giant canvas, 4 feet 2 inches (1.27 m) by 6 feet 3 inches (1.9 m), of the banquet at the Guildhall to celebrate the end of the wars against France, which involved portraits of 100 guests. It was while engaged on this project that Clennell had a mental breakdown that necessitated his committal to an asylum. He never recovered. Eventually he moved back to Northumberland, but again he had to be moved to an asylum, where he died in 1840.

COAL INDUSTRY (see GREAT NORTHERN COALFIELD)

CODEX AMIATINUS

The *Codex Amiatinus* is one third of perhaps the most ambitious religious and artistic undertaking of the eighth century, which was commissioned by CEOLFRITH, Abbot of the twin monastery of Monkwearmouth/JARROW. It was no less than the production of three *pandects* (complete Bibles) on best-quality vellum and to the highest calligraphic and artistic standards. Ceolfrith intended that two of the books should remain at home, one at Jarrow, the other at Monkwearmouth, while the third was to be a present to the pope. The work was done in the *scriptorium* at Jarrow and was complete by 716, the year Ceolfrith set off for Rome with the papal copy. Unhappily, he failed to reach his destination: already in poor health when he began his journey, he died at Langres in France. What then happened to the Bible is not certain, but eventually it found its way to Florence, where it is now in the Biblioteca Medicea-Laurenziana, in a former monastery on Monte Amiatino. Such is the quality of the work that until recently it was assumed to be from an Italian *scriptorium*. However, research has revealed Jarrow to be its true provenance. The other two copies have not survived, although in 1901 a fragment of one of them was discovered in a Newcastle bookshop by CANON WILLIAM GREENWELL. We cannot be fully certain why Ceolfrith commissioned these massive copies. One reason was that they would be regarded as holy objects in their own right and as such would enhance the places where they were housed. The papal copy, however, may have had a political purpose: to demonstrate the commitment of the Northumbrian church to the leadership of the Holy See and to emphasise its break with its Celtic origins.

The *Codex Amiatinus* is over ten inches thick and weighs 75 lb (34 kg). It contains 2,060 pages of vellum, which consumed 1,550 calf skins. It was written by hand in ink made of lamp black and gum or a mixture of tannic acid, copperas (green vitriol) and gum, using pens which had to be sharpened up to sixty times daily, made of the dried and descaled flight feathers of geese or swans, preferably those of the left wing for right-handed scribes. Like the LINDISFARNE GOSPELS, it was also illustrated in colour. Multiply these figures by three and the monumental nature and expense of the exercise becomes apparent, which in turn proclaims its importance to both makers and recipients.

COLLIERS

Colliers were the ships that took coal by sea from North-East ports to distant markets. Initially, coal was exported in 'foreign' ships that came from elsewhere and were also used for other purposes. In the eighteenth century, however, the region increasingly built its own ships specifically for the coal trade. As with the development of shipping generally, colliers moved from being made of wood and propelled by sail to being of iron (later steel) construction and driven by steam. This transition began with the famous *JOHN BOWES*, launched in 1852.

Until then, the typical collier was about 200 gross registered tons, capable of carrying about 300 tons of coal. Most were brigs (two-masted and square rigged) or snows (brigs with an additional mast aft of the mainmast). Although coal was exported to many places, the staple of the trade was supplying London and its hinterland, around 300 miles (480 km) from where the coal was mined. The voyage down and up the North Sea was made hazardous by two problems beyond human control. One was the wind, which, if contrary, could double the time for the round trip from a month to two months. In fact, the virtual certainty of severe winter gales meant that the transport of coal was essentially a summer activity. The other hazard was the offshore sand banks from the Wash southwards. As a result, every year colliers and their crews were lost. Iron steamships brought two great advantages: a reduced round-journey time of a week, and reduced vulnerability to contrary winds. This did not mean that there were no fatalities, and these increased during the two world wars, when 433 seamen lost their lives as the result of colliers being sunk by German naval action. Throughout the history of the North Sea coal trade it is possible that as many men lost their lives getting the coal to London as were killed winning it.

The coal trade reached its peak in the early and middle decades of the twentieth century. The continued growth of London meant an ever-expanding domestic market, added to which was the growth of the town gas and later the electricity industries, both consuming large quantities of coal. In the later years of the twentieth century the trade declined with the growing use of oil and natural gas. By the time the colliers ceased to run south, they were capable of carrying over 20,000 tons, over sixty times more than their eighteenth-century predecessors.

COLLIERY DISASTERS

Coal mining is a hazardous occupation, with the ever-present possibilities of injury or death arising from human carelessness or accidents of nature, such as roof falls. Almost all the worst disasters, however, stemmed from three causes. One was inundation, often by water that had built up in disused and forgotten workings, hence the growing concern to prepare accurate plans of all workings. The other two related to the gases locked into the coal measures as they formed. The more violent was *firedamp*, a mixture of methane and air, which exploded when in contact with a naked light. More insidious were *afterdamp* and *chokedamp*, respectively carbon monoxide and carbon dioxide resulting from an explosion, both of which caused asphyxiation.

Until the nineteenth century death in the pit was, and to a large extent had to be, accepted as inevitable and unavoidable, but after 1800 there was a growing belief that accidents could be prevented and that many of those involved in accidents could be brought to safety. Increased scientific knowledge and technical expertise, backed by legislation with an effective inspection regime and the creation of rescue organisations, gradually resulted in the substantial realisation of these ambitions. This success is revealed in the statistics of accidents in which there were five or more fatalities.

Between 1800 and 1951, the year when the last of such incidents occurred, accidents in which five or more men died numbered 112 with 2,937 fatalities. Of these, 29 incidents and 785 deaths occurred in Northumberland pits and 83 accidents and 2,152 deaths happened in those in Durham. The figures broadly reflect the geographical balance of the coalfield.

Much more significant are the differences between the successive half-centuries between 1800 and 1951. Between 1800 and 1849, the number of accidents was 64, in which 1,530 men died. In the following fifty years, the number of accidents fell to 34 and the total deaths to 1,004. From 1900 until 1951, the number of incidents dropped to 14 and the number of deaths to 403. The difference between the first and second halves of the nineteenth century is the more impressive when the increase in the number of pits and miners is taken into consideration. It serves to underline the growing effectiveness of the safety measures devised and enforced by legislation and a qualified inspectorate. In explaining the absence of accidents with five or more fatalities after 1951, the accelerated closure of pits must be added as a factor to the improvements in mine-safety measures.

In the course of the 150 years for which we have reliable statistics, there have been four major disasters in which the number of deaths exceeded 100: Wallsend in 1835 (102), New Hartley in 1862 (204), Seaham in 1880 (164) and West Stanley in 1909 (168), to which should be added other major disasters at Felling in 1812 (92), Haswell in 1844 (94), Trimdon Grange in 1882 (74) and EASINGTON in 1951 (81). Mercifully, none of the North East's disasters reached the magnitude of that in 1913 at Senghenydd Colliery near Caerphilly in South Wales when 429 men died.

Two of these tragedies had beneficial consequences. The first was the Felling disaster, caused by a double explosion of gas as the result of the use of naked candle flames for illumination. The impact of the great loss of life was a competition to find a 'safety lamp', one where the flame was insulated from gas and so unable to trigger an explosion. Within three years, three lamps were produced, two in the region, by WILLIAM CLANNY and GEORGE STEPHENSON, the third by the eminent scientist Sir Humphrey Davy. Although many miners preferred the Clanny Lamp or the 'Geordie' Lamp, it was the Davy version that became most widely adopted.

The other disaster which had two salutary consequences was that at New Hartley. There, the cause was the breaking of the 42-ton iron beam of the pumping engine, half of which crashed down the shaft. Because there was only one shaft, now totally blocked, it took the rescue team led by the eminent sinker William Coulson (who had sunk the shaft fifteen years earlier) over a week to reach the two affected seams, where they found that all the emtombed miners were dead. Most were buried in the churchyard at Earsdon, where their memorial still stands. The inquiry that followed came rapidly to two obvious conclusions: that, had there been a second shaft, the only deaths would have been the five men who were plunged to their deaths as the broken beam crashed down the shaft; and that these too might not have occurred had the beam been made of wrought iron rather than cast iron. The legislative reaction was immediate: an act of August 1862 required all future pits to have two shafts and all one-shaft pits to sink a second shaft within three years. The New Hartley disaster had one other benefit, the setting up of the Northumberland and Durham Miners' Permanent Relief Fund to support the dependants of miners killed at the pit and miners no longer able to work.

COLLING, ROBERT (1749–1820) and CHARLES (1751–1836)

The Colling brothers did not work together and for some parts of their lives they were not on good terms. Yet they were both interested in the same aspect of farming and both made significant contributions to the development of stockbreeding. They were the sons of Charles Colling and his wife, Dorothy Robson, who farmed at Ketton, three miles north of Darlington. Robert, the elder brother, was originally apprenticed to a grocer at South Shields, but was forced to abandon this career as the result of ill health. Returning home, he rented a farm at Barmpton, about a mile south of Ketton. There he developed a first-rate herd of Shorthorn cattle, based upon a foundation bull called Hubback. When the Shorthorn breed became popular after 1810, Robert Colling was able to sell his herd for nearly £7,853. His best-known beast was a heifer, which weighed 1,820 lb (825 kg) at four years old and was bought by two butchers, who exhibited it at the Three Crowns in Piccadilly in London, by which time its weight had risen to 2,448 lb (1,110 kg).

Charles Colling, however, was the more dynamic and ambitious of the two brothers. On the death of their father in 1782, he took over the farm at Ketton and followed Robert into the business of breeding Shorthorn cattle. He immediately spent three weeks with the famous advocate of selective breeding, Robert Bakewell, at his farm at Dishley in Leicestershire, learning the principles by which Bakewell operated. He also bought his brother's foundation bull, Hubback, which he mated with the cows at Ketton. It was from Charles Colling's herd that the famous DURHAM OX came, which did much to advertise the Shorthorn breed and the benefits of controlled breeding of domestic animals. Charles Colling was, therefore, the more successful of the brothers: he lived longer, enjoyed better health and had the active support of his wife, Mary Colpitts, who was equally interested in the development of the Shorthorn breed.

The Colling brothers were not responsible for devising the concept of contolled breeding, but they did practise the principles effectively and made the Shorthorn one of the most popular breeds of cattle, providing the stock on which the Scottish Shorthorn was based.

COLLINGWOOD, VICE ADMIRAL CUTHBERT, LORD COLLINGWOOD OF HETHPOOL (1748–1810)

The giant statue of Vice Admiral Collingwood by J.G. LOUGH that stands on the cliff at TYNEMOUTH overlooking the mouth of the river, and the bust in St Nicholas's Cathedral by J.F. Rossi, together with the plaque placed on the wall of Milburn House (the site of Collingwood's birthplace) near St Nicholas's Cathedral by Newcastle City Council, bear silent witness to the esteem and respect in which Collingwood is held in his native land. Elsewhere, however, his achievements and reputation have been given distinctly lower rating. In part this is attributable to his having been a northcountryman from a family of modest status. But it is clear that until recently his reputation has been sacrificed to the apotheosis of his great friend, Horatio Nelson.

Ironically, the snobbery relating to his origins missed the fact that, although his father was a Newcastle trader of modest means, he came of a very old Northumberland gentry family. His education at Newcastle Royal Grammar School, as his letters show, was sound and thorough. Among his contemporaries was JOHN SCOTT, the future Lord Chancellor and Earl of Eldon. In 1761 his father paid £30 to a friend, Captain Braithwaite, who took Collingwood as a midshipman on HMS *Shannon*, the 28-gun frigate he commanded. It was Collingwood's good fortune that Braithwaite was a good commander, who gave his friend's son a thorough training in the art of seamanship. On this sound foundation, Collingwood built a successful career that kept him at sea for forty-four of the remaining forty-nine years of his life.

The next fourteen years were Collingwood's apprenticeship, serving as a midshipman in five 28-gun frigates and a 50-gun man-of-war in Home, Atlantic, Mediterranean and the West Indies stations. Except for the first two years of his service, Britain was at peace and consequently Collingwood saw no action. This changed in 1775 with the outbreak of the American War of Independence, when he distinguished himself in ferrying supplies and wounded troops between Boston and Charlestown during the first land battle of the war at Bunker's Hill. His training and character showed to good effect: he was said to have been cool and brave under fire and shown good judgement. It was sufficient to earn him promotion to the rank of lieutenant and in the following year his first command, a 14-gun sloop, *Hornet*. The American War kept him on the West Indies station for the next five years, during which time he met his lifelong friend, Horatio Nelson, who was ten years his junior and of very different temperament. Collingwood was again promoted, to commander, and given a 28-gun frigate, HMS *Pelican*, which unfortunately in 1781 was wrecked in a hurricane off the coast of Jamaica. Collingwood was in no way to blame for this loss; indeed, his conduct in getting his crew safely ashore was exemplary and in 1783 he was given command of a larger ship, the 44-gun HMS *Mediator*.

With the end of the American War in 1783, Collingwood was able (perhaps more accurately forced) to spend a fair amount of time at home, during which he married in 1791 Sarah Blackett, daughter of a prominent Newcastle family. They rented (and subsequently bought) a house in MORPETH that still stands on the north side of Oldgate. In 1793, however, the long war against France began, which was to last with only a short break until 1815, five years after Collingwood's death. In 1794, he took part in the first great naval battle of the war, known as the 'Glorious First of June', in which Admiral Howe defeated the French fleet, although his failure to prevent the convoy it was protecting from making port meant that his victory was only partial. Collingwood was flag captain to Admiral Bowyer on HMS *Barfleur* and distinguished himself in the action. However, he was not mentioned in the dispatch Howe sent to the Admiralty, which resulted in the award of medals to those captains who were. Collingwood felt the omission keenly, as he considered it a slight on his performance and professional competence. The matter was rectified three years later in 1797, when Collingwood, in command of the 74-gun HMS *Excellent*, distinguished himself at the Battle of Cape St Vincent, notably rescuing Nelson from the consequence of his own impetuosity. The fleet commander, Sir John Jervis, recommended all his captains for medals. Collingwood was minded to refuse his, until Jervis soothed his wounded *amour propre* by arranging for the omission of 1794 to be rectified.

In the following years, Collingwood was absent from two battles that added to Nelson's reputation, Aboukir Bay at the mouth of the Nile (1798) and Copenhagen (1801). Instead, he was engaged on the infinitely tedious but equally important duty of blockading French ports. Nevertheless, his performance and ability secured his promotion to Rear Admiral in 1798 and Vice Admiral in 1803. Two years later he was to experience his finest hour at the Battle of Trafalgar. This was the great showdown that the British government and the Royal Navy sought. The Franco-Spanish fleet numbered thirty-three ships of the line, five more than the British fleet, which mustered twenty-seven. Collingwood was second in command to Nelson, who decided to break the enemy line by attacking in two columns, thereby breaking it into three parts. Nelson in HMS *Victory* commanded the windward column; Collingwood in the 100-gun HMS *Royal Sovereign* commanded the leeward column. Collingwood engaged first and the *Royal Sovereign* as the lead ship took a fearsome pounding until she was close enough to open fire. After a desperate fight, he forced the Spanish flagship, the 112-gun *Santa Anna*, to surrender, by which time *Royal Sovereign*'s masts and rigging were shot away to the extent that she had to be towed out of the battle by the frigate HMS *Euryalus*. Collingwood, whose composure under fire was displayed by his eating of an apple as he went about his business, was wounded in the leg by a splinter of wood.

Nelson's death placed Collingwood in command. In the hours following the end of the battle he took the decision to abandon thirteen (four had already been sent to Gibraltar) of the seventeen enemy ships that had surrendered. This not only deprived the Royal Navy of warships that could be repaired and put back into service, it also denied the British crews their prize money. It was not a decision lightly taken, especially as Nelson's last order was for the British ships to anchor once the battle was over. But Collingwood, a supremely competent seaman, knew that a westerly gale was approaching, that all the British ships had suffered severe damage, including in some cases loss of anchors, and that the fleet was perilously close to a rocky lee shore. It was imperative that he took whatever measures were necessary to prevent any British losses, which meant abandoning the enemy ships and moving his own further out to sea. Although Collingwood's decision was vindicated by an Admiralty inquiry, the unwarranted criticism that he wasted Nelson's victory has only now been shown to be the calumny it is.

From Trafalgar, fought on 21 October 1805, until his death at sea in February 1810, Collingwood was in command in the Mediterranean. Here, too, his performance has been derided and compared unfavourably with that of Nelson. Again the criticism is a travesty. It is true that he did not achieve glorious victory in battle, but bringing this about, which he undoubtedly sought, could not be guaranteed, given the uncertainty and inaccuracy of naval intelligence. In any case, great battles were incidental to the Royal Navy's task, which was to deny control of the Mediterranean to the French. In this Collingwood was successful, preventing the French gaining control of Malta,

Sicily and the Balearic Islands, and removing them from Corfu, as well as bottling up their fleet in Toulon for long periods. In pursuit of these needful purposes, Collingwood traversed the length and breadth of the Mediterranean several times and also, which is often forgotten, engaged successfully in diplomatic activity. Throughout these years Britain was on the defensive: on land Napoleon Bonaparte was sweeping all before him and had yet to experience his nemesis in Russia (1812) and the defeat of his marshals in Spain (1809–14).

In the last years of his command, Collingwood was in poor health, yet the Admiralty would not allow him to resign until 22 January 1810. Seventeen days later, he died at sea as he was returning home to retirement. On arrival, his body lay in state at Greenwich and was then buried alongside Nelson in St Paul's Cathedral: if later generations derided his contribution, his contemporaries knew its worth. Collingwood was a very different man from Nelson. He did not have his friend's ambition, his swashbuckling approach, or his capacity for self-advertisement. But he was a caring and well-respected commander with the perception and experience accurately to read and react to the situation in the midst of the chaos of battle. Above all, he was a superb seaman and a trainer of his crews in gunnery, which was *the* advantage to which the Royal Navy owed its victories in battle. British ships were not superior to those of her enemies, but French and Spanish gunners could discharge only one round to the Royal Navy's three. In working the gun crews of his ships up to that pitch of performance Collingwood had no equal.

Although not so intended, Collingwood's statue at Tynemouth is a reminder that over 500 other men of the North East served with him at Trafalgar.

COMMON, JACK (1903–1968)

Jack Common was a North-East author whose work has failed to receive the recognition that many, including George Orwell, believe it deserved. He was born in 1903 in an upper TYNESIDE FLAT in Heaton, Newcastle, son of a driver of a shunting engine in the nearby marshalling yard. His school record was mediocre, except for his ability to write an English essay, which was sufficiently outstanding for the headmaster to read some of his work to the whole school. After leaving school at the statutory age of fourteen in 1917, he went to Skerry's Commercial College, from where he secured employment in a solicitor's office. In his spare time he became acquainted with some of the radical thinking of his time through membership of several political groups. In 1928 he left Tyneside for London, where he made a living in a variety of jobs, including that of assistant editor of a magazine and as a scriptwriter. He also found time to write essays on the social and working conditions of the 1930s, which were published by Secker and Warburg and were well reviewed by George Orwell. After World War II Common's hand-to-mouth existence in London continued, and included such varied occupations as a labourer and writing reports on films.

But it was during these early post-war years that he wrote the two novels for which he is remembered, *Kiddar's Luck* (1951) and *The Ampersand* (1954), both closely autobiographical. In the former, in which he gave himself the name Will Kiddar, he recounted his life as the son of a working-class Tynesider, whose marriage failed, thanks to the mother's injury and subsequent descent into drunkenness and to the father's philandering. In the sequel, which recounts his life in Newcastle after leaving school, he changed his name to the less flattering Will Clarts. In both, he is able to describe the society in which he grew up, with which he identified to a considerable degree, but from which he gradually became distanced as the result of his growing aspiration as an author. Both novels were recognised as works of quality, but they did not bring fame and fortune to Common, partly it has to be said because of his own inability to promote his career. Seven years after Common's death in 1968, his two novels were reprinted in a single volume in Newcastle, but even this failed to secure wider recognition. It is surprising that they were not seized upon as material for film or television scripts.

CONSETT

To the present, the history of Consett has three distinct phases: a pre-industrial phase, about which little is known; the iron and steel years, lasting from 1840 until 1980; and the present phase, which may be called post-industrial.

The origins of Consett are totally obscure. Its original name, Conkesheued, has a Celtic element of unknown meaning and an English word meaning 'headland'. The first record of it is in Boldon Book, when it was in the possession of Arnold the Baker, to whom it was given in exchange for Tursdale, for an annual rent of 24s (£1.20). In area, it probably covered about 2,500 acres (1,000 ha). Who Arnold was is not known, but a reasonable assumption is that he was an important officer in the household of Bishop Hugh of le Puiset. Six and a half centuries later, in 1834, Consett was still a small agricultural community with seven farmers, thirty-nine houses and a population of 195; its most prominent building was Consett Hall, now demolished.

The second phase of Consett's history, the 'iron age', began in 1840, when a small group of entrepreneurs founded the Derwent Iron Co. and sited their works at Consett. This decision was governed by three factors: the presence of good-quality coking coal; the presence of iron ore and limestone in Weardale; and the existence of the Stanhope and Tyne Railroad, built after 1834, which could bring raw materials from Weardale to Consett. Their appreciation at that time was sound and their enterprise prospered to the extent that they soon became the largest producer of iron in the North East. In the 1850s, however, two things happened that wrong-footed them. One was the discovery of huge quantities of iron ore in the Cleveland Hills, which put in doubt the wisdom of electing to operate at Consett. The other was the failure in 1857 of the company's banker, the Northumberland and Durham District Bank. It was fortunate that by that date the Derwent Iron Co. was large and important enough to the North-East economy for its disappearance not to be countenanced. The upshot was that, although with considerable difficulty, in 1864 a new company was formed, the Consett Iron Co., which bought the assets of its predecessor for £295,318.

From then until World War I, the Consett Iron Co. developed to become one of the major producers of iron, and from the 1880s steel, in the North East and in Britain, in spite of the apparent handicap of its location. This handicap was fully recognised by the company, to the extent that in 1899, following the dredging of the Tyne, the building of the Swing Bridge and the coal staithes at Dunston (see Dunston Staithe), a serious study was undertaken to determine whether production should be transferred to a new riverside site at Derwenthaugh. Its conclusion, however, was that the cost advantage would be too slight to offset the high cost of removal. The fact was that in these years Consett's profits were great enough to allow annual dividends paid to shareholders to range from 25 per cent to 45 per cent, while rival firms within the region were paying under 10 per cent.

What was the secret of Consett's success? One was the quality of its management. Between 1869 and 1920, the company had only two general managers, both first-class men: William Jenkins, recruited from the Dowlais Iron Works in South Wales, who held the post until 1893; and George Ainsworth, whom he had trained. Backing them was SIR DAVID DALE, who had great financial expertise and was managing director until 1906. In the hands of these men the company maintained at least parity with its rivals in the technical field. Secondly, the company sat on top of a huge reserve of some of the best coking coal in the world. Sensibly, it acquired mining rights in the vicinity and sank its own pits. Within a few years it was one of the largest coal companies in the region. In 1913 the output of its nine collieries was 2,303,000 tons, of which over half a million tons were coked. Not only did it furnish all the coal and coke it required from its own resources, it made considerable profit from the sale of surplus quantities. Nor at this stage did the distance from its sources of iron ore prove too great a handicap. In fact, most of its ore came from Cumberland (Cumbria) rather than Cleveland, and it began importing from Spain in the 1880s. Nevertheless, the cost of rail transport of a very heavy material had to be borne, and it was fortunate that Sir David Dale was able to negotiate favourable rates with the North East Railway. Finally, Consett came to specialise in the manufacture of iron, and later steel, plates for the shipyards on the Tyne.

The decades before World War I were the great golden years of the Consett Iron Co. But between 1920 and 1980 two conditions developed that gradually ensured its closure. One was the concentration of iron and steel making on coastal sites, which favoured the companies located at Teesside. The other was the gradual erosion of its financial and commercial independence through the gradual imposition of state control. (see IRON AND STEEL INDUSTRY). What finally brought closure, in September 1980, was the rapid decline in the demand for steel and the urgent need for the British Steel Corporation to close plants in order to save money. By that date Consett was one of the smaller facilities and that, combined with its location, made it an obvious candidate for closure. Its site disadvantage, apparent in 1850, in the end was conclusive. While proof of a negative is not possible, it has been argued that had Consett Iron Co. remained outwith state control and able to make its own commercial decisions, it might have been able to survive.

Consett was never a company town in the fullest sense of the word, since the company did not own all the housing stock and other facilities. Nevertheless, Consett Iron Co. was throughout the *raison d'être* for Consett, and consequently the end of iron and steel making was initially a social and economic disaster for its people. But there was worse: in the same year, the last coal mine in North-West Durham closed, as did another major employer in the vicinity, Ransome, Hoffman, Pollard, at Annfield Plain. These hammer blows meant the loss of nearly 7,000 jobs. The unemployment rate in Derwentside District (into which Consett was incorporated in 1974) rose to 15.5 per cent, almost twice the national average.

Massive attempts were made to plug the employment gap by British Steel Corporation's own recovery organisation and the European Social Fund: new roads were built and industrial estates created. But replacement employment came slowly and not all the firms that came stayed or survived. Not surprisingly, the population of Derwentside District declined by sixteen per cent from 102,400 in 1951 to 86,000 at the time of writing and the unemployment rate is over 11 per cent. There is one consolation:

Consett is no longer a 'red town', but has a clean environment, where the former steelworks sites have been cleared and replaced by grassed landscapes.

CONYERS' FALCHION

The Conyers' Falchion is a short curved sword with a blade, broader at the tip than at the hilt, now on display in the Treasury of DURHAM CATHEDRAL. From an unknown date, but certainly from the fourteenth century, until at least 1771, by tradition the head of the Conyers family (and its successor) presented it to the Bishop of Durham on the first occasion on which he crossed the Tees by Neasham Ford or Croft Bridge to enter the bishopric. Having received it, the bishop then returned it to its owner. The legend attached to this ceremony is that a Conyers ancestor slew a worm (dragon), and as a reward for this deed he was given the manor of Sockburn free of all rent, except that of presenting the falchion by which he had slain the dragon on the occasion of the bishop's first entry to the diocese.

This is a fable. The falchion dates from the mid-thirteenth century and almost certainly had a previous owner. On either side of its pommel are the arms of England and the Holy Roman Empire, to neither of which had the Conyers any claim. In fact it has been suggested that the falchion had belonged to Richard, Earl of Cornwall, the younger brother of Henry III, elected King of the Romans (Holy Roman Emperor designate) in 1257. How and when the falchion came into the hands of the Conyers is entirely unclear.

The truth is more prosaic, although without absolute certainty. The first Conyers, Roger Conyers I, was one of eleven Normans granted land in County Durham in the early years of the twelfth century. His estate, bestowed on him by BISHOP RANNULF FLAMBARD, included in addition to Sockburn, Bishopton, Stainton and Dinsdale in Durham, BEDLINGTON in Northumberland and six places in the North Riding of Yorkshire. His son, Roger Conyers II, played a crucial role in the civil war that took place in Durham between 1141 and 1144, occasioned by the attempt of David I of Scotland to impose his Chancellor, William Cumin, on the bishopric following the death in 1141 of Bishop Geoffrey Rufus. The monks of the Cathedral Priory, who were strongly opposed to Cumin and the implied Scottish control, elected William of St Barbe, the Dean of York. The matter was settled in St Barbe's favour after a brief civil war in which Roger Conyers II was St Barbe's leading supporter. Some time between 1149 and 1152 the victorious St Barbara made Roger Conyers II hereditary Constable of Durham and Keeper of Durham Castle.

The falchion may have been the title deed to the office granted to Roger II, or the estate granted to his father, Roger I. Before written records of grants of land and office became the norm, it was customary for a gift, very often a knife, to be handed by the donor to the donee in a public ceremony witnessed by a large number of men. Thereafter that object would be considered to prove the validity of the gift. Conceivably, the falchion (or more likely its predecessor) was the gift made by either Rannulf Flambard to Roger Conyers I or by William of St Barbe to Roger Conyers II as proof of the grant of their estate or hereditary office. It would be natural and appropriate for the head of the Conyers family to show this proof of ownership of an estate that lay on the southern border of the diocese and their claim to the hereditary constableship of Durham Castle on the occasion of the new bishop's first entry.

The Conyers legend of land granted as a reward for the slaying of a dangerous beast is not unique, however. No more than twenty miles to the north, the Pollards of Auckland, a family of lower status than the Conyers, also developed a very similar legend, although in their case the offending beast was a wild boar. And best known of all is the legend of the LAMBTON WORM, involving the Lambton family, made famous in song. Similar tales can be found all over Europe and help to explain the story of St George.

COOKSON, DAME CATHERINE (1906–1998)

Catherine Cookson was arguably the literary phenomenon of the second half of the twentieth century in the English-reading world. Her success, however, was in spite of, but also because of, considerable personal disadvantage and suffering. She was born at Tyne Dock, the illegitimate child of a barmaid working at the Ravensworth Arms at Lamesley, at a time when bastardy was a legal disability and a social stigma. To disguise this fact, her mother, Kate Fawcett, registered her as Catherine Ann Davies. She attended three elementary schools between 1910 and 1919, during which time she learned of her illegitimacy and was sexually assaulted by her mother's man friend. After several short spells in a variety of jobs between 1919 and 1924, she obtained a post at the laundry of Harton Workhouse, rising in three years to be Assistant Laundress. Failure to be appointed Laundress led her, like many North Easterners, to move south. In 1929 she was appointed Laundress at a workhouse near Clacton, but almost immediately she applied for and was offered the much better paid post of Head Laundress at the Hastings Poor Law Institution. Apart from the war years between 1940 and 1945, Hastings was to be her home until 1976.

In 1933 she bought a large house called The Hirst, which she ran as a 'gentlemen's boarding house', while continuing to work for the Poor Law Institution until 1939. In 1936 she met her future husband, Tom Cookson, who was six years her junior and who had joined the staff of Hastings Grammar School after graduating from Oxford University with a degree in Mathematics. They married in the summer of 1940. Paradoxically, this was the start of the worst period of her life. Although it was a happy marriage that lasted for fifty-eight years, its early consequences were traumatic: between 1940 and 1945 she had a stillbirth and three miscarriages, and in the next five years three unsuccessful operations on her womb. By 1950 she knew that she would never bear children. On top of this, in 1940, The Hirst was requisitioned by the government for the duration of the war (and then returned to her in a dilapidated condition) and Tom Cookson was in the RAF from 1940 until 1945, which involved moving several times as he was transferred from one station to another. Finally, by this time she was aware that she had inherited an incurable blood disorder. And in the back of her mind always was the knowledge of her illegitimacy. Not surprisingly, she had a nervous breakdown.

On her own admission it was her depression that drove her to write, although the urge to authorship had been with her since childhood: in 1922 at the age of sixteen she sent a 16,000-word short story, 'On the Second Floor', to the *Shields Gazette*. It was rejected. What her depression gave her was the knowledge that her material was in herself and her background in the North East. Her first novel, *Kate Hannigan*, was written in 1949 and published in 1950. In the course of the next forty-eight years, she was to write another ninety-five books. Seventy-six of these were novels set in the North East and were about life in the region, but she also wrote six more romantic novels under the pseudonym 'Catherine Marchant', ten children's books and four volumes of autobiography. She confessed that, for her, writing was a mania, which is underlined by the fact that in the last eighteen months of her life she published five novels.

By this time she had returned to live in the North East. Tom Cookson retired from teaching in 1969 and in 1975 he and his wife bought a house in Newcastle. The following year they sold their house in Hastings and made their home in the region. In the remaining years of their lives they had three homes, in Corbridge, Langley and finally in Jesmond, Newcastle.

All the while her novels gained and maintained huge popularity. It is estimated that at the time of her death, around 95 million copies of her books had been sold worldwide, and in 1997 sixteen of her novels were among the 100 most borrowed books from British libraries. Four of the novels were turned into plays, while ITV turned sixteen into hugely successful television dramas. The revenue from such output was immense, but with no family the Cooksons had no natural destination for their wealth. The consequence was an increasing outpouring of money to charity. The main beneficiaries were medical causes and hospitals in Hexham, Newcastle and South Shields. Her generosity in this direction is entirely understandable, given that her blood disorder, which caused internal bleeding, necessitated frequent periods in hospital as an emergency admission. By 1977 the requests for help were such that she solved the problem by setting up the Catherine Cookson Charitable Trust to be the vehicle of her giving. Catherine Cookson's death occurred on 11 June 1998, followed by that of her husband seventeen days later. With their passing the Trust became richer by over £15 million. It continues to make grants to those causes Dame Catherine favoured in her lifetime.

In her lifetime Catherine Cookson received many honours. From Newcastle University and Sunderland Polytechnic (now University) she received honorary degrees, and from St Hilda's College, Oxford an Honorary Fellowship. In 1985 she was given an OBE and in 1993 she became a Dame of the British Empire. Hers was truly a rags to riches (and honours) story.

COOKSON FAMILY

The Cooksons have been prominent in the economic life of the region since the early eighteenth century. They arrived in the person of Isaac Cookson I (1679–1743), the son of a Penrith brazier, who migrated to NEWCASTLE before 1704. Like many industrialists of his day, he was in religious terms a Dissenter and a member of the notable chapel in Hanover Square, later headed by the Reverend William Turner, the friend of MRS GASKELL. His business interests were various, including brass and iron, but particularly glass in partnership with Joseph Airey (see BEILBY, WILLIAM, RALPH AND MARY). His success was such that he was admitted into the prestigious Merchant Adventurers Company.

He was succeeded by his eldest son, John Cookson I (1712/13–1783), who was arguably the most dynamic and successful businessman of his day in the region. As well as continuing with his father's businesses, he became involved in alum refining and in coal and lead mining. Following his father's death, he bought the Whitehill estate on the western outskirts of Chester le Street, which had belonged to the Mylott family since the fourteenth century, where he set up one of the region's earliest blast furnaces. His wealth was such that he was able to set up with three partners, including Airey, Newcastle's first bank, known as the 'Old Bank'. An indication of his wealth was his ability to provide each of his three younger sons with £10,000 and his unmarried daughters with £5,000. In his will he left the bank to his son, Isaac Cookson II (1745–1831), with the proviso that he inherited the industrial businesses on the death of his mother.

In the next generation, however, the family bifurcated. Isaac Cookson II's eldest son, Isaac Cookson III (1776–1851), bought in 1832 the Meldon estate comprising 2,070 acres (820 ha) from the Commissioners of Greenwich Hospital, in whose possession it had been since its forfeiture by James Radcliffe, 3rd Earl of Derwentwater (see JACOBITE UPRISING OF 1715). The purchase included an enclosed park of 466 acres (189 ha) in which Cookson built at a cost of £7,000 a house in neo-classical style, designed by JOHN DOBSON. His eldest son, John Cookson II (1812–88), moved into the house after his father's death. Like so many industrialists, he used his wealth to turn himself into a landed gentleman. His descendants have been resident there ever since.

His younger brother, William Isaac Cookson, as was common with younger brothers, had to make a living in trade. He went into partnership with William Cuthbert of Beaufront Castle (also designed by John Dobson) and developed a highly successful business empire, in which lead manufacture (see LEAD MINING AND MANUFACTURING INDUSTRIES) was prominent. Thereafter, the Cookson businesses (which included lead, coal, iron and steel, and banking) prospered under the direction of his descendants: Norman Charles Cookson (1842–1909), Clive Cookson (1879–1971) and Roland Anthony Cookson (1908–91).

COQUET ISLAND

Coquet Island covers an area of about fifteen acres and lies about a mile and a half off the mouth of the River Coquet. Like many offshore islands, it has attracted religious men. One story recounts that in 684 ST CUTHBERT met Aelfled, sister of KING ECGFRITH OF NORTHUMBRIA, on the island and told her that her brother had only twelve months to live. Sure enough, Ecgfrith was killed in battle in 685. There is also archaeological evidence that the island was occupied after this date. After the Conquest, the Earl of Northumberland, Robert de Mowbray, gave it to Tynemouth Priory (see TYNEMOUTH AND NORTH SHIELDS), and from then until the Priory closed in 1539, the monks maintained a small cell there. Its most interesting resident, however, was a Danish nobleman, later called St Henry of Coquet, who, with the Prior of Tynemouth's permission, settled there in the first years of the twelfth century and led a life reminiscent of that led by Cuthbert on the Inner Farne until his death in 1127.

After the closure of Tynemouth Priory, ownership of the island passed through several hands, until 1753, when the BOWES FAMILY of Streatlam sold it to the 1st Duke of Northumberland. In recent times it has had two distinct roles. The first was as the site of a LIGHTHOUSE, created in 1841 by superimposing the light on a BORDER TOWER built before 1415. More recently, the island was designated as a bird sanctuary, managed since 1970 by the RSPB. Around 10,000 pairs and eighteen species of seabird breed there and it is the most southerly breeding place for the Eider Duck, known locally as Cuddy's Duck. The island is able to discharge this latter role thanks to the failure to implement a proposal, put forward in 1883, to incorporate it into one of a pair of giant piers that would create a large harbour at the mouth of the Coquet.

CORBRIDGE / CORSTOPITUM / CORIA

There have been two towns that may be called Corbridge. The first was Roman.

Although today known as Corstopitum, it is believed that it was known to its Roman inhabitants as Coria. For the first hundred years of its existence, however, Corstopitum was not a town but a military establishment. The first fort was built near Red House Farm, probably in AD 79 as part of the intended conquest of the island by Julius Agricola. It was in being for a mere five years and in AD 84 it was replaced by another fort on the present site. It was built of turf and timber and its purpose was to guard and control the river crossing. It was destroyed in a fire in the year AD 105. Its replacement, also of turf and timber, not only commanded the crossing of the Tyne but was also one of a series of forts that punctuated the road that ran west to Carlisle and which formed the northern boundary of the Roman province of Britannia. In the 120s, however, its role changed with the building of HADRIAN'S WALL: now it was to house one of the garrisons that were to be stationed immediately behind the Wall. But, with the decision to build forts on the Wall, it became superfluous. Then, in 140, the Roman government decided to move the frontier of the province north to the Forth–Clyde isthmus and build the Antonine Wall, and it was at this point that Corstopitum was rebuilt in stone, with the intention that it would be a major control point on the road to the new frontier. The Antonine frontier, however, lasted little more than twenty years. When, in the 160s, the Roman government decided to pull back to the previous Hadrianic frontier, Corstopitum again became largely redundant for military purposes. It now began its transformation into a town. Its growth (it eventually covered 27 acres: 11 ha) and prosperity derived from its role as an off-duty centre for troops and a market for local natives and its involvement with the mining of coal, lead and iron. Since most of the site has yet to be excavated, we know almost nothing of its history. In particular, we do not know when or how the town fell out of existence.

What is certain is that its replacement, Corbridge, was located on the western edge of Corstopitum. This new town was the centre of an estate belonging to the King of Northumbria, probably comprising Corbridge and five other townships north of the Tyne: Aydon, Clarewood, Halton, Thornbrough and Whittington. The estate also included a large stretch of moorland without settlements south of the Tyne as far as Dipton Burn. The importance of Corbridge was underlined by the foundation of a monastery. The lower part of the tower of the present church and other fragments of early masonry point to its being very similar to the churches at ESCOMB and Monkwearmouth. It was in existence from at least 786, since in that year a bishop was consecrated there. When this monastery ceased to exist is not known, but its church continued as a parish church and in the early eleventh century the porch at its west end was heightened to become a tower, as also happened elsewhere in the Tyne valley.

The importance of Corbridge in the immediate post-Conquest decades is evident from its continued royal ownership and its function as the base for the royal reeve responsible for Northumberland between the Coquet and the Tyne. However, some time between 1107 and 1118, Henry I replaced the Corbridge reeve (and also his counterpart at BAMBURGH, who was responsible for the county north of the Coquet) with a single sheriff. He pensioned off the reeve, an Englishman named Aluric, by creating for him a small barony, comprising a new township carved out of Corbridge Moor south of the Tyne to which the name Dilston was given. About the same time, Henry also gave the church, together with those at Newcastle and Newburn, to his chaplain, Richard d'Orival (Golden Valley). In 1122, by which date d'Orival was an old man, Henry granted the reversion of these churches after d'Orival's death to the newly founded Augustinian Priory at Carlisle, which became the cathedral Chapter when the diocese of Carlisle was created in 1133.

Corbridge remained a royal property until 1205, when King John gave it to Robert Fitz Roger, Lord of Warkworth. By that date Corbridge must have been a borough for some time, since in 1200 its burgesses were leasing it from the Crown for the not inconsiderable rent of £45. The evidence is that Corbridge continued to grow and prosper throughout the thirteenth century. Commercially, it had the right to hold a market, hence the triangular marketplace and the remains of the market cross. It also had one of the most important fairs in Northumberland, held at midsummer, which, although proclaimed in the marketplace, was held on the moor adjacent to Stagshaw Bank (the present A68) just south of the MILITARY ROAD at Portgate. Its major purpose was the trade in livestock. It was finally discontinued in 1930, by which date it had become a funfair with a reputation for rowdy behaviour.

Evidence from the 1290s reveals the wealth and importance of Corbridge at the end of the thirteenth century. In 1295 it was one of two towns in Northumberland required to send two members to parliament, the other being Newcastle. The reason is made clear by the taxation assessments of the following year. These show Newcastle, with 297 inhabitants sufficiently wealthy to be taxed, as the biggest borough in Northumberland, but Corbridge, with seventy-seven, was in second place. The same record reveals the existence of a thriving textile industry and the presence of a goldsmith. The town's expanding size and wealth was expressed in its church. In three building campaigns in the course of the thirteenth century, it was transformed from what must then have seemed an old-fashioned Anglo-Saxon church into the large cruciform building we see today.

The years around 1300 were probably the pinnacle of Corbridge's medieval prosperity. Thereafter it shrank in significance. Never again did it send members to parliament and its economy must have been adversely affected by its position on one of the main invasion routes from Scotland. The three-storey stone tower (see BORDER TOWERS) built for the vicar in the mid-fourteenth century that still dominates the churchyard testifies to the continuing fear and insecurity that haunted North-Eastern society until the seventeenth century. Along with this was the decline of population because of disease: unless Corbridge's fortunes were out of line with those of other places in the region, its inhabitants in the late fifteenth century would have numbered little more than half of those living there in 1296.

Unlike its neighbour, HEXHAM, Corbridge failed to maintain itself as a borough. Although it still displays all the topographical characteristics of a town, it is classed as a village. Its present prosperity is founded upon its considerable attractions as a place to live, enhanced by being close to the A68 (to and from Scotland) and A69 (between Newcastle and Carlisle) and a stop on the Newcastle–Carlisle railway line.

CORBRIDGE, BATTLE OF, 918

The Battle of Corbridge was an important event in the period between 850 and 950, when Scandinavian invasions and conquests created huge political and social upheaval and disruption throughout Britain. Although our knowledge of the event is sketchy, it is clear that it had long-term consequences for the region. The key player was the Viking leader Ragnall, who seized control of Yorkshire in 911, expelling its Danish ruler. About two years later he invaded Northumbria, still at that date extending from the Tees to the Forth, and defeated its ruler, Earl Ealdred. He and his brother, Uhtred, sought refuge with Constantine I, King of Alba, the part of modern Scotland between Fife and the Moray Firth.

Constantine recognised that Ragnall also posed a threat to his kingdom and so, in alliance with Ealdred, invaded Northumbria in 918. Where the Alban/Northumbrian army and that of Ragnall met is not known for certain. It was said to have been on the moors near the Tyne, which points to Corbridge, since Constantine and Ealdred would have advanced south along the Roman road, now the A68. Neither side could claim victory, but Ragnall's losses were such that he was forced to abandon his conquests and withdraw into Yorkshire. This had two important consequences. One was that Northumbria's native dynasty retained political control for another hundred years (see NORTHUMBRIA, KINGDOM AND EARLDOM OF). The other was that Ragnall's removal ensured that heavy Scandinavian colonisation remained south of the Tees.

COSIN, JOHN (1591–1672)

John Cosin, who was one of the most notable bishops of Durham, was born at Norwich. He was educated at Norwich Grammar School and then at Gonville and Caius College, Cambridge. A dedicated and able scholar, he graduated MA in 1617 and later was awarded the higher degrees of BD in 1624 and DD in 1630. Meanwhile he was ordained a priest in the Church of England and was recruited by John Overall, Bishop of Coventry and Lichfield, and after his death in 1619, by Richard Neile, Bishop of Durham from 1617 until 1628.

Overall and Neile were two of the outstanding clerics of the early seventeenth century and were among the leaders of a movement away from the severe Puritanism that had pervaded the Church of England in the reign of Elizabeth I. Influenced by the Dutch theologian, Jacobus Arminius, they sought to mitigate the rigidities of the doctrine of predestination, emphasising the importance of personal endeavour and of the sacraments as the means of salvation. The latter led them inevitably to give a central role to the liturgy of the church, in which they believed music should play a major part. And because the liturgy was so important, they also favoured elaborate priestly vestments and the beautification of churches. Cosin's thinking was entirely in tune with these ideas. The same was true of Charles I, who became king in 1625; consequently men like Richard Neile were advanced into the most important posts in the Church of England.

Through the patronage of Neile and the favour of the king, Cosin prospered. In 1624 he became a canon of DURHAM CATHEDRAL and Master of Greatham Hospital (see MEDIEVAL HOSPITALS), although he immediately exchanged this post for that of Rector of Elwick. Two years later he relinquished Elwick for the larger and richer parish of Brancepeth. In 1635 he became Master of Peterhouse, Cambridge and five years later, Dean of Peterborough. With the onset of civil war in 1642, however, his career crashed. His views were anathema to the Puritan leaders of the Parliamentary cause and as a result he was deprived of his livings. At some time in the 1640s he went into exile in France, where he acted as chaplain to the court of Charles I's queen, Henrietta Maria. His exile lasted until the restoration of the monarchy in 1660. Within a few weeks of his return to England, he was made Bishop of Durham, a post he held until his death in 1672. Much of his time in those twelve years was of necessity given over to the repair of the damage done during the civil war and under the Commonwealth, when the diocese was abolished. This included regaining all the powers exercised by his predecessors, both spiritual and temporal, and repairing the physical damage done to many of its buildings.

Cosin's legacy to the North East was substantial, although unfortunately much of it is not readily visible or accessible. This is particularly the case with the music manuscripts in the possession of the Dean and Chapter. These include not only works acquired from the Chapel Royal, but also compositions by local composers such as William Smith, Henry Palmer and Richard Hutchinson. During the early seventeenth century, Durham probably came to be the most musically advanced cathedral in the country. Its large surviving collection of manuscripts of church music produced between 1540 and 1640, which owes much to Cosin's promotion of music in the cathedral, is one of the most important in Europe.

Rather more visible is the library he built in the late 1660s towards the end of his life. It is located near the gateway to the castle between the Bishop's Exchequer (built *c.*1430) and the University Library. Cosin built it to house his personal collection of books, which he had amassed since the 1620s and which at the time of his death amounted to 5,500 volumes. Although works of liturgy and theology were most prominent, the collection includes works on geography, history, law, literature, medicine, philosophy and science, and is a witness to the breadth of Cosin's scholastic interests. The legend above the door to the library proclaims the value Cosin placed upon books: *Non minima pars eruditionis est bonos nosse libros* ('Not the least part of learning is the acquaintance with good books'). The library, with its extension (known as Little Cosin) built in 1671, has remained virtually unchanged since Cosin's time. Since 1937 it has been in the care of Durham University.

More accessible too are some of the major works of restoration that Cosin undertook. Perhaps the most splendid is the choir stalls of Durham Cathedral, thought to have been the work of a local man, John Clement. They replaced the medieval stalls destroyed by the Scottish prisoners of war in the winter of 1650–51. But equally impressive is the chapel of AUCKLAND CASTLE, which he not only restored but also at the same time converted from its original use as a banqueting hall. His massive grave slab in the middle of the chapel floor tells of the man's pride in his attainments and achievements. Also impressive is the Black Staircase in Durham Castle, which cleverly links its north and west wings. This and the cathedral choir stalls are made of black oak and in the style that has come to be associated with Cosin's name. Woodwork in this style has survived in seven major churches in County Durham and is known to have existed in three more. However, it would be a mistake to think that Cosin was personally or even primarily responsible. Much of the work was done in the years before 1640, when Cosin's authority extended only to the parishes of which he was rector. The only woodwork that can be safely credited to him is the choir stalls and the font cover in Durham Cathedral and that in the church at Brancepeth, which was so tragically destroyed by fire in 1998.

Cosin also made an important contribution to a national institution, the *Book of Common Prayer.* Charles I planned a revision of its form and content before the civil war and had involved Cosin in the project. During his exile in France, Cosin continued to annotate his copy of the Prayer Book with his ideas for changes and improvements. This copy, which came to be known as *The Durham Book* and is still in Cosin's library, was among the most formative influences on the *Book of Common Prayer* issued in 1662.

COTESWORTH, WILLIAM (1668–1726)

William Cotesworth, one of the most dynamic businessmen in the North East in the late seventeenth and early eighteenth centuries, began life in relatively humble circumstances, the younger son of a small farmer at Eggleston in Teesdale. In 1683, then aged fifteen, he was apprenticed to Robert Sutton, a Gateshead tallow chandler. His first advancement opportunity came early, in 1686, through the death of his master, which placed the business in the hands of his widow and incompetent son. Cotesworth was soon the driving force of the business, in which he bought a partnership for the tiny sum of £20 and which, it was said, he used to finance his other business interests. Then, in 1699, he further enhanced his prospects by a very advantageous marriage, to Hannah Ramsay, the daughter of the wealthy Newcastle goldsmith with coal mining interests, Alderman William Ramsay.

In the course of the next twenty years Cotesworth achieved prominence and prosperity. In 1706 the partnership with the Suttons was dissolved, leaving Cotesworth free to trade on his own account. He did so energetically. In addition to the fiercely competitive tallow and candle trades, which continued to feature prominently in his business activity until 1717, he traded successfully in coffee, tea and cocoa, dyestuffs, flax, glass, grindstones, hemp, lead (in 1711 he became agent for Lord Powlett's lead mines), but above all in salt, leasing in 1710 ten pans (later to rise to eighteen) at North Shields. He also entered the coal industry, principally through his friendship with the Liddell family of Ravensworth Castle. In 1704 he secured exclusive rights to the wayleaves over the lands of the Dean and Chapter of DURHAM CATHEDRAL; in 1709 he was made agent for a cartel of five major coal owners known as the Regulation; two years later, in 1711, he persuaded his brother-in-law, William Ramsay, to purchase the manors of GATESHEAD and Whickham in order to control the transport of coal to the Tyne from the growing number of collieries sunk on the estates further south; and in 1715 he and four partners leased Gateshead Park Colliery.

During the same years he also became a landed proprietor, largely through the death in 1716 of his childless brother-in-law, William Ramsay, who bequeathed Cotesworth the bulk of his estate. This included Park House in Gateshead, which he made his home. Three years later, in 1719, he and a partner, Joseph Banks, purchased the Shipcote estate in Gateshead, and also the Stella and Widdrington estates, forfeited by Lord Widdrington for his part in the JACOBITE UPRISING OF 1715. By the early 1720s his annual income from land was reckoned to be in the region of £4,500.

In the last six years of his life, however, his fortunes faltered. The reasons were various. One was his declining health and another was that some of his investments proved to be far less successful than he expected. But more than this was the determination of his enemies to thwart and, if possible, destroy him. Their hostility had several causes. Fundamental was Cotesworth's business methods, which were considered to be unscrupulous and confrontational and earned him the sobriquet of 'Black William'. What made matters worse was his actions during the tense time following the death of Queen Anne in 1714 and the accession of the German Elector of Hanover as George I. Cotesworth, acting out of conviction, became the government's agent in the region and was considered in London to have been largely responsible for preventing a serious Jacobite uprising in the North East. None of this endeared him to the large number of influential Roman Catholics and Jacobite sympathisers in the region. But in addition to everything else was simple snobbery: disdain and dislike for a man they regarded as an upstart, who had risen too high and too quickly from an unacceptably base starting point. Salt was rubbed into their social wounds when in 1719 a grateful government made Cotesworth a JP and High Sheriff of Northumberland.

Despite this, in his last year of life Cotesworth achieved a notable business triumph, bringing together George Bowes, Sir Henry and George Liddell and Edward Wortley to form a major producers' cartel known as the 'Grand Alliance' (see GREAT NORTHERN COALFIELD). By this agreement, which was to run for ninety-nine years, the members would co-operate, not compete, in all matters relating to the mining, transport and marketing of coal.

COTTON, MARY ANN (1832–1873)

Mary Ann Cotton, one of the most notorious 'serial killers' in the history of British crime, was born at Low Moorsley, near Hetton le Hole, the daughter of a miner, Michael Robson, who was killed in the pit when she was fourteen. There was nothing in her early years, however, to hint at what was to come. By all accounts she was a pretty girl, a member of a Methodist church and a teacher at its Sunday School.

But in the twenty years between 1852 and 1872, her progress was littered with death. During that time, she had four husbands and a partner. Of these five men, only one avoided death: James Robertson, whom she married in 1867 and who threw her out when he discovered her taking his savings. The others husbands, William Mowbray, George Ward and Frederick Cotton, and her lover, Joseph Nattrass, all died. Moreover, she managed to dispose of numerous children, some her own and others inherited as stepchildren through marriage. All the while she moved between Sunderland, the south coast of England, North Walbottle and West Auckland.

In the end she was caught by a combination of factors. Then living in West Auckland, she tried to get her one remaining relative, a seven-year old stepson, Charles Edward Cotton, taken into the local workhouse. On being refused by the assistant overseer, Thomas Riley, she hinted that the boy would not live long. This aroused Riley's suspicions, which he reported to the police. But when Charles died shortly afterwards, a perfunctory inquest revealed no evidence of foul play and so the jury returned a verdict of natural causes. However, the pathologist took away for later examination parts of the boy's intestines and these showed that he had been poisoned by arsenic. The same was found in the cases of four other people she had buried, whose bodies were exhumed. These and the fact that Cotton had bought arsenic (to kill bed bugs, she said) left little room for doubt. Found guilty, Mary Ann Cotton was hanged in Durham Gaol on 24 March 1873.

The fact that the investigation of her career was less than complete and scrupulous means that the exact number of people she murdered will never be known, but the lowest estimate is fourteen. Since in many cases the cause of death was recorded as 'gastric fever', the use of arsenic must be suspected. Why she did it is also uncertain, but pecuniary gain and getting rid of children who had become a social encumbrance would seem to be prominent.

COVENTINA'S WELL

Coventina's Well, located on HADRIAN'S WALL a few yards west of the fort at Carrawburgh, was one of the most remarkable non-Christian religious sites in Britain. Although identified as early as 1732 by JOHN HORSLEY, it was not uncovered until 1876, when lead miners prospecting for sources of ore came across it. The discovery was reported to the landowner, JOHN CLAYTON, who organised an excavation. The well consisted of massive walls, 8 feet 6 inches by 7 feet 9 inches (2.6m by 2.4 m), around a spring, resting on the natural gravel over 7 feet (2.1 m) below ground level. This structure lay within a rectangular enclosure formed by a wall 3 feet (90 cm) thick and measuring 43 feet by 41 feet (13 m by 12.5 m), with an opening 18 feet (3.5 m) wide in the western wall. There is no evidence that either the well or the enclosure was ever roofed.

The shrine was dedicated to a goddess called Coventina: altars bearing her name were deposited in the well. Originally, it was thought that her 'catchment area' was very local, but since then shrines dedicated to her have been found in Spain and France. It is clear that she was associated with water and consequently, it is thought, with healing. That she was regarded as an important goddess is reinforced by one of the altars found in the well that describes her as *sancta* (holy), while another deposit describes her, uniquely outside Rome, as *Augusta*.

The Carrawburgh shrine cannot be dated with absolute precision. It was constructed around the time of the foundation of the fort in the year 133, and it appears to have been abandoned in the 390s. The latter date suggests that it was a casualty of the edicts issued by the Emperor Theodosius in 391 and 394 outlawing pagan worship and practices. It is now thought that the altars and other material were deposited in the well in the hope that this would prevent their destruction under these edicts.

But the most remarkable class of objects recovered from the well is coins. No fewer than 13,490 have survived, but the true total is reckoned to have been 16,000, the difference being those removed during the excavation, which was hastily done one Sunday afternoon by a group of thirty or forty workmen hired for the purpose. This is one of the largest coin deposits ever discovered. Mostly of low denomination, they are from every imperial reign between that of Augustus (d.28) and that of Gratian (d.383), an indication that the goddess retained her appeal for over two hundred and fifty years.

COWEN, JOSEPH (1829–1900)

Joseph Cowen was perhaps the most dynamic left-wing politician in the North East during the middle decades of the nineteenth century. He was the son of Sir Joseph Cowen, a wealthy coal owner and manufacturer of firebricks and clay retorts, who lived at Stella Hall, Blaydon. Cowen senior was prominent in local affairs as an Alderman of NEWCASTLE and one of the town's MPs from 1865 until his death; he was knighted for his chairmanship of the Tyne Improvement Commission.

Cowen junior was educated privately at Ryton and then at Edinburgh University, where he was President of the Debating Society. As the product of a wealthy middle-class family, it would not have been surprising had he been a mainstream politician and, like his father, played leading roles in local life. In fact, he used his wealth and his time to support and promote the most radical and revolutionary causes of his day, to the extent that he was the subject of the attention of the spies of both the British and foreign governments. Their concern arose out of Cowen's befriending of a wide range of European revolutionaries, particularly those who had been involved in the numerous failed revolutions of 1848. Those to whom he gave succour included the Italian Mazzini, the Frenchmen Blanc and Ledru-Rollin, the Hungarian Kossuth, the Pole Mieroslawski, and the Russians Herzen and Bakhunin. And there is a suspicion that he may have been involved in the attempt (which nearly succeeded) in January 1858 by an Italian revolutionary, Felice Orsini, to assassinate the French Emperor, Napoleon III. It was in the 1850s during the aftermath of the 1848 revolutions and the failure of the Chartist movement in Britain that he founded a short-lived radical paper, *The Northern Tribune*, and was heavily involved with an organisation that called itself 'The Republican Brotherhood of Newcastle upon Tyne'. He was also active in the Northern Reform League, which advocated a wide range of political and social reforms: secret ballot, equal electoral districts, universal adult suffrage, the disestablishment of all churches, compulsory state-run education, reform of the game laws and tightening of the licensing laws.

His great influence, however, came through his ownership of the *Newcastle Chronicle*, which he bought in 1859. With the help of his editor, James Annand, he made the paper the most widely read in the region, with a circulation greater than that of better-known provincial papers, such as the *Manchester Guardian* and the *Birmingham Post*. The *Newcastle Chronicle* was a publicity organ for his reform programme and the causes he espoused. The articles on serious subjects were well and fully argued and trenchantly written. But the paper was also designed to appeal to more than those interested in the political issues of the day, hence the ample coverage given to sport. The apogee of its success came in 1871, when the *Chroncle*'s backing did much to secure victory for the Tyneside engineers in their battle to secure a reduction of hours per week from fifty-nine to fifty-four without loss of pay. Two years later Cowen was able to take his concerns to Westminster when, on the death of his father, he won a by-election and became a Liberal MP for Newcastle.

He was not, however, a party man, being too determined to follow his own agenda. This led to his falling out with THOMAS BURT and the Durham Miners' Association, and at the end of the 1870s with the Liberal Party and his own editor. The cause was the Bulgarian Atrocities, the brutal suppression of the revolt of its Bulgar (Christian) subjects by the Turkish (Muslim) government, which provoked Russian intervention. As a Radical, Cowen was naturally hostile to the corrupt and tyrannical government of Constantinople, but his difficulty was that he was even more hostile to Russia, which he regarded as the great menace to everything he believed in. Russian intervention, he was convinced, would result in a puppet state and Russian control of the Straits and thereby access to the Mediterranean, which meant giving some support to the hated Turkish regime. A compromise solution was found in 1878 at the Congress of Berlin, but in the election of 1881 Cowen fought (and won) in Newcastle as an Independent Liberal.

A year earlier, however, he had been badly injured in a crush at a public meeting. He never fully recovered and in 1886 he decided not to seek re-election. In the remaining sixteen years of his life he took little part in public life.

CRAWFORD, JACK (1775–1831)

Jack Crawford was an illiterate seaman whose one memorable action has given rise to a widely used saying in the English-speaking world. He was born in SUNDERLAND in 1775 and as a boy worked as the 'pee-dee' on his father's KEEL. But in 1786 he went to sea as an apprentice seaman on board a South Shields boat. Five years later he became a naval rating. By that date Britain was at war with France and her allies. Crawford was a member of the crew of HMS *Venerable*, flagship of Admiral Adam Duncan, and took part in the Battle of Camperdown, off the coast of Holland, in October 1797. By defeating the Dutch fleet commanded by Jan van Winter, Duncan prevented a Franco-Dutch invasion of Ireland in support of the nationalist uprising.

It was by his action in the course of this battle that Crawford earned his place in history and the English language. The story is that the admiral's flag, the display of which was essential to show the rest of the fleet that he was on board, in command and still fighting, was brought down together with the spar on which it flew. To prevent uncertainty and confusion, Crawford climbed the mainmast, through a hail of musket shot, one of which went through his cheek, and nailed the flag to the topgallant head. Whether he acted under orders or volunteered is not clear, but his act made him famous. He was presented to the king, George III, walked in the procession at Nelson's funeral, and was presented with a commemorative silver medal by his native town, and on leaving the Royal Navy, he was granted an annual pension of £30. But he declined an offer of £100 a week to repeat his feat as a circus act at the Vauxhall Pleasure Gardens in London. Crawford settled in Sunderland and died of cholera during the outbreak of 1831. A statue to him was erected in Mowbray Park in Sunderland in 1890, but wider fame has been guaranteed by the saying 'nailing one's colours to the mast' to describe commitment and determination.

CREIGHTON, MANDELL (1843–1901)

Mandell Creighton was born in Carlisle, but educated at Durham School from 1857 until 1862 and then at Merton College, Oxford. There he enjoyed a distinguished academic career, which included nine years as Fellow and Tutor following his graduation in 1866. In 1875, however, he became Vicar of Embleton in Northumberland, of which parish his college had been patron since the late thirteenth century. He was to remain at Embleton until 1884, when he went to Cambridge as Dixie Professor of Ecclesiastical History, an appointment that recognised the importance of the first two volumes of his monumental *History of the Papacy.* During his six years in this post he completed volumes three and four of *History of the Papacy* and also acted as editor of the newly founded *English Historical Review*, which established itself as the foremost historical journal in Britain. In 1890 he returned to ecclesiastical duty as Bishop of Peterborough, but this did not prevent his completing his *History of the Papacy*, the fifth and final volume being published in 1894. His final role was as Bishop of London, to which he was appointed in 1897. He died in post in 1901, aged fifty-seven, and was buried in St Paul's Cathedral.

CREWE, NATHANIEL, LORD (1633–1722)

Nathaniel Crewe (he succeeded to his father's title of Lord Crewe of Stene in Northamptonshire in 1697) was Bishop of Durham from 1674 until 1722. He rose to this position through the patronage of Charles II, and more particularly of Charles's brother, James, Duke of York, who succeeded as James VII and II in 1685. These attachments were advantageous, but it is clear that Crewe's opinions were close to those of the royal brothers. He held a strong belief in the theory of the 'divine right of kings', the belief that as the king received his authority from God, it was to Him alone that he was answerable for his actions. And he was sufficiently 'high church' not to be troubled by James's public conversion to Roman Catholicism, to the extent that he solemnised the marriage of James and his second wife, Maria d'Este, daughter of the Duke of Modena.

The revolution of 1688–89, which removed James II from the throne and replaced him (jointly) with his Protestant son-in-law, William of Orange, the Stadtholder of Holland, and William's wife, Mary, posed a problem for Crewe. Was he, as many did, to oppose what to him was a blatantly unlawful act, or, in the word of the time, to 'trim'. Like the Vicar of Bray, he chose the latter course and so managed to hang on to his bishopric.

But he was no longer welcome in the corridors of power. Consequently, it was in his later years, when perforce confined to his diocese, that his actions benefited the region. In 1700 he married for the second time. His bride was Dorothy Forster, who with her nephew, Thomas Forster, was joint heir of her father, Sir William Forster of BAMBURGH. The fortune of the once wealthy Forster family had been dissipated, and when Sir William died in 1704, his estate was so encumbered with debt that it had to be put up for sale. Crewe, now a wealthy man, stepped in and bought it for £20,679 10s (£20,679.50). When all the debts were paid, his wife and her nephew were left with less than £2,000.

Nathanial Crewe died in 1722. By his will, his estates in Northumberland and Durham were placed in the hands of trustees for charitable purposes. The largest beneficiary was to be Lincoln College, Oxford, where Crewe had been a student and of which he had been Rector from 1668 until 1672; but in addition a wide variety of persons and institutions were to receive grants. As regards the North East, the most notable beneficiaries were Blanchland (see BLANCHLAND ABBEY) and Bamburgh, the places from which the trust drew much of its money. This was thanks to two men, Thomas Sharp and his son, John Sharp, who were the driving forces of the trust between, respectively, 1736 and 1758, and 1758 and 1792. Both men held several benefices in the diocese, canons of DURHAM CATHEDRAL and Archdeacon of Northumberland.

Thomas Sharp was responsible for creating the village of Blanchland as we see it today, including the bridge across the Derwent. His son, however, accomplished much more at Bamburgh. He began by renovating the castle, initially as the venue for the manorial court. But he then made it the home of a boys' school, with two masters, one to teach English, Latin and Greek, the other to teach writing, mathematics and navigation. To help the poor, he set up an abattoir to supply meat, and a store of grain (for the grinding of which he built a windmill, which still exists) to provide flour in times of dearth and high prices. He also set up a cheap shop in the village to provide essentials and hired a surgeon to attend the sick on Sundays in a small hospital. After his death in 1792, a boarding school for thirty poor girls was also set up in the castle and considerable sums were spent on the harbour at North Sunderland Seahouses.

But in the nineteenth century the administration of the trust became slack and in 1862 was investigated by a Charity Commission inspector, who was severely critical. As a result, changes were made to the scheme of administration. Also the castle ceased to be used, one by one, for the various purposes that John Sharp had set up, and in 1894 it was sold for £60,000 to LORD ARMSTRONG.

The trust still flourishes, although its terms were revised in 1974 to allow the trustees more flexibility and it is now administered from the Durham Cathedral Chapter Office. The most notable of recent beneficiaries is Durham University, which in 1958 was given the Sharp Library on long loan. This contains many rare and ancient books that were accumulated by Thomas and John Sharp and by Thomas's father John Sharp, who had been Archbishop of York.

CROWLEY, AMBROSE (1658–1713)

Ambrose Crowley, one the pioneers of North-East industry, was born in Stourbridge, Worcestershire, of a Quaker family.

His father was a successful nail maker, ironmonger and forge master, with works in Pontypool in Wales as well as Stourbridge. Instead of entering the family business, Ambrose was apprenticed to a London ironmonger. After completing his time, he decided to set up his own business, recognising that there was a rising market for iron goods. He also recognised the business potential of the North East. In 1685 he set up a business in Sunderland, but shortly after transferred it to Winlaton and bought out competitors at Swalwell. By 1707 he had two slitting mills, two forges and four steel furnaces, using bar iron imported from Sweden into Newcastle and from Stourbridge. Crowley was fortunate in his timing. Between 1689 and 1713 Britain was almost continuously at war with France, and during these years he became the chief supplier of ironmongery to the Royal Navy, including anchors, screws, bolts, hinges, latches, files and 108 different sorts of nail. But he did not rely solely on this single market; he sold to other people and also exported his wares.

Crowley's was a large and well-organised business, which he ran from his warehouse in Greenwich. He had several works in the West Midlands and warehouses in London and Blaydon, and in 1690 he produced the *Law Book of the Crowley Ironworks*, in which he laid down the scheme of his business and the rules by which he required it to be run. Part of his business success stemmed from his membership of the Quaker nexus and also from his being active in politics (he was a Tory and became MP for Andover), where his contacts helped him in the matter of securing contracts.

Crowley's firm long outlived him, lasting until the middle years of the nineteenth century. In the mid-eighteenth century it was probably the largest iron-making enterprise in Europe, employing over 1,000 workers. He also had some influence, albeit indirect, on the development of British banking in that one of his great-grandsons, Sampson Lloyd, was one of the founders of Lloyds Bank.

CRUDDAS, GEORGE (1788–1879) and WILLIAM DONALDSON (1831–1912)

George Cruddas and his son William were the backbone of the firms created by WILLIAM ARMSTRONG. George was one of Armstrong's financial backers when he decided to forsake the law for business in 1845. His ability to do so was based upon his wealth, derived from his linen and shipping businesses. Thereafter, he was a partner in Armstrong's original firms (Newcastle Cranage Co. and W.G. Armstrong & Co.) and then of the Elswick Ordnance Co. of 1859 and finally Sir W.G. Armstrong and Co., the firm that combined Armstrong's armaments and engineering concerns in 1863. Cruddas's specialism was finance, and the stability and success of these enterprises was largely due to his financial ability and perspicacity. He was also a director of the Newcastle and North Shields Railway.

William Cruddas succeeded his father as Armstrong's financial expert, becoming finance director when Sir W.G. Armstrong & Co. became a limited liability company in 1882, a post he retained until his death. In addition, he was a director of the Newcastle and Gateshead Water Co. from 1873 until his death, and its chairman from 1894. He was also chairman of the *Newcastle Journal*. He was a wealthy man and he used some of that wealth to benefit the city. He gave the land in Scotswood out of which Cruddas Park was created, and he paid for the building of two churches, St Stephen's in Elswick and St Mark's in Byker, practical examples of his support for the Church Extension Movement. He was briefly an MP, representing Newcastle as a Conservative from 1895 until 1900.

CULLERCOATS ARTISTS' COLONY

The ASHINGTON 'PITMAN PAINTERS' and the artists arising from the SPENNYMOOR SETTLEMENT all painted what they had personally experienced: they painted from the inside. In contrast, the artists of the Cullercoats colony were, as the word implies, intruders, who painted what they had not experienced: they painted from the outside. The colony, which flourished from the 1880s until the outbreak of World War I, was not unique, for there were several others in coastal situations in Britain (Staithes in Yorkshire, Walberswick in Suffolk and Newlyn in Cornwall) as well as on the continent.

The artists who came to paint in these locations were not basically concerned with the sea and the shipping on it, as was the case with earlier marine artists, but with the people who lived and earned their living by the sea. Initially they were inclined to see their subjects as living a basic way of life that had managed to survive the industrialisation and urbanisation that had overwhelmed nineteenth-century Britain. Men were depicted as strong, hardy and brave in their contest with an unforgiving environment, while the women were often depicted as waiting for their men to return from the sea or grieving when they failed to do so. Without intending to, for they developed friendly relationships with their subjects, the artists were to some degree patronising them. They were not merely a British phenomenon but part of a Europe-wide artistic movement to portray peasant life and society. Gradually their rather didactic approach gave way to a more illustrative one of the seaside as a place of pleasure and relaxation or to the earlier tradition of seascapes.

Twenty-two major artists have been identified as having spent time painting in or near Cullercoats. Most were of local origin, who continued to work in the region, essentially because they had a local market for their products in the form of the wealthy middle-class collectors of the region who attended the exhibitions of their work at the Bewick Club or the Central Exchange Gallery in Newcastle. The most prolific were JOHN CHARLTON, Henry Emmerson, RALPH HEDLEY, George Horton, Robert Jopling, Arthur Marsh, John Slater and Isa Thompson. But not all came from the North East. The most notable incomer was the American painter, **Winslow Homer** (1836–1910), who spent twenty months in Cullercoats in 1881 and 1882 and many of whose Cullercoats paintings are in the USA in art galleries and private collections. Homer, who is regarded as one of America's greatest artists, was profoundly influenced by his Cullercoats experience, to the extent that when he returned to America he built a studio at Prout's Point on the coast of Maine, where he lived for the rest of his life and produced most of his best work.

CULLEY, MATTHEW (1739–1804), JAMES (?–1794), GEORGE (1734–1813)

The Culley brothers were among the most notable improvers of farming practice in the so-called 'Agricultural Revolution', the misleading title given to the evolutionary changes in farming methods that developed from the late seventeenth century, stimulated by the growth of the population and the inflation of food prices during periods of war.

The Culley brothers were the younger sons of Matthew Culley, who in 1722 bought a 200-acre (80 ha) farm at Denton in south Durham. Prior to his death in 1762, Culley senior had arranged for Matthew junior and George to study with Robert Bakewell, at his farm at Dishley, near Loughborough in Leicestershire. Bakewell was already well known for his selective stock-breeding system that had produced an improved sheep, the New Leicester. The brothers appear to have been with Bakewell from 1762 and 1763 until 1765. Returning home, however, they were unable to put their ideas into practice, since the farm at Denton was now in the hands of their eldest brother, Robert. It was for this reason that they had to move elsewhere, although there was the added incentive in the need for a larger establishment in which to practise their ideas.

The result was that in 1766 or 1767 they moved to north Northumberland and took a 21-year lease of a 1,000-acre (400 ha) farm at Fenton, near Wooler. Thirty years later their enterprise had expanded hugely: they were renting from various landlords nine farms in Crookham, Wark, Thornington, Longknowe and Shotton, totalling nearly 4,000 acres (1,620 ha), for which they paid £4,000 in rent and from which they made £9,000 profit. Their financial success was such that between 1795 and 1807 they bought Akeld and Humbleton, Easington Grange and Fowberry Tower for £82,000. From this it is evident that the Culleys were first and foremost businessmen, who adopted new methods to enhance output and profit.

What were the new methods? Basically, they covered all aspects of farming. On the pastoral side, the Culleys practised the breeding techniques learnt at Dishley, notably importing New Leicester tups and crossing them with Teeswater ewes to produce the Border Leicester breed, which they later crossed with the local CHEVIOT breed. They also bred improved Shorthorn cattle. They altered the agrarian regime by adopting a modified version of the Norfolk rotation system, which involved the use of turnips and artificial grasses as the means of eliminating fallow and providing better feed for stock. The new crops also rejuvenated the soil, which helped to increase the yields of cereals, a process aided by sowing with the use of drilling machines instead of by the ancient broadcast method. In addition, they drained their land, produced their own lime, went in for extensive manuring, and created water meadows. In none of these matters were the Culleys inventors, but rather the successful adopters (and adapters) of methods devised by others.

Another aspect of their activities was publicity. Both Matthew and George made frequent and extensive visits to other parts of Britain, where they met and exchanged ideas with like-minded farmers and landlords. In this way they not only gained knowledge, but also disseminated their own experience. George Culley was particularly expert in this field. In 1786 he published a book, *Observations on Livestock; containing hints for choosing and improving the best breeds of the useful kinds of domestic animals* (usually shortened to *Culley on Livestock*), which ran to four editions. Such was his reputation that in 1793 he was commissioned by the Board of Agriculture, created in that year by the government, to produce a survey of agriculture in Cumberland (Cumbria) and, with John Bailey, the Earl of Tankerville's factor, a similar survey of Northumberland and Westmorland (Cumbria).

CUTHBERT, SAINT (c.634–687)

It is without exaggeration to say that no one has had a greater influence on the North East than Cuthbert. Without him, arguably there would not have been the LINDISFARNE GOSPELS, DURHAM CATHEDRAL and DURHAM COUNTY, and as recently as 1942 the failure of German bombers to conduct a successful 'Baedecker Raid' on Durham was popularly attributed to Cuthbert's arranging for the city to be hidden by mist. Explaining this is not easy, especially as there is a thick overlay of myth and legend, much of it deliberately fabricated at different times by people wishing to make the saint and his reputation work for them. There are in fact two Cuthberts, the man and the legend.

Cuthbert the man was one of the first of the dynamic generation of Northumbrian Christianity, which also produced the highly influential figures of WILFRID and BENEDICT BISCOP. He was born, probably in 634, in the valley of the Tweed (or perhaps the Leader) in what is now the Scottish Borders Region. His composite name (meaning well-known + bright) may indicate membership of the upper level of Northumbrian society, which in turn implies early training directed to making him a warrior. But in 651, when he would have been in his late teens, he opted for a religious vocation. It was said that he was drawn to this by a vision of the death in that year of AIDAN. A more plausible explanation is the influence of Boisil (from whose name derives St Boswells), the prior of the monastery at Melrose, a satellite of the monastery of Lindisfarne (see HOLY ISLAND) founded by Eata, one of Aidan's pupils. The monastery was not at the present town, but at Old Melrose, about two and a half miles to the east in a sharp bend in the Tweed close to the former Roman fort at Newstead.

In the early 660s, by which time Cuthbert was a priest, he accompanied his abbot, Eata, to the newly founded monastery of Ripon. Their stay was short, largely because they found themselves at odds with the monastery's owner, Wilfrid. Shortly after his return to Melrose, Cuthbert became prior on the death of Boisil. How long he remained there is uncertain, but by 670 he had moved or been transferred to the parent monastery at Lindisfarne, where again he became prior. It was during these early years that Cuthbert gained a reputation as a sensitive and perceptive teacher. He also gained religious stature, which enabled him to eradicate laxness at Coldingham, another of Lindisfarne's satellites, and at Lindisfarne itself.

But by the middle of the 670s Cuthbert's religious inclination was moving away from the peripatetic and socially engaged life of a missionary and monastic disciplinarian towards the solitary existence of a hermit. Here perhaps is evidence of the rift between the two notions of church life that was officially resolved in 664 at the famous Synod of Whitby, when KING OSWIU pronounced in favour of the Roman style and against that of the Celtic church. Cuthbert conformed, but his attraction to the eremitic life argues a hankering for the Celtic ways in which he was nurtured, including the belief that a life of solitude and asceticism was second only to martyrdom as the highest form of Christian life. The hermit's life may have been attractive to him in that it allowed him to sidestep the new style of churchmanship. Initially, he tested himself by periods of solitude on an islet (now known as St Cuthbert's Isle), which is cut off from Lindisfarne twice a day by the tide. But in 676 he secured permission to live a fully eremitic life on the Inner Farne (see FARNE ISLANDS), seven miles south of Lindisfarne and two miles offshore from BAMBURGH.

It is an irony of Christian history that many who have gained high reputation for holiness through a life of solitude and self-abnegation are persuaded to play a more active role in the life of the world. And so it was with Cuthbert. In 684, after much importuning by KING ECGFRITH, Cuthbert agreed to become Bishop of Hexham. Not only did this take him from his true vocation, but also from his familiar surroundings. Almost immediately he contrived to arrange an exchange of dioceses, whereby his old mentor, Eata, went to HEXHAM, while he took Eata's place as Bishop of Lindisfarne. As bishop, he was no longer his own master but a leading member of the Northumbrian court, and in this role he advised Ecgfrith against invading Ireland

and attacking the Picts. His advice was not taken. Although Ecgfrith waged a successful campaign in Ireland, his attack on the Picts ended in disaster and his death at Nechtansmere in Angus in the summer of 685.

To Cuthbert, membership of the establishment must now have seemed doubly pointless and in the following year he managed to resign the bishopric and return to his cell on the Inner Farne. There he died on 20 March 687. It is significant that, although he wished to be buried near his cell, he agreed that his body should be taken back to Lindisfarne. He would have been well aware of his reputation as a holy man and that in death he would be the subject of a cult.

And so it proved. As was usual with men cast in the role of saint, his body was interred so that the flesh could decay in preparation for the reburial of his bones, suitably cleaned and clothed, above ground, to be the object of pilgrim veneration. This second stage was reached in 698. But when his stone coffin was opened, it was discovered that his body had not decayed. To the Lindisfarne monks it was a miracle, incontrovertible proof of Cuthbert's holiness. Today, it is more likely that the preservation of his flesh will be seen as an accident of nature or the product of human action. Whatever the truth, the event marks the start of Cuthbert's second life, his life after death, which was to last a thousand years.

The Cuthbertine cult was no accident but the deliberate work of the monks of Lindisfarne, who immediately reburied his body in a more sumptuous fashion. It was placed in a special wooden coffin, on the sides and lid of which were carvings of saints, together with a pectoral cross, made of gold thread, and a portable wooden altar overlaid with silver. The remains of these artefacts, preserved and on display in the Durham Cathedral Treasury, are strangely incongruous: their use of gold, silver and jewels speak of high status and wealth, but they contrast starkly with the life of extreme self-denial valued and lived by the man with whom they were buried. The new coffin was then sited above ground to the right of the high altar of the monastic church, where it could be accessible to pilgrims.

The powerful attraction of the saint, inadvertently helped by the Vikings, turned the monastery of Lindisfarne into something quite different. In 793 sea raiders sacked the monastery and from that time Lindisfarne was no longer entirely safe. Consequently, around 840 they moved inland to NORHAM, but then returned to Lindisfarne, only to leave for good in 875, taking with them Cuthbert's coffin and other treasures. From this time they ceased to be monks in the normal sense of that word. Instead, they were now the **Congregation of St Cuthbert**, whose purpose was the service and defence of their revered saint.

For the next seven years the Congregation had no fixed abode, but spent short periods in a number of places, until in 883 they settled in the ruins of the Roman fort at CHESTER LE STREET. Later accounts portray their journey in almost biblical terms, as though they were latter-day Israelites wandering in the desert. Today, historians are more inclined to see this phase not as a flight from danger in search of a safe haven, but as a deliberate decision by a powerful corporation to relocate towards the new centres of political power, the Scandinavian kingdom of York and the expanding English kingdom of Wessex. The Congregation of St Cuthbert had become a powerful institution: in its miracle-working saint it had a feared psychological force, and its very extensive estates were considerable economic and military assets. The monastery of Lindisfarne had achieved salvation by and through a metamorphosis into something significantly different. Its accomplishment is underlined by the fate suffered by other Northumbrian monasteries (Coldingham, NORHAM, HEXHAM, Monkwearmouth/JARROW, HARTLEPOOL, Whitby, Ripon), all of which were destroyed. Lindisfarne alone survived, although far from home and significantly changed, thanks largely to the status of its saint and the ability of his guardians to utilise the power he conferred.

The sojourn at Chester le Street lasted 112 years, during which time the Congregation's estate was enlarged by gift and purchase to comprise almost all the land between Tyne and Tees. In 995, however, Bishop Aldhune (987–1016) decided to move the Community from Chester le Street to a much more readily defended site at Durham, seven miles to the south. It was not a unilateral decision, but taken in conjunction with (and perhaps at the insistence of) his son-in-law, Uhtred, Earl of Northumbria. This underlined the fact that at this date political power north of the Tees and east of the Pennines was in the hands of these two offices, a duality given further emphasis by Earl Uhtred's injunction to all men between the Tees and the Coquet to assist Alhune and the Community in the work of the building of the new cathedral. This, the first Durham Cathedral, was consecrated in 998, and on 4 September St Cuthbert was 'translated' into his new resting place.

This was the situation when the Norman kings, William I and his son, William II, gradually imposed their control over the region in the years between 1070 and 1095. By that time, the structure of the Congregation of St Cuthbert is a little clearer. At its head was the bishop, who was already a monk or who became one. There were also other monks, although how many is uncertain. But there were also secular clergy, headed by a dean, who were married and whose positions were hereditary. Most prominent of these were the seven men who claimed descent from the Porters of St Cuthbert, the men who had carried St Cuthbert's coffin on its departure from Lindisfarne in 875, four of whose names are known: Edmund, Franco, Hunred and Stitheard. The Congregation was therefore a unique hybrid that had developed in response to circumstances. Certainly, it was beyond the experience and comprehension of the bishops that William I imposed on Durham in 1072 and 1080.

By coincidence, the Norman takeover took place at a time of religious revival and ecclesiastical reform. Hence, the bishops imposed by William I saw the Durham arrangement as incongruous, outmoded and in need of a thorough overhaul to bring it into line with current practice. The first of these bishops, Walcher, was intent on a restructuring exercise, but he was murdered at GATESHEAD in 1080 before his plan was far advanced. It was his successor, WILLIAM OF ST CALAIS, who effected the transformation. In 1083 he replaced the Congregation with a Benedictine monastery, a not surprising move in that he had been brought from Le Mans, where he had been the abbot of the monastery of St Vincent. He is reported to have offered the members of the Congregation the opportunity of becoming fully fledged monks, but all but one declined, although recently it has been suggested that more than one may have made the transition. To fill the vacancies, he brought the monks from the newly refounded monasteries at Jarrow and Monkwearmouth.

St Calais's 'revolution' meant that the guardianship of St Cuthbert was again vested in a fully monastic body. And it is clear that the new Benedictine monastery assumed with deep commitment the role their predecessors had discharged. What did not survive was the unity that characterised the pre-Conquest Congregation.

Although St Calais was a monk, most of his successors were not, and as a result bishop and cathedral priory became separate institutions and the great estate, the **Patrimony of St Cuthbert**, was divided between them, the lion's share assigned to the bishop.

As well as transforming the Congregation, St Calais also began building the second Durham Cathedral, to be a more splendid home for the saint, whose remains were 'translated' into what has proved to be their final resting place on 29 August 1104. Five days earlier, Prior TURGOT and a group of nine senior monks opened the coffin to check that the body was still undecayed. It was, but among the invited guests to the 'translation' was a certain abbot (thought to be of St Mary's, York or Selby) who complained that the opening had taken place at night and in private, implying fraud or deceit on the part of the Durham monks. Naturally, they were incensed and refused the request for another opening, fearing, they said, St Cuthbert's wrath. The situation became heated, and it required the emollient tact of Ralph, Abbot of Séez in Normandy (who later became Archbishop of Canterbury), to smooth ruffled feathers and persuade Turgot to permit a second and more public daytime opening for a small select group of independent scrutineers. The new shrine did not mean that St Cuthbert's former resting places were abandoned. In both the cloister behind St Calais's cathedral and the church of the cell at Lindisfarne the Durham monks founded in the early twelfth century, cenotaphs were maintained on the spot where the coffin had lain. Even though removed, the power of the saint was thought still to reside where he had rested.

The coffin remained unopened until 1537, when Henry VIII's commissioners despoiled the shrine, removing the great quantity of valuables deposited there. In the process, they reportedly discovered that the saint's body was still incorrupt. However, it was rescued from desecration by the monks and was kept in the vestry until 1542, when it was re-interred by the new dean and chapter in a tomb below the place where the coffin had rested. There is, however, an alternative account that claims that the body interred was not that of St Cuthbert but an unknown substitute. Instead, Cuthbert was secretly buried at some time between 1542 and 1558 elsewhere in the cathedral. The whereabouts of this grave is known at any time only to a small number of Benedictine monks. This version will be credible only if this body is produced.

The alternative version was argued at length and in detail in the nineteenth century by a number of Roman Catholic writers. What urged them to do so was the opening of the tomb in 1827 by the eminent historian, CANON JAMES RAINE, which revealed not a body but a skeleton. It was on this occasion that the remains of the coffin, St Cuthbert's portable altar, pectoral cross and comb, now on display in the Treasury, were removed. Not found, however, were a gold chalice and a pair of scissors that were reported in 1104. A second and more scientific investigation of the tomb was conducted in 1899. This included a medical analysis of the skeleton, which showed St Cuthbert to have been a muscular man about five feet eight inches in height and with a dolichocephalic skull. It also made clear that the saint had a poor medical record, having contracted but survived bubonic plague and suffered considerably from osteoarthritis.

Since then, St Cuthbert has rested in peace, disturbed only by the thousands of tourists that gaze down on the large slab of marble on which is engraved (pointlessly in Latin) *CUTHBERTUS*.

'DAINTY DINAH'

'Dainty Dinah' had a life of fifty years, from 1911 until 1961, during which the toffees that bore her name became known throughout Britain and were exported to 150 countries, the USA and Canada being particularly lucrative markets. They were made by a firm founded in 1911 by a Norfolk man, George Horner, who started his business on a 5-acre (2 ha) site in CHESTER LE STREET. Horners expanded rapidly after World War I and additional factories were opened in Edinburgh and at East Ham in London. Over the course of its existence, they made a variety of confectionary products, but the one for which they are remembered is 'Dainty Dinah' toffees, launched in 1914. The famous picture that decorated their tins, of an Edwardian girl wearing a bonnet, was introduced around 1915 and patented as a trademark in 1917. Its designer was a London artist, William Barribal, but whether he used a model and, if so, who she was, is uncertain, although unsubstantiated claims have been made on behalf of several ladies in the Chester le Street area. Inevitably, the firm suffered as a result of severe restrictions imposed during World War II. This, the death of George Horner in 1947, poor management decisions by his successor and the growing competition from larger firms led to the business closing in 1961. The works were demolished in 1989, but the statue of 'Dainty Dinah', which had been fixed to the factory chimney, was rescued and is now in the Chester le Street Civic Centre.

DALE, SIR DAVID (1829–1906)

David Dale was born in 1829 in Bengal, India, where his father was a judge with the East India Company. A year later, as the family was returning home, his father died at sea. His mother intended to settle near her family in Scotland, but at DARLINGTON the breakdown of the coach in which she was travelling resulted in her being given shelter by the local Society of Friends and this in turn led to her decision to make her new home in the town. After private education in Stockton, Durham and Edinburgh, in 1847 Dale became a clerk in the offices of the Stockton and Darlington Railway and in 1852 secretary to its subsidiary, the Middlesbrough and Guisborough Railway.

Thereafter he rose to become one of the North East's leading industrialists, occupying important offices in a broad range of industries: director of the Stockton and Darlington Railway and then of the North Eastern Railway; managing partner in J.W. Pease & Co. and later of Pease and Partners (see PEASE FAMILY); and an active interest in shipbuilding firms in STOCKTON (Richardson, Denton and Duck) and in HARTLEPOOL (Denton and Gray and Thomas Richardson and Sons). But his greatest involvement was with the Consett Iron Co. (see CONSETT), of which he was a founder. By 1869 he had become managing director and in 1884 he was made chairman, a post he held until his death. This involvement with iron and steel led to his helping to found the Iron and Steel Institute in 1869 (acting as its Treasurer until 1895, when he was elected President); in 1881 becoming chairman of a company mining iron ore at Bilbao in Spain; and in 1902 becoming chairman of the Sunderland Iron Ore Co. And since the Consett Iron Co. was a major coal owner, he also was active in the affairs of the Durham Coal Owners' Association, founded in 1873.

As well as running businesses, Dale was also passionately keen on devising means of maintaining good industrial relations. To this end, he favoured the creation of well-organised trade unions and a policy of co-operation with them. He also advocated the settlement of industrial problems and disputes by conciliation and arbitration, and he visited Nottingham to study the conciliation procedures in the hosiery industry introduced by A.J. Mudella. In 1869 he set up the Board of Arbitration for the North East Iron trades and was active in founding the National Iron Trades Conciliation Board. Behind this was the firmly held conviction that co-operation within industry should be based upon the mutual recognition that wages and salaries as well as profits had to reflect the state of trade. His reputation as a leading industrialist led to his appointment to three Royal Commissions, on Trade Depression (1885), Mining Royalties (1889) and Labour (1891), and as a British representative to the Berlin Labour Conference in 1890. Unlike many other leading industrialists, he never found time for a parliamentary career. He was created a baronet in 1895 and three years after his death, Armstrong College, Newcastle (the forerunner of Newcastle University) established the Sir David Dale Chair of Economics.

DALTON, EDWARD HUGH NEALE (1887–1962)

Hugh Dalton, who was born near Neath in South Wales, was an unlikely socialist. His father, John Dalton, was a canon of St George's Chapel, Windsor and tutor and companion of two of the sons (one of whom became George V) of the then Prince of Wales. His childhood was therefore spent in Windsor Castle, after which he went to Eton and then King's College, Cambridge, where he acquired socialist convictions and, in 1910, a degree in Economics. He then went to the Middle Temple to read for the Bar, for which he qualified in 1914. Following World War I, in which he served in the army and saw active service in Italy, he pursued an academic career as Reader in Economics at the London School of Economics. In this role he produced a number of well-regarded books, notably *Principles of Public Finance* and *Inequality of Incomes.*

His connection with the North East began in 1929, when he was elected Labour MP for Bishop Auckland. Apart from the years 1931 to 1935, he held the seat until 1959. During World War II he was in the Ministry of Economic Warfare until 1942, and then the Board of Trade. It was in the latter role that he secured the passage of the Distribution of Industry Act, giving government powers to dictate the location of industrial development. His perceived need of this arose directly from his awareness of the plight of his North-East constituency, which in the inter-war years became one of the most economically blighted in the country. When Labour came to power in 1945, Dalton became Chancellor of the Exchequer, although his heart's desire was the Foreign Office. As Chancellor, he was required to take unpalatable decisions dictated by the parlous state of Britain's post-war finances. In 1947, however, he left office in some disgrace as the result of an unfortunate slip he made in the Palace of Westminster. As he was walking across the lobby to give his Budget speech in the Commons, he was approached by a journalist from the London *Evening Star,* to whom in answer to a question he outlined the tax changes he was about to announce. Immediately, the journalist phoned these through to his editor and within minutes they appeared on the streets in the 'stop press' section of the paper. Dalton had committed the unpardonable 'sin' of telling the press before parliament. In fact, the timing was such that no harm was done, but Dalton felt he must offer his resignation, which was accepted. Such has been the fall in standards in political life since then, in which 'leaking' has become an accepted tactic, that it is hard to imagine the same fate befalling a modern minister.

Dalton continued as an MP for a further twelve years and again held office, but his reputation never recovered.

DALZIEL BROTHERS

The Dalziel brothers, or as they called themselves in their account of their careers, the Brothers Dalziel, became the dominant figures in the mid-Victorian wood-engraving trade. They were born in Wooler, the sons of a Wooler man, Alexander Dalziel (1781–1832), who in middle age forsook a horticultural career to become an artist. His artistic talent and inclination were inherited by all but one of his eight sons.

The brothers of the title were George (1815–1902) and Edward (1817–1905). Their rise to fame and fortune began in 1835, when George went to London and trained as a wood engraver. In 1840 he set up his own business, in which he was joined by Edward. Their business had two parallel strands: they worked on commission for established publishers, such as George Routledge and Frederick Warne; but in 1857 they set up their own publishing house, Camden Press, which gave them scope to commission works, which they then illustrated. Their most ambitious project, which was not completed, was an illustrated Bible.

The quantity and range of their work was enormous. Their credits include *Punch,* founded in 1842, *The Illustrated London News,* the poetry of Tennyson, several novels by Trollope, the paintings of Rossetti, Holman Hunt, Millais, Burne Jones, Lord Leighton and Madox Brown, and the 'Alice' novels of Lewis Carroll. They also exhibited at the Royal Academy, a testimony to their standing as artists. Their success, however, was of short duration. From the 1880s the development of photography spelled the end of wood engraving as the main form of printed illustration. This aspect of their business ended in 1893 and the Camden Press ceased trading in 1905.

The one son of Alexander Dalziel who did not become an artist was Davison Octavian Dalziel, who became a successful businessman. His son, Davison Alexander Dalziel (1852–1928), built upon his success, most notably linking the two major firms engaged in sleeping-car transport on the railways, the British Pullman Palace Car Co. and the Compagnie Internationale des Wagons-Lits, and as chairman of the General Motor Cab Co. introducing the famous black taxi cab to London streets. His only connections with the North East were his involvement with Broomhill Collieries Ltd and their development of Warkworth Harbour (see AMBLE), and the choice of his father's birthplace for his title when he was ennobled as Baron Dalziel of Wooler in 1927.

DARLING, GRACE HORSLEY (1815–1842)

The story of Grace Darling is really twofold: first, the part she played in the event off the FARNE ISLANDS on 7 September 1838, and then the public reaction that followed, some of which was unedifying.

Grace was the daughter of William Darling, then fifty-two years of age, the keeper of the newly built Longstone Light (see LIGHTHOUSES). On 7 September 1838, then twenty-two years of age, she was alone in the lighthouse with her father and mother, all of her brothers being ashore following their respective trades. That night a south-easterly gale was blowing, which caused the cargo ship, *Forfarshire,* on passage from Hull to its home port, Dundee, to get into difficulties. The ship, which was carrying either sixty-one or sixty-three passengers and crew, was an early type of steamship with sails as well as two steam engines. The latter broke down off St Abb's Head, forcing the master to resort to sail and to retreat south to find shelter in harbour at Holy ISLAND. It was his misjudgement that led to the ship's hitting the rock known as Big Harcar and breaking her back.

Grace spotted the wreck at 4.45 a.m., but it was not until about 7 a.m. that it became clear that there were survivors clinging to the rock. William Darling decided that he and Grace would attempt a rescue, because he calculated that the sea state and the three-mile distance would prevent the Seahouses lifeboat at North Sunderland from making an attempt. In this he was wrong: the lifeboat did put out, and its crew, which included Grace's younger brother, William, did reach the rock to find the rescue had been completed by his father and sister. Unable to return to Seahouses, the lifeboat sought shelter at the Longstone light.

William Darling's decision was not one of foolhardy bravery, but a carefully calculated risk. And it was his decision: the story that Grace persuaded her father against his better judgement is not true. Darling calculated that with wind and tide in their favour, and by keeping in the lee of Cove Car rock, he and Grace could row the 21-foot (6.5 m) coble the 400 yards (370 m) to Big Harcar, where they would find men able to help with the more arduous return journey. This proved to be the case. Nine people were alive, including two members of the *Forfarshire*'s crew, who were able to help get the coble back to the Longstone and then make a return journey with William Darling to take off the remaining survivors. The episode was bravery and seamanship of the highest order, based upon accurate perception of risk, in which the young Grace Darling had played a vital part.

Thanks to the region's newspapers, there followed the sort of media-induced publicity frenzy with which we are familiar today. Many artists came to the Farnes to paint their version of the scene and the portraits of William and Grace, including two by the best in the region, JOHN WILSON CARMICHAEL and HENRY PERLEE PARKER, while William Wordsworth, the poet laureate, wrote one of his more forgettable poems. China models and mugs were produced as souvenirs and there were offers of stage appearances in London and Edinburgh and also perhaps of marriage. More appropriately, father and daughter were awarded gold medals by the Royal Humane Society and silver medals by the forerunner of the RNLI. And, more practically, a subscription fund was opened, to which the new monarch, Victoria, contributed £50, which eventually amounted to just over £1,000, which was put into trust. Fame and wealth did not change Grace Darling's life, which was tragically short. She accepted none of the offers or the money, but remained with her parents on the Longstone, until tuberculosis led to a move to the mainland. She died, aged twenty-six, on 20 October 1842 at her sister's house in BAMBURGH. She was buried in Bamburgh churchyard and a memorial to her was erected close by. Her bravery is undoubted, but what followed made her the quintessential 'heroine'.

DARLINGTON

Darlington came into existence well before the Norman Conquest. Its name incorporates an Old English personal name, *Deornoth*, while the second element, *ing*, indicates that he was a person with a substantial following. Almost certainly, it was the central place of a pre-Conquest estate or 'shire', the extent of which is not known, although it would have included Blackwell and Cockerton, members of the medieval parish of Darlington. It is possible, however, that these settlements were only the core of a much larger 'shire'. Like similar 'shires', it had a church, which was important enough to be one of the four to which BISHOP WILLIAM OF ST CALAIS dispersed those members of the Community of St Cuthbert who declined his invitation to become monks in 1083 (see CUTHBERT, SAINT). The estate had come into the possession of the Community of St Cuthbert in the first quarter of the eleventh century, gifted to it by a major Northumbrian landowner, Styr Ulfson. Darlington also gained importance from its nodal position in the communications network: it was there that the roads from Northallerton and Ripon to Durham and beyond, having crossed the Tees at Croft three miles to the south, bisected the main routes up and down Teesdale.

The layout of central Darlington was the work of HUGH OF LE PUISET, Bishop of Durham from 1154 until 1195, although the stages by which he accomplished it are not clear. His first act, said to have been in 1164, was to build a manor house on the site now occupied by the present Town Hall. Its purpose was not solely to provide accommodation for the bishop and his large household; it was also intended to be one of the main administrative centres of the episcopal estate. Next to this manor house, at some date before 1180, he created a borough, which took the form of a square marketplace surrounded on three sides by rows of burgage tenements. On the fourth side, bordering the River Skerne and between the manor house and the marketplace, was the church with its extensive churchyard. Towards the end of his pontificate, Puiset began the reconstruction of the church, which by 1250 had resulted in the splendid building that still exists. Puiset also modified the unsatisfactory arrangement created in 1083 by instituting a college comprising a vicar, with responsibility for pastoral care, and four prebends (Darlington, Blackwell, Cockerton and Archdeacon Newton), whose holders were not required to be resident.

But long before the borough was founded, an agricultural community existed. From Puiset's time this was located in Bondgate and it is likely that it had always been there, although its funnel-shaped structure, so typical of North-East farming villages, was probably a product of Puiset's reorganisation. Where the road is now would have been an open green, with steadings laid out on either side of it. Despite later additions and modifications, Puiset's layout is still intact.

The medieval records show that Darlington was large as well as complex. In the early 1180s, BOLDON BOOK records the Bondgate community comprising seventy tenant farmers of various categories, principally the forty-eight *villani*, later known as *bondmen*, hence the name of the street. The 1381 survey of the episcopal estate carried out by Bishop Thomas de Hatfield reveals a much larger and more diverse population, despite the losses caused by the Black Death in 1349 and subsequent outbreaks of plague. The progress of the borough was equally substantial: in 1181 it was leased for £5; by the early fourteenth century this had increased tenfold to £50; and in 1381 it stood at over £90, making it more valuable than Durham. The economic development implied by these figures was in part based upon a weekly market and five annual fairs, the latter attracting grain and cattle from a wide area. There is also evidence of cloth working, including fulling and dyeing, and also of Darlington merchants prominent in the international wool trade. Economic activity explains the improved access to the borough in the form of the bridge across the Skerne, built in the thirteenth century.

The Reformation in the sixteenth century occasioned some changes. One was to the staffing of the church. In 1439 Bishop Robert Neville had elevated the vicar to the status of dean and secured him a larger income by splitting the Darlington prebend into two parts, attaching one to the Deanery. In 1547 this improved scheme was swept away and

Darlington parish was again served by a vicar. In contrast, the town gained a grammar school in 1563, its charter granted by Elizabeth I, although it is probable that this school was a refoundation of that founded in 1530 in conjunction with a chantry by Robert Marshall. Unfortunately, in 1585, a serious fire in the borough destroyed 273 properties, including almost all of Darlington's medieval buildings. The size of the population at this date can only be guessed, but it is unlikely to have exceeded 2,000. Thereafter, it grew slowly, reaching 4,670 by the time of the first decennial census in 1801. For most of that time Darlington had remained essentially a market town.

From the last years of the eighteenth century, however, it developed into an important industrial town, beginning with the woollen cloth industry, begun by the PEASE FAMILY. The great boost came with the opening of the Stockton and Darlington Railway in 1825, its rapid expansion in the following years, and the creation of the East Coast Main Line through the town in the 1840s (see RAILWAYS). This led to the North East Railway works in 1863, which was followed in 1901 by the transfer of the Robert Stephenson and Hawthorn works from Newcastle (see STEPHENSON, GEORGE AND ROBERT). By the beginning of the twentieth century, Darlington was a 'railway town'. But not exclusively, since other heavy engineering firms such as Darlington Forge (1853), Rise Carr Rolling Mills (1868), Cleveland Bridge and Engineering (1878) and Whessoe Ltd (the origins of which can be traced back to the ironmonger's shop founded by William Kitching in Tubwell Row in 1790) were also founded in the town. These, together with an enlarged woollen industry and the continuing role as a market centre, resulted in a population of 50,000 by 1901, a tenfold increase in 100 years. Its growing size and economic importance led in 1867 to constitutional change: Darlington became both a municipal borough and a parliamentary borough, the latter comprising Darlington, Cockerton and Haughton le Skerne.

If Darlington was a 'railway town', it was also a 'Quaker town', thanks to the wealth and importance of a number of families who belonged to the Quakers (the Religious Society of Friends). The most notable were the Pease family and the BACKHOUSES, but also important were the Cudworths, the Hodgkins, the I'Ansons and the Kitchings. The most demonstrable evidence of their distinctive affiliation is the Friends' Meeting House in Skinnergate. The part of the building fronting the street was erected in 1839 on a site associated with the Society since 1678, the rear part of which is a Quaker Burial Ground. The many other buildings that also testify to the wealth and dominance of the Pease family include Darlington Library, Elm Ridge Methodist Church (originally a house), Grange Hotel, Hummersknot (now a school), Mowden Hall (now offices), North Lodge, Polam Hall (now a school), and 146 Northgate.

However, in the course of the twentieth century, both 'Railway Town' and 'Quaker Town' became invalid designations. The dominance of the Peases did not survive the enfranchisement of a larger percentage of the population for both local and national government: after World War I, the Quaker families ceased to rule Darlington. The railway lasted longer, but it too succumbed in the 1960s to the contraction of the railway network and to the replacement of steam locomotives by diesel and then electric traction. Darlington, however, remains a major junction on the East Coast Main Line, and its important place in the British communications network has been reinforced by the building of the A1(M), which skirts its western suburbs, and the M66/A66 linking it with the conurbation at the mouth of the Tees; and also with the Durham Tees Valley Airport, developed on the site of the World War II aerodrome at MIDDLETON ST GEORGE. The woollen industry and heavy engineering also faded away, so that by the last quarter of the twentieth century Darlington had ceased to be a place of heavy industry. Some lighter industries came in, although not all have survived. Like other industrial towns in the region, it is in the process of restyling its economy.

Running parallel with its changing economy was the town's constitutional development. In 1872 and 1915 it took in more land on its northern edge and in the latter year it became a county borough, which in 1930 absorbed a swathe of land beyond its eastern boundary, including Haughton le Skerne and Blackwell Grange. Blackwell was acquired in 1967, and finally, in 1974, as part of the fundamental restructuring of British local government, the borough was massively enlarged by the addition of Darlington Rural District. Darlington now had a wide rural hinterland, covering nearly 50,000 acres (20,000 ha) and containing twenty-five civil parishes. Its population, which before 1974 had risen to 86,000, was increased to nearly 120,000. By the most recent change, in 1997, Darlington became a 'unitary authority'.

DAVIES, SARAH EMILY (1830–1921)

Emily Davies, who was one of the leading pioneers of women's education, was the daughter of an Anglican clergyman, Dr John Davies, who was vicar of GATESHEAD from 1839 until his death in 1861. Her father's traditional view on the subsidiary and subordinate role of the wives and daughters of the clergy meant that she received almost no formal education. Her trivialised upbringing in Gateshead engendered in her a deep sense of frustration, which turned her into a forceful and persuasive campaigner.

In 1860 she founded the Durham and Northumberland branch of the Society for Promoting the Employment of Women, which argued that women should be educated and be allowed to work. But her real campaigning began in 1862, when her father's death freed her from parental restraint and allowed her to move to London. She was successful in securing the right of girls to take the same public examinations as boys, which would qualify them for university entrance, and at university for women students be allowed to take the same courses and examinations as their male counterparts. Her memorial is Girton College, Cambridge, for the foundation of which in 1869 she was largely responsible.

DAVISON, ALEXANDER (1750–1829)

Alexander Davison was the son of the tenant, and subsequently the owner, of the Lanton estate in north-east Northumberland, who became a highly successful but fraudulent businessman and a friend of Vice Admiral Lord Nelson. At the age of seventeen he went to London to learn the arts of business with a leading merchant company and from there went to Canada in 1772, where he, his brother George, and a Scotsman, John Lees, took advantage of the opportunities afforded by Britain's recent conquest of the French province of Quebec. Their success was substantially derived from supplying the army, the needs of which grew rapidly with the outbreak of the American War of Independence (1776–83). It was during these years that he met Horatio Nelson, then commander of the frigate HMS *Albemarle* serving in American waters, and the two men became lifelong friends. He returned to Britain in 1786, leaving the management of his Canadian interests to his brother. Back home, his business career followed the same pattern: private ventures alongside lucrative government contracts. With the outbreak of war against France in 1793, the latter grew considerably in number, size and value. Then, in 1795, Colonel Oliver De Lancy, the Barrack-Master General, appointed him sole agent to build, furnish and supply the large number of barracks that had to be built for the expanding army. His business successes made him wealthy enough to buy the Swarland estate in Northumberland and a house in St James's Square, London's most exclusive address, and to indulge his passion for fine art and furniture.

Further financial advantage accrued in October 1798, when Nelson appointed him, with the consent of his fleet and at an agreed percentage, their sole prize agent. Since this followed Nelson's overwhelming victory over the French fleet at Aboukir Bay near the mouth of the Nile, Davison was guaranteed a fortune. He celebrated by commissioning (at a cost of £2,000) from the firm of Boulton and Watt commemorative medals struck for every man in Nelson's fleet. These bore Nelson's profile on a shield held by Britannia on the obverse and a picture of the battle on the reverse with his own name on the rim. He also redesigned the park at Swarland in the shape of Aboukir Bay with clumps of trees to represent Nelson's ships.

But disaster struck in the first decade of the nineteenth century. In 1804 he was imprisoned for a year following a conviction for bribery and corruption in an attempt to gain control of two parliamentary seats for the Somerset borough of Ilchester. The following year Nelson was killed at Trafalgar, and in 1806 Davison's own son, whom he had christened Alexander Horatio Nelson and whom he hoped would have a naval career, died. Then in 1807, following a commission of inquiry into his handling of public money, he was found guilty of fraud. His punishment was twenty-one months in prison and a requirement to repay nearly £9,000: not until 1826 was a final settlement agreed between him and the Treasury.

Although his change of fortune made necessary the sale of the house in St James's Square, Davison held on to Swarland. Its subsequent history, however, would have saddened him. The estate was sold in 1873 and its subsequent owners showed no concern for the Nelson connection. In the 1930s part of the park was sold to create the Swarland Settlement, seventy-four houses, some with land, built for unemployed Tynesiders. Of the original fourteen clumps of trees, only four now remain. Then in 1947 the hall, which had been subject to considerable abuse in the early twentieth century, was finally demolished. All that remains of Davison's splendid commemorative work is an obelisk. It bears Nelson's famous signal before Trafalgar, 'England Expects Every Man To Do His Duty', but also states that its purpose was to commemorate a private friendship, not the famous victory. Even this, which he placed prominently by the side of the old Great North Road, has languished unseen since the line of the A1 was shifted several yards to the east. Instead, and ironically, his most visible memorial is an obelisk erected by his brother on top of Lanton Hill overlooking his birthplace.

DAVISON, EMILY WILDING (1872–1913)

Emily Davison was a militant suffragette, the daughter of a Morpeth man, Charles Davison. She caused a national sensation on 4 June 1913 when she threw herself under the hooves of the King's horse, Anmer, ridden by Herbert Jones (1881–1951), the King's jockey, as the field rounded Tattenham Corner in that year's Derby. The horse was uninjured, but Jones had a nasty fall, which seems to have undermined his confidence, so that he retired in 1923. Emily Davison, however, suffered a fractured skull and she died five days later in Epsom Cottage Hospital, without regaining consciousness.

At that date she was forty-one years old and was described as having red hair and green eyes and being tall and slim but also rather gawky. She was also well educated, having been awarded a BA degree by London University and achieving high marks in the English Language and Literature course at Oxford University.

On Saturday 14 June her body was taken from Epsom to Victoria Station in London and thence to St George's Church in Bloomsbury for a funeral service. Throughout the journey through London, crowds lined the streets and fellow members of the Women's Social and Political Union (WSPU) dressed in white accompanied the hearse. After the service, her coffin was taken to King's Cross Station, where it was put on a train for Morpeth. There the London scenes were repeated. The town was so crowded that it took three-quarters of an hour for the hearse to make the short journey from the station to St Mary's Church, where she was interred next to her father: not only did local people line the route, but a special train brought people from Newcastle. Again, members of the WSPU dressed in white escorted the hearse, holding white ropes attached to each of the black horses.

How should Emily Davison be regarded? Her sacrifice was undoubtedly heroic, but, in spite of the publicity it engendered, it was not fully appreciated by the leaders of the WSPU, who saw Emily Davison as an erratic and reckless member, unwilling to conform to their tactics. And their concerns would no doubt have been heightened by the more sober editorials in the national press, which pointed out that the state could not give in to this sort of terrorism. It is not too fanciful to see Emily Davison as akin to the fanatical suicide bombers of our time.

In fact, there is little doubt that Emily Davison was emotionally very unstable and that she had been intent on suicide for some time. This is not only clear from her actions in the previous years, but is supported by things she wrote, discovered after her death, showing that she was convinced that the movement's success required a martyr. In 1909 she attempted suicide in Strangeways Gaol, Manchester, by barricading herself in her cell to prevent the warders from force-feeding her. Late in 1911, of her own volition, she started to set fire to post boxes, for which she was given a six-month sentence. While in prison, she threw herself from the corridor running in front of the cells, and was only saved by the net strung across the well of the prison 40 feet (12 m) below. Subsequently, she tried again by throwing herself down the stairs. Then, at the beginning of 1913, she (together with others) severely damaged by means of a bomb the house being built for the Chancellor of the Exchequer, David Lloyd George, at Walton Heath in Surrey.

It is easy to conclude that she went to Epsom on 4 June with the intention of doing what she did. But there are doubts. The policeman who attended her on the course found two purple, white and green flags (the suffragette colours), one of which she waved as she dashed on to the course; the other was found under her coat. She also had a return ticket to London, suggesting that her intention was to ruin the race by waving flags so as to distract the horses. Her suicide, therefore, may have come from a sudden impulse, or it may even have been an accident. This might be more convincing had she been alone. But she was with another woman with whom she shared lodgings, who was not party to the incident. The return ticket may therefore have been intended to deceive her companion.

As with other suicides that do not leave a note, her intention will remain in doubt. What is certain is that her sacrifice did not secure 'votes for women'.

DELAVAL FAMILY (see SEATON DELAVAL)

DENT, JOSEPH MALLABY (1849–1926)

Joseph Dent rose from humble beginnings to become one of the most successful businessmen of the early twentieth century. His father, George Dent, was a house painter in Darlington whose business failed, forcing him to earn a living as a music teacher and salesman of musical instruments. Because of this, Dent's formal education did not progress beyond the elementary school. Nevertheless, he was a voracious reader and, because of lameness resulting from an accident, he had ample time to indulge his interest. After leaving school in 1862 at the age of thirteen, he was apprenticed to a Darlington printer, but after a short while transferred to a bookbinder. When his master's business failed, Dent moved to London, where he successfully completed a London apprenticeship in 1872.

In the following fifteen years he developed a reasonably successful bookbinding business. In the late 1880s, however, he turned his hand to publishing and it was in this trade that he made his fortune. He began with a series on medieval towns and followed it with another on eighteenth-century novelists. With this he found a niche in the American market and to it he added in the 1890s the 'Temple Pocket Shakespeare' and the 'Temple Classics'. These successes proved to be the prelude to the series that gave him huge and international success: the Everyman Library. This was launched in 1904, with the ambitious aim of publishing the world's classics in pocket editions retailing at 1 shilling a volume. It was not Dent but his literary editor, Ernest Rhys, who suggested the title for the series and the idea that each volume should carry the quotation, 'Everyman, I will go with thee, and be thy guide.' The formula was a winning one: Dent offered a population now literate thanks to compulsory elementary education the chance to buy handy-sized books at a price that was within the reach of most incomes. Thanks to him, the possession of a library was no longer to be the preserve of the well-to-do.

Success was rapid. Despite the practical problems involved, 158 titles were published in the first year and by 1907 it had become necessary to move the business out of London to a purpose built-factory in the 'garden city' of Letchworth. The interruption of World War I, in which two of Dent's three sons were killed, meant that Dent did not realise his ambition of publishing 1,000 titles in the Everyman series. Nevertheless, the Everyman Library attained huge popularity throughout the world where English was spoken and brought high literature within the reach of millions of people.

DERE STREET (see ROMAN ROADS)

DIXON, JEREMIAH (1733–1779)

Jeremiah Dixon was, with Charles Mason, the unintentional deviser of one of the world's most famous boundaries, the Mason-Dixon Line. He was born at Bishop Auckland, the son of a Quaker coal owner in Cockfield. After attending school at Barnard Castle, with the help of Thomas Wright he trained as a surveyor. It was through this and other influential contacts that in 1760 he was recommended as an assistant to Charles Mason, who had been commissioned by the Royal Society to go to Sumatra (now part of Indonesia) to study the Transit of Venus. Because of war, they never reached Sumatra, but managed to accomplish their task at the Cape of Good Hope in what is now South Africa.

It was their success that brought an invitation to go to America to settle a boundary dispute between Thomas Penn, the owner of Pennsylvania, and Frederick Calvert, 7th Lord Baltimore, the proprietor of Maryland. The crux of the matter was that the southern boundary of Pennsylvania, as recorded in Charles II's foundation charter of 1681, conflicted with the northern boundary of Maryland in its foundation charter issued in 1632 by Charles I. The two men took four years, between 1763 and 1767, to arrive at a solution, which was that the dividing line should be latitude 39° 43′ North. This decision was ratified by the Crown in 1769.

The Mason-Dixon Line also defined the southern boundary of Delaware and Virginia. Less tangibly, it was not long before it was seen as the symbolic divide between two economic and social cultures: the southern plantation economy with its dependence on slave labour; and the northern economy with its commitment to commerce, industry and 'free soil'. However, when these two cultures clashed in the Civil War of 1861–65, the Mason-Dixon Line did not become the boundary between the Union and the seceding Confederacy. Maryland, along with Delaware, Kentucky and Missouri, chose to remain in the Union.

After collaborating with Mason in observing the Transit of Venus, this time in Norway, Dixon settled in Durham, where he worked as a surveyor until his death.

DIXON, JOHN (1835–1891)

John Dixon was born and educated in Newcastle, where he qualified as an engineer through an apprenticeship with the firm of ROBERT STEPHENSON. After qualifying, he worked briefly for the Derwent Iron Co. at CONSETT and then for the Bedlington Iron Co. (see BEDLINGTON). When the latter folded in 1867, he went to London and began a very successful engineering career. Among his many achievements were designing a bridge over the River Nile and building the first railway in China. His most renowned success, however, was in devising the means of bringing the Egyptian obelisk known as 'Cleopatra's Needle' from Alexandria to London for erection on the Embankment. The obelisk, which was bought for £15,000 raised by public subscription as a belated commemoration of the defeat of Napoleon, was made around 1460 BC, nearly a millennium and a half before Cleopatra lived. It got its title because it was brought from Alexandria, Cleopatra's capital, in a barge designed and built by Dixon named *The Cleopatra*. The barge was 93 feet (38 m) long and had a beam of 53 feet (16 m) and was towed by a steamship. The journey, lasting several months in 1877, was nearly a disaster because of bad weather in the Bay of Biscay. *The Cleopatra* finally arrived in the Thames in January 1878, to cheering crowds and an artillery salute. The 'Needle' was erected later that year and a bronze plaque noting Dixon's contribution was fixed to its plinth.

DOBSON, JOHN (1787–1865)

John Dobson is arguably the best architect produced by the North East and he was certainly the first to achieve national status. He was also impressive in his range of architecture, which included industrial as well as domestic and ecclesiastical buildings. The son of a successful market gardener at Chirton, near Tynemouth, he revealed an early aptitude for drawing. Consequently, in 1804 at the age of fifteen, he was apprenticed to DAVID STEPHENSON, then the leading architect in NEWCASTLE, and at the same time took lessons from Boniface Musso, the Italian refugee, who also taught JOHN MARTIN. In 1809, on completion of his articles, he went to London for further instruction in the art of watercolour from John Varley. His skill as a watercolourist was a factor in his ability to 'sell' his designs to patrons. Later, as he became busy, he employed John Wilson Carmichael to do this work.

Returning to Newcastle in 1810, he built up a highly successful practice: in the course of his career, he produced 450 designs, although not all of these were executed. Most of his commissions were for North-East clients, but his services were used as far afield as Glasgow, Edinburgh, Liverpool, Leeds, Carlisle, Warrington, Middlesbrough and Whitby. The underlying reason for this was that, unlike earlier architects, such as his master, David Stephenson, he was not a builder as well as a designer. Inevitably many of his commissions were for buildings in Newcastle. These range from the outstanding Central Station (1847–48), together with its hotel (1851) and later *porte cochère* (1861–63), to St Thomas's Church at Barras Bridge and the small Lying-in Hospital in New Bridge Street, later to become (until 1990) the regional headquarters of the BBC.

Also in Newcastle, he is commonly linked with John Clayton and Richard Grainger as the third man in the great central development of the town in the grounds of the former nunnery and friary. This, however, is a misconception: Dobson was not the sole architect, but only one of several who were employed on this huge project. His contributions were Eldon Square, part of the east side of Grey Street, the Royal Arcade and what is known as the Grainger Markets.

Dobson was fortunate in that his career coincided with a rapid growth of population and a religious revival, including Catholic Emancipation, which stimulated a demand for new churches and for repair and extension of old ones. In the course of his career he designed thirty-one new churches, mostly for non-Anglican denominations, and alterations to thirty-two others. Almost all were in one form or another of the Gothic style, since in the first half of the nineteenth century the use of Gothic for ecclesiastical buildings became virtually *de rigueur*. This was not so much the case with domestic architecture. In the course of his career, Dobson built, extended or altered 114 houses and in many cases he used classical forms: of the twenty-three major commissions, seventeen were executed in classical style, compared with only six in Gothic style. Almost three-quarters of his domestic commissions were in Northumberland, the outstanding examples being Doxford Hall (1817), Mitford Hall (1823), Longhirst Hall (1824), Nunnykirk (1825) and Meldon Park (1832), which were in classical style, and Beaufront Castle (1836), where he used a mixture of Perpendicular and Tudor Gothic.

At least thirty-six of Dobson's buildings have been demolished, and in other cases what he built has been obscured or altered by later modifications. His largest project not to be realised was the design for the 3rd Marquess of Londonderry of a new town at Seaham (see New Towns of the Nineteenth Century) to house the people working at the new harbour built by the Marquess for the export of coal. Unfortunately, lack of money prevented the Marquess from executing Dobson's plans and in consequence the development of the town proceeded in a more ad hoc fashion.

Dobson died in 1865, but his career was ended three years earlier by a severe stroke.

DORMAN, SIR ARTHUR JOHN, Bt (1848–1931)

Arthur Dorman, who was one of the major figures in the North-East iron and steel industry in the late nineteenth and early twentieth centuries, was born in Ashford in Kent, the son of a currier, who later became a coal and timber merchant. After education at Christ's Hospital, Horsham,

Dorman was apprenticed in 1866 to an iron manufacturer in Stockton. He was ambitious, and so at the end of his apprenticeship in 1873 he set up as a metal broker. In 1876 he went into partnership with Albert de Lange Long and in the next four years they created a substantial business by taking over a defunct iron-making enterprise at West Marsh in Middlesbrough and leasing the neighbouring Britannia Works from SIR BERNHARD SAMUELSON. During the 1880s they converted from iron to steel, making use of the Gilchrist-Thomas process, and by the end of the decade their enterprise had grown to the point where they moved from being a partnership to being a limited company, Dorman, Long & Co.

From the 1890s the company began to expand by means of mergers and takeovers. In 1899 they merged with one of the North East's major producers, Bell Bros of Port Clarence (see BELL, SIR ISAAC LOWTHIAN), a development completed in 1902, when Dorman acquired the Bell family's shares in exchange for 225,000 Dorman, Long shares. The merger with Bell Bros gave Dorman, Long control of important coking collieries at South Brancepeth, Browney and Tursdale. At the same time as he merged with Bell Bros, Dorman also acquired Cleveland Wire and Steel and the North East Steel Co. By 1914 the combined firm was employing over 20,000 men. The war years of 1914 to 1918 were a boom period for steelmakers and Dorman, Long were one of the major British producers and also one of the leading suppliers of artillery shells. It was also in the war years that Dorman, Long acquired three more North-East producers, Sir Bernhard Samuelson's works at Newport, Middlesbrough, the Ferryhill Iron Co., and the Carlton Iron Co. of Stockton. It also acquired Mainsforth Colliery and the coke ovens at Stillington, ironstone mines in Cleveland, and an interest in a Brazilian iron ore company. The end of the war was followed by a long decade of commercial difficulty and crisis, which saw all steel manufacturers struggle and many cease production. It was also a situation that favoured mergers, and in 1929 Dorman, Long merged with another major North-East steelmaker, Bolckow, Vaughan & Co.

The expansionist thrust of the company's policy must be credited to Dorman, and his achievement in creating one of the largest iron and steel concerns bears witness to his ambition and hard work. But, while he is recognised as being good at empire building, Dorman is seen as being less good at managing what he had created. Basically, he failed to take the necessary steps to integrate the companies he brought together and to weed out old and inefficient management. It was not until he went from the scene that the urgently needed restructuring was undertaken. Nevertheless, Dorman was one of the giants of the British steel industry and a major contributor to victory in 1918, facts that were recognised by his knighthood in that year and a baronetcy in 1923.

DOXFORD, SIR WILLIAM THEODORE (1841–1916)

William Doxford was arguably the most energetic and successful of the entrepreneurs who made Sunderland one of the world's leading shipbuilding centres (see SHIPBUILDING INDUSTRY). He was born to the trade in that his father was a shipwright who began to build wooden ships at Washington in the 1840s, but moved downriver to Pallion in 1858, where in 1864 the decision was made to concentrate on iron. On his father's death in 1882, William assumed the direction of the yard's business, although it remained a family partnership that involved his three brothers until 1891, when it was converted into a limited company with a capital of £200,000. William Doxford became chairman and managing director, posts he held until his death. It was in the year after the change to company status that the first 'turret' ship was launched. Based upon an American design, it brought Doxford fame and fortune. Between then and 1911, 176 'turret' ships were built in the Doxford yard, with another six built elsewhere under licence. The Clan Line of Glasgow bought thirty 'turrets', more than any other shipping company. By 1911 the Doxford yard was the biggest on the Wear, having doubled its capacity in 1902, and between 1905 and 1907 it was the most productive shipyard in the world. In addition, from 1878, Doxfords also built their own engines, and between 1907 and 1913 they developed a marine diesel engine, although this did not become a commercial success until after World War I.

William Doxford was an advocate of conciliation processes in industrial relations, and he held high office in the Royal Institute of Naval Architects and the North East Coast Institution of Shipbuilders and Engineers. He was also politically active, being Conservative MP for Sunderland between 1895 and 1906. On his death, control of the company passed to his son, Albert Ernest Doxford, who three years later in 1919 sold the business to the Northumberland Shipbuilding Co.

DUNSTANBURGH CASTLE

The ruins of Dunstanburgh Castle, perched on the outcrop of the WHIN SILL with a sheer drop of 100 feet (30 m) onto rocks and the sea, is one of the most spectacular sights on the North-East coast. It was built by Thomas, Earl of Lancaster, the son of Edmund (nicknamed Crouchback), the younger brother of Edward I, who had acquired the Barony of Embleton, of which the township of Dunstan was a member, in 1269 after the death of its previous owner, the rebel, Simon de Montfort. Building began in 1313 and was completed around 1325. Essentially, the castle was a formidable twin-towered gatehouse, built in conformity with the most up-to-date principles. From it, a wall ran around the perimeter of the clifftop to create a large ward or bailey, 11 acres (4.5 ha) in area.

Later in the century, the castle was substantially remodelled by the Durham architect JOHN LEWYN for John of Gaunt, Duke of Lancaster, third son of Edward III, who inherited the Lancaster estate in the late 1360s. Responsible at that time for the defence of northern England, Gaunt considered the castle's defensive capability needed upgrading. Between 1372 and 1383 the original entrance between the twin towers was blocked up and a new gate was inserted into the south wall. In addition, a small inner ward or bailey was constructed behind the original gatehouse. In effect, the castle became old-fashioned in style with a keep and an inner and an outer bailey.

Splendid though it was, the castle had an artificial quality. Even its name (*Dunstan* with the word *burgh* added) had to be concocted, since there was nothing on the site before it was built. Nor did it serve any practical purpose. It was well away from the Border and also from the routes taken by invading Scottish armies. Nor was there a good domestic reason: the Barony of Embleton was small, and neither Thomas of Lancaster nor John of Gaunt had any other property in the region. It was, it would seem, little more than a status symbol. It is appropriate, therefore, that the castle, with its dramatic situation, has been used as a film set.

DUNSTON STAITHE

Dunston Staithe is a Grade I listed structure, which before it suffered severe fire damage, was one of the most spectacular monuments to the North East's industrial past. It was built of American pine between 1890 and 1893 by the North Eastern Railway to a design by the company's Northern Division Chief Engineer, C.A. Harrison, later responsible for the King Edward VII Rail Bridge, opened in 1906. The decision to build the staithe, close to where the Team enters the Tyne, was the product of two conditions. One was the ability of ocean-going COLLIERS sailing upriver of Newcastle, thanks to the dredging of the river by the Tyne Improvement Commission and the opening of the Swing Bridge in 1876. The second was the rising demand for coal on Thamesside for the expanding gas and electricity industries.

Opened in 1903, at a cost of £210,000, it was then the largest wooden structure in Britain and one of the largest in the world. It was 1,709 feet (521 m) long, 50 feet (15 m) wide and with a minimum clearance above high water of 35 feet(11 m). It had two rail tracks along the entire length of its outer (north) side, where there were berths for three colliers, and two shorter tracks along its inner side. Such was its success (one and a half million tons of coal were exported in its first full year) that almost immediately an extension was begun. This involved widening the staithe to accommodate two additional rail tracks and shifting the river bank 150 feet (46 m) to the south so as to create a large pear-shaped basin covering 9 acres (3.6 ha) between the staithe and the land. The changes doubled its annual capacity to 3 million tons. This in turn encouraged the North Eastern Railway to build the West Staithe a mile further upstream near the mouth of the Derwent. Opened in 1914, this was not a success and it was closed in 1930.

The gradual decline of the coal trade in the decades after the end of World War II eventually led in 1977 to the end of the staithe's working life and to closure in 1980. Ten years later the land south of the staithe, cleared of the railway siding, coal yards and gas works, became the site of the National Garden Festival.

DURHAM, COUNTY

County Durham was a late creation. It arose out of what was called 'St Cuthbert's Land' or 'The Land of the Haliwerfolc', this latter term meaning the People of the Holy Man. Later this land was designated the PALATINATE OF DURHAM, the franchise belonging to the bishops of Durham. What became County Durham in fact began as the collection of estates given or sold over many centuries to the Community of St Cuthbert (see CUTHBERT, SAINT), the guardian of the saint's body and trustee of his property, which settled in Durham in 995. A hundred years later, St Cuthbert's property within the region comprised all the land south of the Tyne and its tributary, the Derwent, and north of the Tees, but with two exceptions. Included was the parish of Ryton, lying north of the Derwent in the angle between that river and the Tyne; excluded until 1189 were three discrete areas along the north bank of the Tees known collectively as the WAPENTAKE OF SADBERGE.

Also included were two important areas north of the Tyne–Derwent line: NORTH DURHAM and Bedlingtonshire. These areas remained part of County Durham until an act of parliament in 1844 abolished this anomaly and incorporated them into Northumberland.

After 1844 the boundaries of the county remained unchanged until the local government reorganisation of 1974. This deprived Durham of its north-eastern districts, which became part of the new county of Tyne and Wear, and its south-eastern districts, which were allocated to another new county, Cleveland. On the other hand it gained a small part of what had been the North Riding of Yorkshire in upper Teesdale. The truncated County was divided into seven Districts: Chester le Street, Derwentside, Durham, Easington, Sedgefield, Teesdale and Wear Valley. These arrangements were short-lived: Cleveland County was abolished in 1997, Hartlepool and Stockton becoming 'unitary authorities'; the seven Districts were also abolished, in 2009.

Durham was also distinctive in being denied the right to elect two 'knights of the shire' to the House of Commons, as all other counties did from the fourteenth century. The reason was that the bishop's palatine status exempted his territory from taxation, and consent to taxation was the prime reason why parliament, particularly the House of Commons, had come into being. James I, however, abolished this valuable privilege in 1610, thus undermining the argument against Durham's parliamentary representation. The rising demand for representation in the following years was successfully resisted by successive bishops. The county was briefly enfranchised between 1653 and 1656 in the several constitutions devised by Oliver Cromwell, but the restoration of the monarchy in 1660 restored the previous arrangement. Not until 1675 was Durham enfranchised, thereafter returning two members, like all other counties, until the Reform Act of 1885 created the present system of single-member constituencies.

From the late seventeenth century, Durham had the appearance of a normal county, thanks to the transfer of the Bishop's palatine powers to the Crown by an act of parliament in 1536, the abolition of tax exemption in 1610 and the enfranchisement in 1675. The word appearance needs to be stressed, however, since it was only recently that the last institutions of the Palatinate were finally abolished.

DURHAM AGED MINERS' HOMES ASSOCIATION

The Durham Aged Miners' Homes Association (DAMHA) was the brainchild of Joseph Hopper, a miner and Methodist lay preacher from Sheriff Hill, who recognised the need to provide for retired miners. Ironically, the need arose through one of the more beneficial arrangements for miners obtaining in the Great Northern Coalfield, namely, the provision of free housing by the coal owners. While in work, this arrangement was to the miner's benefit; when he could no longer work, he was at a disadvantage in having to find his own accommodation. Hopper launched his idea at a meeting of the Northumberland and Durham Permanent Miners' Relief Fund in 1896, hoping that the Fund would be the agency for providing housing for retired miners. When the Fund declined to do so, he set about creating a separate and dedicated organisation. His initiative won the immediate support of several influential and wealthy people, such as Lord Ravensworth, Sir Charles Mark Palmer, and Bishop Westcott of Durham, as well as the Durham Miners' Association, and the DAMHA came into being in 1898.

By 1920 homes existed in almost every Lodge area and at the end of what proved to be the Association's most productive period, 1,800 homes had been created. Many were purpose-built, comprising one-bedroom bungalows, often on land provided by, and using materials supplied by, the coal owners. Otherwise, the Association took over and converted miners' houses that had become redundant.

The decades after World War II were the lean years, with no new homes built between 1957 and 1983. Worse still, some were sold while many others became substandard as the Association lacked the financial resources to effect the necessary improvements. The solution, adopted in 1981, was for the DAMHA to become a Registered Housing Association, whereby it got access to public funds, although at the cost of some loss of independence. Government money enabled it to embark upon a sixteen-year comprehensive development scheme, involving the modernisation of its existing homes and the completion of a programme of new construction, including a number of sheltered housing schemes. This target was achieved by 1998, the Association's centenary year: all homes had been modernised and 204 new homes completed in thirteen places.

But in the 1980s the Association also made three disastrous moves: one was to set up a business to take over the NCB's redundant housing stock; another was to open a factory to make windows; and the third was to build in 1989 an enlarged headquarters, appropriately named Joseph Hopper House, in Durham City. All three proved to be errors of judgement and led to the Association's reverting to its original role, selling Joseph Hopper House and moving the head office to Chester le Street. At present, the Association has 1,250 homes in seventy-five places.

It was Joseph Hopper's initial intention that his Association, like the Permanent Relief Fund, should cover Northumberland as well as Durham. Northumberland, however, declined to join and in 1900 set up its own organisation, the Northumberland Miners' Aged Homes Association, which by 1950 had built 575 homes in forty places.

DURHAM CATHEDRAL

What we see today is the second cathedral to be built on the loop of the River Wear known as the Peninsula at Durham. The first was begun in 995, almost immediately after the Community of St Cuthbert (see CUTHBERT, SAINT) settled there, and was consecrated in 998, when the saint's body was 'translated' from its temporary resting place. Nothing of that building remains, and even its whereabouts are in doubt, although it is probable that it was a much smaller building and lay under the present cloister, close to the south wall of the nave of the present church. It continued in use until the chancel and crossing of its successor had been built as far as the first bay of the nave. At that point, in 1104, the body of St Cuthbert was 'translated' into the new cathedral.

The decision to replace the old cathedral was taken by BISHOP WILLIAM OF ST CALAIS in 1093. Construction, which was pushed on after his death in 1096 by St Calais's successors, RANNULF FLAMBARD and Geoffrey Rufus (1133–40), took forty years. The result was not the longest cathedral in England; any ambition St Calais may have had was thwarted by the nature of the site. However, he did have the distinction of achieving a 'first': at Durham, for the first time, a vault was built across the whole width of a nave and chancel. Who was the architect? The answer has to be St Calais, simply because there is no record of any other name, although it is reasonable to think that he worked in close co-operation with his master mason.

In its basic structure (though not in detail), the cathedral today is substantially as it was in 1133, with the exception of its extremities. At the west end, the great west door, the deliberately impressive entrance to so many cathedrals, is masked by the Galilee Chapel, built in the 1170s by BISHOP HUGH OF LE PUISET. Puiset's first intention was to add a Lady Chapel at the east end, but he was prevented either by technical problems or the opposition of the monks, who, it is said, proclaimed St Cuthbert's displeasure. Splendid though the Galilee Chapel is, it was the second-best way Puiset found of leaving his mark. Had building on a north–

south axis been allowed, instead of the required east–west axis, Durham Cathedral would almost certainly now have a splendid front facing Palace Green. Instead, entrance is by the north door, still largely the original twelfth-century timber. Fixed to this door is a replica of the famous sanctuary knocker (the original is preserved in the Treasury). By grasping it fleeing criminals were (or should have been) saved from summary justice at the hands of a lynch mob. If they confessed their crime to the Coroner, they were allowed forty days in which to arrange their affairs and abjure the realm by the nearest port.

The east end, however, had to be rebuilt in the thirteenth century, because by that time serious cracks had appeared in the fabric. The cause was the failure of the original builders to go deep enough to secure adequate foundations at a point where the base rock sloped steeply away towards the lip of the peninsula. Construction began in 1242 and took about forty years to complete. The new east end was radically different in form and size. St Calais's chancel ended in an apse, the outline of which is marked on the floor of St Cuthbert's shrine. In its place a T bar was built in the Early English Gothic style across the chancel end. Known as the Chapel of the Nine Altars, its floor is lower than that of the rest of the cathedral, a testimony to the builders' recognition of the need to dig further down to get a secure foundation. The much greater floor area of the extension allowed for more altars, needed partly because of the increase in the number of monks, but also because more of them were priests, who celebrated mass daily.

The third major change was the gradual heightening of the central tower. We do not know how high the original tower was, but surviving examples of this period suggest that it would have been comparatively low and squat. It appears to have been raised in the thirteenth century, when the western towers also were heightened; but the present tower is the result of the damage caused by lightning strikes in 1429 and 1459. Building began *c.*1465 and was complete by *c.*1490.

Several smaller but important alterations and additions were made in the third quarter of the fourteenth century. Five windows were enlarged by Prior John Fossor (1341–74) and given tracery in the Decorated Gothic style. Bishop Thomas de Hatfield (1345–81) built an episcopal throne, reputedly the highest in Europe, with his tomb beneath it. And the screen between the high altar and the shrine of St Cuthbert was replaced, largely at the expense of John Neville, Lord of Raby. The Neville Screen is made of stone brought from Caen in Normandy to London, where it was carved in sections, probably between 1372 and 1376. These were transported by sea to Newcastle and by cart to Durham for installation, although not until 1380. The designer may have been Henry Yevele, the most renowned English architect of his day. Originally it was painted and had 107 alabaster statues in the niches. Probably also of this period are the tombs of Ralph, Lord Neville (d.1376), one of the English commanders at the BATTLE OF NEVILLE'S CROSS, and his son, John, Lord Neville (d.1388), and their wives, which were placed in the Neville Chantry, created in the south nave aisle in 1417 (see NEVILLE FAMILY).

The cathedral was home to two institutions. It was the Bishop of Durham's church and the centre of his diocese, of which he was the spiritual ruler. But it was also home to its chapter, the body of clergy who lived there and manned it. From 1083 until 1539 this was a Benedictine monastery. This fact explains the existence of the cloister and its surrounding buildings attached to the south side of the nave and beyond that a further range of buildings enclosing a large square of land, known as the College. All were purpose-built for a monastic community. The claustral ranges were the living quarters of the forty or so monks resident at any given time, while the outer ranges of buildings served a variety of purposes, such as the infirmary, guest accommodation, storehouses and brewery. The most noteworthy of these buildings is the monastic kitchen, built between 1366 and 1374 by a local mason, John Lewyn.

The medieval centuries of the cathedral's existence ended on 31 December 1539, when the Benedictine priory formally surrendered to the king, Henry VIII. Seventeen months later, on 12 May 1541, a new type of chapter was instituted, comprising a dean and twelve canons, all secular clergy, who, unlike their monastic predecessors, were permitted to marry and have children. The change was not quite as radical as at first appears, since the new dean, Hugh Whitehead, was the last prior, and the twelve canons had all been senior monks. Nevertheless, the monastic quarters became redundant and the buildings in the College were remodelled into family accommodation for the canons. The dean, however, occupied (as he still does) the hall of the former priors in its own enclosure at the east end of the College. The cathedral church was also affected: the stone screen across the width of the cathedral on the west side of the crossing that had divided it into two halves was removed. Other changes included whitewashing the walls to cover the pictures painted on them and the smashing of some of the stained glass by the iconoclastic deans, Robert Horne (1551–53 and 1559–60) and William Whittingham (1563–79).

Far greater disaster befell the cathedral as the result of the triumph of the Parliamentary opponents of Charles I in the 1640s. In 1646 the Bishopric of Durham was abolished, and in 1649 the dean and chapter was suppressed and the cathedral closed. The ultimate indignity followed in the winter of 1650–51, when around 3,000 Scottish prisoners of war, captured by Oliver Cromwell following his victory at Dunbar in September 1650, were housed in the church pending transportation as indentured servants to sugar plantations in the West Indies. In the weeks of their incarceration they were maltreated and in consequence they broke up all the woodwork for use as fuel, smashed the statues in the Neville Screen and defaced the Neville tombs. Consequently, when the monarchy and the Church of England were restored in 1660, the incoming bishop and chapter faced an urgent task of repairing fourteen years of neglect and abuse. Their response to the challenge gave the cathedral its present black oak choir stalls and font cover. Although this work is conventionally attributed to the new bishop, John Cosin, considerable credit ought to be given to Dean Thomas Sudbury (1662–83), who was also responsible for converting the monastic refectory into a library, which it still is.

The eighteenth and nineteenth centuries were generally unkind to the cathedral, although this time the indignities it suffered were self-inflicted. During the course of the eighteenth century virtually all the surviving medieval glass was lost and at the end of the century, with the building clearly in need of urgent attention, the chapter hired the fashionable architect, James Wyatt. Had he had his way, the cathedral would have been very different to what it is. As it was, before he was stopped, he managed to pull down the porch at the north door, replace the lead roofing with slates and destroy the apse of the chapter house, although this was accurately restored in 1890. Happily, he was stopped before he could add a spire to the central tower, raise the floor of the

Nine Altars, demolish the Neville Screen and Hatfield's Tomb (and use the stone to build a canopy over the high altar), and knock down the Galilee Chapel, in order to construct a driveway up to the west door, which he proposed to reopen.

In the 1840s, however, Dean George Waddington (1840–69) moved Cardinal Bishop Thomas Langley's tomb from its place in the Galilee Chapel and reopened the west door. In conjunction with this, the Restoration woodwork across the chancel (the 'return' stalls and the chancel screen with the organ on top) was removed. The organ, the case of which stands by the south door of the Galilee Chapel, was one of the forty or fifty built by 'Father Smith', the German, Bernard Schmidt (*c.*1630–1708), who was responsible for the finest organs of his day and to whom Durham paid £800 for the instrument he built for the cathedral between 1683 and 1685. These changes, which many will regard as vandalism, were made with good intent: to create an uninterrupted view down the length of the cathedral from the west door to the high altar. This, it was believed, would not only be a 'grand vista' but would give an illusion of greater space. Unexpectedly and disastrously, it had the opposite effect and in the early 1870s Sir George Gilbert Scott was employed to put matters right. The result is in its own way equally disastrous, the marble of his chancel screen looking entirely out of place and jarring badly with the Cosin woodwork. The same criticism applies against the pulpit Scott made, which stands on the south side of the chancel steps. On other other hand, Waddington is to be given credit for removing the whitewash applied to the walls during the Reformation (and in doing so revealing fragments of medieval wall painting) and also the late medieval tracery from the Romanesque windows.

Two nineteenth-century changes may be considered to be far less controversial. One is the replacement of the plain glass in many windows with stained pictorial glass. The other is the conversion of the monastic dormitory on the west side of the cloister to accommodate the ever-expanding number of books in the cathedral library. This area has also seen developments in the late twentieth century: the undercroft beneath the dormitory has been converted into the Cathedral Treasury, in which are displayed some of the cathedral's priceless possessions, notably the remains of St Cuthbert's coffin and the items recovered from it, and a facsimile of the LINDISFARNE GOSPELS. Also in the undercroft, to the south of its cross-passage, is a small café. Next door, the monastic kitchen, which for many years housed the dean and chapter muniments, is now a bookshop. Earlier in the century the cathedral acquired two important memorials: to the men of the Durham Light Infantry who died in World War I (1924), in the south transept, and to the miners killed in the county's pits in the south nave aisle (1947).

These recent changes, together with the ongoing programme of replacing decayed stonework in the exterior walls, underlines the fact that repairs, renewal and adaptations are unavoidable. None, however, has destroyed the profound majesty of Durham Cathedral, which is now the centrepiece of a World Heritage Site.

DURHAM CITY

Durham City, like its cathedral, can trace its origins to the arrival of the Community of St Cuthbert (see CUTHBERT, SAINT) in 995, although there is evidence of pre-existing settlement within the loop of the River Wear (locally known as the Peninsula), as there certainly was across the river around the church of Elvet. Indeed, it is possible that the original centre of what is now Durham was near the present St Oswald's Church in Elvet. This said, by 1006, the settlement on the Peninsula had developed sufficiently to have a wooden wall that proved capable of repulsing a major Scottish attack. However, it was in the following century that it developed the physical shape that is still recognisable today. This was largely the work of three bishops: WILLIAM OF ST CALAIS, RANNULF FLAMBARD and HUGH OF LE PUISET. What emerged was not, however, a unity but a collection of eight distinct communities.

The first of these was the Peninsula, the northern neck of which was dominated by the castle, begun for the bishops in 1072 by William the Conqueror. From the castle a stone wall was built by Flambard around the rim of the Peninsula. Within the enclosure so formed lay the cathedral and its monastic precinct. Immediately north of this area was the Borough of Durham, the product of Flambard's decision to remove the population from what is now Palace Green (the land between the cathedral and the castle) and relocate it around the Market Place, which was enclosed by a wall in the early fourteenth century, formed by the convergence of Saddler Street, Silver Street and Claypath. The Borough of Durham ended where Claypath becomes Gilesgate. Flambard also created the Borough of Gilesgate, which he attached to the hospital, later known as Kepier Hospital (see MEDIEVAL HOSPITALS), next to the parish church, which he built *c.*1112.

These three communities lay within the two 'arms' of the River Wear. On the outside of the 'arms' were five others. To the west was Crossgate Borough (also known as the Old Borough), founded by the cathedral priory following Flambard's construction of Framwellgate Bridge *c.*1112. It comprised South Street, Crossgate, Allergate and Milburngate. Its northern boundary was the Mill Burn, now running into the river by means of a culvert. To the north of the Mill Burn was Framwellgate, a suburb of the Borough of Durham, comprising Framwellgate, Castle Chare and Sidegate. Extending Durham Borough on the outer bank of the river was made unavoidable by Gilesgate Borough, which had blocked Durham's natural line of expansion. On the eastern side of the river was the Elvet Borough (also called the New Borough), created by the cathedral priory in the later twelfth century after Puiset had built Elvet Bridge. This borough comprised Old Elvet, New Elvet and Ratten Raw, now Court Lane. Immediately to the south of Elvet Borough the area around St Oswald's Church was the Barony of Elvet, which had all the appearances of a borough without being so called. Finally, adjacent to the Borough and the Barony of Elvet was Elvethall Manor, a farm, part of the steading of which still exists in Hallgarth Street. Durham Borough and Framwellgate were owned by the bishop; Gilesgate Borough belonged to Kepier Hospital, although its Master was an episcopal appointee; and the other elements were in the lordship of the Cathedral Priory.

Durham's medieval form remained unchanged until recent times. Physically, the first significant change was North Road, the construction of which in the 1830s involved culverting the Mill Burn, which still discharges into the river. There were no further changes until the period 1965–74, when an inner bypass was built. This involved two new Bridges, Milburngate Bridge and New Elvet Bridge, an underpass under Claypath and a road parallel to Claypath to join a dual carriageway leading to the Durham Motorway. This solution to the city's bottleneck was very much on the line proposed by Thomas Sharp in the 1930s. The last major change (so far) to the medieval structure was the creation of

'High Street', a completely new pedestrian shopping mall between Saddler Street and Claypath. In addition, the river has acquired three additional pedestrian crossings: Baths Bridge (1855/1898/1962), Kingsgate Bridge (1963) and Pennyferry Bridge (2002).

Constitutional change also came slowly. In 1565 Bishop James Pilkington (1561–76) issued a charter joining Durham and Framwellgate into a single incorporated city to be governed by an alderman and twenty-four burgesses, twelve holding for life and twelve elected annually. However, all these were to hold office at the bishop's pleasure. This charter was replaced in 1602 by Bishop Tobias Matthew (1595–1606), who made significant concessions. The city government was now to comprise a mayor (elected annually), twelve aldermen and twenty-four burgesses chosen annually by the aldermen from the city's trade guilds. These thirty-seven men were to constitute the Common Council. This arrangement, confirmed by James I in 1605, lasted with slight modification in 1780 by Bishop John Egerton (1771–87) until replaced by that imposed by the Municipal Reform Act of 1835. Although there were subsequent boundary changes, they were minor compared to the radical restructuring imposed as part of the 1974 major overhaul of the national system of local government. In place of the small city that had developed organically over the centuries, the new Durham District was a much enlarged local government unit that included a ring of nineteen surrounding townships that hitherto had been Rural Districts. In 2009 this District, along with all the others in the county, was swept away in favour of a single County Council.

Durham's parliamentary history has also been eccentric. Unlike similar towns, the city, along with the county, was denied members of parliament until 1678. The reason was simply the rearguard resistance of successive bishops based upon their palatine status (see Palatinate of Durham). Durham was, in fact, the last borough to be enfranchised before the Reform Act of 1832. From 1678 until 1832, the city returned two MPs, elected by the freemen, many of whom were non-resident. The 1832 act maintained Durham's over-representation, although it did bring its franchise into line with that of other boroughs. Although the city's representation was reduced to one in 1885, it continued to be classified as a borough seat until 1918, when it was redesignated as one of the divisions of the county. As with all constituencies, Durham has undergone regular boundary changes. At present, however, its boundaries coincide with those of the enlarged city.

DURHAM COUNTY CRICKET CLUB

Durham County Cricket Club was founded in 1882 and was one of the founding members of the Minor Counties League in 1894. In the following ninety-eight years it was the most successful of the Minor Counties, winning the title on nine occasions and having great success in other competitions open to it and against overseas touring sides. The County Championship, which ran parallel to the Minor Counties, was inaugurated in 1890 and by 1905 comprised sixteen counties. No further additions were made until 1921, when Glamorgan was admitted. Thus, throughout almost the whole of the twentieth century first-class cricket extended no further north than the Tees, despite the fact that the region's numerous leagues regularly produced cricketers of the requisite standard. The campaign to rectify this began in the early 1980s, initially taking the form of a proposal that 'Northumbria', combining Durham and Northumberland, should apply for admission. For various reasons this possibly ideal solution did not prove feasible and in 1990 Durham applied alone. The application was successful and Durham County Cricket Club began life in the County Championship in the 1992 season. Initially, it played its matches on a number of existing grounds, until its new, purpose-built ground at the Riverside, CHESTER LE STREET, was opened in 1995. In 2008, after only sixteen years in existence, Durham CCC won the County Championship.

DURHAM MINERS' GALA

The Durham Miners' Gala, also known as the 'Big Meeting', began in 1871 and has taken place every year since, except in the war years of 1915–18 and 1940–45, and also in 1921–22 and 1984, when it was cancelled because of industrial action. Its origin was a direct consequence of the formation in 1869 of the Durham Miners' Mutual Association, which itself stemmed from the ending of the much-hated yearly bond, whereby each year miners contracted themselves to their employers for the duration of a twelve-month period. The Association was organised democratically: every colliery was a branch, known as a lodge, which had an elected chairman, secretary, treasurer and committee.

Very shortly after the foundation of the Association, it was decided to hold an annual mass rally of lodges. The first was held on 12 August 1871 at Wharton Park in Durham. Thereafter the venue has always been the Racecourse in Durham (now a Durham University playing field) and the date has usually been the third Saturday in July. From the outset every lodge provided itself with a banner (almost all of them made by the London firm founded in 1837 by George Tutill) and a brass band. The format of the event has changed little throughout its history. From early in the morning banners with their bearers, accompanied by their band, and members of the lodge with their families arrived at Durham by public transport. They then marched through the narrow streets of Durham (where shops had to be closed and boarded up because of the press of the crowds) to the Racecourse, banner raised and band playing. They converged at the junction of Old Elvet and New Elvet to greet and be greeted by the people who had been invited to address the rally looking down from the balcony of the Royal County Hotel.

By noon all were assembled and speeches were delivered, usually from two platforms. Initially, the speakers included local dignitaries and sympathetic clergymen, as well as miners' leaders and political figures committed to the miners' cause. From about 1900, however, speakers have been exclusively Labour politicians and leaders of the miners' union, although other non-speaking invited guests also sat on the platforms. The speeches were about matters of current concern to the Labour movement in general and to the mining industry in particular.

The remainder of the day was devoted to enjoyment: families had picnics; some hired boats on the river; and the city's pubs were open all day, with some inevitable consequences. The only significant addition to the programme was made in 1897, when the then Bishop of Durham, Brooke Westcott (1889–1901), known as the Miners' Bishop, persuaded the Association to support a special service in the cathedral attended by selected banners and bands. Late in the afternoon, the lodges began to start on their return journeys, each making its own arrangements, as they did for their journey to the city.

In its heyday, the Gala was attended by over 150 lodges, and this meant that to get all lodges on to the Racecourse by midday the first arrivals were required to be in Durham early in the morning. But, as pits closed, so the number of lodges attending the Gala shrank, until the event was a shadow of its former self. With the closure of the last Durham pits, EASINGTON, Monkwearmouth and Westoe in 1993, the original purpose of the Gala ceased to exist. The decision was taken, however, to keep the event going, parading the banners of a number of long-closed collieries. As to the speeches, the Gala is no longer about mining and miners and has become a platform for advocates of old-fashioned Socialism.

DURHAM OX

One of the most famous individual animals commemorated on many a pub sign, the Durham Ox was a Shorthorn bred in 1796 at Ketton near Darlington by CHARLES COLLING. From the start, it was recognised as an exceptional animal and at five years old it weighed 216 stones (1,371 kg). It was in 1801 that Colling sold it to man named Bulmer, who lived near Bedale in Yorkshire, for £140. Within five weeks Bulmer realised a huge profit by selling it to a John Day of Rotherham for £250. Day could have been even more successful financially had he accepted offers made to him, the largest of which was £2,000. Instead, he held on to the beast and exhibited it throughout the country for six years, thereby ensuring its fame. In 1807, however, following a dislocated hip, the ox had to be put down. Its carcass weighed 168 stones (1,066 kg).

DURHAM REGATTA

Durham Regatta has some claim to be the oldest regatta in England. It can trace its origin to 1834, but little is known about its early years, other than that it was an established feature of the summer 'season' in the city. Why it was started is not certain, although its coincidence with the founding of the University is probably significant. From mid-century it took on a recognisable form: by 1854 the Grand Challenge Cup, the Wharton Challenge Cup, the Oswald Plate and the Corporation Challenge Cup existed, and by 1900 the Durham City Plate, the Mayor's Plate, the Lady Ann Lambton Plate and the Lady Herschell Plate had been added. There were two courses: the Short Course of 700 yards (640 m) from Pelaw Wood to a point between Baths Bridge and Brown's Boat House, and the Long Course of a mile and a quarter (2 km), starting at Pelaw Wood and ending at the Count's House, the Greek Doric garden house belonging to the house (now demolished) near Prebends' Bridge that was occupied between 1791 and 1837 by the 3 foot 3 inch (1 m) tall Polish dwarf, Count Joseph Borulawski. Then, as now, the regatta was a two-day affair, although in the 1960s it was moved from midweek to the weekend. This change notwithstanding, a returning oarsman from 1900 would have found the whole event very familiar.

The late twentieth century, however, brought many changes. The length of the two courses had to be redesignated in metres and the number of competitions increased considerably: for women, for veterans, for eights and quadruple sculls, and as a result of the Amateur Rowing Association's dividing the traditional three classes of oarsman. By 2007 there were no fewer than 104 separate events. Although the Regatta has always attracted a number of long-distance entries, the bulk of entries has always come from Durham Amateur Rowing Club, Durham University Boat Club, the boat clubs of the growing number of Durham University colleges, and the rowing clubs, civic and academic, based on the rivers Tyne and Tees.

DYKES, JOHN BACCHUS (1823–1876)

John Bacchus Dykes was one of the foremost composers of hymn tunes in the nineteenth century. He was born in Hull in 1823 and was sufficiently musically precocious to be appointed assistant organist at one of the town's churches at the age of twelve. Between 1843 and 1847 he was at Cambridge, where he took a leading part in reviving the University Music Society and almost single-handedly re-created the University Orchestra. Upon graduation he took holy orders in the Church of England and became a curate at Malton in the North Riding in 1848. The following year, however, he moved to Durham, where he spent the rest of his life. From 1849 until 1862 he was the Precentor of the Cathedral, in which post he did much to raise the standard of its music. In 1862 he resigned the Precentorship to become the Vicar of St Oswald's Church, Elvet, the living he retained until his death.

While he was Precentor, he composed a large number of hymn tunes, fifty-five of which eventually were included in *Hymns Ancient and Modern*, including seven in the first edition of 1861. Many are among the most popular and enduring of all those used by the Church of England: 'Holy, Holy, Holy' (Nicaea), 'Jesu Lover of my Soul' (Hollingside), 'Eternal Father Strong to Save' (Melita), 'Lead Kindly Light' (Lux Benigna), 'The King of Love My Shepherd Is' (Dominus Regit Me), 'Praise to the Holiest in the Height' (Gerontius) and 'Through the Night of Doubt and Sorrow' (St Oswald).

Dykes belonged to the High Church wing of the Church of England, and the differences he had with his more evangelical bishop, Charles Baring (1861–78), may have helped to undermine his health and hastened his death in 1876 at the comparatively early age of fifty-three. He is buried in St Oswald's churchyard in Durham.

EASINGTON

During the medieval centuries, Easington was a place of considerable importance. As well as being a township of over 5,000 acres (2,000 ha), which by the 1180s had produced a subsidiary offshoot, Little Thorp, it was the centre of Easington Ward, one of the four wards into which Durham was divided for administrative purposes. It was also important ecclesiastically. Easington parish was large, covering nearly 14,000 acres (6,000 ha) and including Hawthorn, Horden and Shotton. In addition, in 1256 it was decreed by the then Bishop of Durham, Walter de Kirkham, that henceforth the Rector of Easington was also Archdeacon of Durham, the office that developed in the twelfth century and was of major importance in diocesan administration. Consequently, the holder of the two offices enjoyed a huge income, as rector from the tithes paid by his parishioners and his large glebe farm of nearly 600 acres (200 ha), and from the various fees and dues to which he was entitled as archdeacon. Evidence of his wealth is his residence, the large house known as Seaton Holme, which dates from the thirteenth and fourteenth centuries. Located opposite the church at the centre of the village, it was a three-sided stone-built complex, arranged around a rectangular courtyard. One of the sides was demolished in 1950, but the other two were restored between 1988 and 1992 and this now houses the parish council offices.

Easington's importance as a local government centre has been maintained in the modern era. In the late 1830s, following the Poor Law Amendment Act of 1834, it became the centre of the Easington Poor Law Union, comprising the parishes of Easington, Castle Eden, Dalton le Dale, Monk Hesleden and Seaham, and parts of those of Bishop Wearmouth, Hart and Kelloe. In 1894, as a result of the restructuring of local government, it became the seat of Easington Rural District Council. And in 1974 another major reordering of local government arrangements saw Easington Rural District and Seaham Urban District united to form Easington District, one of the seven Districts of the truncated DURHAM COUNTY, which were abolished in 2009.

Easington continued as a rural village until the sinking of the colliery between 1899 and 1909. It was one of the last pits to be sunk in Durham and with Monkwearmouth and Westoe was the last to be closed, in 1993. It was also, tragically, the last colliery in the GREAT NORTHERN COALFIELD to suffer a major disaster. This occurred on 29 May 1951, when at 4.20 a.m. a spark from a coal cutter detonated firedamp released from the goaf (the area from which the coal has been extracted and into which the roof is allowed to fall) and then dry coal dust. The explosion occurred in the Five-Quarter Seam, 1,000 yards (900 m) below the ground and a mile and a half in-bye, that is, from the shaft bottom. Rescue teams, numbering 291 men, worked for 256 hours to get through 120 yards (110 m) of fallen roof to reach the scene of the carnage, losing two of their number as the result of inhaling gas. The eighty-one dead miners were buried together in a single grave over which stands a memorial, on Saturday 22 June (see COLLIERY DISASTERS).

ECGBERHT, BISHOP (639–729)

Ecgberht was one of the first generation of Northumbrian Christians who, like many others, was of noble parentage. Although most of the details of his life are missing, it is clear that he trained at Lindisfarne (see HOLY ISLAND), but then spent most of his life out of Northumbria, firstly in Ireland, and later at Iona. He was not alone in sojourning in Ireland: after the Synod of Whitby in 664, when KING OSWIU decided that Northumbria should conform to the ways of the Roman church, a number of Northumbrian clerics migrated to Ireland in search of scholarship and a more ascetic lifestyle. For most, their sojourn was temporary, but the consequence of their visits to the home of Northumbrian Christianity resulted in fruitful interchange between Celtic and Anglo-Saxon cultures. Ecgberht, however, never came home but deliberately imposed permanent exile on himself in penance for the sins of his youth, although what these were he did not divulge.

It was as an exile that Ecgberht accomplished three major achievements. Like Bede, he was concerned to bring the churches in all the English and Irish kingdoms into conformity with Roman ways. His endeavours came to a triumphant conclusion in 716, when he persuaded the powerful and influential monastic community of Iona (where he spent the rest of his life) to adopt the Roman method of calculating Easter. On the same front, he appears to have been instrumental in securing the adherence of the Kingdom of the Picts to Roman forms. He thus played a major role in creating religious and cultural uniformity between the kingdoms of the British Isles and those of the continent.

His third important contribution was secondhand. While still in Ireland, he formulated a plan to assemble a team of missionaries to evangelise Frisia (modern Holland/Belgium), at that date still heathen. However, his close associates persuaded him not to go, arguing that his work in Britain and Ireland was more important and urgent. Rather than abandon the scheme, Ecgberht found a substitute leader: Willibrord (658–739), the son of a Northumbrian nobleman from Deira south of the Tees. Willibrord's monastic life began at Ripon, but in 678 he migrated to Ireland, where he became one of Ecgberht's pupils, becoming a priest in 688. In 690, after two years' preparation supervised by Ecgberht, he set out for Frisia. Backed by the Frankish king Pepin II, who was annexing this area, the mission was a success and by 695 it had become sufficiently important for Pope Sergius I to grant Willibrord the title of Archbishop of the Frisians, with his base at Utrecht. Willibrord's other great accomplishment was founding the monastery at Echternach (in modern Luxembourg), which became one of the great monastic houses of medieval Europe.

ECGFRITH (?–685), KING OF NORTHUMBRIA 670–685

Ecgfrith was the son and successor of Oswiu and the continuator of his policy of territorial expansion. By virtue of victory in a battle, probably fought somewhere between the modern towns of Stirling and Alloa, Oswiu had established some sort of hegemony over the Kingdom of the Picts, which extended from the Forth to the Moray Firth. Subsequently, he and Ecgfrith attempted to enhance Northumbrian dominance by means of a bishopric for Pictland established at Abercorn on the Forth. But under its new king, Bridei, Pictish resistance to Northumbrian hegemony increased, which in turn led Ecgfrith to invade Pictland in the spring of 685. Instead of giving battle immediately, Bridei lured Ecgfrith further into Pictish territory and into a trap near the modern town of Forfar. The battle fought at Dunnichen on 20 May was catastrophic for the Northumbrians: their army was annihilated and Ecgfrith slain. This battle, also known as the Battle of Nechtansmere, marks the end of Northumbrian attempts to subjugate the Picts. Although Lothian, the land between the Forth and the Tweed, was to remain part of Northumbria for another 300 years, the River Avon (still the boundary between West Lothian and Stirlingshire) was its northern frontier.

Six miles north of Dunnichen in the churchyard at Aberlemno on the B9134 between Forfar and Brechin there is a carved upright stone depicting a battle scene with infantry and cavalry. It has been dated to a generation after the battle and it is generally believed that it was erected to commemorate the victory. If so, the significance of the battle was recognised at an early date.

EDEN, GEORGE, EARL OF AUCKLAND (1748–1849)

George Eden was responsible for one of the worst military disasters to befall the British Army. He was the second son of WILLIAM EDEN, LORD AUCKLAND, but succeeded to the title as the result of the death of his elder brother. Like his father, he was educated at Eton and Christ Church, Oxford, graduating with a BA in 1806 and an MA in 1808. Almost immediately, he embarked on a political career, becoming MP for the borough of Woodstock in 1810, retaining the seat until, on the death of his father in 1814, he entered the House of Lords. As a Whig, he was in opposition until his party came to power following the election of 1830. During the next five years, he was in government, first as President of the Board of Trade and Master of the Mint (1830–34) and then as First Lord of the Admiralty (1834–35).

In the later 1830s, however, his career took a marked turn: in 1835 he was made Governor General of India and in 1839 Earl of Auckland. It was his decision, although on the advice of Sir William Macnaughton, to invade Afghanistan in 1839. Ostensibly to restore its Shah, Shuja, to the throne (he had been deposed in 1809), the real purpose was to establish a puppet regime in Afghanistan to prevent the country falling under Persian (Iranian) or Russian influence. Unfortunately, Shah Shuja proved to be too incompetent and unpopular to be able to re-establish his authority.

Initially the invasion by an army numbering 21,000 was a success. Garrisons were placed in Kabul, Kandahar and Jallalabad and towards the end of the year all but 8,000 troops were withdrawn. But it soon became clear that Shuja was completely dependent upon British arms: he commanded little native support and much of the country remained under the control of local chiefs, who had no intention of surrendering their power to a central government.

The sensible decision would have been withdrawal, but this Auckland would not allow. Instead, he sent Major General William Elphinstone, a sick man without experience of warfare in the Far East, to take command in Kabul. The situation deteriorated towards the end of 1841: in November a revolt broke out in Kabul and on 23 December Sir William Macnaughton was murdered at a conference with the rebels. The situation was now critical and on 6 January 1842 a convention was agreed by which the British troops would be allowed to withdraw to India, leaving behind all the guns and most of the remaining stores, as well as Elphinstone with some officers and all the women and children as hostages. The column that left Kabul included 4,500 troops of whom 690 were British, and 12,000 Afghans. But the agreement proved worthless. The party was subject to constant attack and was finally overwhelmed in the Jagdalak Pass, the Afghans allowing only a Dr Brydon to survive in order to report the disaster at Jallalabad. A few weeks later, Auckland's successor as Governor General, Lord Ellenborough, arrived and took control. The situation was retrieved during the course of 1842, principally by the garrisons at Kandahar and Jallalabad, who secured the release of ninety-five prisoners and made a successful withdrawal to India.

By the time Auckland got back to Britain his party, the Whigs, were out of office.

When they regained power in 1846, he was again made First Lord of the Admiralty, a post he was still holding at the time of his death in 1849. As he had no sons, on his death his title became extinct.

EDEN, SIR ROBERT ANTHONY, 1st EARL OF AVON (1897–1977)

Anthony Eden was Prime Minister from April 1955, when he succeeded Sir Winston Churchill, until January 1957. He was born at Windlestone Hall, County Durham, the third son of Sir William Eden, 6th Baronet. The Eden family had been the owners of Windlestone and parts of West Auckland since the reign of Elizabeth I and been granted a baronetcy in 1672 as a reward for their support for Charles I during the Civil Wars. Eden was at Eton College until 1915, by which date Britain was at war with Germany. Consequently, he went from there straight into the army. He saw active service in France, winning the MC in 1917. Only twenty when the war ended in 1918, he was the youngest brigade major in the British Army. After demobilisation he went to Oxford University, where he gained a first-class honours degree in Persian and Arabic in 1922.

His intention at that time was to enter the Diplomatic Service, but he decided instead to enter politics, seeing it as a faster route to the top. After failing to win in the 1922 general election the hopeless (for a Conservative) constituency of Spennymoor, in which Windleston Hall was situated, he was elected to the safe seat of Warwick and Leamington in 1923, which he retained through eight elections until 1961. As an MP he specialised in foreign affairs and after a number of junior posts, most of them to do with foreign affairs, he became a member of Stanley Baldwin's cabinet in 1935, initially as minister without portfolio responsible for the League of Nations affairs, but then as Foreign Secretary, following the resignation of Sir Samuel Hoare. He remained in post until 1938, when he resigned because of policy differences with the Prime Minister (since 1937), Neville Chamberlain, and because Chamberlain was conducting foreign policy behind his back. At the end of 1940, after Winston Churchill had succeeded Chamberlain as Prime Minister, Eden again became Foreign Secretary, following the appointment of the Earl of Halifax as Ambassador in Washington. He remained in that post throughout the war, attending all the great wartime conferences, except for that at Casablanca, from which foreign ministers were excluded.

Following the victory of the Labour Party in the 1945 election, Eden was out of office. Although in poor health, burdened by the death in action of one of his sons and a failing marriage, he was nonetheless seen as Churchill's political heir. But Churchill, despite old age and health problems, held on to become Prime Minister again in 1951. It was not until 1955 that he retired and allowed Eden to succeed.

The highest office, so long hoped for and expected, turned out to be a poisoned chalice. In little over a year, Eden precipitated what has come to be known as the 'Suez Crisis': the invasion of Egypt by an Anglo-French force in collusion with the Israelis following the nationalisation of the Suez Canal by the Egyptian dictator, Gamal Abdul Nasser. Eden's action had wide popular support in Britain, although the Labour opposition refused to back the use of force, unless it had the blessing of the United Nations. This was not forthcoming, and neither was support from the USA. It was the opposition of President Eisenhower and his Secetary of State, John Foster Dulles, that led to the invasion being aborted, leaving Nasser in power and the Canal in Egyptian hands.

Eden had been defeated by his most important ally. His health, which was never robust, broke down and he resigned the premiership, being replaced by HAROLD MACMILLAN. In 1961 he left the Commons with a peerage as the Earl of Avon. He died in 1977. By that time the connection of the Eden family with County Durham had been broken with the sale of Windlestone Hall, built in the 1830s by his ancestor Sir Robert Johnson Eden and probably designed by IGNATIUS BONOMI, to Durham County Council in 1958.

EDEN, WILLIAM, 1st LORD AUCKLAND (1744–1814)

William Eden, who played an important part in British public life in the last quarter of the eighteenth century, was the third son of Sir Robert Eden, Bt of Windlestone Hall and his wife, Mary Davison of Beamish. In the early years of his life he showed considerable academic promise, at Eton College and then at Oxford University, graduating with a BA in 1765 and an MA in 1768. He then trained as a lawyer and was called to the Bar in 1769. His academic ability was revealed three years later with the publication of a scholarly book, *Principles of Penal Law.*

In 1774, however, he entered political life. From 1774 until 1793 he was successively MP for Woodstock (Oxfordshire) and Heytesbury (Wiltshire). Throughout, his main interest was economics, being a strong believer in the benefits that would accrue from freeing trade from inhibiting controls, fiscal or otherwise. In the early years of his career he was attached to Frederick Howard, 8th Earl of Carlisle, whom he accompanied to America in 1778 and then to Ireland as Chief Secretary, when Carlisle was Viceroy between 1780 and 1782. During these years he sat in the Irish parliament as MP for Dungannon and he was responsible for setting up the Bank of Ireland on lines similar to those of the Bank of England.

On his return to Britain, he became closely allied with William Pitt the Younger, who became Prime Minister in 1784. Pitt's urgent problem on taking office was finance. The total income of the government was about £18 million, of which half was needed to service the national debt, largely as the result of the American War of Independence (1775–83), which had cost £100 million. Pitt's solution had two dimensions. One was the reduction of government expenditure by reforming departments and cutting out waste. The second was to raise more revenue through taxation. This could be (and was) done painfully by imposing new taxes, but also less painfully by increasing trade, which would automatically increase revenue from customs duties. It was in this that Eden showed his worth, between 1785 and 1787 negotiating a free trade agreement with France and settling the disagreements between the French and English East India Companies. By the terms of the treaty, signed in 1786, customs duties on a wide range of products were greatly reduced, to the benefit of British industries, French wine producers and the Treasury.

After this, Eden continued to be used in the diplomatic field until 1793, when he retired with a pension and the title of Lord Auckland of West Auckland in the County of Durham. He died in 1814, having never really recovered from the death of his eldest son, drowned in the Thames in 1810.

EDWINE (?–633), KING OF NORTHUMBRIA 616–633

Edwine was King of Northumbria from 616 until 633. He acquired the throne through the support of Raedwald, King of East Anglia, with whom he had found refuge after his father, Aelle, King of Deira, had been killed and his kingdom annexed by Aethelfrith, King of Bernicia in 604 (see

NORTHUMBRIA, KINGDOM AND EARLDOM OF). In 616 Raedwald and Edwine ambushed and killed Aethelfrith in what is now north Nottinghamshire, allowing Edwine to regain his inheritance.

The significance of Edwine's seventeen-year reign lies in conversion from paganism to Christianity in 627. His decision to do so stemmed from his second marriage, in 625, to Aethelburh, a daughter of Aethelberht, King of Kent. Both father and daughter had been converted to Christianity by St Augustine, the leader of a mission sent by Pope Gregory I that landed in Kent in 597. As a condition of her marriage, Aethelburh was allowed to practise her religion and to have the services of Paulinus, one of Augustine's monks, who was consecrated as a bishop. It took two years of pressure and persuasion, which included letters from Pope Boniface V, before Edwine and his chief advisers were convinced that the queen's god was more powerful than theirs. But having made the decision, Edwine backed Paulinus's conversion drive, which involved a series of mass baptisms throughout Northumbria, notably one lasting thirty-six days at the royal centre at YEAVERING.

This proved to be a false start. In 633 Edwine and his eldest son, Osfrith, were killed at Hatfield near Doncaster by a military alliance of Cadwallon, King of Gwynedd (North Wales), who was British and a Christian, and the Mercian prince, Penda, who was English and pagan. Edwine's queen, Aethelburh, together with her children and Paulinus, managed to escape to safety in Kent, but the consequence of the debacle appears to have been a widespread reversion to paganism in Northumbria, Edwine's defeat and death seemingly casting doubt on the power of the Christian god. However, it proved to be a prelude to the greatest period of Northumbrian history, initiated by Edwine's successor, OSWALD.

ELSTOB, ELIZABETH (1683–1756)

Elizabeth Elstob was born in September 1683 in the parish of St Nicholas, Newcastle upon Tyne, and from an early age showed a liking and an aptitude for languages. Such academic leanings were then not generally encouraged in girls and Elizabeth's development was halted, albeit briefly, at the age of eight when her mother died and she was placed under the guardianship of her uncle. Fortunately, this was a brief interlude, for she was allowed to go to Oxford to live with her brother, William, who was a student there throughout the 1690s. With his encouragement, she appears to have mastered eight languages, including Latin.

But her principal attraction was to Anglo-Saxon, and in 1709 she published an edition, with an English translation, of a work entitled *Homily on the Birth of St Gregory*, which she dedicated to Queen Anne. By this time she would have been living in London, where, from 1702, her brother was rector of two parishes. Elizabeth's achievement was sufficiently impressive for her to secure the patronage of the Earl of Oxford, who secured from the queen the promise of financial support for an edition of the *Catholic Homilies* by the tenth-century monk and scholar, Aelfric. The importance of this book, which was basically a set of sermons written for parish priests to deliver on the major feast days of the Christian year, lies less in its theology than in the quality of its Anglo-Saxon prose. Regrettably, although completed in manuscript form, it was not published. She did, however, secure publication in 1715 for one other scholarly work: *Rudiments of Grammar for the English-Saxon Tongue*.

In that year, however, her circumstances were changed for the worse by the death of her brother, on whom she was economically dependent. Instead of the leisure to pursue her scholarship, she now had to earn her living. She did so by opening a school in Evesham. Unfortunately, although it was a success in other respects, the fees that she was able to charge were inadequate for a decent living. Friends came to her rescue with subscriptions that gave her an annuity of £20, and Queen Caroline, the wife of George I, agreed to double this by giving her £100 every five years. The queen's death in 1737, however, meant that only one donation was made. In 1738 she found financial security as governess to the children of the Duchess of Portland, in whose service she remained until her death in 1756.

ENO, JAMES CROSSLEY (1820–1915)

James Eno was born the son of a shopkeeper in Newcastle and on leaving school was apprenticed to a druggist. In 1846 he was appointed dispenser at the Infirmary, but four years later he set up on his own as a chemist and druggist in the Groat Market. It was about this time that he concocted the mixture that made his name and fortune. 'Eno's Fruit Salts', which were to become a household name and among the most widely known patent medicines of the late nineteenth and twentieth centuries, were a combination of tartaric acid, various citric acids and sodium bicarbonate, which became effervescent when added to water. Eno claimed that it alleviated biliousness, feverishness, sleeplessness, headache and stomach upsets. For about twenty years, Eno made and sold his product on a modest scale in Newcastle, but in 1876 he moved to London to commence manufacture and marketing on a commercial scale. The enterprise was a great success: when Eno died in 1915 at the age of ninety-five, he left a fortune of just over £1,600,000. In moving south, however, he did not forget his birthplace: in 1899 he promised to make up the difference between the money raised to build the Royal Victoria Infirmary in Newcastle and its total cost, which in the end came to £1,500.

ESCOMB CHURCH

Despite being small and in an out-of-the-way village close to the River Wear, Escomb church is a building of national importance, in that it is one of only a handful of complete Anglo-Saxon churches in England. When it was built cannot be determined with complete certainty, but a reasonable guess is between 690 and 730. Nor is it clear why it was built. At that date, stone churches were normally monastic, but no evidence has come to light of the necessary associated buildings. Nor was Escomb an important parish centre later in the Middle Ages. In fact, until modern times it did not have parochial status but was a chapel of ease of the parish of Auckland. One possible clue to its antiquity is its circular graveyard. Graveyards of this shape are seen as *prima facie* evidence of early, pre-Christian religious sites, adopted and adapted for Christian purposes, thereby suppressing previous pagan associations. There is no evidence to support this hypothesis, however. Perhaps the only clues are the fragments of window glass found during recent excavations, which hint at some form of association with the monastery at JARROW, built a few years earlier.

Its form is typical of pre-Conquest Northumbrian churches, being narrow and tall. Its external dimensions are 60 feet (18.3 m) in length, 19 feet 4 inches (5.9 m) in width, and 36 feet (11 m) in height. There is clear evidence that the builders brought all or much of the stone from the abandoned Roman fort at Binchester, about three miles downstream. This is particularly noticeable in the chancel arch, but is fully confirmed by a dedication stone of the VIth Legion, set upside down high up on the north nave wall. What may not be reused Roman masonry are the large quoins at the corners and the cobbles, which are thought to be original, in the north-west corner of the nave. Also probably original is the sundial on the south wall of the nave, over which is a fish-tailed serpent, the import of which has never been satisfactorily determined.

Escomb has undergone relatively little alteration, and certainly not enough to obscure its original appearance. A porch was built at the south door in the thirteenth century, possibly at the same time that the lancet windows were inserted in the south chancel and south nave walls. Happily, five of the tiny original windows have survived intact to show how little natural light could enter the church. Three new windows were also inserted in the nineteenth century at the east and west ends and in the south nave wall. There have also been some removals: at the west end there was a chamber or *porticus*, which may have been an entrance to the church; another chamber on the north side of the chancel is thought to have been a vestry. Neither was bonded into the church walls and therefore must be seen as later additions. When they were taken down is not known. Also gone is the harling of the exterior walls, which would have been limewashed and would thereby have given the building a striking and impressive appearance.

The church had a narrow escape in 1863, when it was abandoned in favour of a new church, built about half a mile to the south. It fell into decay and was in danger of demolition, but was saved by the determination of the vicar, through whose efforts it was re-roofed in the late 1870s. In 1970, however, it was the Victorian church that was demolished and the Anglo-Saxon church, fully restored in 1965, again became the parish church.

ESSOLDO CINEMAS

The Essoldo chain, comprising 196 cinemas, was the third largest in Britain. It was built up by Sol Sheckman (1891–1963), who began as a boxing promoter at St James's Hall, NEWCASTLE, and then started to acquire cinemas in 1923. When the company, which was based in Newcastle, was formed in 1931, its name was devised by combining the first letters of the names of himself and his wife and daughter: ESther, SOL, DOrothy. The Essoldo chain eventually succumbed to the popularity of bingo, its main cinema in Newcastle being sold in 1972.

EVETTS, LEONARD CHARLES (1909–1997)

Leonard Evetts was born in the Welsh town of Newport, where his father had a building business, to which he was apprenticed on leaving school at the age of fourteen. He had a natural talent for drawing, which he developed by constant practice, attending classes at Newport College of Art and winning a Berger Paints Scholarship for three months at the Royal College of Art. Two years later, at the age of nineteen, he won one of the four prestigious three-year National Scholarships at the Royal College.

In 1933, after completing his training in London, he joined the staff of the Edinburgh College of Art, where he taught drawing and calligraphy. Four years later, in 1937, he came to King's College, NEWCASTLE (since 1963 Newcastle University), where he remained, apart from war service, until he retired in 1974 as Head of the School of Design. Although he was a delicate watercolourist and had a considerable reputation for lettering – he produced a book on Roman lettering that ran to ten editions, and completed 140 commissions for such things as memorials and books of remembrance – his artistic reputation rests primarily on the quality of his work as a stained glass designer. Between 1941 and his death, he completed 240 commissions for stained glass windows, three-quarters of them in the North East. The outstanding display of his work is the forty-six windows he designed for the church of St Nicholas, Bishop Wearmouth. He also designed the window (known as *Stella Maris*) in the Galilee Chapel in DURHAM CATHEDRAL that was commissioned by the American Friends of Durham Cathedral to commemorate the 900th anniversary of the laying of the foundation stone. He contributed three windows to Newcastle Anglican Cathedral, notably the Ascension Window, and the designs for three altar frontals.

FALKNER, JOHN MEADE (1858–1932)

John Meade Falkner was a man who lived two parallel but equally successful lives, as an industrialist and as a poet and novelist. He was the son of a clergyman, who moved from Fleet, near Weymouth in Dorset, to Wearmouth. He was educated at Marlborough College and Hertford College, Oxford, graduating in 1882. Early in the following year, he took a job as tutor to John Noble, the son of SIR ANDREW NOBLE, the effective head of the great armaments firm of WILLIAM ARMSTRONG at Elswick. From that seemingly unlikely position he became secretary, then director and finally in 1899 chairman of the company. In that same year he married Evelyn Adey and bought the Divinity House, close to DURHAM CATHEDRAL (of which he became Honorary Librarian), where he lived until his death in 1932.

It was Durham that was the setting for his other life. His education had given him a passionate interest in the Middle Ages, which his increasing wealth enabled him to indulge. He purchased a large number of medieval manuscripts and other artefacts, which were auctioned at Sotheby's after his death. He also paid for the statues at either side of the high altar and reredos and stone screen around the Lady Chapel in the church at Burford in Oxfordshire, to which he had become very attached while a student, and in which his ashes are buried.

But Falkner is best remembered as the author of the classic and still widely read adventure novel *Moonfleet*, a tale of smuggling set in his native Dorset. His other novels, *The Lost Stradivarius* and *The Nebuly Coat*, have been largely forgotten, as has his *History of Oxfordshire*.

FARNE ISLANDS

There are twenty-eight islands in the Farne group at low tide, dropping to fifteen at high tide. Geologically they are outcrops of the WHIN SILL and lie two to three miles off the Northumberland coast. Most important by far is that known as Inner Farne. Large enough to support life, it was made famous by ST CUTHBERT, who spent much of his later life there as a hermit. In later centuries it remained a possession of the Community of St Cuthbert and thus of DURHAM CATHEDRAL Priory. As a result, it attracted a number of men who wished to emulate St Cuthbert, the most notable of whom was ST BARTHOLOMEW. Over fifty years later in 1246, the Cathedral Priory guaranteed permanent religious occupation by establishing a cell there for two monks. This was to last until the Cathedral Priory was dissolved in 1539.

The consequence of this was the buildings that are still extant. One is a chapel dedicated to St Cuthbert. Most of its fabric dates from *c.*1370, but there is evidence of twelfth- or thirteenth-century masonry in the lower stages of its walls. The chapel was restored in the mid-nineteenth century and supplied with seventeenth-century furniture from Durham Cathedral. Also extant are the foundations of another chapel, dedicated to St Mary. The need for two places of worship on a tiny island seems incongruous and is not readily explained. One possibility may be that it is a distant echo of the very earliest days of Christianity when monasteries frequently had more than one church.

Near the two chapels is a two-storey BORDER TOWER, attributed to Prior Thomas Castell (1494–1519), although there is evidence of fabric of an earlier period. Its purpose may have been to provide defensible living quarters for the monks, similar to the several vicars' peles that are to be found in Northumberland. The only other building on the island is the LIGHTHOUSE, erected in 1809 for Trinity House, Newcastle.

Apart from Inner Farne, there are only three other islands of significance to humans: Longstone, where the lighthouse made famous by GRACE DARLING was built in 1826 and later enlarged; Brownsman, on which a lighthouse was built in 1810, but abandoned when the Longstone Light was built; and Staple Island, where a beacon was erected in the eighteenth century but destroyed in 1783 (see LIGHTHOUSES).

After the Reformation the ownership of the Farnes remained with the new Dean and Chapter of Durham Cathedral, until they were bought by Charles Thorp, Archdeacon of Durham, who was responsible for the restoration and refurnishing of St Cuthbert's Chapel. In 1925 the Farne Islands were sold to the National Trust by LORD ARMSTRONG. Inner Farne and Staple Island are among the most important sanctuaries in Britain for breeding seabirds and are used by twenty different species, including Razorbills, Guillemots, Puffins, Arctic Terns, Sandwich Terns, Shags, Kittiwakes, Fulmars and Eider Ducks, known as Cuddy's Ducks, because of their association with St Cuthbert.

FENTIMANS

For the first two-thirds of the twentieth century, Fentimans was famous in the North East for ginger beer. The business had its origin in a loan made by Thomas Fentiman on the security of a recipe for botanically brewed ginger beer. Since the debt was never repaid, Fentiman became owner of the recipe. The process involved fermentation of the product in the bottle for a week, which gave it a very low alcoholic content. The ginger beer was made in a factory in King Street, Gateshead and sold door-to-door in large stone bottles, known as Grey Hens, which customers returned when empty. From the 1930s every bottle carried as a logo a picture of the head of an Alsatian dog. This was in fact Fentiman's own dog 'Fearless', which was twice the winner of the Cruft's obedience test. The original factory in King Street, which is a listed building, still bears a mosaic of Fearless.

Unable to withstand the competition of the expanding supermarket chains, the business closed in the 1960s. In 1988, however, it was revived by Thomas Fentiman's great-great-grandson, Eldon Robson. It markets, and not only in the North East, Victorian Lemonade, Mandarin and Seville Orange Jigger, Curiosity Cola, Dandelion and Burdock, and Shandy, as well as Traditional Ginger Beer. The recipes of all the drinks accord with the original recipes, namely, a combination of herbs, natural flavourings, sugar, brewer's yeast and spring water, which are fermented for seven days in wooden vats. The only updating is mild carbonation, necessary to replace the carbon dioxide lost through pasteurisation required by current health regulations.

FENWICK, COLONEL GEORGE (1603–1657)

George Fenwick was a member of the Fenwick family that acquired and made their home in BRINKBURN PRIORY following its closure in 1537. He was educated at Queen's College, Cambridge and Gray's Inn, London, where he qualified for the Bar in 1631.

His first achievement was in America. Between 1636 and 1645 he was a leading figure in the founding and ruling of the small colonies that eventually coalesced as the State of Connecticut and also in formulating the articles of confederation of the United Colonies of New England. His time in the New World ended with the death of his first wife, Alice, in 1645.

At the time of his return to England, the country was in the throes of the Civil Wars. Almost immediately he joined the Parliamentary army and in the following five years displayed the military competence that led to his appointment as Governor of

BERWICK in 1649. It was in this office that he was responsible for the building of the present parish church of Holy Trinity. A new church had been badly needed. For about a century, ever since the demolition of the original parish church of St Mary, which lay outside the Elizabethan ramparts, Berwick had been forced to make do with a small and increasingly dilapidated chapel dedicated to the Trinity. This was demolished to make way for the new church. The new Holy Trinity has been described as 'of quite exceptional architectural interest', particularly as it is one of the very few churches in Britain built from scratch in the seventeenth century. The building was completed between 1650 and 1652 to the design and under the supervision of a London mason, John Young. In style it combined Gothic and Classical elements, akin to the work of JOHN COSIN and his contemporaries. It was given a more Classical appearance during the 'restoration' carried out in 1855.

George Fenwick's involvement with Berwick included his election as its MP in 1655 and 1656, although as the result of a quarrel with Oliver Cromwell, he was denied his seat on the latter occasion.

If Fenwick's involvement with Berwick was significantly philanthropic, his interest in SUNDERLAND was not. Like so many civil war victors, he was concerned that their triumph should yield material gains. His great success was to purchase in 1649 for £2,851 9s. 6d. the town of Sunderland, that is, the rights formerly enjoyed by the bishops of DURHAM, whose diocese had been abolished in 1646 and its property 'nationalised'. Three years later, in 1652, he purchased a third of the Monkwearmouth estate on the north bank of the river opposite Sunderland from the widow of a convicted Royalist. Fenwick died in 1657, leaving no male heir and so his estate was divided between his daughters. He therefore did not live to see the loss of Sunderland to the restored Diocese of Durham in 1660. But the Monkwearmouth investment was retained by his younger daughter, Dorothy, who married a Nottinghamshire man, Sir Thomas Williamson of Great Markham. Over time the family came to possess the entire Monkwearmouth estate.

FENWICK, JOHN JAMES (1846–1905)

John James Fenwick was a grocer's son, born and raised in the North Riding town of Richmond, who moved to Middlesbrough in 1861 to begin a seven-year apprenticeship as a draper. On completion in 1868, he moved to NEWCASTLE and secured posts as a shop assistant, first with Moses and Brown in Blackett Street and shortly afterwards with Charles Bragg, a silk mercer, in Pilgrim Street. He rose to be its manager, but in 1882 he was dismissed for running a private business as an insurance agent on the side. He retaliated by bringing an action for wrongful dismissal against Bragg, which he won, and secured damages of £1,000. This windfall helped him to open his own shop in Northumberland Street, then largely an upper middle-class residential area. Over the years he acquired more houses in the street, each of which he turned into a separate shop. He also opened a shop in SUNDERLAND in 1888 and in London, in New Bond Street, in 1891. In 1897 his firm became Fenwick Ltd. Following this he demolished several of his houses in Northumberland Street and built a large store on the site, modelled on Bon Marché in Paris. In doing this, he moved away from the individual shop towards the department store. Fenwick's success was due to a number of factors, among them assiduous attention to customers, while forbidding his staff to accost them while they browsed, a determination to attract the wealthiest clients and a growing reputation as a designer of fashionable clothes.

Today, Fenwicks is still based in Newcastle and remains a family firm. It no longer has a branch in Sunderland but has branches in Canterbury, York, Leicester, Tunbridge Wells, Brent Cross Retail Complex and Bond Street in London and Windsor.

FINCHALE PRIORY

Finchale, one of the nine cells (distant branches) created by DURHAM CATHEDRAL Priory, came into being in contentious and protracted circumstances arising from the death in 1170 of ST GODRIC. As soon as Godric's death was known, the Cathedral Priory sent two of its members to occupy the hermitage, claiming that Godric had bequeathed it to them. The Cathedral Priory's motive, apart from a wish to acquire more property, was to prevent a rival cult beyond their control developing on their doorstep. The anxiety of the monks may have been heightened by the awareness that Godric's benign attitude to women might attract female pilgrims alienated by the widespread belief that Cuthbert was a misogynist.

However, they were thwarted by the bishop, HUGH OF LE PUISET, who, although willing to allow Durham monks to occupy the hermitage, was not prepared to concede ownership, since it was on his land and through his generosity that Godric had been allowed to settle there. It was not until twenty years later that, late in life, the bishop finally gave the monks what they wanted.

But at around the same time an even bigger threat appeared in the person of Bishop Hugh's son, Henry, who in the early 1190s attempted to found at Haswell a cell of the Augustinian Canons of Guisborough. This location proving uncongenial, Henry secured from his father as an alternative site 120 acres (48 ha) of wasteland at Baxterwood, a sheltered spot on the banks of the River Browney between DURHAM and BEARPARK. To counter this new threat, the monks used all their persuasive powers, threatening Henry with the dire anger of ST CUTHBERT, to persuade him to back down. They were successful: shortly after his father's death, Henry handed over to the Cathedral Priory all the endowment he had accumulated for the Guisborough cell, which the monks used to endow the cell they created at Finchale.

The monks could not afford to dismiss St Godric, and so they erected their new church around the chapel Godric had built and dedicated to St John the Baptist, which when demolished left St Godric's tomb close to the high altar. The cell was occupied and served by ten monks sent from Durham under the headship of a prior. In fact, to be Prior of Finchale was one of the most prestigious offices to which a Durham monk could aspire. The Black Death reduced the size of the Cathedral Priory and consequently the number of monks sent to its cells had to be reduced. Finchale's complement was normally four plus a prior, to which could be added a few short-term residents on retreat.

Finchale Priory was closed in 1538 under the act to suppress smaller monastic houses. Thereafter buildings gradually fell into decay until the early twentieth century, when they were taken into the guardianship of the Office of Works, the forerunner of English Heritage.

FINCHALE TRAINING COLLEGE

Finchale College is one of only four similar institutions in the country, whose role is 'to meet the needs of those hardest to help' and for whom other sources of help may not be appropriate or fully adequate. The others are St Loy's at Exeter, Queen Elizabeth's at Leatherhead and Portland at Mansfield. Its premises were not in origin purpose-built but began life as a 'road house', opened in

1934 by a local consortium and called the 'Finchale Abbey Hotel'. This development was based upon an expectation that the road by which it stood was to be upgraded to carry the rising volume of A1 traffic. This did not materialise and in consequence the 'road house' proved a business failure and was closed a few years later. As a vacant property of some size, it was considered by the Durham Orthopaedic Association, which was looking for premises to house a training facility for the disabled. In the end, however, the Association opted to go elsewhere and the hotel remained unoccupied until the middle of World War II.

Then, in 1943, it was opened as a facility for the rehabilitation of men in the armed forces disabled in the war. Shortly after the end of the war, it was finally taken over by the Durham Orthopaedic Association and named the Sir John Priestman Hospital for the Disabled, in recognition of the substantial grant made by the trust set up by Sir John Priestman. New residential accommodation was added in 1947. Subsequently, the name of the institution was changed, first to Finchale Abbey Training Centre and then to Finchale Training College. At present the College has at any one time about 250 students, about 125 of whom are resident. In the course of a year, about 400 students pass through the College. Although roughly 60 per cent of students come from the north of England, the College is not rigidly regional and admits men and women on a suitability basis from all parts of the UK. Operational costs are met by government, but the College is a registered charity and as such raises its own funding for building and other purposes.

Over the years since 1943, its role has evolved. Although started to cater for men disabled by the war, this problem inevitably faded away and increasingly students were men seriously injured in the heavy industries that then dominated the North-East economy. As these declined, and as British society has become more complex, unstable and fast-moving, the problems with which the College has to deal have come to include those of mental stress and personal inadequacy exacerbated by poor social conditions and inadequate qualifications, as well as those of physical injury. Because of this, the College has developed links with the prison and probation services. Perhaps its most fundamental change has been the recognition that disability was not an exclusively male problem, which led to the College becoming mixed in the 1960s.

Evolution has also been driven by changes and advances in technology and by the requirements of the law and the needs of employers. At the outset, courses were offered in Gardening, Watch and Clock Repair, Typewriting Mechanics, Boot and Shoe Making and Repair, Carpentry, and Storekeeping. While courses on the whole range of building maintenance skills are still offered, Gardening has developed into Horticulture, Computer Technology and Electrical Engineering have replaced the technology of watches, typewriting mechanics and boot/shoe making have been replaced, and courses on Office Administration and Accountancy are now available. Attention is also given to the basic literacy, numeracy and computer skills now essential in so many areas of employment and an 'outreach' programme has been initiated to provide help to people in their own areas who lack the confidence at present to travel to Durham.

FISHER, ANN (1719–1778)

Ann Fisher continued to work under her maiden name, although in 1751 she married Thomas Slack, a Newcastle publisher and owner of the *Newcastle Chronicle*. She was born at Oldscale in the Cumberland

(Cumbria) parish of Lorton, where her father was a farmer. In the light of her later achievement, he must have seen that she received a very sound education. Education was, in fact, her lifelong interest. In 1746 she started a school, which gave her the necessary experience of teaching on which to base her clearly held views, which would not be out of place today. These first appeared in *A New Grammar: Being the Most Easy Guide to Speaking and Writing the English Language Properly and Correctly*, which first appeared in 1745 and had gone through thirty editions by 1800. Subsequent publications, all popular, were *The Pleasing Instructor* (1756), *The New English Tutor* (1763), *A New English Exercise Book* (1770) and *An Accurate New Spelling Dictionary* (1773). However modern her ideas of how children best may learn were, she was adamant that they should master correct grammar, syntax and spelling. Her achievement is the more remarkable in that she also amply discharged her wifely duty, having nine children (all daughters) and giving her husband a great deal of help in his business. In all, she appears to have exemplified the feminist ideal.

On Thomas Slack's death in 1784, the business passed to Ann's daughter Sarah, who in the following year married Solomon Hodgson, THOMAS BEWICK's publisher.

FLAMBARD, RANNULF (?–1128)

Rannulf Flambard was Bishop of Durham from 1099 until his death in 1128 (see DURHAM CATHEDRAL). He was in many ways a sharp contrast to his predecessor, WILLIAM OF ST CALAIS, who was a monk and an ecclesiastical reformer. Flambard was neither. He had made his reputation as a financial expert who had helped William II to make money, not least by defrauding the church. His arrival in Durham must have filled the monks of the cathedral with considerable apprehension. Up to a point, their fears were justified in that Flambard did remove certain properties from them, only restoring them on his deathbed. However, it would be risky to accept the monastic version at face value, since there may have been genuine uncertainty as to the ownership of these properties.

In the North East, however, Flambard should be remembered not for his financial chicanery or his differences with his chapter, but for his work in creating DURHAM CITY as we know it. He certainly pushed on with the construction of the cathedral, work on which had flagged in the three years between St Calais's death in January 1096 and Flambard's arrival. At the time of his death, the cathedral was close to completion. He also strengthened Durham's defences by building a stone wall around the rim of the Peninsula. Of more fundamental importance was his decision to remove the inhabitants from the area between the castle and the cathedral. In so doing, he created the open square known as Palace Green. Those dispossessed were settled north of the castle around what is now the present Market Place. Flambard also built Framwellgate Bridge over the River Wear. This enabled a new road towards the royal castle of Newcastle to be created and a start to be made on colonising the huge stretch of moorland between DURHAM and CHESTER LE STREET. He also founded Kepier Hospital (see MEDIEVAL HOSPITALS) and the borough of St Giles, with the unfortunate effect of barring Durham's eastward development. Apart from the construction of Elvet Bridge by BISHOP HUGH OF LE PUISET in the later twelfth century, which facilitated the development of the Elvet area, after Flambard's death there was no major change in the morphology of Durham City until the nineteenth century.

FLODDEN, BATTLE OF, 1513

The Battle of Flodden, fought on 9 September 1513, was the last major battle of the long Anglo-Scottish conflict to take place on English soil, and it was the bloodiest and most disastrous for Scotland. At the end of the day, the King of Scots, James IV, lay dead, together with his natural son, Alexander, Archbishop of St Andrews and Chancellor of Scotland. Also killed were the earls of Argyll, Bothwell, Caithness, Cassillis, Crawford, Erroll, Lennox, Montrose and Rothes; the Bishop of the Isles and the abbots of Inchaffray and Kilwinning; and fourteen lords and numerous knights and esquires. It is no exaggeration to say that almost every family in the Scottish political nation lost at least one member. And the losses of rank and file were equally huge: in all, probably 8,000 of them died that day. There is a statue in Selkirk of a man named Fletcher holding the flag of Sir Christopher Savage of Macclesfield, which his company had captured. It would seem to celebrate a triumph. In fact, Fletcher was the only member of the town's contingent, which numbered eighty, to return alive. And the Scottish losses were not only human: the very large train of artillery that James had painstakingly built up at great expense was transferred to the arsenal of the English king.

The explanation of this calamitous event is to be found in the international politics of the day. The young Henry VIII of England, in contrast to his cautious father, was anxious to win fame and glory on the battlefield. To this end, he joined an alliance put together by the pope (consequently known as the Holy Alliance) directed against France. In the hope of emulating his ancestor Henry V and winning another Agincourt, he invaded France with a large army at the end of June 1513. His expedition did not have the desired outcome. In return for great outlay, Henry won one skirmish when the French ran away so fast that it was derisively dubbed the Battle of the Spurs, and captured the towns of Thérouanne and Tournai.

Invaded by England, the French invoked their 'auld alliance' with Scotland. James IV willingly complied, hoping that by inflicting a decisive defeat on an English army he would bring a weakened English government to the negotiating table and to secure the return of BERWICK, the last Scottish town still in English hands. The English government was fully aware that an invasion through the 'back door' was likely and so Thomas Howard, Earl of Surrey remained in England with a commission to raise forces in the north to oppose any Scottish invasion.

The Scottish army crossed into England on 22 August. Within six days James's siege cannon had battered the great fortress of NORHAM into surrender, and shortly afterwards the other Tweedside castle at Wark and the smaller inland fortresses at Etal and Ford were subdued. Having achieved a major success in destroying England's first line of defence, James deliberately chose not to advance further south. Instead, he elected to await Surrey's arrival with the intention of forcing what he hoped would be a decisive battle. To give himself the best chance of victory, he established his army in a camp on top of Flodden Edge. From this position he could not only see his enemy approaching but would force him into launching a frontal attack up a steep slope against his well-prepared defences. Meanwhile, Surrey at his headquarters at Pontefract in Yorkshire was preparing to act as soon as he learned of the Scots offensive. Once he had this news, he set off north, reaching his mustering point, Bolton, near ALNWICK, on 4 September.

It did not take long for Surrey to become aware of the strength of the Scottish position. To attempt a frontal assault on the

Scottish camp would be suicidal and he was not prepared to play the role James IV had written for him. Instead of heading straight for the Scottish camp via Wooler, he took a more easterly route so as to use the cover of the high ground of Doddington and Barmoor moors to hide his movements. He then crossed the River Till by means of the bridge at Twizel and Heaton Mill Ford, which brought him behind the Scots and between them and their homeland. James had been outflanked and it was now he who had to react to his opponent's actions. Rapidly, he had to break camp and reposition his forces on the brow of Branxton Edge.

With the English between the Scots and their homeland, battle was now unavoidable. Although forced into changing his ground, James probably had the larger force and the potential advantage of more modern weaponry. His artillery train was among the most advanced in Europe and his troops were equipped with the latest weapon, the pike, an eighteen-foot spear whose effectiveness in battle had been convincingly demonstrated by the Swiss. But beneath these apparent advantages lay concealed weaknesses. To be effective, the pike had to be used in tightly linked formations. The Scots, however, had not had sufficient training to ensure the necessary degree of cohesion in all circumstances. And the artillery, while up-to-date, was essentially for siege work. In contrast, the English guns were smaller but built for action in the field, while their infantry was armed with either the longbow or the bill, a much shorter weapon (only eight feet in length) but with a point, a hook and a blade: it was altogether a more versatile and wieldy weapon than the pike.

The outcome of the battle was determined by two factors. The first was the accuracy of the English artillery, which put the Scottish guns out of action and then began to cut holes in the ranks of their infantry. This forced James to abandon the upper ground and to order an advance down the hill so as to get to grips with the enemy. Here the second factor came into play, the marshy ground at the foot of the hill, exacerbated by the recent wet weather. This disrupted still further the cohesion of the Scottish ranks and gave the advantage to the English billmen. The battle, which started around four in the afternoon, lasted about four hours and ended with the king and his nobles dead and those who could escaping across the Tweed and into Scotland.

The Battle of Flodden achieved no immediate or obvious political result. But it deeply scarred the Scottish psyche: for the next ninety years, until the regnal union, the Scottish political class remained reluctant to risk a full-scale invasion of northern England; in the late eighteenth century, Jean Elliot of Minto would pen the haunting poem 'The Flowers of the Forest', a lament for the desolation of the Scottish Borders in the days that followed the catastrophe; and in 1910 a granite memorial cross was erected on the site by the Berwickshire Naturalists' Club, which is still the focus of an annual remembrance ceremony.

FOOTBALL

The North East has long had a reputation for being passionate about football and has a tradition of producing outstanding players. Its clubs, however, have only intermittently lived up to the hopes and expectations of their supporters. The two dominant clubs have been Newcastle United and Sunderland, with Middlesbrough a close third.

Newcastle United FC: Newcastle United came into existence in 1892, when two rival clubs in the city, Newcastle West End and Newcastle East End, merged to become Newcastle United. At that moment the former was virtually defunct, but a balance of pride was maintained by the new club moving to West End's ground, which was renamed St James's Park, and retaining West End's colours, black and white stripes, hence the nickname 'Magpies'. The union was accompanied by the decision to become a professional club and to apply for admission to the Football League, founded in 1888. Successful application led to Newcastle United entering Division II of the League in 1893. Six years later, in 1899, they won promotion to Division I. From then until the outbreak of World War I, United were one of the most successful clubs in the Football League, thanks in no small measure to their ability to attract talented players from the Scottish League. In those years they were League Champions in 1905, 1907 and 1909 and won the FA Cup in 1910. This run of success continued in the inter-war years, until the mid-1930s. The League Championship came to Tyneside again in 1927 and the FA Cup in 1924 and 1932.

But in 1934, for the first time, the club was relegated to Division II, and from this date until the present time the club's fortunes have fluctuated. United remained in Division II for fourteen years until 1948, although for five of those seasons League football was in abeyance because of World War II. Promotion was followed by another period of success, notably in the FA Cup, which United won in 1951, 1952 and 1955. This period was short-lived, and between 1961 and 1965 the club had another spell in Division II. Their return to Division I led to another round of success: FA Cup finalists in 1974 and 1976 and winners of two European Competitions, the Inter-Cities Fairs Cup in 1969 and the Anglo-Italian Cup in 1973. Between the late 1970s and the early 1990s, the club was again in trouble: they were relegated to Division II in 1978 and 1989, with a record of poor management, sale of the best players and declining attendances, although they did regain Division I in 1984.

Rescue came in 1992 in the person of Sir John Hall, who acquired control of the club, sorted out its financial problems, and oversaw the rebuilding of St James's Park following the resolution of long-running differences with the City Council that in 1971 had threatened to take the club to a new ground at Gosforth. The new St James's Park, which is capable of seating 56,000 people, is now a prominent feature of the Newcastle skyline. Newcastle also secured entry to the Premiership when it broke away from the Football League in 1993 and has maintained its presence there. But success otherwise has proved elusive, amounting to no more than second place in the Premiership in 1996 and beaten FA Cup finalists in 1998 and 1999.

Sunderland AFC: Overall, Sunderland AFC has not enjoyed quite as much success as its great Tyneside rival. It is, however, the older club, having been founded in 1879 as Sunderland and District Teachers' Association Football Club. It remained a closed club for only two years: in 1881 the club became open to non-teachers and changed its name to the one it has had ever since. The club became professional and joined the Football League in 1890, and in 1898 it moved to Roker Park (which it bought in 1908 and enlarged in 1912, 1925, 1929 and 1936), the ground it was to occupy for ninety-nine years. In these early years Sunderland enjoyed great success in the League, winning the championship on five occasions: 1892, 1893, 1895, 1902 and 1913, although for many years it had no success in the FA Cup, the closest it came being beaten finalists in 1913. This finally came in 1937, the year after it won the League Championship for the sixth time. Unlike its great Tyneside rival, Sunderland retained its place in Division I until after World War II.

Until 1945 Sunderland was arguably marginably more successful than Newcastle United. Since that date, however, this has not been the case. Although they were not relegated to Division II until 1958, this experience was repeated in 1970, 1985, 1991 and 1997. Worse occurred in 1987, when it was relegated to Division III, although it won immediate return to Division II the following season. Apart from securing promotion to Division I in 1964, 1976, 1980, 1990 and 1999, its greatest triumph was winning the FA Cup in 1973, the first non-Division I side to do so for forty years. Since the inception of the Premiership in 1992/93, it has been promoted to it twice but relegated from it three times.

Unlike Newcastle United, which has never moved from St James's Park, Sunderland moved from Roker Park in 1997, which by that date had a crowd limit of 32,000. Their new home was a brand-new stadium, the Stadium of Light, with a capacity of 41,000, built on the site of Monkwearmouth Colliery. At the same time it also adopted the nickname of the Black Cats, which stems from the gun battery set up at the mouth of the Wear in 1805.

Middlesbrough FC: The North East's third major League club is Middlesbrough. It was founded in 1876, but remained an amateur club until 1899. During that time it won the Northern League championship in 1894, 1895 and 1897 and the English Amateur Cup in 1895 and 1898. These performances encouraged the club to turn professional and to join Division II of the Football League. The decision was justified by early success: promotion to Division I was achieved in 1902; in 1903 the club acquired Ayresome Park, which was to be its home for ninety-two years; and in 1905 it was wealthy enough to buy Alf Common from Sunderland for £1,000, the first four-figure transfer fee. Since 1945, however, Middlesbrough's progress has stuttered. It was relegated to Division II in 1954 and remained there until 1974, and similar relegations occurred in 1982, 1989 and 1993. The ultimate indignity was relegation to Division III in 1986, although promotion back to Division II was gained in the following season. Moreover, the club has never won the League or Premiership titles or the FA Cup, its only major success coming in 2003, when it won the Carling Cup. It has, however, managed to maintain membership of the Premiership since 1995. In that year, like Sunderland, the club moved into a brand-new ground built on a former industrial site: the Riverside Stadium, with a capacity of 32,000, occupies what was the Middlesbrough docks.

Smaller League Clubs: At the present time the region has two clubs in what is now called the Coca Cola League, formerly the Football League, Darlington and Hartlepool United, of which **Darlington** is the older. Formed in 1883 by the amalgamation of several other amateur clubs, in 1889 it was a founder member of the Northern League, which it won in 1896 and 1900. In 1908 the club turned professional and joined the North East League, finishing top in 1913. In 1921, shortly after the end of World War I, when the Football League expanded by adding two third divisions, North and South, Darlington joined Division III North as one of its founder members. It remained a member of that division, except for two seasons in Division II between 1922 and 1924, until 1958/59, when Division III North and Division III South were replaced by Division III and Division IV. In consequence, Darlington found itself in Division IV.

Since then it has enjoyed varied fortunes. In 1966, 1985 and 1991 it won promotion to Division III, but on all three occasions it was relegated after one or two seasons. In contrast, as the result of finishing bottom of Divison IV, it was forced to apply for re-election to the League on five occasions in the 1970s. Worse followed in the 1980s. In 1987 it was relegated from Division III and two years later it was relegated to the Conference (by that date the club finishing bottom of Division IV was automatically replaced by the club that finished top of the Conference League, which was recognised as the senior non-League division). Darlington's time in the wilderness lasted for only one year: in 1990 it regained League status and in 1991 won promotion to Division III, only to be relegated back to Division IV the following season.

As well as mixed fortunes on the field, the club was in financial difficulties for much of the 1980s and 1990s, on one occasion almost going into liquidation. In 1996, however, it was rescued by George Reynolds, a local (and later disgraced) businessman, who was responsible for it moving from Feethams, its home ground since its foundation, to a new stadium in Neasham Road. It is currently in Division III of the Coca Cola League.

The story of the **Hartlepool** club is broadly similar to that of Darlington. It was founded in the 1880s and joined the Northern League shortly after its foundation in 1889. It too became a professional club in 1908 and took over the Victoria Ground, which is still its home ground, although in 1995 it was renamed the Victoria Stadium. Like Darlington, it joined the Football League Division III North when it was set up in 1921, as Hartlepools AFC. It remained in that League until 1958/59, when the two third divisions, North and South, were replaced by Division III and Division IV. Hartlepools, like Darlington, found itself in the lower of the two divisions, where it remained until 1968, when it was promoted to Division III. Its stay there lasted only one season. In 1977 it changed its name to Hartlepool United FC, and in 1985 it replaced the 'temporary' grandstand which was erected after the original stand was destroyed in a Zeppelin raid in 1916. Like Darlington, it experienced almost fatal financial problems, from which it was rescued in 1993 by a local businessman, Harold Hornsby. Two years later, he sold the club to an Aberdeen firm, Increased Oil Recovery. Their financial support resulted in the complete rebuilding of the stadium between 1999 and 2001 and enabled the club to win promotion to Division II of the Coca Cola League in 2003.

In addition, three other clubs within the region were briefly members of the Football League. **Durham City** was a founder member of the League's Division III in 1921, but it survived only until the end of the 1927/28 season. **Gateshead**, however, had a longer run. It came into being as the result of the financial difficulties of another founding member of Division III, South Shields. As a result of these problems, the South Shields club moved to Gateshead's Redheugh Stadium in 1930 and became Gateshead FC. Its time in the League, in Division III, and after 1958 in Division IV, came to an end in 1960, when, having finished in last place, it was forced to apply for re-election. It was unsuccessful, the League deciding to admit Peterborough United in its place. Since leaving the League, both Durham and Gateshead have continued to exist in various non-League leagues.

Amateur Clubs: In addition to clubs in the professional Football League and its successors, the region maintained a strong showing in the amateur game, until the distinction was discontinued in 1974. This was principally through the Northern League, formed in 1889. The prowess of its teams was made evident by their success in the FA Amateur Cup. This was competed for between 1893 and 1974, the final being guaranteed to fill Wembley Stadium. In the years between 1950 and 1969 the Northern League was particularly dominant, with its clubs winning the trophy on ten occasions and beaten finalists on two others. The most successful clubs were Crook Town with four wins and Bishop Auckland with three. The other clubs to win the cup were Willington and North Shields. For the 1974/75 season a new trophy was introduced to replace the Amateur Cup, the FA Trophy. Sad to say, North-East non-League clubs have not enjoyed the same success.

Berwick Rangers: This club does not belong in any of the above categories in that, although based in England, it plays in the Scottish League. Curiously, this arrangement, which began with the club's admission to the Scottish League in 1955, reflects BERWICK's position as a Scottish town that became English. The explanation is that from its foundation in 1881 (or 1884), the club played in Scottish leagues, from 1905 the Scottish Border League. On top of this is that its distance from its potential opponents in England makes it economically unrealistic for it to be in the English League. An additional irony is that its present ground, Shieldfield Park, which it has occupied since 1954, is on the south side of the Tweed on land that was never in Scotland. Because of small attendances, it has never advanced beyond the lower divisions of the Scottish League and it has experienced periods of acute financial difficulty. The most momentous and memorable moment in its history was its 1–0 defeat of Glasgow Rangers in the 1967 Scottish Cup, a game watched by a record crowd of over 13,000.

FORMAN, JOSEPH (see **SMYTHE, REGINALD**)

FORSTER, SIR JOHN (1515–1602)

Sir John Forster was arguably the last great English Borderer, and an object lesson on how a man from a relatively modest beginning could, given ability, energy and the right circumstances, achieve his ambition, which in his case was to replace the PERCY FAMILY as the dominant power in Northumberland and on the Border. His starting point was not propitious: the second son of Sir Thomas Forster of Adderstone, near Bamburgh, a long-established but not very wealthy family of Northumbrian gentry. The circumstances of his early life, however, favoured his ambition. Through personal bravery and military ability, he played a prominent part in what was called by the Scots the 'Rough Wooing', the military attempt during the 1540s by the English government to force their Scottish counterpart to agree to the marriage of Henry VIII's heir (who in 1547 became Edward VI) and Mary, the infant daughter of James V and, since his death in 1542, Queen of Scots. During these years, the Percy family was in disgrace on account of their participation in the uprising against Henry VIII's religious reforms known as the PILGRIMAGE OF GRACE.

Forster's success had two aspects. One was the acquisition of land from two sources. The first was the estates land that came on to the market through the closure of the religious houses in the late 1530s: Forster acquired lands that had belonged to Alnwick Abbey and Hexham Priory, and those in BAMBURGH of the Dominican Friary and of the Yorkshire Abbey of Nostell, to which the parish church had belonged from the twelfth century until its closure in 1538. The other was the estates forfeited by participants in the unsuccessful RISING OF THE NORTHERN EARLS against Elizabeth I in 1569, to which he could lay some claim, since he was largely responsible for ensuring the loyalty of Northumberland.

Forster's other success was in securing and holding on to public office, which also brought income as well as conferring power. His public career began in 1556 with his appointment as Deputy Warden of the Middle March, and he used his time in office to create an entrenched position so that he was able to withstand the attempt of Henry Percy, 7th Earl of Northumberland, who was restored to his estates and to the Wardenship by Mary I, to oust him. Not long after the accession of Elizabeth I in 1558, Percy was again removed and in 1560 Forster became Warden of the Middle March, a post he was to retain until 1596, except for a brief interlude in 1587–88. Two years later he became Justice of the Peace, and more importantly, Custos Rotulorum, that is, the head of the Bench. He was also made a member of the Council of the North, which sat in York and was in effect the regional government of northern England, and he served on numerous government commissions and on six occasions on embassies to the Scottish court.

His success and the means by which he achieved it, which were at times unscrupulous, meant that he made enemies. The most persistent was the Earl of Huntingdon, the President of the Council of the North, who worked through another Northumbrian squire, Sir Cuthbert Collingwood of Eslington. It was their persistent criticism that led to Forster's being briefly removed from office in 1587. Of the criticisms levelled against him, four were particularly serious. One was that he was responsible for what was called the 'decay of the Borders', that is, the decline in the number of men sufficiently armed to discharge their obligation to defend the Border. There is no doubt as to the fact: between the 1550s and 1590s the number of effective light horsemen had halved. The reason for this, however, had little to do with Forster's stewardship. There was probably more truth in the claims that he neglected his duties and that he was partial in his justice. Most serious, however, was that he colluded with the Scots, that is, committed March Treason. This too was true, but in his defence it can be argued that, with the military power at his disposal declining, Forster knew that negotiation would achieve more than military action. His reappointment in 1588 was an acknowledgement that there was no adequate alternative to him.

There is no doubt that Forster was a grasping, devious and unscrupulous character. In religion he was a contradiction: he appears to have been a convinced Protestant at a time when among the Northumbrian gentry to show Catholic sympathies might have been more advantageous. On the other hand, his personal morals were far from those of the prevailing Puritan ideal: he had several mistresses by whom he had at least five illegitimate children, although to his credit he did his best by them.

Forster's career ended in 1596 with his final removal from office, by which time he was too old and infirm to discharge his duties properly. He died in 1602 at the very advanced age of eighty-seven. How much his estates were worth is not known, but the fact that £454 was lavished on his funeral, and that his goods were valued at over £1,000, demonstrates the success with which he had pursued the acquisition of wealth. However, his irregular marital performance meant that he failed to produce a legitimate heir.

FORSTER, JOHN (1812–1876)

John Forster, who was one of the most influential figures in the world of literature in the middle decades of the nineteenth century, was born in Newcastle, the son of a butcher and cattle dealer. Although his parents were not wealthy enough to afford him a good education, a rich uncle paid for him to attend the Royal Grammar School in the town, where he prospered and became head boy. In 1828 he went to Jesus College, Cambridge, but left after a month to study law in London. Although he qualified and eventually was called to the Bar in 1843, he never practised as a barrister. His legal training, however, helped him secure the secretaryship of the Lunacy Commission (the government body responsible for lunatic asylums) in 1855 and membership of that commission between 1861 and 1871.

But Forster is to be remembered for his contribution to literature, not as a writer but as a promoter of the work of others. This he was able to do through his journalism, notably with *The Examiner*, where he was drama and literary critic from 1833 until 1855 and also editor from 1847. His favourable reviews of their work did much to further the careers of such writers as Alfred, Lord Tennyson, ELIZABETH GASKELL and Walter Savage Landor, which he also promoted by using his social and business contacts to introduce writers to publishers. He was, in effect, their literary agent, driven by a strong desire to see writers and actors awarded the high status considered to be their due.

His most important 'protégé' was Charles Dickens, to whom he was friend and adviser from 1837 until Dickens's death in 1870, representing him in negotiations, proof-reading his work, persuading him to excise matters he thought would injure his reputation, and generally helping to widen the range of Dickens's social and political acquaintance. The two men were not alike (for example, Forster disliked Dickens's reading tours) and as Dickens grew in fame and Forster moved from journalism to government service, the two men became less close, although to the end Dickens continued to consult Forster on all matters of importance.

Forster was himself a writer, who published some mediocre poetry and several works of history and biography. But his major contribution was his monumental *Life Of Charles Dickens*, written between 1872 and 1874, still consulted by students of the novelist's work. Forster himself might have been better known had his widow and later his literary executor not destroyed so many of his papers. Fortunately, they did not touch his library and his collection of Dickens's manuscripts, which he bequeathed to the Victoria and Albert Museum.

FOSTER, ALFRED JAMES (1864–1959)

Alfred Foster was the son of James Foster, founder and managing partner of Foster, Blackett and Wilson, paint manufacturers in Newcastle. After education at Rugby School, he joined the family firm and took over its management following his father's death. In 1890 he converted the partnership into a private limited company and diversified into the manufacture of both red and white lead and lead sheets and pipes. Between 1911 and 1915 he became prominent on the national stage through his election to the chairmanships of the White Lead Convention, the Red Lead Convention and the UK Lead Manufacturers' Association. The purpose of these organisations was to control the output and prices of lead carbonate, lead oxide and sheet and pipe lead. Given these roles, it was natural that he should have been chosen to head the UK delegations that helped to set up an international cartel and to become president of the consequent International Convention. To have become so prominent in what were in effect the politics of the lead industry almost certainly owed something to his role as Assistant Controller in the Ministry of Munitions during World War I. The International Convention did not survive the outbreak of World War II, but Foster remained Chairman of the UK Convention until 1946.

FOSTER, JOSEPH (1844–1905)

Joseph Foster was born at Bishopwearmouth, Sunderland, the son of a prosperous draper. His uncle was the artist MILES BIRKET FOSTER. After private education, he moved to London to embark on a career as a printer. His real interest, however, was genealogy, to which he devoted most of his life, to his financial detriment. He was one of a number of men (the most famous being Sir Bernard Burke of *Burke's Peerage*) committed to producing authoritative family trees of the titled members of British society. Foster's contribution, published in 1879, was *Peerage, Baronetage and Knightage.* It was written in collaboration with Edward Bellasis, who held the office of Bluemantle Pursuivant (one of the nine third-rank officers of the College of Heralds) and was essentially an improved and corrected version of the work of Edward Lodge, published in 1866. Foster also published detailed studies of the PEASE FAMILY and BACKHOUSE FAMILY and evidence of the region's gentry families derived from the records of the late sixteenth- and seventeenth-century Visitations by the Norroy King of Arms (the Herald responsible for England north of the Trent) to determine whether those claiming coats of arms were entitled to them.

Foster was equally active in producing accurate transcripts, annotated for publication, of institutional membership lists. The most important of these were the eight volumes (1887 and 1891) of *Alumni Oxonienses*, members of Oxford University from 1500 until 1886, for which the University conferred on him the degree of MA. Other similar publications were *Members of Parliament, Scotland 1357–1859* (1882), *Register of Admissions to Gray's Inn 1557–1886* (1889) and *Alphabetical Lists of Ecclesiastical Dignitaries in England and Wales since the Reformation* (1890).

Although Foster lived, died and was buried in London, a memorial to him was erected in Bishopwearmouth churchyard.

FOSTER, MILES BIRKET (1825–1899)

Miles Birket Foster was one of the most popular British artists of the nineteenth century. He was born in North Shields, but except for the first five years of his life he lived in and around London, following his family's move south in 1830. He was educated as a draughtsman at schools in London and Hitchin, after which he was apprenticed to an engraver. In the ten years following the end of his apprenticeship in 1846, he earned his living as an illustrator, although his ambition was to be a landscape artist in watercolours. It was not until the early 1860s that he was able to realise this ambition, partly as the result of a growing reputation, but also through the financial security provided by a substantial inheritance. Perhaps as the result of his early training as an engraver, most of his work was on a small scale and finely executed.

FROSTERLEY 'MARBLE'

The stone known as Frosterley marble, quarried in Weardale, has been used in DURHAM CATHEDRAL and other churches within the region. It is not, however, a marble but a limestone formed 325 million years ago during the Carboniferous period through the hardening by compression of the ooze on the bed of a shallow sea, in which fossil corals, *dibunophyllum bipartitum*, had become buried. The stone is dark grey in colour and the fossil corals almost white with fine markings. It has proved ideal for use in situations where a highly polished stone is required.

FURNESS, CHRISTOPHER, LORD FURNESS OF GRANTLEY (1852–1912)

Christopher Furness was one of the most dynamic and successful businessmen of the late nineteenth and early twentieth centuries. He was the son of John Furness, a West Hartlepool provisions merchant, and his wife, Averill Wilson of Nesbit Hall. He was educated at a school in West Hartlepool (see NEW TOWNS OF THE NINETEENTH CENTURY) and then joined the family firm. In 1872, having proved his ability, particularly by his performance as the firm's buyer in Sweden, he was made a partner, and in the same year married Jane Suggett of Brierton. As the firm expanded the scope of its trade, it began to hire its own ships, and this led in 1882, following the death of their father, to the division of the firm between Furness and his brother. Thomas Furness continued to operate as a provisions merchant, but Christopher concentrated on shipping. Rapidly he acquired liners and tramp steamers and in 1891 amalgamated with another West Hartlepool firm, the shipbuilders Edward Withy & Co., becoming, Furness, Withy & Co. with a capital of £700,000. Thereafter, his fleet grew rapidly: by 1914, it had over one million gross tons of shipping.

He also expanded laterally, acquiring control in 1898 and 1899 of the Moor Steel and Iron Works, the Stockton Malleable Iron Works, the West Hartlepool Steel and Iron Co., and the Weardale Steel and Iron Co., which were merged to become the South Durham Steel Co. (see IRON AND STEEL INDUSTRY). The acquisition of the last named gave him control of eight collieries: Thornley, Wheatley Hill, Tudhoe, Croxdale, Black Prince (at Tow Law), West Thornley, Hedley Hill and Middridge. Five years later he linked his firm with the Cargo Fleet Iron Co., which gave him access to the south bank of the Tees, and in 1910 he bought Palmer's Shipbuilding and Iron Co. of JARROW.

Like many other successful businessmen, Furness entered politics, holding the seat at Hartlepool as a Liberal MP between 1891 and 1895 and between 1900 and 1911, when he was raised to the peerage. And also like other successful businessmen, he became a country landowner with an estate extending to 30,000 acres (12,000 ha). When he died, his estate was valued at £1 million.

GASKELL, MRS ELIZABETH (1810–1865)

Born Elizabeth Cleghorn Stevenson in Chelsea in 1810, Elizabeth Gaskell was the daughter of William Stevenson, a Berwick man, formerly a Royal Navy captain and then employed as Keeper of the Records at the Treasury. In 1832 she married William Gaskell, a Unitarian minister in Manchester, and it was as Mrs Gaskell that she published her writings. She is best known for her novels *Mary Barton* (1848), *Cranford* (1851–53) and *North and South* (1854–55).

She had, however, a brief experience with NEWCASTLE and Tyneside, which she subsequently used in two of her novels. In the winter months of 1829 and 1830, following her father's death, she lived in Newcastle at the home (13 Cumberland Terrace) of the Reverend William Turner, the minister of the Unitarian chapel in Hanover Square. He was one of the town's leading intellectuals, who kept a school with a considerable reputation and was one of the prime movers in the foundation in 1793 of the LITERARY AND PHILOSOPHICAL SOCIETY OF NEWCASTLE UPON TYNE.

The earlier novel, *Ruth*, published in 1858, she called 'my Newcastle novel'. Its central theme is the fate of a seduced woman (a daring subject at that time) and it is set in 'Eccleston', which some believe can be identified as Newcastle. This is probably incorrect: the name Eccleston is taken from a village near Chester, and it is portrayed as a more industrial town than Newcastle then was. The Newcastle link is more likely to be the characters of the Reverend Thurston Benson and his sister, Faith, who rescue Ruth, the 'fallen' woman, and are clearly based upon William Turner and his daughter, Ann, of whom Elizabeth was very fond. When the cholera epidemic swept through Newcastle in the early months of 1831, Elizabeth and Ann Turner were packed off to Edinburgh, but Turner stayed in Newcastle to help with the relief of suffering in the town. Newcastle and Tyneside are more clearly identifiable in a later novel, *Sylvia's Lovers*, published in 1863. Here Elizabeth reveals her fascination with the Northumbrian dialect and accent, which was spoken by Charlie Kinraid, the object of the heroine, Sylvia Robson's, desires; Kinraid is the chief harpooner on a whaler, sailing out of 'Monkshaven', a fairly obvious reference to Tynemouth.

GATESHEAD

The origins of Gateshead are obscure. There is just enough evidence to prove the existence of a community at the south end of Pons Aelius, Hadrian's bridge across the Tyne, although what it was called is not known. Thereafter, there is silence, until BEDE, writing *c.*730 mentions a certain Utta, Abbot of Gateshead in 653, showing that Gateshead already existed under its current name and that in the earliest days of Northumbrian Christianity it was an important ecclesiastical site. Following this, again there is silence until 1080, when Gateshead became the scene of a notorious murder. In May of that year, a meeting was arranged in the church at Gateshead between the Bishop of Durham, Walcher, and his entourage, and members of the Northumbrian ruling class. Walcher had been made Bishop of Durham in 1072 and Earl of Northumbria in 1076 by William the Conqueror. Despite his high offices, his power base was very narrow, consisting of little more than the garrison of Norman troops in Durham Castle. It is clear that Walcher's men's abuse of power drove the natives to revolt. The meeting at Gateshead, Walcher assumed, was to be a conference to resolve problems. The Northumbrians, however, were intent on a bloodier solution. Because the church was holy ground, they could not enter and drag Walcher out. They therefore set fire to the building (which would have been of wood) to force Walcher and his companions to leave. As they did so, they were cut down. The immediate consequence of this act was that Northumbria was severely ravaged and a castle built on the north bank of the Tyne, opposite Gateshead.

From this time on Gateshead was to be overshadowed by the royal borough that grew rapidly next to the royal castle across the river. Not that Gateshead was neglected: the bishops of Durham had a manor house and hunting ground there, and in the 1160s BISHOP HUGH OF LE PUISET established his own borough, comprising Hillgate, Oakwellgate and Bottle Bank and he allowed the development of another urban nucleus along Pipewellgate. But the bishops were not resident and had many other concerns and so they carved up most of the territory of Gateshead into estates, granting them to people other than their burgesses. The largest of these estates were Redheugh, Saltwellside, Field House and the lands of St Edmund's Hospital, which became the Shipcote Estate after the Reformation.

NEWCASTLE, on the other hand, was not an absentee, and as its ruling elite grew in power and wealth, one of their main aims was to secure complete control over the bridge and of all commercial activity on both sides of the river. In the main, the bishops were able to thwart Newcastle's intrusive acts and so preserve their 'liberty', including control of the southern third of the river and the bridge, the limits of their jurisdiction being marked by the Cuthbert Stones. Even so, in 1454 the Mayor and Burgesses of Newcastle were granted conservatorship of the entire river, a role they were to have until the mid-nineteenth century.

As the Newcastle Corporation saw it, the ideal solution was for Newcastle to annex Gateshead. And this they succeeded in doing by an act of parliament in 1553, at a time when the Catholic Bishop of Durham, CUTHBERT TUNSTALL, had been suspended by the Protestant government of Edward VI and was thereby unable to defend his 'liberty'. Newcastle's victory was short-lived: with the death of Edward VI later in the year and the accession of his Catholic half-sister, Mary, Bishop Tunstall was reinstated and secured by another act of parliament the restoration of his ownership of Gateshead. But the status quo was not fully restored, since in 1555 Tunstall was persuaded to lease the Saltwellmeadows and the tolls of Gateshead to the Corporation of Newcastle for 450 years. The land involved lay immediately east of the end of the bridge and comprised 34 acres (14 ha), which mysteriously grew to 95 acres (38 ha).

But the Newcastle Corporation was nothing if not determined, and in 1576, during the episcopal vacancy at Durham following the death of Bishop James Pilkington, they introduced another bill in parliament to annex Gateshead. Although it failed to pass, victory of sorts was achieved, albeit by an indirect route. In 1577 Elizabeth I forced the incoming Bishop of Durham, Richard Barnes, to hand over to her the lordship of the manors of Gateshead and Whickham with their huge reserves of coal. She did not retain them, but leased them to a southerner, Thomas Sutton, the Master of the Ordnance at Berwick, initially in 1577 for seventy-seven years, but shortly afterwards in 1583 for ninety-nine years. He intended to use his control to force his way into the Newcastle merchant oligarchy. They were having no truck with a 'foreigner', whom they were able to thwart through their control of the Tyne. Eventually Sutton gave up the fight and transferred what had come to be known as the Grand Lease to two leading members of the Newcastle Merchant Adventurers Company, Henry Anderson and William Selby. They were supposedly acting on behalf of a larger consortium, but they attempted to secure exclusive ownership, even though most of the money to secure the lease had come from the borough's funds. In 1599, however, they were forced to concede, and the Grand Lease came into the hands of a wider, but nonetheless exclusive, group of Newcastle merchants.

Gateshead, however, managed to survive this subordination. In 1679 BISHOP NATHANIEL, LORD CREWE recovered the lordship, although rather than exercise it directly, in 1684 he leased it for an annual rent. This arrangement continued until Bishop Charles Longley surrendered it to the Ecclesiastical Commission in 1857, which held it until its abolition in 1924. Gateshead's independence was confirmed by the nineteenth-century reforms. In 1832 it became a parliamentary borough with one MP, and in 1835, as a result of the Municipal Reform Act, a municipal borough. In 1889 it became a county borough, and in 1974, as a result of the radical reordering of local government structures, one of the five metropolitan districts that made up the new metropolitan county of Tyne and Wear. The metropolitan district was much larger than the county borough it replaced in that it included, in addition to Gateshead county borough, the urban districts of Blaydon, Felling, Ryton and Whickham, and Birtley, previously in Stanley urban district. In 1986 metropolitan county councils were abolished, leaving Gateshead as a unitary authority.

These advances reflected the growth of the town's population, which rose from under 9,000 in 1801 to about 120,000 on the eve of World War I, through industrial expansion. Notable were coal mining, revived by the growing technical ability to reach lower seams, and iron making, especially the firms of Hawks, Crawshay (1757–1889) and John Abbott (1835–1909). The Greenesfield Works of the North East Railway Co. was a major locomotive manufacturer from 1852 until 1909, when it was moved to DARLINGTON. Chemicals too were of huge importance, notably ALLHUSENS, in its heyday the world's largest chemical factory, and the Friar's Goose Works. Other important industries included glass (Sowerby's), ropes (Hood Haggie and R.S. Newell) and pottery. Some of the largest of these enterprises were located on the Saltmeadows site from which Gateshead drew a paltry income until it was recovered from Newcastle control in the 1930s. The dates quoted show that almost all the industries that developed in the eighteenth and nineteenth centuries were dead or moribund by the time of World War I, the notable exception being the engineering firm of Clarke, Chapman, founded in 1864. As a consequence, Gateshead became a depressed town, recovery from which was to begin with the creation of the TEAM VALLEY TRADING ESTATE in 1936.

Gateshead has, to mix metaphors, been an ugly duckling, forced to play second fiddle to Newcastle. Yet despite all its larger neighbour's efforts, it has managed to retain its independence and in recent years has upstaged its rival with such notable cultural icons as the ANGEL OF THE NORTH, the Baltic Arts Centre (see ART GALLERIES), the Millennium Bridge (see BRIDGES) and THE SAGE GATESHEAD, as well as, in METROCENTRE, one of Europe's largest out-of-town shopping centres. These, however, should not obscure the enduring Little Theatre, situated near Saltwell Park and built between 1939 and 1943, the only theatre to be built in Britain during World War II. Its purpose was and is to be the home of the Progressive Players, a theatre group founded by three sisters, Hope, Ruth and Sylvia Dodds, in 1919. It continues to flourish, putting on ten plays every year to almost full houses. Gateshead is also prominent in the Jewish world as the home of Britain's largest Yeshiva (College of Talmudic Studies), founded in 1929.

GEORDIE

The term 'Geordie' is frequently applied loosely by outsiders to the inhabitants of the North East and to their distinctive ways of speech, which are clearly different from those of adjacent regions. Within the North East, however, the term has a geographically more restricted application: 'Geordies' and 'Geordie' are and belong to Tyneside. The earliest known use of the term is in the early eighteenth century and probably relates to the fact that Newcastle remained loyal to George I during the JACOBITE UPRISING OF 1715. Since then, however, it has also been applied at various times to describe pitmen, colliers and golden guinea coins.

GILPIN, BERNARD (c.1510–1583)

Thanks to hagiographical accounts of his life written in the seventeenth and nineteenth centuries, Bernard Gilpin has acquired a reputation as the 'Apostle of the North', a reputation not entirely warranted. Born into a Westmorland (Cumbria) gentry family, he was educated at Oxford University and then embarked upon a clerical career under the patronage of CUTHBERT TUNSTALL, Bishop of Durham, to whom he was related. Unlike Tunstall, he gradually moved in a Protestant direction, both in doctrine and in the matter of the need for the church to raise its standard of personnel and performance. Having studied abroad in the early 1550s, he settled in DURHAM in 1556 as Archdeacon of Durham, attached to which office was the rich Rectory of EASINGTON. The following year he became also Rector of Houghton le Spring, another very valuable living. As a result, he was guilty of 'pluralism' (holding more than one benefice with cure of souls), an offence he had publicly condemned. To his credit, in 1560, after Tunstall's death, he lived up to his professed beliefs and resigned the Archdeaconry, retaining only the parish of Houghton.

He remained Rector of Houghton for the rest of his life, declining offers of the Provostship of The Queen's College, Oxford and the Bishopric of Carlisle. His decision did not involve financial hardship, since Houghton was one of the largest parishes in the diocese and yielded a very substantial income. He discharged his duties as rector meticulously and conscientiously, employing a sufficient number of able and well-qualified curates to meet the spiritual needs of his parishioners and his obligation to provide for the material needs of the poor. And, in conjunction with John Heath, a wealthy Londoner who bought the estate of Kepier Hospital (see MEDIEVAL HOSPITALS) when it was dissolved in 1547, he founded Kepier Grammar School at Houghton. Its purpose was to educate boys, who could then go to Oxford and after graduation become effective parish priests. In this, he recognised the urgent need of the church for many more well-qualified and conscientious priests like himself. This devotion to Houghton has led to the belief that he was in some way responsible for the annual 'Houghton Feast', which still takes place at the end of September. However, it is more likely that this event pre-dates Gilpin's time and that it was held on or near the feast day of the patron saint of Houghton church, St Michael (29 September), to raise money for the maintenance of the fabric of the nave.

But what earned Gilpin his 'title' were his annual preaching tours through TYNEDALE and REDESDALE. This was the heyday of the BORDER REIVERS, when strangers entering these dales were at some risk. Provision of religious services was almost nil, since most of the beneficed clergy were non-resident and neglectful of their duties. In consequence, the changes in doctrine and religious observance imposed by the government of the new queen, Elizabeth I, to which Gilpin was fully committed, were largely ignored. Gilpin had the backing of his bishop, Richard Barnes (1577–87), who also, on Gilpin's urging, eradicated the corruption in his own administration. However, although commendable, Gilpin's tours had limited success: they could not be an adequate substitute for well-qualified and committed resident parish clergy.

GILROY, JOHN THOMAS YOUNG (1898–1985)

John Gilroy was born in Newcastle, the son of a painter, John William Gilroy. He was trained, initially by his father, then either side of World War I at Armstrong College in Newcastle, the Royal College of Art in London, and finally by means of a travelling scholarship in France and Italy. This long apprenticeship was the basis of an outstandingly successful career, but in two very different spheres. For thirty-five years from 1928 he worked for an advertising agency, for which he produced the famous and popular Guinness adverts; and during World War II, he contributed to the war effort by designing posters such as those urging us to *Dig for Victory* and warning us that *Careless Talk Costs Lives*. But he had equal success as a portrait painter. He painted the leading members of the Royal Family: the Queen, the Queen Mother, Princess Anne and Princess Margaret and the Prince of Wales; and many other equally famous subjects, including Pope John XXIII, Winston Churchill and Lord Mountbatten.

GODRIC, SAINT (c.1066–1170)

Godric is a relatively minor saint, but one with an unusual history, the detail of whose life was recorded shortly after his death by his friend Reginald, a monk of DURHAM CATHEDRAL Priory. He was born probably in Norfolk and probably in the mid-1060s. From early manhood until the first decade of the twelfth century, he led a secular life notable for its lack of permanence. He made his living as a merchant, which took him around the North Sea and the Baltic, but in between commercial voyages he made three visits to Rome, one to the shrine of St James at Compostela in Castile and one to the Holy Land, where he may have been the English 'pirate' (the term may not then have had such a sinister meaning), 'Gudric', who ferried the King of Jerusalem from Asuf to Jaffa.

Clearly, his visits to holy places would seem to indicate a spiritual side to Godric's nature that sits rather oddly with his maritime activity. It was the spiritual urge that eventually overcame his wanderlust, although not entirely in the first instance. In 1104 he renounced the sea and became a hermit near Carlisle, but soon moved to Wolsingham in County Durham to share a cell with an older hermit. When his companion died in 1106, Godric made a second journey to Jerusalem, settling briefly at Whitby on his return. Then in 1112 he came to Durham, where BISHOP RANNULF FLAMBARD gave him permission to settle in the bend of the Wear three and a half miles downriver from Durham on what was then a huge tract of undeveloped moorland.

There he built a church, dedicated to St Mary, and basic living accommodation a short distance downstream from the later FINCHALE PRIORY. Some time around 1150 he added a second church dedicated to St John the Baptist following a lucky escape from drowning in a flood. He lived there for the rest of his life, initially with his mother, brother and sister. Following their deaths, he continued to live as a hermit, practising the most rigorous forms of asceticism. He also acquired a reputation in the North East as a guide and adviser in a wide range of spiritual and personal relationship matters and consequently his help was sought by a wide variety of troubled people. At first he did not welcome these intrusions, but slowly he came to accept his role within the community. When he died on 21 May 1170, he was almost certainly over 100 years old. He was buried in St John's Church.

GOOCH, SIR DANIEL, Bt (1816–1889)

Daniel Gooch, one of the most influential British industrialists of the nineteenth century, was born in Bedlington. His father, John Gooch, was the bookkeeper at the Bedlington Ironworks and his mother was the daughter of Michael Longridge, the manager and later owner of the firm. Between 1831 and 1837 he trained as an engineer at the Forth Street Works of ROBERT STEPHENSON at Newcastle. His talent and competence were such that Isambard Brunel appointed him locomotive superintendent of the Great Western Railway a week before his twenty-first birthday.

Over the next forty years he was responsible for three major engineering and financial successes. One was the creation and development of the GWR's works at Swindon, opened in 1843. Gooch was responsible for the planning, tooling and management structure of the new enterprise and in the years that followed, he developed the Swindon works to the point where it could supply almost all the GWR's requirements in locomotives, rolling stock and rails, thus realising Brunel's 'in-house' procurement policy. In doing so, he introduced such important concepts as standardised design and interchangeable parts.

He also rescued the GWR from the financial crisis resulting from the over-ambitious policies of its chairman Richard Potter. In 1864 Gooch resigned over the board's criticism of aspects of his management of the Swindon works. His absence was brief. With the GWR on the verge of bankruptcy, he was invited to return in 1865, not to his former post but as Potter's replacement as chairman of the board. His rigorous financial measures brought the GWR back into profitability by 1872 and established it as perhaps the most famous and one of the most successful railway companies in Britain.

Gooch was also responsible for creating between 1860 and 1866 the transatlantic telegraph link, a project that required both his engineering skills and business acumen. Essential to its success was his membership of the boards of the three companies, the Great Eastern Steamship Co., the Telegraph Construction and Maintenance Co. and the Anglo-American Telegraph Co.; and overseeing the repair and fitting out as a cable layer of Brunel's monster ship, *Great Eastern*, badly damaged by a boiler explosion in 1859. The success of this project earned him a baronetcy.

Like many successful businessmen, Gooch established himself as a landowner, with an estate in Berkshire, and secured election to parliament. He was MP for Cricklade (in which his railway town of New Swindon was situated) from 1865 until 1885, although unlike many of his kind he was a Conservative, not a Liberal. In line with his political affliliation, he was a staunch member of the Church of England and a firm opponent of trade unions.

Gooch's younger brother, Thomas (1808–82), was also involved with the development of the railways, assisting Robert Stephenson with the London–Birmingham Railway and GEORGE STEPHENSON with the Manchester–Leeds Railway. His career was cut short by the breakdown in his health in 1847 and after a brief recovery he retired in 1851.

GRAINGER, RICHARD (1797–1861)

Arguably, more than any other individual, Richard Grainger was responsible for the present appearance of central NEWCASTLE, the area now designated 'Grainger Town'. His origins were humble, the youngest of six children of Thomas Grainger, a quayside porter. After an elementary education at St Anthony's Charity School, in 1809 he began an apprenticeship as a carpenter, which lasted until 1816. He then set up as a jobbing builder with his brother, George, but through his connection with the Methodist church, he attracted the attention of William Batson of Higham Dykes, near Ponteland, who recognising his potential, commissioned him to build the houses in Higham Place, Newcastle, some of which still stand. On the successful completion of this contract, Grainger married Rachel Arundale, the daughter of Joseph Arundale, a wealthy Newcastle tanner. It is likely that Grainger owed his introduction to the Arundales to Batson, who clearly saw his protégé as a man likely to go far. Rachel brought with her a dowry of £5,000, which helped Grainger to finance the building of several prestigious projects during the late 1820s and early 1830s: Blackett Street; Eldon Square (1825–31), tragically demolished in the 1960s; the Royal Arcade (1829–31), also demolished in the 1960s; Leazes Terrace and Leazes Crescent (1829–34). The virtue of these developments was not solely due to the quality of Grainger's workmanship, but also to the designs of the architects he employed, THOMAS OLIVER for Leazes Terrace and Crescent and the houses in Blackett Street, and JOHN DOBSON for the Royal Arcade and Eldon Square. By 1833 Grainger's achievements were sufficient to merit a public dinner in his honour.

But his successes to date proved to be preliminaries to a greater achievement, the creation of a new town centre. The opportunity was presented by the death of Major George Anderson in 1831, which brought on to the market Anderson Place and the Nuns Field, virtually open spaces void of buildings between Pilgrim Street and Newgate Street. Grainger, who recognised the potential for redevelopment on a grand scale, paid over £50,000 to secure these properties and others close by. His plans were approved by the Town Council, and between 1834 and 1839 nine new streets, centred on Grey Street (known until 1836 as Upper Dean Street), were built. Thanks to the memoir written by his daughter, Margaret Jane Dobson, it used to be thought that John Dobson was the architect of all the buildings in these streets. This was not so. In addition to Dobson, the services of JOHN AND BENJAMIN GREEN, George Walker and John Wardle were extensively used.

The most innovative element in the development, opened in 1835, still known as the Grainger Market, comprised a quadrilateral of buildings between Grainger Street and Clayton Street, and between Nun Street and Nelson Street. The space thereby enclosed, over 80,000 square feet (740 m^2) in area, was roofed to create a covered market, the first of its kind. It still discharges its original function, although the present aisles with individual booths replaced the earlier division into two parts, one for meat, the other for vegetables.

Grainger's monumental achievement would not have reached fruition had it not been for the Town Clerk, JOHN CLAYTON. His contribution was twofold. He was responsible for persuading the Town Council to approve Grainger's daring and ambitious plan. Following this, his influence persuaded a large number of wealthy individuals and the Northumberland and Durham District Bank to advance over £100,000 on the security of mortgages to finance building operations: for many lenders Clayton's reputation for probity and financial and legal sagacity was sufficient guarantee.

Grainger's basic business plan was to buy the land, build houses and other buildings on it, using capital raised on mortgage, and then to lease the properties, repaying the loans out of the accruing income. In 1841, following the completion of the central Newcastle development, he bought the Elswick estate from John Hodgson Hinde for the sum of £114,000, with the intention of developing it on an equally large scale. In doing so, however, he over stretched himself and was saved from bankruptcy only by the loyalty and financial acuity of Clayton. One aspect of his salvation was the sale of parts of the Elswick estate, notably the land bordering the Tyne, to William Armstrong, on which Armstrong built his great armament works. Despite this, when Grainger died in 1861, he had an estate worth just short of £17,000 but debts of over £128,000. In the end, however, his business plan paid off: by the end of the century, when all debts had been cleared (largely thanks to Clayton's financial skill), the Grainger Estate was worth £1.2 million.

GRAND ALLIES (see GREAT NORTHERN COALFIELD)

GRAY, SIR WILLIAM (1825–1898)

William Gray was probably the most successful of the North East's many shipbuilders (see Shipbuilding Industry), which is all the more surprising in that neither his family nor his own original business was in any way connected with the sea. He was born at Earsdon, near Blyth, where his father had a successful drapery business, which he joined after an education at Dr Bruce's Academy in Newcastle. However, on completing his apprenticeship, he moved south in 1844 and set up his own drapery business in the newly founded town of West Hartlepool (see New Towns of the Nineteenth Century). Four years later, in 1849, he became more closely acquainted with the sea through his marriage to the daughter of a Royal Navy captain.

His involvement with shipbuilding did not begin until 1863, when he entered into an informal partnership with a Hartlepool shipbuilder, William Denton, whereby the profits were to be divided 55–45 per cent in Denton's favour. However, as Denton's health declined (he died in 1872), Gray gradually took control of the business. In the twenty-six years between then and his own death in 1898, Gray created one of the UK's and the world's leading shipyards: four times, in 1878, 1882, 1888 and 1898, Gray's yard launched more tonnage than any other shipyard in the world. Not only did Gray build ships, he also supplied them with their engines from his Central Marine Engineering Works, opened in 1884. His success was founded on quality. His tramp steamers were innovatively designed, very well built and very economical to run, the last factor owing much to his pioneering of the quadruple expansion engine. He also formed a close association with Marcus Samuel, founder of Shell Petroleum, for whom he built much of his tanker fleet. Gray's shrewdness in business also extended to the shipping business: he owned twelve cargo ships outright and had a financial interest in seventy others.

GRAY OF HEATON, SIR THOMAS (?–1369)

Sir Thomas Gray (or Grey) was a member of the long-standing north Northumberland family which prospered through engagement in royal service in the wars against France and Scotland. Gray's military career began in the late 1330s and he is known to have fought at the BATTLE OF NEVILLE'S CROSS in 1346 and to have been with Edward III's son, Edward, the Black Prince, in France in the late 1350s. In this he was indistinguishable from many other members of the landowning gentry and nobility. What has given him his place in history is the book he wrote, entitled *Scalachronica*. The second part of the title is self-explanatory, but the first part refers to a *scala* or scaling ladder, which was the emblem above his family's crest. He began to compose it in 1355–56 while a captive in Edinburgh Castle pending his ransom. Following many known models, he began his account with the Creation and eventually took it up to the year 1362. Only one copy exists, and that is defective in that the folios covering the years 1341–55 have disappeared, although something of what they contained is known through an abstract made in the sixteenth century by the antiquarian John Leland.

Scalachronica is important as the earliest history written by a member of the English ruling classes, revealing that, although primarily military men, they were by no means lacking in education. It is in French, at that time still the language of the upper strata of English society; had it been written a generation later it is likely that it would have been in English. More important, as recent research has shown, is the valuable information it furnishes about most of the notable incidents in the Anglo-Scottish war of which he had first-hand knowledge, and also about the attitudes and ambitions of the men of the Marches (see MARCHES OF ENGLAND TOWARDS SCOTLAND), for whom war and its attendant brutalities were an accepted and acceptable fact of life.

GRAYSTANES, ROBERT (c.1290–1334)

Robert Graystanes was briefly Bishop of Durham. He was probably born around 1290 and appears to have been from the family that owned Morton Tinmouth in South-West Durham. Some time between 1300 and 1310 he became a monk of DURHAM CATHEDRAL Priory. Academically able, he spent much of his time at the Priory's cell at Oxford (see OXFORD UNIVERSITY COLLEGES), for which he is known to have acquired at least nine books, seven of which survive. By 1332, however, he had come back to Durham to be the Priory's Sub-Prior and in July of the following year he was made Prior of Coldingham (Berwickshire), the Priory's wealthiest cell. Had it not been for what followed, it is likely that he would have in due course been elected Prior of Durham.

In October of the same year, however, he returned to Durham, again to be Sub-Prior. The urgent reason was the death of the Bishop of Durham, Lewis de Beaumont. The monks in their role as cathedral chapter immediately exercised their canonical right to choose the new bishop, and on 15 October they elected Graystanes. The matter then proceeded in correct legal fashion: his election was confirmed by Durham's ecclesiastical superior, the Archbishop of York, William Melton, who consecrated him in the chapel of the archiepiscopal palace on 14 November; and on 18 November he was installed in Durham Cathedral. All that remained was for Edward III to restore to him the episcopal temporalities (secular properties), which, also in proper fashion, had been taken into the hands of the Crown immediately following the death of his predecessor. But this Edward refused to do, claiming that the pope, John XXII, had already 'provided' (appointed on his own authority), at royal request, RICHARD DE BURY. The matter was settled by the arrival in England of the papal bull of provision, which, conveniently, was dated 14 October, the day before Graystanes's election. Graystanes chose not to contest the matter. Within a year he was dead.

Graystanes may have been one of the monks who compiled the chronicle kept in the Priory, in which was recorded matters, local and national, considered to be of importance to its welfare and which is now a valuable source of information about the North East. Graystanes, it has been claimed, was responsible for putting together a coherent account of the years 1215 to 1334. However, there is no proof of his authorship, although, given his erudition, it is entirely conceivable.

Recently, the acquisition by the Dean and Chapter of a Bible, lost when the Priory was dissolved, that had belonged to Graystanes, in which he had inscribed his name and which he had used for his devotions and studies, has increased our contact with one of Durham's more distinguished monks.

GREAT FIRE OF TYNESIDE, 1854

The Great Fire of London of 1666 may have been more destructive, but the Great Fire of Tyneside in 1854 was pyrotechnically more spectacular. It began about midnight on 6 October 1854 in the eight-storey worsted factory of J. Wilson & Son in Hillgate, GATESHEAD. With the fire raging out of control, two hours later the building's roof collapsed and the fire spread to an adjacent bonded warehouse, from where a large quantity of sulphur flooded out and was set alight. Shortly afterwards the fire spread to another warehouse used by a number of firms to store various materials, including arsenic, copperas, naphtha, pyrites, salt, sodium nitrate and sulphur. Up to this point, the fire was a spectacular event that drew hundreds of spectators.

At 3.10 p.m., however, it became a tragedy. Around 3 p.m. two explosions were heard, but these were followed by a third massive explosion that shook nearby St Mary's Church, stopping its clock, rocked the foundations of the newly built High Level Bridge, blew out the windows of buildings in and around Grey Street, and was heard as far away as Alnwick and Hartlepool and ten miles out to sea. But the real damage was caused by the blazing debris that was flung across the Tyne, setting fire to buildings on the NEWCASTLE Quayside. By the time it had run its course, the fire had destroyed the properties in sixteen ancient chares that ran down from Akenside Hill (then Butcher Bank) and Dog Bank to the Quayside between the bottom of the Side and the Customs House.

Fifty-three people died in the conflagration, including the son of the architect JOHN DOBSON, 800 families were made homeless and sixty-four businesses were destroyed. The cause of the explosion was never conclusively explained. On the Newcastle side, the buildings we see today in the devastated area are largely the result of rebuilding after the fire, while on the opposite side of the river THE SAGE GATEHEAD stands on the site of Wilson's factory.

GREATHEAD, HENRY (1757–1816)

Henry Greathead, who has a good claim to be the inventor of the lifeboat, was born in Richmond, North Yorkshire, where his father was an exciseman. Upon his father's promotion, the family moved to SOUTH SHIELDS in 1763 when Henry was six years old. Having served an apprenticeship as a boatbuilder, he spent the years 1777–83 at sea as a carpenter's mate. These were the years of the American War of Independence, and in 1778 while in West Indian waters he was captured by an American privateer. However, he was freed as a result of a prisoner exchange and as a consequence was impressed into the Royal Navy. He spent the next five years on two sloops of war. With the end of the war in 1783, he came out of the service and two years later began his own boatbuilding business in South Shields.

What led to the development of the lifeboat was the wreck in March 1789 of a collier, the *Adventure*, at the mouth of the Tyne, with the loss of the entire crew. This event led a group of men headed by Nicholas Fairles, then the most prominent man in South Shields, to meet at the Lawe Coffee House. The upshot was advertisements in local newspapers offering a two-guinea prize for the design of a boat capable of holding twenty-four people and of negotiating heavy seas. This elicited two serious responses, by Greathead and another local boatbuilder, William Wouldhave, who offered a radical design built of tinplate and lined with cork. The Lawe House Committee did not adopt either model; instead they retained Greathead to build a boat to their specifications. This he did, but added a significant modification, a curved keel. What he produced was a boat weighing seven hundredweight that was 28 feet 6 inches (8.7 m) long, with a beam of 9 feet 6 inches (2.9 m), and 3 feet 2 inches (1.1 m) deep amidships and propelled by ten oars. There was much discussion as to the influences that produced the design, but one was almost certainly what was called the Moses Boat, with which Greathead would have become familiar in American waters, which was used as a lighter to take laden sugar barrels through heavy surf to waiting ships. He also added a belt of cork to give greater buoyancy. This also was derivative, from the 'unimmersible' boat designed and patented in 1785 by the fashionable London coachbuilder, Lionel Lukin.

Nicholas Fairles refused to acknowledge Greathead as the 'inventor of the lifeboat', and in this was to a degree justified. Greathead, however, worked assiduously to substantiate his claim. In this he was successful, getting the backing locally of the 2nd Duke of Northumberland and Sir John Swinburne of Capheaton and recognition in the form of monetary rewards totalling 250 guineas (£262.50) from the Royal Humane Society, Trinity House of London and Lloyds of London; and no less than 1,200 guineas (£1,260) from the government. Equally to the point were the thirty-one boats he built for places around the British coast from Findhorn to Ayr and the ten others built to his design, several of which were for foreign customers. Although Greathead should not be credited with being the sole inventor of the lifeboat, it was his design that proved successful, was widely adopted and was therefore the starting point for lifeboat evolution.

GREAT NORTHERN COALFIELD

For centuries the North East was synonymous with coal and coal mining: the adage 'Taking Coals to Newcastle' is still known and used wherever English is a native language. Maps of the coalfield usually show it covering the south-east quarter of Northumberland and most of central and eastern Durham north of the Tees lowlands. There are, however, extensive coal deposits under western and northern Northumberland that have been only marginally exploited. The coalfield also had depth, with up to eighteen exploitable seams, once the means of reaching them had been discovered. The history of coal mining may be said to have ended with the closure of Ellington Colliery in 2005. Some opencast extraction continues, but this is classified as civil engineering. When the industry began, however, cannot be pinpointed with equal accuracy. It probably existed in the twelfth century and there is evidence, some of it circumstantial, that it expanded considerably in the thirteenth century.

In the fourteenth century, however,

extant records provide a reasonably clear, if broad, picture of the industry. Coal was extracted across much of County Durham, for use as domestic fuel and for such industrial purposes as lime burning and salt boiling. Pits are recorded at Aldin Grange, Broom, Coxhoe, Evenwood, Felling, Ferryhill, Heworth, Lumley, Railey, Softley, Tow Law, Whickham and Winlaton; and in Northumberland at Elswick near Newcastle and around BEDLINGTON and BLYTH. More significantly, coal was exported in ships to London and to ports along the North Sea coast of Europe and the south coast of the Baltic. Production figures can only be approximate, but an annual output of around 50,000 tons seems likely, of which 20,000 tons were exported.

Moreover, most of the arrangements that characterised the industry until the mid -ineteenth century had been devised and put in place. It was established that the legal ownership of the coal belonged to the lordship of the manor. The owner of the lordship, individual or corporate, could exploit the asset directly, or lease the right to do so to another individual or partnership. If the records of the bishops of Durham and the Cathedral Priory are an accurate guide, it would seem that medieval landlords preferred the indirect method of exploitation. Extraction in many places would have been by means of a drift, that is, following an exposed seam into the side of a hill; but there is evidence of vertical shafts sunk to reach the uppermost seam, which was then exploited horizontally until the danger of roof collapse became acute. The greatest depth recorded is 36 feet. Also the means of transporting coal once it had been brought to bank were in place. The term 'wayleave' had been coined to describe the permission granted to those who mined coal by the owners of adjacent properties to allow its carriage across their land, at a price. Where coal was intended for export the destination of the routes was the 'staithes' built on the river bank (at this stage the Tyne), from which coal could be more easily loaded into KEELS, which moved it downriver to COLLIERS.

More accurate figures from the sixteenth century indicate that 45,000 tons were exported around 1510, rising to about 60,000 tons by 1570. Since some coal was also extracted for local use, total production would have been significantly greater, perhaps as much as 90,000 tons. In the next hundred years, output increased fourteenfold to over 1 million tons. Broadly, two factors account for this upsurge. One was growth of demand. Here the explanation is basically singular: in the last years of the sixteenth century and for most of the seventeenth century the population of London grew at a phenomenal rate, requiring increasing quantities of fuel for domestic and industrial purposes, a demand that could not be met from the country's wood resources. This expanding market was served mainly from pits in the parishes of GATESHEAD, Whickham and Ryton, although some came from Benwell, Elswick and Newburn on the north bank of the river and from pits around BLYTH; and it was during this period that the Wear became significant, with coal exported through SUNDERLAND from collieries at Harraton, Lambton and Lumley. By 1680, 600,000 tons were exported annually from the Tyne and 185,000 from other North-East ports, principally Sunderland. Again, to this total of nearly 800,000 tons must be added an uncertain quantity mined for local use, which almost certainly drove up the region's output to perhaps 1,250,000 tons. In all, the North East produced nearly half of all the coal mined in England in 1700. The expansion and importance of the export trade led to the distinction between 'seasale' and 'landsale' collieries, the former much larger and concerned with exports, the latter smaller and catering for local needs.

Increased output could not have been accomplished without a considerable development of extraction techniques and an increase in capital input and organisation. Little is known about techniques, but the organisational aspect is clear. The mining of coal for export from the Tyne became a monopoly of the NEWCASTLE merchant company known as the Hostmen. The term was derived from the practice of requiring the would-be purchaser to acquire his coal not from the producer but from a middleman, his 'host'. The Hostmen's Company emerged in the early sixteenth century, but it did not secure complete control of the coal trade until the end of the century. The events that led to this began in 1577, when Queen Elizabeth I forced the newly appointed Bishop of Durham, Richard Barnes (1577–87), to grant her a seventy-nine year lease of the rights to the coal in the episcopal manors of Gateshead and Whickham for the paltry annual rent of £118. In 1583 she increased the lease to ninety-nine years and transferred it to her favourite, Robert Dudley, Earl of Leicester, who in turn handed it over to his associate, Thomas Sutton. Sutton's ambition was to become a member of the Hostman's Company, but they were having none of it and in the end forced him to sell the lease to them.

In 1600 the Hostmen became an incorporated company with a membership of forty-eight and the possessor of the remaining years of what became known as the Grand Lease. Those excluded were resentful and in 1604 they managed to secure an ordinance allowing any burgess of Newcastle to become a Hostman upon payment of the prescribed fee. This right, however, proved to have little substance. The policy of the Hostmen's Company, now a monopoly cartel, was to acquire leases of more collieries, in some cases to stop production (the rent they paid was known as a 'dead rent') and to use Newcastle's control over the commerce of the Tyne to exclude all but themselves from the coal trade. In this they succeeded: even the region's most powerful aristocrat, the Earl of Northumberland, was forced out. The Hostmen's power gave them the ability to fix the price of coal, which in turn helped to guarantee their profits. The justification for this profitable monopoly, which had some validity, was the great input of capital required to 'win' (sink) a pit, the continued risks inherent in mining, and the uncertainty of the market. Although London might grumble, the Crown was reluctant to disrupt the arrangement, since it profited by the imposition of a duty of 1 shilling per chaldron (53 cwt: 2,693 kg). In 1677 Charles II granted this charge to his illegitimate son, the Duke of Richmond and Lennox, and it was known thereafter as the 'Richmond Shilling': it was not abolished until 1831. The government also imposed other duties on coal exports, which it varied from time to time. Not for nothing was the North East known as 'England's Peru', a reference to the riches derived from the silver mines of that country by the Spanish Crown.

In the last quarter of the seventeenth century, the grip of the Hostmen on coal production was loosened. In the early 1680s the Grand Lease came to an end and the most accessible seams near the Tyne were becoming exhausted. Consequently, new producers entered the industry, sinking pits on land they owned or leased further from the Tyne. The lengthening distance from the river meant a growing transport problem, which was solved by the development of WAGONWAYS. Since these required the construction of lines over other people's property, the negotiation of wayleaves became an acute matter, often leading to physical violence and legal conflict. Also the depth of pits was increasing and with it came a number of problems, most urgently that of expelling water, which was solved by the Newcomen Engine, twenty-six of which were installed by the early 1730s. All these factors drove up the cost of starting a colliery: an outlay of £6,000 was normal and up to £40,000 possible. Consequently, the risk takers sought a maximum guarantee of returns. Hence the various attempts at 'regulation' in the early years of the eighteenth century that culminated in the Grand Alliance formed in the summer of 1726 by George Bowes (see BOWES FAMILY), Edward Wortley, Sir Henry and George Liddell and WILLIAM COTESWORTH. By its terms, the signatories agreed for a term of ninety-nine years to co-operate rather than compete in the matters of wayleaves, acquisition of collieries and output of coal. In forming an alliance and working whenever possible with other producers they hoped to control output and so keep up the price of coal. Recent research has suggested that they were primarily motivated by the need to gain maximum bargaining strength in dealing with the powerful Newcastle Hostmen, through whom they had to export their coal, and the equally powerful ring of London coal merchants, who by 1770 controlled the London Coal Exchange, a grip they retained until 1831.

This cartel was only partially successful and its influence weakened in the third quarter of the century, although it continued to function until 1777. Its decline was in part due to the exhaustion of the pits opened around 1700, but also to the development of the local banking system, which made it impossible to prevent newcomers entering the industry. In the second half of the century over thirty new collieries, most of them with greater capacity, were opened, a high proportion north of the Tyne. By 1800 there were fifteen 'seasale' collieries north of the river and only ten south it, of which half were east of the Team. These developments enabled the Tyne collieries to keep pace with the growth of the London market, which increased by a quarter between 1770 and 1800. The need for co-operation, however, remained, and in 1771 a new regulatory organisation, the Limitation of the Vend, was formed with the same objectives, namely, the management of output and the maintenance of high and stable prices. This was the last attempt by the North-East coal owners to manage the market and it lasted until 1845.

The same period also saw the growth of coal mining in the lower Wear valley, using Sunderland as the export outlet. Indeed, one of the major developments of the eighteenth century was the growth of Sunderland as a supplier of the London market, which the North East continued to dominate, supplying over 80 per cent of the needs of the capital and its hinterland. In 1725 Newcastle's contribution was 71 per cent (680,000 tons), compared with Sunderland's 25 per cent (247,000 tons). By 1815 the balance had shifted in Sunderland's favour, the port supplying 35 per cent (982,000 tons) against Newcastle's 61 per cent (1,730,000 tons). Although these figures are impressive, it needs to be borne in mind that by 1815, although the North East was still the largest coalfield in Britain and since 1700 had more than tripled its output to 5,395,000 tons, the expansion of other coalfields meant that its share of the nation's total output had dropped from 43 per cent to 24 per cent.

In the ninety-nine years between the Battle of Waterloo and the outbreak of World War I, the Great Northern Coalfield changed in almost all respects. Most obvious was the rise in output, which in

1913 reached 54,200,000 tons, representing 19.6 per cent of Britain's total output of 271,000,000 tons. This growth was achieved by various means, two of which began in the 1820s. One was the exploitation of the area around BISHOP AUCKLAND. Here the coal was not hard to reach; the problem was distance from the sea. This was solved by the construction of railways after 1825 to the new ports at Hartlepool, Seaham and Middlesbrough (see NEW TOWNS OF THE NINETEENTH CENTURY). The other was the start of mining in East Durham, where the problem was the difficulty in getting to the coal, partly because the seams sloped downwards and so were further from the surface, but mainly because east of the Wear they were below a cap of magnesian limestone up to 1,000 feet (400 m) in depth. Neither the technology nor the capital required to sink pits through the limestone was available until the early 1820s. The breakthrough was achieved in 1822 with the winning of Hetton pit. Thereafter, the development of the East Durham coalfield continued until the first decade of the twentieth century. In addition, improvements in boring and shaft sinking techniques made possible the exploitation of deeper seams in the older districts of the coalfield.

Technology was, in fact, key to expanded production. In all aspects of mining the period saw important changes that facilitated the mining process. These included shaft sinking, winding gear, underground haulage, ventilation, the cutting of coal at the face, and the increasing use of the motive power of steam and later of electricity. Here the North East made two notable contributions. The more famous was the safety lamp. In the second decade of the nineteenth century, three such lamps were invented, two of them in the North East, by WILLIAM CLANNY and GEORGE STEPHENSON, although that by Sir Humphrey Davy was the most widely adopted. The other contribution, by THOMAS HALL, was an improved shaft haulage system to replace wicker corves fastened to chains. His solution was iron cages in which tubs carrying coals and men could be carried up and down the shaft on guide rails. The North East, however, lagged behind many other coalfields in two respects. One was the continued use of the 'stall and pillar' method of extraction, that is, the retention of pillars of coal to support the roof, instead of the more widespread and efficient 'longwall' system, in which all the coal along a face was extracted. The other was the reluctance to adopt mechanical coal cutters. However, in neither case was it blind conservatism, but rather considered reasons based upon knowledge of local conditions.

Production growth was a response to expanding and diversifying markets. The region continued as a major supplier of London's needs, particularly to the burgeoning gas and electricity generating industries. But an equally important market developed on its doorstep: the IRON AND STEEL INDUSTRY, which experienced huge expansion on Teesside after 1850. There the need of this industry was coke, the demand for which is revealed by the Durham sector of the coalfield, where 6,800 ovens at fifty-seven collieries produced over 25,000,000 tons of coke by 1913. Overseas markets also grew. Although these had always been significant, by 1913 the region was exporting 23,000,000 tons, 31 per cent of Britain's total export trade, second only to South Wales with 40 per cent. The growth of exports, stimulated by the growth of industry on the continent, was facilitated by the abolition in 1850 of the export duty on coal.

These developments were accompanied by changes in the organisation of the industry. A survey carried out in 1843 reveals the existence of eighty-two collieries, twenty-four in Northumberland and fifty-eight in Durham, although, significantly, they were not so recorded. Instead, they were listed under headings of the river from which their products were exported: forty-five were classed as Tyne collieries, thirty-two as Wear collieries and seven as Tees collieries. At mid-century, the coalfield was still viewed in traditional terms. Total output was 5,823,967 tons, an average of 71,000 per colliery, and at only nine collieries did production exceed 100,000 tons. The labour force totalled 27,770, with very few collieries employing more than 500 men and boys.

The contrast with 1913 is striking. The creation of the separate Durham and Northumberland Coal Owners' Associations in the early 1870s split the coalfield into two halves. The predominance of Durham, already evident in 1843, was more accentuated: of the total output of 54,200,000 tons, 41,750,00 or 77 per cent were produced in Durham. The Durham sector was now so large that it was divided into three districts: North (north of the River Deerness), Auckland (south of the Deerness) and East. There were now 197 pits, nine of which produced over 500,000 tons a year. In place of the forty-four private owners or partnerships of 1843, there were forty-nine limited liability companies and only five private owners. Sixteen companies each produced more than 1,000,000 tons annually, with the Lambton and Hetton Co. heading the list with 4,100,000 tons. The Northumberland sector's production, 12,450,000 tons, was only 23 per cent of the coalfield total. It was the product of fifty collieries, largely concentrated in the area south of Amble and east of the Great North Road.

The owners' associations were preceded by, and a necessary response to, the emergence of permanent miners' trade unions. In 1863 moves were made to create the Northumberland and Durham Miners' Mutual Confidence Association, but this came to nothing, and like the owners a few years later, their employees formed unions on a county basis; the Northumberland Miners' Association was founded in 1864 and the Durham Miners' Association in 1869. These were the fourth attempt at union creation, those of 1810 and 1831, by TOMMY HEPBURN, and that of 1844 having been crushed following unsuccessful strikes.

The attempt of 1844 had had as its main object the ending of the 'bond'. For centuries miners had been hired on an annual basis, the hiring sealed by a binding fee that varied according to the shortage or abundance of labour. Once taken, however, the fee established a legal contract. The 'bond' system was not peculiar to mining, but was the traditional means of hiring farm servants. Although apparently as binding on the employer as on the employee, its terms were written by the former so as to give him greater scope to terminate the contract if he so wished and to expose the latter to abuses, such as payment in kind and obligation to buy at the owner's shops. The legal validity of the 'bond' was finally ended by the decision in a court action in 1869 in a case involving miners at Monkwearmouth Colliery won by the advocacy of the solicitor William Prowting Roberts (1806–71), who had been the legal adviser to the 1844 union and was known as 'the miners' attorney general'. The ending of the 'bond' system together with the emergence of permanent and successful unions turned miners from indentured servants into waged employees.

The Northumberland and Durham associations retained the undivided loyalty of most of their members until after 1900, despite the emergence of a rival organisation with a seemingly most appealing wages policy, the Miners' Federation of Great Britain (MFGB), formed in 1888 and dominated by Yorkshire. The leaders of North-

East associations accepted and advocated the principle of the 'sliding scale', that is, that miners' wages should reflect the price obtained for the coal they mined. In contrast the MFGB argued that miners' wages should be independent of the price of coal and the first charge on whatever income the owners earned. The attraction of the MFGB view gradually infiltrated the North East as younger and more radical leaders came to the fore and led to the two associations affiliating with the MFGB in 1908.

In addition to the collapse of the Limitation of the Vend, the coal owners suffered another setback in the 1840s. This was the 1842 Mines and Collieries Act, which outlawed the employment of women and children underground. The importance of this legislation was of far greater significance than the modest adjustment in employment practice it prescribed. What it did was to establish the principle that the state had the right to devise and impose on the owners and employers regulations governing the workings of the coal industry, a process that ended in the nationalisation of the industry on 1 January 1947. Between 1842 and 1914 there were seven further acts of parliament relating to coal mining: in 1850, 1860, 1872, 1887, 1896, 1908 and 1911. Two especially met with resistance in the North East. One was the 1842 act, on the grounds that women had never worked underground in North-East pits but that boys needed to work underground from an early age if they were to mature into fully trained and efficient miners. The other was the 1908 act, which imposed an eight-hour day. In this the owners and unions were at one, since the seven and a half hour shift was already the norm in Northumberland and Durham.

The years immediately before the outbreak of Word War I proved to be the apogee of the Great Northern Coalfield, but there was already evidence of economic problems. In Durham from the 1890s until 1907 output per man/year was over 800 tons for faceworkers and over 300 tons for all employees. By 1913, although output had risen, the figures per man/year had fallen to 764 and 262 tons respectively. The industry's problems were exacerbated by World War I, which saw Durham's production fall from nearly 42,000,000 tons in 1913 to 28,500,000 tons in 1918 and manpower reduced from nearly 160,000 to 128,000, largely as the result of miners joining the armed forces. The problem of falling output led to the industry being taken under government control at the end of 1916.

The economic crisis of the coalfield became apparent in the early 1920s. During the war, coal company dividends had been 12 per cent or more. By 1924 they had fallen to under 2 per cent. The owners' solution was cost cutting, by lowering wages and/or extending hours. This the unions would not accept, demanding instead the nationalisation of the industry. The root of the problem was undoubtedly manpower. In Durham in 1924 output was 37,000,000 tons, over 5,000,000 tons less than in 1913, but the number of men employed was 170,000, almost the same as the pre-war total. Consequently, output per man/year fell to 219 tons, down from 262, which was already much lower than in 1900. The crisis came in 1926, with the General Strike and the much longer strike in the coal industry. The miners' defeat transformed the manpower situation. The Durham figures for 1928 show that nearly 36,000,000 tons were produced by a much-reduced workforce of 127,500, giving an output of over 280 tons per man/year. Indeed, the output by face workers had risen to 959 tons per man/year.

Then came the great depression of 1929 to 1933. By the latter year in Durham there were only thirty-six mining companies and only 108 pits at work. Total output was down to a little over 28,000,000 tons and the number of miners had dropped to 98,500. The unemployment rate in Durham stood at over 30 per cent. Northumberland was rather better, but even there 21 per cent of miners were out of work. Not all parts of the coalfield were equally affected. The most severly depressed was South-West Durham, where of the 42,000 male workers 66 per cent were miners, of whom over 70 per cent were permanently unemployed. Indeed, in some villages the male unemployment rate was over 90 per cent. The main cause was the depression and the declining demand for coal, but it was exacerbated by the fact that many pits were old and had thin seams not susceptible to mechanisation. Although there was some recovery in the late 1930s, the coalfield was again adversely affected by war: in Durham output fell from 31,700,000 tons in 1939 to 24,700,000 tons in 1945, by which date the number of miners was still around 98,000.

When the act of nationalisation came into force on 1 January 1947, there were 139 collieries in Durham and 70 in Northumberland. The compensation paid to the colliery owners totalled just over £55,800,000, only two-thirds of which was for the pits, the rest being for the ancillary industries attached to them. Of the total sum, £39,000,000 came to Durham and £16,800,000 to Northumberland. Calculations have indicated that the industry in the North East was considerably overvalued, particularly as the government had already acquired control of coal deposits and royalties by the act of 1938 that came into operation in 1942.

Since the early years of the century, miners had seen nationalisation as the panacea for all their troubles. And for a few years after 1947 it seemed to be so. More coal was needed and modernisation, which to a large degree meant mechanisation, was undertaken. Then in the late 1950s the demand for coal began to decline. A national output of 240,000,000 tons by 1959 was planned; when that year arrived, demand was less than 192,000,000 tons. And it continued to fall in the face of a continuing decline in exports and at home the rising preference for oil, and the arrival of natural gas and of nuclear-generated electricity. Instead of expansion, contraction was required. Already the antiquity of the coalfield had resulted in the closure of twenty-eight pits before 1957, sixteen in Durham and twelve in Northumberland. This was the prelude to the avalanche: between 1957 and 1969, 124 pits were closed, eighty-five in Durham and thirty-nine in Northumberland, an average of over ten a year. After this, the closure rate slowed, but between 1970 and 1984, when the year-long miners' strike began, a further twenty-five pits in Durham and ten in Northumberland were shut. When mining resumed in the spring of 1985, there were only sixteen working pits in the coalfield, ten in Durham and six in Northumberland, and nine of these (Ashington, Bates, Brenkley, Eppleton, Herrington, Horden, Sacriston, Seaham and Whittle) were closed within two years. The remaining six were located on the coast and were mining several miles under the North Sea, an indication of the exhaustion of the inland regions of the coalfield after centuries of exploitation. Five of the six (EASINGTON, Monkwearmouth, Lynemouth, Vane Tempest and Westoe) were closed in the 1990s, leaving Ellington to survive, but under private ownership, until 2005. It was the last survivor of the industry that had dominated the region.

GREAT NORTH RUN

The Great North Run takes place annually in the early autumn and is the world's most popular half marathon. First run in 1981, its course is just over 13 miles (21 km) long, starting at Newcastle and finishing at South

Shields. Those taking part raise thousands of pounds for charity.

GREEN, JOHN (1787–1852) and BENJAMIN (1808–1858)

John and Benjamin Green, father and son, were architects working in the region in the first half of the nineteenth century. John was born at Nafferton and in early life joined his father as a carpenter and maker of agricultural implements. They then moved to CORBRIDGE, where they developed a business as general builders. In 1820 John Green felt confident enough to move into NEWCASTLE and set up as an architect and builder and to apprentice his son, Benjamin, to Augustus Pugin senior to get a proper architectural training. Father and son then formed a partnership shortly after 1830.

Over the period of their collaboration they built or repaired twenty-one churches and designed thirty-three other public and private buildings, all but three in the North East. Their most notable works were PENSHAW MONUMENT, the Theatre Royal in Newcastle, the column for the Grey Monument, also in Newcastle, and the stations for the Newcastle and Berwick Railway. They were also bridge builders. The wrought iron suspension bridge over the Tees at Whorlton still stands, but those over the Ouseburn and Willington Dene were partially of laminated timber, an invention for which John Green was awarded the Telford Medal by the Institute of Civil Engineers. They were also employed by the Duke of Northumberland to design farmhouses. The elegant results still grace the Northumberland countryside.

GREENWELL, CANON WILLIAM (1820–1918)

William Greenwell was the son of a gentry family that had been settled on the Greenwell Ford estate at LANCHESTER for around three hundred years. He was educated at Durham School and the newly founded Durham University, where he took a BA degree in 1839 and MA in 1843. His subsequent career was spent entirely in Durham in the service of the University and the Cathedral. In the 1840s and 1850s he held a number of minor University posts but by the mid-1860s he had become permanently bedded in the Durham ecclesiastical world: in 1854 he was made a minor canon of DURHAM CATHEDRAL; in 1863 he became the Cathedral Librarian, a post he held until 1908; and in 1865 he became Rector of St Mary the Less, the tiny parish behind the Cathedral.

Greenwell's fame rests on three foundations. He was a stalwart of the Surtees Society, acting as its Vice-President from 1890, and editing several of its volumes, notably BOLDON BOOK and *Feodarium Prioratus Dunelmensis*. The latter was a selection of important documents relating to the estate of the Cathedral Priory, including what purported to be its earliest title deeds issued by William the Conqueror and several of his eminent contemporaries, which Greenwell demonstrated were forgeries. He also discovered in a Newcastle shop in 1909 a leaf from one of the pandects (complete Bibles) written in the early years of the eighth century in the scriptorium of the monastery of JARROW/Monkwearmouth on the orders of its abbot, CEOLFRITH. He was even more prolific as an archaeologist, although his technique was crude by current standards. He was particularly interested in prehistoric burial mounds and the remains they contained. These, which he gave or sold to the British Museum, are one of its most important collections of artefacts of British prehistory. He amassed a large collection of Greek coins, which was sold in 1901 for £11,000, and he also built up a collection of seventy carved stones of the Anglo-Saxon period discovered in the region, which are now housed in Durham Cathedral Library.

Ironically, however, perhaps his most enduring memorial is neither historical nor archaeological but recreational. It is 'Greenwell's Glory', one of the most famous British trout flies, which he invented.

GREY, CHARLES, 2nd EARL (1764–1845)

No visitor to the centre of NEWCASTLE can fail to see Grey's Monument. It is a hollow column, Doric in style and 135 feet (41 m) high with 164 internal stairs leading to a square platform on which stands a statue 13 feet (4 m) high, carved by E.H. Bailey. The column, designed by BENJAMIN GREEN and erected in 1838, has at the bottom a plaque inscribed with a florid eulogy composed by the early nineteenth-century raconteur, bon viveur and co-founder of the influential *Edinburgh Review*, the Reverend Sydney Smith.

The man extolled is Charles, 2nd Earl Grey. He was the eldest surviving son of the distinguished military man, General Sir Charles Grey, 2nd Baronet (1729–1807) of HOWICK, whose services were rewarded by elevation to the peerage as Lord Grey of Howick (1801) and Viscount Howick and Earl Grey (1806). The younger Grey's career was political, not military. Educated at Eton, Trinity College, Cambridge and the Middle Temple, and through the Grand Tour, in 1786 he entered the Commons with the courtesy title of Viscount Howick as one of the two MPs for Northumberland, a seat he retained until his father's death in 1807. Throughout these years, he was a staunch Whig, a committed supporter of Charles James Fox, the most radical politician of the day, and a committed opponent of the Prime Minister, William Pitt the Younger. He took a leading part in the impeachment of the Indian *nabob*, Warren Hastings; opposed going to war with revolutionary France in 1793; spoke against the restrictions of civil liberties, such as the suspension of the Habeas Corpus Act, which Pitt's government considered necessary in the 1790s; favoured Catholic emancipation; and opposed the 1801 act that enforced the union of Ireland with Great Britain. He was briefly in office as Foreign Secretary between September 1806 and March 1807.

In the latter year he not only lost office and but also his seat in the Commons, becoming 2nd Earl Grey on the death of his father. Now a member of the Lords, his active involvement in politics waned, partly through a necessary concern with his Northumberland estates, but also because Tory domination of political life under, successively, Lord Liverpool, George Canning, Viscount Goderich and the Duke of Wellington diminished the attractions of life at Westminster. Following the 1830 election, however, Grey, now sixty-six years old, found himself the leader of the Whig party and of the Opposition. Almost immediately Wellington's government was defeated and, upon his resignation, the king asked Grey to form a government.

The foremost issue facing Grey's administration was the reform of parliament. This matter had been festering for decades, but the rapid growth of the population and economic power of the Midlands and the North made a solution ever more necessary, while the fears aroused by the 1830 revolution in France added anxiety and urgency. Wellington and the Tory party were totally opposed, but the Whigs, among whose ranks there had always been advocates, were prepared to drive a measure of reform through parliament. They were successful, considerably thanks to Grey's determination, but it was a fraught process lasting from March 1831 until June 1832, essentially because of the Tory majority in the Lords. This was finally overcome by civil unrest and violence in many parts of the country that many feared was a prelude to revolution, and by an election that gave the Whigs a clear Commons majority, but above all by the king (William IV), who agreed to create, if necessary, enough new peers to produce a Whig majority in the Lords.

What did the act accomplish? As regards seats, fifty-six English boroughs with tiny electorates lost both members and another thirty lost one. These seats were redistributed: twenty-two new boroughs got two members, twenty got one and sixty-five seats were distributed among the most heavily populated counties. The effect was to enhance the representation of the Midlands and the North at the expense of the South. The franchise was also changed. In boroughs the vote was given to all men with buildings with an annual rent value of £10; and in the counties, in addition to the traditional freeholders with land reckoned to be worth 40 shillings (£2) per year, copyholders and leaseholders paying £10 a year and tenants at will paying £50 a year were enfranchised. The overall effect was to increase the size of the electorate by 50 per cent. But elections continued to be open affairs since the demand for secret ballots was turned down.

To what extent does Grey deserve credit for this? He was not one of the primary authors of the proposed changes, which were devised by a small working party whose members were probably keener on reform than he was. But he was prepared to use all his political skills to secure a significant redistribution of seats and extension of the franchise, even though he was a member of a class that ran the state. The reason he did so was a conviction that, were reform to be denied, the consequence would be revolutionary and catastrophic. In other words, he saw moderate reform as necessary if his class was to retain political control. This explains his refusal to end open elections. Finally, it needs to be noted that Grey did not see the reform of 1832 as the first step towards the system we now have. Yet this is what it proved to be, as his Tory opponents said it would. Nevertheless, when all the caveats have been entered, Grey deserves his place on the high pedestal that dominates and is the focal point of Newcastle's city centre as much as Nelson is entitled to his place of honour in London's Trafalgar Square.

Grey's other claim to fame is the blend of tea that still bears his name. It was the result of a present from a Chinese mandarin whose life had been saved by a British diplomat. In gratitude, the mandarin sent Grey, at the time Prime Minister, a sample of the tea, and, more importantly, the recipe, which includes a special ingredient, oil of bergamot. Grey liked what he tasted and gave Twinings permission to produce and market the product. 'Earl Grey Tea' is drunk in nearly 100 countries and the 2nd Earl Grey is therefore more widely known and appreciated for an afternoon beverage than for his contribution to the advance of democracy.

GREY, SIR EDWARD, Bt, VISCOUNT GREY OF FALLODON (1862–1933)

Edward Grey was the great-grandson of a younger brother of the 2ND EARL GREY and the grandson of Sir George Grey, Bt, from whom he inherited his baronetcy. Given the Grey family's involvement in politics, it is not surprising that in 1885, shortly after leaving Oxford University, he entered parliament as Liberal MP for the new constituency of BERWICK UPON TWEED, a seat he retained until his elevation to the peerage in 1916.

His made foreign affairs his speciality, and in the short-lived Liberal governments of Gladstone and Lord Rosebery (1892–95), he was a promising Under-Secretary of State for Foreign Affairs. But with the Conservatives in power under the Marquess of Salisbury (1895–1902) and then Arthur Balfour (1902–06), Grey was out of office until the Liberal landslide victory of 1906. He then returned to the Foreign Office as Foreign Secretary, retaining the post for ten years in the cabinets of Henry Campbell Bannerman (1906–08) and then Herbert Asquith (1908–16). Thus it fell to Grey to steer Britain's foreign policy through the difficult years leading up to the outbreak of World War I in August 1914.

Although Grey hoped to avoid war, he recognised that if a general conflict broke out in Europe, Britain's interest would not allow her to remain neutral but would require her to ally with France and Russia against Germany and Austria-Hungary. In this he faced considerable political difficulty since a great many Liberals were isolationists, holding the traditional belief that Britain should not become involved in a European war, while others were anti-French and pro-German. On both counts Grey could not openly avow the policies he thought right for the country because of the crisis that would ensue within his party. In the end Germany's determination to go to war resolved the issue, although it was only her violation of Belgium and the open support of the Conservatives and the Irish members that enabled the Cabinet to take the country into the war, though not without four resignations from it.

Grey retired from active politics when David Lloyd George replaced Asquith as Prime Minister in 1916. By that time he was in his mid-fifties and beginning to go blind. His political commitments apart, Grey was a countryman, who wrote books on fly-fishing and bird watching. He was also passionately attached to Northumberland and spent as much time as he could at Fallodon.

GREY, HENRY GEORGE, 3rd EARL (1802–1894)

Henry George Grey was born at Howick, the eldest son of the 2nd Earl Grey. Although a politician like his father, he played a less significant part in public life. From 1826 until he succeeded his father as 3rd Earl Grey in 1845, he had the courtesy title of Viscount Howick and was an MP, successively, for Winchelsea, Higham Ferrers, Northumberland and Sunderland. He was the junior Secretary for War in Lord Melbourne's government from 1835 until 1839. Being of a high-minded disposition and having no interest in using office for personal gain, his aim was to improve army administration. Vested interests, however, thwarted him, although he did secure the passage of several measures (good conduct pay, regimental savings banks, sports facilities) designed to improve the soldier's lot. Since the Secretary of State for War was also (until 1854) the Secretary of State for the Colonies, Lord Howick (as he then was) was involved in colonial matters. He favoured the policy urged by Edward Gibbon Wakefield, which was to discontinue free gifts of land in the colonies in favour of its sale by auction, the hope being that this would ensure a better class of migrant, make emigration self-financing and generally promote colonial development. He also began the withdrawal of financial support for the Church of England in the colonies and he campaigned to end slavery in British territories, resigning over the decision to compensate slave owners.

He was again Secretary of State for War and the Colonies in the Whig ministries of Lord John Russell (1846–52) and the Earl of Aberdeen (1852–55). He was responsible for the development of Australia by severing South Australia, Tasmania and Victoria from New South Wales and launching them as separate colonies. In

New Zealand, he sponsored a system of elected government for the white settlers, although he was forced to suspend this with the onset of the Maori Wars. The most difficult area with which he had to deal was South Africa, where he had to try to reconcile four different factions: British settlers; Dutch settlers (Boers), many of whom had migrated across the Orange River and out of Cape Colony; the black natives; and the person of Sir Harry Smith, the Governor of Cape Colony. With the latter there was a difference of ambition, Smith wanting to extend the area under British control, a policy Grey did not favour. Unfortunately, his ability to control the situation was severely hampered by distance and the lack of ready means of communication. Overall, he did not enjoy great success. He did manage to secure an elected upper house for the Cape legislature, but in Natal, which had been separated from the Cape in 1843, he failed to impose his policy of integrating the black natives into a single economic regime and was forced to see them confined to 'special areas'. It is conceivable that had Grey's policy prevailed, the twentieth century might have been spared the policy of apartheid. The other problem was the Boers who had migrated north of the Orange River in the late 1830s (the Great Trek). By the Sand River Convention in 1852, Grey conceded to them a large measure of self-government and freedom of allegiance to the Crown. In this lay the seeds of the South African War of 1899–1902.

His experiences in office soured Grey's view of political life and after the fall of Lord Aberdeen's ministry he played no further part in national affairs. It is clear that Grey was too highly principled to ever be at ease with the less salubrious aspects of political life.

GREY, JOHN (1785–1868)

John Grey, who was one of the foremost agricultural reformers and improvers of the first half of the nineteenth century, came of minor Northumberland gentry distantly related to the Earls Grey. Born at Milfield in Glendale and educated at Richmond in North Yorkshire, he had to take over the management of the family estate at an early age. Ambitious and energetic, he immediately associated himself with the improving farmers in north Northumberland, notably the Culley Brothers, from whom he acquired a great deal of knowledge. But Grey also involved himself in politics. A staunch Whig, he supported causes such as Catholic emancipation and parliamentary reform and through this activity became acquainted with the 2nd Earl Grey and other grandees of that party, including Lord Althorp, a fellow enthusiast for agricultural improvement. This political involvement bore fruit in 1833, when he secured the management of the Northumberland and Cumberland (Cumbria) properties of Greenwich Hospital. These largely comprised the estates that had been confiscated after the Jacobite Uprising 1715 uprising and in 1735 were assigned to the Hospital to finance the completion of the building and thereafter the support of the inmates. Based at Dilston, the centre of the Radcliffe estate, he held the post for thirty years, eventually resigning in 1863. Over that period, by the imposition of better farming methods and shrewd (and sometimes sharp) commercial activity, he transformed the estate from a rundown condition and financial underperformance to a modern enterprise yielding a 50 per cent increase in rental income. He used his position to increase his own wealth and to enhance the social status of his family. One of his children was the social reformer Josephine Butler.

GULLY, JOHN (1783–1863)

John Gully had a highly successful if rather shady career. He was the son of a butcher in Bath, who by the age of twenty-one was in prison. He was rescued from a life of crime by his prowess as a boxer: between 1805 and 1808 he won a series of fights, one of which went to sixty-four rounds, and made a great deal of money through betting on the outcome. Retiring from the ring, he devoted himself to betting and to the ownership of thoroughbred horses. Between the late 1820s and 1854 he won six classics: the Two Thousand Guineas (with Ugly Busck and Hermit); the Derby (Pyrrhus the First and Andover); the Oaks (Mendicant); and the St Leger (Margrave). His winnings allowed him to buy Ackworth Park near Pontefract and to become its MP from 1832 until 1838.

His connection with the North East began in the 1820s and lasted until his death. Over a period of about forty years he invested heavily in the East Durham coalfield, which was being opened up following the successful penetration in 1822 by the Hetton Coal Co. of the limestone cap that overlies the coal measures. He began by purchasing shares in the Hetton Company; then in 1838 he invested in the company that sank Thornley Colliery and shortly afterwards Trimdon Colliery; and finally in 1862 he bought the Wingate estate with its colliery.

HACKWORTH, TIMOTHY (1786–1850)

Timothy Hackworth was born at Wylam, where his father, John Hackworth, was the master blacksmith at Wylam Colliery. He left school in 1800 at the age of fourteen and after serving his apprenticeship was appointed to his father's position. While at Wylam he collaborated with WILLIAM HEDLEY in the development of steam locomotives, helping to build the famous *Puffing Billy*. In 1817, however, he moved to Walbottle Colliery, not for professional reasons but because his strong Methodist convictions would not allow him to work on Sundays. From there in 1824 he was seconded for six months by his employer to manage the newly opened locomotive works of Robert Stephenson & Co. at Forth Street in Newcastle during the time when ROBERT STEPHENSON was working in South America and his father, George, was busy with the Stockton and Darlington Railway.

Although Hackworth returned to his job at Walbottle, his ability had been noted by GEORGE STEPHENSON, who in 1825 offered him the post of superintendent of the Stockton and Darlington Company's engines at New Shildon, but with an understanding that he could also work on his own account. This enabled him to build his best-known engine, *Royal George*, in 1827, which proved to be more efficient and powerful than the locomotives then used by the Stockton and Darlington Railway; and also the *Sanspareil*, the only serious rival to *Rocket* at the Liverpool and Manchester Railway Company's Rainhill trial in 1829, which its directors subsequently bought for £500. By 1833 Hackworth was confident enough to renegotiate his relationship with the Stockton and Darlington company: instead of being a salaried employee, he undertook to build and maintain the Company's locomotives on a contract basis. This enabled him to develop his own business, the Soho Works, where he built nineteen more locomotives of the *Royal George* class, two of which were exported, to Russia (1836) and Canada (1838). In 1840 he broke completely with the Stockton and Darlington Railway Co. to concentrate exclusively on his own Soho Works.

Other than locomotives, Hackworth's other passion was the Methodist church. He was an active lay preacher until the end of his life and he gave of both his wealth and his time to the service of his church, which thanks considerably to him and his wife was able to create and sustain a new circuit centred on BISHOP AUCKLAND.

HADAWAY, THOMAS (1922–2005)

Tom Hadaway, who engendered huge affection and respect in Tyneside theatrical circles, is considered by many to be the North East's best playwright. His origins, however, were far from propitious. He was born Thomas Hunter to a working-class family in North Shields, but was adopted at the age of five, following the death of his mother and the desertion of his father. He took the surname of his adoptive father, a fishmonger on what is now the Meadowwell Estate, into whose business he went on leaving school. He remained in that business throughout his working life, apart from a period of service in the Royal Navy.

He did not start writing seriously until the late 1960s, after attending a writers' workshop. His first play was *What is the Colour of the Wind?*, but the first to be performed publicly (at the People's Theatre in Newcastle) was *A Quaker at Cullercoats*. In his early years as a writer, his mentor was C.P. TAYLOR, who instantly recognised his natural talent and gave him a great deal of encouragement and help. He became known nationally as the result of *God Bless Thee Jackie Maddison* (1974). Two years later he wrote, together with SID CHAPLIN, a number of scripts for the renowned television series *When the Boat Comes In*. His best-known plays are *The Filleting Machine*, *The Long Line* and *Francie Nichol*. He had a long and happy association with Newcastle's Live Theatre, for whom he was a major writer. He was also writer-in-residence in 1986 at Durham and Frankland prisons, out of which experiences came two long and two short plays, published collectively as *The Prison Plays*.

It is widely held that Tom Hadaway did not achieve the recognition the quality of his work merited. This may have stemmed from his continuing to live in North Shields and to the essentially North-East subject matter of much of his work. This included in *Seafarers* (1993) the experience of Jim Slater, an official of the Seamen's Union, who was arrested in the United States on account of his Geordie accent, which led the authorities to believe that he was a Soviet spy.

HADRIAN'S WALL

Hadrian's Wall, which bisects the region, was not the only physical frontier boundary the Romans created, but it was the most splendid and substantial. For the Roman imperial government it was the end-product of a period of experiment that lasted nearly a hundred years. The earliest attempt at a formal frontier was made in AD 83 by the Governor of Britain, Julius Agricola (77–84), who built a road studded with forts up Strathmore in what is now Scotland, the purpose of which was to block the exits from the Highland glens. Within three years it was decided to withdraw to the Forth–Clyde line, the narrowest isthmus in Britain, and to construct a similar road with forts. This frontier lasted less than twenty years. Around the year 100 the frontier was moved even further south to the Tyne–Solway isthmus, and again it consisted of a road (the Stanegate) with forts.

About twenty years later, in 122, the Emperor Hadrian, then visiting Britain, decided on a more substantial boundary, a wall, most of which was constructed during the governorship of Aulus Platorius Nepos (122–27). But almost immediately after Hadrian's death in 138, his successor, Antoninus Pius (138–61), decided to advance the frontier northwards again to the Forth–Clyde line. The Antonine Wall, which was of turf not stone and in length 37 miles (60 km) only half that of the Hadrianic wall (73 miles: 118 km), ran from Old Kilpatrick on the Clyde to Carriden on the Forth. Building work had scarcely finished when the next emperor, Marcus Aurelius (161–80), opted again for Hadrian's frontier. This 'Grand Old Duke of York' policy now ended: Hadrian's Wall became the 'final frontier' until the Roman imperial government abandoned Britain early in the fifth century.

As originally conceived, Hadrian's Wall was to be 8 feet (2.4 m) wide and was to run from what is now Newcastle to Bowness on the Solway Firth. As far as the River Irthing it was made of stone; west of the Irthing initially it was made of turf, later replaced by stone. Its height was between 15 and 20 feet (4–6 m), and it may have had a battlemented wall walk; but both of these statements are speculative, since nowhere has the wall survived intact. Every Roman mile (1,600 yards: 1,463 m) there was a gateway defended by a small fort (the modern word is milecastle); and between each milecastle there were two lookout towers or turrets. In front of the wall, where the ground permitted, a ditch 10 feet (3 m) deep and 30 feet 9.1 m) wide at the top was dug.

This plan was never fully realised. During the course of construction, several modifications were introduced, the most fundamental being the incorporation of forts into the wall. Also designed to strengthen the arrangement was the ditch known as the *Vallum*, 10 feet (3 m) deep and 20 feet (6.1 m) wide, dug on the south side of the wall, the excavated earth being used to form mounds on either side of it. Because of these extra measures and the manpower needed to create them, the sections of the Wall constructed subsequently were only 6 feet (1.8 m) in width. The Wall was also lengthened by the addition of a four-mile (6.5 km) extension eastwards from Newcastle to Wallsend. Finally, in the 170s the Military Way, a road between the wall and the *Vallum*, was constructed. Virtually all the construction work was done not by slave labour but by the troops of the IInd, VIth and XXth legions, a total workforce of about 18,000 men.

Legionary troops did not garrison its seventeen forts. These were manned by auxiliary troops, non-Roman citizens recruited in the provinces of the empire. The units into which they were formed were of two sorts: the infantry *cohors* of six *centuriae* with a total strength of 480 men; and the cavalry *ala* of *turmae* with a total strength of 512 men. Although military establishments, the forts did not continue to exist in isolation. Around each a civilian settlement (*vicus*) grew up outside its south gate to meet a number of needs: accommodation for travellers, services for the garrison in its off-duty time, and a place where time-served troops might wish to retire. This last point is easier to understand when it is recognised that, although a unit was raised in a distant province and bore a name to indicate that fact, from an early date it drew its recruits from the local population.

What purposes did the Wall serve? Contrary to widespread belief, it was not a defensive barrier in constant action against aggessors from the north. That this was not so is clearly indicated by the existence of a gateway every Roman mile. Moreover, it is by no means certain that it had a battlemented parapet that would have allowed it to be used as a fighting platform. Its primary role was to mark the boundary of the empire and act as a filter to control the ebb and flow of peaceful traffic. For long periods relations with the British peoples living north of the wall were regulated by treaties: in return for subsidies, native rulers allowed roads to be maintained and troops to be stationed in their territory in forts at High Rochester and Risingham.

Nevertheless, there were times of disturbance, when the wall saw serious military activity, and then, presumably, the forts on the wall were the first line of defence. The worst of these was in the early third century in the time of the Emperor Septimius Severus (193–211), and that at the beginning of the following century, when the Emperor Constantius (293–306) and his son, Constantine, conducted campaigns against the Picts. Later in the fourth century there were two further major incursions in 367 and 382. After this what happened is unclear, but twenty-five years later the Romans effectively deserted Britain and the wall ceased to be part of an integrated defence system.

After the departure of the Romans the Wall was never again a state frontier. Contrary to widespread belief, particularly among Scots, it was never the boundary between Scotland and England, since neither country existed until many centuries later. Ironically, it is the Antonine Wall that can claim to be an ethnic boundary, separating the Scots and Picts to the north from the British and English to the south.

HAIR, THOMAS HARRISON (1810–1875)

Thomas Hair was born at Scotswood, then a village west of Newcastle. Of his education and training we know little, but by the time he was twenty years old he had become a competent watercolourist and engraver. Although he produced many pictures of various scenes in the region, his importance lies in two books he published in 1839 and 1844: respectively *Sketches of the Coal Mines of Northumberland and Durham* and *Views of the Collieries of Northumberland and Durham*. These are the most valuable source of information about the appearance and buildings of the region's collieries in the first half of the nineteenth century.

HALIDON HILL, BATTLE OF, 1333

On 19 July 1333 an English army commanded by Edward III annihilated a Scottish army led by Sir Archibald Douglas, the grandfather of the victor of the BATTLE OF OTTERBURN, on the slopes of Halidon Hill two miles north-west of BERWICK. The English victory had two important consequences, one permanent, the other of shorter duration. The permanent consequence was that from this date Berwick, which had first fallen to the English in 1296, but had been retaken by the Scots in 1318, effectively ceased to be a Scottish town and became part of Northumberland. Although the Scots captured it again on several occasions after 1333, they were never able to retain it for very long. The second consequence relates to the art of war. The English victory was achieved by a combination of bodies of heavily armed men-at-arms fighting on foot, not as cavalry, interspersed with groups of archers armed with longbows. This new tactic was essentially defensive, but it made English armies all but invincible in Britain and in Europe for over a hundred years.

The train of events that culminated in this battle began in 1328, when Edward's mother, Queen Isabelle, and her lover, Roger Mortimer, having deposed his father, Edward II, agreed a peace treaty with Robert Bruce, whereby they recognised him as the rightful sovereign of Scotland (see BALLIOL AND BRUCE FAMILIES). Edward III overthrew Isabelle's illegitimate regime in 1330, denounced this agreement and gave his support to Edward Balliol, the son of John, King of Scots, who was deposed in 1296 and died in 1314. Edward Balliol invaded Scotland in 1332, supported by a group of nobles known as the 'Disinherited', members of families who had owned estates in both England and Scotland, but had been deprived of their Scottish lands when they gave their allegiance to the King of England. The invaders won a victory at Dupplin Moor in Fife and had Edward Balliol crowned at Scone. Their success was short-lived: by the end of the year they had been driven south of the Border. Edward III's invasion was intended to restart their attempted conquest.

The immediate occasion of the battle was an agreement between the English king and the Scottish garrison in Berwick, who promised to surrender the town and its castle, unless they were relieved by 19 July. The Scottish army therefore had to fight or allow Berwick to be lost by default. Edward did not pursue his success: four years later his interest diverted from Scotland to pursuing his claim to the French throne.

HALL, THOMAS YOUNG (1802–1870)

Born into poverty at Greenside and with almost no formal education, Thomas Hall rose to be one of the giants of the GREAT NORTHERN COALFIELD. That he did so was considerably thanks to JOHN BUDDLE, who recognised his exceptional ability and trained him to be a colliery viewer. Between 1825 and 1832 his ability secured him the post of under-viewer at North Hetton Colliery, work for Jonathan Backhouse (see BACKHOUSE FAMILY), surveying East Durham to establish the possibility of mining at Coxhoe, Shadforth and Sherburn, a directorship of the company that reopened the old harbour at HARTLEPOOL, and finally the post of mining engineer at South Hetton Colliery.

It was at South Hetton that he made his great technical innovation. Hitherto coal had been brought to the surface in wicker corves attached to chains, and men and boys descended and ascended the shaft by clinging to the chain. The system was inefficient and dangerous: the corves were small, soon wore out and were expensive to maintain, while for the miners travel to and from their work was extremely hazardous. Hall's solution was the iron cage, cubic in form, in which miners could be carried and into which wheeled iron tubs filled with coal at the face could be run for haulage to the surface. To give it stability during transit, the cage was controlled by iron guide rods. Although this was his major contribution to the advance of mining technology, Hall also invented an adjustable coal screen, several improved safety lamps and a gauge for steam boilers.

In 1836 Hall went into ownership, joining forces with his mentor, John Buddle, and a Newcastle man, Addison Potter, to create the Stella Coal Co., which remained a major mining concern in North-West Durham until nationalisation. Three years later, in 1839, he went to the USA at the invitation of the owners of a coal mining company in Virginia to find the solution to a gas problem. His success led to the company being bought by an English firm and Hall spent five years in Virginia as resident superintendent.

His American venture was very highly rewarded and this, together with his income from the Stella Coal Co., enabled him to retire in 1844 to live a social life. He never married and when he died he left money to fund a scholarship at the Newcastle College of Physical Science, the forerunner of Newcastle University.

HALTWHISTLE

Haltwhistle in upper South Tynedale has one claim to fame: it is the geographical centre of Great Britain.

HANCOCK MUSEUM (see LITERARY AND PHILOSOPHICAL SOCIETY OF NEWCASTLE UPON TYNE)

HARBUTT, WILLIAM (1844–1921)

William Harbutt, who invented the modelling material known as 'Plasticine', was born at North Shields, where his father was a galvaniser. Nothing is known of his early education, except that he trained as an artist at the National Art Training School at South Kensington in London. In 1874 he was appointed head of the Bath School of Art, but remained in post for only three years, resigning in 1877 after a disagreement with the management. After a period as a peripatetic teacher, he and his wife set up their own school in Bath, the Paragon Art Studio. It was here that he conducted experiments to devise a substitute for modelling clay. Eventually he produced a product whose main ingredients were petroleum jelly, a calcium salt and fatty acids, to which he gave the name 'Plasticine'. The original colour was grey; only later were coloured varieties produced.

He began to market 'Plasticine' in 1897, publishing at the same time a book, *Harbutt's Plastic Method and the Use of Plasticine*, which was intended to promote sales, and two years later he registered Plasticine as a trademark. His success was sufficiently rapid to encourage him to produce Plasticine on a commercial scale and to this end he acquired a redundant mill at Bathampton. Harbutt proved to be an assiduous entrepreneur and by 1912 the business had grown to the point where it became advisable for it to have limited liability status. He also found time to be active in local government and church affairs. Harbutt died in New York at the age of seventy-seven, while engaged in promotional activity in the USA.

Almost certainly he would have been pleased, both as an artist and as a businessman, at the publicity given to his product by the success of the recent *Wallace and Gromit* films.

HARDYNG, JOHN (1378–1464)

John Hardyng was born somewhere in the region in 1378 and in 1390 at the age of twelve entered the household of Sir Henry Percy (1364–1403), known as 'Hotspur', the eldest son of the 1st Earl of Northumberland. He remained a member of that household until Hotspur's death in 1403 and with his master took part in the battles of HUMBLETON HILL and Shrewsbury. With the collapse of the Percy Family's fortunes, he entered the service of another Border chieftain, Sir Robert Umfraville (see UMFRAVILLE FAMILY), with whom he saw service in France, including the Battle of Agincourt. He remained in Umfraville's service until his master's death in 1436.

Hardyng has two claims to fame, both dubious. The first is that during the reign of Henry V and again in that of his son, Henry VI, he spent a great deal of time in Scotland acquiring documents purporting to prove the subordination of Scotland to England. These he presented to the English government, for which he received modest rewards. In the nineteenth century, however, all of the surviving documents were shown to be forgeries. His other 'achievement' was the composition of a verse chronicle in English about the events of his own time. This record, which he dedicated to Henry VI, might be considered a most important source of information about the events that led to the deposition of Richard II in 1399, since both 'Hotspur' and his father were leading actors. However, after Henry VI's deposition in 1461, he produced two revised versions, the second of which he presented to the new king, Edward IV. His early account favours the 'Lancastrian' version of events; the second version conflicts with the first in many respects; consequently, neither version is considered trustworthy.

HARRISON, THOMAS ELLIOT (1808–1888)

Thomas Harrison, one of the most eminent civil engineers of the nineteenth century, has been overshadowed by ROBERT STEPHENSON, for whom and with whom he worked for many years. He was born at Fulham, but came to Sunderland with his family while still in infancy. After an education at Kepier Grammar School in Houghton le Spring, he served an apprenticeship in Newcastle with WILLIAM CHAPMAN, which he completed as railway development was gathering pace.

He began his professional life assisting Robert Stephenson survey the line for the London–Birmingham Railway. He then surveyed the line of the Stanhope and Tyne Railroad and was involved with surveying the line from Newcastle to Carlisle. He became the resident engineer for the Durham Junction Railway and as such was responsible for the construction of the Victoria Bridge, opened around the time of Victoria's coronation in 1838, over the Wear near Penshaw. The design, which was influenced by the Roman bridge at Alcantara in Spain, was 800 feet (244 m) in length and had four arches, each spanning 160 feet (49 m) (see BRIDGES AND RAILWAYS).

In the 1840s he was chief engineer for the Newcastle and Berwick Railway, built between 1845 and 1847, and the surveyor of its branch from Tweedmouth to Kelso. He was also heavily involved in the building of the High Level Bridge over the Tyne between Newcastle and Gateshead. Although he publicly acknowledged the design of the bridge to be Stephenson's, it seems clear that the work was largely carried out under Harrison's supervision. Harrison's role in building one of the greatest engineering structures of the nineteenth century was acknowledged at the time on the dedication plate affixed to the bridge on which his name appears after that of Robert Stephenson as its engineers.

In 1849 he became chief engineer of the York, Newcastle and Berwick Railway and five years later secured the same post with the North Eastern Railway, formed in that year by the merger of the York, Newcastle and Berwick with two other companies. It was as chief engineer that he was involved with the negotiations that led to the merger of the North Eastern Railway with the Newcastle and Carlisle Railway in 1862 and the Stockton and Darlington Railway in the following year. Towards the end of his career, he was responsible for the Team Valley line from Gateshead to Newton Hall via Birtley and Chester le Street, which straightened the East Coast Main Line (opened in 1868) and Wearmouth Bridge (opened in 1879) to carry the railway over the Wear into Sunderland Central Station, the train shed of which he also designed. He was also responsible for the design of the docks at JARROW and HARTLEPOOL. His reputation for reliability and competence earned him the sobriquet 'Honest Tom' and his election in 1873 to the presidency of the Institute of Civil Engineers.

HARRISON AND HARRISON

The firm of Harrison and Harrison of DURHAM CITY has been at the forefront of organ making and restoration since the mid-nineteenth century and is now the largest organ-building firm in the country. Its founder was a Londoner, Thomas Hugh Harrison (1839–1912). His father, himself an organ maker, apprenticed him, together with his brother, James, to the famous London organ maker, 'Father' Henry Willis. Upon completion of his apprenticeship, Thomas left London, worked briefly for a William Allen in Bristol, and then in 1861 set up on his own in Rochdale. Why he chose this particular town in unclear, but in the eleven years he was there he developed a successful business, initiated by his impressive renovation of the organ of The Queen's College, Oxford. During his years in Rochdale he built thirty-six organs, including six for the North East.

Then, in 1872, he transferred his business to Durham City. The reasons for this move appear to have been threefold. One was a disagreement with his partner in Rochdale; another was the urgings of the Precentor of DURHAM CATHEDRAL, JOHN BACCHUS DYKES, who was impressed with the instruments he had built for North-East churches. To these personal reasons may be added a shrewd perception that there was a dearth of organ makers in the far north of England and Scotland at a time when new churches and chapels were being built to cater for a rapidly rising population. On moving to Durham, he was joined by his brother, James, and thereafter the firm was Harrison and Harrison. Thomas Harrison retired to near London in 1896, leaving the management of the firm in the hands of his two sons, Arthur and Harry. Arthur, who was an outstanding 'voicer', died in 1936, but Harry continued to run the firm during the difficult times between 1939 and 1945. Shortly after the end of World War II, he was able to hand over to his son, Cuthbert, following the latter's demobilisation from the army. In 1975 Cuthbert retired and direction of the firm passed to Mark Venning, who had joined three years earlier. In 1996 the firm moved from its original premises in Hawthorn Terrace near the centre of Durham City to new, purpose-designed premises in Meadowfield on the outskirts of the city.

Under the three generations of Harrisons, between 1872 and 1975, the Durham firm built or renovated 725 organs, of which 235 or 35 per cent were in the North East. Their market was far from being local, however. They supplied organs to churches and other buildings in eighteen overseas countries, including the USA and China, as well as those in the Empire and Commonwealth. In the course of the twentieth century Harrison and Harrison built or restored organs in twenty-six cathedrals, including those in Lagos (Nigeria), Shanghai (China) and Auckland (New Zealand), as well as the Royal Albert Hall, the Royal College of Music, the Royal Festival Hall and Westminster Abbey in London.

HARTLEPOOL

Hartlepool lies within the district known as Hartness, which was probably an ancient estate or 'shire', with its centre at Hart, where parts of the fabric of the church indicate an eighth-century origin. Hartness was part of the WAPENTAKE OF SADBERGE, which was in Northumberland until 1189, when Richard I sold it to BISHOP HUGH OF LE PUISET. Hartlepool's history falls into three clear phases.

The first began in 647, when a woman whom BEDE calls Heiu founded a monastery at a place called Heruteu, meaning Hart Island. Excavations have established that the site of this monastery was about 150 yards (140 m) south-east of the present church of St Hilda. Bede claims Heiu was the first nun in Northumbria and that her decision to found the monastery was blessed by ST AIDAN. Shortly afterwards, however, she made way for a person of much higher rank, Hild, the niece of KING EDWINE of Northumbria, who was baptised with him in 627 and subsequently trained as a nun at the Frankish royal monastery at Chelles in France. Her appointment brought the monastery at Hartlepool under state control. In 657 Hild founded another monastery thirty miles south of Hartlepool at what was then called Streanaeshalch, now known by its later Scandinavian name, Whitby. The monastery at Hartlepool ceased to exist late in the eighth century, although not, apparently, as the result of destruction by Vikings.

The second phase of Hartlepool's history started over three hundred years later in the first decade of the twelfth century, when King Henry I (1100–35) granted a large estate in Cleveland and the district of Hartness to his supporter, Robert Bruce. Robert Bruce also became a major landowner in Scotland through the grant to him by the Scottish king, David I, of the lordship of Annandale. The estate did not remain united: after the death of Robert Bruce it was divided between his elder son, Adam Bruce, who got the lands south of the Tees, and his younger son, Robert Bruce II, who had Hartness and Annandale (see BALLIOL AND BRUCE FAMILIES).

Robert Bruce I built a castle at Skelton and founded a monastery at Guisborough. He may also have founded a borough at Hartlepool, although it is more likely that this was the work of his successors, who some time between 1162 and 1185 issued a charter to the men of Hartlepool giving them the same privileges as the burgesses of NEWCASTLE. In 1201 King John confirmed (for a fee of £6 13s 4d = £6.67) this charter, which in 1230 was amended in favour of the burgesses by the Bishop of Durham, Richard Poore (1229–37). These charters gave the men of Hartlepool the right to elect a mayor and to form a merchant guild, privileges that gave them a degree of independence. They also gave them the right to hold a weekly market on Tuesdays and an annual fair lasting fifteen days from the Feast of St Lawrence (10 August). Commercial activity, which grew considerably in the course of the thirteenth century, was centred on a marketplace laid out between Middlegate and High Street and Southgate. At the south end of the market a harbour covering 12 acres (5 ha) with a dock was created and sea defences erected, while at the north end was the church of St Hilda. Until after the Reformation the church did not have parochial status, but was a chapel of ease dependent on the parish church at Hart. Originally built in the twelfth century, probably when the borough was founded, it was reconstructed and enlarged in the thirteenth century and is basically the present church. One pointer to Hartlepool's size and importance is the presence in the town from 1259 of a Franciscan friary. Others are the receipt in 1306 of £200 from the custom duty on wool exports and the annual rent paid to the Crown by the burgesses for the right to manage their own affairs fixed in 1314 at £84, a figure that put the town on a par with DURHAM and DARLINGTON.

The early years of the fourteenth century saw considerable changes. In 1306 Edward I confiscated Hartness from Robert de Bruce VII, now styling himself King of Scots, and granted it to his most able army commander, Robert de Clifford, lord of Brougham in Westmorland (Cumbria). Bruce exacted his revenge nine years later when in 1315, the year after the Battle of Bannockburn, in which Clifford lost his life, Bruce's lieutenant, Sir James Douglas, sacked Hartlepool during a raid into Durham. This led to the building of a stone wall across the isthmus on which the town stood and along the beach to the cliffs near Sandgate. The wall was 1,050 yards (960 m) long, 7 feet (2.1 m) thick and 25 feet (7.6 m) high, and it crossed the harbour, leaving two gaps protected by towers and booms to allow access for fishing boats and commercial vessels. It was probably complete by 1350, although it was reinforced with square and round towers and bastions in the later fourteenth century. The wall replaced an earlier defensive system, comprising a ditch 16 feet (4.9 m) wide and 13 feet (3.9 m) deep, with an earthen bank on its inner side between 6 and 7 feet high. In 1353 Hartlepool's economy was damaged by the Crown's decision to require all wool from the four northern counties to be exported through Newcastle.

The sixteenth century brought one important change: in 1587 George Clifford, 3rd Earl of Cumberland, a descendant of Robert de Clifford, sold the lordship of the town to Lord Lumley (see LUMLEY FAMILY AND CASTLE). In 1593 the new owner restructured the borough's constitution. Henceforth the burgesses of Hartlepool were to have corporate status and the right to elect a mayor and a governing council. But in return for handing over his powers to the new corporation, Lumley demanded that they pay him half the annual income from court fines and commercial dues. This was the only significant change until the second quarter of the nineteenth century. By then Hartlepool was in a stagnant state, as indicated by the fact that the harbour had silted up and in 1808 was enclosed for farming. At that date, the town's population was no more than 1,000.

The third phase of Hartlepool's history began in the 1830s. Constitutionally, matters did not start well. In 1835 commissioners were appointed to investigate all existing boroughs in preparation for the Municipal Reform Act, which was to replace ancient, individual and in many cases corrupt corporations with standardised elected municipal councils. Hartlepool was not among the 178 boroughs reformed under the act because it was so decayed that the commissioners concluded that it no longer qualified as a corporate borough. There were only thirty-eight freemen, of whom twelve were non-resident, and the mayorality was confined to the owners of only nine burgages, of whom no more than six ever attended the mayor-making ceremony. Fifteen years elapsed before Hartlepool reached the standard required for borough status: by 1850, however, the increase in population from 1,500 to 9,500 made Hartlepool's claim undeniable and as a result it became a corporate borough ruled by a mayor, four aldermen and twelve councillors.

Hartlepool's change of fortune was the consequence of the setting up in 1831 of the Hartlepool Dock and Railway Co. (taken over by the North Eastern Railway in 1854). By 1835 it had reopened the old harbour and by 1840 had constructed the Victoria Dock. To these facilities coal was brought for export by the Hartlepool Railway, a 23-mile (37 km) railway line linking the town with pits in the Thornley and Wingate area. By the early 1840s Hartlepool was handling annually nearly 2,500 ships, in which nearly 500,000 tons of coal were exported.

Success bred emulation. In 1838 the Stockton and Hartlepool Railway Co. was formed. Its purpose was to divert coal coming from pits in the BISHOP AUCKLAND area destined for Middlesbrough via the Stockton and Darlington line to Hartlepool by a new eight-mile stretch of railway. From there it would be exported from a new dock the company intended to build on the south shore of Hartlepool Slake. To prevent this happening, the Hartlepool Dock and Rail Co. bought the Middleton Estate, thereby gaining control of the land to the south of the Slake and the sea entrance to it. Thwarted, the Stockton and Hartlepool Co. had no option but to ship its coal from the Hartlepool Dock and Rail Co.'s dock. This arrangement lasted no more than four years. In 1844 the Stockton and Hartlepool Co. terminated the agreement and reverted to its original plan to build its own dock, this time in the neighbouring township of Stranton. So began the town of West Hartlepool (see NEW TOWNS OF THE NINETEENTH CENTURY).

The development of West Hartlepool meant that Hartlepool was hemmed in to a small area, which restricted its scope for expansion. By 1881 the area of the old borough had a population of over 12,000. The situation became easier in 1883, when the borough was allowed to absorb Middleton to the south and Throston to the east, an expansion that allowed the population to rise to over 20,000 by 1891. It also led to the enlargement of the corporation to a mayor, six aldermen and eighteen elected councillors. In 1901 Hartlepool's population reached its highest level, 22,723, but by that date it had been far outstripped by West Hartlepool. Thereafter, the number declined to under 18,000 in 1961. Six years later, in 1967, the history of the ancient Borough of Hartlepool as an independent borough ended with its merger with West Hartlepool to form the new Borough of Hartlepool. Curiously, the union of Hartlepool and West Hartlepool (which had been proposed but rejected in 1902) was anticipated exactly one hundred years earlier, when in 1868 Hartlepool and West Hartlepool were united as a single-member parliamentary constituency.

Over its history, Hartlepool was prone to attack and occupation. In 1153 it was sacked by pirates and in 1315 devastated by the Scots. In 1569, during the RISING OF THE NORTHERN EARLS, it was occupied by Christopher Neville, the uncle of the Earl of Westmorland, with a force of 300 men in the hope that it would facilitate the landing of a Spanish army from the Netherlands. This did not happen (nor was it ever going to happen) and the rebels soon abandoned the town. The next occupation lasted much longer.

Like all other main towns in the North East, Hartlepool was occupied by a garrison from the Scottish army between 1644 and 1647 (see SCOTTISH OCCUPATION). The most unexpected attacks, however, occurred shortly after the outbreak of World War I. On 16 December 1914 three units of the German fleet (the battlecruisers *Seydlitz* and *Moltke* and the heavy cruiser *Blücher*) shelled Hartlepool for nearly three-quarters of an hour, firing 1,150 shells, which killed nine soldiers and 112 civilians and wounded another 400 people. They did not get away unscathed, however, as a 6-inch and two 4.7-inch shore guns returned fire and inflicted some damage.

In one important respect, the history of Hartlepool has come full circle: with the closure of the West Hartlepool docks and their conversion into a marina, Hartlepool has regained its status as a port. Currently, the Victoria Dock has three operational quays, with a 'ro-ro' facility and a quay to service the offshore oil industry close by.

HARTLEPOOL ART GALLERY (see ART GALLERIES)

HARTLEY, JAMES (1811–1886)

James Hartley, one of the foremost glass-makers of the nineteenth century, was born in Dumbarton, where his father, John Hartley, was the manager of a local glassworks. Family moves took Hartley to Bristol and then to Birmingham, where John Hartley became the manager of the crown glass firm of Chance. James Hartley was thus bred to the trade of glass manufacture. During the 1830s he pioneered a number of economies in the glass-making process and moved to SUNDERLAND to found his own business, the Wear Glass Works at Deptford. Success did not come immediately and for a time he returned to Birmingham to work for another concern. However, in 1847, he patented a new type of glass, rolled plate glass, and this proved to be a huge success. In 1854 he granted licences to Chance in Birmingham and Pilkington in St Helens to manufacture rolled plate glass, and these firms, together with Hartley, came to dominate the flat glass market.

As was common with successful businessmen, Hartley took on several public roles. He was Mayor of Sunderland in 1851 and 1862, Deputy Lieutenant for County Durham, a Justice of the Peace in both Sunderland and County Durham and MP for Sunderland from 1865 until 1868. He retired in 1869. Thereafter the firm he had founded failed: his son was an incompetent businessman, there was a damaging strike in 1891 and 1892, and in 1916 the Wear Glass Works was destroyed by fire.

HATTON GALLERY, NEWCASTLE UNIVERSITY (see ART GALLERIES)

HAWKS, GEORGE (1801–1863)

George Hawks was the fourth generation of an industrial dynasty that created one of the North East's early industrial empires. The business was begun by William Hawks I (1708–55), who having worked for AMBROSE CROWLEY at Swalwell, set up on his own on the GATESHEAD shore to manufacture iron goods, using scrap metal brought into the Tyne as ballast. The business was vastly enlarged by his son, William Hawks II (1751–1803), in partnership with a Sunderland man, Thomas Longridge (1751–1803). Not only did they enlarge the Gateshead enterprise, they also started other works at Beamish and Lumley in Durham, Ouseburn in Newcastle, and at the mouth of the River Blyth. The most lucrative sector of their business was supplying a variety of iron parts to the Royal Navy, which explains their decision to call the Gateshead works New Greenwich.

On William's death the business was divided between his sons: George I (1766–1820), Sir Robert (1768–1840) and John (1770–1830), but it was his grandson, George II, who, concentrating on the Gateshead works, gained the firm an international reputation for engineering, especially bridge building. In the North East its most famous accomplishment was a double-decker bridge, the High Level Bridge over the Tyne, opened in 1849 (rail) and 1850 (road). After 1840, however, control of the company was gradually lost as the result of the sale of Sir Robert Hawks's shares to the South Wales ironmaster, George Crawshay (1794–1873), who became the driving force after George Hawks II's death. The firm, now Hawks, Crawshay and Sons, went into liquidation in 1889.

A testimony to the status and standing of the firm in the early years of the nineteenth century is the tale, humorous and entirely apocryphal, of the Duke of Wellington having to send for the 'Haaks Men' to help him defeat Napoleon.

HEDLEY, RALPH (1848–1913)

Ralph Hedley was born in the village of Gilling West in North Yorkshire but lived all but his school years in NEWCASTLE. He came to the city as an apprentice woodcarver, but during his years in training also attended evening classes in painting and drawing given by WILLIAM BELL SCOTT at the Government School of Design. He was thus able to pursue two careers. In 1869 he began his own woodcarving business, which over the next decades discharged numerous commissions, although most of the work was not done by Hedley but by members of his workshop. The work for which he is best known was in St Nicholas's Church in Newcastle, which became a cathedral in 1882. Alongside this he became widely popular within the region as an artist. Today his most appreciated works are his paintings of scenes from local life.

HEDLEY, THOMAS (1809–1890)

Thomas Hedley was the son of a sheep farmer at Harnham, Northumberland, who in 1826 secured employment as a junior clerk in the office of John Greene & Sons, wine merchants and tallow chandlers in GATESHEAD. With an aptitude and liking for figures, he rapidly improved his financial skills through evening classes at the Gateshead Mechanics' Institute, so that when in 1839 Greenes expanded into soap making in NEWCASTLE, Hedley became a partner in the new enterprise. Eventually, in 1861, he bought control of the business, at which point he took into partnership his brother, Edward and his son, Armorer. Thereafter he raised the quality of his products by using palm oil as the basic ingredient in preference to tallow, and the success he enjoyed led to the firm becoming a limited liability company in 1897. However, the brand name for which the firm became world-famous, 'Fairy', with its logo of a small boy in a nappy striding purposefully from right to left, was not invented by Hedleys, but by a Birmingham firm that Hedleys took over in 1898. Hedley did not confine his business interests to his own firm: at various times he was chairman of the Newcastle and Gateshead Gas Co., the Solway Haematite Co. of Maryport, and the Tyne Shipping Co., and he was a director of the Consett Iron Co., Clelands Slipway, and the North East Banking Co. He was also involved in local politics, becoming a member of the Newcastle Town Council in 1853 and serving as sheriff in 1860–61 and mayor in 1863–64.

Ten years after his death, however, a controlling interest in the company was bought by Lord Kylsant, the chairman of the shipping company, the Elder Dempster Line. This phase of the company's history lasted until 1930, when financial difficulties forced him to sell to the American firm Procter and Gamble of Cincinnati, Ohio. This company had been formed in 1837 by two immigrants, an English candle maker, William Procter, and an Irish soap maker, James Gamble. Their acquisition of Hedleys was their first in Europe and they continued to trade in Britain under the name Thomas Hedley until 1962. P&G are now a huge international corporation with operations in fifteen European countries in addition to the UK. Of their eighteen research centres, five are in Europe, one of which in Newcastle specialises in fabric and home care products.

HEDLEY, WILLIAM (1779–1843)

William Hedley was born at Newburn on Tyne, the son of a grocer. He was among the group of men working to develop a viable steam locomotive in the first decades of the nineteenth century. His work was done at Wylam Colliery, to where he moved as viewer after serving in the same role at Walbottle. Hedley's major contribution to railway development was his demonstration that 'friction adhesion' would allow smooth wheels to act on smooth rails. He built his most famous engine, *Puffing Billy*, in 1813 with the help of TIMOTHY HACKWORTH and a John Forster and with the backing of the colliery's owner, Christopher Blackett. It had a working life of almost fifty years and is now in the Science Museum in London. Its sister engine, *Wylam Dilly*, is in the Royal Museum of Scotland in Edinburgh.

In the 1820s, however, Hedley resigned his position as viewer at Wylam in order to pursue his business interests, which included leasing collieries at Callerton, Shield Row and South Moor. He died at his home, Burnhopeside Hall, near Lanchester.

HEMY, CHARLES NAPIER (1841–1917)

One of the best maritime painters of the nineteenth century, Charles Hemy was born in Newcastle, the eldest of the three sons of Henry Hemy, a music teacher and composer. Although he had early lessons from WILLIAM SCOTT BELL at the Government School of Art, his proper training was delayed until the 1860s, largely thanks to the decision of his parents to migrate to Australia. Hemy found his new home uncongenial and worked his passage home to Tyneside. In the years that followed, he oscillated between an inclination towards the Roman Catholic priesthood, which led to his spending some time at USHAW COLLEGE, and working as a sailor on the colliers plying between Newcastle and London. His experience in this work, together with that of the long voyages to and from Australia, gave him an abiding passion for the sea. It was probably this that drove him to undergo training as a painter at the Antwerp Academy. On his return he settled in London and rapidly gained a reputation as a maritime artist. In 1880 he moved to Falmouth in Cornwall to live next to the subject he loved. His reputation was based on his composition skill, but also on the accuracy with which he depicted both the water and ships upon it, in both oils and watercolour.

Both of Hemy's brothers became artists and like him specialised in marine subjects. Thomas Maria Madawaska Hemy (1852–1937) was born at sea on the ship, *Madawaska*, that took the family to Australia. He too returned to the North East, but moved to London in the 1890s. The youngest brother, Bernard Benedict (1855–1915), was born in Australia but returned to his family roots in the North East, where he continued to live, apart from a period spent at the Antwerp Academy.

HENDERSON, ARTHUR (1863–1935)

Arthur Henderson, who was a major figure in the early years of the Labour Party, was born in Glasgow, the illegitimate son of a domestic servant who moved to Newcastle in 1872 when Arthur was aged nine. On leaving school in 1875, he trained at the Forth Banks works of ROBERT STEPHENSON and Hawthorns, but in 1893 moved to work at the Newcastle *Evening News*. During these years he became active in trade union affairs and in local politics. In both fields he was a moderate, convinced, as were many politically active workers of his generation, that conciliation and co-operation were both right and sensible. This belief was closely linked to his staunch Methodism, which also resulted in a lifelong abjuration of drinking, smoking and gambling. In politics he was what was then known as a 'Lib-Lab', a workingman in the Liberal Party, and it was as such that he was elected to the Newcastle City Council.

In 1895, however, he moved to DARLINGTON to become political agent for Sir Joseph Pease, the Liberal MP for BARNARD CASTLE. Three years later he was elected to Darlington Borough Council and in 1903 was chosen as mayor. That same year, he was elected as Labour MP for Barnard Castle upon Pease's retirement. The change of label was not the consequence of a change of political philosophy, but of his union's decision to adhere to the recently formed Labour Representation Committee: as their delegate for the North East, he was bound to follow its lead, since it paid his salary until 1911, when MPs became state salaried. From this time until his death he was one of the central figures in the emerging Labour Party, at any given time holding the office of Secretary, Treasurer or Chairman, as well as acting as its Chief Whip in the Commons.

He also became prominent in government. In May 1915 he joined Asquith's coalition ministry, nominally as President of the Board of Education, but spending most of his time on Lloyd George's munitions committee, whose purpose was to galvanise industrial production for the war effort. When Lloyd George replaced Asquith as Prime Minister in December 1916, Henderson became a member of his small war cabinet. He resigned, however, following Conservative objections to his open support for the Socialist International, believing that this was the necessary means of helping the moderate Russian leader, Alexander Kerensky, to resist the Bolshevik extremists.

Henderson severed, unnecessarily, his links with the North East at the end of World War I. As his work was mainly in London and as boundary changes had made his Barnard Castle seat marginal, instead of opting for the newly created and safe seat of Spennymoor, he chose to fight the London constituency of East Ham, only to be defeated. Although he was briefly MP for Newcastle East in 1923, between 1919 and his death he represented Widnes (1919–22), Burnley (1924–31) and finally Clay Cross, Derbyshire (1924–33).

It was during these years that he gained national and international prominence. He was Home Secretary in the short-lived Labour government of 1924 and Foreign Secretary in the second Labour government that came to power in 1924. When in 1931 the Labour Prime Minister, RAMSAY MACDONALD, chose to form a National Government, Henderson replaced him as leader of the Labour Party. His tenure ended less than three months later when he lost his seat in the October election of that year. His international reputation arose from his efforts to secure world peace through negotiation. He strongly supported the League of Nations, negotiated normal diplomatic relations with the new USSR, and from 1932 until 1935 he was chairman of the World

Disarmament Conference. His efforts won him the Nobel Peace Prize in 1934, the year before his death.

HEPBURN, THOMAS (1796–1864)

Tommy Hepburn was the earliest leader of the Durham miners (see GREAT NORTHERN COALFIELD). He was born at Pelton into a mining family and was orphaned early when his father was killed in a mine accident. He started work at the age of eight at Urpeth Colliery and by the late 1820s he was working at the recently opened Hetton Colliery, having been at Fatfield and Jarrow: like most pitmen, he moved from pit to pit. During the same years he found time to acquire some education, sufficient to become a Primitive Methodist preacher. By the time of the event that brought him to the fore, he was a man who commanded respect and had leadership qualities.

The crisis that blew up in the Durham coalfield in 1831 and 1832 centred on two grievances: one was the long hours that boys were forced to work; the other was the bond, the contract that miners were required to sign that bound them to an employer for an entire year. In April 1831 there was widespread refusal to sign the bond. The coal owners' response was a lockout. Hepburn emerged as the organiser of the resistance, and by insisting that the miners conducted their dispute with restraint and within the law secured a wide measure of public support. In the end, the coal owners conceded the principle of shorter hours for boys.

Such was Hepburn's prestige after this victory that he was able to give up work in the pit in order to be the full-time organiser of the pitmen's union, earning his living by running a school. But in the following year his inability to control the members became fatefully apparent. The strike that broke out in 1832 was marred by violence and at least two murders. Public opinion was alienated and this stiffened the resolve of the owners. 'Black legs' were brought in and by the end of the summer the strike collapsed.

As the leader of a broken union, Hepburn could expect to remain unemployed indefinitely. That he found work was due to the magnanimity of Thomas Forster, the manager of Felling Colliery, who offered him employment, but only if he agreed to forsake union activity. In the years that followed Hepburn was a deputy, an overman, a lamp inspector and a master wasteman. Although he was a supporter of the struggle for the People's Charter, because of his promise to Forster, he declined to take part in the next great attempt to form a miners' union in 1844. The fact that a later generation of miners begged him to become their leader was testimony to the reputation he had acquired in 1832.

Sadly, in his last years he became mentally incapacitated. He died in 1864 and was buried at Heworth.

HEPPLEWHITE, GEORGE (?1727–1786)

Almost nothing is known about this George Hepplewhite, who was one of the three most influential British furniture designers of the eighteenth century (the others being THOMAS SHERATON and Thomas Chippendale) and whose designs have stood the test of time. Although born in Ryton, there is no record of him thereafter until 1768, when he has been identified as living in Clerkenwell in London, then a major furniture-making location. It is reasonable to assume that at some time and somewhere in the previous thirty years he had been successfully apprenticed to the trade. The only other information we have about his life is that he married (his wife's name was Alice) and that he had two sons. His fame rests on his *Cabinet-Maker and Upholsterer's Guide*, which was published in 1788, two years after his death. It contained 300 designs and 126 illustrations and its influence spread to the USA and Europe.

HESILRIGE, SIR ARTHUR, Bt (1601–1661)

Arthur Hesilrige (there are various spellings of his name) was a major figure in the life of the North East in the six years after the end of the 1st Civil War (1642–47). He was the son of a substantial Midland landowner, Sir Thomas Hesilrige of Noseley, Leicestershire. He was educated at Magdalene College, Cambridge and Gray's Inn and succeeded to his father's title and estate in 1630. By that date he had come to hold very radical political and religious opinions, which alienated him from Charles I and his policies to the extent that he considered emigrating to the American colonies.

He was deflected from this by the summoning of parliament in 1640, the first time since 1629. Elected as one of the two members for his county, he took an active part in the subsequent revolution that deposed Charles I, abolished the monarchy and established a republic. His distinguished military career in the 1640s led to his appointment as Governor of NEWCASTLE in 1647, following the departure of the Scottish army of occupation (see SCOTTISH OCCUPATION). When war flared up again between 1648 and 1650, he was again active in the field, accompanying Oliver Cromwell's invasion of Scotland in 1650. After Cromwell's decisive victory at Dunbar, Hesilrige was put in charge of the Scottish prisoners of war, which he housed in DURHAM CATHEDRAL, pending their dispatch to the colonies.

His office enabled him to dominate North-East life and, like so many others, he worked to the adage 'to the victor the spoils', using his power to purchase the former episcopal estates of EASINGTON and Wolsingham, and also BISHOP AUCKLAND, where he began demolishing the bishop's palace preparatory to building a modern manor house (see AUCKLAND CASTLE). This scheme was halted in mid-course by his fall from power in 1653 as the result of his quarrel with Oliver Cromwell, with whom he differed on two fundamental issues. Firmly committed to the concept of a republic governed by an elected parliament, he opposed Cromwell's assumption of the title Lord Protector with its quasi-regal overtones and powers. As a Presbyterian, he was equally hostile to Cromwell's favouring of Independency, the tolerant religious policy that allowed, within broad limits that excluded Roman Catholicism and Anglicanism, independent sects to devise their own forms of worship.

When Charles II and the monarchy were restored in 1660, Hesilrige's name was among those exempted from the Act of Indemnity, even though he was known to have opposed Charles I's execution. However, he died in the Tower in 1661, before the new regime could exact vengeance.

HESLETINE, JAMES (c.1672–1763)

James Hesletine was born in Durham but was trained as a musician at the Chapel Royal by Dr John Blow, a leading English composer of his day. In 1711 he was appointed organist at DURHAM CATHEDRAL, a post he held until his death fifty-two years later. Like all of his kind, his duties included composing for choir and organ. Unfortunately, very few of his compositions have survived: for reasons not known, he tore all of his works out of the cathedral choir books some time after 1750. However, *A Collection of Anthems*, published in 1749, and a few other surviving pieces, show him to have been a composer of considerable merit.

HESLOP, HAROLD (1898–1983)

Harry Heslop, a virtually forgotten novelist, has been credited with inventing the mining novel and influencing the better-known Sid Chaplin. He was born at New Hunwick, near Crook, where his father was a colliery overman, and was sufficiently intelligent to win a scholarship to King James's Grammar School, Bishop Auckland, but was unable to continue with his place as in 1911 his father moved to North Yorkshire to become the manager of an ironstone mine at Boulby. Shortly afterwards, however, his mother died and his father remarried, a move that broke up the family, Harry moving to South Shields to work at Harton Colliery. This experience over the next twelve years turned him into a radical: he became active in the Durham Miners' Association (DMA) and a member of the Independent Labour Party. His political stance became more extreme between 1923 and 1926, when, as the holder of a DMA scholarship at the Central Labour College in London, he was exposed to an essentially Marxist curriculum.

On completion of the course in 1926 he returned to South Shields and Harton Colliery. He resumed his activities in the DMA and was one of a group of extremists who wanted the union movement to work for the overthrow of the capitalist system. In the following year, however, he was made redundant in the aftermath of the 1926 strike. Early in 1928 he returned to London with his wife, a Londoner from a politically left-wing family, whom he had married in 1926. That year saw the publication of his first novel about mining, entitled *Goaf*, not in Britain but in translation in Russia, where it sold over half a million copies. During the inter-war years, Heslop continued to live in London, earning a living through a variety of low-grade jobs, including work for Arcos, the Russian trade mission. He also wrote and had published three further mining novels: *The Gate of a Strange Field* (1929), *Journey Beyond* (1930) and *The Last Cage Down* (1935). In addition, *Goaf* was published in Britain in 1934, as was a thriller he wrote, *The Crime of Peter Ropner*, which was praised by the popular crime writer, Dorothy L. Sayers; and he co-authored a book on the abdication of Edward VIII. These were not the only products of his pen: he also wrote articles, some of which appeared in print, and novels, plays, scripts for the radio and biographies, none of which were published or performed. The one exception was a futuristic novel, *Red Earth*, which was published in translation in Russia in 1942.

By that time he had followed his wife and two children to Taunton in Somerset, where they had gone as evacuees. He was to live there until his death in 1983, again earning his living in low-grade jobs. He continued to write until 1960, including his autobiography, *Karl Marx* and *The Class Nature of English Society*, but without finding a publisher. Although he continued to be very left-wing in his politics, at some point in the post-war years he ceased to be a Communist and joined the Labour Party.

Unlike many of the inter-war alumni of the Central Labour College who became prominent trade union leaders and Labour politicians, most notably Aneurin Bevan, Harry Heslop appears not to have been moved to carve out a high-flying career for himself. Nor did thirty years of literary effort yield other than modest profit and critical recognition, except in the USSR: like many prophets, he was more appreciated in foreign parts than in his own country.

HEXHAM, BATTLE OF, 1464

The Battle of Hexham, fought on 15 May 1464, ended the struggle of Edward IV, son of Richard, Duke of York, to overthrow and replace the Lancastrian king, the feeble Henry VI. Edward had effectively gained the throne by his victory at Towton in Yorkshire in 1461, but Henry VI and his determined French wife, Margaret of Anjou, held out in Northumberland, where the leading families supported the Lancastrian cause. Their attempt to recover Henry's throne, organised and led by Henry Beaufort, Duke of Somerset, ended in failure. On 25 April, he was defeated at Hedgeley Moor about a mile and a half north of the Breamish at Powburn on what is now the A697, by John Neville, Lord Montagu, the brother of Richard, Earl of Warwick (Warwick the Kingmaker).

Somerset escaped, retreated into the Tyne valley and raised more troops. But he was pursued by Montagu, and the two armies again met, but exactly where is not certain. The most detailed study of the battle has located its site on Swallowship Hill on the west side of Devil's Water, about two hundred yards above Linnels Bridge. The clash of the two armies, neither of which exceeded 4,000 men, was soon over, with the Lancastrian cause totally defeated. Somerset was captured and beheaded in Hexham the same day. Another notable Lancastrian, Sir William Tailbois, managed to escape, but he was caught later with a large sum of money (not his, but Henry VI's) hiding in a coal pit near Newcastle. While all this was happening, the hapless Henry VI was in the castle at BYWELL, whence he escaped, leaving behind his sword and his crowned helmet. He was captured some days later at Clitheroe in Lancashire. The Battle of Hexham, though not on a large scale, was one of the decisive military engagements in the dynastic and power struggles that have been given the fanciful title, the 'Wars of the Roses'.

HEXHAM, JOHN OF (?–1189×1209)

Both Richard and John (see following article) were natives of HEXHAM, both joined the Augustinian Canonry founded there in 1114, and both became prior, Richard in 1141 and John in 1160. And both wrote invaluable accounts of the important events that took place in the region during their lifetimes and which influenced its future.

John of Hexham's *History of the Church of Hexham* covers the years 1135 to 1154. Although some of its material derives from his predecessor's work, John's book is an important source for the events after 1139, particularly the failed attempt by David I to secure the bishopric of Durham for his Chancellor, William Cumin, and the civil war that ensued between 1141 and 1144.

HEXHAM, RICHARD OF (?–1155×1167)

Prior of Hexham from 1141, Richard of Hexham wrote a work, entitled *De Gestis Regis Stephani et de Bello Standardii* (*The Deeds of King Stephen and the Battle of the Standard*), recording in detail the invasions in 1136 and 1138 of the region by David I, King of Scots (1124–53), whose purpose was to bring Northumberland, Durham, Cumberland and Westmorland (Cumbria) under his rule. His second invasion was crushingly defeated on 22 August 1138 at the Battle of the Standard, so called because of the presence of the banners of several major Yorkshire churches. Despite this setback, David secured from the English king, Stephen, weakened by civil war further south, a major concession: by the Treaty of Durham, agreed in 1139, David acquired the Earldom of Northumbria, comprising Northumberland, Cumberland and Westmorland.

Richard also had a cultural purpose, to proclaim the virtues and values of the pre-Conquest church of Hexham stretching back to its founder, ST WILFRID, while extolling the Augustinian Canonry to which he belonged. Like SYMEON at Durham in the previous generation, for Richard reconciling the present Anglo-Norman with the previous Anglo-Saxon world was a necessary task.

HEXHAMSHIRE AND HEXHAM

Hexhamshire straddles the Tyne: to the north, it extends as far as the Erring Burn and includes the fertile townships of Bingfield, Cocklaw, Wall, Fallowfield, Portgate, Acomb, Anick and Sandhoe; the area to the south is larger, stretching as far as Nookton Edge, the boundary with County Durham. But apart from Hexham itself, which unlike other early Tynedale settlements lies on the south side of the river, this area was originally almost devoid of settlement, being open and less attractive moorland.

The origins of Hexhamshire are not known, but it was probably an estate before *c.*674, when Queen Aethelthryth, the first wife of KING ECGFRITH of Northumbria, gave it to ST WILFRID. Because it was she who made the donation, it may have been part of her dowry, given to her by her father-in-law, KING OSWIU. It has been further argued that the estate may originally have been within the British kingdom of Rheged, centred on Carlisle, and that it became a Northumbrian possession as the result of the marriage of Oswiu and the Rhegedian princess, Rienmellth. If so, Hexhamshire was a border estate that changed hands as part of a marriage agreement.

All this is conjecture. What is certain is that Wilfrid's purpose, for which Queen Aethelthryth gave him this extensive property, was to found a monastery. This he did to some effect, since his church was described at the time (almost certainly with exaggeration) as the finest north of the Alps. What made it special was its construction in stone, a building material not normally used at this date by the Anglo-Saxons. For this, there was a ready-made source close at hand, the ruins of the Roman fort at CORBRIDGE, three miles to the east. Since nothing of this church remains above ground, its precise form cannot be known. The latest archaeological view is that there were two separate churches on the same east–west axis. The larger stood over the crypt (rediscovered in 1725), the entrance to which is in the nave of the present church. The smaller was a separate chapel, roughly where the so-called *frith stool* stands in the chancel of the church. This sort of arrangement is known elsewhere in England and on the continent. In addition to the church and its chapel, there would have been an extensive range of domestic buildings within an enclosure.

Hexham was not merely an abbey. For 240 years from 681 it was also the centre of a diocese, covering the central sector of Northumbria between the Aln and the Tees. To the north of it, stretching as far as the River Forth, was the Diocese of Lindisfarne, and to the south, between the Tees and the Humber, the Diocese of York. This arrangement continued until the early years of the ninth century, when all aspects of Northumbrian society were being disrupted or destroyed by the Vikings. After 821, there are no further references to the bishops of Hexham.

For the next 200 years we have no knowledge of Hexham and its 'shire'. When the mist clears in the eleventh century, it is evident that Hexham had fallen under the control of the Bishop of Durham, whose diocese now stretched from the Tees to the Tweed. In his hands lay the right to appoint the two officers who controlled the 'shire': the Provost, who administered the estate and had authority in secular matters, and the Priest, whose authority was over spiritual life. When this arrangement was devised is not known, although it was in existence by the beginning of the eleventh century. In 1070 the posts were in the hands of two Englishmen, respectively, Uhtred and Eilaf, who was also the Treasurer of the Community of St Cuthbert in Durham (see CUTHBERT, SAINT).

In the following thirteen years the ownership of Hexham and its 'shire' changed hands. The early 1070s were a time of chaos in northern England following the violent suppression of native resistance by William the Conqueror in the winter of 1069–70 and the deposition in 1070 of Bishop Aethelwine of Durham. When the king delayed appointing a new bishop until 1072, Uhtred transferred his allegiance to the Archbishop of York, Thomas of Bayeux. Thirteen years later, in 1083, the Priest of Hexham, Eilaf, did the same. Then the cause was the decision of BISHOP WILLIAM OF ST CALAIS to replace the old Community of St Cuthbert with a Benedictine priory. As a married member of the Community, Eilaf had no place in the new dispensation. The Archbishop, however, allowed him to carry on at Hexham, without putting his wife away.

The consequence of these two acts was that for centuries Hexham and Hexhamshire were an anomaly: surrounded by Northumberland, this was an 'alien territory', owned by and governed by the Archbishop of York. In secular matters the Archbishop's rule continued until 1545, when Henry VIII's government confiscated the estate and made it Crown property. Twenty-six years later, in 1571, Hexhamshire was made part of the COUNTY OF NORTHUMBERLAND. Between 1071 and 1545, however, Hexhamshire was governed, not by the officers of the Crown, but by the Archbishop's Bailiff, whose fourteenth-century headquarters, the Moot Hall and the Old Gaol, are still prominent features of Hexham's landscape. These lay within a walled compound, access to which was, and still is, by a passage under the Moot Hall from the Market Place.

In ecclesiastical matters the authority of York lasted even longer. Hexhamshire continued to be a detached part of the diocese of York until 1837, when the sweeping reform of the Church of England did away with this and similar anomalies, which were known as 'jurisdictional peculiars'. Hexham rejoined the diocese of Durham after an interval of 766 years. With the division of the diocese of Durham in 1882, Hexham became part of the new diocese of NEWCASTLE.

The dominant building in Hexham is the abbey. This is not Wilfrid's church but that of the house of Augustinian canons founded in 1114 by the Archbishop of York, Thurstan (1114–40), who believed that this order, which allowed its members to work as parish priests, could rejuvenate the religious life of the region. The church was erected between *c.*1180 and *c.*1250, but only a part of it has survived. The east end of the chancel was rebuilt between 1856 and 1858, while virtually the whole of the nave was built afresh but on the original foundations between 1905 and 1908. This was necessary as a result of events following the decision to close the canonry in 1537 as part of the general suppression of monasteries. The move to close Hexham provoked armed resistance, which helped to trigger the PILGRIMAGE OF GRACE. After the resistance ended, the nave was demolished, but the chancel was retained as the parish church. Given all of these vicissitudes, the survival of Wilfrid's episcopal seat, the frith stool, and of the fifteenth-century pulpitum and the choir stalls with their misericords and two chantries is remarkable. Although much of the church survived, most of the claustral and domestic buildings have not, the only substantial exception being the prior's house, which was occupied by successive lords of the manor to whom Hexham was granted by the Crown. What can be seen today, however, is largely the rebuilding that followed a major fire in 1819.

The town of Hexham was transformed by the building of the Augustinian canonry. The moorland south of the town was also changed, but in less spectacular fashion by means of gradual colonisation. This process was under way by 1114 when the canons arrived, since Thurstan endowed them with the small townships of Yarridge and Dotland. The following two hundred years were a period of population growth and the result was the creation of about forty farms or small hamlets, carved out of the moorland. Enough evidence has survived to show that this process was sanctioned if not promoted by the archbishops of York, who would benefit from the rents paid by their tenants. Most of this colonisation took place on the western bank of Devil's Water and its tributaries, but farms were also established along the West Dipton and Darden burns. Although about 7,000 acres (2,800 ha) were enclosed and brought under cultivation, this was less than a third of the available moorland, which was not enclosed until the late eighteenth century.

The basic shape of Hexham on the day the abbey closed remained unaltered for over three hundred years. Then in 1864 the lord of the manor, William Beaumont, and the local authority co-operated to create Beaumont Street, a broad, tree-lined road linking the Market Place and Battle Hill. In the process many crowded sub-standard dwellings and narrow vennels were swept away and the Market Place opened up. It also made possible the building of the Town Hall and Corn Exchange.

Since the closing of the abbey, Hexham has been a local market town, gradually increasing in size and serving the valleys of the North and the South Tyne, which meet a few hundred yards above the town. The bridge over the Tyne, built in 1799, has served to link the town with the main road system which always has, and still does, run on the north side of the river, while the railway, built in the 1830s, links it with Newcastle and Carlisle.

HICKS, WILLIAM SEARLE (1849–1902)

William Hicks was one of the most highly considered late Victorian church architects in Britain, at a time when the continued growth of population meant a demand for new churches and the enlargement of existing buildings. In tune with the ideas of his day, he was an exponent of Gothic Revival, favouring whenever possible the perpendicular style. He was born in Dorset, the son of a clerical family, from whom he acquired a lifelong commitment to the Church of England. His connection with the North East began in 1866 when, at the age of seventeen, he became a pupil of R.J. Johnson, whom he later succeeded as Diocesan Architect to the Newcastle Diocese. After completing his training, he set up in NEWCASTLE and in 1888 took a partner, H.C. Charlewood. Much of his work was the repair, embellishment or remodelling of existing churches. But he did design thirteen new churches in the region, seven with his partner. The most notable are St Matthew, Summerhill in Newcastle, Holy Sepulchre in Ashington and St James Shilbottle.

HODGKIN, THOMAS (1831–1913)

Thomas Hodgkin was born in Tottenham, London, into a Quaker family. His father, John, was a barrister, and his mother, Elizabeth, the daughter of Luke Howard, a meteorologist. As a Quaker, he was barred from entry to Oxford or Cambridge and so he took his degree at University College, London. Initially he was set to follow his father into the law, but poor health forced him to move out of London and into the provinces and to a career in banking, first at Pontefract and then at Whitehaven. His arrival in NEWCASTLE followed the failure in 1857 of the Northumberland and District Bank, which left an opportunity for a new bank in the town. The result was the formation of Hodgkin, Barrett, Pease and Spence, which in 1902 became part of Lloyds.

Long before that, however, Hodgkin had retired from active participation in banking in order to devote himself to history. This was largely the result of a holiday in Italy in 1868, which fired him with enthusiasm for that country's history. His great work, published in four volumes in 1870, but expanded to eight volumes for the second edition in 1892, was *Italy and her Invaders*, a study of what happened in the Italian peninsula during the collapse of the Roman Empire. He also produced the translated letters of the late Roman Christian intellectual, Cassiodorus, who was responsible for preserving much of the scholarship of the ancient world (1886), *The Life of Theodoric*, the Ostrogothic King of Italy between 493 and 526 (1891), and *The History of England from the Earliest Times to the Norman Conquest* (1906). But his importance for the North East lies in his successful move in 1890 to reawaken interest in the idea of completing JOHN HODGSON's *History of Northumberland*, which had lain dormant since 1858. In addition he was a stalwart contributor to *Archaeologia Aeliana*, the organ of the Society of Antiquaries of Newcastle upon Tyne (see LITERARY AND PHILOSOPHICAL SOCIETY OF NEWCASTLE UPON TYNE), which published over fifty of his articles and notes.

From the late 1850s Hodgkin's home was in Northumberland at Benwell, then Bamburgh and finally at Barmoor Castle. He died suddenly while on holiday and is buried at Budock in Cornwall.

HODGSON, REVD JOHN (1779–1845)

Broadly, it may be said that John Hodgson is to the history of Northumberland what ROBERT SURTEES is to Durham, but more so. He was not a Northumbrian but was born in the parish of Shap in Westmorland (Cumbria) and educated until the age of nineteen at Brampton Grammar School. At that point he should have gone to university, but his family was unable to bear the cost. Consequently, he became a schoolteacher, first at Matterdale and then at Stainton near Penrith in Cumberland (Cumbria), and subsequently at Sedgefield and Lanchester in Durham. In 1804, at the second attempt, he passed the Church of England ordination examination and became curate of Esh and Satley in Lanchester parish where he was already working. Two years later he became curate at Gateshead and joined the LITERARY AND PHILOSOPHICAL SOCIETY OF NEWCASTLE UPON TYNE. After two years in Gateshead, he got his first parish, Jarrow, which included Heworth, where he built the church of St Mary, partly to his own design.

By then his antiquarian interests were well developed and in 1810 he was commissioned to write an account of Northumberland for a traveller's guide entitled *The Beauties of England*. In 1812 he was one of the seventy men brought together by the Newcastle bookseller, John Bell, to found the Society of Antiquaries of Newcastle upon Tyne (see LITERARY AND PHILOSOPHICAL SOCIETY OF NEWCASTLE UPON TYNE), which came into formal existence the following year. The same year he further enhanced his literary reputation by producing a full and accurate account of the Felling Colliery disaster (see COLLIERY DISASTERS). All this was by way of preparation for his great work, *A History of Northumberland*. This was published in six volumes between 1820 and 1840: three comprised histories of families, landownership and churches presented in a parochial framework; the others were complementary compilations of transcribed original documents. By 1840 Hodgson's health did not permit him to continue, but in 1858, long after his death, his great project was completed in one respect when John Hodgson Hinde brought out a general history of the county. But only up to a point: Hodgson's intention had been to cover the whole county, but he managed to deal with only twenty-one of the county's sixty-four ancient parishes. His ambition, while wholly laudable, was beyond one man's capacity.

Nevertheless, his achievement was monumental, and it stood as a standing reproach to the following generations of those interested in the county's history, until they were provoked into action in 1890 by THOMAS HODGKIN. The outcome was the formation of a committee to oversee the completion of Hodgson's work. It is a measure of Hodgson's achievement that it required a further fifteen volumes and took nearly fifty years to complete, and without Alnwick, Berwick and North Durham, which were thought to have been sufficiently covered by other publications. The Northumberland County History was finally completed in 1940, exactly one hundred years after Hodgson laid down his pen. One consequence of the revival of Hodgson's project was that Northumberland opted out of the Victoria County History project, the only English county to do so.

Hodgson did not work entirely unaided. Although he went to London to consult the national records, he was given great support by Sir John Swinburne of Capheaton, who made available his large collection of manuscripts, and by Walter Trevelyan of Wallington (see TREVELYAN FAMILY AND WALLINGTON HALL). All the while he was a clergyman with parochial duties, and it is to their credit that his diocesans, Shute Barrington and WILLIAM VAN MILDERT, helped him financially and by providing him with the comfortable livings of Kirkwhelpington in 1823 and Hartburn in 1833, the latter a kindly move to assuage his bereavement at the deaths of his wife and child.

Hodgson's volumes contain a wealth of information and are still consulted by historians. Their structure is now dated in its focus on church, land ownership and landed families, but these were the concerns of those who bought his books and were central to a largely pre-industrial and pre-urban society.

HOLY ISLAND

Holy Island, also known as Lindisfarne, is not a true island in that it is accessible from the mainland twice daily at low tide. It is most widely known as the home of the monastery founded in 635 by ST AIDAN where the LINDISFARNE GOSPELS and other notable biblical works were produced in the late seventh and eighth centuries, and as the home of ST CUTHBERT. Regrettably, as Aidan's monastery was of wooden construction, all trace of it has disappeared. Recent studies have suggested that there were two churches and that they lay under the present parish church and the ruins of the later priory, and that between them was a tall carved cross. Further detailed excavation may yield more clues as to the buildings and the compound in which they were located. This monastery was abandoned in 875, on account of its exposed situation and the threat from seaborne raiders.

Thereafter virtually nothing is known about the island until after the foundation of Durham Cathedral Priory in 1083 and the building of the second cathedral at Durham, which began ten years later. Not long afterwards, probably some time in the first two decades of the twelfth century, the monks of the Cathedral Priory decided to revive monastic life on Holy Island. They did so because Holy Island was the first resting place of the body of St Cuthbert, of which they were trustees, and their titular head, the Bishop of Durham, was the successor of the bishops of Lindisfarne. The architectural remains of the church they built show that it closely resembled DURHAM CATHEDRAL in style. From then until the closure of the monasteries by Henry VIII, this church was the focal point of a cell, an outstation of the Durham Cathedral Priory, staffed by up to twelve of its monks. The church is almost certainly built over that in which St Cuthbert's body was buried, and a cenotaph was erected over the spot, doubtless in the hope of attracting pilgrims.

Close by was the parish church of Holy Island, which served not only the island community, but also over twenty townships on the mainland, although by 1157 there were chapels of ease at Ancroft, Kyloe, Lowick and Tweedmouth. This church, which probably is of Anglo-Saxon origin, continues to serve the community of the island, but not those on the mainland, where new parishes were created in the nineteenth century.

The closing of the monastery did not end the island's importance, since it had one of the best harbours on the North-East coast. Consequently, in both the sixteenth and the seventeenth centuries several defensive measures were undertaken. The first was the construction of three earthen bulwarks in the 1540s, a time when the government was upgrading defences along the eastern and southern coasts. However, nothing of these remain, and not even their whereabouts is certain. In contrast, the castle constructed on the outcrop at the south end of the island, known as Beblow or Biblaw, is a prominent and much photographed and painted building. It was built between 1557 and 1571 thanks to the insistence of Sir William Read, the man responsible for the island's defence. It was essentially an artillery platform from which the harbour, then covering a larger area than it does today, could be dominated. As the dangers receded, the castle became obsolete and eventually ruinous. It was saved and reconstructed to its present state in the first decade of the twentieth century by Sir Edwin Lutyens for Edward Hudson, the founder of *Country Life*. At the same time the famous designer Gertrude Jeykell created a walled garden on the flat ground below the castle.

Further defensive works were built in the late seventeenth century to combat the perceived threat from Dutch maritime raiders. Known as Osbourne's Fort, it was constructed at the south end of the Heugh in 1675 by a military man, Major Daniel Collingwood, and the architect ROBERT TROLLOPE. The plans show that it comprised upper and lower platforms with gun emplacements and a central two-storey blockhouse. Almost nothing of this construction remains, in part because of the action of the sea.

HORSLEY, JOHN (1685–1732)

John Horsley can be regarded as the first, and certainly one of the foremost, in a line of scholars who have made the study of Roman Britain their special interest. His origins are entirely obscure and the search for them has been hindered by the existence of two contemporaries of the same name. It is likely, however, that he was born in Newcastle. What is certain is that he was educated at the Royal Grammar School in Newcastle and afterwards at Edinburgh University, graduating MA in 1701. Some time later, but by 1709 at the latest, he was a Presbyterian minister in MORPETH, where he also ran a school. He was deeply interested in natural science and his work was considered sufficiently distinguished for him to be elected a Fellow of the Royal Society in 1729. At the time of his death he was engaged on a course of public lectures in Morpeth and Newcastle.

Today, however, his reputation rests upon his monumental three-volume *Britannia Romana or The Roman Antiquities of*

Britain. He had been compiling materials for this for many years but began the task of assembling them into publishable form in 1727 with the help of a friend, Richard Cay, and George Mark, his assistant at his school in Morpeth. He is known to have penned the dedication (to Sir Richard Ellys) a few days before his death in January 1732 at the early age of forty-six. He therefore did not live to see it published in April of the same year.

The first volume, in ten chapters, provides a general history of the Romans in Britain, but is largely concerned with a description of the military stations and the Hadrianic and Antonine walls. The second volume has three chapters and records, with interpretive notes, all the surviving inscriptions and sculpture then known in Britain. The last volume, which has five chapters, deals with the geography of Roman Britain. Appropriately for a Northumbrian, he did much to clarify the layout and construction of HADRIAN'S WALL, although like most contemporaries, he attributed it not to Hadrian (117–38), but to a later emperor, Septimius Severus (193–211), believing that Hadrian was responsible only for the vallum.

Nonetheless, *Britannia Romana* was the foundation of all subsequent study of Roman Britain and the quality of Horsley's research and presentation has earned the respect and recognition of later scholars.

HOWICK

Although only a small hamlet, Howick has four important distinguishing elements. Most obvious is Howick Hall, one of the finest pieces of country house architecture in the North East. It was built in 1782 on the site of an earlier house for Sir Henry Grey, father of the 1st Earl Grey (d.1808), to the design of the Newcastle architect WILLIAM NEWTON. A little over twenty-five years later, however, it was 'turned round' in that a new front entrance was built on its north side, replacing the original entrance on its south side, which now faces a garden running down to Howick Burn. The main body of the house is currently unoccupied, although there are plans (as yet at a very early stage) to restore the ground floor to house an exhibition to illustrate the history of the house, the Grey family, the 1832 Reform Act, and the garden and the natural history of the vicinity.

This would clearly relate to the arboretum, development of which began in 1988. Extending to about 65 acres (26 ha), it contains at present about 11,000 trees and shrubs covering about 1,800 'taxa' or scientific classifications. The principle underlying the collection is that the plants are grown from seeds collected in the wild to ensure that they are products of nature, not of man. In some cases, seeds were gathered by expeditions from the arboretum; in others, seeds or seedlings have been acquired from similar institutions, including the Royal Botanic Gardens at Kew and the Royal Botanic Garden in Edinburgh. Since the trees grow in natural conditions out of doors, the collection is confined to species from the temperate regions of the world. Almost all European countries are represented, as are sixteen in Asia, Africa and the southern hemisphere. The arboretum has been developed according to strict scientific principles and is of growing importance.

The church is small and as a building not especially distinguished, being a Victorian remodelling of the eighteenth-century replacement of the medieval church. However, the historical interest lies not in the building but in the fact that the parish was one of the smallest in the North East, comprising no more than Howick township, yet it was attached to the office of the Archdeacon of Northumberland and provided him with a very small income.

The fourth aspect of Howick is at the same time the oldest and the youngest. It is the site of the mesolithic house, excavated in 2000 and 2002, on the edge of the cliff overlooking the shore. Carbon dating of the remains show that it was built around 8000 BC and that it was occupied for about a hundred years. The house was a circular hut about 20 feet (6 m) in diameter and about 23 feet (7 m) high, the height being the consequence of its conical construction. It was made of roughly hewn timbers covered with thatch. Its other noteworthy feature was its floor, which was sunk below ground level. This settlement is one of the earliest discovered in Britain and has increased our knowledge of the way of life of people at a much earlier stage of human development.

HUDSON, GEORGE (1800–1871)

George Hudson was one of the most influential figures in the development of the British railway system, particularly in the North East (see RAILWAYS), but also one of the more dubious businessmen of the nineteenth century. He was born the son of a farmer at Howsham, twelve miles north-east of York. In 1815 he was apprenticed to a drapery partnership in York, Bell and Nicholson. At the end of his apprenticeship he got a share of the business, which he consolidated by marrying Elizabeth Nicholson. By 1827 he was a wealthy man, but became more so upon inheriting £30,000 from a great-uncle. His fortune enabled him to engage in local politics and in 1837 he served as Mayor of York.

In the same year he became the chairman and largest shareholder of the York and North Midland Railway Co., whose engineer was GEORGE STEPHENSON. It was in partnership with the Stephensons that he was able in the 1840s to create a railway from York to Berwick, partly by buying up existing railway companies, but also by forming new ones and laying new lines. Without doubt, much of what he did could have been done better; however, but for him, the completion of the East Coast Main Line from London to Edinburgh would probably have been considerably delayed.

Hudson's other association with the North East was with SUNDERLAND, which he represented as a Tory MP from 1845 until 1859. To a great extent he owed his election to his promise to provide Sunderland with a much-needed expansion of its dock facilities. This he began in 1846 by acquiring the Durham and Sunderland Railway Co. and the Wearmouth Dock Co., which would link Sunderland and its new dock with the main line being created through County Durham as well as offering competition to Seaham Harbour (see NEW TOWNS OF THE NINETEENTH CENTURY) in the export of coal. Designed by John Murray, the engineer of the River Wear Commission, and requiring the efforts of 13,000 men, the South Dock was built and covered 47 acres (19 ha), with an exit to the sea into Hendon Bay. Almost immediately it was decided to extend the dock and by 1856 its surface area was 66 acres (27 ha).

By the time the South Dock was opened in the summer of 1850, Hudson's dubious finances had been exposed and he had been forced to resign all his directorships. His status as the MP shielded him from prosecution, however. Consequently, when he failed to be re-elected in 1859, he fled abroad. He returned to England in 1865 in order to seek election as the MP for Whitby, but he was arrested and endured several months in prison in York Castle. For many, Hudson's personality outweighed his defects of character, and in 1869 a banquet in his honour was held in Sunderland and a subscription raised enough to provide him with an annuity of £600. He died two years later at Whitby.

HUMBLETON HILL, BATTLE OF, 1402

This was one of the major battles of the long Anglo-Scottish war. It was fought on 14 September 1402 between an invading Scottish army commanded by Murdoch Stewart, Earl of Fife (heir of Robert Stewart, Duke of Albany, younger brother of the King of Scots, Robert III) and Archibald, 4th Earl of Douglas, and an English force led by Sir Henry Percy, known as Hotspur (heir of Henry Percy, 1st Earl of Northumberland) and a Scotsman, George Dunbar, Earl of March. The place was the lower slopes of Humbleton Hill, a little over two miles north of Wooler and just south of the junction of the A697 and the B6351. The outcome was a crushing defeat for the Scottish invaders, in which Fife and Douglas and two other Scottish earls, Moray and Angus, together with two lords and twenty-one knights were captured.

To explain why this invasion took place and why a Scotsman was one of the leaders of the English army it is necessary to go back to the late 1390s, when George Dunbar negotiated the marriage (for which he paid a large sum of money) of his daughter, Elizabeth, and the heir of Robert III, David, Duke of Rothesay. But the arrangement was made without the approval of the Scottish parliament and consequently it was suspended until the situation could be regularised. At this point, Archibald, 3rd Earl of Douglas (known as Archibald the Grim) stepped in and secured (for a larger sum) the marriage of the Duke of Rothesay to his daughter, Marjorie. Dunbar's response was to demand either Rothesay's marriage to Elizabeth or the return of his money. He got neither. In reaction to this gross insult, he renounced allegiance to Robert III and decamped to England with his family and many of his followers.

Over and above this quarrel over the right of the respective daughters to be the future Queen of Scots was an ongoing struggle between the Douglas and Dunbar families for dominance in the Scottish borders. Once in England, Dunbar immediately became an ally of the PERCY FAMILY, who also were in a feud with the Douglas clan. The result was raid and counter-raid.

Meanwhile, the situation in the Scottish government changed dramatically. In 1400 the 3rd Earl of Douglas died and was succeeded by his son, also Archibald, as 4th Earl (he was known as the Tyneman, meaning 'loser') and the old and feeble king, Robert III, was forced to hand over the reins of government to his heir, the Duke of Rothesay. This threatened the prospects of the king's brother, the Duke of Albany, who would succeed Robert III, were Rothesay out of the way. The upshot was an alliance between Albany and the new Earl of Douglas: in return for Douglas turning a blind eye to Albany's murder of Rothesay, Albany agreed to join Douglas in an invasion of England, designed to destroy Dunbar and Percy: hence the presence of Albany's son in the invading army.

The English victory had important consequences. The English king, Henry IV, ordered that the Scottish leaders should not be ransomed but handed over to him, albeit with suitable compensation. Hotspur refused to comply and retained the Earl of Douglas. In doing so, he flouted the accepted rules of war. Why he did so can be traced back to 1399, when he and his father played a crucial role in Henry's deposition of Richard II. For this they were amply rewarded, but for a variety of reasons their relations with the new king turned sour. Ten months after Humbleton Hill, in July 1403, Hotspur rebelled against Henry IV, but he was defeated and killed near Shrewsbury.

HUME, GEORGE HALIBURTON (CARDINAL ARCHBISHOP BASIL HUME) (1923–1999)

Archbishop Basil Hume was born in NEWCASTLE, the son of Sir William Errington Hume, Professor of Medicine at Durham University and Consultant Physician at Newcastle's Royal Victoria Infirmary. Hume's father was English and a nominal Anglican, but his mother was French and ardently Roman Catholic, and it was her religion that he followed. He was educated at Ampleforth College, where he appears to have been more impressive on the sports field than in the classroom. His time there ended in 1941, when he was aged eighteen. Unlike most of his contemporaries, who immediately joined up, Hume decided to enter Ampleforth Abbey, the Benedictine monastery to which his school was attached, adopting Basil as his religious name. His decision, taken at a critical time in World War II, exposed him to some harsh criticism. His took his final vows in 1945, after which he spent two years at Oxford reading History and a further three years at the Catholic University at Fribourg in Switzerland studying Theology. Towards the end of his time there he was ordained a priest.

For the next thirteen years he was on the staff of Ampleforth College. Then, in 1963, the pattern of his life changed radically with his election as Abbot of Ampleforth Monastery. He remained in that post until 1976, when, on the death of Cardinal Heenan, he was chosen to be the Archbishop of Westminster (*ex officio* head of the Roman Catholic Church in England) and Cardinal, with the titular church in Rome of San Silvestro in Capite. In this role he maintained cordial and co-operative relations with successive archbishops of Canterbury and, with his quiet demeanour, won the admiration of many who were not of his faith. He was made an honorary freeman of Newcastle in 1980. A statue of him now stands outside St Mary's Roman Catholic Cathedral in Newcastle.

HUNT, ISOBEL VIOLET (1862–1942)

Violet Hunt (who, because of her quick temper, was nicknamed 'Violent' Hunt) was born in a house in Old Elvet, Durham, a daughter of the Liverpool-born landscape artist Alfred Hunt. Her mother was Margaret, the daughter of JAMES RAINE THE ELDER, while her godfather was WILLIAM GREENWELL, who had proposed to her mother but been rejected. Four years later, the family moved to London, hoping to secure Alfred's election to the Royal Academy.

Violet grew up to be a vivacious and sexually liberated woman, who wrote seventeen novels and also became the lover of a number of literary men, notably Somerset Maugham, H.G. Wells and Ford Madox Ford. Her writing, although at the time well received and highly rated by D.H. Lawence for its 'new woman' approach, is now considered second-rate. But she deserves to be remembered as the co-founder in 1921 of PEN (Poets, Editors, Novelists), the international writers' organisation that defends freedom of speech and expression.

HUNTER, CHRISTOPHER (1675–1757)

Christopher Hunter, who was a meticulous antiquary and one of the earliest field archaeologists, was born at Medomsley and educated at Kepier Grammar School, Houghton le Spring, and St John's College, Cambridge, where he took a degree in Medicine in 1698. Initially he practised as a doctor in Stockton, but moved to Durham, where he was better able to pursue his interest in the past. This took two forms, one of which was archaeology, where his particular interest was the remains of the Roman occupation. He traced the course of ROMAN ROADS in the county and the outlines of the ROMAN FORTS at LANCHESTER and Ebchester, and paid several visits to HADRIAN'S WALL. He also built up a collection of Roman coins and altars and other inscribed stones and records of inscriptions on stones he left in situ. His discoveries were of considerable value to JOHN HORSLEY as he assembled the evidence for his monumental *Britannia Romana*. Hunter also contributed to two other works of scholarship: *History of Newcastle upon Tyne* (1736) by Henry Bourne; and, more importantly, *Concilia Magnae Britanniae et Hiberniae* (1737), a work of reference still widely used today by historians. Compiled by David Wilkins (1685–1745) and published in four volumes in 1737, it comprises abstracts from the records of church councils held between the years 446 and 1717, together with papal bulls, letters and other documents that applied to Britain and Ireland.

In 1743 Hunter mooted the idea of a two-volume history of County Durham, based upon the records belonging to the Diocese and the Cathedral Priory and its successor, the Dean and Chapter, of Durham. This was a massively ambitious undertaking, which he did not achieve but which was largely realised in the following century by ROBERT SURTEES.

Hunter died at Unthank near Shotley, leaving behind a large library, twenty-one volumes of accumulated evidence and a large collection of Roman materials. Unfortunately, all were dispersed and largely lost, except for two volumes of transcribed documents relating to the cathedral estate and his collection of Roman materials, which were bought by the Dean and Chapter.

HUNTER, SIR GEORGE BURTON (1845–1937) and SIR ERNEST JOHN (1912–1983)

Sir George Hunter and Sir Ernest John Hunter, the latter the grandson of the former, presided over, respectively, the rise and the decline of one of the world's greatest shipbuilders (see SHIPBUILDING AND INDUSTRY).

George Hunter was born in SUNDERLAND, the son of a shipowner, Thomas Hunter. After a sparse education, he became a pupil of the engineer of the Wear Commission and then an apprentice with the Sunderland shipbuilder William Pile, rising to be acting manager. To widen his experience, he spent the years 1869 to 1871 at the Clyde shipyard of Robert Napier & Co. at Govan, but returned to Sunderland in the latter year to become manager of Pile's yard. Unfortunately, two years later, Pile died and the business collapsed.

This led Hunter to set up on his own in partnership with another Sunderland shipbuilder, S.P. Austin. This lasted until it was dissolved in 1879, when Hunter moved to the Tyne to form a partnership with C.S. Swan to create a new shipyard on a 7-acre (2.8 ha) site in what was then the village of Wallsend. The business expanded rapidly, particularly as it moved with the times, converting from iron to steel, adopting the triple-expansion engine and being willing to design and build new kinds of ships, such as oil tankers and refrigerated cargo vessels. By 1895 the business had become large enough to acquire private liability company status, with Hunter as its chairman. In the years between then and the outbreak of World War I, it continued to expand. In 1897 it took control of the neighbouring yard of Schlesinger, Davis & Co. Ltd., which enabled it to build passenger liners. It was ambition in this field that led in 1903 to the merger of C.S. Swan and Hunter with Wigham Richardson and Co. Ltd to form Swan, Hunter and Wigham Richardson & Co. Ltd in order to build the great liner, *MAURETANIA*. Almost immediately, the new firm enterprise expanded further by taking over two more Tyneside firms, Tyne Pontoons and

Dry Docks Co. Ltd, and Wallsend Slipway and Engineering Co. Ltd. Nine years later, in 1912, it extended its interests beyond the Tyne, acquiring the Clydeside firm of Barclay Curle & Co. Ltd and opening a new yard at Southwick in Sunderland. Hunter retained the chairmanship of the enlarged company until 1928, when he resigned following the death of his wife, although he continued as a director.

Almost inevitably, Hunter was involved with a range of organisations concerned with maritime matters: he helped to set up the North-East Coast Institution of Engineers and Shipbuilders in 1884; and he was for many years on the councils of the Institution of Naval Architects, Lloyd's Register of Shipping and the Merchant Shipping Advisory Committee. His honours included a DSc, awarded in 1906 by Durham University in recognition of his support for Armstrong College, its science arm in Newcastle, and a knighthood in 1918, which recognised his services during World War I.

The growth of his firm was largely responsible for transforming Wallsend from a village into an industrial town, which became a chartered borough in 1901 and in whose government Hunter was much involved. Perhaps his most eccentric philanthropic act was to found and support financially the Wallsend Café, which provided non-alcoholic drinks. This stemmed from his lifelong hostility to alcohol, which led him to the presidency of the National Temperance Federation and support for the campaign for outright prohibition. He was an enthusiast for spelling reform and was the chairman of the Simplified Spelling Society.

John Hunter, who eventually succeeded his grandfather, was the son of George Ernest Hunter (1875–1957). He was educated at Oundle School then at St John's College, Cambridge and Durham University, from which he graduated in 1935. He then joined the company, rising to become a director in 1945 and chairman and managing director in 1957. He did so at a time when the commercial situation for the industry was becoming increasingly difficult. One solution was to expand overseas, which the company did by taking over dockyards in Malta, Singapore, South Africa and the West Indies. A more drastic cure followed the government-sponsored Geddes Report of 1964, namely, the merger of Swan Hunter with the other major Tyne firms: Smith's Docks (which also had a yard on the Tees), Vickers Armstrongs, Readheads and Hawthorn Leslie; and also the Tees yard of Furness. This process, which was complete by 1969, made the Swan Hunter group the largest shipbuilder in Britain (see SHIPBUILDING INDUSTRY). This solution worked for a short time, but in the 1970s the firm failed to secure orders for warships and the demand for oil tankers virtually collapsed. The *coup de grâce* came in 1977, when the Labour government nationalised the shipbuilding industry, making the group part of British Shipbuilders. By that date Hunter was no longer managing director, having retired in 1972.

Hunter also discharged leading roles in many organisations. Some, such as the North-East Coast Ship Repairers' Association, the North-East Coast Institution of Engineers and Shipbuilders, the Shipbuilders and Repairers National Association and the Dry Dock Owners and Repairers Central Council, were part of the industry. Others had wider implications: the Central Training Council, the Confederation of British Industry and the National Economic Development Council. He also held directorships of other companies, notably British Railways, the Glasgow Iron and Diesel Co., the Hopemount Shipping Co., and the brassfounder, M.W. Swinburns & Sons.

HUNTING, SIR PERCY LLEWELYN (1885–1973)

Percy Hunting was the son of a Newcastle shipowner, Charles Hunting (1853–1921). He was educated at Loretto School in Edinburgh, followed by time in Paris to improve his French. He then undertook an apprenticeship with the North East Marine Engineering Co. and then went to study marine engineering at Armstrong College, the Newcastle end of Durham University. On completing his training in 1910, he joined the family firm, which two years later sent him to the USA to investigate possible business opportunities there, particularly in oil. During World War I he served in the Northumberland Fusiliers and then in the Royal Flying Corps, seeing action in Mesopotamia. After demobilisation in 1918 he returned to the family firm, which had suffered greatly during the war. With his brother, he took control in 1921 and based its revival on tankers and the transport of oil. Success was sufficient for the firm to become a private liability company in 1926, with Hunting as chairman. Huntings remained a shipping company until they were badly affected by the worldwide slump between 1929 and 1932.

It was this that drove him to diversify and to do so he moved south, relocating his family from Edmundbyers to a village in Sussex. The diversification followed two courses. On the one hand, he retained his involvement in the transport of oil to the extent of remaining chairman of the British Chamber of Shipping's Tanker Committee until 1943 and deputy chairman of the International Tanker Owners' Association until 1950. But at the same time he became involved in oil production through two companies, one British, the other American, and petrol sales through ownership of a chain of filling stations in Lancashire and Yorkshire.

In complete contrast, from the late 1930s he became increasingly involved in aircraft manufacture. This began in 1938 with the acquisition of Rollasons, an aircraft repair firm in Croydon, and Aircraft Operating Company and its subsidiary, Aerofilms. To these he added a new factory in North Wales to manufacture airframe parts and then in 1944 acquired Percival Aircraft Ltd of Luton. In the post-war years this firm specialised in the design and construction of trainers, which culminated in the Jet Provost, the RAF's basic trainer in the 1970s and 1980s. When he retired in 1960 it became part of the British Aircraft Corporation. Also in the post-war years, Hunting developed the Airfilms subsidiary he had acquired before the war into a larger enterprise, Hunting Aerosurveys, and founded his own airline, Hunting Air Travel. This enjoyed considerable success, but mainly in Africa, as the consequence of hostility on the part of government and the two nationalised airlines, BOAC and BEA, to private enterprise in the air travel industry.

HUTCHINSON, WILLIAM (1732–1814)

William Hutchinson was the son of William Hutchinson, a lawyer who practised in Durham, and his wife, Hannah Doubleday of Butterby. After attending Durham School, he followed his father into the law. In 1756, shortly after qualifying, he married a Stockton woman, Sarah Marshall, and set up as a solicitor in BARNARD CASTLE, where his house in Galgate still stands. His real interest, however, was not in law but in history. His great achievement was to produce the first detailed history of Durham, *The History and Antiquities of the County Palatine of Durham*, which he was commissioned to write in two volumes by Solomon Hodgson, the Newcastle printer and owner of the *Newcastle Chronicle*. A serious disagreement between author and publisher arose, however, because between 1786 and 1794 Hutchinson wrote three volumes, the last of which Hodgson was not disposed to print. The matter came to court, but was resolved by arbitration. Hutchinson also wrote a two-volume history of Cumberland (Cumbria) and several descriptive tours, but it is on his history of Durham that his reputation is based. Although to a considerable extent superseded by ROBERT SURTEES's history of Durham, it was Hutchinson's pioneering work that made possible Surtees's superior study.

HUTTON, CHARLES (1737–1823)

Charles Hutton was the quintessential lad of parts, the local boy who made good. Born in NEWCASTLE on 14 August 1737, the son of a pitman, Henry Hutton, he was destined to follow his father's trade, but his life as a miner was ended by injury at a very early age. This enforced retirement enabled him to gain an education in which he revealed a high degree of mathematical ability. Such was his academic progress that in 1760, at the age of twenty-three, he opened his own school and was soon tutoring pupils from the Royal Grammar School. During his thirteen years as a schoolmaster in Newcastle he produced at the request of the corporation a very accurate plan of the town, published several mathematical tracts, and in 1773 a book, *The Principles of Bridges*, a detailed study of the mathematics of bridge engineering prompted by the destruction of the Tyne bridges the previous year.

That year was his last in Newcastle. In the face of stiff competition, he secured the post of Professor of Mathematics at the Royal Military Academy, Woolwich. This and his previous work led to his being elected FRS in 1774, although he was to resign his membership ten years later, following a quarrel with the then president, Sir Joseph Banks. This in no way diminished his scholarly output. In addition to papers on various aspects of mathematics and also on the teaching of the subject, in 1795 he published his *magnum opus, A Mathematical and Philosophical* [i.e. scientific] *Dictionary.* He also was a member of the group of scholars who co-operated on *Abridgement of the Philosophical Transactions of the Society of London*, which was published in eighteen volumes in 1806. In addition, he was regarded as a leading expert on bridge construction and as such on several occasions was consulted about London bridges, actual and proposed.

Charles Hutton died on 27 January 1823 aged eighty-three. Throughout his life in Woolwich, which lasted almost fifty years, he lived a bachelor existence. His wife and his three children, all of whom were born before he went south, remained in Newcastle, well maintained by the husband and father, but at a distance.

IDA (?–587) (see NORTHUMBRIA, KINGDOM AND EARLDOM OF)

IRON AND STEEL INDUSTRY

Considerable quantities of iron ore, albeit not of the highest grades, that underlie many of the upland parts of the North East have been mined and smelted from at least Roman times. During the medieval centuries, the monks of DURHAM CATHEDRAL Priory acquired quantities of what they termed 'Weardale' iron, although it was in fact smelted in Derwentdale. They supplemented this with Spanish iron, imported through NEWCASTLE, possibly because it was of higher quality but also because local supplies may have been inadequate. It is reasonable to think that other landowners did likewise.

During the eighteenth century, however, the North East became Britain's most important steelmaking district: it has been calculated that towards mid-century roughly half of the 1,000 tons of steel made in Britain was made in the North East. Moreover, contemporaries considered that Newcastle and Blackhall Mill produced the country's finest steel. Manufacture was mainly in the Derwent valley, where between *c.*1690 and 1740 steelmaking furnaces were set up at Allensford Mill, Derwentcote, Blackhall Mill, Winlaton Mill and Swalwell; facilities were also created further east at Teams and Newcastle. Although some steel was made from locally produced iron, the bulk of the raw material appears to have been bar iron imported from Sweden. The impetus for this development came from a number of sources, including Newcastle merchants, but the input of two incomers, AMBROSE CROWLEY and the German immigrant Wilhelm Bertram, was crucial. From the last quarter of the century, the North East lost its pre-eminence to Sheffield.

During the same century attempts were made to make iron using local ore, coal and limestone, notably at Whitehill, west of CHESTER LE STREET, and at BEDLINGTON. But it was the rising demand and rising prices caused by the long war against France between 1793 and 1815 that led to ironworks being started on the Tyne at Lemington in 1801 and at Newburn in 1810, both using local coal and iron ore. In the post-war years, iron was in demand for pipes for the expanding water and gas industries, but it was the onset of railway building after 1825 that led to a soaring demand for iron. Railways required huge quantities of iron, and since the early railway works were located in the North East, there was an obvious market for locally produced iron. In 1829 the Birtley Iron Works began production, followed by those at Wylam in 1836, Walker in 1842 and Wallsend in 1845: all close to, or on, the Tyne.

During the same years, other enterprises were started well away from that river, also based upon local supplies of coal and iron ore. Two were in the uplands of North Tynedale and Redesdale. In 1839 an ironworks was started at Hareshaw near Bellingham, but because of transport difficulties, financial problems and outdated technology, it had a life of only ten years. What remains of it constitute picturesque ruins in a completely non-industrial setting. The other upland, but unrelated, enterprise was started at the same time in Redesdale, on the A68 about two miles south of West Woodburn. Because of its isolated location, a completely new village, Ridsdale, was built for its workers. It had a longer life, although its pig iron was taken to Tyneside for further smelting.

More successful were three enterprises started in the 1840s in the Pennine foothills in mid-western Durham. The earliest was at CONSETT, founded by the Derwent Iron Co. in 1840, followed in 1846 by the ironworks at

Tow Law, founded by CHARLES ATTWOOD and at Witton Park by HENRY BOLCKOW and John Vaughan. All three were located where they were because of the ready availability of coal, limestone and iron ore, or so it was believed. In fact, the optimism was well founded as regards coal and limestone, but the local iron ore proved to be limited in both quantity and quality. The life of all these enterprises was fairly brief: Witton Park closed in 1884, Tow Law in 1882 and the Derwent Iron Co. in 1857. The last, however, was successfully refounded as the Consett Iron Co.

By the late 1840s, the North East had developed an iron industry, although relatively modest in size. What transformed the situation radically was the discovery in 1850 of the existence of huge quantities of iron ore in the Cleveland Hills in North Yorkshire. The consequence was an 'iron rush' that brought a variety of men to Teesside to set up ironworks. By 1875 twenty-five iron companies were in operation on Teesside, twelve on the Yorkshire side of the river at Middlesbrough, South Bank, Ormesby, Lackenby, Newport and Thornaby, and thirteen on the Durham side at HARTLEPOOL, Port Clarence, Carlton, STOCKTON and DARLINGTON. Between them, they operated 109 furnaces and produced annually nearly two million tons of pig iron, about 20 per cent of Britain's output. Teesside supplied virtually all the rails laid down in Britain and many of those abroad, as well as plates and angles for ships, by then increasingly built of iron. Alongside the growth in the output of pig iron went that of wrought iron: by the mid-1870s, there were nearly 1,200 'puddling' furnaces at work.

The boom in the iron industry was not confined to Teesside. Elsewhere in the North East, thirteen other iron companies had been founded, at Ferryhill, BISHOP AUCKLAND, Fencehouses, CHESTER LE STREET, CONSETT, SUNDERLAND, Newcastle, GATESHEAD and JARROW. Between them, they had forty-five furnaces, the largest number being ten, at Consett. However, these figures clearly underline the gravitational pull exerted by the Cleveland ore field that drew the iron industry south to Teesside. The fact was that transport costs made it economically sensible to move coal (in the form of coke) and limestone to where iron ore was mined, rather than vice versa.

However, by the 1870s iron was beginning to give way to steel, which for most purposes was a superior metal, as the result of the process invented by Henry Bessemer in 1859 and subsequently improved by Alphonse Mushet. Unfortunately, Cleveland ore, because of its high phosphorus content, was unsuited to the Bessemer process. What was required was haematite ore, which had to be imported from either Cumberland (Cumbria) or Spain. Consequently, the turnover to steel on Teesside was delayed until the 1870s. Steelmaking on Teesside was begun by Bolckow, Vaughan & Co., who in 1872 bought a share in a Spanish haematite ore mine and in 1874 the necessary plant from a bankrupt firm near Manchester, which they dismantled and brought to Eston. Nevertheless, the problem could have had serious long-term consequences for Teesside had it not been for the solution devised in 1879 by Percy Gilchrist and Sidney Gilchrist Thomas, which involved lining the converters with dolomite to absorb the phosphorus from the ore.

The late nineteenth and early twentieth centuries saw the fairly rapid reduction in the number of firms, partly through business failures during periods of trade depression, but mainly through mergers and buyouts. By 1929 iron and steel making in the region was in the hands of three giant concerns. One was Consett Iron and Steel Co., in North-West Durham, which had managed to survive and grow, despite its disadvantageous location. The others were a result of the business dynamism of two men. One was SIR ARTHUR DORMAN, who starting in 1876, created the firm of Dorman, Long, which dominated the industry on the south bank of the Tees. A similar phenomenon occurred on the north bank of the river, thanks to CHRISTOPHER FURNESS, who brought all the major facilities together as South Durham Steel. The final act in this development came in 1929, when Barclays Bank forced Bolckow and Vaughan, one of the great pioneers of the Teesside industry, into union with Dorman, Long.

By that date the steel industry was losing control over its affairs. During World War I, it was subject to government control to ensure maximum commitment to the war effort. With the return of peace, it entered its most depressing period, thanks to Britain's continuing commitment to free trade in the face of the European Iron and Steel cartel, which undercut the British industry at home as well as abroad. Relief came in the early 1930s: in 1932 the Import Duties Advisory Committee was set up, which imposed a duty of 33⅓ per cent on foreign imports; and two years later the British Iron and Steel Federation came into existence, charged with modernising the industry. Thanks to rearmament, the industry revived in the late 1930s, but during World War II it again came under government control, with the aim of maximising output, to which urgency the modernising of plant had to be deferred.

The victory in the 1945 election of the Labour Party, with its ideological commitment to nationalisation, made it certain that the industry would be brought into state ownership. This occurred in 1950, but lasted only until 1953, when the Conservative government handed it back into private ownership. Denationalisation, however, did not free the industry of government oversight, since investment in new plant remained under the control of the Iron and Steel Board. Two results of this in the region were South Durham Steel's new integrated plant on the former airfield at Greatham and a similar development by Dorman, Long at Lackenby. The industry was again nationalised in 1967, when all the region's firms became part of the British Steel Corporation. This time, state control was of longer duration, lasting until 1988, when it was again privatised as British Steel. By that date, however, it was contracting rapidly in the face of a falling demand for steel. In 1980 this resulted in the closure of Consett, whose disadvantageous location finally counted against its continuation. The undeniable fact was that with the closure of the last Cleveland iron ore mine in 1964, all the iron ore processed in the region came from abroad, which dictated that steelworks should be located on the coast. It was this consideration that lay behind the decision to build a completely new works, with a capacity of twelve million tons, at Redcar. Steelmaking north of the Tees was no more.

In 1999 British Steel merged with the Dutch firm Koninklyke Hoogovens to form Corus.

IRVIN, RICHARD (1853–1920)

Richard Irvin was born at North Shields and after a very basic education began work in his family's marine store business. Then in 1871, when only eighteen, he bought a second-hand trawler and began a career in fishing. Five years later he acquired a paddle tug, which he converted into what was probably the first steam-powered trawler. From this modest beginning, over the next ten years he built up a substantial fleet and operated over an increasing area of the North Sea.

In 1887 he opened an office in Aberdeen, shrewdly recognising that that city was the closest fishing port to the farthest extent of the North Sea grounds and that it had a good rail link to the London market. By landing catches at Aberdeen he could steal a two-day march on his rivals based upon Hull and Great Yarmouth. He also built a new fleet of purpose-built steam 'side-winder' trawlers with steam winches. By the end of the first decade of the twentieth century he owned eighty vessels, although some of these were the consequence of takeovers, and he had acquired bases at Scarborough and Milford Haven.

Alongside his own fishing interests, he also acted as a supplier of equipment to other fishing companies and he acquired interests in a local ice factory, fish canning factory, offal works and a ship repair yard. His enterprise was a major factor in the growth of the North Shields economy (see TYNEMOUTH AND NORTH SHIELDS). In 1907 his business interests had become so diverse that a major reorganisation was undertaken and converted into a limited liability company, with local offices in Aberdeen, Fraserburgh, Peterhead and Great Yarmouth. Two years later he looked abroad for further expansion, entering into partnership with C.O. Johnson of Capetown to engage in whaling and sealing in the Southern Ocean. This did not prove to be a particularly profitable venture and was sold to Lever Bros in 1920. By that year, the year in which he died, Irvin owned 120 vessels.

Irvin was a staunch Presbyterian in religion and a Liberal in politics. He was a member of Tynemouth Borough Council from 1890 and served as mayor in 1897 and 1898.

ISHERWOOD, SIR JOSEPH WILLIAM, Bt (1870–1937)

The son of a grocer, Joseph Isherwood was born in Hartlepool and educated there until the age of fifteen. He was then apprenticed in the shipyard of Edward Withy, first in the drawing office and then in several other departments. The extensive knowledge of ship design and construction he acquired from his wide-ranging training enabled him to secure a post as a ship surveyor with Lloyd's Register, his role being to examine and classify the plans of ships submitted to it. In the course of his work, he developed ideas for a stronger, safer and cheaper longitudinal girder, which he patented in 1906 and which became known as the Isherwood System. The following year he left Lloyd's and started his own business as a naval architect, which enabled him to devise and patent other improvements in ship design. By the year of his death, 2,500 ships had been built incorporating his design features. In 1921 he was given a baronetcy in recognition of his work for the government during World War I.

JACKSON, RALPH WARD (1806–1880)

Ralph Ward Jackson, who was responsible for the creation of West Hartlepool (see New Towns of the Nineteenth Century), was born at Normanby Hall, son of a North Yorkshire landowner. He was educated at Rugby School and then trained as a solicitor at Preston in Lancashire. He developed a successful legal practice in Stockton, married and settled at Greatham Hall. But his real ambition lay not in the law; rather it was to rival and outdo the Pease Family in the fields of commerce and urban development. To this end, he founded the Stockton and Durham County Bank as a device for raising the necessary money for his ambitious projects. These included not only the construction of railways, docks and a new town, but also steamships and coal mines. In forcing the pace, he overstretched himself financially, which led him to engage in dubious practices. His downfall stemmed from a legal action against him by a Benjamin Coleman, whose motive was personal, not altruistic. Although Jackson was guilty of financial malpractice, it was recognised that his aim was not personal gain, but the completion of his ambitious projects. Between 1868 and 1874 he was the first MP for the Hartlepools, the new constituency created in 1868 by linking Hartlepool and West Hartlepool.

JACOBITE UPRISING OF 1715

Jacobites were those who opposed on principle the removal from the throne in 1688–89 of the Roman Catholic James VII and II and his replacement by (jointly) his Protestant daughter, Mary, and her husband, William of Orange, Stadtholder of Holland. After his death in 1701, they transferred their loyalty to his son, who for them was the rightful king, James VIII and III. Broadly, Jacobites were of two sorts: Roman Catholics, for whom James represented their only hope of complete freedom of worship and removal of civil disabilities, and Anglicans who subscribed to the doctrine that as God's appointed rulers, kings could not be removed, no matter how unsatisfactory they were.

The Jacobite uprising in the autumn of 1715 was occasioned by the accession of George I, after the death of Queen Anne in 1714. She had been just acceptable to many in that she, like her predecessor, Mary, was James VII and II's daughter. George, the Elector of Hanover, however, was a German who spoke no English. Although his maternal great grandfather was James VI and I, it was difficult to argue the legitimacy of his right to the throne on grounds of heredity. The purpose of the uprising was, therefore, to remove George and replace him with 'James VIII and III', whose hereditary claim was unimpeachable. It would be wrong to dismiss the 1715 uprising as a forlorn hope, but its success required the coincidence of two factors: the landing of a substantial force of French troops, with James at their head, and the co-ordinated uprising of large numbers of those committed to the project. Neither happened, with the result that the uprisings were easily put down.

The main uprising was in Scotland, led by the Earl of Mar. In England, the only region where the project gained any support was the North East, more particularly Northumberland. There were two reasons for this. One was the existence in the county of a relatively large number of resident Roman Catholic gentry. The other was the arrival in the region in 1709 of James Radcliffe, 3rd Earl of Derwentwater, who in 1705 inherited a large estate with its centre at Dilston, near Corbridge. Born in 1689, he was sent to France in 1703 to the court of the exiled James VII and II at St Germain to be a companion for James 'VIII and III'. The result was that Derwentwater, an ardent

Roman Catholic, became a close friend of the young James and totally committed to the cause of restoring him to the throne. His presence in the county was the focus of Jacobite action.

The Northumberland uprising began on 6 October with a gathering at Greenrigg. Immediately, it became apparent that the Jacobites had considerably overestimated the number prepared to turn out. Perhaps most significant was their failure, thanks to the prompt action of loyalists such as WILLIAM COTESWORTH, to gain control of Newcastle. But there was also a notable absence of gentry. Careful analysis of the surviving records has shown that only eighty-four of those who were 'out' were gentlemen, of whom only five came from Durham. Of the remaining 266 participants, no fewer than 180 were described as servants, who we must assume were 'out' because their masters required them to be. Nevertheless, they constituted a small army, military command of which was entrusted to Thomas Forster of Adderstone, a man without military experience, but who was one of the MPs for Northumberland and also an Anglican.

For the rest of the month this small force moved around Northumberland, too small to accomplish anything of significance and therefore forced to wait on events. Eventually its leaders decided to link up with Jacobite insurgents in the Scottish borders, who had been reinforced by 2,000 Highlanders. Again there was uncertainty as to what to do, but in the end, on the receipt of intelligence that massive support would be forthcoming in Lancashire, the decision was taken to invade England via Cumberland (Cumbria). Thereupon half the Highlanders deserted and went home. When the Jacobite force reached Preston it numbered no more than 1,600. But again the Jacobites were deceived: there was no mass turnout of Lancastrians; instead they learned of the proximity of a larger force of government troops. On 9 November there was fighting as the government troops attacked the Jacobite defences around Preston, but were repulsed. The following day, however, the government forces were reinforced and were able to completely surround the whole town. This led Forster, without the agreement of the other leaders, to meet the commander of the government troops and agree to an unconditional surrender on 14 November. The campaign had lasted six weeks and accomplished nothing.

The aftermath was not one of mass executions. On 24 February 1716 Derwentwater was beheaded on Tower Hill, despite the pleas of his wife and several other important people: being the senior nobleman, he was deemed to bear primary responsibility for the uprising. The nearest to him in social seniority in Northumberland, William, 4th Lord Widdrington, was also condemned, but reprieved at the last moment. Three other men were executed because they held offices under the Crown: John Hall of Otterburn was a JP, and John Shafto and John Hunter were commissioned officers in the army. As an MP, the same fate would have befallen Thomas Forster, but thanks to the loyalty and daring of his sister, Dorothy, he escaped and lived out his days as Steward of the Jacobite court in exile at Urbino in Italy, dying in 1738. He was not the only escapee: in fact twenty-one of the gentry managed to escape abroad. Ostensibly, this was the result of carelessness, although it is hard not to believe that the government may have been quietly relieved not to have to carry out so many executions.

Eleven Northumberland men forfeited their property as the result of being convicted of treason, but only two families were entirely and permanently dispossessed. One was that of the Earls of Derwentwater, whose property was transferred in 1735 to the portfolio of estates owned by Greenwich Hospital. The other was George Collingwood of Eslington, who was executed at Liverpool and whose estate was sold in 1719 to Sir Henry Liddell of Ravensworth for £21,000. The others managed to retain portions or to recover all in the end, thanks to the legal arrangement of their estates and to the skill of their lawyers.

There was a belated postscript. Charles Radcliffe, the Earl of Derwentwater's younger brother, was among the escapees. Bolder and more swashbuckling than the Earl, he would probably have been a much more daring and imaginative commander. Having married (at the eleventh time of asking) a rich widow, he survived abroad until 1745, when he was captured at sea on his way to Scotland to take part in the last Jacobite rising. This time he did not escape: on 8 December 1746 he was beheaded, defiant to the end in his regimental uniform.

These events formed the basis of a novel, *Devil Water*, written by Anya Seton (1904–90) and published in 1962. Although living in the USA, the author was very fond of Northumberland and had strong regional connections: her father was born in South Shields; some of her relations lived at Felton in Northumberland; and her roots extended, as those of so many Northumbrians did, into the Scottish border country.

JARROW

Jarrow is one of the earliest English names in the region; its name means 'fen dwellers'. In its long history it has had two periods of fame and importance. Although very different in character and separated by over 1,000 years, both were short-lived and ended in disaster. In the first, which may be termed the 'Age of Bede', it was a famous monastery and a major centre of European art and scholarship. It was founded in 681 by Benedict Biscop on the west bank of the River Don at its juncture with the Tyne, not as an independent house, but as the twin of the monastery at Monkwearmouth he had founded in 674. It was renowned as the place where Bede lived and worked and where the *Codex Amiatinus* and its companion volumes were produced. It was also a craft centre where the working of stone and the making of glass attained high levels of excellence. Its existence ended, however, in or about 800, when it was sacked by the Vikings.

Jarrow's other age of greatness, which may be called the 'Age of Palmer', lasted from 1851 until 1933. In that time Jarrow grew from a colliery village into an industrial town. Its transformation was the work of one of the most dynamic and far-sighted nineteenth-century industrialists, Sir Charles Mark Palmer (1822–1907). In 1851 Palmer and his brother, George, set up a shipyard on the site of an earlier yard that made wooden ships. The Palmer brothers were committed to the new technology of iron-hulled and steam-driven ships, in the first instance Colliers to transport coal to London. These immediately proved to be faster and more reliable than their wooden-hulled and sail-driven predecessors, improvements that were needed to meet the competition of inland coalfields further south that could get their product to the capital by train. Their insight was fully vindicated by their first launch, the *John Bowes*.

Between 1851 and 1913 Palmers achieved two major accomplishments. The first was to widen its range of products to include all varieties of both merchant and naval vessels. Perhaps the apogee was reached in 1913 with the launch of the 27,000-ton battle cruiser, *HMS Queen Mary*, sunk three years later at the Battle of Jutland. The other achievement was turning Palmers into a fully integrated business. The iron (later steel) needed for ships' hulls was produced on site from ore shipped in Palmers' vessels from Port Mulgrave, the port on the North Yorkshire coast Palmers built to load the iron ore from its own mines. The coal required in the making of iron and steel was obtained from its own pits. And the engines fitted into their ships were manufactured on site. What they did not do was to provide adequate housing for the huge number of men who flocked to Jarrow to work in their yards and workshops, although Charles Mark Palmer did build a hospital for his employees as a memorial to his first wife, Jane, who died in 1870. Almost inevitably, Palmer became involved in public life, being an MP, first for North Durham and then for Jarrow, where he was also the town's first mayor.

The disaster that overtook Jarrow and brought the Age of Palmer to an end was the Great Depression of 1929–33. No longer the dynamic firm of the late nineteenth century, Palmers was unable to ride out the economic storm. The last of the 982 ships the firm produced, the destroyer HMS *Duchess*, was launched in July 1932, and in June the following year the company went into receivership. The fall was made all the harder by the very integration that had made Palmers such an advanced enterprise: by 1933 Palmers was Jarrow, and its closure meant the ruination of the town's economy, with all the attendant social consequences. Jarrow became the most blighted industrial community in Britain, a circumstance that produced the famous JARROW MARCH, to many the best-known fact about the town.

Between the first and second periods of prominence, Jarrow was a small rural village, with a close connection to DURHAM CATHEDRAL. This began in 1074, when a small group of English monks, led by one named ALDWINE, with the blessing of the Bishop of Durham, Walcher, restarted monastic life in Jarrow and Monkwearmouth. In 1083 Walcher's successor, WILLIAM OF ST CALAIS, having failed to persuade all but one of the members of the Congregation of St Cuthbert (see CUTHBERT, SAINT) to become monks in his newly founded Benedictine monastery, brought the monks from Jarrow and Monkwearmouth to Durham to be the founding fathers of the new venture. This gave Durham Cathedral Priory ownership of Jarrow. Thereafter, until 1537, Jarrow was two things: a small cell of the Cathedral Priory, staffed by a handful of monks sent from Durham, and the centre of a very large parish comprising nine townships that stretched from the boundary of GATESHEAD to the sea. The closure of the monasteries by Henry VIII in the 1530s meant the end of the monastic presence, but Jarrow continued as a possession of the Dean and Chapter of the Cathedral until the estates of the Church of England passed into the control of the Ecclesiastical Commission in the 1830s.

In its struggle to recover from the catastrophe of the inter-war years, Jarrow has in one respect come full circle, to the second Age of Bede: his name is carried by an industrial estate set up to attract new industries; and the excavation of the Anglo-Saxon monastery and the opening of Bede's World Museum (see MUSEUMS) have created a major tourist attraction.

JARROW MARCH, 1936

The Jarrow March was an imaginative response, born of desperation, by the people of Jarrow to their condition. This was no less than the collapse of the town's economy, as the result of the closure of Palmers shipyard in 1933, which resulted in 80 per cent unemployment. The March began on 5 October 1936, when 207 men, each provided with a waterproof groundsheet that could double as a cape, set out to march to London. They carried two banners, each bearing the legend

JARROW CRUSADE. Their purpose was not only to highlight the town's plight, but also to present to the House of Commons a petition bearing 11,572 signatures, asking that the government provide work for Jarrow. Their journey of 280 miles (450 km) took four weeks, and as they moved south they were encouraged and provided with food and accommodation by people in the towns that they passed through. They arrived in London in pouring rain on 3 November, headed by the town's MP, ELLEN WILKINSON.

What had triggered this dramatic act was the collapse of moves to create a large integrated steelworks on Palmers' site, which it was claimed would provide 4,000 jobs. In 1933 the site was sold to National Shipbuilders Security Ltd., the company created to buy up and close down redundant shipyards and then offer them for sale on condition that they would not be used for shipbuilding for forty years. However, the idea of a steelworks was given active and detailed consideration by both the government and the steel industry from the middle of 1934, and there was a belief in Jarrow that the development would go ahead. But in the summer of 1936 the idea was abandoned, largely because of the opposition of the other North-East steel firms, particularly those on Teesside, who were unwilling to defer their own expansion plans to accommodate the Jarrow development. It was the feelings of anger, despair and betrayal that led to the idea of the March and also to Ellen Wilkinson's book, *The Town that was Murdered*, published in 1939. Although the steelworks was not built, the March was not entirely a failure. At the time, it aroused a great deal of sympathy and moral support for Jarrow; and in 1940 a smaller and more limited version of the 1934 concept was opened. By that time World War II was under way and rapidly curing the problem of chronic unemployment.

JOHN OF BEVERLEY, SAINT (?–721)

Little is known for certain about the origins and early life of St John of Beverley. Later tradition gives his place of birth as Harpham, near Beverley, and claims that he was educated at Canterbury in the household of Archbishop Theodore of Tarsus (d.699). BEDE, however, says that he was trained at St Hild's abbey at Whitby. What is certain is that he was appointed Bishop of HEXHAM after WILFRID had been expelled from Northumbria and that he held that office until he was translated to York, where he served as bishop until his retirement in 714 or 718. Following his death, miracles were claimed for him and he was canonised in 1037.

During his time at Hexham he ordained Bede as a priest and he is commemorated by the church of St John Lee in the township of Acomb to the north of the town.

JOHN BOWES

The *John Bowes* is widely regarded as the first purpose-built, iron-hulled, steam-propelled COLLIER. There is considerable truth in this, in that she was purposely designed to provide a quicker and more reliable means of transporting coal from the Tyne to London at a time when the threat to the coal trade from the rapidly developing rail network was very apparent. Nevertheless, she had precursors in the form of the *Bedlington*, built at SOUTH SHIELDS in 1841 to bring coal from BLYTH to the Tyne; and the *Experiment*, built in SUNDERLAND in 1845 but wrecked the following year. It was the *John Bowes*, however, that finally demonstrated that the future lay with iron and steam. She was 150 feet (45.7 m) long and had a beam of nearly 27 feet (8.2 m) and a depth of 15 feet 6 inches (4.7 m). Her gross tonnage was 485 and she was capable of a speed of 9 knots. She was built by Charles Mark Palmer in his newly opened shipyard at JARROW and fitted with an engine made at the Forth Street works of ROBERT STEPHENSON. Her maiden voyage, when she carried 500 tons of coal, began on 27 July 1852 and she was back in the Tyne in a mere seven days. Sailing colliers, who were at the mercy of the weather, took up to a month for the round trip to London. The *John Bowes* continued as a working ship, although not as a collier and with several changes of name, until 1933, when she developed a leak and sank off the coast of northern Spain.

JOICEY, JAMES, LORD (1846–1936)

James Joicey, who was ennobled in 1906, was the last of the great coal 'barons' of the GREAT NORTHERN COALFIELD. He was born at Kip Hill near Stanley, the son of George Joicey and nephew of James Joicey, the heads of a family firm with an engineering works in Newcastle and coalmines at Tanfield. In 1863, at the age of seventeen, following an education at Gainford School, he joined the family firm. Within four years he had become a partner, from which position he rose to become chairman and managing director in 1881 on the death of his uncle. At that date Joicey & Co. owned seven collieries in North-West Durham: Tanfield Lea, Tanfield Moor, East Tanfield, South Tanfield, Beamish, Twizell and West Pelton. The aggregate annual output of these collieries was 1,400,000 tons.

Joicey's earliest leadership move, made in 1886, was to make Joicey & Co. a limited liability company with a nominal capital of £500,000. Ten years later, in 1896, he vastly expanded his enterprise by buying the Earl of Durham's collieries: Sherburn House, Sherburn Hill, Littletown, Lady Durham, Houghton le Spring, Margaret, Dorothea, Harraton, Lumley, Lady Ann, Lambton and Herrington. It was a shrewd move, since the severe depression in the coal industry allowed Joicey to buy cheaply. These collieries had an annual production of around 2,200,000 tons, which roughly doubled the coal output of Joicey's enterprises. The acquisition necessitated a new business structure: the former collieries of the Earl of Durham now became Lambton Collieries Ltd, a limited liability company with a nominal capital of £1,200,000.

This remained the situation until 1911, when Joicey made further acquisitions. He bought Silksworth Colliery from the Marquess of Londonderry, and the Hetton Coal Co., which had three collieries at Hetton, Elemore and Eppleton. Silksworth had an annual output of over half a million tons, while the three Hetton pits produced over a million tons. The new collieries were bought by the Lambton Co., which now became Lambton and Hetton Collieries Ltd. The additions did not so much add to Joicey's capacity as compensate for the decline of older collieries: those at Tanfield Moor, East Tanfield, South Tanfield and Twizell were in the latter stages of their productive life, while three of the Lambton pits – Littletown, Lady Durham and Lady Ann – had already closed. The final business reorganisation came in 1924, when Joicey Collieries Ltd was acquired by Lambton and Hetton Collieries Ltd to become the Lambton, Hetton and Joicey Collieries Ltd. At the time of his death in 1936, James Joicey's company was the largest coal producer in Durham, with an output of around 3,800,000 tons a year. His nearest 'rival', Horden Collieries Ltd, had an output of 2,600,000 tons.

Joicey's mining interests included shares in the colliery at Shirebrook in Derbyshire and he was also a director of several other companies, notably the North Eastern Railway (later the LNER), GEORGE ANGUS & Co., the Montevidean and Brazilian Telegraph Co. and the Dunrobin Shipping Co. In public life he was a Deputy Lieutenant and a JP in Durham and from 1885 until he became Baron Joicey in 1906 he was Liberal MP for Chester le Street. In his later years, however, he moved far to the right politically, to the extent that he voiced his support for the Italian dictator, Benito Mussolini. Like many other successful businessmen, he became a country landowner, buying land at Longhirst Hall near Morpeth, and in 1907 and 1908 the Ford and Etal estates amounting to 15,000 acres.

JUDE, MARTIN (1803–1860)

Martin Jude was one of the leading lights in the Miners' Association, formed in late 1842, which came to grief in a failed strike in 1844 (see Great Northern Coalfield). Nothing is known about his place of birth, his parentage or his education, although his reasoning and public speaking abilities point to formal schooling. Nor was he a miner, but a publican. Nevertheless, he was one of Tommy Hepburn's associates in the previous attempt to form a miners' union in the early 1830s. The 1842 venture was initially an instant success, with an estimated membership of 100,000 within six months of its foundation. Jude was among its leading figures, not surprisingly perhaps, given that the North East had the largest number of miners, and he was chosen as its treasurer. His stance was cautious and moderate, in particular in resisiting demands for a strike, possibly because the memory of the 1832 failure was fresh in his mind. But once the strike was called he gave it his full support.

After the predicted failure, which left many miners out of work and the rest on reduced wages, Jude became an active Chartist and in 1847 was elected to the Chartist Grand Council. He was also a member of the Northern Political Union, whose purpose was to expand the franchise so as to give workingmen political rights. But he also remained committed to the miners' cause, playing a leading role in 1847 in devising the Mines and Collieries Bill, which although it failed to become an act, set out in clear terms the demands and aspirations of the mining community. In this his voice continued to be one of moderation. He felt that a miners' union ought to be concerned with more than better wages and striking to achieve their aspirations, although he argued that better wages and shorter hours would lead to miners becoming better men and creating better families. His wider concerns included the setting up of a mines inspectorate, to be an independent body with access to necessary scientific advice. This ambition was gradually realised following the 1850 act.

Martin Jude did not get the recognition he deserved and died in severe poverty in North Shields. He was buried at Elswick.

KEELS, KEELMEN AND THE KEELMEN'S HOSPITAL

Keels were a distinctive form of boat used on both the Wear and the Tyne to take coal from riverside staithes to COLLIERS at or near the rivers' mouths. In this role they flourished from at least the fourteenth century until the mid-nineteenth century. Tyne keels were 40 feet (12.2 m) long and 15 feet (4.6 m) wide, and although equipped with a square sail and two oars, one of which acted as a rudder, they were propelled considerably by the tides. Each keel had a capacity of 20 tons and was manned by a crew of three or four men and a boy, known as the 'pee-dee'. Keelmen were not self-employed but were hired by the members of the Hostmen's Company on an annual contract, which they entered into around Christmas.

In NEWCASTLE they formed a distinctive community. Most of them lived in Sandgate and were visually distinguished by their dress, comprising blue bonnets, short blue jackets, yellow waistcoats and grey trousers. They were also distinguished by their origins: large numbers came from Scotland and from the English border regions of Tynedale and Redesdale. Their employment was seasonal in that bad weather prevented colliers sailing in the winter months. It was also rendered precarious by the fluctuations in the coal trade. Consequently the keelmen's income fluctuated, which in part may explain their readiness to go on strike. They were also renowned for their 'ferocity and savage roughness'.

Their distinctive trade and ghetto existence was not without advantage, however. This is most manifest in the Keelmen's Hospital, which still stands above Sandgate overlooking the Tyne. It was completed in 1701 to care for poor, sick and destitute keelmen. Built of brick, it is quadrangular in form and it cost £2,000, a sum raised by means of a levy, begun in 1699, of 1d. (one old penny) per tide on all keelmen's pay. The history of this charity was chequered until 1787, when it was refounded by act of parliament. Its funds were then amassed through a levy of 1d. per chaldron (53 cwt: 2,650 kg) and managed by a board of trustees made up of Hostmen and city magistrates. Their remit was the relief of poor, sick, aged and disabled keelmen.

In the course of the nineteenth century, advances in technology gradually made the keelmen redundant. The first was the development of the spout, which enabled wagons coming down the WAGONWAYS to discharge directly into the holds of colliers. The use of spouts began below the Tyne Bridge, but the opening of the Swing Bridge in 1876, together with the dredging of the river by the Tyne Improvement Commission after 1850, made it possible for colliers to sail upriver as far as DUNSTON STAITHE. In the late nineteenth century the keelmen disappeared from Sandgate to be replaced by Irish immigrants.

Much less is known about the keelmen of the Wear, except that they performed the same function and that their boats were smaller because of the shallowness of their river.

KIELDER FOREST PARK

Kielder Forest Park is a consequence of the Forestry Act of 1919, which set up the Forestry Commission. Covering 150,000 acres (60,000 ha), it is the largest man-made forest in Europe and includes the forests of Kielder, Redesdale and Wark in Northumberland (78 per cent) and Kershope and Spadeadam in Cumbria (22 per cent). The initial area was small, but was substantially expanded between 1932 and 1960 by purchases from the Duke of Northumberland (47,000 acres: 19,000 ha), the Church Commission, Sir John Swinburne of Capheaton and Lord Redesdale.

About 85 per cent of the park is now forested. Of the twenty-five species planted, Sitka Spruce accounts for 75 per cent, other varieties of conifer for a further 17 per cent, and broadleaves for 8 per cent. Since 1990 this last category has been expanded at the expense of conifers other than the Sitka Spruce. But it is likely that the Sitka will always predominate, since the park's primary economic purpose is timber production and the Sitka grows quickly and is the variety most suited to the poor soils that cover most of the park. Planting began in 1926 and was rapidly expanded in the years after the end of World War II. Felling, which began in 1948, now produces 14 million cubic feet (400,000 m^3) of timber or 5 per cent of timber grown in Britain. The forest's product goes for building timber, fencing, pallets, chipboard, cartonboard and newsprint. To compensate for the felled timber, 1,800,000 saplings are planted annually. The forest has now achieved a condition of maturity and equilibrium: input and output are in balance. The park gives direct employment to 80 people and uses 180 outside contractors.

Although growing timber is the basic reason for the forest, since 1974 it has consciously served two other purposes. One is wildlife conservation. There are 175 species of birds in the forest, 600 species of insects and 6,000 roe deer; and there are nine designated Sites of Special Scientific Interest (SSSI) covering 18,500 acres (7,500 ha). The other is the tourist industry: the forest currently attracts half a million visitors a year, many basing their activities on the Kielder Castle Visitor Centre. This building was never a real castle, but a hunting lodge built between 1772 and 1775 by the 1st Duke of Northumberland. It was enlarged in the mid-nineteenth century by the 4th Duke, for whom it was a favourite weekend retreat. Wildlife conservation and the needs of the tourist industry are now an integral part of the forest's planning strategy, which also involves liaison with the Northumberland National Park, since almost all of it lies within the park's boundary.

Such was the scale of the development that the Forestry Commission had to create two new villages to house its employees, at Stonehaugh near Wark on Tweed and Byrness in Redesdale.

KIELDER WATER

Kielder Water (which originally was to have the far more mundane name of Otterstone Reservoir) is the largest man-made lake in Europe. It is also the culmination of a process of reservoir construction that began with the Whittle Dean reservoir, opened in 1848. It was the response to a number of needs that became gradually more urgent in the course of the nineteenth and twentieth centuries: the rapid growth of population; the proliferating uses of water in the home; the increasing demand for water for an expanding number of industrial purposes; and the scientific discovery that clean water is necessary for public health, and particularly the prevention of cholera, which ravaged the region in 1831–32, 1848 and 1853.

Kielder Water was the result of a long period of investigation and discussion involving thirty-eight sites. The decision was made in 1973, after a two-year inquiry (which heard 188 objections), when it was established that no further reservoirs could be built on the Tees, that there was not enough water for a reservoir in upper Weardale and that other possible solutions, such as mine water, would be insufficient. Construction began in 1974 and was complete by 1980, after which it took two further years for the reservoir to fill. This was not accomplished without disruption: most significantly, forty-two families, whose land was to be flooded, had to be moved and rehoused; and also 1,500,000 trees were felled and a stretch of what had been the Border Counties Railway between Riccarton and Hexham was lost forever.

The dam contained nearly 6 million cubic feet (170,000 m^3) of clay and was 170 feet (52 m) high and 3,740 feet (1,140 m) long. The resulting lake is 7 miles (11 km) long, has a shoreline of 27 miles (44 km) and a surface area of 2,684 acres (1,090 ha). Its catchment area, with an average rainfall of 48 in (122 cm), covers 60,000 acres (24,000 ha). As well as the dam, two other facilities were constructed: a hydro-electricity generator capable of producing up to 6.2 megawatts, which came into operation in 1984; and a 37 km long underground pipe 3 m in diameter between the Tyne at Riding Mill and the Tees. Its twelve pumps are capable of lifting 1,136 million litres of water a day from the North Tyne for delivery to the Derwent, the Wear at Frosterley or the Tees at Eggleston. The urgent reason for building the reservoir and the links to the Wear and the Tees was the estimated expansion of the needs of heavy industry on Teesside. This forecast proved to be inaccurate, industry contracting rather than expanding. However, Kielder Water has become an important asset to the tourist industry in conjunction with KIELDER FOREST PARK.

Since 1995 Kielder Water has been owned by Northumbrian Water PLC, a product of the privatisation of water supply companies after 1989. It includes the former Newcastle and Gateshead and Sunderland and South Shields water companies, nationalised in 1974 and privatised in 1992 as North East Water, and the Durham County Water Board. The company owns thirty-two reservoirs, but Kielder's immense size is revealed in the fact that its capacity, 44,000 million gallons (200,000 million litres), exceeds the aggregate capacities of the other thirty-one. Its nearest rival, the Derwent Reservoir, built jointly by the Durham County Water Board and the Sunderland and South Shields water companies and opened in 1966, has a capacity of only 110 million gallons (500 million litres). Other major reservoirs serving the region, with their completion dates, are: Balderhead (1965), Burnhope (1936), Catcleugh (1905), Colt Crag (1884), Cow Green (1971), Hallington (1872 and 1889) and Selset (1960).

KIRKPATRICK, JOHN SIMPSON (1892–1915)

On 18 May 2003 a service was held at St Hilda's Church, SOUTH SHIELDS, to honour the memory of a man born in the town, who was killed at Gallipoli on 19 May 1915 while serving with the Australian forces. John Simpson Kirkpatrick's story is curious and interesting in that it shows how legends are made. He was born in July 1892 in South Shields, the son of a seaman. After a basic schooling and four years as a milkman, he joined the merchant navy in 1909. The following year, however, he jumped ship at, appropriately, Newcastle, New South Wales. During the next four years, he did a variety of labouring jobs, until August 1914, when he volunteered for the Australian Imperial Force under the name of Simpson. His motive was not so much patriotic as a means of returning to Europe and to his mother and sister in South Shields, with whom he had kept in touch. However, his unit went not to Britain, but to Gallipoli, where he landed on 25 April 1915. Kirkpatrick was not a fighting soldier, but a member of 3rd Field Ambulance, Australian Army Medical Corps. The job he found himself doing was bringing wounded men from the front, down what was called Shrapnel Gully to dressing stations on the beach. To help him with men with leg wounds, he acquired a donkey. His career was short, for on 19 May he was killed by a bullet through the heart and was buried on the beach.

In his short time at the front his performance, although worthy of a mention in dispatches, was in no way exceptional. Yet he became a national hero in Australia and a symbol of that country's manhood. Statues of him with his donkey stand at the Shrine of Remembrance in Melbourne and at the Australian War Memorial in Canberra. He has appeared on postage stamps, a film has been made about him, and there was even a petition for the award of a posthumous Victoria Cross. A statue by a South Shields artist, Robert Olley, stands in Ocean Road, South Shields, near the centre of the town.

John Kirkpatrick was an ordinary and undistinguished man, who did his duty bravely but briefly and paid the ultimate penalty, as did thousands of others. It remains a mystery why this simple and worthy reality should have been inflated into a legend.

KNOTT, SIR JAMES, Bt (1855–1934)

One of the most successful North-East businessmen of the nineteenth century, James Knott was a classic case of rags to riches. He was born in January 1855, in Howden on the north bank of the Tyne, the eldest of ten children of a butcher. In 1869, at the age of fourteen, he started work as a clerk in a shipping office on the Newcastle quayside. Nine years later, in 1878, he bought an old collier for £185. This was the start of a meteoric business career: by the end of the century, he was the owner of the Prince Line, a shipping company that did trade all over the world, and he also had acquired interests in coal mining in Northumberland and South Wales. Not only did he succeed in business, but he also found time to study law and become a barrister, although the pressure of business life meant that he practised only for a few years. The launch of his business career coincided with his marriage, which produced three sons. His two younger sons were killed in France in 1915 and 1916, and it was thought that his eldest son, with whom he had quarrelled, had also died, although this was disproved in 1918 when he returned on leave from Egypt. By that time, however, Knott, believing that all his family was lost, sold his shipping interests to Furness, Withy & Co. (see FURNESS, CHRISTOPHER) and retired from public life. In the same year, 1917, he was made a baronet and went to live at Samares Manor, a property he had bought in Jersey.

In retirement James Knott became a noted philanthropist. His benefactions were eclectic, ranging from the gift of a section of HADRIAN'S WALL to the Newcastle Society of Antiquaries (see LITERARY AND PHILOSOPHICAL SOCIETY OF NEWCASTLE UPON TYNE) to the building of the Memorial Flats for Trawlermen at North Shields; and donations towards the welfare of those who had suffered in the war. What they all had in common was that they were in the North East. In 1924 this charitable work was placed in the hands of a company he formed, Samares Investments Ltd, which had wide discretion as to who might benefit, but again with a stress on the needs of the North East. The consequence of his decision to move his assets offshore was that when he died in 1934, he was reviled in both the local and the national press as a tax dodger.

Time has shown this to be a calumny: Sir James Knott's fortune has been used to the benefit of his native region and not dissipated by later generations or taken by the Treasury. The focus on the North East became firmer in 1990, when the directors of the Samares Investment Company diverted over half its capital to fund the 'Sir James Knott Trust' based in Newcastle. Since then it has distributed over £1 million every year to a very wide variety of North-East bodies and causes, including youth organisations, churches, sheltered housing, hospitals and medical research, the region's universities, and community services.

In addition, the Samares Company is the owner of two important Northumberland properties. Arguably the more important is Chillingham Park, bought in 1982. Its aim is to preserve the unique herd of white wild cattle, the management of which is in the hands of the Chillingham Wild Cattle Association (see CHILLINGHAM WILD CATTLE). The other property is much larger, the 13,000 acre (5,000 ha) College Valley Estate, which was bought in 1952. Although a commercial enterprise, the estate management policy aims to balance sheep and forestry with the conservation of wildlife and the abundant archaeological heritage.

KNOX, JOHN (c.1513–1572)

John Knox, one of the prime movers of the Scottish Reformation and still for many the embodiment of Scottish Calvinism, had a brief but personally influential connection with the North East. Following an abortive revolt in 1547 against Mary of Guise, the widow of James V and regent for their infant daughter, Mary (Queen of Scots), Knox became a prisoner and served for nearly two years as an oarsman on a French galley. Following his release, he came to England, where the situation was congenial in that the government of the underage Edward VI was pursuing a positive Protestant policy. He was briefly a licensed preacher in BERWICK, and then for a longer spell in NEWCASTLE. From there he went to London, where he became involved in revising the Book of Common Prayer and was offered, but declined, the bishopric of Rochester. However, on the death of Edward VI in 1553 and the accession of his ardently Catholic half-sister, Mary I, he returned to Newcastle, from where he fled abroad to Geneva.

While in Northumberland he met Elizabeth Bowes, the wife of Richard Bowes (see BOWES FAMILY), then serving on the Border as Captain of Norham. From their meeting two things sprang. One was the marriage of Knox and Marjory, Elizabeth's daughter, a marriage strongly opposed by the rest of the Bowes family. The other was Elizabeth's complete reliance on Knox as a spiritual adviser. From her letters to him (his replies have not survived), it would appear that she had serious concerns about forsaking the religion in which she had grown up in favour of the new Protestant version. In this there was nothing exceptional – Knox was discharging the role ministers of religion have held down the centuries. What was unconventional was that when Knox fled to Geneva, Elizabeth deserted her husband to go with him. When Knox returned to Scotland in 1559, so, shortly afterwards, did Elizabeth. However, by that date she was a widow, Richard Bowes having died the previous year, and her daughter had two young children to care for. But the association continued after Marjory died in 1560 and lasted until Elizabeth's own death eight years later. This dogged devotion caused tongues to wag, to the extent that in 1572 Knox deemed it prudent to issue a public statement that their 'great familiarity' was 'neither flesh nor blood but her troubled conscience'.

LAING, SIR JAMES (1823–1901)

James Laing was born at Deptford House, Sunderland. His father, Philip Laing, came from Pittenweem in Fife in 1793 to join his brother, John, in developing a shipbuilding business at Monkwearmouth. In 1818 the partnership was dissolved and Philip moved to Deptford, where James was trained to succeed to his father's business, which he did on Philip's death in 1843. At this stage, the firm was building in wood, in which he was an innovator in that he was the first to use teak. Ten years after succeeding his father, wood began to give way to iron and Laing built his first iron ship in 1853. But he also continued to build in wood until 1866, his last and most famous wooden vessel being the clipper *Torrens*, on which the novelist Joseph Conrad served as second mate. And he continued to build composite ships (wooden hulls on iron frames) until 1875. His speciality, both in wood and iron, was the passenger-cargo ship. Laings merged with three other yards in 1954 to form Sunderland Shipbuilders Ltd and closed in 1985 (see SHIPBUILDING INDUSTRY).

As a leading shipbuilder, Laing was on the governing bodies of several appropriate organisations: Lloyd's Register, the Institution of Naval Architects and the UK Chamber of Shipping. He also had many other business interests, including a controlling share in the Ayres Quay Bottle Works and directorships of the Sunderland Gas Co., the North East Railway Co. and the Suez Canal Co. He was a member of the River Wear Commission from 1859 and its chairman for thirty-three years from 1868 until his death in 1901, and chairman of the Hendon Dock Co. He was knighted in 1897, but is said to have declined a peerage. He was followed in the firm by his son, Philip (1849–1907) and grandson, Hugh (1871–1930).

LAING ART GALLERY, NEWCASTLE (see under ART GALLERIES)

LAMBTON, ANTHONY CLAUD FREDERICK (1922–2007)

Anthony Lambton was at the centre of one of the major social and political scandals of the late twentieth century. He was the second son of the 5th Earl of Durham, who became heir to the title on the death of his elder brother. In 1951, as Viscount Lambton, he became Conservative MP for BERWICK UPON TWEED and during the next twenty years he proved to be a very able member, seemingly destined for high office. His progress was halted briefly in 1970, when on the death of his father he became 6th Earl of Durham. He immediately took advantage of the recent legislation permitting a peer to renounce his title (but without prejudice to his heir) in order to continue to sit in the Commons. Thereafter, he was Mr Lambton, although he fought to retain his pre-1970 courtesy title, Viscount Lambton, but this was denied to him by the argument that the title now attached to his son as the heir to the earldom. It was three years later, when Parliamentary Under-Secretary for the RAF in Edward Heath's government, that he fell from grace, as a result of the publication of photographs of him in bed smoking cannabis with two prostitutes. Although there was no evidence that his behaviour had resulted in blackmail or the leakage of state secrets, he was convicted for the possession of illegal drugs. He immediately resigned his office and his seat in parliament, which in the 1974 election was won by the Liberal candidate.

Thereafter, Lambton lived in Tuscany with his mistress, returning only for the annual shooting in August. Still a wealthy man, he bought the Villa Cetinale, near Siena, which in the seventeenth century had belonged to a cardinal, and restored its neglected garden to a splendid condition. His other activity was writing. Here, his ability to cause upset and disturbance showed no sign of abating, most notably with the first part of a two-volume study, *The Mountbattens*, which caused such a stir through its highly unflattering portrayal of Earl Mountbatten, hitherto presented as a war hero, that he was persuaded not to proceed with the second volume.

LAMBTON, JOHN GEORGE, 1st EARL OF DURHAM (1792–1840)

In 1797 Lambton succeeded his father as the head of an ancient Durham gentry family. Although permanently in indifferent health, he played an important part in the politics of his day, which secured his elevation to the ranks of the nobility. Following a short spell in the army between 1809 and 1811, he launched his political career in 1813 by securing election as one of the MPs for County Durham, a seat he held until his elevation to the peerage as Lord Lambton in 1828. Throughout his life he was a strongly committed Whig, firmly ensconced on the radical wing of that party. During the early years of his career the Whigs led the rising demand for the reform of parliament, and Lambton, despite a very distinct autocratic streak in his personality, held democratic views, advocating equal electoral districts, household suffrage and triennial parliaments. As early as 1821 he introduced a reform bill, but this was defeated. Following this, his health precluded a fully active participation in political life and he spent some time in the warmer climate of Italy. He returned to full activity with the fall of the Tory government and the electoral victory of the Whigs in 1830. The new Prime Minister, the 2ND EARL GREY was the father of his second wife and it is therefore not surprising that he became a member of the government as Lord Privy Seal. Throughout the hard struggle to secure the passing of the Reform Bill in 1832, Lambton consistently favoured the more radical proposals, which earned him the popular sobriquet of 'Radical Jack'. Throughout, he was frustrated by the need to compromise, which resulted in an act that delivered far less than he wanted. The effort of these years, however, again undermined his health and he resigned from the government in 1833. As a reward for his work, he was created Viscount Lambton and Earl of Durham.

His radical stance and irascible nature meant that he was far from being the ideal party man. In fact, he was a nuisance to his party. The solution was to get him out of the country. In 1835 he went as ambassador to St Petersburg, to the displeasure of Tsar Nicholas I. After two years he resigned and returned home, but almost immediately another overseas opportunity arose. In 1837 disturbances broke out in Canada's two provinces, Upper Canada (Ontario), with its rapidly growing British population, and Lower Canada (Quebec), where the population was of French origin. In both provinces there was great dissatisfaction with the constitutional arrangements that had been put in place in 1791.

Lambton was sent to find a solution to the problems and he spent six months in Canada between May and November 1838. His treatment of the ringleaders of the insurrection was typically autocratic, notably acting *ultra vires* in exiling some to Bermuda. Nevertheless, the *Report on the Affairs of British North America* that he presented to the Colonial Office provided the solution to the Canadian problem. Although known as the Durham Report, it was written almost entirely by Lambton's friend and associate, Charles Buller. It did, however, reflect Lambton's typically radical views, namely that Upper and Lower Canada should be united and be given genuine home rule based upon a democratically elected assembly. Adopted, this arrangement remained in force until the Canada Act of 1867 united all the Canadian provinces into a federation, the Dominion of Canada.

Although his elevation to the peerage was for political services, account was also taken of his great wealth. His estate in land extended to 17,000 acres (7,000 ha), but the greater part of his income came from coal. He not only mined the coal under his own land, but also leased mining rights from other landowners, notably the church. He had six working collieries (Newbottle, Cocken, Harraton, Lumley, Littletown and Sherburn) and four others (Shadforth, Ludworth, Sherburn House and Cassop) that were not being worked. The hub of this 'empire' was Philadelphia, linked to his pits by railways, which also carried the coal to Sunderland for export. Although away from home for long periods, he did not neglect his business interests. In his absence, matters were supervised by his capable agent, Henry Morton. Their correspondence shows both fully commited to running all elements of the estate efficiently and to maximum profit.

Like other wealthy titled landowners, the Lambtons were determined to have a country seat of suitable opulence. The result was Lambton 'Castle'. Quotation marks are needed because 'castle' is a misnomer. The family's original home, Lambton Hall, lay on the south side of the Wear and was demolished in 1797, when the new 'castle' was under construction. The 'castle' was in fact a rebuilding of Harraton Hall, situated on the north side of the river, which the family had acquired by marriage a century earlier. Turning Harraton Hall into 'Lambton Castle' was begun by the Earl's father. During the Earl's minority work ceased, but was resumed when he attained his majority, using the services of IGNATIUS BONOMI, and continued until 1828. The life of this edifice was brief: much of it, including parts built later in the nineteenth century by JOHN DOBSON and his son-in-law, Sydney Smirke, was pulled down in 1932. The family home is now Biddick Hall.

The career of John George Lambton needs to be seen alongside that of the 3RD MARQUESS OF LONDONDERRY. Both were politicians, but widely separated on the political spectrum, Londonderry the reactionary Tory, Durham the radical Whig. In other respects they were much alike and were consciously rivals. Unlike many aristocrats with access to mineral wealth, they actively exploited their assets personally and directly, rather than simply collecting rents and royalties, and both sought to dominate the North-East coal trade. Much of the wealth that coal brought them they put into creating grandiose dwellings. Both peerages survive, but they no longer possess the monuments in stone to their former wealth and importance.

'THE LAMBTON WORM'

Now one of the North East's best-known and frequently sung folk songs, 'The Lambton Worm' was first performed in 1867 at the Old Tyne Theatre in Newcastle by its composer, C.M. Lumaine. It tells of how Sir John Lambton, while fishing in the Wear one Sunday morning, caught a strange fish, which he mindlessly threw down a well. Shortly afterwards, and without further thought, he joined a group of knights and went abroad on crusade. While he was away, the strange creature grew into a serpent (worm) of immense size and proceeded to terrorise the neighbourhood. On his return, Lambton slew the serpent in a fight in the middle of the River Wear, a necessary venue in order to prevent the reuniting of the two halves into which he cut the beast.

As related in Lumaine's song, the story is a jolly version of a much older and darker legend. In it, Lambton's act in fishing on a Sunday (perhaps Easter Sunday) contravened his spiritual and social obligations, for which the 'worm' was a punishment. Also, his strategy for defeating the 'worm' was given to him by a 'wise woman' or witch he consulted. She advised him to stud his armour with razor-sharp knife blades on which the serpent would lacerate itself, as well as to fight the contest on a rock in midstream. Finally, she told him that, following victory, he must kill the first living thing he saw, otherwise succeeding generations of the Lambton family would not die peacefully. To fulfil this commitment, Lambton arranged that once the serpent was dead he would sound his horn, a signal to his father to release his son's hound for Lambton to kill. However, in his joy the old man forgot, and on hearing the sound of the horn, rushed out of the house to be seen by his son. Although Lambton repeated the exercise, this time killing the dog, the curse was activated.

This legend, or variants of it, is found in many parts of the world. It bears a close resemblance to far older and universally known versions, the ancient Greek fable of Theseus and the Minotaur and the biblical account in the Book of Judges of Jephthah's victory over the Ammonites. There are 'worm' legends in other places within the region, such as the Laidly (Loathsome) Worm of Spinleston and the Dunstanburgh Serpent. Elsewhere, the serpent is replaced by a wild boar, as at Brancepeth and in the story of the Pollard family near BISHOP AUCKLAND.

LANCHESTER

Now a large residential village, Lanchester, like Ebchester six miles to the north, has had two histories. The first was the ROMAN FORT, Longovicium, built *c.*122 and in use until the fourth century. The remains of its outer wall are visible on the south side of the B6296 about 900 m from the village. Longovicium, however, was more than a military establishment on Dere Street, the Roman road from the Tees to CORBRIDGE; it was also a substantial civil settlement that grew up outside its gates. Virtually nothing is known of either since very little excavation has taken place.

What happened to the fort and its village after the end of the Roman occupation is unclear, in particular whether there was any continuity between them and the medieval village that grew up below the Roman settlement, close to the confluence of Newhouse Burn and the River Browney. The new settlement became a large and important member of the episcopal estate, with a church that served one of the most extensive parishes in the country. Its size meant that its tithe revenue was immense and this led to its reorganisation by Bishop Anthony Bek in 1284. Instead of a single rector, the church was to have a college comprising a dean and seven prebendaries. Bek's purpose was not altruistic, but to enable him to pay an increased number of clerks in his administration: the holders of the prebends were to have no parochial duties, other than to provide and pay four vicars to serve as the parish clergy. However, this early form of team ministry may, incidentally, have provided an improved service to the parish. The arrangement disappeared after the Reformation.

LAUREL, STAN (1890–1965)

Stan Laurel, the world-famous comedy actor, was born Arthur Stanley Jefferson, the son of Arthur Jefferson, an actor, playwright and theatre manager, and his wife, Madge, who was a talented set designer. At the time of his birth, his father was manager of the Theatre Royal in BISHOP AUCKLAND, but Madge went back to her family home in

Ulverston, Cumbria for the birth. Fourteen months later, she returned to Bishop Auckland, where Stan was christened. The family remained in Bishop Auckland until 1896, when Arthur Jefferson became manager of the Theatre Royal in North Shields, where he remained until he took over the Metropole Theatre in Glasgow. Stan's education was consequently disrupted: Gainford School, King James's Grammar School at Bishop Auckland, and schools at Tynemouth and finally Glasgow.

Whether intentionally or not, he was bred to theatrical life, and after some time in the box office of his father's theatre, he found work as a bit-part actor, eventually joining Fred Karno's group, where he understudied Charlie Chaplin. It was with Fred Karno that he went to the USA in 1910 and 1913, and he eventually settled there in 1917. It was at this time that he took up with an Australian actress, Mae Dahlberg, who persuaded him to adopt the stage name Stan Laurel. Moving to Hollywood in the 1920s, he found work with Hal Roach and in 1927 he made his first film with Oliver Hardy (1892–1957), the start of what proved to be an internationally successful comic partnership. In the course of his film career between the late 1920s and the late 1950s he made nearly 190 films, and in 1961 he was awarded a special Oscar for his services to the film industry. His private life, however, was turbulent. In addition to his common-law wife, Mae Dahlberg, whom he ditched in 1925, he was married five times, including twice to the same woman. A statue of him in a characteristic pose stands in Dockwray Square, North Shields and a 'Stan Laurel' tourist trail has been laid out in Bishop Auckland.

The other well-known twentieth-century theatrical star with North-East connections is **Dame Flora Robson (1902–1984)**, who was born at South Shields during the time when her father, a marine engineer, was working there. The theatre at South Shields is named in her honour.

LAWSON, DOROTHY (1580–1632)

Born Dorothy Constable, she was the daughter of Sir Henry Constable of Burton Constable in the East Riding of Yorkshire. In 1597 she married Roger Lawson, the heir of Sir Ralph Lawson of Brough, also in the East Riding, with whom she had fourteen children. It was the expansion of their family that led to them move to another Lawson property, Heaton Hall near Newcastle. Two years after Roger Lawson's early death in 1614, Dorothy and her children and household moved to a house she had built at St Anthony's, immediately south of Heaton on a sharp bend in the Tyne.

It was there that she gained her reputation as a zealous Roman Catholic. She brought up her children in that faith and is said to have converted her mother, the members of her household and most of the population of the neighbourhood, where she was well known for her religious devotion and her charitable work. More than that, her house was the landing place and a refuge for priests sent to England to minister to members of the Catholic church and to make converts. Both activities were illegal: to be a practising Roman Catholic was to incur financial penalties; and to aid and give shelter to a priest was a capital offence. Yet Dorothy Lawson's name was never placed on any recusancy list, nor was she ever fined, and her house was never searched. Why she had a charmed life is uncertain, but her social status, having friends in high places and the relaxed attitude on the part of the local authorities in an area where many landed families remained committed to the old religion were probably sufficient to explain her peaceful survival.

Alnwick Castle (above)
Since 1309, the castle has belonged to the Percy family, who have been responsible for most of its development and for whom it has been the main country home since the middle of the eighteenth century. The view is from the north bank of the River Aln and it was on the rising ground behind the camera that Malcolm III, King of Scots, is said to have been killed on 13 November 1093. (Mike Kipling Photography)

Holy Island (Lindisfarne) (below)
The view is from the rocky outcrop known as the Heugh and shows the parish church of St Mary on the left and to its right the ruins of the early twelfth-century monastery, founded as an outpost of Durham Cathedral Priory. Its church enclosed the site of the church where St Cuthbert was buried in 687. Between the two churches (not visible) is the base of a tall cross, now lost, which may have been similar to that at Ruthwell.
(Mike Kipling Photography)

Collingwood Statue, Tynemouth
Overlooking the mouth of the River Tyne, the 10 metres high statue of Admiral, Lord Collingwood, the victor of Trafalgar, by John Lough, stands on a plinth designed by John Dobson. It was erected in 1847. The guns, from Collingwood's flagship, *Royal Sovereign*, were added the following year.
(Mike Kipling Photography)

Newcastle Central Station
The train shed, covering about 1.5 hectares, is 407 metres long and curved on a radius of 245 metres. Incorporating important innovative engineering, it was built between 1845 and 1850 to a design by John Dobson. (Mike Kipling Photography)

St Mary's Lighthouse, Whitley Bay
Rising to 33 metres, the lighthouse was built in 1897–98 on a small rocky island, accessible on foot only at low tide.
(Mike Kipling Photography)

Grey's Monument, Newcastle
The monument is at the hub of the town centre development carried out by Richard Grainger and John Clayton in the 1830s. It faces south down Grey Street towards the steep bank of the Tyne. To the right is Grainger Street leading to the Central Station. Visible in the middle distance to the left of the column is the tower and lantern of St Nicholas (CofE) Cathedral. (G. Peacock / Mike Kipling Photography)

Bamburgh Castle (above)
Dominating both land and sea from its position on top of an outcrop of the Whin Sill, the castle was for centuries a major political and military centre. Visible today are the keep and the three baileys, built in the twelfth century but subject to subsequent modification and alteration. The most recent restoration was carried out around 1900. What can no longer be seen are any of the Anglo-Saxon buildings of what was the 'capital' of the Kingdom of Northumbria. (Mike Kipling Photography)

Hadrian's Wall (below)
This section is about a mile north of Vindolanda. The picture shows the Wall running east along the ridge of the Whin Sill, at the foot of which is Crag Lough, in the direction of Housesteads (Vercovicium) Fort.
(G. Peacock / Mike Kipling Photography)

The Chapel, Gibside
Designed by James Paine, the Chapel at Gibside was begun around 1760 but not completed until 1816. It is the best preserved of the buildings commissioned by George Bowes (1701–60) for his remodelled Gibside Estate. It stands at the west end of a tree-lined Grand Walk, 800m in length with a distant view of a Column to Liberty, which is almost as tall as Grey's Monument and is crowned with a statue of a female figure holding the Staff of Maintenance and wearing a Cap of Liberty. It is a bold statement of Bowes's adherence to the Whig Party.
(G. Peacock / Mike Kipling Photography)

Brinkburn Priory (above)
The Augustinian priory was founded in the early 1130s, but its church (fully restored in 1858–59) was built between *c.*1190 and *c.*1220 in a mix of Romanesque and Early English styles. To its left is the Manor House, created after the priory was closed in the later 1530s out of the south range of the monastic cloister. It was given its present form by John Dobson in the 1830s. (G. Peacock / Mike Kipling Photography)

Turbinia (below)
Turbinia, the ship that in 1897 revealed the superior driving power of the steam turbine, is now fully restored and housed in the purpose-designed well of the Discovery Museum, Newcastle upon Tyne.
(G. Peacock / Mike Kipling Photography)

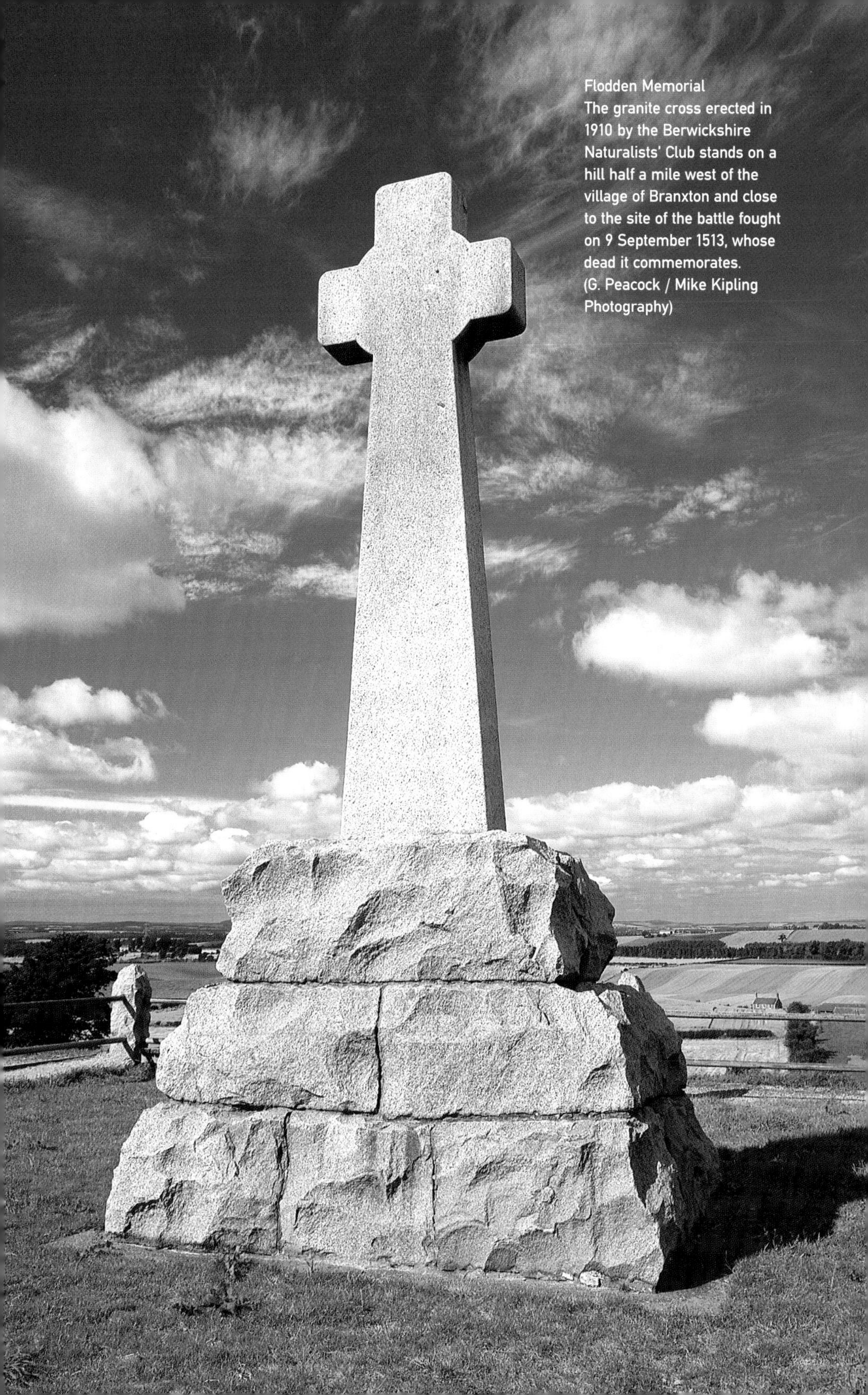

Flodden Memorial
The granite cross erected in 1910 by the Berwickshire Naturalists' Club stands on a hill half a mile west of the village of Branxton and close to the site of the battle fought on 9 September 1513, whose dead it commemorates.
(G. Peacock / Mike Kipling Photography)

Woodhouse Bastle (above)
Situated a mile and a half from Holystone, Woodhouse is arguably the most complete example of a two-storey bastle. The ground floor entrance, just visible in the gable end, carries the date 1602. The main deviation from the standard bastle design is that access to the upper floor is by an internal stair, instead of through a door in the upper part of one of the long walls reached by an external stair parallel to it.
(G. Peacock / Mike Kipling Photography)

Auckland Castle (below)
Although called a castle, it was never designed for defence and is more correctly described as the episcopal palace of the bishops of Durham. Facing is the chapel created by Bishop John Cosin (1660–1672) by converting the twelfth-century banqueting hall of Bishop Hugh of le Puiset (1154–1195). To the left are the oriel windows of the sixteenth-century extension begun by Bishop Thomas Ruthall (1509–1523). The bishops of Durham still live in part of the castle. (Mike Kipling Photography)

Bowes Museum, Barnard Castle (above)
Designed by the French architect, Jules Pellechet, Bowes Museum was built between 1869 and 1892 to house the fine art collection of John and Josephine Bowes, neither of whom lived to see it completed. Looking like a French chateau, its style contrasts sharply with that of other buildings in the town. It faces southwards across the River Tees towards the Pennine Hills of North Yorkshire. Its founders are buried in the graveyard of the Roman Catholic church just to the left of the 'monkey puzzle' tree at the bottom left of the picture. (Mike Kipling Photography)

Durham Castle (below)
Durham Castle, begun by William the Conqueror in 1072, has undergone a long and complex development. Its keep, which stands on the earthen motte, the earliest part of the castle, was built in the fourteenth century but rebuilt in 1847 after the castle passed into the ownership of Durham University. The castle is the main building of University College and the keep is now used for student accommodation. (Mike Kipling Photography)

Belsay Castle (above)
Probably the finest and most sumptuous example of a three-storey border tower, Belsay Castle was built *c.*1370 for the Middleton family. To its right is the façade of the more comfortable and convenient Jacobean extension begun shortly after the end of the Anglo-Scottish war in 1603. (G. Peacock / Mike Kipling Photography)

Durham Cathedral (below)
The cathedral was built between 1093 and 1133, but subsequent alterations have significantly changed its appearance. The western towers (on the right) were heightened in the thirteenth century, as was the central tower, which was raised again in the fifteenth century; and in the middle decades of the thirteenth century the original apse at the east end was replaced by the Chapel of the Nine Altars in the form of a T Bar. In addition, a number of its windows were enlarged in the fourteenth and fifteenth centuries and given elaborate tracery. (Mike Kipling Photography)

Tyne Bridges: Gateshead and Newcastle (above)
The photograph highlights three splendid (in both architectural and engineering terms) solutions to the problem of spanning the Tyne gorge. In the foreground is the Tyne Bridge, opened in 1928; beyond is the double-decker High Level Bridge, opened in 1850; and between them the (red) Swing Bridge of 1876.
(G. Peacock / Mike Kipling Photography)

Washington Old Hall (below)
Built in the first quarter of the seventeenth century on the fashionable H plan, Washington Old Hall was one of perhaps forty similar projects across the region. These signalled the move away from the need for defensive buildings occasioned by the Union of the Crowns in 1603, which brought the long Anglo-Scottish war to an end. Other good examples are Westholme Hall, near Barnard Castle, and Denton Hall, Newcastle.
(G. Peacock / Mike Kipling Photography)

Tornado (above)
Built in Darlington by the A1 Steam Locomotive Trust set up in 1990, the *Tornado* is a Peppercorn Class A1 Pacific locomotive, which in 2009 reintroduced the 'age of steam' to the East Coast Main Line. The picture shows the locomotive without its name-plate but already painted in the green livery of the old LNER Company. (G. Clarke / Mike Kipling Photography)

Lumley Castle, Chester le Street (below)
The castle is situated on the east side of the River Wear opposite Chester le Street and overlooks the Riverside ground of the Durham County Cricket Club. It was built in the last twenty years of the fourteenth century and comprises four towers (two shown here) linked by buildings to form a quadrilateral. It was altered, though not fundamentally, in the early eighteenth century by Sir John Vanbrugh. Still owned by the Lumleys, Earls of Scarbrough, it is now a hotel. (Mike Kipling Photography

National Glass Centre, Sunderland
Opened in 1998, the Centre occupies the site on the north bank of the River Wear of the former North Sands shipyard and is a prime example of post-industrial redevelopment. Immediately to the west is the church of St Peter, Monkwearmouth with the remains of the Anglo-Saxon monastery, where glass making by foreign craftsmen brought to the region by Benedict Biscop began in the late seventh century. The view is southwards across the river and seawards towards the entrance to South Dock. (Mike Kipling Photography)

Penshaw Monument (above)
Designed by John and Benjamin Green and based upon a Greek temple in Athens, Penshaw Monument was erected in 1844 as a memorial to John Lambton, First Earl of Durham. It stands on top of Penshaw Hill, which features in the song 'The Lambton Worm'. It is visible from a considerable distance in all directions.
(Mike Kipling Photography)

Transporter Bridge (below)
Built between 1907 and 1911 by the Glasgow firm of Sir William Arrol to a design by the Cleveland Bridge and Engineering Company, the bridge spans the River Tees between Port Clarence and Middlesbrough.
(Mike Kipling Photography)

LAWSON, JOHN JAMES, LORD LAWSON OF BEAMISH (1881–1965)

Jack Lawson was one of the best-liked of the miner MPs to represent North-East constituencies. He was born in Whitehaven in Cumberland (Cumbria), but in 1893 aged twelve he moved to Boldon Colliery to rejoin his father, who had become a miner there in 1890. Thirteen years later, by which time he was a hewer, a married man and a staunch Methodist, he won a scholarship to Ruskin College, Oxford. On completing his studies, he returned home to resume work in the pit, but also to become very active in Labour politics. In 1913 he was elected to Durham County Council, on which he sat until 1923, and in 1919 he was elected MP for CHESTER LE STREET. He was to hold this seat until 1949, rarely securing less than 70 per cent of the votes cast.

As an MP, Jack Lawson's foremost concern was the welfare of his constituents, particularly demanding government aid to alleviate suffering in mining communities in his constituency that were badly affected by the depression in the industry in the inter-war years. At the same time he held minor office in the two Labour governments of this period: parliamentary private secretary to RAMSAY MACDONALD in 1924; and parliamentary secretary to Margaret Bondfield, the Minister of Labour, in 1929–31. With Labour out of power between 1931 and 1945, Lawson was again a backbencher. He finally achieved high office in the Labour government of 1945, appointed to the Cabinet as Secretary of State for War, with the particular remit of organising the smooth and equitable demobilisation of Britain's huge national service forces. Ill health, however, forced his retirement after only one year. He remained a backbencher for another three years, retiring in 1949 and then entering the House of Lords with a peerage in the following year.

Apart from his political life he was also active as an author, both as a journalist and in writing his autobiography, *A Man's Life*, and biographies of PETER LEE and the miners' leader, Herbert Smith. The respect in which he was held was indicated by the honorary DCL from Durham University in 1947, by the Freedom of Sunderland in 1950 and by the Lord Lieutenancy of County Durham from 1949 until 1958. These awards also demonstrate his capacity for friendship across the political spectrum, made possible by the fact that Lawson was not a doctrinaire Socialist, but a man for whom politics was the means of achieving sensible solutions to social problems.

LAWTHER, SIR WILLIAM (1889–1976)

Will Lawther was born at Choppington, Northumberland, where his father was a miner. In 1901, at the age of twelve, he joined his father in the pit and six years later went with him and the rest of his family to Chopwell. There he became active in both politics and trade union work. His opinions were fiercely radical and from 1907 until 1911 he was secretary of the Chopwell branch of the Independent Labour Party (ILP). In this he followed the family tradition: his father was an early supporter of the ILP, while his grandfather had been an active Chartist in the middle decades of the nineteenth century. Moreover, his radical outlook was in tune with that of the Chopwell community, which from its early days was a hotbed of left-wing politics, becoming known as 'Little Moscow'. Political commitment, combined with intelligence, won him a scholarship at the Central Labour College in London for the years 1911 and 1912. On his return to Chopwell, he helped to found a Socialist Sunday School and branches of the Plebs League at Chopwell, South Shields and Consett. His left-wing convictions drove him to being a conscientious objector in 1914, even to the point of refusing to serve in the Red Cross.

Not long after the end of World War I he became a checkweighman at Victoria Garesfield Colliery and also very active in the Labour Party, serving on the National Executive from 1923 until 1926. During the General Strike in the latter year, he went to prison for two months rather than pay a £50 fine for intimidating the police and interfering with food distribution. At this stage his ambition was to become an MP, but he was thwarted in 1922, 1923 and 1924 elections by defeats at South Shields at the hands of the Liberal candidate, Edward Harney. Success finally came in 1929, when he won Barnard Castle. But it was short-lived, ended by the comprehensive defeat of the Labour Party in the 1931 election. In the same year he also resigned from the Durham County Council, on which he had served since 1925.

He now turned his energy and ambition away from politics to the miners' union. In 1933 he became a full-time union official as Treasurer of the Durham Miners' Association and in the following year he was elected Vice-President of the national body, the Miners' Federation of Great Britain, succeeding to the presidency in 1939. When the Federation was restructured as the National Union of Mineworkers in 1945, he was elected as its first president and retained the office until his retirement in 1954. In the immediate post-war years he was one of the dominant personalities of the trade union movement.

By the time of his retirement his ideological stance had undergone a marked rightward shift. During the 1930s he remained far to the left, expressing fervent admiration of the Soviet Union, staunchly supporting the Republican cause in Spain (for which one of his brothers, Clifford, died in 1937 fighting in the International Brigade) and advocating the affiliation of the Labour Party to the Communist Party. But towards the end of World War II, and particularly after the Labour victory in the 1945 election, he moved to the right. Thereafter, he used his undoubted authority and reputation to thwart the machinations of the Communists in the TUC and to argue against the left-wing views of Aneurin Bevan in the Labour Party. His ideological shift did not go down well with his remaining brothers, all of whom were active union officials and retained their left-wing outlook. He was knighted in 1949 and died in 1976.

LEAD MINING AND MANUFACTURING INDUSTRIES

The exploitation of the North Pennine lead ore field was one of the North East's most important industries until the last years of the nineteenth century. Roughly, the field extended from the Tyne Gap in the north to Stainmore in the south and from Wolsingham in the east to Alston in the west. Almost all the lead extracted was in the form of galena (lead sulphide), although there were small quantities of cerusite (lead carbonate). The field also had a number of other minerals in commercial quantities: iron (spalhose or rider ore); fluorite (calcium fluoride), largely in the central areas of the field; and barytes (barium carbonate) in its outer fringes; calamine (zinc carbonate); and blende (zinc sulphide).

These minerals were formed millions of years ago by the cooling of warm water that welled up into fissures in the earth's crust. These fissures, known to the miners as *veins*, were up to 12 feet (3.6 m) wide and essentially vertical in their orientation. While some veins were mined downwards from the surface, the most widespread method was for horizontal tunnels, known as *levels*, to be driven into the hillside until the veins were reached. These were then mined upwards towards the surface. The levels were constructed on a slight upward slope, to allow gravity drainage. What the miners extracted was *bouse*, a mixture of minerals and stone from which the galena was extracted by crushing and then sieving in water. The resulting lead concentrate, which was between 40 and 60 per cent lead, was then removed for smelting.

When lead mining began is uncertain. There may have been some during the Roman era, but firm evidence becomes available only in the twelfth century, following King Stephen's confirmation in 1154 of mineral rights in the WEARDALE FOREST to BISHOP HUGH OF LE PUISET. Thereafter exploitation was on a modest scale until the end of the seventeenth century. The modern lead-mining industry developed in the hundred years after the repeal of the 1568 Royal Mines Act in 1693, which gave landowners greater freedom in the exploitation of minerals under their properties. Within a few years it was dominated by two concerns. One was distant from the region, the London Lead Co., formed in 1705 by the merger of three other companies, all founded in the 1690s. Dominated by Quakers, its main areas of operation were Teesdale and Alston Moor, where its operational bases were, respectively, at Middleton in Teesdale and Nenthead. In Middleton, the company's mid-nineteenth-century head office, Middleton House, and company housing designed by IGNATIUS BONOMI remain notable architectural features of the town.

The other major concern was the Wentworth Beaumont Co., a family enterprise with a complex history. It was started by the wealthy Newcastle merchant, Sir William Blackett (*c.*1620–80), but fully developed by his son, also Sir William (*c.*1657–1705). In 1688 the latter bought the Manor of HEXHAM, which included East and West Allendale estate, from the impecunious Sir John Fenwick. In the following decade, he gained control of much of lead mining in Weardale by leasing large tracts of the dale from the Bishop of Durham and in 1696 becoming the bishop's Moormaster, the office created in the late sixteenth century to administer the episcopal mining interests in the Forest of Weardale. After the death without a male heir of his son (another Sir William) in 1728, control of the estate and its lead mines passed through successive heiresses to three families: Calverley (who adopted the Blackett name), Wentworth, and finally Beaumont. Their headquarters was at Allenheads. By 1850 these two companies between them employed nearly 4,000 men. The only other major institution with a significant interest in the industry was the Commissioners of the Royal Naval Hospital at Greenwich, to which was assigned many of the estates forfeited by the Earl of Derwentwater following the collapse of the JACOBITE UPRISING OF 1715.

Mining conditions differed from those in the coal industry. The mines themselves were not gaseous and consequently the lives of miners were not at risk from explosion, although bad air was a serious problem as the consequence of ventilation difficulties. Mining was carried out by small teams of between four and six miners on three-monthly contracts. Their pay was determined by the amount of galena they produced and was generally lower than in coal mining. Consequently the economy of lead-mining communities had a dual nature, miners combining mine work with farming smallholdings on which they kept a cow, pigs and poultry and grew vegetables.

After the crushing and separation processes were completed, the galena was moved to central smelters. The sites of thirty-seven of these have been identified, the last in operation being three at Eggleston (closed in 1903), owned by the London Lead Co., and Rookhope (closed in 1883) and Allendale (closed in 1896), owned by the Wentworth Beaumont Co. By the early nineteenth century, two sorts of smelter were in use: the ore hearth (where ore and fuel were heated together), and the reverberatory furnace (where fuel and ore were separate). Also in the early nineteenth century long underground flues were added to smelt mills. Their purpose was to remove the gases generated during the smelting process, not for health and safety reasons, although they did have such benefits, but to allow lead to condense on to the walls of the flue, from which it could be scraped from time to time. The smelted lead then went to Tyneside for manufacture (see below), initially by packhorse. This mode of transport was gradually superseded by railways, which were extended into the lead-mining districts between 1834 and 1895.

The Pennine lead extraction industry dwindled almost to nothing between 1860 and 1914. The underlying reason was cheap imports, particularly from Spain, but also from Australia and the USA. In 1865 the price of lead was £24 a ton; by the late 1880s it had dropped below £10 a ton. British manufacturers could not compete. On top of this, by the late nineteenth century most of the best veins had been discovered and worked out and attempting to exploit poorer veins meant higher production costs. By 1870 Britain had lost its export markets and ten years later it was losing its home market. Foreign competition had become permanent and unbeatable.

The Wentworth Beaumont Co. gave up their Weardale leases in 1883, although the London Lead Co. soldiered on until 1904. The disappearance of the two giants did not bring mining to an abrupt end, however. A new company, the Weardale Lead Co., took over the Wentworth Beaumont leases from the Ecclesiastical Commissioners for a period of sixty years. They found new sources of lead and on the eve of World War I they were still extracting annually over 5,000 tons of lead ore, which was about a fifth of that mined in Britain. More importantly, it benefited from the growing demand for the two ancillary products, fluorite (for use as a flux in steelmaking) and barytes (required by the paint, paper, rubber and textile industries). By 1914 production of fluorite ore had risen from around 3,000 tons a year to over 22,000 tons, and that of barytes from about 7,000 tons a year to over 14,000 tons. The Weardale Lead Co. continued until 1962, when it sold out to Imperial Chemical Industries, who in turn sold their interest to the Swiss Aluminium Co. in 1977. Other successor companies included the Nenthead and Tynedale Lead and Zinc Co., which passed into the hands of the Belgian company Vieille Montagne Co. in 1895.

The most abundant evidence of this once major industry are the numerous villages, with their nineteenth-century stone houses, in the upper reaches of the rivers Tees, Wear and the Allen. These apart, most remains are not readily visible to the untutored eye, which is perhaps surprising given that 148 mines have been identified as well as the many smelters. The most visible remains are Stublick Colliery, which supplied coal for Allendale smelters, and more particularly the Park Level Mine (opened in 1853 and closed in 1916) at Killhope in Upper Weardale (see MUSEUMS).

As well as mining lead, the North East became a major centre for lead manufacture. This, however, was a separate activity as regards ownership and management, geographical location and period of time. Whereas lead mining took place in the western upland dales, lead manufacture was concentrated on Tyneside around NEWCASTLE and GATESHEAD and did not begin to develop until the late eighteenth century. By the outbreak of World War I, however, Tyneside had become one of the country's main centres for the manufacture of lead products: sheet, shot, pipe and paint. It was dominated by three firms, with two others of lesser stature.

The earliest was the firm that came to be known as Walkers, Parker & Co. It was founded at Elswick in 1778 by the famous Rotherham ironmaster, Samuel Walker (1715–82) in partnership with two Hull merchants. When they died, a Walker nephew, Samuel Walker Parker, became a partner. Despite this, the partnership was Walker-dominated and the Parkers sold their interest in 1871. In 1889, as the result of an internal family feud, the partnership was converted into a limited liability company as Walkers, Parker & Co. Although the Elswick works were their largest, they also had facilities at London, Chester, North Wales and Glasgow.

The second firm, founded in 1795, was a partnership of a London merchant, John Locke, and Christopher Blackett, the owner of Wylam Colliery and the Newcastle agent for the Blackett, Beaumont Lead Mining Co. Its first premises were in Gallowgate in Newcastle, with an additional site acquired shortly after in The Close. In 1846, however, a third and more suitable location was found at St Anthony's, close to the Tyne. The success of the firm, which by 1850 rivalled Walkers, Parker, was due to the dynamic leadership of an Alston man, James Leathart (d.1895), who joined the firm in 1820 and rose to become its driving force. In 1891, shortly before his death, the partnership became a limited company. Leathart, whose other interest was art, built up one of the finest collections of Pre-Raphaelite paintings at his house in Low Fell. Unfortunately, this collection was lost to the region as the result of enforced sales in the depression of the 1880s and dispersal after Leathart's death.

The third major firm was Cooksons (see COOKSON FAMILY), founded by William Isaac Cookson. From 1847 he was engaged in the manufacture of Venetian Red and antimony, but in 1851 he began making lead at a site at Hayhole and then at Howden, near Willington Quay, moving his earlier business to Gateshead. Cooksons, which proved to be the most dynamic and innovative of the Tyneside firms, converted to limited liability status in 1904.

The other two firms were smaller: Foster, Blackett and Wilson, founded in 1862 at Hebburn (see FOSTER, ALFRED JAMES), and James & Co. at Ouseburn.

The main features of the inter-war years were amalgamation and rationalisation. The former was achieved largely under the aegis of Associated Lead Manufacturers, founded in 1919. The process was completed in 1949, when full amalgamation was implemented and the organisation became AML Ltd. Thoughout its history, until the retirement of Roland Cookson in 1974, it was led by a Cookson or one of Cooksons' directors. As regards rationalisation, there was considerable concentration, which involved closures, notably, Locke and Blackett, and Foster, Blackett and Wilson.

The post-World War II years saw the gradual contraction of lead usage as new products, such as titanium oxide and zirconium, replaced lead in various manufacturing processes. This resulted in further closures. That of the Elswick shot tower in 1951 followed by its demolition in 1954 not only ended production but also removed a prominent Tyneside landmark. In 1980 ALM Ltd moved its headquarters from London to far less expensive Newcastle and in 1983 renamed itself the Cookson Group and is now concerned with ceramics, electronics and precious metals, rather than lead.

LEE, PETER (1864–1935)

Peter Lee was the son of a miner at Trimdon Grange, who became the first Labour chairman of Durham County Council and gave his name to one of the new towns built in Durham after 1945. His father was a man of little education, but his mother, Hannah Simpson, was the educated daughter of a mill foreman in Lancashire. This geographical duality meant that Lee's early life alternated between Durham and Lancashire: his first job, at the age of nine, was in a Lancashire cotton mill; a year later, aged ten, he was working at Littletown Colliery. Between 1874 and 1886, he rose from putter to hewer and, as was common, moved from pit to pit on an annual basis. In 1886, however, he went to the USA to join his uncle and worked as a miner in Pennsylvania, Indiana and Kentucky. He returned home in 1888, married and secured a job as a checkweighman at Wingate Colliery. But in 1896 the urge to roam seized him again, and he left his family and went to South Africa to work in the goldmines. Like his spell in America, his stay was short. Returning in 1898, he became a checkweighman at Wheatley Hill Colliery.

This restlessness seems to have burned itself out in the early years of the twentieth century. He gave up smoking and drinking, became widely read, to the extent that a room in his house was set aside as a library, and qualified as a Methodist lay preacher. He also became active in the Durham Miners' Association, rising through various offices to become general secretary in 1930 and in the following year President of the Miners' Federation of Great Britain. Parallel with this was his progress in the field of local government. He was chairman of the Wheatley Hill Parish Council in 1903; in 1907 he was elected to Easington Rural District Council; and in 1909 he secured a seat on Durham County Council, which he retained until 1932. When Labour won control of the council in 1919, he was the natural choice to be chairman.

His primary concern was to improve the health and quality of life of the mining population and because of this his best memorial is not the town named after him (see New Towns of the Twentieth Century) but the Burnhope Reservoir, opened in 1936, the year after his death, which ensured clean water for the county.

LE PUISET, HUGH OF (?–1195)

Hugh of le Puiset (whose name has been corrupted to Pudsey) was Bishop of Durham for forty-one years from 1154 until his death in 1195. His father was Hugh III, Lord of le Puiset, Viscount of Chartres and Count of Corbeil and his mother, Agnes, daughter of the Count of Blois, whose brother, Stephen, became King of England by usurpation in 1135. Hugh was therefore entirely French, highborn and very well connected. He arrived in England around 1130, hoping to prosper through his own ability and the influence of his formidable uncle, Henry of Blois, Bishop of Winchester. His ambition was crowned with success when the monks of the Durham Cathedral Priory elected him as their bishop following the death in 1152 of his predecessor, William of St Barbe. He was not consecrated, however, until after the death in 1154 of his ecclesiastical superior, the Archbishop of York, Henry Murdac, who had strongly opposed his election. The Durham monks knew that they were getting a firm hand, but such was necessary: they needed a protector after the trauma of civil war in Durham during the 1140s, which stemmed from the attempt by David I of Scotland to impose his Chancellor, William Cumin, on them as bishop following the death of Bishop Geoffrey Rufus in 1141.

Puiset's achievements as bishop were considerable and various. Perhaps the most fundamental was his acquisition of the WAPENTAKE OF SADBERGE, purchased in 1189 from Richard I. Until then part of Northumberland, it would now be part of County Durham and make the Tees the county's southern boundary, at least until the Redcliffe Maud 'reform' of 1974.

In the City itself, Puiset inherited two major buildings, the castle and the cathedral, and to both he made significant changes. Those to the castle were enforced, since it suffered considerable fire damage early in his pontificate. He rebuilt the Great Hall and made major repairs to the North Hall: the great Norman doorway that can be seen along the Tunstall Gallery still shows the magnificence of his work. The cathedral offered him less chance of leaving his mark, since it had been completed only twenty years before his arrival. He hoped to add a Lady Chapel at the east end, but was dissuaded by the monks. Instead, he added the Galilee Chapel at the west end and in so doing masked (perhaps unfortunately) the west front of the cathedral.

Although the evidence shows Puiset to have been an ambitious and grasping man, he did provide his diocese with two notable charitable institutions. Sherburn Hospital (see MEDIEVAL HOSPITALS) was entirely his own creation and was intended to house no fewer than sixty-five lepers. Kepier Hospital, however, was the work of BISHOP RANNULF FLAMBARD, but it had been destroyed during the civil war in Durham in the 1140s. Puiset refounded it, but on a less exposed site on the banks of the Wear, a mile below Durham.

The later twelfth century was a time of population growth throughout Europe, which gave landlords both reason and opportunity to develop their estates and enhance their income. Puiset was an enthusiastic developer. He built the second bridge (Elvet Bridge) over the Wear at Durham, which enabled the Borough of Elvet to flourish, and he also stimulated borough developments in Durham, DARLINGTON, Wearmouth (SUNDERLAND) and GATESHEAD. He granted (or sold) for enclosure and cultivation tracts of moorland for which economic rents could be charged. And he appears to have used his muscle to effect property exchanges to his own advantage.

But for us he should be thanked for the survey of his estates he commissioned in the early 1180s, known as BOLDON BOOK, without which our knowledge of economic and social conditions in the North East at this date would be almost nil.

LESLIE, ANDREW (1818–1895)

Andrew Leslie, one of the founders of the Tyneside SHIPBUILDING INDUSTRY, was the son of a Shetland crofter, who moved to Aberdeen after being evicted from his farm. At the age of thirteen, Andrew became an apprentice boilermaker and attended night school with Charles Mitchell, another man who was to make his name on Tyneside. In 1840 he set up his own business in Aberdeen, but in 1853 moved south to Tyneside. This was a gamble, but it was based on an informed awareness of the opportunities opening up on Tyneside for the construction of iron-hulled, steam-driven ships. He began his works on a nine-acre site in Hebburn in conjunction with a fellow Scot, John Coutts, and brought down from Aberdeen many of his skilled workers, to the extent that Hebburn became known as 'Little Aberdeen'. Between 1853 and 1885, when he retired, Leslie built 260 ships, sixty for Russian companies and many for the Liverpool firm of Holts. Following his retirement, his firm merged with the marine engineering firm of R. & W. Hawthorn.

Leslie was an active member of the Tyne Improvement Commission for thirteen years and was careful to provide for his workers, building over 100 houses for them and, in 1872, St Andrew's Presbyterian church, as well as helping to set up the Hebburn Co-operative Society. He died at Coxlodge Hall, but was buried in Edinburgh, appropriately about halfway between Aberdeen, his place of origin, and Hebburn, where he made his fortune.

LEWYN, JOHN (?–1398)

John Lewyn, who was almost certainly a Durham man, was one of the outstanding architects of the later Middle Ages. His style was functional and without frills, probably because most of his commissions were of a military character. During the 1370s and 1380s he is known to have worked on many northern castles: at BAMBURGH, Carlisle and Roxburgh for the Crown; at DUNSTANBURGH for the Duke of Lancaster; and at DURHAM for the Bishop of Durham. He also worked for several aristocratic clients: at Raby, Sheriff Hutton and Brancepeth for Lord Neville (see NEVILLE FAMILY); at Bolton for Sir Richard Scope; and at Lumley for Lord Lumley (see LUMLEY FAMILY AND CASTLE). He is also believed to have designed the great keep at Warkworth commissioned by the 1st Earl of Northumberland. If so, it demonstrates that Lewyn combined great ability as an architect and as a military engineer. His many commissions show that in the last quarter of the fourteenth century he was regarded as the foremost military architect in the north.

He was also engaged by DURHAM CATHEDRAL Priory between 1367 and 1374, to construct a new kitchen. This building, misleadingly called the Prior's Kitchen, is now the cathedral bookshop. It is rightly renowned for its vault, formed by four pairs of parallel intersecting ribs that meet to form an octagon that supported the smoke louvre. This construction combines ingenuity and elegance and reveals Lewyn to have been an architect of the highest quality.

LEYBOURNE, GEORGE (1842–1884)

George Leybourne, who had a brief but dazzling career as a music hall star, was born in Gateshead, where his father was a currier and also a theatre musician. When he was three the family moved to London. There, after what appears to have been a very modest education, he began to work as an entertainer, initially using the stage name of 'Joe Saunders' but reverting to his real name in the late 1860s. This coincided with his sudden fame and fortune, which were based upon two particular songs he wrote in 1866 and delivered on music hall stages with flamboyance and panache. One was *Champagne Charlie,* which was so popular that music hall owners and also wine merchants, who recognised the value of the publicity he provided, were prepared to pay him a sufficient income to enable him to live off the stage in the style he portrayed on it. The other was *The Daring Young Man on the Flying Trapeze.* Like many other meteoric careers, his was brilliant but short. By the late 1870s his health was declining and he could no longer maintain the hectic schedule of his heyday. The cause of his death is uncertain, but may have been excess-related.

LIBERTY SHIPS

'Liberty Ships', so called because the first vessels were named after the signatories of the American Declaration of Independence, were a major factor in securing victory in World War II. Between 1941 and 1945, 2,770 were built in eighteen American shipyards by an organisation headed by Henry Kaiser. They were 7,000 tons deadweight, could carry 9,000 tons of cargo and had a crew of forty-one. For Britain, they helped in replacing losses inflicted by German U-boats and thereby helped to sustain the vital seaborne link with the USA. Such was the efficiency of the Kaiser organisation that by 1943 the time between keel-laying and launch had fallen from 230 days to 42. In part this was due to prefabrication. But underlying this was the fundamental design of the ship, which was consciously based upon that made in 1879 at the SUNDERLAND shipyard of J.L. Thompson (see THOMPSON FAMILY), which in the last quarter of the nineteenth century was the most dynamic, innovative and up-to-date yard on the Wear. Not only did Sunderland build ships for the Merchant Navy during World War II, it also made a vital contribution to victory at one remove.

LIGHTHOUSES

With a coastline of 75 miles (120 km), nine harbours and in places hazardous offshore rocks, the North East had need of lighthouses. Some of these followed the construction of piers at harbour or river entrances and were the responsibility of the harbour commissioners, as were others located as guiding lights for ships coming into port. Additional to these, however, were five lighthouses, all but one built by Trinity House, the organisation in which control of all lighthouses around the coasts of England and Wales was vested by an act of parliament of 1824. The earliest, however, built as a private venture before the 1824 act, was that on Inner Farne (see FARNE ISLANDS), erected to a design of David Alexander in 1809. It was located on top of the defensive tower erected by Thomas Castell, the Prior of Durham, around the year 1500 and it replaced an earlier beacon first recorded in the 1770s. Trinity House sold this lighthouse to the National Trust in 2005. The Farne Islands had a second light, also designed by David Alexander, and built by Trinity House on the Longstone in 1825–26. This was the lighthouse manned by the father of GRACE DARLING. It too was a replacement for an earlier beacon on the Brownsman, erected in 1795, from where the Darlings moved to the Longstone light. The Brownsman beacon was in turn a replacement for an even earlier beacon on Staple Island, destroyed in 1783.

On COQUET ISLAND, about 20 miles south of the Farne Islands and a mile and a half from Amble, Trinity House decided in 1839 to build a lighthouse, which came into operation in 1841. As on the Inner Farne, use was made of the medieval tower built by the monks of Tynemouth Priory (see TYNEMOUTH AND NORTH SHIELDS). A further 18 miles (29 km) south, Trinity House built a lighthouse, which became operational in 1898, on the rocks known as St Mary's Island, which, like HOLY ISLAND, is accessible twice daily at low tide. It was a replacement for the 400-year-old beacon at Tynemouth. The most southerly of the North East's lighthouses, and the only one built in County Durham and on land, is that on Souter Point, near Marsden. It was built in 1871 by a Whitburn builder, Robert Allison, to the design of James Douglas, who was responsible for the Wolf Rock and Eddystone lights. Like the Inner Farne lighthouse, it now belongs to the National Trust.

All five lighthouses were built in the nineteenth century with the intention of preventing maritime disasters. Thanks to more recent technology, in particular radar and GPS, they have become redundant.

LILBURNE, GEORGE (?–1676)

George Lilburne was the younger brother of Richard Lilburne (1583–1667), a landowner of modest means at Thickley Punchardon, near Bishop Auckland. The family was a branch of the Lilburnes of West Lilburne in Northumberland that had moved to Durham in the fourteenth century. As a younger son without prospect of land, he was put into trade in SUNDERLAND. His business associates (Bowes, Bellasis and Hylton) were also of gentry stock and together they did much to promote the town's early economic development. In the 1630s, however, Lilburne's interests were also political, and radically so. He was opposed to the regime of Charles I, with its emphasis on the royal prerogative and its studied refusal to summon parliament. Locally, he was equally hostile to the Bishop of Durham, both as a landlord and as a promoter of High Church forms and usages. In brief, he was strongly committed to a parliamentary constitution and the Presbyterian form of church polity. Consequently, when in 1640 Charles was finally driven to summon parliament, Lilburne was loud in his advocacy of strong action against him. The consequence was incarceration, which lasted until the defeat of the Royalist cause in northern England in 1644.

Then as an ally of the VANE FAMILY, he enjoyed three years as a leading political figure in Durham: County Sequestrator for 'Delinquent' (Royalist) Estates, Surveyor for the Sale of Episcopal Lands, and member of the Militia Commission. Like so many others, he used his power for his own gain, in particular to secure (almost certainly by dubious means) control of the coal mines around Harraton. However, his star waned between 1647 and 1653, when the North East was effectively under the control of SIR ARTHUR HESILRIGE, the Governor of Newcastle. With Hesilrige losing power as the result of his quarrel with Oliver Cromwell, Lilburne's political fortunes revived and he became MP for Durham under Cromwell's short-lived constitution.

Despite being a lifelong opponent of monarchy, Lilburne managed to surivive its restoration in 1660. Not only did he survive but he prospered in Sunderland to the point where in 1669 he could afford to expend £2,750 on buying the manor of Barmston from its long-time owners, the Hyltons.

George Lilburne was the uncle of two other Lilburnes, JOHN LILBURNE and ROBERT LILBURNE, who though very different characters, were active radicals.

LILBURNE, JOHN (c.1614–1657)

John Lilburne was born in Sunderland, the second son of Richard Lilburne (1583–1667) of Thickley Punchardon in Durham. He was educated at the grammar schools in Bishop Auckland and Newcastle and then apprenticed to a London cloth merchant, with whom he remained until the mid-1630s.

By that time he had imbibed the most radical political and religious ideas then current, which he was to hold and advocate until his death in his early forties. He wished to bring about a society in which there was freedom of conscience in religion and a root and branch reform of the system and organs of government, including the introduction of extensive (though not universal) manhood suffrage. He was opposed to monarchy and to an established church supported by tithes, and he fiercely championed the concept of equality before the law. His advocacy was exaggerated and passionate in the extreme, and he was vindictive towards those who did not agree with him, sometimes to the point of falsehood. His writings led to prosecutions so that he spent roughly half of the last twenty years of his life in prison or in exile. The authorities found him impossible to deal with, since his popularity would have made his execution for treason very risky.

His career falls into three phases. The first was his association with the radical opponents of Charles I's religious policy, part of which was the ban in 1624 (repeated in 1637) of the publication or importation of writings on religion, church government and state matters, unless they had been officially approved. For this he was fined £500, whipped, pilloried and imprisoned. He was not released until 1642, by which time Charles I had lost control of London to his Parliamentary opponents. The second phase, 1642 to 1647, was the period of the 1st Civil War, in which Lilburne distinguished himself as a soldier, taking part in two of its major battles, Edgehill and Marston Moor, and rising to the rank of lieutenant-colonel.

Ironically, Lilburne got into the most serious trouble after the New Model Army in which he had fought had won the war and made Charles I its prisoner. In the post-war years, two fundamental issues became urgent: what to do with the king, and what sort of constitution should replace the monarchy. Both provoked furious debates. Lilburne was among those demanding a radical solution, a view prevalent among the lower ranks of the Army and which led to his becoming a leading member of the so-called Leveller Movement. But their views did not prevail, and a series of more conservative regimes was contrived and imposed by Oliver Cromwell, who after the execution of Charles I in 1649 became *de facto* ruler of England. Lilburne felt bitterly that Cromwell and the other Army leaders had 'betrayed the revolution', but his anger was also personal, driven by a belief that the state had defrauded him of what he was owed for his services.

Lilburne's final clash with authority was also motivated by personal considerations, in his intemperate support for his uncle, GEORGE LILBURNE, in his quarrel with SIR ARTHUR HESILRIGE, the man appointed to rule the north of England. The issue was certain collieries confiscated from Royalists and acquired by George Lilburne from which Hesilrige had ejected him in 1649. John Lilburne's attack on Hesilrige and on the parliamentary committee set up to examine the matter (which found in Hesilrige's favour) was so extreme that he was subject to heavy pecuniary penalties, both fine and damages, and then banished for life in 1651. He took up residence in Bruges, but returned to England in 1653, despite having been refused permission. He was arrested and imprisoned in a castle on Guernsey and then in Dover Castle, until in 1655 he was released with a weekly pension on account of his broken health. He lived for a further two years, dying in August 1657.

'Free-born John', as he was known from his emphasis on his rights as a free-born Englishman, was born to trouble, since he was incapable of compromise. His quarrelsome nature led a contemporary to exclaim that if he were the last man on earth 'John would quarrel with Lilburne and Lilburne with John'. Most of his ideas, then so radical and dangerous, now seem uncontroversial.

LILBURNE, ROBERT (1613–1665)

Robert Lilburne was the eldest son of Richard Lilburne of Thickley Punchardon in County Durham. Like his more famous younger brother, JOHN LILBURNE, he strongly opposed Charles I and his style of government. Also like John, he had a successful military career as a member of the New Model Army and was among those who resisted the attempt of parliament at the end of the 1st Civil War in 1647 to disband the Army without arrears of pay or to ship it over to Ireland. In contrast to John, however, he chose to continue a military career and played a prominent role in the 2nd Civil War between 1648 and 1651. In 1648 he defeated a Royalist force assembled in Coquetdale and then joined Oliver Cromwell to defeat a Scottish army that had invaded England at Preston. In the following year he took part in the siege of Pontefract Castle and was in Cromwell's army that invaded Scotland in 1650 and comprehensively defeated a Scottish army at Dunbar.

Finally, in 1651, when again a Scottish army invaded England, he defeated a supporting English force commanded by the Earl of Derby at Wigan.

His close association with Cromwell led to his becoming a 'regicide', his name being the twenty-eighth of the fifty-nine signatures on Charles I's death warrant. Subsequently, he was MP for County Durham, East Riding of Yorkshire and Malton in Cromwell's parliaments, and when in 1655 England was subjected to military rule in the form of eleven districts, each controlled by a Major General, he was appointed deputy to John Lambert with responsibility for the North East. Lilburne was also at ease with Cromwell's religious policy, which favoured Independency, that is, allowing Protestant sects freedom to devise their own forms of organisation and worship. Lilburne, personally, was a Baptist and he is credited with founding the first Baptist congregation in Newcastle.

When the Commonwealth regime began to disintegrate after Cromwell's death in 1658, Lilburne continued his allegiance to John Lambert in his attempt to prevent the return of Charles II and the restoration of the monarchy, which increasingly was seen as the only viable solution to a disintegrating political situation. As a 'regicide' he was inevitably excluded from the Act of Indemnity. But because at his trial he pleaded guilty and asked for pardon, the death sentence was commuted to imprisonment for life. He died in prison near Plymouth in 1665.

LINDISFARNE (see HOLY ISLAND)

LINDISFARNE (BAND)

'Lindisfarne' was, with The Animals (see CHANDLER, CHARLES), the most famous pop group to come out of the North East. It was formed in 1970: a group comprising Simon Cowe (guitar), Rod Clements (bass guitar), Ray Jackson (vocals and harmonica) and Ray Laidlaw (drums) were joined as frontman by the singer and songwriter Alan Hull, and changed their name from 'The Brethren' to 'Lindisfarne'. They enjoyed tremendous popularity during the next three years, particularly with their second album, *Fog on the Tyne*. In 1973, however, they broke up, their members forming two new bands. As neither proved particularly successful, in 1977 they came back together and 'Lindisfarne' was reborn. There were no further changes until 1984, when a sixth musician, Marty Craggs (saxaphone and flute) joined them. The band endured until the 1990s when it again broke up: in 1990 Ray Jackson left the band; in 1993 Simon Cowe emigrated to Canada to run a brewery; in 1995 Alan Hull died of a heart attack at the age of fifty; and in 2000 Marty Craggs dropped out. Although replacements were brought in, they decided to disband. Their last concert was in May 2004.

LINDISFARNE GOSPELS

The book known as the Lindisfarne Gospels has been described as 'one of the great landmarks of human cultural achievement'. Although it has been subjected to intense examination, historians do not yet claim to have conclusive answers to all of the questions it raises. However, although some have raised doubts, most scholars are convinced that it was produced in the *scriptorium* of the monastery at Lindisfarne (see HOLY ISLAND) between the 690s and 725. Who wrote it is a question that at first glance appears to have an easy answer: between 950 and 970 a monk named Aldred inserted a *colophon* (statement of authorship) to the effect that the script and the illustrations were the work of Eadfrith (Bishop of Lindisfarne between 698 and 721), that it was bound by the monk Aethelwald (his successor as bishop between 721 and 740), while a hermit named Billfrith ornamented the cover with jewels. Although there is no way of verifying Aldred's statement, there is no internal evidence to cast doubt upon it. What is certain is that with very few and minor corrections, the script and the illustrations were the work of one hand and in a single campaign that may have lasted up to ten years. The occasion of its commission was almost certainly the reburial in 698 of the body of St Cuthbert, although whether before or after that event is undetermined. The lavishness of its production, however, leaves no doubt that it was intended to be itself an object of veneration and to be part of the cult of St Cuthbert.

The book comprises 259 leaves of calf-skin vellum measuring 13½ inches by 9¾ inches (34.3 cm by 7 cm). They are of the highest quality and required the skins of 150 animals, which may have been supplied by the monastery's own estates, but also may have included gifts from pious donors. The core of the book comprises the texts of the four gospels based upon the translation into Latin by St Jerome in the 390s known as the Vulgate. The writer, however, was not simply a slavish copyist, but a scholar actively seeking to produce an improved version, since he is known to have worked from at least two gospel books that came from southern Italy, probably the vicinity of Naples. Where he obtained these copies is not known, but the most likely source was the monastery at Monkwearmouth/JARROW, which had an extensive library of imported books. The script he adopted, a form of uncial known as *Insular Majescule,* was not from the Mediterranean but from Irish *scriptoria.* In addition to the texts of the gospels, there are a number of prefatory entries, including a copy of a letter from St Jerome to Pope Damasus and ten Canon Tables, a system of cross-referencing devised by a fourth-century theologian, Eusebius, Bishop of Caesarea.

The book is not merely a beautifully executed text. This is embedded in, and embellished by, illustrative matter, which has been described as 'an aesthetic encyclopaedia of the post-Roman world'. Each of the gospels begins with three pages of illustration, two of which are readily understandable: a picture of the gospel author with his traditional symbol; and an *incipit* ('Here begins the gospel of ...') page with a highly complex initial letter. The third, called the 'cross-carpet page', consists of intricate geometric patterns that form a central cross. The name was given to these pages because of their resemblance to carpets, and it may be that they were intended to represent the sorts of prayer rug in use at that time. Almost certainly, the crosses had a dedicatory function. The forms and shapes within the patterns in these and other illustrations derive from many sources: the Iron Age Celtic world of Ireland; the Pictish world of northern Britain; the Germanic world of the Anglo-Saxons; and the Mediterranean world, including Gaul, Italy and Byzantium. The artist achieved a complex and subtle synthesis of a wide and diverse range of cultural influences. The script is in black ink, but the illustrations are in colour, derived from a variety of local animal, vegetable and mineral sources, but not, as was once thought, lapis lazuli from the Himalayas. It is very obviously a work of the highest quality, on which no expense was spared.

The history of the book has many gaps. As far as can be discerned, it remained in the possession of the Community of St Cuthbert (see CUTHBERT, SAINT) throughout its various moves after it left Lindisfarne in 875. It may have been the book that was washed overboard and then 'miraculously' recovered when the Community made an abortive attempt to sail to Ireland. It was certainly at Chester le Street, since it was there that Aldred added his *colophon* and also, in a different script to the one used for the texts, an interlinear translation into English. Today this would be regarded as a desecration and an act of vandalism. In fact, Aldred has our thanks since the words he used have given us an insight into tenth-century Northumbrian English. Thereafter, there are virtually no references to the Gospels until after 1600, although there are no reasons to think that the book did not remain in the possession of the Community and of its successor, the Cathedral Priory, until the latter was suppressed by Henry VIII in 1539 and its treasures removed to London. By 1605, however, it was in the Tower in the possession of the great seventeenth-century collector, Sir Robert Cotton (d.1631). His descendants gave it to the nation in 1703 and fifty years later, in 1753, it was one of the foundation deposits at the British Museum. Since then it has undergone one major modification. The binding work of Aethelwald and Billfrith disappeared at some unknown date in the past. In the 1850s the then Bishop of Durham, Edward Maltby, financed the present binding, much to the disgust of some purists.

It remains in the British Museum (since 1972 a component of the British Library), despite the hopes of many that it might be brought home to the North East.

LITERARY AND PHILOSOPHICAL SOCIETY OF NEWCASTLE UPON TYNE

The 'Lit and Phil' has been one of the North East's outstanding educational and cultural institutions, both in its own right and, perhaps more importantly, as the parent of other organisations. Founded in 1793, it was very much a child of its age, which saw like societies founded throughout Britain with the aim of advancing knowledge, particularly in the field of science. The 'Lit and Phil', however, was not the first attempt to found a serious intellectual society in Newcastle: in 1775 and in 1786 respectively the Philosophical Society and the Philosophical and Medical Society had been founded, but both were short-lived. Although the move to found the 'Lit and Phil' had the support of many of the leading figures, social and intellectual, of the region, the man deserving of most credit is the Reverend William Turner, the minister of the Unitarian Chapel in Hanover Square between 1783 and 1841 and a close friend of the novelist Mrs Gaskell.

The founding purposes of the Society were fourfold: monthly meetings at which members would present papers, the contents of which would then be discussed; to build up a collection of natural history specimens; the creation of a library; and lecture courses to promote scientific knowledge. Knowledge to be pursued, however, was restricted: religion, politics and the practical aspects of law and medicine were excluded from the monthly papers, and the library would not acquire novels. These restrictive rules were not rescinded until 1891, by which date interest was shifting to the humanities. Almost inevitably, the balance of activities changed: monthly papers fell out of favour in the 1840s, while greater prominence was given to lectures and lecture courses, which culminated in the University Extension Scheme under the aegis of Cambridge University, vigorously promoted in the 1870s by the Secretary, Robert Spence Watson.

At the outset, the Society had no home of its own, but held its meetings in a series of four venues, the last being (from 1809) the concert hall of the Turk's Head Hotel in the Bigg Market. This unsatisfactory situation was resolved in the 1820s with the acquisition in 1822 of the grounds of the former town house of the Nevilles (see Neville Family), Earls of Westmorland, in Westgate

Road, which the Nevilles acquired in the early fifteenth century as part of the Barony of Bolbec (Styford). On this site the Society built between 1822 and 1885. The building, in Neo-Grecian style, was designed by the local architect JOHN GREEN and cost £13,000. An extension, appropriately named Bolbec Hall, was added in the first decade of the twentieth century. Earlier, in 1893 and almost coincident with the Society's centenary, a fire seriously damaged the library and destroyed about a quarter of its books. Remarkably, it took only two years for the Society to restore its collection to its previous condition.

The Society continues to flourish, and membership, which peaked at about 5,000 (which from 1856 included women) immediately after the end of World War I, is now around 1,400, but rising. The annual lecture series remains popular. The themes and subjects are serious in nature and the lectures of high academic quality and not infrequently the vehicles of original research. The library continues to expand and now has nearly 150,000 volumes. In addition, it has the best collection of music scores in the North East and a collection of 10,000 LP records and 6,000 CDs. However, with the advent of the public library system and of the ever-expanding libraries in the region's institutions of higher education, its importance has declined. But not entirely: as well as serving its rising membership and being a popular and appropriate venue for poetry readings, book launches and recitals, it has, as the oldest library in Newcastle, books that no other library in the city possesses, which assures its continued value to the world of scholarship; and as an almost complete collection, it reflects the evolving pattern of scholarly interest.

It may be argued that the expansion of educational provision means that if the Society did not exist, it would not now be founded. But this should not diminish its standing. Rather, it is a testimony to its success in helping to bring into being more specialised institutions that have taken on the role of the advancement of knowledge that drove its founding fathers in 1793.

The Society of Antiquaries: The earliest of the 'breakaways' was the Society of Antiquaries, founded in 1813. Its prime movers were two members of the Society, the bookseller John Bell and the lawyer John Adamson, and its purpose was to expand the knowledge of the region's history and archaeology. The new society was housed at the 'Lit and Phil' until 1848, when it moved into the Black Gate of the castle, which it leased from the city council. In 1822, 1832, 1844 and 1855, the Antiquaries published volumes of papers under the title *Archaeologia Aeliana*. From 1857, however, occasional volumes were replaced by an annual publication, which has appeared every year since. Throughout its existence, the Society of Antiquaries has been run by, and has attracted the work of, scholars of the highest standing and *Archaeologia Aeliana* rightfully enjoys an international reputation.

The Natural History Society of Northumberland, Durham and Newcastle upon Tyne (now Northumbria): The second breakaway, which occurred in 1829, was of those members who through an exclusive interest in natural history had, in effect, formed a society within the Society. Added to this was the practical problem of housing the important natural history collection of Marmaduke Tunstall of Wycliffe in North Yorkshire, who died in 1790, bought by the Society from George Townsend Fox for £500 in 1822. Through the sponsorship of the Trevelyans of Wallington (see TREVELYAN FAMILY AND WALLINGTON HALL), the new society was able to buy from the 'Lit and Phil' land behind its library, on which it built its museum. It occupied these premises until 1884, when it sold them to the North Eastern Railway Co., using the money to build a new museum at Barras Bridge.

In 1890 this was named the Hancock Museum in recognition of the work of the two Hancock brothers, Albany (1806–73) and John (1808–90), who were the sons of a Newcastle businessman, John Hancock. They were members of the 'Lit and Phil', leading advocates of the new society and notable natural historians, particularly Albany, whose work (in collaboration with John Alder), *A Monograph of the British Nudibranchiate Mollusca* (shell-less slugs), published between 1845 and 1855, gained him an international reputation. John Hancock's major work was more local, *Catalogue of the Birds of Northumberland and Durham*, published in 1874. In the course of the nineteenth century other members of the society were responsible for the accurate classification of the region's flora and fauna. Their discoveries were, and continue to be, published in the society's *Transactions*, which has appeared annually since 1831. In addition, the society holds a large number of collections of international importance, including the largest collections of the original drawings of birds by THOMAS BEWICK. The society also manages the 140-acre nature reserve in Gosforth Park, with its lake, which has been designated as a Site of Special Scientific Interest, and is active in ringing birds both there and on the FARNE ISLANDS and COQUET ISLAND.

In 2006 the Hancock Museum closed for major renovation in preparation for reopening as the Great North Museum in 2009.

The North of England Society for the Promotion of the Fine Arts: This was formed in 1836 within and by members of the 'Lit and Phil'. Its aims were to create a library and mount exhibitions, but above all to set up a School of Art and Industrial Design, as was common in continental cities, but not in Britain. In 1842 the School secured a government grant, which permitted the appointment of a full-time master, the post held for twenty years by WILLIAM BELL SCOTT. The School functioned in rooms in the Natural History Society's museum, until that was sold to the North Eastern Railway Co. in 1884. At this juncture the School ceased to have an independent existence, becoming the art department of the Newcastle College of Science.

North of England Institute of Mining and Mechanical Engineers: Usually called the Mining Institute, it was formed in 1852, largely through the efforts of NICHOLAS WOOD, who had been a member of the 'Lit and Phil' since 1814. Between 1869 and 1872 the Institute built its own premises on land adjacent to the 'Lit and Phil', which it named Neville Hall, commemorating the medieval owners of the ground. Its design was by a prominent local architect, A.M. Dunn, whose father, Matthias Dunn, was an important figure in the North-East coal industry. Its purpose being to advance scientific and technical knowledge, it built up an impressive library of appropriate works housed in the purpose-built Wood Memorial Hall, which is dominated by a statue of the man it commemorates, Nicholas Wood. It also housed the offices of the Coal Owners' Associations of Durham and Northumberland, formed in the 1870s. These Associations stored the considerable quantities of data sent to them annually by their member companies, which constitute valuable information about the industry between *c.*1870 and 1946. With the demise of mining, the role of the Institute has faded and these and other records have been transferred to the care of the respective County Record Offices.

College of Physical Science: The gestation period of the College of Physical Science was long and difficult, lasting from 1852 until 1871. The final success owed a great deal to the determination and lobbying of the Society's secretary, Robert Spence Watson, and was finally achieved as the result of negotiations between the Warden of Durham University, William Lake, who was very sympathetic to the proposal, and Nicholas Wood. Until the College acquired its own premises and facilities, its home was in the Mining Institute and it was allowed the use of the Society's library, lecture rooms and scientific apparatus. Also, the Society handed over the running of its evening classes to the new institution. Subsequently, the College of Physical Science became Armstrong College (1904), then King's College (1935), both within Durham University, and finally in 1963, the University of Newcastle upon Tyne.

LONDONDERRY, CHARLES WILLIAM VANE-TEMPEST-STEWART, 3rd MARQUESS OF (1778–1854)

The only son of the 1st Marquess by his second wife, Charles Stewart had three distinguished careers, the last of them in the North East. His first career, lasting twenty years from 1794 until 1814, was military and it coincided with the long war against the France of the 1st Republic and then of Napoleon Bonaparte. The first phase, when Londonderry (then Lord Stewart) was a young officer, took place in the Netherlands in the 1790s and was a campaign in which the British army did not distinguish itself. Then, between 1808 and 1813, Stewart served with both Sir John Moore and Wellington in Portugal and Spain. During these years, he took part in several of the notable engagements in that campaign: the battles of Talavera, Busaco, Fuentes d'Onoro and the storming of the frontier fortress of Ciudad Rodrigo. Wellington described him as 'a very gallant and very able officer of cavalry', although he took a bit of the shine off this accolade by adding that he was 'more impetuous than wise'. Nevertheless, he became Wellington's Adjutant General with the rank of Major General and the two men became friends as well as comrades in arms. Towards the end of the Peninsular campaign, Stewart was appointed British Minister in Berlin, the capital of Prussia, but this did not interrupt his military activity, since he took an active part in the series of battles in Germany that finally brought Bonaparte to his knees.

With the end of the war, Stewart embarked on a short diplomatic career, largely thanks to the fact that his half-brother (the 2nd Marquess, better known as Lord Castlereagh) was Foreign Secretary. In 1814 he accompanied Castlereagh to the Congress of Vienna, the principal peace conference, and in 1820 and 1821 he was sent by his half-brother as an official observer to congresses held at Troppau and Laibach, at which the autocratic rulers of central and eastern Europe were determined to proclaim their right, as a matter of principle, to intervene with force to suppress popular revolutions wherever they broke out, on the grounds that they threatened European stability. His final role was to accompany Wellington to the Congress of Verona, where their job was to thwart the wishes of the conservative governments of Russia, Prussia, Austria and France to help the King of Spain suppress his liberal constitution.

This was Stewart's last diplomatic role. As he was about to leave for Verona, his half-brother committed suicide. As Castlereagh was childless, Stewart became 3rd Marquess of Londonderry. Three years earlier, in 1819, he had married Frances Anne, the sole heir of Sir Harry Vane-Tempest and his wife, the Countess of Antrim, who had large estates in County Durham and Ireland. As a result,

Londonderry now began his third career, that of the manager of a huge portfolio of properties. Unlike many wealthy aristocrats, from the outset he adopted a vigorous hands-on approach, in particular to the exploitation of his wife's coal assets. As one historian has put it, 'he had a passion for industrial activity, long after most grandees had abandoned this irksome responsibility'. It so happened that his neighbour, JOHN LAMBTON, 1ST EARL OF DURHAM, was imbued with the same enthusiasm, which led to keen competition between the two men.

Londonderry's Durham estate was strictly not his property, but that of his wife. He was merely its life tenant and as such he was not allowed to sell any part for his own profit and was responsible to a set of trustees for the good management of it. The Durham element comprised 12,000 acres of land, much of which is six townships in the south-east of the county centred on Wynyard, and ten collieries, all but one on the south side of the Wear between Durham and Sunderland. To these he added Seaham, bought in 1822 from the Milbanke family. In the management of these assets he hired as his chief agent JOHN BUDDLE, whose primary responsibility was with the mining element. This was of vital importance, since coal was responsible for about three-quarters of the estate's income.

In this third phase of his life, Londonderry's concerns were threefold. His chief industrial ambition, apart from being the dominant voice in the coal trade and thwarting the ambitions of Lord Lambton, was the construction of the new coal port at Seaham, which was the reason for his purchase of the Seaham estate (see NEW TOWNS OF THE NINETEENTH CENTURY). In this he was successful, the port opening for business in 1835. He was also anxious to establish political control. In contrast to his rival Lambton, who was a Whig, Londonderry was a high Tory, who was intensively individualistic and chafed at any form of restraint on his freedom of action. Buddle was probably the only man able to dissuade him from pursuing his inclinations. It was his misfortune that for much of his time as a landowner, government was in the hands of the Whigs. His third absorbing concern was with Wynyard Park, where he set out to build on a grand scale. The house was designed by Philip Wyatt, who based his plans on those of his brother, Benjamin Wyatt, for Wellington's palace at Stratfield Saye. It was completed between 1822 and 1828, but was two-thirds destroyed by fire in 1841. Not deterred, Londonderry rebuilt using Philip Wyatt's original drawings, the work supervised by IGNATIUS BONOMI. Not content with a magnificent country seat, Londonderry also acquired by purchase in 1825 an equally sumptuous London home, Holdernesse House in Park Lane. When his accounts are examined it becomes clear that a very high percentage of Londonderry's income went on conspicuous consumption on and in these two properties. His style of living left no one in doubt of his place in society.

LOSH, JAMES (1763–1858)

James Losh, the son of a wealthy Cumbrian landowner, was born in the parish of Wreay six miles south of Carlisle. He went to Trinity College, Cambridge, graduating in 1786, and then to Lincoln's Inn, from which he was called to the Bar in 1789. In 1792 he had a lucky escape: while in Paris he was arrested and was saved from execution as an aristocrat only by the intervention of JEAN-PAUL MARAT, who had spent several years in Newcastle. Also in these early years he became a friend of the poets Wordsworth, Coleridge and Southey.

In 1799 he settled in NEWCASTLE and rapidly developed a reputation as a man of unimpeachable integrity and high competence as a barrister. In religion, however, he was a Unitarian and as such barred by the Test and Corporation Acts, passed in the reign of Charles II, from holding civic or political office, qualification for which was membership of the Church of England. He became a vigorous participant in the campaign for the repeal of these acts, which achieved success in 1828. It was a measure of the respect in which he was held that he was immediately made Recorder of Newcastle, the highest legal office in the borough's gift. He held the post from 1828 until 1832.

But his desire to foster change was not merely singular and personal. He actively campaigned against the slave trade and in favour of Roman Catholic emancipation; above all, he advocated the reform of parliament and in this he became a friend and supporter of the 2nd EARL GREY and other reformers in the region. He was a noted philanthropist, with special concern to reduce poverty and to provide better health care and education for the poor. And he was a strong supporter of the Newcastle–Carlisle railway, built between 1829 and 1838.

LOUGH, JOHN GRAHAM (1798–1876)

John Lough was the best sculptor produced in the North East in the nineteenth century. He was born at Geenhead near Consett, the son of a farmer. He had natural artistic talent, which he was encouraged to develop by the nearby landowner, George Silvertop of Minsteracres, and which enabled him to secure an apprenticeship with a local mason. Shortly afterwards, he moved to NEWCASTLE to assist in carving decorations for the Literary and Philosophical Society's building (see LITERARY AND PHILOSOPHICAL SOCIETY OF NEWCASTLE UPON TYNE). Still not satisfied, he secured free passage on a collier to London, where in 1826 he became a student at the Royal Academy. The following year he came to the notice of the sculpture-buying public with a sculpture of Milo, and for the next eight years he executed several commissions and exhibited at the Royal Academy and the British Institution. In 1834, however, he took what would now be thought of as a four-year career break to study in Italy. On his return to Britain, he secured commissions from the aristocracy, his most constant patron being Sir Matthew White Ridley. In fact, much of Lough's best work is at the Ridley country house, Blagdon Hall, and includes *Milo*, resited by Sir Edwin Lutyens in the artificial lake west of the hall. Lough's two best-known works, however, were the result of public commissions. That of ADMIRAL, LORD COLLINGWOOD, 23 feet in height, was paid for by public subscription and erected in 1847. It stands on the cliff at TYNEMOUTH overlooking the entrance to the Tyne on a pedestal designed by JOHN DOBSON. On the base on which the statue and its pedestal stand are four cannon from Collingwood's flagship at Trafalgar, *Royal Sovereign*, the first guns to be fired in the battle. The other statue is of GEORGE STEPHENSON, at the junction of Neville Street and Westgate Road in Newcastle.

LOVELACE, ADA AUGUSTA, COUNTESS OF LOVELACE (1815–1852)

Ada Lovelace was the only offspring of the short and disastrous marriage of Anna Milbanke, the daughter of Sir Ralph Milbanke of Seaham, and the poet George Gordon Noel, 6th Lord Byron, the father she never knew. Freed from marital distractions by Byron's desertion, Anna devoted herself to her daughter's education, teaching her personally as well as hiring private tutors. The thrust of Lady Byron's syllabus was towards mathematics and science, in part because of her own keen interest, but also, it is said, because she feared that otherwise Ada might acquire her father's love of poetry. In consequence, Ada became a highly competent mathematician. She was also fortunate in that she received the support and encouragement of her husband, William King (1805–93), whom she married in 1835 and who became Viscount Ockham and Earl of Lovelace in 1838. She corresponded on equal terms with the best mathematical minds of the age, but she is best remembered for her close association with Charles Babbage, whom she met in 1833 and who is often described as the 'father of the computer'. Her ability went beyond a basic understanding of Babbage's thinking: she had a depth of knowledge and perception that enabled her to make her own original contributions. This was revealed in *Sketch on an Analytical Machine invented by Charles Babbage*, which she published in 1843. Basically, this was a translation of an article written by Luigi Menabrea (later Prime Minister of Italy) following Babbage's visit to him in Turin in 1840. What revealed Ada as more than a mere translator, however, were the copious explanatory notes she added to this article. The originality of her thinking was further revealed in her correspondence with Babbage, who valued her friendship highly.

Ada Lovelace's life ended tragically. She died at the age of thirty-eight of uterine cancer and in debt as the consequence of her addiction to gambling on horses. In 1979, however, she received belated and posthumous recognition of her contribution to the development of the computer when the United States Department of Defense gave the name ADA to the new computer programming language that it had commissioned.

LOWRY, LAURENCE STEPHEN (1887–1976)

L.S. Lowry was one of the most widely known and highly appreciated artists of the post-World War II decades, best known for his pictures of 'matchstick' people set in working-class and industrial districts in or near his native city of Manchester. Although he lived throughout his life from 1909 in Salford and Mottram, he became strongly attracted to the North East. His visits began in 1936, but it was after his retirement in 1952 from his job as chief cashier of a property company that his visits became frequent and prolonged, partly as a result of his growing fascination with the sea. Although he painted in Berwick, from 1960 until his death he made SUNDERLAND his base, always staying at the Seaburn Hotel (now the Marriott Hotel) and always occupying room 104. Sunderland, its industry and maritime activities were the inspiration and the subject of much of his later work.

LUCOZADE

Lucozade was invented in 1927 in a pharmacy bearing the name W. Owen and Sons at the corner of Barras Bridge and Claremont Road, Newcastle. The inventor was William Hunter, a pharmacist, who had bought the business from Mr Owen. Initially, it was called 'Glucozade', its purpose being to give an energy boost to sick and convalescent people. It was made in premises behind the shop and was rapidly adopted in hospitals throughout the UK. In 1929 its name was changed to 'Lucozade', a name suggested by William Hunter's wife, when it was decided to manufacture the drink on a commercial scale in a new factory. In 1938 the patent and the factory were bought by the large pharmaceutical firm, Beechams (now Smith Kline Beecham). Beechams continued to market Lucozade as an aid to recovery until 1985, when they rebranded it as a general energy drink.

LUMLEY FAMILY AND CASTLE

Lumley is one of the most complete 'quadrangular' castles built in England in the late fourteenth century. It comprises a courtyard 100 by 75 feet (30 m by 23 m), with towers at the corners, those on the west measuring 60 by 35 feet (18 m by 10.7 m) and those on the east 50 by 35 feet (15.2 m by 10.7 m). Between the four towers are ranges of buildings, including a gatehouse on the east side facing the deep gorge of the River Wear. The castle was the work of Ralph, 1st Lord Lumley, consequent upon 'licences to crenellate' granted to him by the Bishop of Durham in 1389 and the Crown in 1392. Since then the castle has undergone relatively little alteration. John, 6th Lord Lumley modernised it in the 1570s and the 2nd Earl of Scarbrough employed Sir John Vanbrugh between 1721 and 1728 to remodel the interior. Vanbrugh was also responsible for the only substantial modification by moving the main entrance from the east range to the west range and in so doing turning the medieval great hall into an entrance hall.

Although the family had been in possession of the Lumley estate for many generations, it was Ralph Lumley who brought the family to national prominence. Richard II granted him a baronage and he repaid his benefactor with his life: following Richard II's deposition in the autumn of 1399, he joined a conspiracy to rescue and restore him to the throne by assassinating his usurper, Henry IV. The plot was betrayed and the conspirators fled westwards from Windsor. They were recognised at Cirencester and lynched by the townsfolk. This was not the end of the family, however: Ralph's fourth son, Marmaduke, became Bishop of Carlisle in 1429 and of Lincoln in 1450 and was the Lord Treasurer between 1446 and 1449; his grandson, Thomas Lumley, was restored to the barony as the 2nd Lord Lumley in 1461 by Edward IV. Thereafter the family prospered, until the Reformation. In 1536 John, the 5th Lord Lumley, took part in the PILGRIMAGE OF GRACE, the northern rebellion triggered by the radical changes in religious practice imposed by Henry VIII's government. Fortunately, he did not take part in the renewal of the revolt in 1537, but his brother George did, for which he was executed.

John, the 5th Lord Lumley, died in 1545 and was succeeded by his son, also John, who regained the family lands and title in 1547. The 6th Lord Lumley had been educated at Oxford, which may explain his extraordinary addiction to the history of his family. This led him in the 1590s to confect a series of effigies purporting to be those of his ancestors that still line the west side of the nave of the church at CHESTER LE STREET. This obsession also produced one of James I's well-recorded outbursts. While staying at Lumley Castle on 13 April 1603 as he travelled from Edinburgh to London, James was treated to a lengthy discourse on the Lumley pedigree. James, finally tiring of this, cut it short with the sarcastic remark, 'I didna ken that Adam's name was Lumley.' A more important consequence of Lord Lumley's interest in learning was his library, said to have been the finest in England. Lumley gave some of his books to the university libraries at Oxford and Cambridge, but after his death the bulk was bought by James I and in the end, thanks to the generosity of George II, came into the possession of the British Museum.

His library apart, the 6th Lord Lumley made one important contribution to the region: in 1593, he secured for HARTLEPOOL a charter of incorporation. And, although he spent money on renovating the castle and buying land in the county, he lived most of his time at Nonsuch Park, near Cheam in Surrey, bequeathed to him by his first wife's father, the Earl of Arundel. The 6th Lord

Lumley had no sons and upon his death in 1609 his title became extinct. The estate and the castle passed to his cousin, Richard, who in 1628 was created Viscount Lumley of Waterford.

Waterford's grandson, also Richard, played a prominent, astute and personally advantageous part in British politics between 1680 and 1707. He was a Catholic and was favoured by the crypto-Catholic Charles II and his overtly Catholic brother and successor, James II. Consequently he joined the army raised to defeat James, Duke of Monmouth and Buccleuch, the illegitimate son of Charles II, who in 1685 tried to overthrow James II. Monmouth's small army was routed at Sedgemoor in Somerset and he surrendered to Lumley a few days later. Two years later, however, sensing that the mood of the country was hostile to the radical catholicising policy of James II, Lumley converted to the Church of England. His desertion of James was completed in June 1688, when he was one of the seven signatories of the letter inviting William of Orange, Stadtholder of the Netherlands and husband of James II's elder daughter, Mary, to invade England and replace his father-in-law. During Orange's successful invasion in 1689, Lumley was active in the North East, ensuring that Durham and Newcastle supported the regime change. His reward was the titles Viscount Lumley of Lumley Castle and Earl of Scarbrough.

Thereafter he had a successful army career, retiring in 1699 with the rank of Lieutenant General. He continued to play an active role in politics: he was chosen as one of the English commissioners to negotiate with their Scottish counterparts the terms of the Treaty of Union by which the two countries were united on 1 May 1707; and in 1714 he was a member of the committee that decided upon the order of seniority of the regiments of the British army, an order that is still recognised.

The Lumley family's home (the present head is the 13th Earl of Scarbrough) is now in Yorkshire. They still own Lumley Castle, but since the end of World War II have not lived there, leasing it first to Durham University as a student residence and more recently as a hotel.

MACARTHUR, REVD ARTHUR LEITCH (1913–2008)

Arthur Macarthur was born in Newcastle, the son of a linotype operator in the print section of a local newspaper who was also session clerk at his local English Presbyterian Church (EPC). After taking a degree at Durham University, he trained as a minister of religion at Westminster College, Cambridge and was then ordained as a minister in the EPC in 1937. His first appointment was as minister at the Clayport Church in Alnwick, where he remained until 1944: as a confirmed pacifist he was not involved in World War II. Between 1944 and 1950 he was a minister in London, after which he returned to the North East to a church at North Shields.

Thus far his career was conventional, but in 1960 he was appointed General Secretary of the EPC and it was through this office that he was to advance his ecumenical beliefs. These had become apparent as early as 1948, when he was chosen as the EPC's representative at the inaugural meeting of the Assembly of the World Council of Churches, held in Amsterdam. In 1971 as Moderator of the EPC he took the lead in persuading his church to agree to merge with the Congregationalists to form the United Reformed Church (URC). Macarthur was appointed General Secretary of this new church, a post he held until 1980. He was also a leading figure on the Free Church Federal Council, acting as its Moderator in 1980.

MACDONALD, JAMES EDWARD HARVEY (1873–1932)

James Macdonald was a landscape painter whose work is highly regarded in Canada, examples hanging in the National Gallery of Canada and the Art Gallery of Ontario. He was born in DURHAM CITY, but at the age of fourteen in 1887 emigrated to Canada with his family. On leaving school in 1889 he trained as a lithographer with a firm in Toronto and also took art courses at the Central Ontario School of Art and Design. In 1903 he returned to England, where he stayed until 1907 working as a book designer and illustrator. On his return to Canada he took up similar work in Toronto.

His conversion to landscape painting followed a visit to northern Canada in 1908, where he was overwhelmed by the majesty of the wilderness. Thereafter he concentrated on becoming a painter. In the years after World War I he made annual trips in the autumn when colours were at their most brilliant, to Algoma, Michigan in the USA. In 1921 he joined with six other artists (A.Y. Jackson, F.H. Varley, Franklin Carmichael, Lawren Harris, A.J. Casson and Arthur Lisner) to form the 'Group of Seven', who were later joined by an outstanding artist, Tom Thomson. Their conscious purpose was to paint the landscape of Canada and in so doing to heighten in Canadians an awareness and appreciation of the natural beauty of their country.

MACDONALD, JAMES RAMSAY (1866–1937)

Ramsay Macdonald was the classic case of a Scottish 'lad o'pairts', who made good by his own industry, although also helped by an advantageous marriage. He was born at Lossiemouth on the Moray Firth, the illegitimate son of a ploughman and a farm servant, and became Prime Minister while representing a North-East constituency. His formal education did not extend beyond the parish school, but he supplemented it by his own efforts. At the age of eighteen he moved south, first to Bristol and then to London, all the while sampling the various left-wing political ideas then current. Finally, in 1893, he joined the Independent Labour Party. In 1896, despite his humble origins, he entered the middle class through his marriage to the daughter of a distinguished scientist, J.H. Gladstone. Thereafter his political progress was steady. In 1906 he became secretary of the Labour Representation Committee, the forerunner of the Labour Party, and in the election of that year won West Leicester to become one of twenty-nine Labour MPs. He retained his seat in the subsequent election, and in 1911 he was elected chairman of the parliamentary group.

His career faltered as a result of his opposition to Britain's declaration of war in 1914, which led to his being branded a pacifist and pro-German. As a result, he lost his seat in the 1918 election. Four years later he re-entered the Commons as MP for Aberavon. In the general election of 1923 Labour won more seats than the Liberals, and consequently these two parties were able to outvote the Conservative government. Macdonald had no hesitation in forming the first Labour government. But the even balance of the three parties made another general election inevitable, and in it Labour lost forty-one seats and power. Labour was in opposition until 1929, when the general election of that year returned them as the largest party, with 287 seats. Macdonald was returned for the County Durham mining constituency of Seaham. There was no reason why the Labour government, with Macdonald as Prime Minister, should not have completed a full term. In 1931, however, it was overwhelmed by the worldwide depression. To meet the crisis, Macdonald formed an all-party National Government, which won the election with an overwhelming majority. By his action Macdonald became politically isolated, disowned by his own party, which elected another leader. He continued as Prime Minister and MP for Seaham until 1935. In June of that year, with his health declining, he resigned the premiership and in the November election he was defeated at Seaham by EMMANUEL SHINWELL. Early in 1936 he returned to the Commons, elected in a by-election as MP for the Scottish Universities, but late in the following year he died suddenly.

His son, Malcolm Macdonald (1901–81), late in life renewed the Macdonald association with region. After a long career in which he oversaw the transition of many of Britain's colonies to independence and membership of the Commonwealth, he was made Chancellor of Durham University in 1970, a post he held until his death.

McGUINNESS, THOMAS (1926–2006)

Tom McGuinness was born at Witton Park and lived most of his life in nearby BISHOP AUCKLAND. He became a miner in 1944 as a 'Bevin Boy', an alternative form of National Service to the armed forces, made necessary by the declining number of miners at a time when coal was urgently needed. Apart from a brief period after his release in 1947, he remained a miner until he was made redundant in 1983. In doing so, he spurned the opportunity of becoming a professional artist.

His natural ability as an artist was developed in the mid-1940s through evening classes at Darlington School of Art, which he was persuaded to attend by his training officer in his early days as a 'Bevin Boy', and membership of the Sketching Club at the SPENNYMOOR SETTLEMENT. By 1948 his work was sufficiently advanced for it to be exhibited at the Shipley Art Gallery in Gateshead (see ART GALLERIES), which in 1949 bought one of his drawings. By 1960 he was having one-man shows and in the 1970s his work attracted the attention of the London art world, as the result of which he had exhibitions in the capital and was the subject of TV programmes and a full-scale book. In 1983–84 he was appointed Artist in Residence at the new nuclear power station at Hartlepool. In the course of his career he expanded the range of his techniques and of his subjects, but the abiding impression he left was as a portrayer of miners and mining. With the demise of deep mining, his like will not be seen again.

MACKAY'S CARPETS (1908–2005)

Mackay's Carpets, also widely known as Durham Carpets, were of the highest quality and world-famous. Carpet making in Durham City was started in 1820 by a Gilbert Henderson, using Brussels-type looms he had surreptitiously acquired from Kidderminster, which then had a monopoly of the trade. Henderson's business, based in his factory in Freeman Place, grew and prospered under his management and, after his death in 1824, that of (successively) his widow, Ann, sons, John and William, and grandson, John Henderson's son, Arthur. In 1903 Arthur Henderson sold out to the Halifax firm of Crossley, which promptly closed the Durham factory: their purpose in taking over Hendersons was to eliminate a competitor and acquire their patterns and access to their foreign customers.

That Crossley's asset stripping did not mark the end of carpet making in Durham was due to the enterprise of Hugh Mackay, Henderson's works manager, who leased part of the Henderson factory and restarted manufacture. Between then and 1930 he gradually acquired the rest of the Freeman Place premises and created a world-famous business. Following the destruction of the factory by arson in 1969, the works were relocated from the centre of the City to Dragonville on its outskirts. Its final location, from 1999, was on the Meadowfield Industrial Estate beyond the City's western boundary. By that date it was no longer in Mackay family ownership, having been taken over by Allied Textiles in 1990. They too relinquished ownership in 2004, to a management buyout. All these changes were the consequence of declining business: in 1968, the year before the fire, Mackay's employed 750 people; by 1992 the number had shrunk to 350; and at the time of closure in 2005 it was only 138.

This was a sad end to a distinguished history, which included the issue of a royal warrant in 1972. In their time, 'Durham' carpets were trodden on in royal palaces in London (Buckingham Palace, Kensington Palace, The Tower), Sandringham, The Hague, Riyadh and Oman; the Library of Congress in Washington DC; the liner *Queen Elizabeth II*; the Savoy Hotel in London, Caesar's Palace in Las Vegas and EuroDisney near Paris; and the Millennium Stadium in Cardiff and the football stadiums in Newcastle and Middlesbrough; as well as thousands of less notable buildings and homes throughout Britain.

MACKENZIE, ENEAS (1777–1832)

Eneas Mackenzie was a prolific author who did a great deal to bring the history of the region to a wider public. Although born in Aberdeen, he lived in NEWCASTLE from the age of three, as a result of his parents' migration from north-east Scotland. Little is known of his education or early life, except that he tried without success a number of occupations as diverse as minister of religion, schoolmaster and shipbroker, before forming in 1810 a partnership with a John Dent, with premises in St Nicholas's churchyard, to print and publish educational works. Between then and his death he wrote six massive volumes covering the three counties of the region: *An Historical and Descriptive View of the County of Northumberland* (1811), *A Descriptive and Historical Account of the Town and County of Newcastle upon Tyne* (1827) and *An Historical, Topographical and Descriptive View of the County Palatine of Durham* (completed after his death by Metcalf Ross and published in 1834). While his approach and early historical material are now dated or superseded, these books are still of considerable use to contemporary historians. He also wrote other books, including a similar work on the USA and Canada, a History of Egypt and a Life of Napoleon. Mackenzie was a political radical, concerned to see an improvement in the condition of the working class. It was this that led to his taking the lead in founding the Newcastle Mechanics' Institute in 1824. He died of cholera in the great epidemic of 1832.

MACLAUCHLAN, HENRY (1792–1882)

Henry Maclauchlan was born at Felixstowe, Suffolk, son of a storekeeper working for the Board of Ordnance. His father died in 1795 and later Henry was enrolled as a cadet in the Royal Corps of Military Surveyors, with which he remained after completing his training until it was disbanded in 1817. Thereafter, until he retired in 1844, he was employed by the Ordnance Survey, working in the south of England.

His connection with the North East began in the late 1840s and was due to the 4th Duke of Northumberland's enthusiasm for archaeology, particularly his ambition to have all prehistoric and Roman sites in his county accurately recorded. The upshot was the series of commissions he gave to Maclauchlan, out of which came five substantial publications between 1850 and 1867. They dealt with four subjects: Watling Street (now called Dere Street) from Piercebridge to Chew Green on the Border; East Watling Street from Beuclay near Corbridge to Low Learchild; HADRIAN'S WALL; and prehistoric remains. Each publication comprised detailed notes accompanied by maps, both produced to the highest standard as regards accuracy, precision and detail. The quality of Maclauchlan's work has been fully acknowledged by modern scholars, who continue to use his volumes as the base for their own research and are grateful for his record of sites that have since disappeared.

Perhaps Maclauchlan's only error was his continued conviction that the Wall was the work of Septimius Severus (193–211), not Hadrian (117–38).

MACMILLAN, MAURICE HAROLD, 1st EARL OF STOCKTON (1894–1986)

Harold Macmillan, who was Prime Minister from 1957 until 1964, was the third son of the wealthy publisher Maurice Crawford Macmillan and his American wife, Helen Belles. After Eton he went to Balliol College, Oxford, but his studies were interrupted by the outbreak of World War I in 1914. He immediately joined the army and was commissioned into the King's Royal Rifle Corps, but then transferred into the more socially prestigious Grenadier Guards. His active service was ended in 1916 by serious wounds.

After the war he entered politics and in 1924 he was returned as the Conservative MP for STOCKTON ON TEES. He remained the town's member until 1945, except for the years of the Labour government of 1929–31. Stockton would not have seen much of him during World War II, since from 1942 he was in Algiers as Minister Resident and political adviser to General Eisenhower. Almost inevitably, he lost his seat in the 1945 election, but later secured the safe Conservative seat of Bromley, in Kent. It was as MP for Bromley that he succeeded SIR ANTHONY EDEN as Prime Minister in 1957. Ill health forced him to retire in 1964. He declined the earldom, then the traditional perk of a retiring Prime Minister, because he did not wish to place a block on the parliamentary career of his son, Maurice. It was only in 1984, when it was known that Maurice Macmillan was terminally ill, that he became Earl of Stockton. His choice of title was governed by the fact that, although he had no connection with the town before or after he was its MP, he had always valued his association with it, through which he said he had come to knowledge of, and sympathy with, the difficulties and hardships experienced by the North East during the inter-war years.

MANNERS FAMILY

The Manners family, like the Percys, were of Norman origin, but in other respects were their mirror image: the Percys came north into Northumberland from elsewhere, but rose to become earls then dukes with that county as their title; in contrast, the Manners began in Northumberland, but achieved an earldom and then a dukedom by moving south.

Their name derives from Mesnières, a village in the *département* of Seine-Maritime. The earliest reference to them in Northumberland occurs in the late twelfth century, when Robert de Manners was recorded as holding an estate of the Barony of Wooler. That this was the Manor of Etal is confirmed by a more precise reference in 1232. When this estate was granted to the family is not known, but possibly shortly after the Barony of Wooler was created in the first decade of the twelfth century by Henry I for his supporter, Robert de Muschamp.

Over the next seven generations the Manners family continued in Northumberland as county gentry. In four generations between the mid-fifteenth and the mid-sixteenth century, however, they climbed the social scale, vastly increased their wealth and migrated from the North East to the Midlands. This advance began with the marriage of Sir Robert Manners (d.1495) to Eleanor, the daughter of Thomas, 10th Lord Roos, whose extensive estate lay mainly in Northumberland and Yorkshire. It was not he, but his son, George Manners (d.1513), who reaped the benefit, inheriting the entire Roos estate in 1508 and 1509. He also made a prestigious marriage, to Anne St Leger, a niece of King Edward IV. It was doubtless these advantages that convinced him that living close to the Border was unhealthy and that a move to Rutland was advisable.

Sir George Manners was succeeded by his son, Thomas, who raised the family's status still further. He was a very active member of Henry VIII's regime, particularly during the dangerous political circumstances of the 1530s, when he backed the royal divorce and the subsequent religious changes; he also played an active role in suppressing the PILGRIMAGE OF GRACE in the winter of 1536–37. His reward was the land of ten suppressed monasteries in Leicestershire, Lincolnshire and Yorkshire, one of which, Belvoir, he converted into his home. These services apart, he also benefited from his link with the royal family through his mother, a link publicly acknowledged by Henry VIII in allowing him to add the royal lion passant and the fleur-de-lis to his coat of arms. It also explains why he was made Earl of Rutland in 1525. These advances, economic and social, allowed the family to sever its connection with the North East. In 1547 Thomas's son, Edward, who succeeded as 2nd Earl of Rutland in 1543, handed over to the Crown, in exchange for land elsewhere, all his Northumberland property, comprising 5,000 acres, 2,000 of which were in Etal and the remainder in ten neighbouring townships.

The Crown's concern to possess the Manners estate centred on the castle at Etal, which had been sadly neglected as a result of the family's southward migration. The castle, now a substantial ruin maintained by English Heritage, is an interesting example of how the Anglo-Scottish war that began in 1296 transformed living arrangements in the Border zone. In the late thirteenth century, before war began, the Manners family built a stone hall-house and probably surrounded it with a wooded palisade. In 1341, however, they secured from the Crown a 'licence to crenellate', that is to fortify their house. The changes, which included the addition of a fourth storey, turned it into a BORDER TOWER. Before 1368, however, Etal became a castle. This involved the building of a towered gatehouse and two further smaller towers, which were all linked by stone walls to form a square enclosure. Although not comparable with BERWICK and NORHAM, Etal was an important element in the second line of defence against Scottish invasion.

In 1703 the family reached the top of the social ladder when the then Earl became Duke of Rutland.

MANSELL, SIR ROBERT (1570–1652)

Robert Mansell, who pioneered glassmaking in the North East, was the eighth son of a Welsh landowner, Sir Edward Mansell of Margam, Glamorgan. At the age of fifteen, through the patronage of Lord Howard of Effingham, he embarked on a successful naval career, which included taking part in the defeat of the Spanish Armada in 1588 and culminated in 1604 in his appointment as Treasurer of the Navy, a post he was alleged to have used corruptly to enrich himself.

In 1618 he resigned his post in order to concentrate on his business interests, particularly the manufacture of glass. He did so because a major manufacturing problem had been recently overcome: in 1610 Sir William Slingsby, the lessee of mines at Seaton Delaval, had demonstrated the possibility of using coal in place of wood, a process that was considerably improved shortly afterwards. This led in 1614 to the award of a patent to Sir Edward Zouche and three other men granting them the monopoly of glassmaking in England. The following year the patent was reissued in order to admit Mansell, who almost immediately bought out the others to become sole patentee. The patent was comprehensive: it forbade the use of wood in making glass, the importation of glassware and a twenty-one-year monopoly of glassmaking (to include window glass, bottles and crystal) throughout England. In return, he agreed to pay the Crown £1,000 a year.

At the time of the patent, the factory was in Broad Street, London, an expensive location, and so Mansell began to look for a place where costs would be lower. After considering places as far apart as Dorset, Pembroke and Nottingham, he decided on Tyneside, because of its cheap coal. In the next few years, Mansell expended £28,000 on developing the business, manufacturing glass for the London and east coast markets on Tyneside but supplying other parts of the country through other manufacturers working under licence. His business was so successful that he secured a renewal of the patent in 1635, agreeing to increase his annual payment to the Crown to £1,500 in return for an extension of the patent to Ireland. In the early 1640s, however, the business ran into difficulties. In 1640 the Scottish invasion of Northumberland and the BATTLE OF NEWBURN caused his workmen and their families to flee, and two years later a now hostile parliament revoked his patent. He did manage to restart the business but by then he was an old man struggling with adverse conditions, and he sold out in 1645.

MARAT, JEAN-PAUL (1743–1793)

Jean-Paul Marat, who became one of the most violent and extreme of the early leaders of the French Revolution, was briefly a member of North-East society. He was born in Switzerland but moved to France in 1759 to study medicine. In 1768 he came to Britain with the same purpose and remained here until 1777. During that time he completed his training and from 1770 until 1775 lived and practised in NEWCASTLE. It was while he was there that he wrote *The Chains of Slavery*, a diatribe against what he saw as the despotism of the kings of France and in favour of popular sovereignty and 'human rights'. He returned to France in 1777 and continued to practise as a doctor. But as the Revolution got under way, he forsook medicine for political journalism, founding an influential newspaper, *L'Ami du Peuple*, in which he demanded ever more executions of opponents or lukewarm supporters of the new order. He was murdered in his bath in July 1793 by the daughter of a minor Norman noble, Marie-Anne Charlotte Corday D'Armans, an event immortalised in the painting by Jacques-Louis David.

MARCHES OF ENGLAND TOWARDS SCOTLAND

A 'march' is a defined frontier district with special military and administrative arrangements to deal with the inherent extraordinary circumstances and situations that are likely to arise within it. The 'Marches of England towards Scotland' were essentially the response to the unresolved state of hostility between England and Scotland that lasted from 1296 until 1603. Originally they were two in number, the East March and the West March. The latter comprised the counties of Cumberland and Westmorland (Cumbria); the former was the COUNTY OF NORTHUMBERLAND. Durham was not included because it was a PALATINATE, where the Bishop of Durham enjoyed quasi-regal powers. Occasionally the East March was split into two, the East March and the Middle March, a division that became permanent in the sixteenth century, the boundary between them running from the summit of the Cheviot, through Bewick and then following the north bank of the Aln to the coast. The East March was much the smaller, while the Middle March, as well as being much larger in area, also included the notoriously lawless districts of TYNEDALE and REDESDALE. The English Marches were mirrored by Scottish equivalents.

As war became endemic in the course of the fourteenth century, a command structure developed. Initially, this took committee form, temporary commissions of local men appointed by the Crown to deal with crisis situations. However, in the last quarter of the century this gave way to permanent single officials, the Wardens of the Marches, whose duties and remuneration (smaller in time of truce, larger in time of war) were set out in a contract. Of the two marches, that of the East was regarded as more important and its Warden had larger fees. With the Wardenship of the East March frequently, but not invariably, went the office of Keeper of Berwick. From the time of its creation, the office of Warden of the East March was a permanent object of ambition for the PERCY FAMILY. Although they had some success in their attempts to monopolise it, appointment to it always remained in the king's gift and between 1537 and 1557 their ambition was fatally wounded with the (temporary) loss of their estates to the Crown and their domination of Northumberland society to SIR JOHN FORSTER; and after 1572, the royal requirement that they live on their estate at Petworth in Sussex.

The primary duty of an English warden was to defend his march against the Scots and to this end he had command of the military forces in his wardenry. These were, or should have been, adequate to repulse small-scale incursions. But not major invasions: on these occasions, which were rare, the warden would lead his contingent, but under the command of a royal officer.

In addition, the warden had the civil responsibility of policing the Border and dealing with cross-border crime. He did so in accordance with March Law, first codified in 1249 by a commission of twelve men from each nation, but subsequently modified and elaborated. Justice was dispensed at meetings known as 'days of truce', when an English warden met his Scottish counterpart at traditional places along the Border. What we know of these events comes largely from sixteenth-century evidence, that is, when the system had reached maturity. Then, it seems, 'days of truce' were by custom always held on Scottish soil and attended by large numbers of men. What was supposed to happen was that aggrieved persons put their accusations to their warden, who notified his opposite number of them. The two wardens were then expected to bring their respective sets of accused to the next 'day of truce', when they would be tried. If it was agreed that an accused man should have a jury trial, his case went before a pre-selected jury of his *own* countrymen. Alternatively, his case could be decided by the oath of the warden or that of an 'avouer', an agreed third party who was believed to know the facts of the matter. In most cases, the consequence of a guilty verdict was the payment of compensation, but to avoid any festering resentment, at the end of each meeting, the two wardens attempted to ensure that the total sum paid in compensation by each nation should be roughly equal. However, not all crimes got to a 'day of truce', since raiders caught in the act could be pursued across the Border (the right of 'hot trod') and if caught might lose not only what they had stolen, but also their lives through 'Jeddart justice', execution in place of trial. This right of pursuit extended to six days after the offence had been committed, when it was known as 'cold trod'. The whole system was open to abuse and to all manner of prevarication, so that it came nowhere near suppressing crime.

A warden also had to deal with cases of March Treason within his own wardenry, that is, of persons accused of aiding the enemy. Commonly this was selling arms or horses to the enemy, but it could include passing helpful information to them and even riding with them. The very existence of this problem highlights the fact that there was cross-border friendship and alliance as well as enmity, so that there were occasions when the men of the borderlands were Borderers first and Englishmen or Scotsmen second.

The accession of James VI of Scotland to the English throne in 1603 rendered Marches obsolete and James declared that henceforth the English and Scottish Marches should be known collectively as the Middle Shires of Britain. For good or ill, this designation has failed to find favour.

MARLEY, SIR JOHN (1590–1673) (see under SCOTTISH OCCUPATION 1644–1647)

MARR, SIR JAMES, Bt (1854–1932)

James Marr, who became an influential figure in the shipbuilding industry, was born in Newcastle, where he had only an elementary education. In 1868, at the age of fourteen, he joined the SUNDERLAND shipbuilder Thomas Oswald, but transferred to J.L. Thompson (see THOMPSON FAMILY) when Oswald's business folded in 1876. By 1882 he was Thompsons' general manager. Thereafter he rose to be a director when the firm became a public liability company in 1894, and in 1901 was made Chairman and Managing Director. Such was his reputation that in 1909 he was invited to take control of Laings, another major yard in Sunderland that was in financial difficulties. There is no doubt that Laings survived and thereafter flourished as a result of Marr's time on its board. During World War I he played a leading role in organising British ship production to answer the crisis in merchant shipping. For his services, he was made a baronet in 1919.

MARSHALL, FRANCIS CARR (1831–1903)

Along with SIR BENJAMIN BROWNE and SIR HERBERT ROWELL, Francis Marshall played a major part in creating and sustaining the shipbuilders Hawthorn Leslie as a builder of merchant vessels but also a leader in the design and building of destroyers. He was born at BEDLINGTON, where his father worked as a smith in the Bedlington Iron Works, but shortly afterwards the family moved to Newcastle, where his father secured employment with R. & W. Hawthorn. Marshall attended the Westgate Academy for seven years and then went to Hawthorns as an apprentice, first in the workshops and then in the drawing office. In 1860, however, he left them to become manager of Sir Charles Palmer's Marine Engine Works at JARROW. Ten years later he became a partner of Benjamin Browne, who had bought Hawthorns and would merge it with the shipbuilder ANDREW LESLIE in 1885. Marshall was very closely involved with the marine engine works at St Peters at the mouth of the Ouseburn, which became noted for warship engines. He also spent much time in Russia, securing orders.

MARTIN, JOHN (1789–1854)

John Martin was one of the most popular and widely known British artists of the early nineteenth century. He is sometimes, but entirely erroneously, referred to as 'Mad' Martin, through being confused with his brother, Jonathon, who set fire to York Minster, for which he was confined for many years in a lunatic asylum. John Martin was born into very humble circumstances in a cottage near Haydon Bridge, but moved with his family to Newcastle in 1803, when he was fourteen. After being briefly apprenticed to a coach painter, he secured a place in the studio of an Italian artist, Boniface Musso, where JOHN DOBSON was also a pupil. In 1806 he left the North East with Musso and his son, Charles, and settled in London. For the next few years he earned a precarious living as a glass and porcelain painter, working first for Musso, then after Musso became bankrupt, for a William Collins. All the time, however, he was honing his skills as a painter.

In 1812 his fortunes changed: he decided to break with Collins and set up on his own, and he painted a huge canvas, entitled *Sadak in Search of the Waters of Oblivion*, which he exhibited at the Royal Academy. This established the style for which he became famous: huge canvases illustrating, in wild colours and lurid light, catastrophic or dramatic events from the Bible or classical literature. Perhaps the best-known example of this genre is *Belshazzar's Feast*, for which he was paid £200, and which drew huge crowds when exhibited at the British Institution. Many of these paintings are reminiscent of several of Turner's pictures, which is not surprising given that both men were living and working at the height of the Romantic Movement. In addition, it has been said that his dramatic landscapes owe something to the hill country of his youth and the colours to the industrial world of Tyneside.

Martin enjoyed widespread fame in the 1820s, but not universal critical acclaim, and for this reason he did not submit anything to the Royal Academy between 1825 and 1836. Nor did his pictures make his fortune, since they were not easy to sell on account of their size. What did give him both wealth and international fame were his mezzotint prints, particularly the twenty-four in 1824 he did for an edition of Milton's *Paradise Lost*. In fact, his prints were so popular and so widely sold throughout Europe that he was knighted by the King of the Belgians and awarded decorations by the kings of France and Prussia and the Tsar of Russia. Like 'the prophet in his own country', however, he was never made a Fellow of the Royal Academy. Because of his mezzotint business, he painted few large canvases after 1830, concentrating instead on producing smaller works in watercolour as well as oil. But very near the end of his life he did paint one of his best-known cataclysmic scenes, *The Destruction of Sodom and Gomorrah.*

Martin was not only interested in art. He also was something of an amateur engineer, usually working with his brother, William. His designs, none of which was put into effect, included those for the improvement of London's water supply, an inner London railway system, sewage removal and the ventilation of mines.

MAURETANIA

The *Mauretania,* named after the Roman province in North Africa, was launched on 20 September 1906 and began her maiden voyage to New York on 16 November 1907. She was built by the firm of Swan Hunter and Wigham Richardson (see JOHN WIGHAM RICHARDSON), the product of a merger agreed in 1903 with the express purpose of bidding for the contract. *Mauretania* (and her sister ship, the ill-fated *Lusitania,* built by John Brown of Clydebank) was ordered by Cunard, but with considerable financial support from the government, with the intention of wresting the Blue Riband of the Atlantic from the Germans, who had held it with four successive ships since 1897.

Mauretania was not the first or only liner built on the Tyne, but, at just under 32,000 gross tons, she was the largest. Her overall length was 790 feet (241 m) and her maximum beam was 88 feet (27 m). She was driven by four propellers, initially of three blades, but almost immediately changed to four. These were turned by Parsons turbines (see PARSONS, SIR CHARLES ALGERNON), built by Wallsend Slipway and Engineering Co. Ltd, and powered by twenty-five boilers heated by 192 furnaces. Originally, these were coal-fired, but they were converted to oil in 1922.

The two sister ships succeeded in what they were built to do. *Lusitania,* which entered service a month before *Mauretania,* struck first, capturing the coveted Blue Riband for both eastward and westward crossings. But it was *Mauretania* which was the ultimate winner. She captured the eastward record in December 1907, with an average speed of 23.69 knots; in September 1909 she secured the westward record, with an average speed of 26.06 knots. Both records were to stand until 1929, the longest periods, twenty-two and twenty years respectively, for which they have been held.

Mauretania's heyday was the years before World War I. She was capable of carrying 2,335 passengers and had a crew numbering 812, although this reduced considerably when she was converted to oil. During the war she was requisitioned for use as a troop ship and as a hospital ship, and the hard use and lack of maintenance of these years were not fully rectified until 1922. Her records were finally broken in 1929 by the new German ship, the 51,000-ton *Bremen,* with average speeds of 27.37 knots (westwards) and 27.92 (eastwards). *Mauretania* tried to regain the Blue Riband, and indeed improved on her own pre-war averages, but with only 68,000 horse-power compared with 100,000 of the *Bremen,* the attempt was doomed to failure.

Also by this time, *Mauretania* was too out-of-date and old-fashioned for modernisation to make economic sense. In September 1935 she made her last run from New York, still capable of an average speed of over 24 knots. In the following year she was sent to the breakers at Rosyth. On this her last journey she hove to at the mouth of the Tyne to receive the farewells of thousands of the people of the river where she had been born.

MEDIEVAL HOSPITALS

A medieval hospital differed from its modern counterparts in two respects. One was that it was an ecclesiastical institution: it had a chapel; it was run by men in holy orders; and it had a chantry function, that is, to pray daily for the souls of the founder and any other persons named in the foundation document. The other was that its function was to care, not cure. Some hospitals were founded to house lepers and were akin to the isolation hospitals of more recent times. Others were founded as what would now be called hospices to care for the aged and infirm, and some were designed as hostels to give shelter to travellers, particularly pilgrims.

In the North East, forty-six hospitals were founded, although information about most of them is very scanty. On the other hand, there were three that were among the richest in England. All were in Durham and all were founded and substantially endowed by bishops of Durham. Two of them still function, as does another smaller one in GATESHEAD. The earliest episcopal foundation was **Kepier Hospital** on the outskirts of Durham, founded in 1112 by BISHOP RANNULF FLAMBARD and dedicated to God and St Giles. It was located on top of the hill overlooking the town on the road towards Houghton le Spring and it remained there until it was severely damaged in the civil war that raged in the county during the early 1140s. About 1180 it was refounded by BISHOP HUGH OF LE PUISET, not on the original site but below on the banks of the River Wear. Flambard's church, however, remained on the hill to become the parish church of the Borough of St Giles.

The original function of the hospital may have been as a hostel for pilgrims visiting the shrine of ST CUTHBERT, but Puiset's intention appears to have been that it should cater for indigent persons as well as pilgrims. Its establishment comprised a Master (appointed by the bishop) and thirteen Brethren, of whom six were to be chaplains. The intended number of inmates was not prescribed, but in 1535 it stood at ten. In addition, it is clear that outdoor relief was also part of the hospital's obligation. Flambard and Puiset together ensured that the hospital was lavishly endowed. Among its possessions were the neighbouring villages, Clifton and Caldecotes, which were depopulated and turned into farms, respectively, Low Grange and High Grange. It was also entitled to Gillycorn, that is, two sheaves from every thrave (twenty-four sheaves) from the corn tithes of fifteen villages in the county, and in 1443 it was allowed to appropriate the parish church of St Nicholas, Durham, which gave it possession of the parish glebe, the village of Old Durham. In addition, the Master of the hospital was also the immediate lord of the Borough of St Giles, also founded by Puiset.

Kepier Hospital was the richest in the diocese, with an annual income reckoned in 1535 to be £186. It was surrendered to the Crown in 1545. Its estates were sold and passed rapidly through the hands of two speculators, until in 1555 they were bought by a Londoner, John Heath, who turned the hospital into his home. In the early 1570s Heath's son, also John, conveyed the right to Gillycorn to the Dean and Chapter to endow the grammar school founded by BERNARD GILPIN at Houghton le Spring, which consequently bore the name Kepier. The Heaths owned Kepier until 1629. In 1674 it came into the possession of the Musgrave family, in whose hands it remained until 1941, when it was sold to the

North East Electricity Board. Their intention, announced in 1944, was to build a power station with thirteen cooling towers on the site, but they were thwarted by a local campaign supported by the national press. Most of the buildings have been destroyed, the most notable survivor being the gatehouse built by BISHOP RICHARD DE BURY.

Hugh of le Puiset not only refounded his predecessor's hospital, but about the same time also founded another, **Sherburn Hospital** in the township of South Sherburn. To be run by a Procurator, three priests and four clerks in holy orders, its function was to house and care for sixty-five lepers. The large number is an indication of the prevalence of the disease, but also perhaps of Puiset's intention that it should serve the whole of his diocese between the Tweed and the Tees. In 1535 its annual income was reckoned to be £142. By that date, however, its function had changed radically. In 1434 Bishop Thomas Langley issued a new constitution, which prescribed that the hospital should admit two lepers, 'if such could be found', and thirteen poor persons. Reform had become necessary as a result of mismanagement, but also because of the drastic decline in the incidence of leprosy.

The third major hospital, **Greatham Hospital**, was a later foundation. Its founder was Bishop Robert de Stichill (1260–74) and the circumstance was the fallout from the defeat of the rebellion of Simon de Montfort in 1265. Greatham had belonged to Peter de Montfort, one of the rebels, whose lands were therefore forfeit to the Crown. Shortly afterwards, Henry III gave it to a Thomas de Clare. Stichill protested, arguing that the lands of traitors within the PALATINATE OF DURHAM should be forfeit to the bishop, not the Crown. Henry III accepted this argument and handed over Greatham to Stichill. In 1272 Stichill decided to use his windfall to endow a hospital, but also perhaps as security against a change of royal mind. The hospital he founded was to be run by a Master, five priests and two clerks, all in holy orders, and was to care for forty poor persons from places on the episcopal estate. In 1535 Greatham's annual income was reckoned to be £97.

Neither Sherburn nor Greatham fell victim to the closure of religious establishments in the 1530s and 1540s. Subsequently they experienced necessary reorganisation on a number of occasions, but are still in existence and continue to perform the functions assigned to them by their medieval founders. Currently Sherburn has sixty-two residents and sheltered housing for a further twenty-five, while Greatham has twenty-seven residents in the hospital and also thirty-nine almshouses in the village, with a capacity to house double that number.

A smaller foundation in Gateshead has also survived to the present day. Confusingly, two hospitals dedicated to St Edmund were founded in the town. One, dedicated to **St Edmund, Bishop and Confessor,** was founded *c.*1250 and dissolved in 1540; the other was to **St Edmund, King and Martyr,** founded some time before 1315. Its endowment was small, consisting mainly of small parcels of land in the Friars Goose area of Gateshead. In 1535 its income was reckoned to be a little over £6. Yet it managed to survive the upheavals of the Reformation years and was refounded in 1611 as the Hospital of King James. Subsequently income from its modest endowment grew: coal beneath it was mined until 1880; urban development produced increased house rents; and occasional sales (including compulsory purchase by the local authority) raised capital that was judiciously invested. The hospital currently accommodates up to sixty people in its thirty almshouses, built in 1973.

The medieval period is usually thought to end in the sixteenth century. However, in the matter of provision for the aged and infirm, it may be argued that the Middle Ages were prolonged to the end of the seventeenth century, since, until 1700, hospitals very similar to those of the twelfth and thirteenth centuries were being founded. The best-known example is the **Holy Jesus Hospital** in Newcastle, which although intact has been crushed between two arms of the central motorway. Founded in 1682 by the corporation of Newcastle for the accommodation of poor and infirm freemen and their widows and unmarried children, its initial endowment comprised property in Etherley in Durham and Whittle in Northumberland. When this proved inadequate, the two estates were sold and the manor of Walker, with an estimated annual yield over three times greater, was purchased for £12,200. The hospital was in the charge of a Master appointed by the Corporation, and the inmates were known as brethren and sisters. In all respects it resembled a medieval hospital, except that it was a secular, not an ecclesiastical, foundation. The hospital was located on the ground occupied until 1539 by the Augustinian Friars, which after the friary closed in the late 1530s became the King's Manor, where the Council of the North was to meet. The building, in brick, is three storeys high and has forty-two rooms, each measuring 13 feet by 12 feet. It continued to perform the function for which it was founded until 1937, when it was replaced by a new Holy Jesus Hospital at Spital Tongues.

MERRIMAN, HENRY SETON (see SCOTT, HUGH STOWELL)

MERZ, JOHANN THEODORE (1840–1922) AND CHARLES HESTERMAN (1874–1940)

Theodore and Charles Merz, father and son, together with Joseph Swan, Charles Parsons and Alphonse Reyrolle, made the North East the leader in the manufacture of electricity-generating equipment and in the use of electricity in the home, in transport and in industry.

Theodore Merz was a naturalised Briton of German origin, who by trade was an industrial chemist but by inclination a philosopher. He married Alice Mary Richardson, daughter of John Wigham Richardson and thereby became a member of the influential Tyneside Quaker nexus. His contribution to the growth of the use of electricity was twofold. In 1881, together with Joseph Swan, William Armstrong and Robert Spence Watson, he founded the Swan Electric Light Co., with a factory at South Benwell and headquarters in Mosley Street, Newcastle. Five years later, however, the enterprise was moved to London. More permanent was NESCO, the Newcastle upon Tyne Electric Supply Co., which he founded in 1889, again with Spence Watson, his brother-in-law. Merz senior was an enthusiastic member of the Literary and Philosophical Society, where he lectured on many occasions, usually on philosophical subjects. A less ephemeral product of this interest was his four-volume work, *A History of European Thought in the Nineteenth Century*, published between 1896 and 1914. He also wrote a study of the German philosopher Leibnitz, and a book entitled *Religion and Science*.

Charles Merz, who had a more influential career than his father, has been described as 'the premier electrical engineer of the first half of the twentieth century'. He was born at Gateshead and as a result of his Quaker upbringing was educated at the Friends' School at York. He was then briefly a student at Armstrong College, but in 1892 he became an indentured pupil at the Pandon Dene Generating Station, owned by the British Thomson Houston Co., of which his father was a director. Subsequent training took place in Lincoln (Robey Engineering) and London (Bankside Power Station). It was in the south that he made his reputation in 1897 as the manager and engineer of the system installed to provide Croydon with electricity. This led to his being invited to Cork to perform the same role. It was in Cork that he met William McLellan (1874–1934), with whom he formed a partnership, Merz McLellan, Consultant Electrical Engineers, in 1902.

His skill as a designer of power stations was fully established in 1904. In that year the advanced Carville Station at Wallsend which he designed for NESCO was opened and the paper he wrote with McLellan, *Power Station Design*, which laid the foundation of future large-scale power station design, was published. Merz McLellan also set up a London office, from which they secured orders from many parts of the world, not only for power stations, but also for schemes to electrify railways. Such was Merz's stature in the industry that in World War I he was appointed Director of Electric Power Supply.

During the inter-war years, Merz McLellan were recognised as the leading consultants in the field of electrical engineering, eventually having seven partners and 200 employees. It was Merz McLellan that supplied the technical data for Lord Weir's report that led to the creation of the National Grid, which in turn led to the Central Electricity Generating Board. In supporting this, Merz went against the grain of his principles, which favoured individualism against collectivism; but he was prepared to accept that personal beliefs should not be placed before what he saw as the best solution to the country's needs.

Charles Merz came to a tragic end: he and two of his children were killed in October 1940 during the London Blitz by a bomb that hit his home in Kensington.

METROCENTRE

MetroCentre, located between the Newcastle/Gateshead Western Bypass and the railway line running along the south bank of the Tyne, occupies 120 acres of land previously used as a dump for power station ash. It was conceived by its developers, Cameron Hall, as a comprehensive retail and leisure complex in which the needs and aspirations of customers were the guiding development principles. Essential to its development were the taxation advantages that accrued from its designation, in 1981, as an Enterprise Zone, and the decision by central government and the local authority (GATESHEAD) to pay most of the cost of installing services and access roads. Building began in 1985 and the Centre was formally opened in the following year, since when expansion has been continuous and is still not fully complete. At present there are over 300 shops of all sorts, ranging from national department stores to individual shops, including some that are foreign and unique to it. It attracts 24 million customers from all parts of Britain and from abroad, assisted by free parking for 9,000 cars and dedicated bus and railway stations. It employs over 7,000 people and the income it generates has helped to regenerate Gateshead. In addition to its shops, it has over fifty bars, cafés and restaurants, an eleven-screen cinema and a bowling facility.

Although similar developments have taken place in other parts of the country, MetroCentre can claim to have led the way, just as the Grainger Market (see GRAINGER, RICHARD) did in the early nineteenth century.

MIDDLESBROUGH (see under NEW TOWNS OF THE NINETEENTH CENTURY)

MIDDLETON, SIR GILBERT DE (c.1280–1318)

Gilbert de Middleton was a minor Northumberland landowner who committed one of the most notorious medieval outrages in the region. The scene of his crime was Rushyford, ten miles north of Darlington, and the date 1 September 1317. On that day, together with an armed band, he forcibly seized Louis de Beaumont and his brother, Henry, and two cardinals as they were proceeding towards Durham. The victims were men of importance. Louis de Beaumont had been recently appointed Bishop of Durham and was on his way to his consecration and enthronement in the cathedral, while the two cardinals were papal envoys on their way to Scotland. The two cardinals were allowed to travel on to Durham, although stripped of most of their valuables, but the Beaumont brothers were taken to Mitford Castle, where they were held until mid-October, when ransoms were paid. Meanwhile, Middleton appears to have compounded his offence, which was both a crime and sacrilege, by engaging in a protection racket. His career, however, was short-lived: in December 1317 he was captured and taken to London, where he was tried and convicted as a traitor and hanged, drawn and quartered.

Middleton's motives are far from clear. Superficially, the fact that when he was captured he is reckoned to have had cash, jewels, furs, horses and plate with an estimated value of close on £3,000 suggests the basest of motives. But to dismiss him as a mere brigand may be too simple. Although a minor Northumberland landowner, he was also a King's Knight and therefore had a special loyalty to the Crown. Consequently, other motives have been sought. Perhaps the most convincing is that his actions were a desperate protest against the failure of Edward II's government to protect the far north of his realm against Scottish raids, which were especially severe in 1315 and 1316 following the disastrous English defeat at Bannockburn in 1314, and which coincided with three consecutive exceptionally wet summers and disastrous harvests.

MIDDLETON ST GEORGE

In the Middle Ages, Middleton St George was the centre of a small parish comprising Middleton St George, Middleton One Row and West Hartburn; the last, which was also known as Goosepool, has disappeared. Its history was agricultural and uneventful until 1934, when 250 of its 2,516 acres (1,018 ha) were acquired for an RAF station. Construction began in 1939 and it was officially opened at the beginning of 1941 as the base of two squadrons in 4 Group Bomber Command, whose headquarters were at Heslington Hall, York. It continued as an RAF station until the first day of 1943, when, together with five other stations in the North Riding of Yorkshire, it was handed over to the Royal Canadian Airforce. Thereafter, until the end of the war in Europe, two (of 419, 420 and 428) Canadian bomber squadrons operated from Middleton, taking part in raids on Germany and German-occupied Europe.

In July 1945 Middleton reverted to the RAF and for the next twenty years it alternated between Fighter Command (1945–47 and 1956–64) and Flying Training Command (1947–56). In 1964, however, its military use ended and almost immediately it acquired a civil role as Teesside Airport. Since then, it has expanded and acquired a dedicated railway station. In 2004 it was renamed Durham Tees Valley Airport.

MILBURN, COLIN (1941–1990)

Colin Milburn was probably the most talented cricketer to have been born in the North East. He was not merely talented:

with a huge physique, a flamboyant and dynamic approach to batting and a genial personality, he was one of the game's outstanding and most attractive characters. He was born in Consett, the son of an electrician, whose own cricketing ability was sufficient for him to play as a professional in a local league. The son, however, was better than the father: at the age of thirteen he was a member of the Burnopfield 1st XI and in 1959 he was chosen to play for Durham while still at Stanley Grammar School. The following year Milburn became a professional with Northamptonshire. He played for them for eight seasons, scoring 13,262 runs (including 23 centuries) and in doing so he displayed huge power and a whole range of shots. He was a useful bowler, taking 99 wickets, and he held 224 catches. During these years he also had winter seasons with Western Australia and he played nine times for England, averaging nearly 48 runs per innings.

In May 1969, however, when he was at the height of his powers, he was involved in a car crash in which he sustained permanent damage to his right eye and lost the sight of his left eye, the lead eye for a right-handed batsman. His cricketing career was over, although he did, unsuccessfully, attempt a comeback. Had he not suffered this tragic accident, he would probably have played at top level for up to ten more years and would have continued to entertain crowds with his swashbuckling batting.

MILBURN, JOHN EDWARD THOMPSON (1924–1988)

Jackie Milburn was one of the greatest footballers produced in the North East. More than that, he was perhaps the most respected and loved. He was born in Ashington, the son of a miner, into a family that had the ability to breed talented footballers. Leaving school in 1939, he became an apprentice fitter at the colliery, an occupation he was required to continue until 1948. Meanwhile, in 1943, he had signed for Newcastle United, initially as a winger on account of his speed. Within a few years, however, he had moved to being a centre forward and took permanent possession of the No. 9 shirt. In that position his hallmark was not only electric speed, but also, more important, a ferocious shot with either foot. Unlike most centre forwards, however, he hated heading the ball, although one of his most famous goals was the one he headed against Arsenal in the first minute of the 1955 cup final.

He played for Newcastle until 1957, making 498 appearances and scoring 200 goals, a record for the club, until surpassed in 2006 by Alan Shearer. With them he won the FA Cup on three occasions: 1951, 1952 and 1955. He also won thirteen caps for England, scoring ten goals. Following his retirement from Newcastle, until 1963–64 he tried management, first with Linfield in the Northern Ireland League, and then with Ipswich Town. But it became clear that he did not have the temperament needed in that role and he returned to the North East to become a football columnist for the *News of the World*, a role he performed for twenty years.

Jackie Milburn was more than a star centre forward; he was also a much-loved and respected man, renowned for his friendliness, loyalty and love for his native region. All this was demonstrated by the 44,000 who turned up for his testimonial match in 1967, in his being made an honorary Freeman of Newcastle in 1981, by the thousands of people who lined the roads as his funeral cortège proceeded to Newcastle Cathedral, and by the statue of him that stands outside St James's Park. For the club's supporters and many others, he was simply 'Wor Jackie'.

MILFIELD PLAIN

The Milfield Plain covers about seven square miles of flat land bordering the River Till north of Wooler. Now seemingly a quiet rural area, early and late in time it has been the scene of important events and developments, most of which, unfortunately, are no longer visible to the untrained eye.

Although evidence reveals that man was active in the area during the Mesolithic period (6,000–4,000 BC), it was during the succeeding Neolithic period, particularly between 2,500 and 2,000 BC, that the Plain became subject to intensive settlement, which resulted in the clearance of woodland for farming by communities such as those revealed by the excavations at YEAVERING and Thirlings. Along with this went important cultural developments, largely revealed by aerial photography, which are now being substantiated by archaeology. The most notable are the henges, ten of which have been identified in and around Milfield. These were enclosures formed by the excavation of a ditch, using the resulting soil to form a bank on its outer rim. Entrance to the enclosure was by means of one or two gaps. Inside, in some but not all cases, was a ring of holes, which may have held posts. What purpose the henges served is also uncertain, but since the ditch was on the inside of the bank, it was not for defence. However, the amount of work required to create them argues a high degree of social organisation and urgent and serious concerns, which may have included beliefs that should be classified as religious. A hint of these is the entrances to the excavated henge known as Milfield North, which are accurately aligned with Yeavering Bell. That this hill had considerable significance for the people of the Plain is also attested by an avenue of holes, which we assume originally contained posts, leading to it. The same people also created three stone circles and a number of single standing stones, which must have been significant, either socially or spiritually. The Milfield Plain is one of the most important areas in Britain for the study of the evolution of our ancestors during the Neolithic period.

The Plain was equally important during the early years of the KINGDOM OF NORTHUMBRIA. A royal palace complex was created at Yeavering, almost certainly an acceptance by the newly created kingdom of the importance to the native inhabitants of Yeavering Bell. The palace at Yeavering had a short and chequered history, being burnt down on two occasions, and this may be one reason why it was abandoned some time after 650. The Milfield Plain, however, was too important to the Northumbrian kings to be left without a royal presence. The upshot was a replacement palace complex, which BEDE says was called Maelmin. The location of this new high-status residence, where the king and his peripatetic court would reside for sufficient time to impress by its presence, conduct important business, and consume the food rents paid by the farming communities, has been revealed by aerial photography to have been in a field between the present village of Milfield and the River Till. The nature of the new location, at the centre of the Plain, and its position controlling a crossing of the Till, may have been additional reasons for the removal from Yeavering. The new complex, which amounted to a small town, was surrounded by a wooden palisade, inside which were a large number of wooden buildings of various sizes, including at least one hall capable of seating 300 people.

Much more recently Milfield gained national importance during World War II. RAF Milfield was the most northerly airfield in England and one of fifteen built for the RAF in the North East. Like several others, it had been a landing ground in

World War I, when it took its name, Woodbridge, from the adjacent farm. The new version, begun in 1941, was opened in the following summer. Its intended purpose (and that of its satellite station, RAF Brunton, eighteen miles to the south-east) was to be the home of 59 Operational Training Unit (OTU) and it discharged this function until the beginning of 1944, training 1,200 fighter pilots for frontline service. Then, in January 1944, it became the home of the Fighter Leaders' School (FLS), to train fighter pilots in the techniques of ground attack, using bombs and rockets, in preparation for the invasion of Normandy, which commenced on 6 June. Six squadrons were involved, one of them American. In all, the School ran eleven courses, each lasting three weeks, with an average of sixty pilots on each course. Two special ranges on Goswick Sands allowed the use of live ammunition, but dummy attacks were also made on villages and transport facilities in the vicinity. In September another training school was added, the Day Fighter Development Wing (DFDW), comprising three squadrons to develop new tactics and techniques. The importance of ground attack formations, virtually all of whose pilots trained at Milfield, in the destruction of the German armies during the war in Europe between June 1944 and May 1945, cannot be over-estimated.

In the last days of 1944, however, both the FLS and the DFDW were transferred to RAF Wittering in Northamptonshire, and Milfield and Brunton reverted to their original role as a conventional OTU. RAF Milfield was closed early in 1946, but the site is still connected with aviation as the home of the Borders Gliding Club, although the ground from which the Club operates is several feet lower than the wartime airfield as the result of gravel excavation. The one reminder of RAF Milfield is a plaque recording the names of the forty-six men killed while based at the station.

MILITARY ROAD

Not to be confused with the Military Way, the road built by the Roman army immediately to the south of HADRIAN'S WALL, the Military Road was built between 1751 and 1757 to meet the need for a modern all-weather link between the towns of NEWCASTLE and Carlisle. The need was exposed by the failure of General George Wade, commander of the army at Newcastle, to move his forces across the country in December 1745 to protect Carlisle and intercept the invading army under Charles Edward Stuart. Although heavy snow was a major factor in Wade's failure, the lamentable state of the road was also significant.

Contrary to what is sometimes thought, Wade played no part in the campaign for the road or in its design and construction, since he died in 1748, the year before the campaign got under way. This was the work of a group of Northumberland landowners, the most prominent of whom appears to have been Lancelot Allgood of Nunnykirk. Wade's experience, however, was indirectly influential in that three officers of his army gave persuasive accounts of their experiences in 1745 to a Commons select committee that considered the matter. Their graphic descriptions, when added to the government's fright in 1745, explains why the bill authorising the construction of the road passed through all its stages in less than a month and became an act in May 1751.

The survey and preparation of estimates were carried out by two army engineers, Dugald Campbell and Hugh Debbeig, between July and December of the same year. The building contract was awarded to a Yorkshireman, Christopher Lightfoot, and his three associates, one of whom was from County Durham, while the appointed surveyor was John Brown, the brother of 'CAPABILITY' BROWN. The cost of construction, set at £22,450, was borne by appointed commissioners, and to recoup their outlay they were to be allowed to charge tolls (except on military traffic) at fourteen toll gates. The roadway was to be 27 feet (8.2 m) wide from ditch to ditch and the road itself was to measure 16 feet (4.9 m) in width and be made of stone, 15 inches (38 cm) deep at the crown, tapering to 5 inches (12.7 cm) at the edges. The road was completed by 1757 and its cost was only £230 over estimate.

For us, the depressing aspect of the project was the decision to use Hadrian's Wall as the base for the road whenever possible, resulting in the destruction of long stretches of it. In fact, between the West Gate of Newcastle and the North Tyne at Chollerford the Wall, because of this decision, has largely disappeared. Beyond the North Tyne, however, there was little destruction of the Wall, although several stretches of the *Vallum* were obliterated. Only between Twiced Brewed and the county boundary at Greenhead was a long stretch of the Wall complex completely spared.

The Military Road is still in use today, although much altered for most of its length. From Newcastle it is the A69 as far as Walbottle, when it becomes the B6528 as far as Heddon. Thereafter, it is the B6318 until the county boundary at Greenhead. In Cumbria it is the A69 as far as Brampton, then the B6264 as far as the River Eden, when it is the A7 into Carlisle.

MONTAGU, ELIZABETH (1720–1800)

Elizabeth Montagu was born Elizabeth Robinson, the daughter of Matthew Robinson, a Yorkshire landowner. In 1742 she married Edward Montagu (1692–1775), a member of the family deeply involved in the GREAT NORTHERN COALFIELD. Montagu's interest increased in 1758, when he inherited Denton, west of Newcastle. The estate included Denton Hall, still standing close to the A1/A69 interchange. If the date it bears, 1622, is correct, it is one of the region's earliest country houses. The estate also included several coal pits, which later coalesced into Montagu Main Colliery.

Elizabeth Montagu deserves to be remembered for three reasons. As regards the North East, her voluminous correspondence includes letters written in Newcastle and Denton in which she casts light on miners, mining and Tyneside life in the later eighteenth century. Nationally, she was instrumental in introducing the word 'bluestocking' into the English language, which was applied to the circle of women with serious intellectual interests, of which she was a prominent member and into which she drew the young Mary Eleanor Bowes (see BOWES FAMILY). Elizabeth Montagu's particular interest was Shakespeare, and in 1769 she published a well-received book, *Essays on the Writings and Genius of Shakespear* (sic), written to refute the criticisms of Voltaire. It ran through seven editions and was translated into French and Italian.

One hundred and thirty-five years after her death what had been her estate provided the evidence for a popular novel, *The Stars Look Down*, in which miners and Tyneside life are again presented. The author, Archibald Joseph Cronin (1896–1981), had been a Medical Inspector of Mines who had investgated the Montagu Main disaster in 1924, when nineteen men were drowned by an inrush of water from workings that may have dated back to Elizabeth's day.

MORPETH

We have very little knowledge about the origins of Morpeth, although it seems almost certain that the basic shape of the town as it is today was the work of the first Norman family to possess the Barony of

Morpeth, one of the largest in Northumberland. It may also be one of the earliest, created by William II (d.1100) or by the then Earl of Northumberland, Robert de Mowbray, who was removed from office by William II in 1095. In all probability, the men responsible were the first three generations of the de Merlay family, who held the barony between the 1090s and 1188. Probably the first building they erected was a castle, the motte of which survives in Carlisle Park as Ha' Hill. It was created by cutting a deep cleft in the ridge overlooking the Wansbeck so as to separate the northern tip of the ridge from the rest. This detached part was then landscaped to form a flat-topped cone. On top of this motte a wooden keep was built, which appears to have been reconstructed in stone at some time in the twelfth century.

This castle was destroyed in 1216 by King John in the course of the war he waged until his death in October of that year against the rebels who had forced him to seal Magna Carta. It was not rebuilt; instead, after they had recovered the barony in 1218, the de Merlays built another castle a few yards to the south. This second castle still existed at the time of the 1st Civil War, when it was occupied by the Scots (see Scottish Occupation) and badly damaged during a siege in 1644. Its keep has entirely disappeared, and all that remains are part of the curtain wall and the mid-fourteenth-century gatehouse, now restored as holiday accommodation.

It was the norm for incoming Norman barons not only to build a castle, but also to found a borough to provide services and stimulate economic development. Curiously, Morpeth borough lies on the opposite bank of the Wansbeck. When it was founded is not recorded. Whether it was on the north side of the river from the outset, or moved there later, is also not known. The selection of the site may have been dictated by strategic need, but equally it may simply have been that the land on the north bank was more suitable.

The borough occupied land within an elongated loop of the Wansbeck and probably at first comprised two streets, Oldgate and Bridge Street, separated by the Market Place. Later, at an uncertain date, a third street, at right angles to the earlier streets and appropriately called Newgate Street, was developed, probably in response to rising population and increased economic activity. These streets, layout of which has remained unchanged ever since, and which are still the central business district of the town, were certainly in being before the end of the thirteenth century.

Another product of that century was the bridge linking the borough and the castle area, presumably replacing a ford or ferry. This was replaced by the present bridge, designed by Thomas Telford and built between 1829 and 1831, although its stone piers carry an iron footway, built in 1869. Associated with the bridge, and probably founded at the same time, was the chapel dedicated to All Saints. Classed as a chantry, it was closed down, as were all the others in England, by act of parliament in 1548. Four years later, in 1552, the endowments of the chapel were assigned to the maintenance of a grammar school (i.e. it taught Latin) to be run by two masters. Morpeth Grammar School was one of twenty-four similar schools founded in different parts of the country that were distinguished as King Edward VI Grammar Schools. Currently, the chapel houses the local Tourist Office, craft shop and a bagpipe museum.

Another puzzling aspect of medieval Morpeth is the location of its parish church, dedicated to St Mary, which is clearly detached from the rest of the town, lying as it does several hundred yards south of the castle. Although its present fabric is essentially fourteenth-century, it is known that there was an earlier church on the site. One possible explanation is that a church was already there when the de Merlays arrived, but in the absence of evidence of pre-Conquest fabric, this remains speculation. The one certain de Merlay ecclesiastical initiative is the Cistercian monastery of NEWMINSTER, begun by Ralph de Merlay in 1138 a few hundred yards east of his castle. The closure of the monastery at the Reformation led to its destruction by the townsmen, who used it as a source of dressed stone.

Another change in the sixteenth century was the arrival of the last family to be lords of Morpeth. The de Merlay family died out in the male line in 1265 and was succeeded by the Greystokes until 1487, when again a failure of male heirs brought in the Dacres. Around the middle of the century, the Dacre heiress, Elisabeth, married Lord William Howard, third son of Thomas Howard, 4th Duke of Norfolk. In 1661 their great-grandson, Charles Howard, was created Earl of Carlisle, Viscount Howard of Morpeth and Lord Dacre. The heir to the earldom has the courtesy title of Viscount Morpeth. Howard control of Morpeth was not finally secure until the early years of the seventeenth century, about the time that the town's most distinctive building, the Clock Tower at the entrance to Oldgate, was erected. It is a very rare example of a free-standing tower, with the clock face having only an hour hand. It still rings the curfew at eight o'clock every evening.

Although the Howards did not live in Morpeth (they resided at Naworth Castle in Cumbria or, later, Castle Howard in the North Riding), they did benefit the town in several ways. In 1662 they secured from Charles II a charter confirming Morpeth's status as an ancient borough. In fact, Morpeth had been returning two members to parliament since 1553 and continued to do so until 1832, when the Reform Act reduced the number to one. Until that time, one of the MPs was invariably a Howard and the other often a relative. Four years later the borough's ancient constitution was scrapped and replaced by one under the terms of the Municipal Reform Act of 1835. Both before and after this change, the rulers of the borough operated from the town hall that was paid for by the Earl of Carlisle and built to the design of Sir John Vanbrugh, the architect of Castle Howard. The Howard influence waned in the late nineteenth century. In part, this was due to the widening of the franchise, which reduced the great landowners' power to command. But there was also a more singular reason. George James Howard, 9th Earl of Carlisle (1843–1911), handed the Morpeth estate over to his wife, Rosalind. She believed that she could make it more profitable, but finding that this was not so, she put it on the market in 1887. Buyers proved hard to find, although in 1915 LORD JOICEY bought the town hall and presented it to the borough. The following year, Countess Rosalind gifted to Morpeth the land that now forms Carlisle Park, which, because of World War I and the post-war depression, was not opened until 1929.

Although a number of manufacturing enterprises were established in Morpeth during the eighteenth and nineteenth centuries, the town never became a major industrial centre, but continued its historical role of market town for the surrounding districts and increasingly served as a commuter town for people working on Tyneside. As regards the latter, it was boosted in the 1840s by the arrival of the York, Newcastle and Berwick Railway (from 1854 the North Eastern Railway) and later by the Blyth and Tyne Railway and the Border Counties Railway (see RAILWAYS). Its lack of growth is evident in the size of its population, which in 1900 was still not much above 5,000. In the twentieth century, however, growth was more rapid, the 2001 census recording a total of 14,400. But this was not due to a huge expansion of industry, but rather to the general rise of population and in particular to Morpeth's increased importance as an administrative centre during the last quarter of the century.

This stemmed directly from the act of parliament that created the new County of Tyne and Wear as part of a fundamental restructuring of local government throughout Britain. The consequence was that a truncated COUNTY OF NORTHUMBERLAND came into formal existence on 1 April 1974. One of the earliest decisions of the new Northumberland County Council was to end its unsatisfactory and uneconomic administrative arrangements, involving departments scattered in nine different locations in NEWCASTLE. Several alternative options were considered, including relocation in Newcastle and moving to Cramlington. In the end, the preferred solution was to build an integrated headquarters at Morpeth, which came into use in 1981 and was officially opened the following year. Morpeth was now effectively the county town of Northumberland. Another consequence of the act was the creation of the Borough of Castle Morpeth, comprising the old borough and large parts of the old Castle Ward of Northumberland. However, this, together with the other Districts of Northumberland, was abolished in 2009.

Morpeth is also an important cultural centre in that its branch of the Northumberland County Library houses the Northern Poetry Library. This is, with the exception of London, the largest collection of contemporary poetry in England. Currently, it has 15,000 volumes, but the number will grow as more poetry is published.

MORRISON, REVD DR ROBERT (1782–1834)

Robert Morrison, who became one of Britain's greatest Sinologists, was born at Buller's Green, Morpeth, the son of a manufacturer of boot lasts and trees. Two years after his birth the family moved to Newcastle, where Robert was required by his father to learn the family trade. Robert, however, had strong religious leanings, and in 1798 he became a Presbyterian and set about learning Latin, Greek and Hebrew with the intention of becoming a minister. To futher this aim, in 1803 he moved to London to attend the nonconformist Hoxton Academy, and the following year he was accepted for training by the London Missionary Society. There followed three years at the Missionary Academy in Gosport, Hampshire, St Bartholomew's Hospital in London, and the Royal Observatory at Greenwich. Also in these years he took lessons in Chinese, since it had been decided that China was where he would work, and it was to that country that he sailed in 1807, shortly after his ordination.

He was to remain in China, mainly in Canton and the Portuguese colony of Macao, for the rest of his life, except for a short interlude in England between 1824 and 1826. In these years he achieved monumental success, but not in his intended field. His missionary success was minimal: the Chinese authorities were hostile, as was the East India Company, which feared that missionary activity would hinder trade. Nevertheless, the Company employed Morrison as a translator and interpreter. It was therefore in the field of language that Morrison was to achieve greatness. His fame rests on three monumental works: *A Grammar of the Chinese Language* (1815), *A Dictionary of Chinese* (1815–23), and *The Bible Translated into Chinese* (1819). As regards the last, which was published in twenty-one volumes, he had begun this task soon after his arrival in China, but in completing it he had the assistance of a Scottish missionary, the Reverend Dr William Milne (1785–1822), who arrived in China in 1813. In addition, in collaboration with Milne, he founded the Anglo-Chinese College at Malacca in 1818 and just before his death he was appointed Chinese secretary to Lord Napier, who came out to Canton as the government's representative following the abolition of the East India Company's monopoly in 1833. When he returned briefly to London in 1824, he brought with him a substantial library, which became the basis of the Chinese section of the library of the London School of Oriental and African Studies.

Morrison also achieved posthumous success through one of his sons, John Robert Morrison (1814–43), who also became a first-rate Sinologist. He mastered the Chinese language, wrote several books, notably *A Chinese Commercial Guide*, and took a leading part in the negotiations that led to the Treaty of Nanking in 1842, which ended the 1st Opium War with China and by which Britain acquired Hong Kong.

MOULTON, STEPHEN (1794–1880)

Stephen Moulton, who played an important part in the development of the vulcanised rubber industry, was born at Whorlton on Tees, the son of a law stationer. Nothing is known of his early life, except that at an uncertain date after 1826 he went to the USA, where he met Charles Goodyear, the inventor of the vulcanisation process. In 1847 he returned to Britain, where he took out a patent for an improved version of the vulcanisation process and, with US financial backing, set up a factory at Bradford upon Avon, where he manufactured a form of vulcanised rubber that was cheaper and of superior quality to that of its rivals. He returned to the USA in 1851.

MUSEUMS

Museums in the North East fall broadly into two categories: those dealing with localities, and those concerned with specific institutions or activities.

Of the former, by far the largest and most ambitious is **Beamish Museum**, which was proposed in 1958 but not opened until 1977. Its purpose was to rescue the physical remains of northern life, occupational, social and domestic, and to re-erect them in an open-air situation. The site for this (acquired from the National Coal Board) was Beamish Hall and its home farm and grounds, extending to over 300 acres. Originally its ambition was to encompass all of northern England, but this proved to be politically unrealistic. Although no time frame was stipulated, almost inevitably the museum became concerned with the period of industrialisation and population growth from the late eighteenth century. Since 1986 visitors have entered by passing under a giant iron arch, the frame of a steam hammer, known as 'Tiny Tim', built in Glasgow in 1883 and used in DARLINGTON in the manufacture of ships' anchors.

The most notable 'rescues' have been: Beamish 2nd pit winding gear; a coal drop from Seaham Harbour; Rowley Station from the Stanhope and Tyne Railroad; a Gateshead tram; a Newcastle trolley bus; a NER J2 locomotive of 1886; a row of miners' cottages from Hetton le Hole; a terrace of Georgian houses from Gateshead; a Board School; a public house from Bishop Auckland; and the bandstand that stood on an island in the middle of the lake in Saltwell Park, Gateshead. In reassembling these items, the museum has created an artificial town, the purpose of which is to give a more realistic understanding and appreciation of North-East life in the nineteenth and twentieth centuries.

Other local museums are on a smaller

scale and cover much more limited areas. Alnwick and the surrounding district has the **Bailiffgate Museum**, housed in the deconsecrated church of St Mary. **Berwick Museum** occupies part of the historic Ravensdown Barracks. Durham has a **Heritage Centre** housed in St Mary le Bow, a redundant parish church, built in the Middle Ages but rebuilt in 1635 and 1702. At Hartlepool, there are two adjacent museums: **Museum of Hartlepool** (free entry) and **Hartlepool's Maritime Experience** (entry charge), which also gives access to *Trincomalee*, the restored Royal Navy frigate launched in 1817. At **South Shields** the museum, created in 1976, occupies a building originally erected in 1858–60 as a Mechanics' Institute and subsequently used by the town's library between 1871 and 1976. Stockton's museum is at **Preston Hall**, built in 1825 and opened as a museum in 1953. It specialises in late Victorian society, but it also possesses *The Dice Players*, one of only three paintings in the country by the great seventeenth-century French artist Georges de la Tour. **Sunderland** is the only purpose-built museum in this category. It was erected in 1877–79 and extended in 1960–64 and includes a Winter Gardens. The **Weardale Museum** at Ireshopeburn was opened in 1985 in the redundant manse, which had been added to High House Chapel in 1804. The chapel itself was built in 1760 as a consequence of John Wesley's visit to the dale in 1752 and is the oldest Methodist chapel in the world in continuous weekly use since its opening.

Of the museums with more specific concerns, the most numerous are those concerned with HADRIAN'S WALL and the Roman frontier. The most widely known is that at **VINDOLANDA**, owned by the Vindolanda Trust and opened in Chesterholm House in 1974, which displays artefacts, largely of a civil nature, excavated from the *vicus* lying to the south of the military fort. The most renowned of these are the documents that have survived and been restored to legibility and give the museum international importance. Further west, at Carvoran, is the **Roman Army Museum**, opened in 1981 and administered since 1997 by the Vindolanda Trust. This museum is particularly concerned to make the Roman frontier intelligible to children. The oldest museum is that at **Chesters**, which houses the artefacts excavated in the nineteenth century by JOHN CLAYTON. Similar but more recent museums exist at three of the Wall sites: **South Shields**, **Wallsend** and **Housesteads**, and also at **Corbridge** south of the Wall. Also in this category is the **Museum of Antiquities**, since 1960 in Newcastle University. Since it began as a joint venture with the Society of Antiquaries (see LITERARY AND PHILOSOPHICAL SOCIETY OF NEWCASTLE UPON TYNE) it houses a collection of finds built up by the Society, which were housed in the Black Gate and Keep of Newcastle Castle, until those locations were found to be unsuitable, as well as artefacts deposited by the Duke of Nothumberland and important finds from excavations in the City. Not all of its material, therefore, is Roman. In addition, this museum has on display a model of Hadrian's Wall and models of the various military establishments along its length, which is of considerable aid to understanding their original structures.

Another single focus group comprises the museums devoted to the region's military associations. Each of the three infantry REGIMENTS has its own museum: the **King's Own Scottish Borderers**, housed in Ravensdown Barracks in Berwick; the **Royal Northumberland Fusiliers** in the Abbot's Tower in Alnwick Castle; and the **Durham Light Infantry**, which has a purpose-built museum, constructed between 1964 and 1968 near County Hall in Durham and which also acts as a local art gallery for temporary exhibitions. In addition, the **Northumberland Hussars** have a small museum in the **Discovery Museum** (see below) in Newcastle. Also in Newcastle is the **Military Vehicle Museum**, housed in the last surviving pavilion of the 1929 NORTH-EAST COAST EXHIBITION, when it was the Palace of Fine Arts. In 1934 it became the Museum of Science and Engineering, which moved to Blandford House in 1978 to become the **Discovery Museum**. Five years later, the pavilion was taken over by the North East Military Vehicle Club as a home for its fifty vehicles and other militaria. At present this museum is closed indefinitely as the result of structural problems.

The history of railways in the region is served by four museums. The best is the **Darlington Railway Centre and Museum**, opened in 1975 in the North Road station, built in 1842 for the Stockton and Darlington Railway. Its two prize exhibits are *Locomotion*, built by GEORGE STEPHENSON for the Stockton and Darlington Railway, and *Derwent*, built for the same firm in 1845 by the local maker, William Kitching. It also houses the Ken Hoole Study Centre, named after Ken Hoole (1916–88), a lifelong railway enthusiast, who was an active campaigner for the museum and donated his books and papers to it. As well as these, the centre possesses a great variety and quantity of material relating to the region's railways from other sources of value to transport historians. At **New Shildon**, a museum that was given the name **Locomotion** was opened in 2004. It combines the museum of 1975 based upon the house and Soho works of TIMOTHY HACKWORTH (which houses *Sanspareil*, built for the Rainhill Trial held by the Liverpool and Manchester Railway in 1829) and the extension of the National Railway Museum at York, which exhibits a selection of locomotives in a purpose-built shed on the former marshalling yard. The third museum is the Stephenson Museum at **North Shields**, which is working to restore a 1939 locomotive that belonged to Ashington Colliery and which has been renamed 'JACKIE MILBURN', with the aim of providing steam train rides from the Museum to Percy Main. The most elegant is the small station at **Monkwearmouth**, built in classical style in 1848 by GEORGE HUDSON. It ceased to be used as a station in 1967 and opened as a museum in 1973.

Surprisingly, the industry for which the North East is most widely known, coal mining, is not well served. Apart from the exhibits at Beamish Museum and the winding engine at the site of **Washington F Pit**, the only museum devoted to coal is on the site of the colliery at Woodhorn, near Ashington. The museum complex, costing £16 million, opened in the late autumn of 2006 and incorporates the Northumberland county archives, along with information on the industrial and socially historic aspects of coal mining. The museum, which took two years to create, is situated in the Queen Elizabeth II Country Park, which was created in the late 1970s on the former pit heaps of Ashington and Woodhorn Collieries and is known as **Woodhorn: Northumberland Museum, Archives and Country Park**. LEAD MINING is served by the **North of England Lead Mining Museum** at Killhope near the head of Weardale. It is at the former Park Level Mine, which was opened in 1853 and last worked in 1916. Since 1968 the site has been gradually developed until it is now the most complete lead mining museum in the country, with permitted access to the mine workings as well as restored surface buildings and machinery. Its most spectacular exhibit is the Killhope Wheel, nearly 34 feet in diameter, which was built in 1859 for a mine at Allendale and was moved to Killhope in 1876–78.

A number of other museums do not fit easily into either of these categories. The largest is the **Discovery Museum** in Newcastle. It came into being in 1934 as the Museum of Science and Engineering and it was the largest museum devoted to scientific matters outside London. It was, in fact, the collection of exhibits brought together in 1929 for the North -East Coast Exhibition held in Exhibition Park, the thirty-five acres of Newcastle Town Moor set aside for recreational purposes by the Town Moor Act of 1870 and used to hold the Royal Jubilee Exhibition in 1887. The pavilions erected in 1929 were to be temporary, but in fact had a life of forty years. In 1978, however, the museum was removed to Blandford House, which had been built in 1899 as the northern headquarters and distribution centre (serving over 1,000 stores) of the Cooperative Wholesale Society. The museum was given its present title in 1993. It is still the best scientific and technical museum outside London, but also illustrates the industrial and social history of Tyneside. Its most notable possession is the restored and renovated ***TURBINIA.***

The **Shefton Museum** in Newcastle University, which began as a collection of materials for use as teaching aids bought by Professor Brian Shefton with money provided by the University, was opened to the public in 1960 and made fully accessible in 1999. It is regarded as one of the most important collections of Greek and Etruscan artefacts in the country. Also in Newcastle is the **Hancock Museum** (see LITERARY AND PHILOSOPHICAL SOCIETY OF NEWCASTLE UPON TYNE).

At the time of writing, the North East's most exciting development is the **Great North Museum**. This will bring together the Museum of Antiquities, the Shefton Museum, the Hancock Museum and the ethnographic collection in the Hatton Gallery (see ART GALLERIES) and will be housed in the refurbished and extended Hancock building. The project, which is the result of a partnership comprising Newcastle University, the Natural History Society of Northumbria, Newcastle City Council and Tyne and Wear Museums, opened in 2009.

Durham University has two museums. That known as the **Oriental Museum**, founded in 1960 as the Gulbenkian Museum, was the consequence of funding by the Gulbenkian Foundation. Its foundation collection comprised the Egyptian artefacts donated by the 10th Duke of Northumberland and the Wellcome Foundation, and the Chinese porcelain purchased from Malcolm Macdonald, the Chancellor of Durham University between 1970 and 1981. Since then there have been further acquisitions by gift and purchase. The museum also regularly mounts temporary exhibitions and has a teaching function within the University. It is the only specific oriental museum in the country and has international standing. The other museum, known as the **Old Fulling Mill Museum**, is housed in a mill whose origins can be traced back to the fifteenth century, when there were two mills on the site, the Lead Mill and the Jesus Mill, both owned by the Cathedral Priory. It has housed the University's museum since 1975, although it had been the original home of a museum from its inception in 1834 until *c.*1870. In its early days the museum had a miscellany of unrelated artefacts, but it is now very much focused on Durham City and its immediate neighbourhood. Like the Oriental Museum, it has a teaching role within the University.

At JARROW, the **Bede's World** museum, unlike most others, does not house excavated artefacts but attempts to illustrate and elucidate the late seventh-century and early eighth-century world in which BEDE lived and worked by means of accurate models (indoors) and houses (outside), and also in a farm with plants and animals akin to those grown and reared at the time. More conventional is the **North of England Aircraft Museum** at Sunderland. It has been so named since 1979, but its origins go back to 1974, when a group of enthusiasts founded the North East Vintage and Veteran Aircraft Association. Its collection now numbers over thirty aeroplanes, including a Vulcan bomber and three items donated by the US Air Force. It is housed at Sunderland Airport, the former RAF Usworth. On a smaller scale is the **Tynemouth Volunteer Life Brigade Museum**. The Brigade was founded at the end of 1864 to assist HM Coastguards rescuing people from ships wrecked at the mouth of the Tyne (see TYNEMOUTH AND NORTH SHIELDS). The museum is in the Brigade's Watch House, built on the top of the cliff in 1887, and is still used as its headquarters and operations base.

MUSTARD

What is now called English Mustard was invented by a Mrs Clements around 1720 in her shop in Saddler Street in Durham City. Her idea was to grind mustard seed in a mill so as to separate the husk from the seed, which was then ground into a fine powder. As well as inventing the process, she popularised the product by acting as her own 'travelling salesman'. Such was her success that King George I is said to have been among her clients. Her process was inherited by her daughter, who married a local miller, Joseph Ainsley. They and their descendants continued to make mustard in Durham City until 1896. But Ainsleys failed to develop mustard making into a major industry in Durham: that took place in distant Norwich and became associated with the name Colman.

NATIONAL GLASS CENTRE

The National Glass Centre, built to an award-winning design, was opened in 1998 on the north bank of the Wear overlooking the river mouth. On the site of a former shipyard, it is a major part of the regeneration of SUNDERLAND's waterside in the post-industrial age. It was made possible by the support and financial backing of local bodies (Sunderland City Council and University, the North East Chamber of Commerce, Northern Arts, Tyne and Wear Development Corporation and One North East); of national bodies (the Arts Council, the Victoria and Albert Museum and the National Lottery); and of an international agency (the European Regional Development Fund).

Its siting in Sunderland is appropriate for two historical reasons. It is next door to St Peter's, Monkwearmouth, the church of the monastery founded in 674 by BENEDICT BISCOP, where he brought glassmakers from Gaul to make the glass for his church windows and to pass on their skills to native workers. Monkwearmouth, therefore, was probably the earliest site of English glassmaking. The second reason is Sunderland's more recent prowess in glassmaking, associated particularly with JAMES HARTLEY and PYREX.

The Centre has a variety of roles. One is to celebrate and record Sunderland's glass heritage and also to explain the nature and developing uses of glass: in these respects it acts as a museum. But it is more than that. It houses the Glass, Architectural Glass and Ceramics departments of the School of Art and Design of Sunderland University, whose St Peter's Campus is close by. In doing so, it not only celebrates the past but also promotes future glassmaking design and techniques. Similar aims are served by the Glass Studio, which offers facilities for resident artists as well as holding classes for those wanting to learn glassmaking techniques. And there is the Glass Gallery, where exhibitions are held and which runs 'outreach' programmes to stimulate and encourage interest in glassmaking in local schools.

If the NGC may be said to celebrate Wearside's place in the history of glassmaking within the region, Tyneside's role has recently acquired an unintended monument: the **Lemington High Cone**. Built in 1797 for the Northumberland Glass Company, it is thought to contain nearly two million bricks and is 115 feet high and 70 feet wide at its base. Although disused from the late nineteenth century, it remained intact and in 1976 was given Listed Building status. It was neglected, however, until the 1990s, when it was renovated and became fully exposed by the demolition of surrounding industrial plant. Like the ANGEL OF THE NORTH, it is visible to all who use the A1 road, standing proud on the north bank of the Tyne above the bridge over the river.

NEASHAM ABBEY

At Neasham, one of the most southerly villages in County Durham, a small nunnery was founded in the 1150s. It had the distinction of being the only independent monastic house, other than DURHAM CATHEDRAL Priory, to be founded in the county in the post-Conquest era. This was no accident: the Benedictine monks of Durham Cathedral Priory jealously sought to prevent any rival monastic house being founded in 'their' territory between Tyne and Tees. Neasham escaped, partly because it was small, far from Durham and for women; but also at that date it was in the WAPENTAKE OF SADBERGE, then part of the EARLDOM OF NORTHUMBRIA. Virtually nothing is known of its history, but it did survive until its closure along with other small monasteries in 1537. At that time it had a complement of seven nuns. Nothing remains of the Neasham nunnery, except for a fine stone cross from its church now in the Durham Cathedral Treasury.

NESCO (1889–1948)

In the late nineteenth and early twentieth centuries, the region led the way in the generation and use of electricity: by 1914 electric power was far more widely available on Tyneside than any other part of the country. This was substantially due to the Newcastle upon Tyne Electric Supply Co. (NESCO), founded in 1889 by THEODORE MERZ and ROBERT SPENCE WATSON. Another company, the Newcastle and District Lighting Co. (DISCO) was founded in the same year, but in the end was far less successful: by 1940 NESCO had over 300,000 customers compared with under 25,000 for DISCO.

NESCO also gained control of the electricity supply in Durham through its acquisition of the power stations of the British Electric Traction Co. and the Cleveland and Darlington County Electric Power Co. In consequence, in 1932 it changed its name to the North East Electric Supply Co., while retaining the name NESCO. It owed its success to several factors: the availability of cheap coal for its power stations; the presence on Tyneside of Parsons and Reyrolles, the world's leading designers and manufacturers of turbines and switch gear (see PARSONS, SIR CHARLES ALGERNON; REYROLLE, ALPHONSE CONSTANT); the guidance of CHARLES MERZ, the internationally renowned electricity consultant; and the quality of its management. In 1928 NESCO opened its new headquarters, Carliol House (named after a notable medieval merchant family) in Newcastle. This building is considered to be one of the outstanding pieces of architecture in the UK built during the inter-war years.

NESCO's independence ended in 1948, as did that of all other electricity supply companies, when the industry was nationalised.

NESFIELD, WILLIAM ANDREWS (1794–1881)

William Andrews Nesfield was renowned in his own day as a watercolour painter and landscape designer but, except in professional circles, this is now largely forgotten. In his early years, however, there were no signs that he would make his career out of these activities.

He was born at Chester le Street, where his father was a curate at the parish church. Four years later, the family moved to Durham City, and then following his mother's death in 1808, to Brancepeth, where his father had become rector. The following year, Nesfield entered the Royal Military College at Woolwich as a cadet. Two years later he passed out and became an Ensign (2nd Lieutenant) in the 95th Foot, in which he saw active service in the later stages of the Peninsular War. In 1814 he transferred to the 89th Foot and went with it to Canada, where he again was on active service in the brief war between Britain and the USA.

It was around this time that he developed his skills as a surveyor and as an artist. In 1816, having returned to Britain, he resigned from the army on half pay, ostensibly on the grounds of ill health, although his wish to devote himself to artistic activities was probably the real reason. Certainly, he began immediately to make a living as a watercolourist, becoming a member of the Old Water Colour Society and over the next thirty years exhibiting his work at their exhibitions. He became particularly noted for his depictions of waterfalls and cascades, probably influenced by what he had seen in North America, which would have included Niagara Falls. His reputation as an artist is indicated by the presence of his works in the Royal Collection, the Wallace Collection, the Victoria and Albert Museum and the British Museum.

In the 1830s, however, he increasingly devoted his time to garden and landscape design, in which his training as a surveyor was to stand him in good stead. Over the course of his career, he built up a highly successful practice, which he ran from his house in York Terrace, Regent's Park. He secured over 230 commissions, ranging from complete landscapes to small parterres. As well as commissions from the aristocracy, including the Duke of Northumberland, he was involved in remodelling royal parks such as Regent's Park and the grounds of Buckingham Palace, as well as the Royal Horticultural Society's gardens in South Kensington and Kew Garden. At the last, where he was in charge of landscape design, he was at loggerheads with the first Director, William Hooker. Despite this, he was responsible for the basic layout of the Gardens as we see them today, notably the vistas and avenues. These are now being restored to their original grandeur, testimony to recognition of Nesfield's genius.

NEVILLE FAMILY

The Nevilles were the most powerful and influential lay family in County Durham from the early fourteenth until the late sixteenth century. Despite their obviously French name, in the male line they were of English origin, a rare example of a pre-Conquest family to survive the Norman Conquest and retain possession of its property. The earliest notice we have of it is in a document dated 1131 or 1132 by which the Prior of Durham confirmed the estate of Staindrop and Staindropshire to a certain Dolphin son of Uhtred. The names may sound outlandish, but they had a distinguished pedigree in pre-Conquest Northumbria. The estate referred to comprised Staindrop and eleven neighbouring townships, including Raby, which was later converted into a park, at the centre of which a castle was built. Dolphin was succeeded by his son, who bore another distinguished Northumbrian name, Maldred. He, however, married a Norman woman, Joanna de Stuteville, and gave his sons French, not English, names. The oldest was Robert and it is with him that the Neville connection began.

Robert married Isabel de Neville, the sole heir of her brother, Henry (who died in 1227) and of their mother, Emma, the daughter and sole heir of Bertram de Bulmer. In marrying Isabel, Robert son of Maldred acquired the Bulmer estates, centred on Brancepeth in Durham and Sheriff Hutton and Raskelf in Yorkshire, and those of the Nevilles in Lincolnshire. Consequently, when Robert died *c.*1242, his son, Geoffrey, became owner of two very large estates in Durham (Raby and Brancepeth) as well as others in Yorkshire and Lincolnshire. He also adopted the name Neville, thus completing his family's transformation from English to Norman.

The Nevilles became increasingly prominent and influential in the fourteenth and fifteenth centuries, although the early years of the fourteenth century were not propitious. The head of the family, Rannulf de Neville, was in disgrace on account of his incest with his daughter, Anastasia, and consequently leadership of the family fell to his eldest son, Robert, known as the 'Peacock of the North'. Just before Christmas 1318, in a scuffle on Framwellgate Bridge in Durham, Robert murdered Richard Fitz Marmaduke, head of the only other family capable of challenging the Nevilles in the county. Luckily for the Nevilles, they got away with both crimes: Rannulf died shortly after the murder, and six months later Robert was killed in a Border skirmish. Leadership of the Neville interest now passed to Robert's younger brother, Ralph, a man of much greater ability than either his father or his brother. Meanwhile the death of Rannulf's mother brought the Nevilles yet another estate, that centred on Middleham in North Yorkshire.

Ralph (d.1367) and his son, John (d.1388), were notable defenders of the Border against the Scots, Ralph being one of the commanders of the English army at the BATTLE OF NEVILLE'S CROSS. Both were benefactors of DURHAM CATHEDRAL, paying for the screen that bears their name and separates the high altar from the feretory where ST CUTHBERT was buried. As a reward they too were buried in the cathedral, their mutilated tombs still to be seen in the south aisle of the nave. But it was John's son, Ralph, who engineered the great upward shift in the family's fortunes.

Ralph de Neville was an active supporter of Richard II, who rewarded him in 1397 with the title of Earl of Westmorland. This did not buy continued loyalty: two years later Neville was among the group of northern nobles who backed Henry of Bolingbroke's successful *coup d'état* that overthrew Richard II and put him on the throne as Henry IV. Richard II and Bolingbroke were cousins, their respective fathers being Edward the Black Prince and John of Gaunt, Duke of Lancaster, the first and third sons of Edward III. Neville's change of allegiance to Bolingbroke was the consequence of his second marriage in 1396 to Joan Beaufort, John of Gaunt's daughter by his long-time mistress and eventual third wife, Katherine Swynford. Neville's second wife was therefore a half-sister of the new king. The close friendship of Henry IV and Ralph Neville was confirmed in the early years of the reign by the crucial part Neville played in defeating the revolts of the PERCY FAMILY in 1403 and 1405.

Between 1396 and his death in 1425, Ralph Neville and his second wife had fourteen children. This is in itself remarkable, but even more so is the way Neville used them in successfully manipulating the marriage market. For his eldest son, Richard, he secured the greatest heiress of the day, Alice Montagu, the only child of the Earl of Salisbury: the bargain came good in 1429, when Richard Neville succeeded to that title. Three other sons did almost as well, through marriage becoming Lord Fauconberg, Lord Latimer and Lord Abergavenny, while another son, Robert, became Bishop of Durham (1438–56). And he was equally successful with his daughters, securing for three of them marriage to the Duke of Buckingham, the Earl of Northumberland and the Viscount Beaumont. The greatest prize, however, went to Cecily, known as the 'Rose of Raby', who became the wife of Richard Plantagenet, Duke of York and the mother of two kings, Edward IV and Richard III.

Ralph Neville died in 1425 and was buried in Staindrop church. He had been probably the most successful marriage arranger in the history of the English aristocracy. But the sting was in the tail. Contrary to all the norms of inheritance, he virtually disinherited his rightful heir, his grandson, Ralph, the son of his eldest son (who died in 1420) by his first wife, Margaret Stafford. All he left him was the title, Earl of Westmorland, which he could not legally deny him, and the Brancepeth estate. All his other properties he bequeathed to his eldest son by his second marriage, Richard Neville, the future Earl of Salisbury. Naturally, Ralph, 2nd Earl of Westmorland contested this outrageous settlement, but with very little success: all he gained (in 1443) was Raby, the other Durham estate, following the death of his stepmother, Joan Beaufort.

As a result of the 1st Earl's actions, there were now two Neville families, but only the senior but poorer branch were settled in the

North East. The junior branch rose higher still and then suffered almost complete destruction. Richard, Earl of Salisbury proved himself to be as good as his father in finding a fortune for his eldest son, also Richard. This came in the person of Anne Beauchamp, heiress of the Earl of Warwick, which in due time passed to Richard Neville. He earned himself the sobriquet 'Warwick the Kingmaker', by his part in helping his aunt Cecily's son, Edward, depose the ineffectual Henry VI and become Edward IV in 1461. Ten years later, however, Edward IV and Warwick fell out. Warwick rebelled and tried to reinstate Henry VI, but was killed in battle at Barnet outside London. As he had no male heir, his line came to an end. And the other sons of the 1st Earl of Westmorland also failed to establish durable families, except for Edward, whose descendant is the Marquess of Abergavenny.

The senior branch with its main bases in County Durham lasted just under one hundred years longer. The 2nd Earl of Westmorland lived a long life, not dying until 1484. Neither he nor his successors regained any of the estates the 1st Earl had bestowed on his eldest son of his second marriage, but through service to the Crown and judicious marriages they greatly enhanced their fortune. The line, however, was brought to an end by Charles Neville, 6th Earl of Westmorland through his participation in the disastrous Rising of the Northern Earls against Elizabeth I in 1569. Although Neville managed to escape abroad, he was never reconciled with Elizabeth and died at Nieuport in Flanders on 16 November 1601. Since he and his countess had no children, the line became extinct and his estates reverted to the Crown.

NEVILLE'S CROSS, BATTLE OF, 1346

Neville's Cross, fought on the western outskirts of Durham on 17 October 1346, was one of the major battles in the Anglo-Scottish war that lasted from 1296 until 1603. It was a disaster for the Scots: the earls of Moray and Strathearn, the Marshal and Constable of their army, and two of the leading members of the Scottish government, the Chancellor and the Chamberlain, were killed, while their king, David II, four more earls and at least twenty barons were captured.

The context was Edward III of England's invasion of France in the summer of 1346 in pursuit of his claim to the French throne. This brief campaign culminated in his complete victory over the French army at Crécy on 26 August. He then commenced the siege of Calais, which fell to him eleven months later and was to remain an English possession until 1558. Before embarking for France, however, Edward commissioned the Archbishop of York, William de la Zouche, to organise the defence of his northern frontier.

David's decision to invade England was driven by a miscellany of considerations: the urgent request of the French king, Philippe VI, under whose protection he had lived between 1333 and 1341; the desire to emulate the military feats of his father, Robert I; the recovery of the parts of his kingdom still in English hands; and the hope that victory would force Edward III to accept him as the rightful and independent King of Scots.

Drawn from most parts of his kingdom, David's army would have been of considerable size. It entered England on 7 October by the western border, forced Carlisle to pay tribute and then proceeded eastwards along the line of the present A69 as far as Corbridge. Turning south, he reached the outskirts of Durham on the 16th, setting up camp in the Prior of Durham's park at Beaurepaire. Meanwhile, anticipating David's move, the Archbishop of York and the leading nobility of northern England, chief of whom were Ralph, Lord Neville and Henry, Lord Percy, mustered their army at Richmond. Evidence suggests that it numbered about 6,000 men. It advanced via Easby, reaching the Bishop of Durham's park next to AUCKLAND CASTLE as the Scots were arriving at Beaurepaire. At this point it seems likely that, while the English knew where the Scots were, the Scots were completely unaware that an English army was in the vicinity.

First contact was made near Ferryhill by William, Lord Douglas and a Scottish foraging party, which ran into the van of the English army as it advanced from BISHOP AUCKLAND. A running fight ensued as far as Sunderland Bridge, ending with the surviving Scots streaming back to camp with the alarming news. The Scottish army was immediately drawn up in battle formation on Beaurepaire Moor (now Arbour House Farm), just to the north of the River Browney and west of the present A167.

After several hours' stand-off, the Scots launched their attack at around 2 p.m. Thereafter, although the exact course of events is not clear, three facts seem to emerge. One is that the English archers, who had become Europe's most successful battle winners, appear not to have played the decisive role they did on other occasions. Consequently, the battle became a mêlée of hand-to-hand combat. Perhaps most crucial was the decision by the king's cousin, Robert the Steward, and Patrick, Earl of March, the commanders of the rearguard, to pull out of the battle and make their escape. The effect of this was to end Scottish resistance, probably at around 5 p.m., and turn the battle into a rout.

The consequence of the battle was a generation of Scottish debility. David II remained a captive in England until 1357, and then until his death in 1371 was saddled with an enormous ransom that crippled the Scottish Crown's finances. The English asserted control over southern Scotland, thereby creating a buffer zone that was to last until the 1370s.

Close to the junction of the A167 and A690 on the western outskirts of Durham City the base of a medieval cross is still extant. This cross, or probably an earlier version, already stood near this spot before the battle, one of at least three crosses on roads in and out of the town. Its name proclaims the fact that a few yards west and below the ridge on which it stands, the road (now A690) out of Durham crossed the River Browney and entered the great Neville estate centred on Brancepeth Castle. Although a more magnificent cross, probably paid for by Ralph Neville as a memorial, replaced the one already there, it may be argued that the cross gave its name to the battle, not vice versa.

NEWALL, ROBERT STIRLING (1812–1889)

Robert Newall was born in Dundee. On leaving school he commenced a mercantile career, initially with his father, and then with a London merchant, for whom he spent two years in the USA. In 1840 he founded, with two partners, a works in GATESHEAD to manufacture wire ropes. Having become aware that such things were used in German coal mines, he went to Germany to study them. Back in Britain, he developed his own manufacturing process, which he patented in 1840. Although the ropes were initially made for use in mines, Newall used his wire rope to make a submarine cable. This comprised a copper core, insulated in gutta-percha and encased in wire rope. His mining experience also enabled him to devise an effective machine for paying out the cable from the stern of a cable laying ship. Throughout most of the 1850s Newall had a monopoly of the manufacture of submarine cables. In the early 1860s, however, having made his fortune, he withdrew from the business in order to devote himself to astronomy, a passion he shared with HUGH LEE PATTINSON, whose daughter he married. In 1862 he bought enough high-quality glass at the London exhibition of that year to make a 25-inch lens. This was then fitted to a telescope 32 feet long and weighing 9 tons by the famous York telescope maker, Thomas Cooke. When complete, it was erected at Newall's Gateshead home, Ferndene. On Newall's death, it was given to Cambridge University.

NEWBURN, BATTLE OF, 1640

The Battle of Newburn took place on 28 August 1640. It was, however, hardly worthy of this designation (at the time it was described as a 'scremedge') since it was a brief and one-sided affair. On the north side of the Tyne seeking to cross by the ford was a large Scottish army that had crossed the Tweed at Coldstream eight days previously; opposing it on the south side of the river was an English force with very little resolution. The 'battle' began with a Scottish bombardment followed by a crossing by a portion of their troops, whereupon the English broke and fled. Two days later, the Scottish troops occupied Newcastle.

But the battle had significance out of all proportion to its size and duration. It was the culmination of the attempt by Charles I, begun in the winter of 1637–38, to impose his version of the Prayer Book on the church in Scotland. This precipitated a revolution in Scotland which had the support of a broad cross-section of the population. To defend itself, the revolutionary government, known as the Covenanters, raised an army. Although the colonels of its regiments were noblemen, many of the other officers were men with serious military experience gained in the war then raging on the continent, including its commander Alexander Leslie (soon to be Earl of Leven), who had been a Field Marshal in the Swedish army. In contrast, Charles I had the utmost difficulty in raising troops and the money to pay them.

The consequences were profound. On 26 October Charles I signed the Treaty of Ripon allowing the Scottish army to occupy the six northern counties of England and receive £850 a day expenses until a settlement was agreed. This did not take place until the following June. Arguably, the victory at Newburn secured the revolution in Scotland. But the battle was equally a prelude to revolution and civil war in England. Charles I could no longer govern without calling a parliament, something he had avoided doing since 1629, except for a very brief period in 1640. The election produced what has come to be known as the Long Parliament, the majority in which forced on the king fundamental changes in the government of England. A year later, Charles began the war to recover his authority, which led to his deposition and execution and the setting up of a republic.

NEWCASTLE BROWN ALE

Newcastle Brown Ale is the region's most famous alcoholic product. Created in 1923 by a man with an appropriate name, Colonel James Porter, it gained an immediate reputation through the award of a gold medal at the International Brewers' Exhibition of 1928. It rapidly became a favourite in the North East, but its reputation and popularity became more widespread after the merger in 1960 of Newcastle Breweries Ltd with Scottish Brewers to form Scottish and Newcastle Breweries. By the 1990s it was the best-selling bottled beer in Britain and Europe and was penetrating markets further afield. Alas, despite its name, it is no longer brewed in Newcastle.

NEWCASTLE DISEASE

'Newcastle Disease' is the name sometimes given to Fowl Pest because the virus was first identified in Newcastle in 1926.

NEWCASTLE LEAD CRYSTAL (see BEILBY, WILLIAM, RALPH and MARY)

NEWCASTLE PROGRAMME

The so-called 'Newcastle Programme' was the set of policies adopted by the National Liberal Association at its annual conference held in the Theatre Royal, Newcastle in October 1891. Later described by Roy Jenkins as 'a capacious rag bag', it was born of the political crisis that arose from the effort in 1885 of the Prime Minister, William Gladstone, to force through the bill granting Home Rule to Ireland. The bill convulsed the Liberal Party and was defeated in the Commons, thanks to a large number of Liberal MPs voting with the opposition.

The consequence was more serious: the desertion of most of the party's aristocratic leaders and a large contingent of its wealthiest middle-class members. The effect, it has been argued, was to turn the Liberals into a radical party, a notion confirmed by the Programme, which included, in addition to Home Rule for Ireland, the disestablishment of the church in Wales and Scotland, triennial parliaments, payment of MPs, employers' liability for industrial accidents, and elected parish, rural district and urban district councils. It is also argued that this ushered in a fundamental political shift: instead of the political divide being vertical, with both parties receiving support from all levels of society, it became horizontal, along class lines. If true, the 'Newcastle Programme' was a significant milestone in the evolution of politics in Britain.

NEWCASTLE UPON TYNE

The history of Newcastle upon Tyne falls, roughly, into two periods: the medieval, from its origins until 1835; and the modern, from 1835 onwards.

Medieval: The origin of Newcastle can be dated with some precision. In the summer of 1080, as he returned from a military expedition into Scotland, Robert, eldest son of William the Conqueror, built a new castle on the north bank of the Tyne, from which the city got its name. His action was part of the suppression of a Northumbrian rebellion that had involved the murder of Walcher, bishop of Durham, at GATESHEAD on 14 May. The castle, which would have been made of wood, was located within the ruins of the Roman fort of Pons Aelius, built to guard the bridge over the Tyne immediately below it. What is unclear is whether there was a settlement of any sort nearby. A hint that there was is contained in references to Monkchester. The *chester* element is the English corruption of the Latin *castra* (fort); *monk*, which indicates monastic possession, may mean that it had belonged to the monastery at TYNEMOUTH, destroyed by Viking raiders in the ninth century. The boundaries of Monkchester, and by implication those of Newcastle, are tentatively identified by those of the surrounding townships of Elswick, Fenham, Gosforth, Jesmond and Byker, whose pre-Conquest English names point to their being in existence in 1080.

What happened in the years immediately following the building of the castle is obscure. But at some time in the course of his reign, Henry I (1100–35) founded a borough immediately to the north of the castle. This occurred about the time BISHOP RANNULF FLAMBARD founded the borough of Durham around the Market Place. It is probably more than a coincidence that both these newly founded boroughs were given a parish church dedicated to St Nicholas, then a popular saint, whose relics had recently been stolen from Myra in Asia Minor (now Turkey) and brought to Bari in Italy. However, nothing is known of the borough of Newcastle until 1158, when Henry II granted to its burgesses a charter setting out their rights and privileges. Its growth would seem to have been rapid. In the reign of King John (1199–1216), the records of a tax imposed in 1205 show that Newcastle paid £158, not far short of the £175 owed by York, a much older and at that date more important town. Further evidence is John's decision between 1205 and 1213 to double the rent (from £50 to £100) paid by the townsmen and known as the 'farm of the borough'. What the burgesses of Newcastle had negotiated was the privilege of paying annually to the Crown the agreed fixed sum of money in return for which they retained in their own treasury all the rents and dues arising in the borough, an arrangement that gave the Crown an assured income, while giving the burgesses considerable control over their own lives and, hopefully, an annual profit.

'Farming the borough' was the first stage in a struggle in which most boroughs engaged to gain even greater control over their affairs, in particular freeing themselves from the clutches of the king's officers, the borough bailiff and the county sheriff. At Newcastle, the next advance was achieved in 1251, when the burgesses secured the right to elect a mayor, five bailiffs and a coroner. Then in 1333 Edward III decreed that the mayor should be *ex officio* the king's escheator, the officer responsible for administering any property that came into the hands of the Crown. Finally, in 1400, Newcastle became a county, separate from Northumberland. Its governing body comprised a mayor and six aldermen (who were to be justices of the peace), an elected council and a sheriff. The Sheriff of Northumberland's authority was confined to the castle and its adjacent land, the Castle Garth. It was a measure of the importance of Newcastle that it was only the fourth borough to achieve county status after London (1121), Bristol (1373) and York (1396). Meanwhile, in 1299, Edward I had granted to Newcastle the township of Pandon within the lordship of Byker, and in 1353 his grandson, Edward III, assigned control over the land adjacent to the town, then called Castle Field and Castle Moor, now the Town Moor. Newcastle's territory was now that of the previous Monkchester.

However, this evolution was far from inevitable and without strife. The Crown may have granted land and powers, but it did not relinquish ultimate control. During the middle years of the century a power struggle within the town between the wealthiest burgesses, organised as the Company of Merchant Adventurers (the Drapers, the Mercers and the Boothmen or corn merchants), and the members of twelve other trade and craft guilds became so violent that it provoked Crown intervention. The outcome was a complex form of election that appeared to give some power to the poorer burgesses while allowing it to remain in the hands of the Merchant Adventurers. The final scheme of government before the Municipal Reform Act of 1835 was embodied in the Great Charter issued to the town in 1600. By its terms, the power to make by-laws and manage all the borough's property and finances was vested in a mayor, ten aldermen, a sheriff and twenty-four councillors, all elected annually, but again by a convoluted arrangement that ensured that power continued in the hands of a small wealthy oligarchy.

This political oligarchy was also the economic oligarchy, the members of the Company of Merchant Adventurers and the Company of Hostmen. This latter group developed in the course of the sixteenth century and secured in 1600 by the terms of its incorporation complete control of the coal trade. At that date, it numbered forty-eight, all but ten of whom were also Merchant Adventurers. The economic power of this small group of men was based upon trade. The major exports were grindstones, coal, hides and wool. As regards the last, in the middle years of the fourteenth century the government imposed regulations on the trade, requiring wool to be exported through specified ports to facilitate the collection of customs duty. From 1363 this port was normally Calais, and the business was placed in the hands of a corporation of twenty-six merchants known as the Company of Merchants of the Staple. The one notable exception to this was the wool of the four northern counties, which was considered to be of inferior quality. This was to be shipped out of Newcastle, which in effect was for northern England what Calais was for the country to the south. The main imports were iron from Spain, wine and salt from France, wine from Germany and sawn timber from the Baltic.

Commercial growth led to an important physical development, the creation of the Quayside downstream of the bridge and the Lort Burn. Previously, ships came in on the high tide, became beached as the tide dropped and then refloated as the tide rose. The solution, which allowed ships to remain afloat at all stages of the tide, was put in place during the thirteenth century. It involved dumping in the river an immense quantity of material brought in for the purpose and held in place by a retaining wall. On the platform this created were built the narrow streets known as the chares that run at right angles to the river, and also a section of the town wall. By shifting the river's edge many yards into the stream, the surface area of the town was increased by over 10 per cent. Above the bridge, private individuals carried out a similar development in what is called the Close. Local trade also had its topographical consequences in the series of markets extending from just north of St Nicholas's Church to Newgate next to St Andrew's Chapel. This market sector had a characteristic shape, wide at its southern end (there were no buildings between the Groat Market and the Cloth Market), gradually narrowing towards Newgate.

Newcastle's commercial success rested upon its claim to a monopoly of the trade of the Tyne. The origin of the claim is obscure, but its extent was not: the port of Newcastle was deemed to extend from 'Sparhawk to Hedwin Streams', that is, from its mouth to Newburn. Newcastle's ability to sustain its exalted position depended upon royal support. This the Crown gave, recognising the value of the town's tax yield and its crucial importance to the defence of the realm against the Scots. Crown backing in the late thirteenth century enabled Newcastle to thwart the attempt by Tynemouth Priory (see TYNEMOUTH AND NORTH SHIELDS) to develop North Shields as a rival port. The other competitor was Gateshead. Although this belonged to the powerful bishops of Durham, they were generally absent from their diocese for long periods and not interested in mounting an economic challenge to Newcastle. Newcastle's fear of Gateshead's potential threat to its commercial activity is clearly revealed in the attempt, which almost succeeded, in the reign of Mary I (1553–8) to annex its cross-Tyne neighbour at a time when the diocese of Durham was in abeyance.

Newcastle's military importance was enhanced by the development and modernisation of the castle in the twelfth and thirteenth centuries. Curtain walls were built in stone; between 1168 and 1176 a stone keep measuring 62 feet by 56 feet and conforming to the highest contemporary standards was erected at a cost of £1,144; and between 1247 and 1250 a complex barbican (now known as the Black Gate, not because of its colour, but because it was owned and occupied for a time by a Patrick Black and his wife Barbara) was added as a more highly protected gateway. The Crown also sanctioned, but did not pay for, the building of the town walls. They were erected between *c.*1260 and *c.*1360 at the town's expense, and covered a length of two miles. Twenty feet high and up to ten feet thick, they had six towered gates and were strengthened at intervals by eighteen towers; and to compound an attacker's problem, they were fronted by a deep ditch. The only occasion on which these defences were overcome was during the Scottish siege of 1647, by which date cannon had made stone walls vulnerable.

Newcastle's military and commercial importance was not matched by equal ecclesiastical status. Until the nineteenth century, it had no cathedral, the diocesan centre being located at Durham, fifteen miles to the south. Nor did it have a major abbey, its only monastic house being the nunnery of St Bartholomew, which occupied a considerable area of land south of what is now Blackett Street. Founded in the twelfth century, its main role was to provide a safe and comfortable home for the unmarried daughters of the wealthier burgesses. When it closed in 1537, it housed eleven nuns. Following its suppression, its grounds (and those of the nearby Franciscan friary) were bought by Henry Anderson, who built on them a large mansion, which he called the 'Newe House', later known as Anderson Place.

The spiritual welfare of the town's population rested with the clergy of the parish church of St Nicholas, adjacent to the castle, and of its three chapels of ease: St Andrew in Gallowgate, St John in Westgate and All Saints near Pilgrim Street. There were, however, up to fifteen other small chapels without parochial status. In the thirteenth century, spiritual welfare provision was boosted by the arrival of the newly founded mendicant orders of friars. The friars concentrated primarily on urban locations and it was therefore a measure of its size and importance that all the mendicant orders settled in Newcastle: the Dominicans (Black Friars) close to St Andrew's chapel; the Franciscans (Grey Friars) in Pilgrim Street; the Augustinians (the Austin Hermits) near the Holy Jesus Hospital; and the Carmelites (White Friars) between the west wall and modern Orchard Street. Originally, the Carmelites had settled in Pandon, but in 1307 they moved across town to allow the town wall to be built through their grounds. Their new home by the west wall was previously occupied by a small order, the Friars of the Sack, which was suppressed by the papacy. Subsequently, in 1360 another small order, the Trinitarians, occupied the old Carmelite site near the Pandon Gate. When the friaries were closed down in the reign of Henry VIII, there were nearly fifty friars still operating in the town.

Welfare was provided by hospitals, all of which were ecclesiastical institutions run by men in holy orders. Twelve have been identified in Newcastle, but not all existed at the same time: their dates of foundation ranged from the early twelfth to the late fifteenth century. The earliest was that dedicated to St Mary Magdalene, founded at Barras Bridge by Henry I (1100–35); the latest was that founded in 1495 by a burgess, Christopher Brigham. St Mary the Virgin (known as the West Spital) in West Gate was the largest and wealthiest of Newcastle's hospitals, with property and land in seventeen places in Newcastle, Northumberland and Durham. Another prominent hospital was the Maison Dieu, founded on the Sandhill in 1412 by the famous Newcastle merchant Roger Thornton. Apart from the Magdalene, which was originally intended for lepers (hence its location well away from the town) the purpose of the hospitals was to cater for travellers and the poor of the town.

The latest important medieval institution to be founded was Trinity House. The date of origin of the 'Guild and Fraternity of Seamen and Mariners dedicated to the Blessed Trinity' is not certain, but was probably 1492. In 1505 it purchased a tenement in Broad Chare in order to build an assembly hall, a chapel and an almshouse for its elderly members. It was a fairly typical parish guild formed to safeguard the professional standing and the material and spiritual welfare of its members. In 1536, however, its status was enhanced by a Crown grant of a charter of incorporation, which imposed on it responsibility for maintaining two lights at North Shields as navigation aids to ships entering the Tyne. In 1584 and 1606 its function was enlarged, so that it became responsible for pilotage and buoyage, as well as lights, in the port, with powers to levy tolls on shipping to finance these purposes and also to support twelve poor members. Its authority was not confined to the Tyne, but extended from Blyth to Whitby. The present building is extremely complex, being the result of many reconstructions, alterations and additions.

Modern: Modern Newcastle may be said to have begun in 1835. The new era was launched by the Municipal Reform Act, which affected all ancient boroughs and which came into force in that year. Its provisions altered the character of the town in two fundamental ways. The first was that Newcastle was physically enlarged by the addition of the neighbouring townships of Westgate and Elswick to the east and Jesmond, Heaton and Byker to the west, the first of four expansions. More radical was the revised structure of the town's government. This comprised a Council of forty-two members elected for three years by ratepaying householders, with a third of the seats being subject to election each year. The Council was to choose fourteen of its number to be Aldermen, who were to serve for six years, and a Mayor, to hold office for one year. No longer was the town controlled by a small, self-perpetuating oligarchy, but by a body elected on a much wider and more logical franchise, the nature of which was dictated, and would henceforth be dictated, by national government according to national considerations.

The year 1835 also saw the start of the major redevelopment scheme undertaken by the Town Clerk, JOHN CLAYTON, and his associate, the builder RICHARD GRAINGER, using the twelve-acre site of Anderson Place, which Grainger bought for £50,000. The result was Grey Street, Grainger Street and Clayton Street and the linking roads, Hood Street, Market Street, Nun Street, Nelson Street and Shakespeare Street. What they created is considered to be one of the finest nineteenth-century town centres in Europe. It is rightly famous, but unfortunately its reputation has served to overshadow the earlier achievement of Nathaniel Clayton (John Clayton's father and predecessor as Town Clerk), Alderman Mosley, and the architect and builder DAVID STEPHENSON, who in the 1780s filled in the noisome Lort Burn and created Dean Street and Mosley Street. The development of Anderson Place, therefore, should be seen as extending and completing the earlier scheme. Also by 1835 Northumberland Street and Percy Street had been laid out north of the walls, converging at Barras Bridge. These developments had the effect of removing the heart of Newcastle away from the river.

The coming of the railway in the 1840s not only put Newcastle on the main east coast line, it also considerably enhanced the town architecturally: the train shed of the Central Station and its fore buildings and *porte cochère* are among the finest examples of railway architecture in the country.

The debit side of growth and modernisation was the loss of some of Newcastle's medieval inheritance. Much of the wall and all its gates were demolished. Fortunately, the most important parts of the castle, the keep and the Black Gate, were saved, bought by the Council in, respectively, 1810 and 1823. The former, no longer needed as a gaol, was renovated, not entirely accurately, and opened up to the public. The latter was eventually sold in 1883 to the Society of Antiquaries (see Literary and Philosophical Society of Newcastle upon Tyne), which restored it as its museum. Between these two events, the good work was spoilt by the Newcastle and Berwick Railway, which was permitted to build a viaduct between the keep and the Black Gate in 1848. This viaduct, however, did much to hasten the clearance of the squalid and insalubrious properties that had enveloped the Castle Garth. All the medieval hospitals and friaries disappeared, except that of the Dominicans (Black Friars), the claustral buildings of which were saved through their use by the town's guilds. The parish church and two of its chapels have retained their medieval fabric, but All Saints was entirely replaced between 1786 and 1796 by David Stephenson.

Newcastle is generally seen as an industrial town, but to a considerable extent this is a misconception. In fact, only one major industrial enterprise arose within its original boundaries, the locomotive works of Robert Stephenson and Hawthorn. Three other major manufacturing enterprises developed in townships added to the town in 1835 and later: Armstongs in Elswick and Walker, Parsons in Heaton, and Malings in Walker. Building outside the ancient boundaries is partially explained by the fact that much of the land within them, namely the Town Moor and Nuns Moor (acquired *c.*1650), were denied to industrial (and domestic) expansion by an act of parliament of 1774, which, while vesting ownership in the Council, reserved grazing rights in perpetuity to resident freemen. Rather than an industrial town, Newcastle should perhaps more correctly be seen as the commercial hub of industrial Tyneside.

Newcastle also lost its monopoly control of the Tyne. The Tyne Improvement Act of 1850 set up a Commission on which, in addition to members from Newcastle, Gateshead, South Shields and Tynemouth had Admiralty representatives. Contrary to fears, this proved beneficial: the river was deepened by dredging, and rocks and sandbanks at the mouth were removed, while the building of the Northumberland Dock in 1857, the Tyne Dock in 1859 and the Albert Edward Dock in 1884 created a modern port that brought prosperity to all sectors of the river. Also in 1884 the Tyne Commission took over the duties performed by Trinity House.

In the nineteenth century, Newcastle at last became a major ecclesiastical centre, with two cathedrals, though neither was built as such. Between 1842 and 1844 the growing Roman Catholic population built a new church, designed by Augustus Pugin, opposite the Central Station. Six years later, in 1850, it became the cathedral of the newly created diocese of Hexham and Newcastle, and in 1872 it acquired its slender spire that rises to 222 feet (67.7 m). At the same time, the Church of England, faced with providing for a rapidly rising population, was considering the division of its ancient dioceses. For various political reasons, it was not until 1882 that the diocese of Durham was split along county lines into the dioceses of Durham and Newcastle. The Church of England did not build a new cathedral for its new diocese, but converted the parish church of St Nicholas.

The twentieth century prior to the end of World War II saw a certain amount of change, notably the extension of the city in 1904 and 1935. In the former year, Benwell, Fenham, part of Kenton and Walker were brought within the city's boundaries, and in the latter year, Denton, Kenton and Benton were added. But it was in the second half of the century that radical change occurred. The earliest was the mutilation of the city centre by the Central Motor Way in the interests of vehicular traffic. This was carried out without much concern on the part of the planners for what was being destroyed, most notably the Royal Arcade and most of Eldon Square. Accompanying this was the demolition of old housing, much of it replaced by high-rise flats, and the insertion in the city centre of Brutalist office blocks. These developments are closely associated with the name of T. Dan Smith.

Then in 1974, as part of the national revision of local government and structures, the city absorbed the Urban Districts of Newburn and Gosforth, almost doubling its area. The enlarged Newcastle was one of five Metropolitan Districts within the newly created Metropolitan County of Tyne and Wear, an arrangement that lasted until 1986, when the Tyne and Wear County Council was abolished, leaving Newcastle as a 'unitary authority'. During these same years, the approach to redevelopment became more sensitive to the inhertance from past centuries. As the Tyne's commercial functions became concentrated close to the river mouth, the Quayside became derelict. This led in the 1980s to excavations that revealed its origins, preservation of its quality buildings and replacement of decayed properties with buildings of architectural merit. The consequence was to give new, but different, life to the area. The conservation programme also included the exposure and presentation of such stretches of the city wall that had escaped demolition and, in less spectacular fashion, the refurbishment of older housing stock.

One major compensation for the demise of earlier industrial and commercial activities has been the expansion of higher education (see Universities). The University of Newcastle upon Tyne became an independent body after its severance from Durham University in 1963, and Newcastle Polytechnic became the University of Northumbria in 1992. In 2009 these institutions between them had 46,000 students, full-time and part-time, undergraduate and postgraduate, from all over the world. Consequently, the two universities are major employers and important to the economy of Newcastle.

NEWMINSTER ABBEY

Newminster was the only Cistercian (from the name of the original monastery at Citeaux, the Latin for which was *Cistercia*) monastery founded in the region. Although the Cistercians, like the traditional Benedictine monks, observed the Rule of St Benedict, they differed in several respects: laying greater emphasis on poverty and austerity (for example, making their habits of undyed cloth, hence their name, the White Monks); concentrating exclusively on worship, leaving the manual work of the monastery to 'lay brothers'; locating in waste places and refusing gifts of tenanted land and parish churches; and imposing a tight organisation with a rigid inspection system and ultimate authority vested in the Abbot of Citeaux.

The Cistercian style rapidly became hugely popular throughout Europe in the first half of the twelfth century. The first house in England was founded in 1129 at Waverley in Surrey. Newminster came only nine years later, founded in 1138 by twelve monks, sent from Fountains Abbey in Yorkshire under the leadership of one Robert. Although not formally canonised, Robert subsequently became known as St Robert of Newminster. The initiative, however, came from Ralph de Merlay, lord of MORPETH, who was deeply impressed by what he saw during a visit to Fountains. The site for the new monastery de Merlay provided lay in the valley of the Wansbeck about a mile west of his castle and borough of Morpeth. Its success was rapid, so much so that before 1150 groups of Newminster monks had been sent out to start new houses at Pipewell in Northamptonshire and Sallay (now Sawley) and Roche in Yorkshire.

In the course of time Newminster, like all other Cistercian houses, broke its own rules by acquiring tenanted land and, in the fourteenth century, the churches of Hartburn, Stannington and Kirkwhelpington, partly as a result of declining zeal, and partly through poverty caused by the ravages of war after 1300. Like Cistercian houses everywhere, Newminster created farms known as granges, worked by 'lay brothers', at Ulgham, Heighley, West Ritton, Sturton, Newton and Kidland.

When Newminster was closed in 1537 in the first wave of dissolutions, there were then fifteen monks in residence. Only fragments of what was once a monastery of some size and substance now remain.

NEWSPAPERS

Currently, fourteen newspapers are published in the North East, five of them daily. Two are morning papers: *The Journal*, published in NEWCASTLE, and *The Northern Echo*, published in DARLINGTON. In addition, there are four evening papers: the *Newcastle Chronicle*, the *Sunderland Echo*, the *Hartlepool Mail* and the (*South*) *Shields Gazette*, the last claiming to be the oldest provincial evening paper. The two morning papers are serious alternatives to the more obviously national papers in that they cover national and international news as well as regional and local matters. Consequently, their circulation extends beyond the region. Complementing them are the eight weekly newspapers: *Berwick Advertiser, Northumberland Gazette* (Alnwick), *Morpeth Herald, Hexham Courant, Durham Times, Darlington and Stockton Times, Teesdale Mercury* and *Weardale Mercury*. These deal with local matters and by definition have a geographically restricted circulation.

These fourteen papers are a small residue of over 100 newspapers launched in the region during the second half of the nineteenth century. Before 1800 the only papers published in the region were the *Newcastle Courant* (1711–1876; the earliest newspaper north of the Trent), the *Newcastle Journal* (1739–1788), the *Newcastle Chronicle* (1764) and the *Newcastle Advertiser* (1788–1814). All were weekly publications, as were the papers launched in the first third of the nineteenth century: the *Tyne Mercury* (1802), the *Durham County Advertiser* (1814), the *Durham Chronicle* (1820), the *Sunderland Herald* (1831) and the *Newcastle Journal* (1832). The newspaper revolution in the second half of the nineteenth century was the consequence of a variety of fiscal, technological and political changes. Between 1853 and 1861 'the taxes on knowledge', as their opponents dubbed them, were scrapped, as were the tax on advertisements in 1853, the tax on paper in 1861, and stamp duty in 1855. These were followed by radical developments in printing technology, culminating in the 'Linotype' machine invented in America in 1886. These financial and technical changes made it possible to publish newspapers daily and to sell them for as little as ½d. or 1d. Other influences were the speed with which news could be gathered by means of the railway and the electric telegraph; the extensions of the franchise in 1867 and 1884, which turned working-class males into voters whose political commitment had to be cultivated; and the spread of literacy, helped by the imposition of compulsory elementary education in 1870.

In this revolution the North East had a number of 'firsts': the *Northern Echo* (morning) and *Shields Gazette* (evening) were the first papers to be sold at ½d., while the *Newcastle Daily Chronicle* was the first to be printed on a 'Linotype' machine. All newspapers were political advocates, in the majority of cases in support of the Liberal Party. Most of them, however, were short-lived; by 1910 only thirty had managed to survive. Since then the shrinkage has continued, often as the result of amalgamation, and some have become free advertising publications. An example of both developments is the *Durham County Advertiser*, which absorbed the *Durham Chronicle*, the *Consett Chronicle* and the *Auckland Chronicle* and is now a weekly free paper.

The region also has one Sunday newspaper, the *Sunday Sun*, published by the firm that owns *The Journal* and the *Newcastle Evening Chronicle*.

NEWTON, WILLIAM (1730–1798)

William Newton, the son of a Newcastle shipwright, Robert Newton, was a highly competent Georgian architect. His achievement was all the more worthy in that he was largely self-taught, although he was fortunate in living at a time when architectural pattern books were becoming readily available. He lived in NEWCASTLE throughout his life and all of his work was within the region. His most notable buildings in Newcastle are the church of St Ann at Battlefield, the Old Assembly Rooms in Westgate Road, and Charlotte Square, the only example of a 'London' square in the city. Also, with DAVID STEPHENSON, he refaced the Exchange and Guildhall. In addition, he built or substantially altered ten country houses, most notably Castle Eden in Durham, and in Northumberland Whitfield Hall, Dissington Hall and the Duke of Northumberland's hunting lodge, Kielder Castle.

NEW TOWNS OF THE NINETEENTH CENTURY

In the course of the second quarter of the nineteenth century three new towns were founded, all in Durham and all with the same purpose, the export of coal. All to varying degrees were associated with ancient settlements and two grew to be large towns.

Middlesbrough: Middlesbrough's medieval antecedent was the cell (distant branch) founded in the early years of the twelfth century by the Benedictine abbey of Whitby. Located close to where the centre of the new town was to be, it was dissolved by Henry VIII's government in 1537 but its ruins survived until the early nineteenth century.

The origins of the new town were twofold, the second closely following the first. The initial move was made by the Stockton and Darlington Railway Co., which within months of commencing operations realised the inadequacy of STOCKTON as a coal port. Therefore, in 1828, the Company obtained an act of parliament allowing an extension of the line from Stockton to Middlesbrough, crossing the Tees by means of a suspension bridge, designed by Captain Samuel Brown, who ten years previously had built the Union Chain Bridge over the Tweed. The project also involved building staithes at Middlesbrough, designed by the locomotive engineer TIMOTHY HACKWORTH and named Port Darlington. The enterprise became operational in 1830, a year before the opening of the Portrack Cut, which shortened the distance between Stockton and the sea by about three miles. This attempt by Stockton to render the railway superfluous came too late, but had improvements to the river been put in hand earlier, Middlesbrough might not have been founded.

No sooner had Port Darlington begun to function than a company was formed to buy a larger area of land in Middlesbrough. Headed by Joseph Pease and his brother Edward, and four other men, three of whom were related to the PEASE FAMILY by marriage, it comprised three small estates, amounting to around 520 acres (210 ha) of land for £30,000. Much of the money was advanced by two fellow Quaker bankers, Francis Baring and Samuel Gurney, and by two Jewish bankers, Nathan Rothschild and Moses Montefiore. In 1839 a further 39 acres (16 ha) were bought, on which Middlesbrough Dock was built in 1841–42 at a cost of nearly £22,000. This was necessary because the volume of coal for export had far outstripped expectations and the ability of Port Darlington to handle it. Between the Port Darlington staithes and the new dock a new town was laid out on a conventional gridiron plan. Initially it was estimated that the town would have a population of 5,000.

Had Middlesbrough continued to be simply a coal port, it might have grown no larger than Seaham Harbour. What transformed it into a major industrial town was the discovery in 1850 of huge quantities of iron ore in the hills south of the town. The result was what may fairly be termed an 'iron rush'. Numerous ironworks were built, using the rapidly extending rail network to draw ore from close by, coal from the BISHOP AUCKLAND area and limestone from Weardale. Very rapidly, Middlesbrough became 'Ironopolis'. The rise of iron making is clearly demonstrated by the population figures. By 1841 the population stood at 5,709, already above the original planning estimate. By 1851 it had risen to 7,893, but in the next thirty years it shot up to 56,588, ten times what the founders had envisioned.

The rapid emergence of the iron industry altered the trade of Middlesbrough as a port: coal declined as its staple export in favour of pig iron, wrought iron, manufactured iron products and chemicals; and the import of iron ore became important. The expansion of trade necessitated successive increases in the size of the dock from its original nine acres to twelve acres in 1869, 15 acres (6 ha) in 1884 and finally to 25 acres (10 ha) in 1898. The ability of ships, which were increasing in size, to reach the dock was facilitated by improvements to the navigation of the Tees. These were the work of the Tees Conservancy Commission, set up by act of parliament in 1852, which gave control of the river from High Worsall to its mouth. Initially, there were fifteen commissioners, five each from Stockton and Middlesbrough, two from the medieval port of Yarm and, significantly, three from the Admiralty. The major change was the straightening of the river's course by means of retaining banks made of slag from the growing number of ironworks. In addition, the channel was deepened by dredging, made safe by the removal of obstacles, and protected by the construction by 1891 of the South Gare and North Gare breakwaters. The breakwaters and the retaining walls increased the speed of the river's flow and thereby its scouring effect. On the eve of World War I, the Tees handled nearly 6,000,000 tons of goods worth nearly £14,000,000. Although Stockton continued to function as a port, its share of this trade was a mere 10 per cent.

By that time, the iron and steel works in

and near Middlesbrough produced around two and half million tons of pig iron from seventy-five blast furnaces and one and a half million tons of steel. In the same year, the river's yards launched seventy ships totalling over 137,000 gross registered tons of new ships. There were also numerous engineering works, catering for, and using the materials produced by, the steel industry.

All this economic activity had driven the population of Middlesbrough up to about 110,000. In part, the rapid rise in population is explained by high fertility rates, but it should also be recognised that Middlesbrough was very considerably an immigrant town and as such would have resembled contemporary cities in the USA. Also contributing were the successive enlargements of the town, which were accompanied by changes in local government arrangements. It is a testimony to the speed of the town's growth that in 1853 it received a royal charter incorporating it as a municipal borough, with a governing body comprising a mayor, four aldermen and twelve elected councillors. In 1866 the Middlesbrough Extension and Improvement Act added parts of neighbouring townships. The following year the Representation of the People Act made Middlesbrough a parliamentary borough, returning one member to the House of Commons. In 1874 another act again enlarged the borough and increased its ruling body to ten aldermen and thirty councillors. In 1889, by which date the population had risen to over 70,000, Middlesbrough became a county borough. In 1913 a further extension order enlarged the borough to 4,159 acres (1,683 ha) and increased its population to 131,000. Five years later, following the end of World War I, Middlesbrough's parliamentary representation was doubled to two members. The town's final expansion came into force in 1932 and enlarged the area of Middlesbrough to 7,205 acres (2,916 ha). The borough now embraced Acklam, Ayresome, Cargo Fleet, Coulby Newham, Hemlington, Linthorpe, Marton, Nunthorpe, Stainsby and Stainton and had a population of nearly 140,000.

Since the end of World War II, Middlesbrough has been affected by major changes in its local government arrangements and in its economy. In 1965 it became part of the new County Borough of Teesside, which combined Middlesbrough, BILLINGHAM, Eston, Redcar, STOCKTON and Thornaby into a giant authority with a population of nearly 400,000. Nine years later, in 1974, a further fundamental reorganisation was imposed with the creation of the new Metropolitan County of Cleveland, comprising the boroughs of DARLINGTON, HARTLEPOOL, Middlesbrough and Redcar, Stockton and Thornaby, the Urban Districts of Billingham, Eston, Guisborough, Loftus, Skelton and Whitby, and the Rural Districts of Sedgefield, Stokesley and Whitby. This lasted until 1986 when, following the government's decision to scrap the metropolitan counties, Middlesbrough became a 'unitary authority'.

In the economic field the key change has been the shift of the centre of gravity eastwards towards the coast. Steelmaking moved to Lackenby and is now confined to Redcar; ICI developed a giant chemical works at Wilton, the estate acquired at the end of World War II; and as the old docks became increasingly inadequate, a new modern port, Teesport, was created close to the river mouth.

Seaham Harbour: Its name suggests that Seaham was one of the earliest English settlements in the region and the oldest parts of the fabric of its church, as revealed by the 1913 renovations, show close similarity to those at ESCOMB, which indicates late seventh- or early eighth-century construction and therefore ecclesiastical importance during the earliest phase of Northumbrian Christianity. This early prominence did not last, however, and throughout the medieval and early modern centuries Seaham remained a small township at the centre of one of the region's smaller parishes.

It was transformed by the construction of what came to be called Seaham Harbour, although this new settlement was not in Seaham but in the neighbouring township of Dalton le Dale. The plan, devised in the late 1810s, was to develop the small rocky cove that fishermen had long used for shelter, and to link it to the hinterland by a railway. The scheme was that of the then owner of the Seaham estate, Sir Ralph Milbanke (the father of Lord Byron's wife) and his agent, William Taylor. Their perception was that, as it became possible to reach the coal seams beneath the East Durham Plateau, additional port facilities would be needed, since those at Sunderland would become inadequate. They also recognised that a new port would provide an outlet for lime and limestone, demand for which was also rising. Consequently, Milbanke commissioned plans from a well-known civil engineer, WILLIAM CHAPMAN, which he submitted in 1820. When complete, the new facility would be called Port Milbanke.

In the following year, however, financial difficulties led Milbanke to sell the entire Seaham estate to LORD LONDONDERRY for £55,000. At the time of purchase, Londonderry was not aware of Milbanke's plans. It was William Taylor, who was convinced of the scheme's great potential, who made him acquainted with it. Londonderry immediately commissioned Chapman to submit revised plans, which he sent to John Rennie and Thomas Telford, the most prestigious civil engineers of the day, for vetting. The result of their revisions was to raise the estimated cost from the original £6,000 to £42,000, plus another £23,000 for a railway linking the port with Londonderry's pits at Rainton and Pittington.

Construction work began in 1828, using stone from the Londonderry quarries at Penshaw. By 1831 the North Harbour was complete and by 1835 the South Harbour was finished, although work continued to effect improvements until 1840. At the same time as the harbour was being built, the railway was constructed, so that the shipment of coal became possible in 1831. As well as the harbour and railway, Londonderry had to build a town to accommodate the families attracted to his enterprise. Typically, he started out with a grandiose ambition, commissioning JOHN DOBSON, the North East's most distinguished architect, to plan a new town on a grand scale. Dobson obliged, producing a scheme that comprised two crescents of houses of various sizes and quality facing the North Sea and a bridge over the railway line as it descended to the harbour, on which would be built the company offices, a hotel and shops. Had it been realised, the result would have been an architectural masterpiece. The cost, however, was prohibitive. Consequently, although one crescent of large houses and the company offices over the railway were built, the rest of the scheme was abandoned in favour of terraces of workers' cottages running parallel with the railway line. In the end, Seaham Harbour cost Lord Londonderry over four times the estimate: £180,00 instead of £42,000. It is worth noting, however, that over his lifetime, he spent even more, £220,000, on his homes, Wynyard Hall in Durham, and Holdernesse House in London.

The prosperity of Seaham Harbour was completely tied to the coal trade. The closure of Seaham (1986), Dawdon (1991) and Vane Tempest (1993) collieries and the end of coal exports appeared to doom the town to long-term decline. This has not happened. The Seaham and Vane Tempest colliery sites on the north side of the town have been reclaimed and new housing estates built on them. At the same time, new life has been given to the harbour by the Victoria Group, who bought the facility in 2002, and who also own four other small ports in Britain. New warehousing has been built on the reclaimed Dawdon Colliery site south of the harbour, which has been modernised, and is able to take ships of up to 8,000 tons. Its trade is largely concerned with handling imports, principally from the Baltic, including, ironically, coal from Poland. And as well as continued commercial activity, it is hoped that a marina will be developed in the North Harbour.

Apart from the three pits sunk in the immediate vicinity, Seaham did not attract other industries and so did not become a large industrial town. Consequently, for local government purposes, it remained an Urban District, until 1974, when the restructuring of local government made it part of Easington District.

West Hartlepool: The origin of West Hartlepool lay in the failure of a commercial agreement. In 1832, the newly formed Hartlepool Dock and Railway Co. secured parliamentary approval to build twenty-three miles of railway from the area around Thornley and Haswell to Hartlepool, reopen the old harbour at Hartlepool and create a much larger dock in the Inner Harbour, which became known on its completion in 1840 as the Victoria Dock. The purpose of the development was the export of coal. Hartlepool's potential, however, attracted other businessmen, headed by Ralph Ward Jackson. In 1839 they formed the Stockton and Hartlepool Railway Co. with the aim of diverting coal traffic from the Bishop Auckland area, which would otherwise be exported through Middlesbrough to Hartlepool, where they intended to build their own port facilities. To thwart this ambition, the Hartlepool Dock and Railway Co. bought the Middleton House estate that occupied the land south of Hartlepool Slake. Initially, therefore, the Stockton and Hartlepool Co. had no option but to ship its coal through its opponent's dock, for which privilege it paid considerable fees.

This arrangement could only be temporary. In 1844 the Stockton and Hartlepool Co. secured an act of parliament allowing them to form another company, the Hartlepool West Harbour and Dock Co., with permission to build a new dock south of Middleton. During the following twelve years they constructed the Jackson Dock, the Swainson Dock, the Timber Dock and the Coal Dock, which allowed them to export coal and import timber. It was this company that as early as 1847 coined the name 'West Hartlepool' and in doing so disguised the fact that it was not in Hartlepool but in the neighbouring township of Stranton. The independent life of the West Hartlepool Harbour and Dock Co., as it was renamed in 1852, ended in 1865 with its acquisition by the North Eastern Railway Co. By 1880 the new owners had added the North Basin, Central Dock, Union Dock and a graving dock, and, because they had already acquired the Hartlepool Dock and Railway Co., they were able to create a single integrated port with seven docks, two tidal basins and four timber ponds. The trade of this port was almost exclusively concerned with the coal trade: exporting coal and importing timber for use as pit props. On the eve of World War I, its trade tonnage amounted to 3,500,000, worth over £4,600,000.

In the inter-war years, when ownership passed to the London and North Eastern

Railway Co., the dependence on coal and timber continued, although both declined by about 50 per cent. In large part this was due to the economic depression, but it was also clear that the port was becoming inadequate: silting and the increasing size of ships posed problems, and warehousing and cranage facilites and road access were poor. The port continued to decline in the years following the end of World War II. In 1967 control, which had passed to British Railways in 1948, was transferred to the newly formed Tees and Hartlepool Port Authority. This change of ownership coincided with the last years of the coal trade, which finally ended in 1971. As a consequence, the Swainson, Coal and Central Docks, the North Basin and the Timber Ponds were closed and filled in. Hartlepool survived as a port, however, thanks to the development of specialised facilities. Ironically, these were in or close to the oldest part of the port, the Victoria Dock at Hartlepool.

Immediately south of its port facilities, the West Hartlepool Harbour and Dock Co. founded a new town. Although carefully laid out, with a large marketplace, an imposing church and terraces of houses on a gridiron pattern, there was no thought of the grandeur that characterised John Dobson's plan for Seaham. But unlike Seaham, West Hartlepool became a large industrial town, primarily thanks to two major industries. One was shipbuilding (see SHIPBUILDING INDUSTRY): from the 1860s until well into the twentieth century, the firm of WILLIAM GRAY was one of Britain's foremost shipbuilding firms, which on six occasions between 1878 and 1900 launched greater tonnage than any other yard. Along with shipbuilding went marine engineering, with Richardson Westgarth rivalling Gray's own Central Marine Engine works. The basic needs of the shipbuilding industry led West Hartlepool to become an iron and steel town, and eventually the base of South Durham Steel, which emerged in the twentieth century as one of the region's three giant steelmakers, employing 10,000 people. Another industrial enterprise for which West Hartlepool became widely known was the Lion Brewery, founded in 1852, by a William Waldon, control of which was acquired on the death of Waldon's son in 1865 by John William Cameron, with whose name it was linked thereafter. By the end of the nineteenth century, Camerons owned 400 pubs throughout the region.

The growth and expanding diversity of industry was sustained by rising population, initially at least hurried on by immigration. The census of 1831 shows Stranton with a population of 391; thirty years later the census recorded a population of 14,515, a 37-fold increase. And the increase continued, until in 1961, shortly before West Hartlepool ceased to be a separate entity, it had a population of 77,035. To some extent, the decennial increases revealed in the census records stemmed from the enlargement of the town to incorporate neighbouring villages, and these in turn related to the development of local government arrangements.

Initially, the local government of West Hartlepool was Stranton parish council. However, the new town grew rapidly to the point where this was inadequate and in 1854 the West Hartlepool Improvement Act created an Improvement Commission, comprising twelve elected members with power to levy rates to finance the solutions to a number of community problems. In 1870 another piece of legislation, the West Hartlepool Extension and Improvement Act, extended the area of the town southwards, enlarged the Commission to fifteen members and gave it wider powers. Twelve years later, West Hartlepool grew still further with the addition of the township of Seaton Carew. This evolutionary process culminated in 1887, when in celebration of Queen Victoria's Golden Jubilee, West Hartlepool became an incorporated borough, with a mayor, eight aldermen and an elected council of twenty-four. In the following years, the rapid rise in population led to West Hartlepool becoming a County Borough in 1902.

Also at that time, the union of Hartlepool and West Hartlepool was proposed, but rejected by local opinion. The union of the two towns was logical and increasingly became harder to oppose. It was finally achieved in 1967. Seven years later, in 1974, the new singular Hartlepool became part of the new Metropolitan County of Cleveland. This short-lived arrangement ended in 1986, when Hartlepool became a 'unitary authority' in the wake of the government's decision to scrap metropolitan counties. In addition to the former Hartlepool and West Hartlepool, the 'unitary authority' includes the ancient settlements of Hart, Thorp Bulmer, Nelson, Amerston, Stotfold, Newton Hanzard, Claxton, Greatham, Newton Bewley, Burntoft and Seaton Carew.

Today, the economy of West Hartlepool (as it was before 1967) is radically different from that of its ninteenth-century predecessor. Shipbuilding ceased with the closure of the Gray yard in 1961; Richardson Westgarth closed in 1981; and by 1994 steelmaking was reduced to a pipemaking facility employing 500 people. What has survived is the Lion Brewery, which in 1955 launched its most famous beer, 'Strongarm', in response to the demand for a stronger than normal beer. 'Strongarm' is still brewed, although the brewery is no longer Camerons, having been acquired in 2002 by the Castle Eden Brewery after a lengthy period during which it had several owners. Also surviving are two docks: the Union Dock is now a marina, while the Jackson Dock is home to a restored wooden frigate, HMS *Trincomalee*. The reclaimed land where the other docks and timber ponds were, is now home to light industry, shops, entertainment facilities and tourist attractions.

NEW TOWNS OF THE TWENTIETH CENTURY

The new towns of the twentieth century differed in one important respect from those of the nineteenth century: they were the product of government planning. They were also products of experiments in, and thinking about, urban development since 1870. The most notable practical examples were Bournville (Birmingham) and Port Sunlight (Birkenhead), both model settlements built for their employees by, respectively, the chocolate manufacturer, Cadbury, and the soap maker, Lever. Both places showed what comprehensive planning and controlled development could achieve. Then, in 1898, Ebenezer Howard published his book *Tomorrow: A Peaceful Path to Reform*, which was a powerful advocacy of 'garden cities' as a better alternative to continued and unregulated urban sprawl. His thinking produced two results: Letchworth in 1903 and Welwyn in 1920. Both, however, were essentially the product of private enterprise and did not lead to further examples.

It was during and immediately after World War II that government adopted the idea of new towns as a means of post-war reconstruction and of eradicating squalor that had become so evident in the inter-war years. Planning began as early as 1940 with the Barlow Report, which led in 1943 to the setting up of the Ministry of Town and Country Planning and two years later to the Distribution of Industry Act, giving government the authority to decide where industrial development should take place. Then in 1946 came the New Towns Act, which vested in the Minister of Town and

Country Planning the power to designate areas for the development of new towns, to set up development corporations to plan and run such towns, and to buy land (if necessary by compulsory purchase) and put in the basic services. The financing of these ventures was by interest-bearing Exchequer loans, and the business of development and administration was placed in the hands of appointed New Town Development Corporations. The result of this policy was the creation of nine new towns around London and a string of five across the central belt of Scotland between the late 1940s and the early 1960s.

The new towns in the North East were, therefore, very much part of a national movement. Nevertheless, each town was the product of a particular circumstance. Of the region's five new towns, three were in Durham and two in Northumberland.

Newton Aycliffe: The origin of Newton Aycliffe lay in the decision taken in 1940 to set up a Royal Ordnance Factory on low-grade farmland located conveniently close to the A1 road and the East Coast Main Line. The result was a site with over 1,000 buildings employing 16,000 people, mainly women, preparing shells. When the end of the war in 1945 made this facility redundant, the factory was handed over to North East Trading Estates to attract and house peace-time industries. In 1947 government took the decision to designate a new town to be developed in conjunction with this situation. It was also seen as a means of stanching emigration from south-east Durham, which had gone on throughout the inter-war years. Durham County Council was not enthusiastic, however: they wanted new industry to be directed to the BISHOP AUCKLAND/Crook area, where coal mining was in decline, and they were also fearful that Darlington would eventually secure control of the new town. Their opposition was not successful; the most they were able to secure was the location of the new town to the north of the ROF site, that is, as far as possible away from Darlington.

Peterlee: In contrast to Newton Aycliffe, Peterlee was the result of local pressure directed upwards to government, rather than government imposing the idea from above. The new town was the brainchild of C.W. Clarke, the Engineer and Surveyor to the Easington Rural District Council. In 1942 the government ordered the Council to draw up plans, to be activated after the war, for the eradication of the large amount of sub-standard housing in EASINGTON, Horden, and Blackhall, villages which were described derogatorily as 'mining camps'. It was Clarke's view, which he put forward in 1943, that rather than adding to or replacing houses in the existing villages, a new town should be built. Clarke persuaded his Council that this was the better solution and subsequently he elaborated his ideas in a book, *Farewell Squalor*, published in 1946.

Translation from theory into reality, however, required formal designation of new town status by the Minister of Town and Country Planning, and this was granted in 1948 by the then Minister, Lewis Silkin. Although Silkin accepted the local arguments in favour of a new town, he was perhaps more influenced by a personal sociological conviction that there was an urgent need to get away from what he saw as the mono-cultural and one-class condition of mining villages. Silkin also agreed that the new town should be called Peterlee, the merger of the forename and surname of PETER LEE, the first Labour chairman of Durham County Council. The area designated for the new town comprised 2,350 acres north of Castle Eden Dene between the coast and the A19.

At the outset, however, the development was hampered by two problems. One was the rearguard resistance of a number of affected parties, particularly the National Coal Board and, above all, the existing villages, which resented being sentenced to a lingering death and denied the right to their own renewal programmes. The other was the style of the new town as proposed in the First Master Plan. This was the work of a team of international architects headed by Berthold Lubetkin, an ardent advocate of Modernist architecture. Lubetkin had migrated in the early 1930s from Europe to London, where he had built up a considerable reputation. His plan was imaginative but far too advanced for local tastes and conditions, particularly in his preference for multi-storey housing. Not a man prepared to compromise, he resigned in early 1950. As a result, the design for Peterlee as set out in the Second Master Plan of 1952 was more conventional. The basic layout was of sections defined by roads radiating from a town centre towards a perimeter road, each intended to house 5,000–7,000 people and to have its own schools and shops. Curiously, when the earliest housing was deemed to be unimaginative in design and poorly constructed, Victor Pasmore, Professor of Fine Art at Newcastle, a man strongly influenced by the same ideas as Lubetkin, was appointed in 1955 to improve the design and aesthetic aspects of the development.

Overall, the building of Peterlee took twenty-five years, from 1950 until 1975.

Washington: There was a gap of nearly twenty years between the designation of Newton Aycliffe and Peterlee and that of Washington in 1964. The town was assigned 5,600 acres (2,200 ha) of land, much of it requiring reclamation. Notable were the spoil heaps of four collieries (Harraton, Washington F, Washington Glebe and Usworth) closed between 1965 and 1972, and those of the Newell Chemical and Insulating Co. In fact, the development of Washington as a new town deliberately coincided with the need to replace old industries with new.

The Master Plan, devised by two architectural partnerships and accepted in 1967, envisaged a comprehensive road system in the form of squares, within which there were to be eleven industrial sites distributed throughout the town but close to the primary road network and also to the A1(M), which formed the town's western boundary. Residential areas were also to be distributed in the form of villages, each with a population of around 4,500. Some of these were already in existence, although in need of upgrading, while others were new creations. While the imperative of a good road system was fully acknowledged, the plan also created a network of footways that made possible pedestrian movement between all parts of the town. Although the underlying theme appeared to be dispersal, there was to be a central business, administrative, entertainment and shopping centre.

The new town corporations no longer exist. Since 1988 their functions have been transferred to the elective local government system: Newton Aycliffe and Peterlee are part of, respectively, Sedgefield District and Easington District in County Durham, while Washington is within the City of Sunderland.

The two new towns in Northumberland were not strictly 'new towns' but Comprehensive Development Areas. The difference was that, although they were so designated by government, they were not financed directly by government and were developed by pre-existing local authorities.

Cramlington: Plans for the development of Cramlington were conceived in 1958, although its designation as a Comprehensive

Development Area was delayed until 1964. Government assistance was confined to clearing derelict land arising from the closure of nearby collieries. The development agencies were Northumberland County Council and Seaton Sluice Urban District Council. The Master Plan envisaged an industrial zone of 170 acres (70 ha), located close to the main railway line, and twelve residential areas, each with its own primary school, shops and social facilities. Basic implementation of the plan was achieved by 1972, although the population target of 90,000 was never achieved.

Killingworth: At the time Killingworth was designated a Comprehensive Development Area in 1958, it, or at least its moor, had already had a significant history. For many years until its enclosure in the early 1790s, Killingworth Moor was the venue of Newcastle Races. More notably, it was the place where GEORGE STEPHENSON made his reputation. From 1804, two years after the West Pit was sunk, until 1821, Stephenson was employed in various capacities at Killingworth Colliery. It was during this time that he invented the safety lamp that bore his name and built a series of locomotives, culminating in the *Blücher* in 1814. During his time at Killingworth he lived at Dial Cottage, its name deriving from the sundial bearing the date 11 August 1816 above the door, said to have been made by Stephenson and his son, Robert.

The Killingworth Master Plan was completed and approved by the Minister of Housing and Local Government. Implementation, which took note of the Ministry guidelines, was in the hands of Northumberland County Council and Longbenton Urban District Council. The land involved lay north of the old village and the new development began with an artificial lake. Immediately north of this a commercial and administrative centre, enclosed by two roads named East and West Citadel, was created. Otherwise, the development comprised new housing, built by the local authority, housing associations and private builders (with the aim of achieving a population of 20,000) and new light industry. The whole was contained between two major north–south roads, the A189 and the A19, both subsequently rebuilt as dual carriageways.

Cramlington is now part of the Borough of Castle Morpeth in Northumberland, while Killingworth is in the Borough of North Tyneside in Tyne and Wear.

NOBLE, SIR ANDREW, Bt (1831–1915)

Andrew Noble was one of the major driving forces in the success of SIR WILLIAM ARMSTRONG's Elswick armaments business. Born in Greenock the son of a retired RN officer, he was educated at Greenock and at Edinburgh Academy and then from 1847 until 1849 at the Royal Military College, Woolwich, from where he was commissioned into the Royal Artillery. He rapidly gained a reputation as a gunnery expert with an active interest in the science of gun design and performance. This led in 1860 to his resignation from the army to become joint manager of the Elswick works. This enabled him to further his research interests, notably into the pressure produced in gun barrels by the explosion of gunpowder and cordite and the means of calculating the velocity of projectiles leaving gun barrels. His discoveries, which constituted major advances in the science of ballistics, earned him an FRS in 1870. In 1865 he became a partner in the firm and during the next twenty years negotiated two important mergers, with the shipbuilder Charles Mitchell in 1882 and the Manchester armaments firm, Whitworths, in 1897. Vice-chairman from 1881, in 1900, as expected, he took over the chairmanship following Lord Armstrong's death, continuing in that role until his own death in 1915. He was knighted in 1893 and made a baronet in 1902.

His succession was not, however, to the company's advantage in that he failed to give the sort of leadership it needed. As a manager, he was an ageing autocrat who stifled debate and resisted the adoption of more modern and appropriate methods, and he was no longer an innovative engineer. Consequently, under him the company tended to stagnate, to the benefit of its main rival, the Sheffield firm of Vickers.

NORHAM

Norham, now a pleasant village with a splendid parish church overlooked by the ruins of its castle, was intended to be a place of greater size and importance. Throughout the medieval centuries it was the 'capital' of NORTH DURHAM. The decision to have Norham as a seat of government was taken by BISHOP RANNULF FLAMBARD (1099–1128), who may have been influenced by the knowledge that Norham had for a short time in the ninth century been the residence of the Community of St Cuthbert (see CUTHBERT, SAINT). What gave Norham its importance, however, was its castle, built by Flambard in 1121 on the orders of Henry I, on the high ground overlooking the Tweed near the point where, until the bridge was built in 1838, it was crossed by means of a ferry. Flambard also attempted to enhance Norham's status further by making it a borough, hoping that it would become a thriving centre of trade. This ambition was unfulfilled, largely because the long war between England and Scotland inhibited economic development.

Norham's fate during the three hundred years of conflict was to be a frontier fortress. In fact, it was the middle castle in a line of three, the others being Wark and BERWICK UPON TWEED. These three castles were England's first line of defence and as such were frequent targets of Scottish aggression. Scottish armies captured the castle on four occasions: 1136, 1138, 1322 and 1513, and they besieged it without success on five more: 1215, 1318, 1319, 1327 and 1497. It is not surprising that Sir Walter Scott made it the setting for his poetic tale of derring-do, *Marmion*.

The last time the Scots took the castle was during the 1513 invasion that ended in their crushing defeat at Flodden (see FLODDEN, BATTLE OF). On that occasion, it was battered into submission in less than a week by James IV's formidable artillery train. The damage to it was so severe, and its inadequacy in the face of modern cannon so apparent, that between 1513 and 1521 it was restructured as an artillery fort. Forty years later, by which time it was Crown property, one of the foremost fortification experts of his day, Rowland Johnson, drew up plans for an even more ambitious modernisation. But his plans were never activated and the castle was allowed to decay. In part this was a matter of cost, but the gradual recognition in both countries that James VI of Scotland would shortly become King of England removed the urgency for up-to-date frontier defence.

In 1209 Norham was the venue of an international peace treaty, agreed between the Scottish king, William I, and the English king, John. The matter it resolved was the attempt by John to build a castle at Tweedmouth opposite that of Berwick, which had provoked a violent response from the Scots. John agreed not to proceed with the castle, but in return William had to accept humiliating terms.

NORTH DURHAM

Until 1844, when it was united with NORTHUMBERLAND, the district known as North Durham was part of the PALATI-

NATE OF DURHAM and then of DURHAM COUNTY. It comprised two contiguous districts, Norhamshire and Islandshire, which formed a triangle of land roughly ninety square miles in area bounded by the North Sea from Tweedmouth to Budle Bay and the River Tweed from Tweedmouth as far as Cornhill. Originally royal estates and administrative units, these 'shires' became parishes following the adoption of Christianity, with parochial churches at, respectively, NORHAM and HOLY ISLAND. Together these 'shires' contained thirty townships. The number should have been thirty-four, but in the first decade of the twelfth century the townships of Barmoor, Bowsden, Holburn and Lowick were abstracted from Islandshire and incorporated into the Barony of Wooler, created by Henry I for Robert de Muschamp so as to give Muschamp control of a continuous arc of land from the Cheviot to Budle Bay. This transfer took place while the Bishop of Durham, RANNULF FLAMBARD, who held the lordship of both 'shires', was out of favour and in exile in Normandy. Although he later regained royal favour, he did not regain his townships, which remained members of the parish of Holy Island.

The reason for their exclusion from the newly created county of Northumberland was that they were part of the estates belonging to ST CUTHBERT, over which the Bishop of Durham as the head of the Community of St Cuthbert was allowed to retain unreduced political and legal authority after the EARLDOM OF NORTHUMBRIA was ended in 1095. And even when the bishop's palatine powers were gradually eroded after the Reformation, the two shires remained part of Durham County until the 1844 act.

NORTH SHIELDS (see TYNEMOUTH AND NORTH SHIELDS)

NORTH-EAST COAST EXHIBITION OF INDUSTRY, SCIENCE AND ART, 1929

The North-East Coast Exhibition of Industry, Science and Art was one of the largest and most ambitious exhibitions of its kind held in Britain and it ran for six months between May and October 1929, attracting nearly 4.5 million visitors. It was held on Newcastle's Town Moor in an area still known as Exhibition Park. Over 400 exhibitors took part, displaying their wares in specially constructed steel and concrete pavilions. The purpose of the exhibition was to demonstrate the huge variety of products and inventions produced by Britain and her Empire, with the hope that it would stimulate and revitalise the North-East economy. The only surviving parts are the entrance gateway and one of the pavilions, the Palace of Fine Arts. From 1934 until recently used as a museum, it now lies empty, having been declared structurally unsafe.

NORTHERN ROCK

Northern Rock, the region's most recent bank, was created as a company in 1964 by the merger of two Newcastle-based building societies, Northern Counties Permanent Building Society, founded in 1850, and Rock Permanent Building Society, founded in 1865. The two societies functioned side by side until 1957, when their approximate equality of size made merger seem logical. However, it took several years for this to be achieved. That it was managed was due considerably to the dynamism and ambition of Fuller Osborn, chief executive of Northern Counties since 1950, who occupied the same post in the merged society from its inception until 1978. Under his leadership, Northern Rock grew in size and geographical range, substantially by absorbing twenty-two smaller societies, a process that culminated in 1994 with the takeover of the Sunderland-based North of England

Building Society. With almost one million members, Northern Rock was now one of the largest building societies in Britain.

'De-mutualisation' and conversion into Northern Rock PLC was the next logical step, and one already taken by other leading societies under the enabling legislation of 1986. The change was effected in 1997, although not without opposition. This, however, was placated by the creation of the Northern Rock Charitable Foundation, which was to receive a percentage of the issued capital and of the company's profits to support worthy causes within the region. In 2007, however, disaster struck: as the world-wide financial crisis began to develop, the bank was driven to apply to the Bank of England for financial support and this triggered a rush of depositors to withdraw their savings. In fact, the problem was not that the bank was insolvent but that it was unable to borrow money in the financial markets to sustain its mortgage business. The outcome was a takeover by the government in 2008, a solution that in the opinion of many would have been avoided had the involved government agencies taken swifter action. The consequence was substantial redundancies and the demise of the North East's largest independent financial institution.

NORTHERN SINFONIA

In the Northern Sinfonia, the North East possesses an orchestra of international standing. It was the brainchild of Michael Hall, a native of the region who, after National Service, was educated at the Royal College of Music and King's College, Newcastle. The Sinfonia's first concert was on 24 September 1958, a time when there was no professional orchestra in eastern England and the best the region could expect was the visits of orchestras such as the Hallé from Manchester. It was not until 1961, however, that the orchestra was placed on a permanent footing. This was made possible by the provision of the necessary funding from local authorities via the North East Association for the Arts (later Northern Arts and now Arts Council England, North East). The injection of public money effected one obvious change. Originally, the orchestra's name was 'The Sinfonia', Michael Hall wishing to avoid any impression of second-rate provincial quality. Pressure from the local authorities, however, forced the addition of 'Northern'.

The high standard of the orchestra's playing was established in the 1960s and 1970s by the then Joint Principal Conductors, the Canadian Boris Brott, and Rudolf Schwartz, the eminent conductor who had re-established the Bournemouth Symphony Orchestra after World War II and had done outstanding work with the City of Birmingham and BBC Symphony Orchestras. The present Music Director is another musician with an international reputation, Thomas Zehtemayer. In the forty-three years of its existence, the Sinfonia has undertaken tours in the United States and most countries in Europe and has invariably received critical acclaim. It has now moved into its new home, The Sage Gateshead.

NORTHUMBERLAND, COUNTY OF

Northumberland as a county within the Kingdom of England came into existence in 1095. Prior to that it had been part of an earldom (see Northumbria, Kingdom and Earldom of) and had never had the system of pre-Conquest local government that obtained further south. For this reason, like the other three northern counties of England, it has never been called a 'shire'. At the end of the eleventh century, it comprised all the land between the Tweed in the north and the Tees in the south, but with large parts excluded from its jurisdiction. Most notable were the Lands of St Cuthbert, which constituted the PALATINATE OF DURHAM under the rule of the Bishop of Durham. These included all the land south of the Tyne and Derwent, except for three enclaves on the north bank of the Tees, known collectively as the WAPENTAKE OF SADBERGE. These, too, were lost to Northumberland in 1189, when Richard I sold them to the Bishop of Durham, HUGH OF LE PUISET. The Lands of St Cuthbert also included NORTH DURHAM. Also exempt was HEXHAMSHIRE, ruled by the archbishops of York from the late eleventh century, and ALSTON, which was attached to Cumberland. There was to be one further loss in the Middle Ages: in 1400 NEWCASTLE UPON TYNE, except for the castle and castle garth, became a separate county.

Hexhamshire was recovered in the late sixteenth century, but it was not until 1844 that North Durham became part of Northumberland. The latest change occurred in 1974. This was the loss of the county's most populous districts in the south-east (Tynemouth, Wallsend, Longbenton, Gosforth, Newburn and parts of Castle Ward) to the new county of Tyne and Wear. What remained of the County was divided into five Districts: ALNWICK, BERWICK UPON TWEED, Castle Morpeth (see MORPETH), Tynedale and Wansbeck. They were abolished in 2009.

NORTHUMBERLAND NATIONAL PARK

The genesis of Britain's national parks was the report issued in 1942 by the Committee on Land Utilisation in Rural Areas chaired by Lord Justice Scott. This led after the end of the war to the National Parks and Access to the Countryside Act of 1949 and to the setting up of the National Parks Commission. The Northumberland National Park, designated in 1956, was the ninth of the eleven so far created. The initial proposal was for a Cheviot National Park covering 197 square miles, but the Northumberland County Council made a counter-suggestion of a park of much greater size, covering 570 square miles (1,476 km^2). The outcome was a compromise: the Northumberland National Park would cover 398 square miles (1,030 km^2), but it would be contiguous with the Border Forest Park of around 200 square miles (500 km^2) to be set up at the same time by the Forestry Commission. The park occupies about one fifth of the present county, but has a resident population of only 2,000. The largest settlements close to it (HALTWHISTLE, Bellingham, Otterburn, ROTHBURY and Wooler) were excluded, since it was not part of the remit of national parks to manage people's lives. Rather, their purpose is 'to conserve and enhance the natural beauty, wildlife and cultural heritage within their boundaries and to provide opportunities for the better understanding and enjoyment of them'. The Park is governed by a 'special purposes local authority', which comprises twenty-two people, six nominated by the Secretary of State for the Environment, Food and Rural Affairs and sixteen from the County Council, the three District Councils (Berwick, Alnwick and Tynedale) and the parishes within its boundaries. This body is required to produce an updated management plan every five years, and in doing so it has to liaise with a wide range of other authorities and interests.

The Park has three major landowners or groups of landowners. Fifty-seven per cent of the land belongs to private individuals, 23 percent to the Ministry of Defence (see OTTERBURN ARMY TRAINING AREA) and 17 per cent to the Forestry Commission: the Park Authority itself owns practically nothing. About 70 per cent of the land inside the Park is moorland and is managed for shooting and low-density grazing, while a further 20 per cent is covered with large blocks of conifers. Current management strategies aim to identify and protect the habitats of wildlife of national or international significance, to reduce the amount of land under conifers and to increase the amount planted with native species, and perhaps to allow tracts to regenerate as wild wood, and to survey and whenever possible to excavate the numerous archaeological sites.

NORTHUMBERLAND PLATE

Compared with Yorkshire, with its nine racecourses and seventy-five trainers with 2,500 horses, the North East is not prominent in the business of thoroughbred racing. It has only three racecourses, two of which, Hexham and Sedgefield, are small National Hunt courses. The exception is Gosforth Park, where races take place under both National Hunt and Flat Race rules and where one of Europe's major handicap races takes place in late June each year. This is the Northumberland Plate, popularly known as the 'Pitmen's Derby'. The plate itself is a shallow dish engraved with the words 'Northumberland Plate Gosforth Park', with a model of the Percy lion, tail extended, at its centre. It was first run in 1833 on the racecourse on the Town Moor, with its grandstand next to the appropriately named Grandstand Road. Then, and ever since, it has been a handicap and the distance two miles. The first winner was Tomboy.

In 1881, however, because of several unsavoury aspects to the event, it was transferred to Gosforth Park. The park, extending to 805 acres, was part of the High Gosforth Estate, bought by two men, Charles Perkins and Fife Scott, from the Brandling family for £60,000. There a new course was laid out and the Plate was run there for the first time in 1882. The winner was Victor Emmanuel. Since then, there have been 112 renewals. The number would have been 123 but for the two world wars (no races 1915–18 and 1940–45) and a waterlogged course in 1982. The transfer was not widely welcomed, especially as it was run on a Wednesday until after World War II, when it was moved to a Saturday.

In the course of its history, there have been two hat-tricks. The first was in the years 1857, 1858 and 1859, when the race was won by a horse named Underhand, until his retirement in 2006 the pen name of the racing correspondent of *The Journal*. The second was in 1954, 1955 and 1956, accomplished by the famous Newmarket trainer, Noel Murless. In each of the three years, however, the winner was a different horse, with a different jockey and a different owner. Murless was not the most successful trainer: that honour belongs to Dobson Peacock of Middleham, who trained five winners between 1904 and 1932. Another owner has won the race four times: R.C. Vyner in 1878, 1880, 1886 and 1898, and the double has been performed on three other occasions: St Bennet in 1838 and 1839; Caller Ou for W. I'Anson in 1863 and 1864; and Tug of War for Mrs Y. Perry in 1977 and 1978.

The Plate has maintained its status and its appeal to owners as the result of the increase in prize money, which currently stands at £100,000 to the winner. Equally, it has retained its popularity as a social and sporting event with racegoers, despite the fact that there are now no pitmen in the region to see it run.

NORTHUMBRIA, KINGDOM AND EARLDOM OF

For nearly 500 years, between 604 and 1095, the modern North East was the heartland of an independent kingdom and then of an autonomous earldom.

The **Kingdom of Northumbria** was a product of the conquest and settlement by English peoples of most of the island of Britain between 450 and 550, following the withdrawal of the Roman government in the year 410. The incomers were Germanic, from the North Sea coastal areas of what are now Holland, Germany and Denmark. Eventually, the only parts of the island not subject to English control and settlement were modern Wales and the parts of what is now Scotland beyond the Forth and Clyde. As the English invasion was protracted and piecemeal, it did not result in a unified state but in seven separate (and warring) kingdoms. Three were large: Northumbria, Mercia and Wessex; while four – Kent, Sussex, Essex and East Anglia – were much smaller.

The Kingdom of Northumbria was the creation of one man, **Aethelfrith** (whose name means, ironically, 'noble peace'), the king of **Bernicia**. Bernicia was the last English and most northerly English kingdom to come into existence, founded by Aethelfrith's grandfather, **Ida**, who with his followers sailed north (probably from what is now the Lindsey district on the south side of the Humber) in 547 and seized the fortress of BAMBURGH. From this base, he and his sons extended their control over a native British kingdom called **Brynaich**. In the year 604, Aethelfrith vastly enlarged his kingdom by forcibly annexing the neighbouring English kingdom south of the Tees, **Deira**, which had been established at an earlier date. Having killed the Deiran king, Aelle, Aethelfrith married his daughter, Acha, thereby ensuring that their sons, **OSWALD** and **OSWIU**, carried the genes of both royal families and thereby the right to rule both Deira and Bernicia. What he failed to do was to capture and kill Aelle's son, **EDWINE**, who escaped and found refuge with the King of East Anglia. This failure proved fatal when, in 616, he was ambushed and killed by Edwine and his backer, Raedwald, King of East Anglia. In the intervening years, however, Aethelfrith had ruled his enlarged kingdom and enjoyed notable military success, winning victories against the native British King of Gwynedd in what is now North Wales, and against the Scots, an Irish people, who had established a kingdom called **Dal Riata** in what is now Argyll. Although early medieval boundaries cannot be identified with total certainty, it would be basically accurate to say that at its fullest extent the Kingdom of Northumbria comprised the central swathe of Britain from the North Sea to the Irish Sea and extending in the east from the River Idle, a tributary of the Trent, to the River Avon, which enters the Forth near Linlithgow, and in the west from the River Ribble in Lancashire to the River Irvine in Ayrshire.

The Kingdom of Northumbria lasted until *c.*900. It was largely destroyed, however, in the great disruption of Britain by the Vikings between 850 and 900. The only English kingdom to survive intact was Wessex, the most southerly state that lay between the Thames and the Channel coast. To the north of it, most of Mercia and the Yorkshire part of Northumbria south of the Tees fell under Viking control. In the course of the tenth century, a new and larger English kingdom emerged out of the wreckage, created by the kings of Wessex, who gradually extended their authority over the Viking areas. By the end of the century this new and enlarged kingdom had acquired the name **England**. Meanwhile, another kingdom emerged in the north: **Alba**, formed by a union of the Scottish kingdom of **Dal Riata** in the west, and the kingdom of the **Picts** in the east. The territory of this new kingdom extended northwards from the north shores of the Firths of Clyde and Forth to the Moray Firth. While the kings of Wessex/England sought to extend their authority northwards, the kings of Alba were equally intent on pushing theirs southwards. What remained of Northumbria, therefore, became the object of ambition for two rival monarchies.

The last reference to a King of Northumbria occurs shortly before 900, but almost immediately, an **Earl of Northumbria** appears. This family, known as the House of Bamburgh, continued to hold the earldom for over a hundred years, which makes it likely that it was a continuation of the Northumbrian royal family, but in reduced circumstances. Although these earls were virtually independent, they were not strong enough to avoid submitting to the overlordship of either the King of England or the King of Alba. In the end, both kings gained. The earls had to acknowledge the overlordship of the kings of England, but the kings of Alba succeeded in annexing the most northerly district of the old kingdom of Northumbria, the land between the Forth and the Tweed. In doing so, they converted Alba into **Scotland**. However, for centuries, the Tweed–Forth district (covering the modern counties of Berwick, Roxburgh, Selkirk, Peebles, and East, Mid and West Lothian) was known as **Lothian**, and although subject to the kings of Scotland, was not considered to be strictly part of Scotland. Moreover, unlike Scotland north of the Forth–Clyde line, its language continued to be English, not Gaelic.

In the course of the eleventh century, the political power of the House of Bamburgh was gradually diminished. The Danish king, Canute, who became King of England by conquest in 1017, treacherously murdered its leading members and replaced them with one of his own men, Siward. However, his authority and that of his successor was essentially confined to Yorkshire, where Viking settlement had been heavy. North of the Tees, power was divided between two men: the Bishop of Durham, who was recognised as the ruler of the lands acquired by St Cuthbert, and the member of the House of Bamburgh, who still bore the title of earl. William the Conqueror retained this arrangement, which might have continued indefinitely, had it not been for the disloyalty of Earl Waltheof, the member of the House of Bamburgh whom he installed as earl in 1072 and trusted sufficiently to marry him to his niece, Judith. William had Waltheof executed in 1076 and assigned the earldom to Walcher, whom he had made Bishop of Durham in 1072. The previous dual arrangement was restored following the murder of Walcher in 1080, when the bishopric and the earldom were again granted to different men, but this time to Normans, not natives. It was terminated in 1095, when William II (who had succeeded as king in 1087) deposed Earl Robert de Mowbray, and did not replace him. Those parts of the region over which Mowbray had ruled became a normal English county, Northumberland, while the rest became the Palatinate of Durham.

NORTHUMBRIA UNIVERSITY ART GALLERY (see ART GALLERIES)

OGLE, SAMUEL (1702/3–1752)

Samuel Ogle was born in Northumberland, the son of Samuel Ogle (1658–1718) of Bowsden, the Recorder of Berwick 1689–98 and MP for Berwick 1690–1708, and also Commissioner of the Revenue in Ireland. Ogle senior's connection with Ireland arose from his second marriage, to Ursula Markham, whose inheritance included estates there. Almost nothing is known about Ogle junior's early life, except that many years were spent in Ireland and that at some stage he joined the army, rising by 1730 to the rank of captain in a cavalry regiment. It was from this situation in 1731 that Charles Calvert, 5th Lord Baltimore, appointed him Governor of Maryland. Maryland was then a proprietory colony founded and owned by the Calvert family, Lords Baltimore, to whom Charles I in 1632 had given a charter awarding them the land between 40° N and the Potomac River with the same rights, powers and privileges over its inhabitants as those pertaining to the Palatinate of Durham. In return, they paid the Crown a token annual rent of two native arrows.

In consequence of this charter, Calvert had complete power to appoint and dismiss officials, which explains why Ogle was appointed as Governor on three occasions (in 1732, 1734 and 1742) and twice dismissed. Baltimore's dissatisfaction with Ogle's performance stemmed from his failure to quell the hostility of the colonists, all of whom were Calvert's tenants, towards him as proprietor, which they voiced in their elected Assembly, their right to which, albeit without significant powers, was enshrined in the 1632 charter. Tenant grievances were various, but underlying all of them was the depression in the tobacco trade. In his last term of office, however, Ogle hit upon the solution, the Tobacco Inspection Act, which imposed an inspection system on the colony's tobacco growers designed to ensure that only the best-quality leaf was exported. This policy, which Ogle persuaded the Assembly to accept, was successful: as the quality of tobacco rose, so did its price, which in turn helped to bring about a pacifying prosperity.

Ogle married and settled in Maryland, persuading his father-in-law to build him a mansion in Prince George County, which he named Belair and which still survives as a splendid example of Georgian architecture. At his death, Ogle had an estate of about 2,500 acres (1,012 ha) in Prince George and Ann Arbor counties and cash and investments of over £7,500. After the USA became independent his son, Benjamin Ogle, was the Governor of the State of Maryland between 1798 and 1801.

OLIVER, THOMAS (1791–1858)

Thomas Oliver, who was one of the architects engaged in the development of central Newcastle by Richard Grainger in the 1830s, was born at Crailing, near Jedburgh in Roxburghshire. After leaving Jedburgh Grammar School, he migrated to Newcastle, where he is believed to have trained under John Dobson. He set up as an independent land surveyor and architect in 1821 and as such he is known to have been involved with the planning of Blackett Street and to have produced the original designs for the first Eldon Square. His reputation, however, rests on his masterpiece, the superb Leazes Terrace, built between 1829 and 1836 for Richard Grainger, which Sir Nikolaus Pevsner compared favourably with the London terraces of John Nash. Unfortunately, St James's Park, the home of Newcastle United FC, now totally overshadows Oliver's terrace.

ORDE, ADMIRAL SIR JOHN, Bt (1751–1824)

John Orde was an almost exact contemporary of CUTHBERT COLLINGWOOD and also a Northumberland man, although as the son of John Orde of East Orde and Nunnykirk, from a much wealthier family. Like Collingwood, he entered the Navy and saw service in the American War between 1776 and 1783 and then against the French and their allies between 1793 and 1815. Although he eventually rose to high rank, the later stages of his career were not as distinguished.

During the American War, however, he made rapid progress up the promotion ladder from midshipman in 1766 to flag captain to Admiral Marriot Arbuthnot in 1783. Shortly after the end of the war, he was appointed Governor of Dominica, the West Indian island returned to Britain in 1783 by the Treaty of Versailles, the peace treaty by which the American War was formally ended and the USA recognised by the international community. During his thirteen years there he restored law and order and civil life to normality and also developed the harbour at Prince Rupert's Bay. For his services, he was made a baronet in 1790.

During the French wars, however, his career was soured by disputes. Recalled to duty in 1793, he was promoted to Rear Admiral two years later. In 1797 he suppressed the naval mutiny at Plymouth and then presided at the court martial in Portsmouth to try the leading mutineers at the Nore. His reward was the command of a major warship, *Princess Royal*, in which he joined Admiral Lord St Vincent as third in command of the fleet blockading Lisbon and Cadiz. However, his relations with his commander rapidly deteriorated as the result of command of a Mediterranean squadron being given to Nelson, who was his junior, and by the arrival of Sir Roger Curtis, who was senior to him, thereby demoting him to fourth in command. His intemperate complaints to St Vincent led to his being ordered home. When St Vincent returned to Britain, Orde challenged him to a duel, which was prevented only by the king's direct intervention, following which both parties were bound over in the sum of £5,000 to keep the peace. In spite of this, Orde became Vice Admiral in 1799. While St Vincent was First Sea Lord, during the premiership of Henry Addington (1801–04), Orde remained inactive. With St Vincent's removal from office after William Pitt the Younger had replaced Addington, Orde was given command of a squadron to strengthen the blockade of the Spanish fleet off Cadiz. Nelson felt that it diminished his authority and consequently he complained frequently about Orde's discharge of his duties. Nelson's low opinion of Orde was neither warranted nor justified. It was Orde, in fact, who perceived Napoleon's strategic plan to have the French fleet sail to the West Indies in the hope of luring the Channel Fleet away so as to allow his army to cross the Channel.

Orde was promoted to the rank of Admiral of the Blue in November 1805 (later Admiral of the White in 1809 and Admiral of the Red in 1814), but his days of active service were over. In 1807 he became the MP for Newport, Isle of Wight, which he retained until 1812. He died in 1824, having outlived both Collingwood and Nelson.

OSWALD, KING OF NORTHUMBRIA AND SAINT (605–642)

To modern eyes, Oswald is a contradiction: a highly effective and ambitious warrior king, yet also a revered saint. Squaring this circle was the work of Bede, whose literary skill created a plausible account, at least at first glance. However, this is less important than the recognition that in his brief reign of eight years Oswald initiated developments that resulted in Northumbria producing some of the finest scholastic and artistic masterpieces in the history of Europe.

Oswald was the elder of the sons of Aethelfrith (see NORTHUMBRIA, KINGDOM AND EARLDOM OF), the King of Bernicia who created the Kingdom of Northumbria in 604 by defeating and killing Aelle, King of Deira (modern Yorkshire) and annexing his kingdom. Oswald's mother was Aelle's daughter, Acha, whom Aethelfrith married as his second wife. He therefore had the genes of both Bernician and Deiran royal families. Aethelfrith, however, was killed in 616 by Aelle's son, EDWINE, who became King of Northumbria. Immediately after this debacle, the eleven-year-old Oswald and his younger brother, OSWIU, were taken for safety to the Scottish kingdom of Dal Riada, with its 'capital' the fort at Dunadd in modern Argyll. Their elder half-brother, Eanfrith (Aethelfrith's son by a previous wife) also escaped, but to the kingdom of the Picts (between the Forth and the Moray Firth). Their separation in exile had an important consequence: Dal Riada, which had been founded by migrants from north-east Ireland, was a Christian kingdom with its religious centre at Iona; the Pictish kingdom was still pagan. Consequently, Eanfrith grew up a pagan while Oswald was baptised and was brought up as a Christian.

Edwine was killed in battle in 633 by a coalition of Cadwallon, King of the British Kingdom of Gwynedd, and Penda, a son of the King of the English Kingdom of Mercia. Aethelfrith's sons, now adult, were bound to attempt to recover their dynastic inheritance. The first to try was, as custom demanded, the eldest, the pagan Eanfrith, but he was lured into a trap and killed by Cadwallon. The obligation now fell on Oswald. In the summer of 634, he invaded Northumbria with a small army of Northumbrians, possibly supplemented by men from Dal Riada. At what was later called Heavenfield, a site commemorated by the church dedicated to St Oswald just north of the B6318 about a mile east of the village of Wall, in a ceremony reminiscent of that by the Roman Emperor Constantine before the Battle of Milvian Bridge in 312, Oswald set up a wooden cross and required his troops to kneel before it. He was calling on his Christian God to grant him victory. And victory was his: in a surprise attack on the invaders camped on the banks of the Rowley Burn, four miles to the south near Whitley Chapel, he wiped out Cadwallon and his army.

Oswald's reign lasted eight years and ended, as did that of most kings of this era, with death in battle. In this period, however, his achievements, political and cultural, were considerable. He established his authority throughout Northumbria (Bernicia and Deira) and added substantially to its territory, notably extending it from the Lammermuir Hills to the Forth and capturing the important fortress of Edinburgh, then known by its British name, Caer Edin. Such were his military successes and his reputation that Oswald was acknowledged as the most powerful and dominant king in Britain. That Edwine's widow sent her sons across the Channel to the Frankish kingdom, fearing that Oswald had the power to persuade her kinsman the King of Kent to murder them, testifies to the length of Oswald's political arm and to the political brutality of his time. Oswald's long-distance influence was further underlined when he married a daughter of the king of Wessex, the most southerly English kingdom. The condition of the marriage was that the West Saxon king become a Christian, that is, to accept his son-in-law's God.

Ultimately more important than his political dominance was his decision, taken immediately after his victory over Cadwallon, to call in missionaries from Dal Riada's religious centre on Iona. The first was not a success and returned home. His replacement, AIDAN, proved to be a missionary of the highest calibre. Oswald gave him as his base the island of Lindisfarne (see HOLY ISLAND), so similar to Iona and conveniently close to BAMBURGH, the political centre of the kingdom. Aidan, aided by more priests from Iona, was not only the spearhead of a successful conversion drive throughout Northumbria, but also a close friend and respected counsellor of the king. And at Lindisfarne he created one of the most important spiritual and artistic institutions in European history: without Oswald there might have been no LINDISFARNE GOSPELS.

Oswald's military luck finally ran out in 642. In August of that year he was killed in battle by the combined army of Penda, now King of Mercia, and the ruler of the British kingdom of Powys. The battle took place at Maserfelth, the whereabouts of which is uncertain, the most widely accepted being Oswestry in Shropshire on the modern Welsh border. Whatever the truth, it seems likely that Oswald met his end trying to extend his authority over his English and British neighbours.

But his death proved to be the prelude to a longer posthumous life. Immediately after the battle his body was dismembered by his enemies, but his brother and successor, OSWIU, succeeded in rescuing parts of it in a raid into Mercia. He deposited the severed arms in the royal chapel at Bamburgh and gave the head to be interred at Lindisfarne, whence it eventually found its way to Durham, where it lies with the remains of ST CUTHBERT behind the high altar of the cathedral. Because of this, the two saints were often represented together iconographically, St Cuthbert holding the crowned head of St Oswald in his arm. The cult of St Oswald became popular enough to result in at least seventy-nine pre-Conquest churches being dedicated to him in Britain as far apart as Cathcart near Glasgow to Paddlesworth in Kent. However, the distribution is very uneven, all but a handful being located between the Tees and the Wash. Significantly, there are only two in Northumberland and one (Elvet) in Durham, almost certainly because the Community of St Cuthbert was not prepared to countenance a rival to its saint within its 'territory'. The cult also spread to the continent, not only in the form of church dedications, but also in claims by four monasteries in Germany, Holland, Switzerland and Luxemburg to possess Oswald's head.

OSWINE, KING OF DEIRA AND SAINT (?–651)

Oswine, who was a contemporary of OSWALD and OSWIU, was the last hope of the royal family of Deira. Following the death of Oswald in 642, he established himself as king in Deira, backed by the Mercian king, Penda. If BEDE is to be believed, he was more personable and more genuinely religious, and more highly rated by ST AIDAN, than Oswiu, who succeeded his brother Oswald as king in Bernicia. Driven by political imperatives, Oswiu contrived Oswine's assassination in August 651 in order to destroy the Deiran dynasty and bring all of Northumbria under Bernician rule. The deed took place at Gilling, North Yorkshire, where Oswiu had to found a monastery in order to expiate his crime. Oswine was not buried in the monastery at Gilling, but at TYNEMOUTH: having removed the living threat, Oswiu was not going to risk the possibility of a posthumous one in the form of a popular cult centre.

This did not prevent the cult of St Oswine developing. Some 414 years later, a body was disinterred at Tynemouth, which it was claimed was that of St Oswine. There are two stories relating to the 'discovery'. One was that it was made by the local priest, Edmund, on the inspiration of a dream in which Oswine appeared to him. The other was that one of the Community of St Cuthbert (see CUTHBERT, SAINT) claimed that he had found the remains of several local saints, including Oswine. The truth of this is immaterial: what was important was that the 'discovery' revived the fame of St Oswine, who was given a splendid tomb in the monastery church at Tynemouth, which became a place of pilgrimage. All this came to an end in the 1530s with the closure of Tynemouth Priory. Excavations took place in 1774, but this time no body came to light.

OSWIU (c.606–670), KING OF NORTHUMBRIA 642–670

Oswiu, the younger brother of OSWALD, succeeded him as king in Bernicia after he was killed in 642. To do so, he may have murdered Oethelwald, Oswald's young son. But his power did not extend into Deira, which with Mercian support fell to OSWINE, a member of the Deiran royal family.

Politically, his reign had two phases. Until the early 650s, his position was weak. By his victory, the Mercian king Penda inherited Oswald's political status. From time to time he raided Bernicia to exact tribute from Oswiu; and he controlled Deira through Oswine, who ruled as a tributary king. All this changed between 651 and 655. In the former year, Oswiu bribed one of Oswine's household to murder him at Gilling, North Yorkshire. The deed deeply shocked ST AIDAN and is said to have hastened his death twelve weeks later. But Oswine's death eliminated the Deiran royal family, which was necessary if Oswiu was to regain his patrimony. Four years later, Oswiu completed his revolution when, on 15 November 655, he defeated and killed Penda in a battle by a river called Winwaed. If, as it is thought, this battle took place in the vicinity of Leeds, it would seem that Penda had invaded Northumbria in order to reassert his dominance. Thereafter, Oswiu expanded his kingdom by imposing his authority on the lands west of the Pennines. By the time of his death he was, as his brother had been, the most powerful ruler in Britain.

But the long-term significance of his reign lay in the cultural field, for it was he who summoned and presided over the conference known as the Synod of Whitby, at that time called Streneshalgh. The venue was the recently founded monastery for men and women, the head of which was Hild, a cousin of the murdered Oswine. The purpose of the meeting was to resolve seemingly intractable differences between two contrasting and conflicting styles of Christianity. The Irish style, brought by Aidan from Iona, was simple and austere, and based upon monasteries, which were both mission stations and cultural centres. The other style came from Rome and the continent. It was more high-profile, glamorous and authoritarian, and with a power structure derived from Roman imperial models. Increasing awareness of this alternative came from those Northumbrians, notably BENEDICT BISCOP, who journeyed to the continent to obtain knowledge, books and relics.

The differences between the two styles found visible expression in clerical tonsure, the haircut that identified the clergy: the Roman form was the shaven crown so that the hair commemorated the crown of thorns; the Irish form was the shaven front of the head. Of more fundamental importance was the difference between the two churches in their method of calculating the date of Easter. This was such that it was possible for the adherents of one style to be celebrating Easter while the advocates of the other were still in the Lenten fast. As Christianity spread and as knowledge of continental ways became widely known, a resolution of the problem became urgent.

At the conference the case for change was put by WILFRID, Northumbria's most ardent 'Europhile'; that for maintaining the status quo by Colman, Bishop of Lindisfarne. After listening to the arguments (and without the benefit of a referendum) Oswiu pronounced in favour of Rome. Whether he was persuaded by the religious arguments or a perception of political advantage or a combination of both cannot be determined, but the consequences of his decision are clear. Some of the Irish monks conformed, but many returned to Iona or to Ireland and the Northumbrian church began to become a more organised and politically involved institution, and to absorb continental influences. Had Oswiu not opted for change, Northumbria might have remained more insular and lacking the cultural infusion that in the decades that followed had the dramatic effects in the fields of art and literature that have been called the Golden Age of Northumbria.

Oswiu owed his success as king to his willingness to act ruthlessly, and his 'reward' was to die in his bed, something that few other kings of his era managed.

OTTERBURN, BATTLE OF, 1388

The Battle of Otterburn was one of the largest military engagements of the long Anglo-Scottish war. It was fought in August 1388, although there is some doubt as to the precise date. Most reports favour St Oswald's Day, that is, 5 August, and also say that it was fought by moonlight. But on the 5th the moon was fully waned, whereas on the 19th, St Oswine's Day, there was a full moon. It is possible, therefore, that the chroniclers confused the two saints. There is an also uncertainty as to the battlefield. The most likely site was the ground north of the village, where the memorial is located.

The two armies were led by noted military leaders: the Scottish commanders were James Douglas, 2nd Earl of Douglas and Patrick Dunbar, Earl of March; the English force was under Sir Henry Percy (known as Hotspur), the eldest son of Henry Percy, 1st Earl of Northumberland (see PERCY FAMILY). Although the battle was important, its fame rests considerably on the Border Ballads. These convey the impression that it was simply an incident in a long-running cross-border feud between the Douglas and Percy families. There is some truth in this. Both families had risen to power during the fourteenth century through land acquisition on their respective sides of the BORDER: to say that in 1388 they were thrusting parvenus, at least in the Border region, is not unfair. And there was rivalry between them over the right to a particularly valuable estate, Jedburgh and Jed Forest, which extended from the Border to the River Teviot, a distance of ten miles. At different times earlier in the century, each family had been given the estate by their respective king. Consequently, both had a good personal reason to take an active part in the war.

But much more lay behind this. The Scottish incursion was in fact part of a full-scale invasion organised by the Scottish government of Robert II and led by his second son, Robert, Earl of Fife. The aim of the offensive was to secure a favourable peace treaty with England, by which the Scots would regain possession of the castles and towns of BERWICK, Roxburgh and Jedburgh, which had been in English hands since the BATTLE OF NEVILLE'S CROSS in 1346. Nor was the timing accidental: since 1386 there had been a political crisis in London during which the young Richard II was all but deposed.

The invasion was intended to take advantage of English weakness. England, however, was not entirely defenceless, since the Wardens on the Marches (see MARCHES OF ENGLAND TOWARDS SCOTLAND) had the authority to raise troops to counter any Scottish incursion. It was in his capacity as Warden of the East March that Hotspur was in command in Northumberland.

The 1388 invasion was not singular in that the Scottish forces were large enough to mount two simultaneous incursions. The main thrust, led by the Earl of Fife, went into Cumberland (Cumbria), with the intention of occupying it and then using it as a diplomatic bargaining counter. The invasion of Northumberland may have been a diversionary feint; or, perhaps more likely, the consequence of differences within the Scottish high command, with Douglas and March deciding to pursue their own agenda and Fife being powerless to overrule them.

Whatever the reason, the western thrust came to nothing, whereas that into Northumberland ended in the greatest Scottish victory on English soil. Douglas's force made an unopposed sweep through Northumberland, and may have entered Durham. Meanwhile, Hotspur was in Newcastle, in front of whose walls Douglas presented himself, daring Hotspur to give battle. Although there may have been a skirmish at Barras Bridge in which Hotspur's pennon was captured, Hotspur, notwithstanding his reputation for impetuosity, was not willing at this stage to risk a pitched battle. The Scottish army therefore headed north unopposed, laden with the spoils of war. But they were shadowed by Hotspur's reconnaissance troops, who reported that they had camped 30 miles (48 km) away at Otterburn.

We can only surmise that Hotspur's decision to go after them was made in the belief that he could move rapidly (his forces would have been mounted) and catch them off guard. His calculation was correct, but in making his move he denied himself the advantage of the reinforcements that the Bishop of Durham, John Fordham, was known to be bringing. As he neared Otterburn, Hotspur also took a tactical decision to send part of his force to the north of the Scottish camp in order to make a flanking attack. Unfortunately, for unclear reasons this failed. The battle itself seems to have been nothing more than a mêlée in which the natural confusion would have been made greater by the lack of light. In the end the Scots were victorious. Hotspur and his youngest brother, Sir Ralph Percy, who was seriously wounded, were captured. With the Durham troops turning back on seeing the remnants of Hotspur's army fleeing the battle, the Scots were able to return to Scotland unopposed with their booty and prisoners. Their only debit was the death of the Earl of Douglas.

The Battle of Otterburn was a major military engagement by the standards of the time. No reliable figures are available, but the large number of male skeletons, carefully arranged in double rows, discovered in the nineteenth century in front of and underneath the north wall of the nave of Elsdon church, may be a clue. Since Elsdon was the parish church and the north wall of the nave was built *c.*1400, it is hard to resist the conclusion that they were the remains of the Otterburn dead. If so, they prove that Otterburn was no mere skirmish.

Major battle though Otterburn was, its outcome did not have a significant consequence. In England, Richard II recovered his authority and therefore no concessions were made to the Scots. Hotspur recovered his liberty the following year, the cost of his ransom being largely met from public funds, to continue his role as defender of the Border.

OTTERBURN, THOMAS (c.1300-c.1350)

Given his importance as a source of information about the dramatic events in northern England in the first half of the fourteenth century, it is unfortunate that we have so little information about Thomas Otterburn. His name points to his having been a native of the North East and we know that he became a Franciscan friar and that he was educated at Oxford University, gaining the degree of D.Th. in 1343. Almost certainly he continued an earlier chronicle written by a Richard of Durham, and his writings were the source of the very important chronicle written at Lanercost Priory, covering events between the start of the Anglo-Scottish war in the 1290s and the BATTLE OF NEVILLE'S CROSS in 1346. His familiarity with all matters military has led to speculation that he may have been a soldier before entering his religious order.

OTTERBURN ARMY TRAINING AREA

The Otterburn Army Training Area (usually referred to as the Otterburn Ranges) covers 57,000 acres (23,000 ha) of land between the rivers Rede and Coquet. Except for 4,000 (1,600 ha) acres of woodland, its freehold is owned by the Ministry of Defence and occupied by thirty-one farms, whose tenants have the same rights in law as those on any other estate. In addition, virtually all the land lies within the NORTHUMBERLAND NATIONAL PARK, whose regulations apply within the military area. The land is used for the training of both regular and territorial troops of the British Army, and also some of our NATO allies, especially the smaller countries that lack sufficient land and the appropriate terrain for training purposes. Two branches of the army train here, the artillery and the infantry. Not the tanks, however: these were tried in 1938, but the ground was found to be too soft for tracked vehicles.

The ranges began life as a training area in 1911, when the then War Office bought 19,000 acres (7,700 ha) from the Duke of Northumberland for use by the artillery elements of the Territorial Army, formed in 1908. Men, guns and horses came by train to the railway station at West Woodburn, and then marched the remaining ten miles to Redesdale Camp, opened in 1912. Periods of training under instruction from regulars lasted a fortnight and covered the better months of the year, from Easter to October. Although intensively used during World War I, it was in 1939 that major developments took place with the doubling of the area by the acquisition of a further 20,000 acres (8,000 ha) and the building of the Otterburn Camp in 1940.

In the years since the end of World War II the area has been twice expanded to reach its present size. In 1959 it was designated an All Arms Training Area, since when it has widened its scope: troops are now trained in integrated fighting in which infantry combine with various forms of artillery and ground attack aircraft. In addition, the quality of accommodation and facilities at both camps has been considerably improved. Otterburn is one of seven Army Field Training Centres and is the largest single live firing area in the country.

As well as playing a vital role in training the British Army, it is of major importance to the local economy. It is not permanently closed to civilians, many of its roads being open, except at times when there is danger from military activity.

OTTERBURN MILL AND THE OTTERBURN RUG

Otterburn Mill, whose products became world-famous, was part of the rapid expansion of industry in the early years of the nineteenth century, which saw the creation of many similar mills on the Scottish side of the Border. Founded in 1821 by a Jedburgh man, William Waddell, it remained in the hands of his descendants until 1995. It was a comprehensive enterprise, taking raw wool and putting it through all the processes needed to turn it into usable cloth. The wool came from local farmers, who took payment in the form of cloth and knitting wool. This barter system was not finally discontinued until 1964, when by law all wool had to be sold to the Wool Marketing Board. Initially, the machinery was powered by water that was brought down a lade dug between the Otter Burn and the River Rede. The existing water turbines, installed in 1890, are still in working order. In 1906 and 1926 these were supplemented by diesel engines, which were replaced in 1940 by two electric motors.

The mill's reputation was based upon its tweeds, a name that was adopted as the result of a clerical error in the early nineteenth century. Originally, Border cloth was known as *twill*, but by mistake a clerk at a mill in Hawick wrote the word *tweed* on an invoice sent with cloth to a London customer, who decided that it would be a better word by which to market the product. Otterburn Mill produced cloth of the finest quality that was highly prized by the great fashion houses of London, Paris, Milan, New York and Tokyo. But it was more widely known for its rugs, which gained fame through their association with the royal family. The story is that Queen Alexandra on a visit to Alnwick Castle was presented with an Otterburn rug. Pleased with it, she enquired whether a quarter-size rug could be made to fit a pram. This was done, and later a similar rug was presented to the royal household on the occasion of the present Queen's birth in April 1926. The surplus rugs were taken by Fenwicks of Newcastle (see FENWICK, JOHN JAMES), where the royal association guaranteed their sale within a week. From that moment, Otterburn rugs graced every possible pram and cot.

Otterburn Mill ceased production in 1976, victim of the failure to invest that characterised the Border textile industry in the decades after World War II. It was not that there was no market for Otterburn tweeds, or that they were out of fashion; it was that the cost of production was too high. It remained closed but intact until 1995, when it was bought by an Inverness company, James Pringle, who turned it into a retail shop with a café and space for the local tourist office. Most of the old machinery has been retained *in situ* to give some indication of the mill's original appearance and purpose. Like so much of Britain's industrial heritage, Otterburn Mill now serves the tourist industry.

OVINGTON, DAVID (1955–2005)

Dave Ovington created a highly successful boat-building business that rapidly acquired an international reputation. He began building boats in his father's yard at Mariners' Lane, Tynemouth in his late teens, but his rise to success really began in 1987, when he won the 'International 14' Prince of Wales Cup in a boat he had built himself. In the same year, the 'Enterprise' championship was won in another Ovington boat. In the years that followed, he built some of the world's fastest dinghies and he designed the '49er', which became an Olympic class in the 2000 Games held at Sydney. Four years later, at the Athens Games, half the boats competing in the '49er' class were built by Ovingtons, including those that won the gold, silver and bronze medals. By that date Ovington had branched out into the manufacture of larger boats, the 'Mumm 30', a thirty-foot, single-keel boat. He was awarded an exclusive contract to build these boats, for which purpose a new yard was developed at Tanners' Bank, North Shields. He died suddenly while on a family holiday, sailing on Windermere.

OXFORD UNIVERSITY COLLEGES

The North East had significant influence on, or involvement with, four of the oldest colleges of Oxford University. Here it should be borne in mind that it was only in the late twelfth and thirteenth centuries that universities as distinctive academic institutions gradually evolved. Oxford University, the oldest in Britain, began its life with the enforced return of English students from Paris during a diplomatic quarrel between the English and French kings. The colleges, which became its hallmark, gradually emerged from the middle of the thirteenth century.

Balliol College: Balliol College arose out of a dispute started by one of the region's most prominent landowners. John Balliol (see BALLIOL AND BRUCE FAMILIES), Lord of BARNARD CASTLE and BYWELL, became engaged in a dispute with the Bishop of Durham, Walter Kirkham (1249–60), and King Henry III (1216–72) over the question of to whom he owed homage for the lordship of Gainford: *he* claimed that the overlordship belonged to the Crown; *they* insisted that it belonged to the bishop as ruler of the PALATINATE OF DURHAM. The story is that in the course of this quarrel some of Balliol's men ambushed the bishop, subjecting him to humiliation and his men to physical abuse. Consequently, Balliol was required to do public penance, which took the form of a ritual chastisement by the bishop at the door of DURHAM CATHEDRAL, and also to make an undertaking to support sixteen poor scholars at Oxford.

Although there is some uncertainty as to the truth of this story, there is no doubt about the quarrel or that from 1263 Balliol was giving financial support to scholars at Oxford, which after his death in 1268 his widow, Dervorguila, the heir to the Scottish lordship of Galloway, continued. In 1282, however, she turned what might be described as a proto-college into a fully fledged institution through the grant to the scholars of a statute of self-government and three tenements in what is now Broad Street, which she had bought for this specific purpose. The following year she provided the college with endowment in the form of land at Stamfordham and Heugh in Northumberland, which she had bought for £200.

In this enterprise she was advised and assisted by **Hugh of Hartlepool**, a Franciscan friar, who in effect was the college's first master. Subsequently he had a distinguished career, rising to become Minister Provincial of his order in England and in this role attending the General Chapters of the Franciscan Friars held at Lyon in 1299 and Genoa in 1301. He died the following year at Assisi, where he is buried. After he relinquished the mastership of the college in 1284, his role was taken by another friar from the North East, **Richard of Slikeburn** (Sleekburn), also known as **Richard of Durham**.

The North-East connection was reinforced in the middle of the following century. In 1340 a Northumbrian knight, **Sir William de Felton** (whose family were lords of Edlingham from 1296 until 1516 and who is buried in Edlingham church) assigned to the college the church of Abbotsley in Huntingdonshire. A few weeks later Sir Philip Somerville, whose family had acquired half of the barony of MORPETH, added the Northumberland church of Longbenton. Behind their generosity lay the persuasive Bishop of Durham, RICHARD DE BURY (1333–45). Their value and the status of their donors occasioned a radical revamping of the college statutes that was tantamount to a refoundation. One of the most significant changes was that vesting the ultimate authority in the college's affairs in the Bishop of Durham: Richard de Bury, it would seem, was seeking to make Balliol College a Durham preserve. Papal intervention in 1363, however, thwarted this by transferring the supervisory role to the Bishop of London.

Balliol College's Northumberland connection lasted until the 1920s, when a reorganisation of its endowments involved the disposal of its North-East properties.

Merton College: The North East was not involved in the foundation of Merton College, which is regarded as the earliest in the University. But in its early days it acquired two very valuable pieces of endowment in the North East, the Northumberland parishes of **Ponteland** and **Embleton**. The patronage (the right to nominate the rector) of Ponteland parish, which contained fifteen townships, belonged to the Bertram family, lords of the Barony of Mitford. In 1262, however, Roger Bertram gave or sold it to a Peter de Montfort, whose son of the same name gave it to Merton in 1268. Merton's intention was to appropriate, that is, to collect all the rectorial income for itself, assigning a fraction to a resident vicar who would carry out the parish priest's duties. This outcome, however, had to be deferred for thirty-five years until the Lords of Mitford gave up their struggle to recover their former rights: not until 1303 did the college gain full control. Events at Embleton, which also had fifteen townships, followed an almost identical course. There the patronage of the parish belonged to Edmund, Earl of Lancaster, the brother of King Henry III, who gave it to Merton in 1274. Like the Lords of Mitford, his successors fought a lengthy rearguard action to frustrate the college's ambition, in this case lasting sixty-seven years: only in 1341 did Merton gain complete control that enabled it to appropriate the rectorial revenues and appoint a vicar. Merton's success not only substantially enhanced its income, but enabled it to provide its former students and fellows with comfortable careers as vicars of Embleton and Ponteland.

Trinity College: This college began life as **Durham College**, founded by the Cathedral Priory in the early 1380s and dedicated to the Holy Trinity, the Blessed Virgin and St Cuthbert. It was for sixteen students: eight were to be monks of the priory, one of whom was to be the head of house with the title of Warden; the other eight were to be non-monastic students, four from the Diocese of Durham and two each from Northallerton and Howden in Yorkshire, places controlled by the Bishop and Cathedral Priory. The foundation owed much to the generosity of the Bishop of Durham, Thomas de Hatfield (1345–81), who bequeathed the sum of £3,000, which enabled the priory to embark upon an endowment and building programme. What emerged was a 'classic' Oxford 'quad', formed by a chapel, a hall at right angles to it with the necessary service rooms, and two sides comprising two-storey accommodation blocks. Between its foundation and the closure of the priory in 1539, the college was the training ground for the brightest monks, one of whom in every generation went on to become Prior of Durham.

However, the college did not start from scratch. For the previous hundred years, Durham Cathedral Priory had sent monks to study at Oxford, accommodating them in premises bought from the Nunnery of Godstow and the Priory of St Frideswide and supporting them financially by subventions from Durham. Hatfield's bequest made it possible to replace this arrangement with a fully endowed college, which was one of the best appointed in late medieval Oxford.

When the new Dean and Chapter of Durham Cathedral succeeded the Priory in the spring of 1541, it retained possession of the college until 1545, when it was surrendered to the Crown. The buildings then lay empty for ten years, except for the years 1547–49, when they were occupied by the University's Vice-Chancellor. But in 1553 they were acquired by Sir Thomas Pope, who two years later refounded the college as 'The College of the Holy and Undivided Trinity in the University of Oxford'. Pope pandered to his own vanity by appending to this title the words 'of the foundation of Thomas Pope' and granting to the college the right to use his coat of arms. Pope had acquired the landed wealth he needed to refound the college through his role as Treasurer of the Court of Augmentations of the Revenues of the King's Crown, the office set up in 1536 to administer and dispose of the lands of dissolved monasteries. Pope took advantage of his position to amass a large portfolio of ex-monastic estates, principally in Oxfordshire. Why did he use his wealth thus? One reason was personal: he and his wife had no direct heirs who would expect to inherit. But there was also a possible political motive. Pope was at heart (appropriately, given his name) a Catholic and welcomed the restoration of the old religion by Mary I (1447–1558), who was concerned to repair the damage done to Oxford University by the ecclesiastical upheavals of the 1530s and 1540s. By restoring a former monastic college, and using ex-monastic property to endow it, he hoped the queen would not hold against him his role in suppressing the monasteries. Since 1555 Trinity College has grown and developed, but it still occupies the site of Durham College, considerable parts of which survive and are still in use.

University College: Although the origins of this college are less clear-cut than those of Trinity, it is clear that it owed a considerable debt to a North-East man, **William of Durham**, about whom regrettably little is known. His name indicates his place of birth, which was probably around 1180; and he is known to have died in 1249. Evidently academically able, he gained an MA degree at Oxford and a D.Th. in Paris, where he was a teacher until 1229. Subsequently, he had a successful ecclesiastical career in France, becoming Archdeacon of Caen. It is also possible that he may have been elected Archbishop of Rouen, although he did not secure tenure of his very prestigious post. At some stage, he returned to the North East and became Rector of Bishopwearmouth.

The ecclesiastical career must have been lucrative, since he bequeathed a large sum to Oxford University with instructions that it should be invested in property, the income from which was to be used to support ten or more men with the degree of MA studying for the degree of D.Th. It was this money that eventually in 1280 was used to found University College. Unfortunately, William of Durham's part in bringing University College into existence has only recently been exposed. For many centuries it was obscured by a ludicrous story that the founder of the college was King Alfred the Great (who died in 899), together with an even more ridiculous fable that the VENERABLE BEDE was one of its alumni.

PALATINATE OF DURHAM

The Palatinate of Durham was a regalian franchise, that is, a defined area of land wherein the franchisee discharged all the functions of government that elsewhere in the kingdom were discharged by the Crown. The franchisee in this case was the Bishop of Durham.

Geographically, the Palatinate comprised a number of discrete areas. The largest was the land between the Tyne/Derwent and the Tees plus the parish of Ryton between the Derwent and the Tyne. Initially it did not include three enclaves on the north bank of the Tees known collectively as the WAPENTAKE OF SADBERGE. These were parts of NORTHUMBERLAND until 1189, when BISHOP HUGH OF LE PUISET bought them from Richard I. North of the Tyne it included North Durham and Bedlingtonshire (see BEDLINGTON), and in the North Riding a small enclave around Crayke.

This franchise was not created formally or at a particular time but evolved in an unplanned fashion from arrangements that pre-dated the Norman Conquest, when the land north of the Tees was not yet fully incorporated into the Kingdom of England. Government was in the hands of two largely autonomous authorities, the Bishop of Durham, who ruled the lands belonging to ST CUTHBERT, and the Earl of Northumbria (see NORTHUMBRIA, KINGDOM AND EARLDOM OF), who controlled the remainder. This situation ended in 1095 when William II deposed the earl, Robert de Mowbray, and did not replace him, thereby effectively abolishing the earldom. Henceforth, Northumberland was to be a regular English county. He did not, however, disturb the arrangement regarding the Bishop of Durham.

Thereafter, successive kings found it useful or convenient to allow the bishops to wield regal power and to permit them to adopt new forms of government devised by the Crown. So comprehensive was the bishop's authority that in 1302 one of his leading administrators, William St Botolph (Boston), remarked, with rather more pride than strict accuracy, that there were two kings in England, the Lord King of England and the Bishop of Durham. Taken at face value, this suggests that the Bishop of Durham was an independent ruler. This impression, however, is deceptive.

It is true that the bishop and the administrators he employed had all aspects of government in their hands. The bishop appointed and controlled all the judicial officers and he kept all the fines, amercements and forfeitures levied in his courts. He also appointed all the local government officials, such as sheriffs, coroners and escheators. He was entitled to the royal rights of wreck and the royal fish (whales, porpoises and sturgeon) and he minted his own coins. Finally, no MPs were sent from the franchise to parliament and the inhabitants of the franchise paid no taxes. But, and it is an important but, there were aspects of government beyond the bishop's reach. He could not develop his own foreign policy. He had no legislative power: the laws of England were those of the Palatinate. And although the coins bore the bishop's mark, they had the same denomination and value as those issued by the royal mints. When stripped of the rhetoric and hyperbole, the bishop was essentially no more than a highly privileged administrator.

Moreover, it was the king who chose the bishop and, although he had no power to dismiss him, he could deprive him of his temporal role and his estates, leaving him with his spiritual authority but very little income. As one historian has aptly remarked, 'The franchise was as long as the king's temper.' This point was amply illustrated by Henry II (1153–89) and by Edward I (1272–1307), who struck down, respectively,

Bishop Hugh of le Puiset (1154–95) and Bishop Anthony Bek (1283–1311), probably the most imperious men to occupy the see of Durham, each of whom twice tried royal patience too far. But neither Henry II nor Edward I was minded to destroy the Palatinate, and consequently both Puiset and Bek were restored after short periods of deprivation that served to remind them where ultimate authority lay.

In fact, the Palatinate was not destroyed, but suffered a lingering death lasting over 400 years. This protracted demise began in 1535–36 with the Act for the Revocation of Franchises, which was directed at franchises generally, not specifically at Durham. At face value it seemed conclusive, but in fact it was more a statement of principle than a restructuring of the mechanisms of government. Henceforth, the franchise continued to function, but in the king's name, not that of the bishop, and to enforce the king's peace, not that of the bishop, so that the bishop no longer had the power to pardon criminals. As regards day-to-day business, however, the inhabitants of the Palatinate would not have been conscious of great changes until the seventeenth century. The most drastic was the total abolition of the Palatinate in 1647. But this proved to be temporary: in 1660, with the restoration of the monarchy, the Palatinate was fully restored to BISHOP JOHN COSIN. In the seventeenth century there were two changes, however, that were permanent. In 1610 the Palatinate became subject to parliamentary taxation, which provoked agitation for the Palatinate to be represented in parliament. This finally succeeded in 1675 and 1678 when, respectively, the County and the City of Durham were each granted the right to elect two MPs.

These changes apart, until 1836 the bishop continued to appoint sheriffs and justices of the peace and through them to control the quarter and petty sessions, to have his own Court of Pleas to deal with civil cases, and to have his own Chancery Court and Temporal Chancellor. In 1836, however, following the death of Bishop VAN MILDERT, the Prime Minister, Lord Melbourne, wished to abolish the Palatinate entirely, but chose to compromise in the face of strong local opposition. The franchise was removed from the bishop, but it was not abolished; instead, it was declared to be a royal franchise vested in the king, but separate from the Crown, a distinction that only a lawyer could appreciate. The Court of Pleas was retained, but its procedures were brought into line with those in the rest of England. The Chancery too was retained, the Temporal Chancellor to be paid by the Ecclesiatical Commission, not by the bishop.

In the late nineteenth century further changes were instituted. In 1873, in the wide-ranging reform of the legal system, the Palatine Court of Pleas was absorbed into the newly created High Court of Judicature. As a result, the Palatinate was reduced to its Chancery. In 1889, however, this was strengthened by a declaration that the Chancellor's decisions should be valid outwith the area of his jurisdiction. The consequence was an increase in the number of cases it dealt with. In 1952 its jurisdiction was extended to include Teesside, which led to a further increase in its business. The end came in 1971. As part of the wide-ranging changes to the judicial system recommended by the Beeching Commission, which saw the replacement of the Assizes and the Quarter Sessions by the present Crown Courts, the Palatine Chancery was abolished. The Palatinate of Durham had become history.

PARKER, HENRY PERLEE (1795–1873)

Henry Perlee Parker spent the middle years of his life in Newcastle. He was born in Devonport, the son of a teacher of drawing, and he inherited his father's skill and benefited from his tuition. By 1815 he was sufficiently confident to set up as a professional portraitist, initially in Plymouth, but almost immediately he moved to the North East, where he believed the opportunities would be greater. His first base was in Sunderland, where he had relations, but after a short time there he moved to Newcastle, which he found more congenial. He remained in the town until 1841, collaborating with THOMAS MILES RICHARDSON, senior, in his attempts to create fine arts institutions. He also enjoyed considerable success as a painter, exhibiting regularly at the Royal Academy, as well as the British Institution. Many of his non-portraits were of smuggling scenes, which secured him the nickname of 'Smuggler' Parker. He also painted two particularly fine portraits, of GRACE DARLING and her father, William Darling. In 1841, however, he left the North East for good, moving first to Sheffield to become drawing master at Wesley College, and then, permanently, to London in 1847.

PARKINSON, CYRIL NORTHCOTE (1909–1993)

Cyril Parkinson was born in Galgate, Barnard Castle, where his father was Art Master at the then Northern Counties School, now Barnard Castle School. He lived there for only four years, until 1913, when his father became Principal of the York School of Arts and Crafts. Parkinson was educated at St Peter's School, York and at Cambridge University, after which, apart from war service, he had a conventional academic career as a historian at Cambridge and Liverpool and in Malaya. All this was changed in 1958 with the publication of his book *Parkinson's Law, or The Pursuit of Progress*, which grew out of humorous articles he had written for *The Economist*. The most famous of the aphorisms in the book was 'Work expands to fill the time available for its completion.' The book made his fortune and allowed him to retire from academic life.

PARSONS, SIR CHARLES ALGERNON (1854–1931)

Sir Charles Parsons was one of the world's greatest innovative engineers, who throughout his life continued to be an inventor and whose interests included sound amplification, helicopters, aeroplanes and compressors, as well as the turbine, the invention for which he is best known. He was the youngest son of William Parsons, 3rd Earl of Rosse, then one of the world's leading astronomers, whose family seat was Birr Castle, County Offaly in Ireland. Family wealth meant that he was not sent to school but educated by private tutors. Thereafter he spent two years at Trinity College, Dublin followed by four years at St John's College, Cambridge, where he took a degree in Mathematics in 1881. As mathematics and science were the core of his education, it was logical that upon graduation he should embark upon a four-year apprenticeship with SIR WILLIAM ARMSTRONG at Elswick (1877–81) to gain first-hand knowledge of engineering practice, which was followed by two years with the Leeds firm of Kitson (1881–83). Fully qualified, in 1884 he became a junior partner in the GATESHEAD firm of Clarke, Chapman & Co., where he was given control of the newly formed department of electrical engineering. It was here that he produced the first of his great inventions, the axial steam turbine. The generator he designed, which was intended to provide lighting in ships, ran at 18,000 rpm, generating 7½ kW. It was so successful that within four years 200 generators had been produced.

Recognising the huge potential of his invention, in 1889 Parsons set up his own company with works at Heaton in

NEWCASTLE, which was to grow to employ 15,000 people. This involved the dissolution of his partnership with Clarke, Chapman, which led to an acrimonious disagreement with them over the ownership of the turbine patents. Parsons, however, needed the freedom his own company gave him to develop turbines for the commercial generation of electricity. To avoid litigation over patent rights, Parsons devised the radial turbine. His first venture was to supply a generator for the world's first power station, that at Forth Banks, Newcastle. The equipment he supplied comprised two turbo-alternators capable of generating 75 kW. The market for electricity generators was instant and worldwide, which Parsons' firm continued to supply for the remaining forty years of his life and beyond. At the time of his death, however, the capacity of his turbo-alternators had risen to 200,000 kW.

In 1894 Parsons turned his attention to the application of the steam turbine to marine propulsion, to which end he set up a separate company, Parsons Marine Steam Turbine Co., at Wallsend. Its first product was the 44-ton vessel *TURBINIA*, which was powered by axial turbines, Parsons having recently purchased the patents to his earlier invention from Clarke, Chapman. This small vessel astonished the naval world at the Spithead Review of 1897 by achieving speeds of over 34 knots. The demonstration had the intended effect, with the rapid adoption of turbine propulsion for all types of ships. By 1901 the first turbine-driven passenger ship was built and the Admiralty was experimenting with the turbine as the means of propulsion in destroyers and cruisers. Four years later turbines were installed in the Cunard liner *Carmania*, and the Admiralty decided that all future warships should be turbine-driven. After the end of World War I, Parsons also pioneered the use of high-pressure steam in marine engines.

Another major area in which Parsons was innovative was optics. He established a separate department at the Heaton works to produce searchlight reflectors. By 1920 this side of his business became fully developed and so over the next five years he bought the well-known London manufacturers of binoculars Ross & Co., Derby Crown Glass Co. and Sir Howard Grubb & Co. These enabled him to set up a new company, Grubb, Parsons & Co., for which he built a new works at Walkergate in Newcastle. There, until its closure in 1983, reflectors for some of the world's most important telescopes were made.

Parsons was honoured by all the nation's scientific institutions, including the Royal Society, and was awarded honorary degrees by seven British universities. He was knighted in 1911 and in 1927 given the OM. He died in 1931 in Jamaica, while on a holiday cruise, and was buried at Kirkwhelpington. Although Parsons' reputation rests on his technological genius, he also created with the help of supporters and backers highly successful businesses that exploited commercially what he had invented in the laboratory.

PASMORE, EDWIN JOHN VICTOR (1908–1998)

Victor Pasmore had a considerable impact on two very different places within the North East during his brief sojourn in the 1950s and early 1960s. He trained as an artist in the inter-war years, becoming a member of a group committed to 'realistic art with social conscience'. In 1940 he was forced to join the army, despite claiming he was a conscientious objector, but was discharged in 1942 after serving a prison sentence for desertion. Thereafter he worked as a teacher at Camberwell School of Arts and Crafts and then at the Central School of Arts and Crafts, where he underwent a conversion to 'abstract' art.

Between 1954 and 1961 he was Director of Painting in the School of Fine Art at King's College, Newcastle, then part of Durham University. During these years he radically transformed the teaching of art at Newcastle and secured for the department a reputation for 'research and experiment in the language of abstract form'. He also made an impact on the development of Peterlee New Town (see NEW TOWNS OF THE TWENTIETH CENTURY), through his appointment as adviser to improve the aesthetic quality and design layout of the housing. His influence is most evident in the south-west area and is still controversial.

After leaving the North East, he became one of the most highly regarded artists of his day. He was made CH in 1981, RA in 1983 and CBE in 1989.

PATTERSON, SIR JAMES BROWN (1833–1895)

James Patterson was born in Alnwick, where his father was an inspector of elementary schools. At the age of nineteen he emigrated to the Colony of Victoria in Australia and in the following twenty years he made a fortune in the abbatoir business. This enabled him to become active in politics and in 1870 he was elected to the Victoria legislature. Between then and 1893 he held several ministerial posts, including that responsible for railways. In 1893 his political career reached its apogee when he became Prime Minister of Victoria. Unfortunately, his arrival at the top coincided with a severe economic depression. The harsh and unpopular but necessary action taken by his government led to its fall the following year. He died in the year after leaving office.

PATTINSON, HUGH LEE (1796–1858)

Hugh Lee Pattinson was born at Alston, the son of a shopkeeper. His parents were Quakers and had their son educated privately. He was deeply interested in, and gave much time to the study of, electricity, chemistry and metallurgy and it was his knowledge of these subjects that led to his involvement in the lead industry (see LEAD MINING AND MANUFACTURING INDUSTRIES). After a short spell with a Newcastle soap manufacturer, in 1825 he was appointed assay master for the Commissioners of Greenwich Hospital, the lords of Alston Manor. He remained in this post for six years until 1831, when he became manager of the Wentworth-Beaumont lead works.

In 1834, however, he made a significant break by going into partnership with two other men, John Lee and George Burnett, to found a chemical works at Felling, later moving to Washington. The basis of this business was his discovery of a simple and inexpensive method of separating silver from lead. He made the discovery in 1825, but was not able to patent it until 1833. His method was viable for lead ores with a silver content as low as 2 per cent, which in turn made viable the opening of hitherto uneconomic mines. It also gave rise to new words in French and German: *pattinsonage* and *pattinsoniren.*

Royalties from his patent enabled him to indulge his interest in astronomy and to buy a 7½-inch refractor, which he installed in his home, Scots House, a property in Boldon that had existed since at least the year 1381. He is also credited with two other scientific discoveries: the simple method of obtaining white lead; and the fact that steam forced through a nozzle becomes electrical, knowledge that WILLIAM ARMSTRONG was to make good use of. He is credited with taking the first photograph of Niagara Falls, published in Paris in 1841.

PEARSON, JOHN LOUGHBOROUGH (1817–1901)

John Loughborough Pearson was one of the outstanding Gothic Revival architects of the nineteenth century. He was born in Durham City, the son of a painter, and lived there until the age of twenty-five. Between 1831 and 1842 he trained as an architect under IGNATIUS BONOMI, but after qualifying moved to London to set up his own practice.

Pearson, who was heavily influenced by the French Gothic style, specialised in ecclesiastical architecture and rapidly gained a reputation for designing large, powerful and hugely impressive churches. Most notably, he reintroduced the stone vault. This began with his courageous decision to create a vaulted ceiling at the parish church of Stow in Lincolnshire, basing his design on clues provided by the vestigial remains of the medieval vault.

Most of his churches are in cities, including several in London. One of these, St Augustine's, Kilburn, is considered to be his finest church and for some it is the finest parish church of any age in the capital. His largest ecclesiastical commission was the cathedral at Truro, one of the many new dioceses created for the Church of England in the later nineteenth century. It was begun in 1880, but not completed until 1910, nine years after his death.

Pearson also had many commissions to repair and restore major churches. The list includes the cathedrals at Bristol, Rochester and Norwich, Shrewsbury Abbey and the socially and politically important church of St Margaret, Westminster. His reputation was such that he was given the prestigious task of renovating one of Britain's most historic buildings, Westminster Hall, following the demolition of the law courts built next to it in the eighteenth century by Sir John Soane. Pearson's scheme involved the construction of two additions to the hall, a proposal that aroused considerable controversy. Pearson, however, was able to demonstrate that they matched their medieval predecessors as closely as could be determined and were necessary to preserve the Norman walling.

In all Pearson designed twenty-nine churches, but only two are in the North East: St Hilda's, Darlington and St George's, Cullercoats. The latter was commissioned by the 6th Duke of Northumberland as a memorial to his father and was intended to stand at the meeting point of two crescents of houses. These were not built and as a result St George's stands like a beacon close to the top of Cullercoats sands.

PEASE FAMILY

The Pease family of DARLINGTON was one of the dominant and determining forces in the society, politics and industrial economy, not only of their home town, but also of South Durham and Teesside, for most of the nineteenth century. The family came to Darlington in the eighteenth century as the result of the marriage in 1706 of Joseph Pease (1665–1719), a small West Riding landowner, and Ann Couldwell, the heiress to a wool-combing business in the town. Their second son, Edward (1711–85), expanded the business by opening a mill in Priestgate in 1752 for weaving and dyeing. Further expansion took place under Edward's son, Joseph (1737–1808), who also started a banking business, not to issue notes, but to be the financial arm of his other enterprises.

Membership of the Society of Friends (Quakers) was one of the distinguishing marks of the Peases. This nonconformity in religion guaranteed their exclusion from public life and the learned professions, and had the result of directing their attention towards business. These early generations laid the foundations upon which their nineteenth-century successors were to build in spectacular fashion, before being overtaken by disaster in the first years of the twentieth century. Although the Pease family was prolific and many of its members participated in its various business enterprises, their great success was primarily the achievement of three men: Edward Pease (1767–1858), and two of his sons, Joseph Pease (1799–1872) and Henry Pease (1807–81).

Edward Pease, who had already made a fortune by the time the Stockton and Darlington Railway was mooted towards the end of the second decade of the nineteenth century, was one of the leading promoters of, and investors in, that enterprise. His decision was a shrewd business move, since by that date he was thinking of retiring, but by becoming involved, he ensured that his son Joseph would be able to play a central role in the developments that followed. Although Edward Pease continued to be active for some years until he retired in 1838, it was Joseph Pease who was the great driving force and one of the century's most dynamic entrepreneurs. His achievements were threefold.

The first was the expansion of the Stockton and Darlington Railway. This began with the purchase of the Middlesbrough Estate (see New Towns of the Nineteenth Century) and the act of 1828 allowing the line to be extended to Middlesbrough and to the coal staithes built there on the banks of the Tees. In 1842 these were replaced by the Middlesbrough Dock, adjacent to which a town with an intended population of 5,000 was laid out. Three years later, the line was extended eastwards from Middlesbrough to Redcar, opened in 1846, and subsequently, in the late 1850s, pushed further along the coast to Saltburn, where the Zetland Hotel was built in the hope of turning a fishing village into a fashionable resort, an ambition that was never fully realised. Much more hard-headed was the decision to promote the Middlesbrough and Guisborough Railway, opened in 1853, to carry iron ore from the rapidly expanding ore field in the Cleveland Hills, a move that was to pay dividends a few years later, when the Peases entered the iron mining industry.

At the same time, the railway was driven north-westwards. The Shildon Tunnel was opened in 1842, linking New Shildon with South Church, and in the following year the line was extended from South Church to Crook. By 1845 the line had reached Waskerley, where it joined the Stanhope and Tyne track. In fact, the Stanhope and Tyne Railroad had become bankrupt in 1839, but in 1842 its assets were taken over by a new company, the Pontop and South Shields Railway. It, however, was interested only in the eastern section, and so it sold the unwanted western section from Stanhope to Consett to the Derwent Iron Co. Three years later, in 1845, this firm leased the line to the Stockton and Darlington Railway. Thus by 1845 the Stockton and Darlington controlled a line that enabled it to service the burgeoning ironworks at Consett. In 1847 the various small railways involved (Bishop Auckland and Weardale, Shildon Tunnel, Wear and Derwent, and Weardale Extension), all of which had been promoted by the Stockton and Darlington, were consolidated as the Wear Valley Railway and taken over by the parent company. Subsequently, some extensions, most notably the Deerness Valley Railway in the late 1850s, were built and improvements made, the outstanding one being the Hownes Gill Viaduct, 700 feet long and 150 feet high, built by Thomas Bouch between 1857 and 1858.

But the main thrust of the Stockton and Darlington's expansion in the late 1850s and 1860s was westwards. The Darlington and Barnard Castle Railway was completed in 1856, and would have been opened earlier had it not been for the perverse opposition of the Duke of Cleveland, who was bent on keeping the railway away from Raby Castle. The completion of this project was followed immediately by the start of the South Durham and Lancashire Union Railway from Bishop Auckland to Tebay (on the west coast main line) via Barnard Castle and Kirkby Stephen. The purpose was to facilitate the transport eastwards of haematite iron ore from Cumberland to Consett and Teesside and the westward movement of coke from the Durham mines to Barrow. At the same time the Eden Valley Railway and the Cockermouth, Keswick and Penrith Railway were built to connect with Workington.

The Peases were heavily involved in all of these enterprises, with Joseph the most prominent. By the time these various projects were complete in 1865, the Stockton and Darlington Railway had merged with the North Eastern Railway Co. (NER). This union was voluntary, both companies recognising that their businesses were complementary and that together they would be better able to resist attempts by other companies to intrude into 'their' territory. Although smaller, the Stockton and Darlington was a well-run and profitable company, and as a result it was able to negotiate very favourable terms: three seats on the NER board and the retention of the management of its former lines for a ten-year period, which was extended to 1879. The Peases were major shareholders in the enlarged NER and in 1894 Joseph's son, Joseph Whitwell Pease, became its chairman.

Joseph Pease's determination to promote and get control of the railway lines from Bishop Auckland into Weardale and up to Consett was a sound business move, given the rapid expansion of the iron industry and ever-increasing demands for coke, iron ore and limestone. But Pease was not content merely to be a transport contractor; he recognised that there was a fortune to be made as a supplier. As a result, between 1830 and the 1860s, he built up one of the largest coal mining enterprises in County Durham. The direction of his expanding mining interests was the same as that of the railway network he was creating. He began in the late 1820s near Bishop Auckland with the acquisition of the Adelaide Colliery, and then added nearby collieries at St Helens Auckland, Tindale and Eldon. In the 1840s he sank seven pits in the Crook area: Roddymoor, Bowden Close, Jobs Hills, West Emma, West Lucy, West Edward and Stanley, known collectively as Peases West. Finally he secured the lease of coal royalty in the Deerness Valley from Lord Boyne, enabling him to open collieries at Waterhouses, Esh Winning, Sunniside and Hedleyhope. In 1883, after his death, Ushaw Moor was added by purchase from another firm.

The records of the Durham Coal Owners' Association show that by 1874 the Pease coalmining concern was the third largest of the fifty in the county. The returns from the pits listed in that year recorded 1,266,518 tons, a total exceeded only by Lambton Collieries and Bolckow and Vaughan. Of this total, just over 600,000 tons was converted to coke, almost every colliery in the group having a bank of 'beehive' ovens. Peases maintained their position in the 'league table' of Durham producers until World War I: in 1913 they were still in third place with an increased output of 2,286,045 tons.

Joseph Pease also entered the iron mining industry. In 1857 the collapse of the Northumberland and Durham District Bank led to the bankruptcy of the Derwent Iron Co. and this gave Pease the opportunity of acquiring the mine at Upleatham, to which were later added mines at Hutton Lowcross, Loftus, Lingdale Brotton and Skinningrove. By the time Joseph Pease died, his company was the largest producer of iron ore in the Cleveland field, with an output of a million tons. As noted above, the Peases already controlled the necessary transport facility. What they did not do was to become major players in the iron-making industry, although they did have major interests in two firms, Gilkes, Wilson and Leatham (later Gilkes, Wilson & Co. of Cargo Fleet) and the South Durham Iron-works of Darlington, where Henry Pease was chairman.

The Peases also became major producers of limestone, the third major element in iron production. Their quarries were at Frosterley and Broadwood in Weardale, which by the time of Joseph's death, were producing 250,000 tons a year. The product was supplied to the Consett Iron Co. and to various ironworks on Teesside.

The Pease economic empire reached maturity by 1860, by which date it had been reorganised into five separate companies: Joseph Pease and Partners (coal, coke and fire clay); J.W. Pease & Co. (ironstone and limestone mining); Henry Pease & Co. (wool manufacture); the Middlesbrough Estate (as of 1858 entirely in Pease ownership); and J.W. Pease (private bank). This was the situation when Joseph Pease died in 1872, but in 1882 there was a further reorganisation, whereby the two firms engaged in mineral extraction were merged as Pease & Partners.

His successor was his eldest son, Joseph Whitwell Pease, who had been associated with him in the business for many years. It was he, however, who was to bring about the collapse of the Pease business empire. Initially, the Peases, despite their growing wealth, only slowly broke free of the constraints of their Quaker background. None left the Society of Friends, but they did gradually abandon its distinctive forms of speech and dress. And they continued to live in or on the edge of Darlington, although in increasingly sumptuous style, as is evident from the large houses with extensive grounds, such as Mowden Hall, that they built or bought. The only sign of upward social mobility was Joseph Pease's decision in 1831 to enter parliament, the first Quaker to do so. Significantly, he chose not to seek re-election in 1841.

All this changed with Joseph Whitwell Pease, who completed the classic metamorphosis from urban industrialist to country gentleman. In 1867 he moved to Hutton Hall near Guisborough, which he completely rebuilt, and bought the neighbouring estates of Nunthorpe and Pinchinthorpe, amounting to 3,000 acres. Like his father, he became an MP, but unlike him he remained in parliament for the rest of his life, representing South Durham from 1865 until 1885, then Barnard Castle from that year until his death in 1903. He was a Liberal and a staunch supporter of Gladstone, and for his loyalty he was rewarded with a baronetcy in 1882. In other respects, too, his lifestyle was not that of a businessman: he was in London when parliament was sitting; otherwise he spent much of his time at Hutton Hall, in Scotland (for the shooting) or abroad on holiday.

It was this diversion from his business role, while continuing to exercise its power that was an underlying cause of the disaster that overtook him. Closely allied to this were the changed economic circumstances of the late nineteenth century, when the boom years of the mid-century gave way to two decades of what economic historians have labelled the Great Depression, characterised by periods of severely depressed trade, low prices and reduced profits and dividends. In such circumstances, men in charge of businesses need to take difficult and unpleasant decisions in order to weed out ailing elements and upgrade others in preparation for better times. Pease failed in these respects. Instead he propped up a large number of loss-making enterprises. This was to a degree forgivable in the case of Henry Pease & Co., since this was the foundation of the family's business empire and its closure would have seriously damaged their standing in the town. The same could not be said for the Middlesbrough ironmaker, Gilkes, Wilson & Co., and the locomotive manufacturer, Robert Stephenson, in which the Peases, although major shareholders, did not exercise immediate managerial control. There was still less reason for his generosity to other firms in which there was no Pease interest, such as the Middlesbrough Pottery and the *Northern Echo*, Darlington's Liberal newspaper. Sir Joseph not only allowed these firms to run up unreasonably large overdrafts at his bank, but he expended nearly £600,000 of his own money in their support. In part, this may have been motivated by a belief that he had the resources to see his businesses and those of others through difficult times, but also by a sense of social obligation inculcated by his religion. Henry Pease & Co., Robert Stephenson and Wilson Pease & Co. were reorganised in 1898, but this was twenty years too late. Sir Joseph's business profligacy weakened the family bank to the extent that it was unable to cope with the crisis it had to face in the 1890s.

As he neared the new century, his finances were in a dangerous condition in that he did not have enough reserves to cover his liabilities to three major public companies that banked with J. & J.W. Pease: the NER, the Consett Iron Co. and the Weardale and Shildon Water Co. To meet his commitments he sold his house in London, mortgaged his estate near Guisborough and resorted to short-term loans from other banks to pay dividends. But it was not his commercial failures that in the end defeated him, but his niece and her husband. Beatrice Pease was the daughter of Sir Joseph's younger brother, Edward, who died in 1880. Pease was the trustee of her inheritance, comprising shares in the family companies, until she was twenty-one or married. In 1885, at the age of nineteen, she married a fortune-hunter, Newton Wallop, Viscount Lymington, who succeeded as 6th Earl of Portsmouth in 1891. From the start, Lymington and his wife were intent on realising her assets in order to invest in higher-yielding stocks. Pease prevaricated, arguing that a depression was not the time to sell. In addition, he saw himself as the patriarch of the family, with a duty to preserve its assets intact. Although there was some validity in both his reasoning and his assumed role, the hard fact was that he had insufficient resources to buy Beatrice's shares. In desperation, the Portsmouths hired a leading London solicitor, Sir Richard Nicholson, whose threat of legal proceedings brought Pease to an agreement in 1898. By this, he agreed to buy Beatrice's shares for £273,000. The bulk of this was for the shares in Pease and Partners, which because of the depressed state of the coal trade, were valued at 33 per cent below par.

But, thanks to his improvident commercial practices, Sir Joseph did not have this amount of money and other banks could not be expected to lend him cash for this purpose. The solution was to raise the money by floating Pease and Partners as a public company. By chance, thanks to a sudden revival of the coal trade, this proved to be a great success, with an eightfold oversubscription. Immediately, the Earl and Countess of Portsmouth claimed that her settlement was less than it should have been. In the case held in the Chancery Court at the end of 1900, the judge found against Pease for failing to declare his intention to float Pease and Partners and in his summing up impugned Sir Joseph's integrity. The new settlement gave the Portsmouths 13,000 shares in the new company valued at £241,000, £66,000 in cash and their legal costs. This outcome, it could be argued, did neither party any favours. Nevertheless, the Earl of Portsmouth became a rich man, his estate being worth over £900,000 gross at the time of his death in 1917.

The Portsmouths had forced a fundamental restructuring of Pease's business, but much worse was to follow. For some time Barclays Bank, formed in 1896 by the merger of Barclays of London, Gurneys of Norwich and BACKHOUSES of Darlington, had been keen to take over J.W. Pease in pursuance of its policy of acquiring private banks with strong industrial connections. With the Portsmouths out of the way, Sir Joseph was willing to proceed with this move. The negotiations in 1902 began in a friendly fashion, natural given the Quaker links between many of the parties involved, but became bogged down by the problem of the loan which Sir Joseph needed to pay the NER dividend on 22 August. Eventually, it was necessary for Sir Joseph and his sons, Alfred Edward and Joseph Albert (Jack), the only other shareholders in the bank, to agree to secure the loan, not only with shares, but also with their personal estates. The final straw was the discovery by the well-known accountant W.B. Peat, hired by Barclays to go through the books of J. & J.W. Pease, that the Middlesbrough Estate had first claim on any money owed to them. With the NER dividend payments amounting to £160,000 due the following day, Barclays revised their offer: they would take over J. & J.W. Pease, but not its liabilities, which would have to be met by Sir Joseph and his sons as best they could. In effect, the Peases were being ruined, although thanks to the support and generosity of friends and other members of the family they were not humiliated by being formally declared bankrupt. Sir Joseph resigned all his directorships and retired to Falmouth, to be looked after by his unmarried daughter, Maud, in the house that had belonged to his wife. It was there that he died in June 1903.

Although the Pease industrial empire was effectively at an end, many members of the Pease family remained active in business, nationally and locally, throughout the twentieth century. Most notable was the continued Pease chairmanship of Pease and Partners, until the nationalisation of the coal industry in 1947: Arthur Pease (Sir Joseph's nephew) 1906–27, Jack Pease (Sir Joseph's younger son) 1927–43, and Sir Richard Pease (Arthur Pease's son) 1943–47. But the firm was a declining force in Durham, in part due to the depressed state of the coal industry until the late 1930s, but fundamentally because of the gradual exhaustion of the coal reserves in south-west Durham: by the time Sir Richard Pease took over in 1943, Pease and Partners had slipped from third place out of fifty-one companies in the year of Sir Joseph Pease's ruin, to twelfth place out of thirty-six companies, and the total tonnage mined by its six collieries had fallen by two-thirds to 745,000 tons. The *coup de grâce* was the nationalisation of the coal industry in 1947.

Of Sir Joseph's two sons, Jack was the more resilient and the more successful. In the inter-war years he remained active in the coal industry, not only as a director and then chairman of Pease and Partners, but also in coal industry politics during one of their bitterest periods. In 1919 he represented the Mining Association of Great Britain before the Sankey Commission, set up by the government to consider the future of the industry. He also served as deputy Chairman of the Durham Coal Owners' Association and vice-chairman of the Durham Coke Owners' Association.

That he came to these roles is not surprising in the light of his successful political career until 1916. He was continuously an MP from 1892: until 1900 for Tyneside; then from 1901 until 1910 for Saffron Walden; and finally until 1916 for Rotherham. In accordance with family tradition, he was a Liberal, and when that party came to power in 1905 he became a junior lord of the Treasury. Subsequently, he rose to be Chief Whip (1908), Chancellor of the Duchy of Lancaster with Cabinet status (1910), President of the Board of Education (1911) and Postmaster General (1915). His time in office came to an end in 1916, when David Lloyd George replaced Herbert Asquith as Prime Minister. In January 1917 he was ennobled as Baron Gainford of Headlam Hall, a property he had managed to purchase. As Lord Gainford, he was appointed in 1922 as the first chairman of the British Broadcasting Company and, had John Reith had his way, he would have been chairman of the reconstituted British Broadcasting Corporation, set up in 1926. His politics, however, stood in the way and he had to be satisfied with the post of vice-chairman, which he held until 1933.

Jack Pease represented the family's liberation from the bonds of a purely family concern and his generation also saw the final emancipation from its Quaker ties as regards education, marriage and religious affiliation. And although many remained active in North-East economic life, they ceased to be dominating forces in the political life of Darlington and South Durham.

In addition to the members of the main line of the family, one collateral branch produced an outstanding businessman, John William Beaumont Pease (1869–1950), the great-grandson of Joseph Pease, the brother of Edward Pease (1767–1858). This branch settled at Pendower Hall in Benwell, Newcastle, but also acquired Nether Grange, Alnmouth. J.W.B. Pease rose to become Chairman of Lloyd's Bank and of the Bank of London and South America, and also President of the British Bankers' Association, and was elevated to the peerage in 1936 as Lord Wardington of Alnmouth.

PENSHAW MONUMENT

Penshaw Monument stands on the top of Penshaw Hill, which features in the famous local song, 'The Lambton Worm'. It was erected in the 1840s, paid for by local subscriptions, to commemorate the life and work of John George Lambton, 1st Earl of Durham, who died in 1840. Designed by John and Benjamin Green, it was a half-size replica of the Theseum (or Temple of Theseus) in Athens, but without the walls, roof and stylobate. It can be seen for many miles in most directions.

PERCY, EUSTACE SUTHERLAND CAMPBELL, LORD PERCY OF NEWCASTLE (1887–1958)

Eustace Percy was born in London, the twelfth child of the 7th Duke of Northumberland. He was exceptionally gifted academically and went from Eton to Christ Church, Oxford, where he was awarded a First in Modern History in 1907. His first career, in the Diplomatic Service, culminated in his playing a major role in drafting the Covenant of the League of Nations. In the same year, 1919, he decided on a career change. He unsuccessfully contested Hull for the Conservatives, but in 1921 he entered the Commons as MP for Hastings, a seat he held until 1937. Although he was an unimpressive performer at the Despatch Box, earning him the unkind and far from accurate sobriquet of 'Useless Percy', his ability could not be gainsaid, and in 1924 he entered the Cabinet as President of the Board of Education. In that role he pushed through a number of important reforms, notably the division of state education into primary and secondary phases, with the break at eleven, and the development of secondary education along lines recommended in the report of 1926, whose author was Sir Henry Hadow, a leading educationalist, Principal of Armstrong College, Newcastle between 1909 and 1919.

Percy's lacklustre Commons performance led to the Prime Minister, Stanley Baldwin, dropping him. Six years later, seeing no future in politics, he resigned his seat to become the first Rector of King's College, the Newcastle division of the University of Durham (see UNIVERSITIES). In this role, he guided the College through the difficult days of World War II, not only as an administrator, but also as temporary Professor of History, and in 1946 he laid the foundation for its post-war future by acquiring the land that enabled it (and after 1963 Newcastle University) to develop on its city-centre site. On his retirement in 1952, he was made Lord Percy of Newcastle. In the following years, he chaired the Burnham Committee, the body that decided teachers' salaries, and the Royal Commission on the law relating to mental illness.

PERCY FAMILY

The Percy family has apparently been forever associated with NORTHUMBERLAND. Yet for the first 240 years of its being in England it had no connection with the county. The first Percy to arrive in England was William de Percy, a member of a not very prominent Norman landowning family, who crossed the Channel in 1066 or 1067. He played a leading part in the suppression of native resistance to William the Conqueror in Yorkshire in 1069 and 1070 and the subjugation of Scotland in 1072, for which he was rewarded with extensive lands confiscated from their English owners. In the Domesday Book, compiled from a survey carried out in 1085, William de Percy's estate was the ninth largest of the twenty-five estates in the hands of Normans in Yorkshire. Its centre was at Topcliffe, a few miles north of York. The Percys remained a Yorkshire family, although in the mid-twelfth century they also acquired an estate in Sussex, centred on Petworth, given by Henry I's second wife, Adeliza, to William de Percy's younger daughter, Agnes, on the occasion of her marriage to Adeliza's half-brother, Jocelin, Count of Louvain.

The Percy connection with Northumberland began in dubious circumstances. In 1309 Henry de Percy (1272–1314), who had become Henry, Lord Percy in 1299, bought ALNWICK, the largest of the twenty baronies that were created in Northumberland between 1095 and 1135. The seller was Anthony Bek, Bishop Durham, into whose possession it had come in 1297, following the death without a legitimate son of William de Vesci, whose family had owned it since the early twelfth century. De Vesci settled his Yorkshire and Lincolnshire properties on his illegitimate son, William de Vesci of Kildare, but had placed the Northumberland estate in the hands of Bishop Bek. Many felt that Bek did not have the right to sell, believing that he was holding it in trust for some future legitimate heir to the de Vesci name. There must have been enough in this for Henry Percy's son to settle out of court the challenge to his title by a Gilbert de Aton, who had secured legal confirmation that he was William de Vesci's nearest legitimate male heir. In 1323, shortly after he came of age, Percy's son, Henry, Lord Percy II paid a large sum of money to Gilbert de Aton for Gilbert's confirmation of the original sale. In effect, the Percys bought Alnwick twice.

As well as securing Alnwick, Henry, Lord Percy II (1301–52) also acquired in the early 1330s two more substantial estates in Northumberland, the baronies of Warkworth and Beanley. Both had been repossessed by the Crown: the former because its owner, Sir John Clavering, had no heirs; the latter because its owner had deserted to the

Scots. The grants underline Henry Percy's importance in the defence of the Border. Henry's son, Henry, Lord Percy III (1320–68) made no additions to the estate, but he married a member of the royal family, Mary, daughter of Henry, Duke of Lancaster, a direct descendant of Henry III.

His son, Henry, Lord Percy IV (1342–1408), however, advanced the family's fortune in two important ways. In 1377, on the occasion of the coronation of the boy king, Richard II, he became Earl of Northumberland. Then in 1381 he married, as his second wife, Maud (née Lucy), the widow of Gilbert de Umfraville (see UMFRAVILLE FAMILY). In doing so he added yet more properties to the Percy portfolio. One was the Northumberland barony of Prudhoe (see PRUDHOE CASTLE), which Umfraville had already sold to him. By marrying the widow, however, he was insuring his gain against claims by her late husband's kin. But Maud was a wealthy heiress in her own right to the small Northumberland barony of Langley and the very much larger Cumberland (Cumbria) estates, the Barony of Cockermouth and a third of the Barony of Egremont. Upon marriage she agreed to disinherit her rightful heirs in favour of the Percys, on condition that they quartered their arms with those of the Lucy family.

Henry Percy was now a member of the nobility and one of the greatest landowners in England. And in the last year of the fourteenth century he and his more famous son, Sir Henry Percy (1364–1403), better known by his nickname, Hotspur, played a crucial role in the deposition of Richard II by his cousin, Henry of Bolingbroke, who ascended the throne as Henry IV. For their support, Henry IV rewarded the Percys handsomely. Yet three years later they had fallen out with the king they had made, to the extent of rebelling against him, with fatal consequences: Hotspur's revolt in 1403 ended with his death at Shrewsbury. His father rebelled in 1405, but without success and fled abroad. Three years later, in 1408, he launched a pathetic invasion from Scotland only to meet his death on Bramham Moor, in Yorkshire.

These calamities, however, did not finish the Percys. The 1st Earl of Northumberland had ensured his family's continued existence by taking his heir, Hotspur's son, to Scotland for safety. When the boy came of age in 1414, Henry IV was dead (1413) and his successor, Henry V, was anxious to heal old wounds. Two years later, Henry Percy (1393–1455) came home, restored to the title as the 2nd Earl of Northumberland and with permission to sue in the courts for the return of his grandfather's properties. In this he was almost completely successful, although the process was long and difficult.

The fifteenth century was the period of the civil conflicts that have been called, or perhaps miscalled, the Wars of the Roses. Throughout, the Percys remained loyal to the Lancastrian dynasty, the successors of Henry IV, although the price was the death in battle of the 2nd Earl (in 1455) and the 3rd Earl (in 1461), and the murder (in 1489) of the 4th Earl, while trying to collect taxes. The following century was also one of conflict following the decision of Henry VIII and all but one of his successors to deny the papal headship of the church and to adopt (and impose) Protestant forms of worship. Three times in the course of the century the Percys met with disaster as a consequence of their continued adherence to the old religion. In 1536–37, Thomas Percy (the brother of the ailing 6th Earl, who died during the uprising) was one of the leaders of the PILGRIMAGE OF GRACE, for which he was executed and the estates forfeit. Both title and estates were restored to his son, Thomas (who became 7th Earl) in 1557 by the Roman Catholic queen, Mary

I. However, the new earl found his influence in Northumberland significantly reduced, thanks to the efforts of SIR JOHN FORSTER during the twenty-year Percy absence. But with the accession a year later of the Protestant Elizabeth I, the Percys were again living with a hostile regime. The upshot was the RISING OF THE NORTHERN EARLS in 1569, which resulted in the 7th Earl's execution in 1572. His brother, Henry, was allowed to succeed as the 8th Earl, but only on condition that he resided in the south. Even so, his loyalty was always in doubt, and in 1585 he was put into the Tower of London on suspicion of involvement with Francis Throckmorton's plot to assassinate the queen. A few months later he was found dead in his room. The official verdict was suicide, but the circumstances made this improbable and unconvincing. The upshot of these tumultuous years was that, while the Percys held on to their estates, they lost their political power in the north.

With the 9th Earl (who was brought up as a Protestant), the Percys apparently had entered calmer waters and through marriage acquired Syon House at Brentford, built on the site of a former monastery. But fate was unkind. The 9th Earl (1564–1632), known as the Wizard Earl on account of his interest in science, was imprisoned from 1605 until 1621 on suspicion of involvement in the Gunpowder Plot to kill James I. There was no evidence of his complicity, but it was his misfortune to employ as the factor on his Northumberland estates a distant relation, Thomas Percy, one of the ringleaders of the plot. Worse still, Thomas Percy had dined with the Earl on 4 November, the occasion being the delivery of the half-yearly rents. The 9th Earl's son was named Algernon, a reference back to the first Percy, whose nickname was *al gernons* ('with the whiskers'). As 10th Earl (1602–68) he faced the dilemma of having to choose between backing Charles I or supporting his Parliamentary opponents in the civil wars of 1638–51. Perhaps surprisingly, he was not a Royalist but a moderate Parliamentarian. But he was opposed to the execution of Charles I and the setting up of a republic, and with the rise to power of Oliver Cromwell he retired from public and political life. The 10th Earl died in 1668, leaving the title and estates to his only son, Joceline, again a reference back to their twelfth-century ancestor. Less than three years later, however, the new Earl was dead and, as his only son had predeceased him, the male line came to an end. There followed an eighty-year interlude, during which it seemed likely that the Percy name would disappear.

The years between 1670 and 1750 are really the story of two women. The first was the 11th Earl's surviving child, a three-year-old daughter, Elizabeth. As heir to an ancient title and a huge fortune, she was the most desirable catch in England. In 1679, when she was twelve years old, a husband was selected for her by her grandmother. That lady, having rejected Charles II's offer of one of his illegitimate sons, chose the sixteen-year-old Henry Cavendish, Earl of Ogle, heir of the Duke of Newcastle. Although married, because of their youth co-habitation was deferred for two years. Unfortunately, the groom died the following year while in Italy. Not long afterwards Elizabeth was abducted and forced into marriage by Thomas Thynne of Longleat (the ancestor of the Marquesses of Bath), the richest commoner in England and because of his great income known as 'Tom of the Ten Thousand'. Happily, she escaped from his clutches and found refuge with family friends, Sir William and Lady Temple. This unhappy situation was resolved not long afterwards when Thynne was murdered by assassins hired by a Swedish count, Charles von Konigsmark, who also had designs on

Elizabeth and her fortune. Finally, in 1682, by which date she was all of fifteen years of age, Elizabeth Percy, it is said with some reluctance, was married for the third time. Her new husband was Charles Seymour, 6th Duke of Somerset, who agreed to change his name to Percy when Elizabeth reached her majority, a promise he was to break.

Elizabeth Seymour, née Percy, who was a close friend and confidante of Queen Anne, died in 1722. She and her husband had twelve children, the oldest of whom was Algernon Seymour, destined to be 7th Duke of Somerset, but until then with the courtesy title Earl of Hertford. After his wife's death, the 6th Duke (who lived until 1748), remarried and had a daughter, who became the wife of a Sir William Wyndham. Meanwhile, Algernon Seymour, Earl of Hertford also married and had two children, George and Elizabeth. Since George appeared to guarantee the future of the Somerset inheritance, there was no objection to his sister Elizabeth marrying in 1740 Sir Hugh Smithson, a Yorkshire baronet. However, in 1742, George Seymour died prematurely, which meant that Elizabeth and Sir Hugh Smithson stood to inherit the Somerset title and estates following the deaths of the old 6th Duke and his son, Elizabeth's father.

The prospect of this happening so horrified the aged 6th Duke of Somerset that he determined to settle the entire Percy estate on Sir Charles Wyndham, the grandson of his second marriage. With the help of George II, the Earl of Hertford and Sir Hugh Smithson managed to prevent this. In 1748 the 6th Duke finally died and was succeeded by the Earl of Hertford as the 7th Duke of Somerset, who arranged, again with the help of the king, a more equitable settlement. It laid down that on the 7th Duke's death, Sir Hugh Smithson would be granted the titles of Earl of Northumberland and Lord Warkworth and inherit the Percy estates in Northumberland and Middlesex (based upon Syon House at Brentford), while Sir Charles Wyndham would become Earl of Egremont and Lord Cockermouth and inherit the Percy properties in Cumberland (Cumbria), Yorkshire and Sussex. The parties did not have long to wait for their respective inheritances: the 7th Duke of Somerset died in 1750. Almost immediately, the new Earl and Countess of Northumberland secured an act of parliament to change their name from Smithson to Percy.

It was only with the implementation of this settlement that the Percys really became a Northumberland family. Until 1309 they had no connection with the county, and even after they had acquired the ownership of large parts of it, they were rarely resident there. In the late Middle Ages, they appear to have lived mainly at their Yorkshire houses at Topcliffe, Spofforth, Leconfield and Wressle; and in the sixteenth century the suspicious government required them to live at Petworth. Consequently, their castles at Alnwick, Warkworth and Prudhoe became neglected and semi-derelict. But with the loss of Leconfield and Petworth, the new Earl and Countess had to find a country seat. In the end they chose Alnwick, which was restored at considerable expense.

The new Earl also gained in status. In 1766 he was advanced two rungs up the ladder of nobility to become Duke of Northumberland and Earl Percy. This was not the reward for some outstanding contribution to the state or national life, but the need for the government of the day to retain his support in parliament. George III in fact gibbed at the double promotion, feeling that Marquess would have been sufficient reward/bribe. Percy, however, had even greater ambitions, demanding the title Duke of Brabant, the province from which his wife's ancestor, Joceline, Count of Louvain had come. He was not obliged.

The 1st Duke of Northumberland did, albeit unintentionally and posthumously, contribute to the good of mankind. In 1765 a Mrs Elizabeth Macie gave birth to an illegitimate son fathered while he was Earl of Northumberland, whom she named James. The boy, who in adulthood changed his name to Smithson, was educated at Oxford, became an eminent scientist and lived most of his life in Europe. On his death in 1829 he left his fortune of £105,000 to his nephew, stipulating that should he have no heirs, the money should pass to the government of the USA to found the SMITHSONIAN INSTITUTION for 'the increase and diffusion of knowledge among men'. Six years later, this came to pass. If, as he is alleged to have said, James Smithson was determined to make his name more famous than that of Percy, he succeeded.

Since the end of the eighteenth century, the Percy situation has remained basically unchanged. Their main residences are still Alnwick Castle and Syon House at Brentford, although their London home, Northumberland House, acquired by marriage in 1642, was sold in 1873 to allow the Strand to be widened. The Alnwick Castle as seen today is not, however, that created by the 1st Duke, but the remodelling by ANTHONY SALVIN for his grandson, Algernon, the 4th Duke (1792–1865). To this has recently been added a new garden, the project of the present duchess (see ALNWICK).

PICKERSGILL, WILLIAM (1847–1936)

William Pickersgill was born at Monkwearmouth. About three years later, his father, also William, founded a shipbuilding firm at Southwick in partnership with a man named Miller, which lasted until 1863. William Pickersgill, senior, was the driving force of the firm until his death in an accident in the yard in 1880. Between 1852 and 1880 he built forty-six ships, all in wood, and was responsible for the last wooden ship built on the Wear, the *Coppermine*, launched in 1880 (see SHIPBUILDING INDUSTRY).

William Pickersgill, junior, learned the trade at nearby Laing's Yard before joining his father. Following his father's death, he took control of the firm and pressed on with the policy of building in iron, which his father was preparing to adopt and to which end he had bought land in order to enlarge the yard. The conversion to iron was not, however, accompanied by the abandonment of sail propulsion. In fact, Pickersgills had a reputation for producing fast clippers for the import of copper ore and nitrate, trades based upon Liverpool. The yard in fact built the largest iron sailing ship, the *Andhorina*, and the last 'tall ship' built on the Wear, the *Marguerita*, launched in 1893. Pickersgills also built steam-propelled cargo vessels, many for local shipping firms such as the Clan Line, the Port Line and the Prince Line.

Unlike many successful industrialists, William Pickersgill was not attracted to public life, although he did serve on the Rural District Council. Instead, he was a keen sportsman, playing both cricket and football for Sunderland.

PILGRIMAGE OF GRACE, 1536–1537

The Pilgrimage of Grace was a very serious rebellion of northern England in the last three months of 1536 that flared up briefly again in the spring of the following year. It was provoked by the radical policies of Henry VIII's government, headed by Thomas Cromwell. The primary discontents related to the government's religious policy, including the assumption of royal supremacy of the church, the closure of smaller monasteries, and changes (and the rumours of changes) to the forms of worship, the most keenly felt being the abolition of the feast days of many saints. Within the region there was particular concern at the likely downgrading of the PALATINATE OF DURHAM, and thereby of ST CUTHBERT.

Although the revolt began in Lincolnshire, its centre was Yorkshire, and it was men from Richmondshire in the North Riding who were instrumental in bringing out around 10,000 Durham men at three rallies held between 16 and 19 October at Oxen le Flatts near Darlington, Bishop Auckland and Spennymoor. Initially, it was a popular uprising, which most of the leaders of society tried to avoid. The Bishop of Durham, CUTHBERT TUNSTALL fled to his castle at NORHAM, while the resident nobility and gentry of Durham came out only under threat of the destruction of their property. Northumberland and Newcastle, however, were excused involvement as they might be required to repulse Scottish incursions. The rebel armies advanced south and united at Doncaster. There they met the king's representative, the Duke of Norfolk, who negotiated a truce and returned to London with two rebel leaders, who were to present the five rebel demands to the king. The royal response was conciliatory: a general pardon and a parliament at York to consider the rebel demands. On the return of the leaders to Doncaster, the king's promises were sufficient to secure dispersal. Not everyone was convinced, however, and in the early weeks of 1537 there was a renewed uprising in parts of Yorkshire and Cumberland (Cumbria), which gave the king the excuse to cancel his promise.

Throughout this affair the role of Sir Robert Bowes (see BOWES FAMILY) was critical. A lawyer by training, he was a protégé of CARDINAL THOMAS WOLSEY, the king's chief minister, who fell from grace and died in 1530. This proved to be a setback to Bowes's career and it is easy to suspect that he used the uprising as the means of regaining royal favour. He claimed that he was captured at Barnard Castle by the Richmondshire rebels, who forced him to join them. This could be true, but it is equally clear that he appeared to be an enthusiastic participant, who rapidly rose to command the Richmondshire and Durham hosts. Further, when the combined host met at Doncaster, it was Bowes who was chosen as one of the two men to present their demands to the Duke of Norfolk and then with Sir Ralph Ellerker to take them to the king.

On his return, he had completely changed his stance and it was he who persuaded the rebels to disperse on the assurance of the king's good faith: both Henry and his minister, Thomas Cromwell, he said, had given their word and it could be trusted. This change brought accusations of betrayal and it is easy to see how this could be true. Since the discussion between Bowes and Ellerker and Henry and Cromwell was secret, there was no way of knowing that Bowes did not undertake to get the rebels to disperse in return for future royal favour. The belief that this is what happened is encouraged by the energy with which in the following weeks Bowes hunted down known participants in the second rebellion and the subsequent revitalisation of his career.

The Durham men, who were among the most belligerent in October 1536, did not get involved in the second uprising and consequently there were few executions. Sixteen inhabitants of Durham City were hanged, but this was for an incident on 29 December 1536, when the Lancaster Herald, returning from a progress through the region proclaiming the royal pardon, was for some reason manhandled in the city: to abuse a royal servant while engaged on royal business was in effect to abuse the king. Also executed were the Rector of Whitburn, Robert Hodges, and two sailors, who had rowed out to the ship, anchored off Whitburn, carrying James V of Scotland home from France and had held with him what was deemed to be a treasonable conversation. Two of the nobility also suffered the death penalty, Thomas Percy, the brother of the Earl of Northumberland, and George, Lord Lumley. These were the most senior noblemen involved and as such they were bound to pay the penalty for failing to secure the loyalty of their social inferiors.

PLACE, FRANCIS (1647–1728)

Francis Place was probably the first artist of significance to come from the North East. He was born in Dinsdale, east of Darlington, but was sent to London at an early age to be apprenticed to a barrister at Gray's Inn. The law, however, was not to his liking. He became a friend of the innovative artist, Wenceslaus Hollar (1607–77), who was born in Prague and worked as an illustrator for publishers in Germany before being brought to England in 1636 by the Earl of Arundel. From Hollar, Place learned the skills of engraving and topographical drawing. Hollar was eventually appointed Royal Scenographer and was the official artist on the expedition to Tangier in 1673.

The two men collaborated until 1668, when Place began to develop his own career. Using his home in Dinsdale as a base, he went on a series of sketching tours. This rather precarious way of life ended around 1675, when the death of his father provided an inheritance that gave him financial security and the scope to extend his artistic range to include portraiture. From this time he became increasingly attached to York, where he settled permanently in 1692, becoming a member of a distinguished group of artists known as the Virtuosi. He also resumed his peripatetic habits, making tours of France as well as all parts of the British Isles. Behind this lay his lifelong fascination with landscape, which he portrayed accurately, in contrast to the contemporary fashion for imaginary scenes. He has been described as 'among the more important anticipators of the English eighteenth-century watercolour style'.

PLACE NAMES

The term 'place names' includes the names of rivers, prominent physical features, farms and pits, as well as towns, villages and hamlets. Present place names cannot be taken at face value, however. Establishing the meaning of a name requires research into its early spellings and knowledge of Latin, Old English, Old French, Old Norse, Old Danish and Old Welsh. Even with these skills, certainty of meaning is not always possible. Moreover, the study of place names in the North East is hampered more than in most other parts of England by its omission from the Domesday Book, which means that pre-1087 spelling of most places remains hidden. Nevertheless, even with these caveats, place names have much to tell about the history of the region.

The names of most of the region's main rivers are, as they are thoughout England, of Old Welsh origin: Aln, Blyth, Tees, Tweed and Tyne, the exceptions being Coquet, Rede and Wansbeck. The same is true of many of their major tributaries: Allen, Alwin, Breamish, Deerness, Derwent, Devil's Water, Font, Glen, Kielder, Pont, Team and Till are of Celtic origin, with Browney, Gaunless and Skerne as the exceptions. Celtic influence has been detected in twenty other names: Alwent, Alwinton, Auckland, Branksome, Branxton, Cambois, Castle Eden, Cheviot, Glendue, Mindrum, Penshaw, Plenmeller, Pontop, Ross, Sedgefield, Tecket, Troughend, Tudhoe, Walworth and Yeavering; and also in the retention of the Old Welsh *luch* (lake or pool), which in Scotland became *loch* and in the North East *lough*, as in Ireland, although today with a different pronunciation.

Overall, however, the paucity of these survivals underlines the extent to which the Old Welsh language succumbed to Old English, the language of the Anglian invaders who took control of the region in the sixth and seventh centuries. It is from this language that a very high percentage of present place names are derived. The most numerous Old English element is *tun* (now 'ton'), meaning 'settlement', of which there are around 200 examples in the region, heavily concentrated in the more easterly, lowland areas. There are, however, another thirty places where the ending *ton* has a different root, either *denu*, meaning 'valley', for example, Ashington, or *dun*, meaning 'hill', as at Eppleton. The next most widespread is the ending 'ley'. In eighty-three of the ninety-seven examples, it derives from *leah*, meaning 'clearing' or 'meadow'; in the remaining fourteen, for example Moorsley, the ending comes from *hlaw*, meaning 'hill'. Places with 'ley' endings are largely found in the westerly, upland parts of the region.

To the generalisation that our place names are of Old English origin there are three important exceptions. The names of many new settlements created in the twelfth and thirteenth centuries have Middle English elements, the most common being *biggin(g)* (building), *riding* (clearance) and *shield* (hut); and also the prefix 'New' or 'Newton'. Of earlier origin, from the ninth century, are names of Scandinavian origin, or which have Scandinavian elements, or betray Scandinavian influence. At least thirty-six examples have been identified with reasonable confidence: Aislaby, Amerston, Auckland, Blakiston, Blaydon, Byker, Carlbury, Carlton, Claxton, Copeland, Coupland, Croxdale, Dotland, Durham, Ingleton, Ireshopeburn, Killerby, Little Thorp, Lucker, Raby, Sadberge, School Aycliffe, Selaby, Sheraton, Stainton, Swainston, Thorp Bulmer, Thorp Thewles, Thrislington, Throston, Tranwell, Trewhitt, Tursdale, Ulnaby, Walker and Waskerley. In addition, the distribution of the Scandinavian word *beck* to small steams is revealing. This word is attached to almost all tributaries of the Tees and to those flowing into the Wear between, roughly, Wolsingham and Durham. But along the upper and lower reaches of the Wear, and all the rivers between the Wear and the Tweed, tributary streams bear the English word *burn*, as they do throughout the rest of the region.

Scandinavian names and names modified by Scandinavian influence consequently form a very small proportion of the total place names of the region and they are almost entirely found in the southern parts of County Durham bordering Yorkshire, where Scandinavian settlement and influence were heavy. Moreover, expert opinion is that north of the Tees, Scandinavian settlement, as opposed to influence, was confined to a handful of places within three miles of the middle sector of the Tees valley. The predominance of Old English within Durham as a whole is further underlined by the presence of eighty-four Old English personal names in the county's place names, compared with only eighteen of Scandinavian origin.

The third exception comprises names of French origin, reflecting the impact of the Norman settlement. Twenty-three can be identified with some confidence: *Beamish, *Bearpark, *Beaumont Hill, *Belasis, *Bellasis (twice), *Bellister, *Bewdley, *Cowpen Bewley, *Newton Bewley, Blanchland, Bulbeck Common, *Butterby, Causey (twice), Durham, Follingsby, Haggerston, Pallion, Plessey, Sacriston and Scremerton, those marked with an asterisk deriving from words meaning beautiful. In addition, in ten places, the influx of French families after the Conquest is advertised by the attachment of a French family name: Coatham

Mundeville, Dalton Piercy, Darras Hall (a simplified and corrupt version of Callerton d'Arenis), Hurworth Bryan, Hutton Henry, Newton Hanzard, Seaton Carew, Seaton Delaval, Thorp Bulmer and Witton Gilbert; and another three, Barnard Castle, Gubeon and Guyzance, are French names of places that may have had no pre-Conquest existence. French influence also explains Chester le Street, shortened from 'Chester en le Street', that is, Chester on the (Roman) Road. Dalton le Dale, Hart le Pool, Haughton le Skerne, Hetton le Hill, Hetton le Hole, Houghton le Side, Houghton le Spring, Howden le Wear, Preston le Skerne, Stainton le Street and Witton le Wear are other examples. All twelve are in Durham, although the significance, if any, of this fact is unclear.

Much more recently the expansion of coal mining in the nineteenth century brought new colliery settlements into being. In most instances, they simply took the name of the township in which they were located, although in some places it was necessary to add a distinguishing suffix, such as 'Colliery', and in the case of Esh, the older word for a pit, 'Winning'. In contrast, a wide variety of names were given to individual pits: simple 1st, 2nd, 3rd, etc.; or A, B, C, etc.; seams, such as Five Quarter or Ballarat; military events, such as Alma, Inkerman and Ladysmith; female names (usually those of the owner's wife and daughters); and indicators of attitude, such as Success, Delight, Adventure and Hazard. In naming the new towns created after World War II (see New Towns of the Twentieth Century), Washington, Killingworth and Cramlington adopted the pre-existing names, while Newton Aycliffe was distinguished from Aycliffe by its prefix. The exception was Peterlee, a name confected by running together the forename and surname of Peter Lee, the first Labour chairman of the Durham County Council.

Farm names fall into three broad chronological groups. A large but as yet uncertain number were medieval creations carved out of moorland between (in most cases) 1150 and 1310. Some are betrayed by Middle English words such as *hag* or *stub*, meaning 'clearing'; and the suffixes 'Hall', 'House' and 'Grange', the last often a pointer to monastic ownership, in many cases indicate foundation in this period. In the later medieval period, after 1350, farms resulted from the contraction of villages due to either population decline or forcible clearance by a landlord, who calculated that one large single-tenancy farm would be more profitable than a community of small farmers. In such cases, the farm retained the name of the previous village. The largest group, however, is comprised of farms arising out of the enclosure of land between (roughly) 1600 and 1850. In most cases the name of the new farm related to some part or feature of the township in which it was located. A few farmers, more original or whimsical, adopted names such as 'Waterloo', 'Canada', 'Peep o' Sea' and 'Make Me Rich'.

POPULATION

In the medieval and early modern centuries, the very meagre evidence we have indicates that Northumberland and Durham were counties of very low population compared with those south of the Tees. By 1801 the first decennial census shows a total population of (in round figures) only 317,000. The census also reveals that the population of Northumberland was slightly larger, 168,000, compared with 149,000 in Durham. Given that Northumberland was the larger county, this difference was to be expected.

One hundred years later the situation was radically different. The total population more than quintupled to 1,791,000 and Durham had become the more populous county, with nearly twice as many people as Northumberland, 1,187,000 as against 603,000. The underlying reason for this is that industry, especially coal mining, had expanded geographically and in other respects to a much greater extent south of the Tyne. Durham was now one of the most heavily populated counties in the country.

Much of the increase was 'natural', that is, people born in the region to parents already living there. The percentage never fell below 73, and from 1880 was rising. This, however, masks the immense contribution of immigrants. In the course of the nineteenth century, Northumberland and Durham were magnets for men and families seeking work and business opportunities. The majority travelled relatively short distances from the immediately adjacent regions. The largest contribution to Northumberland was from Scotland, and to Durham from Yorkshire, and to both counties people migrated from Cumberland and Westmorland (Cumbria). The other major contributor was, of course, Ireland, especially after 1845 with the onset of the devastating famine, and although Irish immigration began to tail off after 1880, it was still contributing to population growth in 1911. The Tyneside Scottish and Tyneside Irish brigades raised in World War I (see REGIMENTS) testify to the large influx from Scotland and Ireland in the preceding decades. Although Ireland and the neighbouring regions accounted for over half the immigrants, small numbers came from all other parts of the country: the contribution of any particular county may have been tiny, but the aggregate was substantial. When World War I broke out, the region's population included people who had come, or whose immediate forebears had come, from all parts of the British Isles.

The expansion and immigration phase of the region's demographic history was coming to an end in the early years of the twentieth century. Although there was some growth, it rapidly decreased in percentage terms. Whereas the population grew by between 15 and 25 per cent per decade in the nineteenth century and up to 1911, thereafter it fell rapidly, so that between 1931 and 1951 the increase was only 1.6 per cent. As a result, the total population, which in 1911 stood at 2,300,000, had risen by only a little over 250,000 to 2,550,000 by 1951. This slowdown stemmed in part from the decrease in the size of families, which was a national phenomenon. But it was assisted by reverse migration: from the end of World War I, emigration gathered pace as the region became one of the most economically depressed in the country. During the inter-war period the region lost around 7 per cent of its population per decade.

Since the end of World War II, the region has had an uphill struggle economically, because of the progressive contraction of its staple industries, and recently of some of those brought in to replace them. Consequently, its unemployment level has consistently been higher than any other part of the United Kingdom, with the exception of Northern Ireland. Not surprisingly, therefore, the North East was not attractive to immigrants from the West Indies and the Indian subcontinent who have come to the United Kingdom since the 1950s. Recent research has shown that in 1961 only 3,023 people of New Commonwealth origin had settled in the region, a mere 1 per cent of the total: only Wales with 2,551 had a lower intake. This pattern still obtains: at present only 1.4 per cent of the North East's population belongs to what are now termed 'ethnic minorities', compared with the national average of 5.9 per cent; and since most of them are concentrated in certain pockets within the region's cities, particularly Newcastle and Middlesbrough, it means that large parts of the North East have almost no inhabitants of recent immigrant stock. For the North East, the 'era of immigration' was the nineteenth century.

PORTER, JANE (1776–1850), **SIR ROBERT** (1777–1842), **ANNA MARIA** (1780–1832)

Jane, Robert and Anna Maria Porter were born in Durham City, the children of an army officer and his wife, but grew up in Edinburgh, where they moved in early childhood after their father's death. Both women achieved fame as writers of novels, or as they called them, 'romances', which were widely popular and were translated into several European languages. Jane's *Thaddeus of Warsaw* (1803) was one of the earliest examples of the historical novel. Her best-known work, *The Scottish Chiefs* (1809), which had as its hero William Wallace, was considered so subversive by Napoleon that it was not published in France until after his overthrow. Sir Walter Scott was a frequent visitor to the family home in Edinburgh and his conversations with Jane Porter are said to have convinced him of the market for historical romances with Scottish and medieval themes. Anna Maria was also a prolific writer of poetry and novels, her best-known work being *The Hungarian Brothers*. Their works would have no appeal to today's readers, but in their day they very successfully met a widespread demand for novels that in recent times has been met by writers such as CATHERINE COOKSON.

Their brother, Robert, was equally if not more successful, but as a painter, particularly of dramatic battle scenes, to which he was attracted as a child on seeing the painting of a battle at the home of Flora Macdonald. His natural talent earned him an early admission to the Royal Academy School. In 1800, when only twenty-three, he burst upon the scene with a picture 120 feet in length (now destroyed) entitled *The Storming of Seringapatam*, which he completed in ten weeks. For most of his life thereafter he lived and worked abroad. Twice (the Spanish campaign of Sir John Moore in 1808 and the Russian Campaign of 1812) he was, in effect, a war artist. He had two spells in Russia, during the second of which he married a Russian princess. He also worked in Sweden, where he received a knighthood, and his illustrated account of the Russian campaign earned him another, from the Prince Regent. With the coming of peace in 1815, he spent three years travelling in the Near East, producing a written and a pictorial account of what he saw. In complete contrast, from 1826 until 1841, he was British consul in Venezuela, where he continued to paint, including a portrait of Simon Bolivar, the 'liberator of South America'. He died, perhaps appropriately, at St Petersburg in 1842.

POTTERY INDUSTRY

Although there are craftsman potters working in the North East, some of them of the highest class, the commercial pottery industry, so prominent in the nineteenth century, came to an end in the early 1960s. The earliest known potteries were founded at Newbottle in the 1720s, but it was not until the last years of the eighteenth century that the industry began to flourish, when four more came into being in and around SUNDERLAND, to be followed at intervals by another seven between 1807 and 1913. Many, however, had short lives, the most enduring being the Southwick Pottery (1788–1986), the Wear Pottery (1789–1881), the Bridge End Pottery, also known as the Jericho Pottery (1844–1941) and the Deptford Pottery (1857–1918). The basis of Sunderland's success was the presence close by of good-quality brown clay and the proximity to the port, which facilitated the import of white clay from Cornwall, Devon and Dorset, and the export of the finished products. Also critical were the expanding markets in London, the near continent and the empire. Sunderland did not attempt to compete for the high-quality, artistic market, but concentrated on producing a wide range of inexpensive products for mass sale to customers of modest income. Nevertheless, Sunderland did become famous for its mottled pink lustreware, which became known as Sunderland Lustre, which was produced by spraying on to the glazed pot a fine mist of oil.

Sunderland also had the distinction of being the place where the region's outstanding pottery, Malings, was founded. It was begun by William Maling, a member of a Huguenot family, who migrated from Scarborough to Sunderland in 1723 and married Catherine, the daughter of Christopher Thompson of Hendon Lodge. By 1750 he was very wealthy, having inherited a considerable fortune from his father in 1743 and his father-in-law in 1749. In 1762 he founded a pottery at North Hylton, not with the intention of engaging personally in the trade, but for his sons, Christopher Thompson Maling (1741–1810) and John Maling (1746–1823). By 1815 the firm was in the hands of Robert Maling (1781–1853), John Maling's son, who took the decision to move from North Hylton to NEWCASTLE and create a factory near the Ouseburn Bridge close to the Tyne. The new works was operational by 1817.

It was Robert's son, Christopher Thompson Maling II (1824–1901), who made the firm Britain's largest pottery manufacturer. In 1859, not long after taking control, he built an additional factory on a two-acre site close to the Ouseburn Bridge works. This became known as the Ford A works and it continued in production until 1926. In 1878, however, he added a giant factory, known as Ford B, on a 14-acre site at St Lawrence. Malings dominated the popular market in two ways. They produced a complete range of domestic wares, all selling at reasonable prices. But in addition they were responsible for 90 per cent of the jam and marmalade jars in Britain, notably for Frank Cooper of Oxford and James Keiller of Dundee, and also considerable quantities of sanitary ware and items for the pharmaceutical industry. They also produced, as occasion demanded, commemorative mugs and plates, and in 1929 they began making pottery for RINGTONS, designed by their art director, Lucien Boullemier.

The reasons for Malings' demise were twofold. One was World War II, during which production virtually ceased, which in turn led in 1947 to the sale of the company to Hoults, the removals and storage firm. Its chairman, Frederick Hoult, effected a considerable revival in pottery production, but this faltered after his death in 1954. The second reason, as with so much of British industry, was the rapid rise of Japanese competition, which was able to produce items far more cheaply than was possible on Tyneside. Pottery manufacture was finally ended at Walker in 1963. Part of the factory was demolished, but a substantial part remains, used for storage and small businesses. Malings was not the only pottery firm on Tyneside, but the others were short-lived and none outlasted the nineteenth century.

PREHISTORIC ROCK ART

Hundreds of what are known as 'cup and ring' carvings have been identified on exposed rocks in the North East, mostly on high ground. They were first recognised in the 1820s on Old Bewick Hill and in recent years assiduous research has considerably increased the number of known sites and examples. A typical carving comprises a hollow 'cup', surrounded by up to five concentric hollowed 'rings' with a hollowed tail running outwards from the cup to beyond the outermost ring. What is evident is the sensitivity of the carvers to the natural form and shape of the rock on which they worked, as if their purpose was to enhance what nature had provided.

About these carvings two questions arise, neither of which can be given a firm answer. The first is when were they made? Here there is broad agreement that most were the product of the Neolithic period, that is, 4000 to 3000 BC, when man became settled as an agriculturalist. However, some may have been created much later in the Early Bronze Age, around 2000 BC. As to the second question, why were the carvings made, the total absence of evidence means a complete reliance on guesswork. Perhaps the only thing that can be said with any confidence is that the long and laborious effort required to produce the carving using stone and bone tools points clearly to their importance for their carvers and, presumably, for the society of which they were a part: they must have been more than doodles. Thoughts about purpose range around three broad possibilities: religion, fertility, and symbols marking boundaries or routes. In future more examples will come to light and increasingly sophisticated archaeological and scientific techniques may give us more certain answers.

PRIESTMAN, FRANCIS (1855–1936)

Francis Priestman was a major figure in the GREAT NORTHERN COALFIELD between 1888 and the 1930s. He was born at Shotley Bridge, the son of Jonathan Priestman, a Quaker and founder of Priestman Collieries. After education at Rugby School, he joined the family business and became chairman on the death of his father in 1888. In Durham, Priestman Collieries comprised six collieries: Victoria Garesfield, Chester South Moor, Blaydon Burn, Axwell Park, Lilley Drift and Watergate. The records of the Durham Coal Owners' Association show that the annual output of Priestman Collieries was nearly 900,000 tons in the late nineteenth century and was still nearly 800,000 tons at the time of Priestman's death in 1936. He was also a partner and majority shareholder in the Ashington Coal Company, which owned one of the largest collieries in Great Britain. In the years before World War I both companies were major exporters.

PRIESTMAN, SIR JOHN, Bt (1855–1941)

John Priestman was a highly successful businessman, who rose from modest circumstances to possess an estate valued at £1.5 million at the time of his death. His father was a master baker in Bishop Auckland, but instead of following the family trade he trained as a draughtsman in the office of the SUNDERLAND shipbuilder John Bulmer. Later he became chief draughtsman with another Sunderland shipbuilder, WILLIAM PICKERSGILL. In 1882 he opened his own shipyard, where he developed three berths with a production capacity of 40,000 tons. Many of his customers were foreign owners. The shipbuilding business was, however, not the sole source of his fortune. In fact, in the slump in shipbuilding that followed the end of World War I, Priestman built no ships between 1922 and 1926, which helps to explain his decision to close his yard in 1933. But he made a great deal of money from investments in the South African goldfields, as well as being chairman or a director of three shipping companies, two collieries, the Sunderland and South Shields Water Co. and Phoenix Assurance. As well as being one of Sunderland's most successful businessmen, he was the town's greatest philanthropist, either directly in person or through the trust he set up. Among his credits are FINCHALE TRAINING COLLEGE, the Sunderland Eye Infirmary, the library of what was Sunderland Technical College, the Earl Haig Homes for disabled servicemen, and the church of St Andrew, Roker, which Priestman had built in 1906–07 in memory of his mother. This church is described by Nikolaus Pevsner as 'one of the architecturally most interesting and successful churches of its date in England'. He also paid for the rebuilding of St Michael's, Bishopwearmouth in the early 1930s. He was made a baronet in 1934.

PRUDHOE CASTLE

In the guardianship of English Heritage since 1966, Prudhoe is one of the most impressive remains of a medieval castle in England. Located on top of a steep cliff over 150 feet above the River Tyne and protected on its east side by a deep ravine, it occupies an eminently defensible site, commanding the land routes up and down the valley as well as the river crossing. It was first erected in the early years of the twelfth century as an enclosure formed by a palisade within which was a wooden tower. It was probably intended as a temporary structure, since in the middle years of the century the palisade was replaced by stone curtain walls forming inner and outer baileys. Within the former, the wooden tower gave way to a stone keep, while the entrance to the latter was given a towered gateway, which was reinforced by a barbican in the thirteenth century.

As well as being a strategic stronghold sixteen miles upriver from Newcastle, it was the heart of one of the largest baronies between which most of Northumberland was divided between 1095 and 1135. The grantee was Robert de Umfraville and his estate comprised twenty-eight townships in the parishes of Ovingham, Chollerton, Thockrington and Kirkwhelpington. The barony remained in the hands of the UMFRAVILLE FAMILY until 1398, when it passed into those of the PERCY FAMILY. They made a number of additions and changes in the late medieval period, but after its military value faded in the seventeenth century it fell into disrepair. It was saved from total ruin by the 2nd Duke of Northumberland, who between 1808 and 1817 cleared away the debris and built a house in the Gothic style between the two baileys. Even though the urban sprawl of Tyneside has encroached upon it, it remains an impressive monument.

PUISET (see LE PUISET, BISHOP HUGH OF)

PUMPHREYS

Pumphreys, renowned for its coffees and teas, can trace its origins to the person of Leigh Smith, who opened a coffee house in what is now the Cloth Market in NEWCASTLE in 1750. In 1800 the business was sold to George Richardson, a member of the Newcastle Quaker family, who included groceries and dealing in tea among his business interests. Eventually he was succeeded by his son, Henry Richardson, who in 1854 brought his nephew, Thomas Pumphrey, into the business. The previous year Thomas's older brother George had bought a grocery business in Blackett Street. In 1911 the two businesses merged. By that date, which also saw the death of Thomas Pumphrey, Pumphreys Coffee was a household brand in the North East.

The business continued on the two sites until the end of World War II, when the Blackett Street operation closed. In 1974 the grocery side of the business was discontinued, and supplying coffee to the catering trade was concentrated on the Old George Yard. What seemed like a moribund business was revived after 1983, when it was bought by C.J. Archer, who moved it to a new factory in Blaydon capable of handling the roasting, warehousing and distribution sides of the operation. Since then, Pumphreys has expanded to serve a nationwide market with eighty different brands of coffee and tea.

PYBUS, FREDERICK CHARLES (1883–1975)

Frederick Pybus was for many years Professor of Surgery in the Newcastle College of Medicine, which became part of King's College in 1935 and then the University of Newcastle upon Tyne in 1963. His claim to fame, however, rests not so much on his professional work as on the huge collection of materials relating to the history of medicine he assembled over a forty-year period prior to 1950 and which he generously presented to the University in 1965. The earliest item is a manuscript of *c.*1380 by the English doctor John of Ardene, but the bulk of the collection comprises printed books, numbering over 2,000 and covering all aspects of the subject, from the late fifteenth century to the early nineteenth century, including early printed editions of the ancient Greek authorities, Hippocrates and Galen, the 'fathers of western medicine', and the Arab writer, Avicenna. The collection also contains much illustrative matter, including 2,000 engravings and fifty portraits. The Pybus Collection, now housed in Newcastle University's Robinson Library, is of international importance.

PYREX

Pyrex is known to everyone as the heat-resistant glass from which a wide range of cooking and tableware is made. It is less well known for its equally wide range of laboratory and industrial uses. It was first marketed under that name in 1915 by the American glass manufacturer Corning, whose laboratories improved upon earlier discoveries by the German scientist and industrialist, Dr Otto Schott of Jena. The heat-resistant quality of Pyrex was achieved by combining 12 per cent boric oxide (and small quantities of other chemicals) with 80 per cent silica.

Pyrex, therefore, was not a North-East invention. But its association with the region began early as the result of the business acumen and drive of Ernest Jobling Purser, who in 1921 secured from Corning the exclusive right to make and market Pyrex products throughout Great Britain and the British Empire, with the exception of Canada. At that date, Purser was working for his uncle, James A. Jobling, the owner of the Wear Glass Works in SUNDERLAND, which he had bought in 1886. Jobling, however, was essentially a Tyneside industrialist, one of whose whose lines of business was supplying chemicals to the glass industry. He appears to have done little to expand the activities of his acquisition and it was left to his nephew to create one of Sunderland's major industrial enterprises.

Jobling's control of the Wear Glass Works, which expanded to cover sixty acres, did not outlive the Purser regime. Just before he retired in 1949, he sold the firm to the famous glassmaker, Pilkington of St Helens. They, however, retained the ownership for only two years: in 1950 they sold a 60 per cent interest to the London holding company, Thomas Tilling, and 40 per cent to Corning. Under this joint ownership Joblings continued to expand, not only in Sunderland, but also by the acquisition of two complementary firms in Staffordshire and South Wales. In 1973, however, Corning secured complete control by purchasing Tilling's 60 per cent interest, and two years later they changed the name of the firm to Corning. What had been a North-East firm was now a wholly owned sector of a giant American corporation with manufacturing facilities throughout the world employing over 300,000 people. The major consequence of foreign control was the ending of the manufacture of laboratory and industrial products in Sunderland and the closing of the research facility at Brancepeth Castle, Durham. From 1995 until production ceased in 2007, Pyrex cooking and tablewares were manufactured under licence from Corning by Newells Ltd.

QUILTS

A quilt comprises two layers of fabric (silk or satin), between which is a layer of wadding, which is divided by sewing into compartments so as to form an intricate pattern. The craft of quilting was widely practised in the region, especially in the western upland dales, primarily to produce bedspreads, but also items of dress. In the course of the eighteenth and nineteenth centuries a number of distinctive patterns evolved, which became traditional.

The craft declined after World War I, but it was revived at a Northern Industries Workshop set up in 1933 in BARNARD CASTLE under the auspices of the Rural Industries Bureau. This facility produced quilts (which became known as Durham Quilts) commercially for the luxury market in London, including the royal family. Although World War II put an end to this enterprise, the craft is still widely practised in the region, where the preservation and dissemination of traditional North Country patterns owes much to Amy Emms (1904–98), a Sunderland woman who settled at St John's Chapel in Weardale, and whose work was recognised by an OBE.

RAILWAYS

Although the North East's claim to be where the railway originated has considerable validity, it is an oversimplified statement. The steam locomotive was not invented there. Nor can the widespread belief that the Stockton and Darlington Railway (S&DR) was the first railway be fully sustained, since it had several of the characteristics and purposes of a WAGONWAY. Arguably, the more valid claim to be the first railway in the modern sense of the word belongs to the Liverpool and Manchester Railway, opened in 1830, five years after the S&DR.

The British railway system was the product of private enterprise, companies raising the necessary finance and deciding where they wished to build their lines and locate their stations. Parliament limited its role to passing or rejecting private acts of parliament necessary to enforce the sale of land on which a railway was to be built and, as the need became apparent, to laying down conditions and regulations governing railway operations. Consequently, what emerged was not a carefully planned national system, but one comprising a large number of separate railway companies, each with its own particular purposes. The most glaring consequence of this policy of minimal state control was the laying of tracks of differing widths: 4 feet 8½ inches by most companies, the notable exception being the important Great Western Railway, which opted for 7 feet. The result was the problem of transferring goods and passengers where the two gauges met. In 1846 government legislation required all future lines to be built with the narrow gauge, but the continued existence of broad gauge lines meant that the problem persisted for several decades. This absence of state direction explains many aspects of British railway history and the consequences, with which we are still living.

Routes and Companies: The success of the S&DR and Liverpool and Manchester Railway ushered in a forty-year period of frantic railway development in the North East. In the earliest phase, lasting until 1840, the underlying impetus was the need to overcome the physical problems and the high cost involved in transporting coal in ever-increasing quantities from the pithead to the expanding number of coastal ports for shipment to the rapidly growing domestic markets of London and southern England and abroad. During these years, fifteen railways came into being: Stockton and Darlington (1825), Clarence (1828), Middlesbrough Extension (1828), Newcastle and Carlisle (started 1829, completed 1838), Hartlepool Dock and Railway (1832), Blaydon, Gateshead and Hebburn (1834), Durham Junction (1834), Durham and Sunderland (1834), Stanhope and Tyne (1834), Brandling Junction (1836), Newcastle and North Shields (1836), Great North of England (1836), Bishop Auckland and Weardale (1837), Stockton and Hartlepool (1839) and West Durham (1839). All but one was licensed by act of parliament; all but two were in Durham; all were on an essentially east–west alignment; and most were short in distance. In the majority of cases their primary purpose was the easier and cheaper movement of goods, especially coal, to the new port facilities at Hartlepool, Middlesbrough, Seaham Harbour, Sunderland and West Hartlepool; passenger services were of secondary consideration (see NEW TOWNS OF THE NINETEENTH CENTURY). After 1850 the need for this sort of railway increased as a result of the rapid development of the iron industry (see IRON AND STEEL INDUSTRY), notably on Teesside and at Consett, which required ore and limestone as well as coal. Movement of minerals was to remain a major role for the railway network in the North East until the late twentieth century and it occasioned the building of a plethora of additional lines, many privately owned by the coal companies.

But after 1840 another and very different objective came to the fore, namely the creation of a trunk route between London and Edinburgh. This sort of scheme, connecting important centres of population and economic activity, had already been achieved on a minor scale by the Newcastle and Carlisle Railway (N&CR), completed in 1838. It was the first cross-country line and it superseded several earlier schemes for linking the Tyne and the Solway by canal (see CANALS). The East Coast Main Line was of greater importance and it was achieved by 1850, largely through the determination of one man, GEORGE HUDSON. It also initiated the process of amalgamation that would leave the railways of Britain in the hands of a few large companies: in the North East by 1850 two companies, the S&DR and Hudson's creation, the York, Newcastle and Berwick Railway (YNBR), controlled almost all the lines.

Hudson began the process of creating the main line through the North East by concocting a line from Darlington (which had been reached from York by 1841) to Gateshead. This was achieved by the summer of 1844. A new line was built from the S&DR tracks a short distance north of Darlington as far as Rainton, about four miles north-east of Durham City, which was to be linked to it by a branch line terminating at a station at Gilesgate, Durham, now part of a hotel. From Rainton, however, the route used the lines of existing companies: Durham Junction Railway, Stanhope and Tyne Railroad and the Brandling Junction Railway, control of which Hudson acquired. As a result, trains followed a roundabout route via Leamside, Penshaw, Washington, Brockley Whins (Boldon Colliery) and Pelaw, a distance of nearly twenty miles. Had a purpose-built line been laid down along the direct route, the distance would have been about eleven miles. But Hudson was a man in a hurry and he was prepared to sacrifice the shortcut in distance for that of time. Fortunately, the absurdity of a route destined for Gateshead extending almost to South Shields was to a large degree eradicated in 1850 by a curve between Washington and Pelaw that shortened the journey by several miles. Nevertheless, from the perspective of the present main line, Hudson's route still appears circuitous.

Having reached the Tyne, Hudson's next objective was the Tweed. Creating a line through Northumberland proved to be more straightforward, although delayed by disputes. Proposals for a Newcastle to Berwick railway were put forward as early as 1837 and 1839, but had come to nothing; but in 1844 two new proposals were made, one by Hudson (and backed by GEORGE AND ROBERT STEPHENSON), the other by Lord Howick (see GREY, HENRY GEORGE, 3RD EARL). These schemes differed as to both route and means of propulsion, Hudson preferring the locomotive, while Howick favoured the system using vacuum pipes. In the end Howick withdrew his scheme, and the railway, which was completed in 1847, was that of Hudson and the Stephensons. Except for a short stretch as far as Heaton laid down by the Newcastle and North Shields Railway, the line was purpose-built, which makes it all the more regrettable that it bypassed Alnwick (thanks to the opposition of the Duke of Northumberland) and, to satisfy the demands of its leading inhabitants, created a very awkward speed-restricting curve at Morpeth.

The completion of the lines through Durham and Northumberland left the problem of engineering the crossing of the Tyne and the Tweed. The former proved to be more difficult, politically and practically.

By 1844 a railway line ran from Carlisle to Redheugh, owned by the N&CR, where it joined the Brandling Junction line, now under Hudson's control, from Redheugh through Gateshead and Pelaw and beyond, either southwards to London or to South Shields and Sunderland. To serve these lines, he built an architect-designed station, complete with hotel, at Greenesfield in Gateshead, which he intended to be the main station for Tyneside. His plan envisaged a high-level road bridge across the Tyne by which Newcastle passengers would have access to the station. Trains to and from the north would cross the river by a bridge between Bill Quay and Walker, where the engineering problem would not be as great as that posed by the deep gorge between Gateshead and Newcastle. The effect of this plan would have been to bypass Newcastle and make Gateshead the hub of the region's rail system. Resistance to it, however, was instant and successful. The combined strength of Newcastle Council and the N&CR forced Hudson to abandon his scheme and accept an alternative, a double-decker high-level bridge between Gateshead and Newcastle carrying both road and rail, the latter leading to a new station built on land provided by Newcastle Council. The outcome was two of the most outstanding pieces of nineteenth-century architecture and civil engineering, Robert Stephenson's High Level Bridge and JOHN DOBSON's Central Station.

The High Level Bridge was opened for rail traffic in 1849 (and for road traffic in 1850) and the Royal Border Bridge carrying the line across the Tweed came into use the following year. By that date, however, trains had been crossing both rivers since the autumn of 1848, thanks to wooden bridges erected in association with the ongoing work in stone and iron. Once across the Tweed, the YNBR linked with the line from Edinburgh to Berwick, completed in 1846 by the North British Railway (NBR). This brought into being an uninterrupted route between the two capital cities. This conjunction in turn made possible the construction of a 24-mile branch line, completed in 1851, from Tweedmouth along the south side of the Tweed to Cornhill and then across the Border to Kelso.

The creation of the YNBR was not the end of amalgamations. Seven years later it merged with the York and North Midland Railway and the Leeds Northern Railway to form the North Eastern Railway (NER), which dominated the North East and Yorkshire until World War I. In the following twenty years the NER expanded its control within the North East, principally by means of four acquisitions. The most important of these, made in 1863, was the S&DR, which since 1825 had expanded considerably, eastwards and westwards (see PEASE FAMILY). By 1863 the merger of the NER and the S&DR made commercial and operational sense for both companies. Not only would each gain by integration, but as a united concern they would be in a stronger position to fend off any attempt by other companies to gain access to 'their' territories. Although the smaller company, the S&DR had sufficient strength to negotiate continued Pease control of the former S&DR elements until 1879.

A year earlier, in 1862, the NER acquired the N&CR. This railway, for which parliamentary approval was secured in 1829, was completed in 1838, with a branch from Haltwhistle to Alston added between 1846 and 1852. Here, too, the motive was the need to prevent a predator company, particularly the London and North Western Railway and the NBR, securing control of a line giving access to the heart of NER 'country'. Three years later, in 1865, they rounded off their control of public railways in County

Durham by their acquisition of the West Hartlepool Dock and Railway Co. This company, created by RALPH WARD JACKSON, the founder of West Hartlepool, was itself an amalgam of three of the small early lines laid down in the north Teesside area. The final acquisition, made in 1874, was the Blyth and Tyne Railway (B&TR), which was founded in 1846 to move coal from pits in the Wansbeck area to the Tyne for outward shipment, Blyth's coal shipping facilities at that date being inadequate. With the movement of coal being the company's core business, it is not surprising that it gradually incorporated and developed several earlier wagonways. But it also developed passenger services in the North Tyneside area, with a terminus at New Bridge Street in Newcastle.

As well as merging with or taking over existing companies, the NER also constructed new lines. Perhaps the most notable was the Lanchester Valley route, which was first mooted in 1857 and completed in 1862. Its purpose was to bring iron ore from the Cleveland field to Consett, but in turn it made feasible new collieries alongside the line at BEARPARK, Langley Park and Malton. The line was subsequently extended from Consett to Newcastle. Although mineral traffic was of prime importance, passenger services were introduced.

Equally important in these years was the major improvement to the East Coast Main Line. This was made possible by the opening in 1857 of a new line from Bishop Auckland to Leamside, which had involved the construction of the viaduct at Durham. The purpose of this line was not to improve the main east coast route but to link the coalfield around Bishop Auckland with the Tyne at South Shields. This Bishop Auckland to Leamside line, however, made possible the two developments that brought the present East Coast Main Line into being. The first was a line (opened in 1868) from Gateshead via Birtley and Chester le Street to join it at Newton Hall. The second was a line (opened in 1872) that left it at Relley Mill and ran to join the old main line at Ferryhill. Although apparently more logical, the new alignment was almost as circuitous as the old one and almost as long. Its major benefit was that it put Durham City on the main line. That the East Coast Main Line through County Durham was not purpose-designed and purpose-built is demonstrated by the Durham viaduct, which lies on an essentially east–west axis while carrying a north–south route. It does, however, afford the most dramatic view of DURHAM CATHEDRAL, one of the most splendid vistas in Britain.

The railway system in the North East may be said to have reached maturity by 1875, but not its fullest extent. From then until World War I, modifications and improvements were made to existing lines and some new lines were created. Two illustrate the nature of railway development. One was a new line along the east coast of Durham to serve the new coastal collieries at EASINGTON, Blackhall and Horden that came into production in the early years of the twentieth century. In complete contrast was a 35-mile line built between 1882 and 1887 across rural Northumberland via Wooler to Cornhill, where it joined the Tweedmouth–Kelso line. It was a single-track railway serving a sparsely populated and essentially agricultural area, and as such was built more in hope than serious expectation.

In spite of these developments, the NER never controlled all the railways in the North East. One exception was the numerous short private lines built and operated by colliery companies, often with second-hand NER engines, to link with the NER network. Essentially, they complemented the public system.

Not so the other exception, the Border Counties Railway (BCR), which fell under the control of the NBR. How this came about illustrates the political scheming characteristic of the British railway industry during its period of growth in the middle decades of the nineteenth century. The genesis of the BCR began in 1854 with a parliamentary act allowing the building of a line from the N&CR line just west of Hexham up the North Tyne valley to Plashetts, a distance of twenty-six miles. It was promoted by a consortium of local gentry, headed by the major landowner in North Tynedale, William Charlton of Hesleyside. It was hoped that the line would facilitate the commercial exploitation of the coal measures at Plashetts. But behind this apparently local scheme was one of the larger railway companies, the Edinburgh-based NBR, whose ambitions were shortly to become clear. Suspicions as to the NBR's involvement are given some credence by the known friendship of Charlton and another Northumbrian, Richard Hodgson, the chairman of the NBR.

Matters came to a head in 1859 with the passage of three acts of parliament: one sanctioned the formation of a company, the Border Union Railway (BUR), to build a line from Hawick to Carlisle, which would complete the rail link between Carlisle and Edinburgh; another permitted the BCR to extend its North Tyne line from Plashetts across the Border to meet the BUR at Riccarton, a distance of fourteen miles; the third sanctioned the Wansbeck Valley Railway to run from Redesmouth on the BCR line via Scots Gap (from where a branch ran north to Rothbury) to Morpeth and there to link with the B&TR system. Since these projects were promoted by the NBR, Richard Hodgson's strategy of securing for the NBR access to Tyneside became clear. The NER reaction was to acquire control of the N&CR, which it feared the NBR would also seek to use to reach Newcastle and the East Coast Main Line. Having secured its back door against the Scottish intruder, the NER was strong enough to negotiate a favourable agreement with the NBR: in return for agreeing to the NBR acquiring the BCR and running its trains between Hexham and Newcastle on the N&CR (now NER) tracks, the NBR granted running rights over its tracks between Berwick and Edinburgh to the NER. This compromise, although letting the NBR into NER 'country', gave the NER a stronger grip on the East Coast Main Line.

After 1875 there were no fundamental changes until World War I, when the government took control of the entire railway system. After the war, the railways were not returned to their original owners but in 1923 handed over to four larger regional concerns, the NER becoming part of the London and North Eastern Railway (LNER). After World War II, when again the railways were under government control, the entire railway system was nationalised in 1948 as British Railways (later British Rail), a situation that lasted until the denationalisation process of the 1990s.

As in other parts of the country, the railway system in the North East is much reduced. Passengers have been lost to other forms of public transport and to private cars, all providing more convenient and/or cheaper services. Equally the movement of a great deal of freight has transferred to the road, the greatest single impact being the demise of the region's coal industry. The contraction of the national rail network began in the inter-war years, but it gathered pace after World War II, culminating in the rationalisation programme drawn up by Dr Richard Beeching in 1963. Today, the rail system in the North East comprises little more than the East Coast Main Line, and of its original thirty-seven stations, only six – Berwick, Alnmouth, Morpeth, Newcastle, Durham and Darlington – are still in use for East Coast Main Line services, although Chester le Street is used by the two companies running cross-country services. Some local services continue to function: on the East Coast Main Line, a few trains daily serve six intermediate stations between Newcastle and Berwick; similarly on the old Newcastle and Carlisle line eleven stations are in use between Newcastle and Haltwhistle; a third system runs from Saltburn through South Teesside to Darlington, and thence one service goes to Bishop Auckland and another heads north to Newcastle; and there is the coastal line from Stockton to Newcastle via Hartlepool, Seaham and Sunderland.

But there has also been an expansion of rail passenger transport on Tyneside and Wearside in the form of the Light Rapid Transit System, known as the Metro. It was created by the Tyneside Passenger Transport Authority, set up by central government in 1970 with the aim of creating an integrated road and rail public passenger service under local government control. The outcome was a combination of old and new. The most striking of the new developments are the underground sections four miles in length under central Newcastle and Gateshead with stations at Haymarket, Monument, and St James's Park, and the dedicated high level bridges over the Tyne and the Ouseburn. The circular line between Newcastle and the coast reuses the pre-World War I suburban loop line brought into being through the merger of the NER and the B&TR in 1874. The Metro system north of the Tyne to a considerable extent revives the electrified suburban service launched by the NER in 1904 to counter the competition of the trams, which ran until 1967, when electricity was replaced by diesel power. The line from Gateshead to Sunderland is that of the early Brandling Junction Railway, while the part of the Ponteland line, closed in 1929, has been reused to extend the system to Newcastle Airport. The most recent extension, opened in 2002, and also making use of a track laid in 1852, runs from Sunderland to South Hylton. Currently, the Metro serves fifty-one stations and provides services for considerable parts of the Tyne–Wear conurbation east of Newcastle and Gateshead.

Rails and Locomotives: Until the end of the eighteenth century, wagonways, the precursor of the railway, had wooden rails. These were of two sorts: 'plate' rails, which were L-shaped and allowed the use of carts with unmodified wheels; and 'edge' rails, which required the wheels of any vehicle on them to be flanged. While the 'plate' rail was popular elsewhere, it was rarely used in the North East and the steam locomotive was to render it obsolete. Between 1797 and *c.*1830, however, wooden rails were replaced by ones made of iron. Initially, cast iron was used, but this, although strong, is made brittle by impurities and therefore liable to crack. This became a serious problem with the introduction of the steam locomotive, the weight of which soon became too heavy for cast iron rails to support. The solution, devised in 1819 and 1820 at Bedlington Iron Works by Michael Longridge (see BEDLINGTON), was rails made of wrought iron. This was in all respects a superior material for the purpose in that it was stronger and lighter and could be rolled into much longer lengths. To complement this, one of his employees, John Birkinshaw, produced a new design of rail similar to that still in use, which was lighter but capable of bearing heavier loads. Wrought iron continued to be used until the advent of steel in the second half of the nineteenth century.

If the invention of the steam locomotive can be attributed to one man, it must be the Cornishman Richard Trevethick, who built the first workable model in 1804. However, it was not for another ten years that this invention was developed to the point that a viable railway system became possible. The breakthrough occurred between 1812 and 1815 at North-East collieries, where the need to reduce the cost of moving coal along wagonways was becoming urgent. Running a wagonway required many men and many horses, the latter consuming large quantities of fodder. During the years of the Napoleonic War (1802–15), rapidly rising transport costs made the idea of the locomotive, which fed on cheap coal and could pull a far greater load than a horse, increasingly attractive.

The development of locomotives capable of running on rails occurred simultaneously at three Tyneside collieries. At Wylam, the owner, Christopher Tennant, employed WILLIAM HEDLEY as his viewer and TIMOTHY HACKWORTH as his master blacksmith. In 1813 these men produced three locomotives that were an advance on the Trevethick model and they validated the idea that the very weight of the locomotive would ensure its adhesion to the rails. Two of these locomotives, *Puffing Billy* and *Wylam Dilly*, have survived, the former in the National Science Museum in London, the latter in the Royal Scottish Museum in Edinburgh. Wylam, however, did not continue long as a pioneering centre of locomotive development: William Hedley became a businessman, while Hackworth left Wylam because Sunday work was contrary to his religious convictions. Although Hackworth continued to design and make locomotives, he did so with ROBERT STEPHENSON, then for the Stockton and Darlington Railway, and finally on his own account.

East of Newcastle, a viable locomotive was created at Wallsend Colliery under the encouragement of the agent, JOHN BUDDLE. Its inventor was WILLIAM CHAPMAN and the engine was called the *Steam Elephant*. But here too development ceased. The third colliery was that at Killingworth Colliery, between Wylam and Wallsend, owned by a consortium, which with their viewer, NICHOLAS WOOD, backed the work of their enginewright, GEORGE STEPHENSON. It was at Killingworth that Stephenson produced his first engines, *My Lord* and *Blücher*, in 1814.

All three collieries were in the North East and three of the four inventors were born in the North East. There were, however, two other inventions, both of which proved to be blind alleys, in which the North East had some involvement. One was by John Blenkinsopp (1783–1831), who was born at Nether Heworth. He believed that smooth wheels would not adhere to smooth rails. His solution was a cog-like wheel that engaged with a toothed rail. His engine was built by the Leeds firm of Fenton, Murray and Wood for Middleton Colliery near Leeds owned by two brothers, Charles and John Brandling of Gateshead, who also owned Gosforth Colliery. The Blenkinsopp system was installed at Orrell Colliery in Lancashire and at Kenton and Coxlodge Colliery on Tyneside, where in 1813 a two-mile track was laid as far as the Ouseburn. But once the premise on which it was based was shown to be false, it had no future.

The other dead end was to modern eyes even more bizarre and even more certain to have no worthwhile future, iron legs moved by steam power to push a train of wagons. It was the invention of William Brunton, who was born at Dalkeith, worked for Boulton and Watt in Birmingham, and became chief engineer of the Butterley Company in Derbyshire. The only connection with the North East was that Brunton's system was installed at Newbottle Colliery in 1813. The life of the system was short: the Brunton engine was destroyed by an explosion in 1815, which killed three bystanders and scalded dozens more.

The rush of railway promotions in the 1830s and 1840s resulted in the emergence of locomotive builders on a commercial scale and the employment by them of engineers who could design and construct bigger and faster models. In these years, the North East rapidly became a major centre for locomotive and rolling stock production.

When railway companies were in their infancy, they bought their locomotives from independent manufacturers. But early on, both the NER and the S&DR opted to build their own engines. Starting in 1854, the NER developed the Greenesfield site in Gateshead, made redundant by the High Level Bridge and Newcastle Central Station, as a locomotive depot and engine building works and using the station hotel as the company's offices. By the end of the nineteenth century, with a workforce of over 3,000, Greenesfield was the largest employer in Gateshead. In 1910, however, the NER decided that the site was too cramped and that engine building should be concentrated at their Darlington works. The Greenesfield shops continued to be used for repair work until they were closed in 1932 by the LNER. The facility was reopened for repair work during World War II, but finally closed by British Rail in 1959.

The NER's facility at Darlington, known as the North Road Works, was opened on the first day of 1863, when still owned by the S&DR. When the S&DR merged with the NER later that year, the decision was taken to concentrate locomotive building at Darlington and this led to the transfer of 150 engineers from the former S&DR works at New Shildon. The post of Chief Mechanical Engineer was given to William Bouch, brother of Thomas Bouch, the builder of the Tay Railway Bridge that collapsed so disastrously in 1879. In all, 2,775 locomotives were built at the North Road Works, the life of which was extended until 1963 by the decision to end production at Gateshead. The NER works at New Shildon continued to function until 1984, making wagons, not locomotives.

The decision of the major railway companies to build their own engines did not, however, mean the end of the independent producer. Several locomotive manufacturers of international importance continued to thrive in the region until the middle years of the twentieth century. The largest was Robert Stephenson, founded in 1823 by George and Robert Stephenson, with the financial backing of Edward Pease and his cousin, Thomas Richardson. Their factory was next to Forth Street in Newcastle, where it remained until it too became too cramped and Stephensons, like the NER, decided to migrate to Darlington. Between 1900 and 1902 they built a new works and a housing estate for their workers on a large site to the east of the main line.

The Stephenson works in Newcastle had a close neighbour in the form of R. & W. Hawthorn (later R. & W. Hawthorn, Leslie & Co.). Robert Hawthorn set up in business as a millwright in 1817 at Forth Banks. It was after 1832, when he was joined by his brother, William, that they entered the locomotive business, opening a factory on the opposite side of Forth Street to Stephensons. In 1937 the two firms amalgamated to become Robert Stephenson and Hawthorns Ltd. Thereafter the new firm built large locomotives at Darlington and smaller engines at Newcastle. The firm was bought by English Electric in 1955, but was closed down in 1961 (Newcastle) and 1966 (Darlington).

Two other Tyneside firms also had considerable success, but over shorter periods. One was Black, Hawthorn & Co. (not related to R. & W. Hawthorn), which flourished in Gateshead from the 1840s until it went into liquidation in 1897, although production continued until 1903 under the management of Chapman and Furneaux. The life of the other firm was even shorter. Armstrong Whitworth came into the locomotive business in 1919, to take advantage of the urgent demand for locomotives, particularly on the continent, to replace those worn out or destroyed in the war. Their involvement in the business lasted no longer than twenty years, ending in 1939.

Two other firms in the south of the region built locomotives until the 1860s. One was that at New Shildon, where from 1825 the S&DR located its first engine works under the direction of Timothy Hackworth. Under the terms of an agreement made with the S&DR in 1833, Hackworth was allowed to build on his own account as well as for them. This lasted until 1840, when he severed all connection with the S&DR and became an independent manufacturer at his Soho Works, named after the famous Soho factory of Matthew Boulton and James Watt in Birmingham. The other maker was William Kitching, one of the group of Quaker businessmen in Darlington, who became a director of the S&DR in 1825. He began building locomotives in the 1830s, most notably *Derwent* (1845), which is now in the North Road Railway Museum at Darlington. His firm ceased to make locomotives in 1862 and became the Whessoe Foundry.

The North East, where arguably the railway began and the viable locomotive was evolved, no longer makes engines or rolling stock, neither role surviving the end of the age of steam.

RAINE, JAMES THE ELDER (1791–1858)

James Raine, who was one of the most prolific historians of the North East, was born at Ovington in the parish of Wycliffe, North Riding of Yorkshire, and educated at Richmond Grammar School. Although he did not hold a university degree, he became second master at Durham School in 1812, a post he held until 1828. Meanwhile, in 1816, the Dean and Chapter of DURHAM CATHEDRAL appointed him as their librarian. Two years later he was ordained priest and in 1822 the Chapter presented him to the Rectory of Meldon in Northumberland. In 1828 he moved to the more convenient living of St Mary the Less in South Bailey, Durham, immediately behind the cathedral close. From 1825 Raine also acted as a judge in the consistory court of the Durham Diocese.

But Raine's real importance sprang from his friendship with ROBERT SURTEES, begun in 1812, who fostered in him an abiding interest in the past of northern England. For many years Raine acted as what would now be called a 'research assistant' to Surtees and to JOHN HODGSON, the historian of Northumberland. Both men valued and paid tribute to his contribution; and both entrusted him, as literary executor, with editing for publication their unfinished work. It was not until 1828 that Raine published on his own account. This was his investigation of the tomb of ST CUTHBERT in Durham Cathedral. Following Surtees's death in 1834, Raine conceived the idea of founding a society in his honour, whose function would be to publish manuscripts relating to the parts of Britain between the Humber and the Mersey in the south and the Forth and the Clyde in the north. Raine is to be remembered not simply as the founder of the Surtees Society, but also as the man who ensured that it was well and truly launched by editing no fewer than thirteen volumes between 1835 and 1856. The Society has published a volume of manuscripts every year since 1835 and it enjoys an international reputation, thanks to its adherence to the highest current standards of scholarship. Its geographical range, however, has become more limited than that proposed by Raine, most volumes now relating to the four northern counties of England. Although the earliest volumes testify to Raine's determination, assiduity and energy, perhaps his finest achievement, suggested to him by Surtees, is *The History and Antiquities of North Durham*, published in 1852, which is an account, supported by transcripts of numerous documents, of the history of those districts of Northumberland that were part of Durham until 1844.

Raine's stature and his work were formally recognised by the University of Durham, which conferred on him the honorary degrees of MA and DCL.

RAINE, JAMES THE YOUNGER (1830–1896)

The younger James Raine's career and interests closely followed those of his father, JAMES RAINE THE ELDER. He was educated at Durham Grammar School and Durham University, graduating in 1851. In the two succeeding years, he gained an MA and then a Licence in Theology, and in 1854 he was ordained priest. Thereafter his career followed two parallel lines. As an Anglican priest, he was Warden of Neville Hall in Newcastle from 1854 until 1856. In the latter year, however, he moved to York to a curacy at All Saints, Pavement, becoming Rector in 1868. He remained in that living until his death. All the while, from 1855 until 1895, he was secretary of the Surtees Society and as such oversaw the publication of its annual volume of historic documents. He himself edited fifteen, all but four of which are related to his adopted home, Yorkshire. Of the others, two are concerned with HEXHAM and contain a great deal of information about the town and the medieval priory and its estates.

RAINE, KATHLEEN JESSIE (1908–2003)

Kathleen Raine, regarded as one of the foremost British poets of the twentieth century, published twelve volumes of poetry between 1943 and 2000. Her reputation was international, recognised by the award of the Queen's Gold Medal and the CBE. She had three connections with the North East. Although born in London, her father, George Raine, was the son of a Durham miner, who won a scholarship to Durham University and became an English teacher at Ilford in Essex. The second, and perhaps the most profound, was her sojourn during World War I at Great Bavington, where her maternal aunt, Peggy Black, ran the small village school. As she revealed in her autobiographical narrative, *Farewell Happy Fields*, published in 1974, these were days of great happiness and contentment, full of deep and abiding experiences, which were to influence her as a poet. In this work she also claimed to have had greater affinity with her mother's Scottish culture than with her father's strong commitment to the tenets of Methodism, of which she became acutely aware when the family settled in Ilford. Her third connection was romantic. Although she married twice, her greatest desire was for the Duke of Northumberland's grandson, Gavin Maxwell, the author of *Ring of Bright Water*. Being homosexual, he did not reciprocate.

RAMSEY, ARTHUR MICHAEL (1904–1988)

Michael Ramsey, considered by many to have been the outstanding Archbishop of Canterbury of the twentieth century, was closely associated with DURHAM. His father was a mathematician and a Fellow of Magdalene College, Cambridge, who in religion was a Congregationalist. Ramsey was educated at Repton School and then at his father's college at Cambridge, where he began reading Law, but transferred to Theology on becoming a committed Anglo-Catholic. After graduating in 1926, he trained for the Church of England ministry at Cuddesdon College and was ordained priest in 1929. Very much the academic, after a brief curacy in Liverpool he became sub-warden and lecturer at Lincoln Theological College. His scholastic reputation was established through his book *The Gospel and the Catholic Church*, published in 1936, in which he attempted to reconcile the Catholic and Evangelical traditions within the church, and it helped to secure the Professorship of Divinity at Durham University in 1939. During his tenure, the Durham Theology Department became one of the most highly regarded in Britain, and his personal reputation, based upon three major theological studies, led to his appointment as Regius Professor of Divinity at Cambridge in 1950.

Two years later he was lured from the academic world by the then Prime Minister, Winston Churchill, who persuaded him to return to Durham as Bishop. This time his stay was much shorter: in 1956 he was persuaded by the next Conservative Prime Minister, SIR ANTHONY EDEN, to become Archbishop of York; and in 1960 Eden's successor, HAROLD MACMILLAN, advanced him to the Archbishopric of Canterbury. Upon his retirement in 1974 he returned to live in Durham for a third time, although he eventually moved back to Cambridge.

Michael Ramsey was widely appreciated for his liberal views. He supported the campaigns to legalise homosexual acts by consenting adults and to abolish capital punishment; he was hostile to the apartheid policy of the South African government; and he was less than fully enthusiastic about the royal family and the Church of England's role as the established church. He had an engaging personality that exuded great warmth and an intense spirituality. At the same time he was congenitally shy and far from easy in social situations, which may explain his facial twitch and hesitancy of speech. These characteristics, however, were part of his charm and seen as evidence of his sincerity and good nature, which made him attractive to many who did not share his views or his faith.

REDESDALE, REGALITY OF

A 'regality' was a designated area of land within the bounds of which the person to whom it was granted was permitted to exercise all or virtually all the administrative and jurisdictional rights of the Crown. The Regality of Redesdale covered about 150,000 acres (60,000 ha) and extended from the watershed with the North Tyne to the southern bank of the Coquet and the whole length of the dale up to the Border. When it was created is not known, but the most likely time is the reign of Henry I (1100–35). Its recipient was the head of the UMFRAVILLE FAMILY, the lord of the Barony of Prudhoe. Unlike almost all other Northumbrian baronies, Redesdale was not burdened with the obligation of military service. Instead its holder had the responsibility of maintaining law and order in a wild upland region bordering a foreign country. Originally the Umfravilles made their 'capital' at Elsdon, but in 1157 Henry II ordered them to build a castle at Harbottle in Coquetdale, the fragmentary remains of which still stand.

The Umfravilles retained the lordship of Redesdale until the Northumberland branch of the family died out in 1436. It then passed to a collateral branch named Tailboys, who held it until they too died out in the main line in 1541. At that date Henry VIII's government was actively seeking to remove what they saw as anomalies obstructing the direct exercise of Crown power. Consequently, the man who should have inherited was persuaded to hand over the Regality to the Crown in return for land in southern England. With this transaction, the Regality came to an end.

Redesdale is almost exclusively upland, fit mainly for pastoral farming, which has continued to be the basis of its economy. However, since 1800, there have been four moves to add other aspects. By this date the land had come into the possession of the Duke of Northumberland, who in 1838 granted permission to a company to exploit the extensive coal and iron ore deposits on a rent and royalty basis. The iron they produced was of such high quality that ROBERT STEPHENSON used it in the construction of the High Level Bridge over the Tyne. Unfortunately, the company was not well managed and in 1849 it ceased to function. Thirteen years later, in 1862, production was resumed by the much larger and well-managed firm of SIR W.G. ARMSTRONG. They, however, did not smelt iron in Redesdale, but merely calcined it before transporting it by rail to their Elswick works, where it was used in the production of armour-piercing shells. This phase lasted only until 1879, when Armstrongs decided that the facility was surplus to their requirements. Subsequently, two small coalmines continued to operate until the end of the century, supplying the local domestic market. The legacy of these failed attempts at industrialisation is the village of Ridsdale on the A68 two miles south of West Woodburn. This was a company village, and remained so until the houses were sold off in 1929. Vestigial remains of spoil heaps can be seen on either side of the A68 just south of the village, and to the north is a building, often mistaken for a BORDER TOWER, which was in fact the housing for a beam engine.

The other enterprises have proved permanent. The first was the construction of the Catcleugh Reservoir, with a storage capacity of 2,345 million gallons (10,660 million litres), by the Newcastle and Gateshead Water Company between 1894 and 1904. Virtually all evidence of the construction phase has disappeared, with the exception of one of the sixty wooded huts that were built for the construction workers and their families. It has been restored, but unfortunately it is almost invisible from the road and can be visited only by special arrangement with Northumbrian Water, the present owners.

The next development was the OTTERBURN ARMY TRAINING AREA, begun in 1911. Then in the inter-war period came the extensive afforestation by the Forestry Commission, which is now a major feature of the landscape of the upper reaches of the dale. Such was the employment generated that in the 1950s the Commission built a village at Byrness to house its employees.

REDESWIRE AFFRAY, 1575

The Redeswire Affray, which took place on 7 July 1575, is sometimes described as the last battle in the long war between England and Scotland, although the term battle greatly exaggerates what happened. The occasion was a 'day of truce', when the respective Wardens of the Marches (see MARCHES OF ENGLAND TOWARDS SCOTLAND) met to deal with accusations of wrongdoing by men of the other country. On this occasion the venue was Redeswire, a few hundred yards east of Carter Bar and one of the traditional meeting places for the wardens of the respective Middle Marches. Leading the English party was the Warden himself, the long-serving SIR JOHN FORSTER. The Scots, however, were not led by their Warden, Sir William Ker of Ferniehirst, but by his deputy, John Carmichael, the Keeper of Liddesdale.

The meeting began in a friendly manner, but gradually turned ugly when Forster refused to deal with a member of the Robson clan from Falstone, against whom Scottish complaints had been laid. Words led to threats and threats to blows. Initially the Scots retreated, largely thanks to English archery, but the battle was turned in their favour by the arrival of reinforcements from Jedburgh. The English, now probably outnumbered, were defeated and fled, leaving twenty-four dead, including the Deputy Warden, Sir George Heron. Sir John Forster, whose intransigence provoked the fight, was captured, and three hundred cattle were lifted from Redesdale.

This incident, perhaps more akin to football hooliganism than a battle, was embarrassing to both governments and led to an investigation by commission, which was unable, genuinely or for political reasons, to come to firm conclusions as to blame. The event is still celebrated annually in Jedburgh in midsummer when the Callant is chosen.

REDHEAD, BRIAN (1929–1994)

Brian Redhead, who was widely known as a broadcaster on radio between the mid-1970s and his death in 1994, was born in Newcastle and educated at the Royal Grammar School there and at Downing College, Cambridge. In 1954 he joined what was then the *Manchester Guardian*, becoming its northern editor following its change of name to *The Guardian* and the removal of its headquarters to London. In 1969 he became editor of the *Manchester Evening News* and was widely expected to become the editor of *The Guardian*, when that post became vacant in 1975. Having failed to be appointed, he developed his career as a radio personality, chairing a programme called *A Word in Edgeways* and co-presenting Radio 4's morning programme, *Today*. His somewhat bumptious personality and his barely disguised political leanings made him a favourite with some but anathema to others. His untimely death in hospital resulting from a burst appendix prevented his becoming Chancellor of Manchester University.

REGIMENTS

Originally the infantry regiments of the British army were known simply by the name of their colonel. In 1751 the potential for confusion this carried was eliminated by giving each regiment a permanent number, the older the regiment, the lower its number. Thirty years later, in 1782, they were further distinguished by being associated with specific counties, a move designed to facilitate and encourage recruiting. These connections were cemented by the army reforms of Edward Cardwell in the 1870s, which gave each regiment two battalions, one to serve at home, the other overseas. These arrangements largely endured until the progressive contraction of the size of the army in the post-World War II years, which resulted in amalgamations and disbandments. Three of the 100 regiments that were raised were closely associated with the North East. In order of seniority they are as follows.

Royal Northumberland Fusiliers: As the 5th Foot, the regiment was one of the oldest in the British army. It traced its origin to one of the four regiments of what was called the English Brigade, raised in England, Scotland and Ireland in the early 1670s, with the consent of the English government, by William of Orange, the Stadtholder of the Netherlands, to help in the defence of his country against Louis XIV of France. Initially it was the Irish regiment, commanded by Daniel O'Brien, Viscount Clare. In 1675, however, he was dismissed and replaced by Sir John Fenwick of Fenwick and Wallington, who converted it into an English regiment and brought in many Northumbrians.

The regiment was summoned to England in 1685 by James II to help suppress the revolt of the Duke of Monmouth. This was put down before it arrived, and as a result its true arrival in England was as part of the army with which William of Orange invaded England in 1688. It was then that Sir John Fenwick lost command because, as a Roman Catholic, he could not acquiesce in the deposition of James II. He was executed in 1697.

The regiment immediately went to Ireland and took part in the Battle of the Boyne, which secured that island for the new regime. Thereafter it was in all the wars fought by Britain until the present time. When regiments were numbered in 1751, it was designated the 5th Regiment of Foot. In 1771 command was granted to Hugh, Earl Percy, the eldest son of the 1st Duke of Northumberland, who held the post until he succeeded his father as 2nd Duke in 1786. As a result, when regiments were allocated to counties in 1782, the 5th became the Northumberland Regiment. The word Fusiliers was added to the title in 1836, and almost one hundred years later, in 1935, on the occasion of George V's Silver Jubilee, it became the Royal Northumberland Fusiliers.

From the year 1774 its members were allowed to wear in their caps a hackle with two colours, red over white. The white was in recognition of the regiment's conduct during the conquest of the West Indian island of St Lucia, during the War of American Independence, when, after one successful engagement in which it defeated a French force ten times its size, the men of the 5th took the white cockades from the French casualties and put them in their own caps.

During World War I the regiment expanded from seven to fifty-four battalions. Eight of these were in effect separate regiments in that they were clearly distinguished by title from the others and were a recognition of the extent to which the region had received a huge influx of people from other parts of the country. The 20th, 21st, 22nd and 23rd battalions were raised as the Tyneside Scottish, and the 24th, 25th, 26th and 27th were raised as the Tyneside Irish.

Both were disbanded at the end of the war. The Tyneside Scottish, however, was resurrected in 1939 as the 12th battalion of the Durham Light Infantry (see below), but the following year was transferred to the Black Watch. For some years after the end of World War II, the Tyneside Scottish was a light anti-aircraft regiment in the Royal Artillery. In 1967, however, the name was attached to territorial units: D Company of the Royal Northumberland Fusiliers TA; and 204 battery of 101 Regiment Royal Artillery (see below). The former was disbanded after two years, but the latter continues, based at Kingston Park in Newcastle.

Like all other regiments, the RNF was affected by the drastic reduction in the size of the army in recent years. In April 1968 it was merged with the Royal Warwickshire Fusiliers, the Royal Fusiliers and the Lancashire Fusiliers to form the Royal Regiment of Fusiliers. As the oldest of these regiments, it became the 1st battalion. Ten of its members were awarded the Victoria Cross: Sergeant R. Grant (1857 Indian Mutiny); Private P. McManus (1857 Indian Mutiny); Private P. McHale (1857 Indian Mutiny); Lance Corporal T. Bryan (1917 World War I); Private E. Sykes (1917 World War I); 2nd Lieutenant J.S. Youll (1918 World War I); 2nd Lieutenant J. Johnson (1918 World War I); Private W. Wood (1918 World War I); Captain J. Jackman (1941 World War II); Major R. Cain (1944 World War II).

Its motto, which it had from its inception, was *Quo Fata Vocant* ('Whither the Fates Call'). Its regimental marches were 'The Blaydon Races' (Quick) and 'St George' (Slow).

King's Own Scottish Borderers: At first glance appearing to be 'foreign' to the North East, the inclusion of the King's Own Scottish Borderers is warranted for two reasons.

The first is that it did not receive the qualifying adjective 'Scottish' until 1887; the second is that its depot from 1881 until 1964 (when it moved to Glencorse in Edinburgh) was in the Ravensdown Barracks in BERWICK UPON TWEED, which is still the regimental headquarters. The regiment was first raised in Edinburgh in 1689 by David Melville, 3rd Earl of Leven, during the crisis of 1688–89 that saw the overthrow of James VII and II. This provoked a brief civil war in Scotland in which the newly formed regiment was involved. On 29 July 1689 it was part of the force commanded by Major General Hugh Mackay of Scourie routed in the Pass of Killiecrankie by the Highlanders loyal to the deposed James, led by John Graham of Claverhouse, Viscount Dundee.

When regiments were numbered in 1751, it became the 25th. When county associations were assigned in 1782, however, the 25th became the Sussex Regiment. One reason appears to have been the refusal of the town council of Edinburgh, the town with which the regiment had always been associated, to allow recruiting there, probably because it wished to avoid competition with the Royal Edinburgh Volunteers, recently returned from America. The Sussex connection, however, was the consequence of its colonel being Lord George Lennox, the younger brother of the Duke of Richmond and Gordon, whose family seat, Goodwood, was in that county. This inappropriate connection continued until 1805, when it was renamed The King's Own Borderers, with permission to recruit within specified limits on both sides of the Border. The word 'Scottish' was added in 1887 as the consequence of the decision to associate the Scottish Borderers Militia, raised in 1864, with the regiment. Upon this change it became a Scottish Lowland regiment and so clad in tartan trews, Black Watch until 1898, but Lennox thereafter.

The regiment has taken part in all the wars fought by Great Britain from the time of its foundation until the Gulf War and it managed to survive all the mergers and disbandments of the past forty years, until all Scottish regiments were merged in 2006. Like all regiments it has acquired traditions, the most notable being the wearing of roses on 1 August, Minden Day. This commemorates a story (for which there is no contemporary evidence) that, as the regiment marched to the battlefield of Minden in 1759, an action in which it distinguished itself, the troops plucked wild roses and stuck them in their headgear. Its cross-border history is symbolised by the fact that it is the royal crest of England, not that of Scotland, that surmounts its regimental badge, an anomaly affirmed as recently as 1961.

Six members of the regiment have been awarded the Victoria Cross: Lieutenant G.H.B. Coulson (1901 South African War); Piper Laidlaw, the famous Piper of Loos (1915 World War I); Company Sergeant Major J. Skinner (1917 World War I); Company Quartermaster Sergeant W. Grimbaldson (1917 World War I); Private W. Speakman (1951 Korea).

Its motto, given to it by George III, was *In Veritate Religionis Confido* ('In True Religion I Trust'). Its regimental marches were Band: 'Blue Bonnets o'er the Border' (Quick) and 'The Garb of Old Gaul' (Slow), and Pipes: 'Blue Bonnets o'er the Border' (Quick) and 'The Borderers' (Slow).

Durham Light Infantry: The DLI was the last of the region's three infantry regiments to be raised. It was one of the twenty-one new regiments (50th to 70th) created in the late 1750s to meet Britain's increased and far-flung military commitments during the Seven Years War. Initially it had no connection with Durham, being raised in 1756 as the second battalion of the 23rd, the regiment that eventually became the Royal Welch (sic) Fusiliers.

Two years later, in 1758, it became a separate regiment with its own number, 68th. It immediately saw action in a commando-style raid on the Brittany coast. Its commander was Lieutenant Colonel John Lambton of the Coldstream Guards, a member of the long-established Durham family. The Durham connection was cemented in 1782, when regimental colonels were asked to name the county with which they wished their regiments to be associated. Without hesitation Lambton opted for Durham: it is said that he had no competitors!

Until 1808 the Durham Regiment was simply one of the ninety-three regiments of the line. In that year, however, it was selected for training as light infantry by Sir John Moore, whose experience in the American War of Independence had convinced him of the need for a special corps of mobile skirmishers who could manoeuvre swiftly in response to bugle calls. The selection of the 68th was due largely to unfortunate chance: the regiment had recently returned from the West Indies, where it had been all but wiped out, largely by disease, and it was probably felt that new recruits would be more easily trained in the use of a different type of musket and in a new mode of fighting than experienced men, who would have to unlearn old ways. The regiment's first action in its new role was in the occupation of the Dutch island of Walcheren, where again losses were due more to disease than to enemy action.

Two years later the DLI was in Portugal to take part in the victorious campaign conducted by the Duke of Wellington. From then until it was disbanded it took part in all Britain's wars, colonial and European. Until the 1870s the regiment had only one battalion, but the reform of the army forced through by Edward Cardwell required all regiments to have two battalions, one to serve abroad while the other remained at home. The solution for the DLI was to attach to it the 106th regiment, the Bombay European Light Infantry, which had been raised in 1839 by the East India Company, but transferred to the British army after the Indian Mutiny. In 1881 this regiment ceased to exist as a separate entity, becoming the 2nd battalion of the DLI. The origins of the 2nd battalion help to explain why it dominated the Indian polo scene in the 1890s, much to the chagrin of the cavalry regiments.

The regiment served with great distinction in the wars of the twentieth century, but eventually fell to a decision taken in Whitehall in 1967. This was that the four regiments forming the Light Infantry Brigade must reduce to three. The DLI was the one to go, since it was younger than the others: the Somerset and Cornwall LI (13th and 32nd), the King's Own Yorkshire LI (51st) and the King's Shropshire LI (53rd). In consequence, in 1968 the regiment ceased to exist. Had the decision been taken on ability to recruit, there would have been no question of the DLI disbanding.

Eleven men of the regiment have been awarded the Victoria Cross: Private J. Byrne (1854 Crimea); Lieutenant Colonel T. Hamilton (1855 Crimea); Sergeant J. Murray (1864 New Zealand); Private T. Kenny (1915 World War I); Brigadier R.B. Bradford (1916 World War I); 2nd Lieutenant A. Lascelles (1917 World War I); 2nd Lieutenant F. Youens (1917 World War I); Private M. Heaviside (1917 World War I); Private T. Young (1918 World War I); 2nd Lieutenant R.W. Annand (1940 World War II); Private A. Wakenshaw (1942 World War II).

Its motto was very simple: *Faithful.* Its regimental march, which of course is a quick march of 120 paces to the minute, was 'The Light Barque' and 'The Keel Row' (Quick) and 'Old 68th' (Slow).

Although cavalry regiments never became formally county-based, one regular regiment recruits in the region, which also has one yeomanry regiment.

15th/19th The King's Royal Hussars: The name goes back only to 1933, when it was granted to the 15th/19th Hussars, the two regiments (15th The King's Hussars and 19th Queen Alexandra's Own Royal Hussars) that were amalgamated in 1922. Both regiments were first raised as Light Dragoons in 1759 during the Seven Years War, but they were restyled Hussars in 1807 and 1861 respectively. In the drastic reductions imposed in 1992, the 15th/19th was merged with the 13th/18th Hussars to form the Light Dragoons: the title had come full circle. The regiment is equipped with light armoured vehicles and has a reconnaissance role.

Four members of the regiment have been awarded the Victoria Cross: Lieutenant H.H. Gough (1857 Indian Mutiny); Quartermaster Sergeant W.T. Marshall (1884 Sudan); Corporal C.E. Garforth (1914 World War I); Private H.G. Columbine (1918 World War I).

Its regimental motto is *Merebimur* ('I Shall Serve'). The regimental marches are 'The Bold King's Hussars' (Quick) and 'Eliott's Light Horse' and 'Denmark' (Slow).

Northumberland Hussars Yeomanry: The regiment was first raised in 1819 in response to the civil disturbances in the years immediately following the end of the Napoleonic War. It was known as the Northumberland and Newcastle Volunteer Cavalry and its commander was Colonel Charles Brandling of Gosforth House. In 1876 it was renamed the Northumberland Hussars, although this belied the fact that its four squadrons were recruited throughout Northumberland and Durham. It first saw serious military action in the South African War (1899–1902) as part of the Imperial Yeomanry. It was fully involved in both World Wars I and II, in the first as cavalry, but in the second in anti-aircraft and anti-tank roles. At some stage, and for unclear reasons, it was nicknamed 'The Noodles', a sobriquet its members cherished with pride. In 1947 it was affiliated with the King's Royal Hussars and in 1971, as the result of contractions, it was linked with three other yeomanry regiments (Ayrshire, Cheshire and Yorkshire) to form the Queen's Own Yeomanry.

Two artillery regiments are associated with the area. **25th Regiment, Royal Artillery**, now disbanded, were known as the 'Geordie Gunners'. **101 Regiment (Volunteers) Royal Artillery** is a Territorial Army unit formed in 1967 by an amalgamation of the Tynemouth Volunteer Artillery (formed in 1859), the Durham Volunteer Artillery (formed in 1860) and the Elswick Battery (formed in 1900), to which were added the Tyneside Scottish (see above).

RENDEL, GEORGE WIGHTWICK (1833–1902)

George Rendel, who was with ANDREW NOBLE one of the mainstays of the great firm founded by WILLIAM ARMSTRONG, was born in Plymouth, the son of a civil engineer. His early schooling was at Harrow, from which, because of harsh treatment, he ran away in 1849. Subsequently he was given on-site training as an engineer by his father, before being apprenticed at the Elswick Ordnance Works of his father's friend, Sir William Armstrong. In 1859 he was made a partner and in 1860 joint manager with Andrew Noble. His success at Elswick was achieved in the field of warship design, which became increasingly important after Armstrong entered into an arrangement with the shipbuilder Charles Mitchell in 1868, which led to the two firms merging in 1882.

Thereafter Rendel concentrated on shipbuilding while Noble focused on ordnance. During his time at Elswick, he was responsible for the introduction of a new type of warship, the cruiser, improving the hydraulic systems required to move heavy guns, improving the power and efficiency of ships' boilers and the design of *Staunch*, Armstrong's first warship. In 1882, however, Rendel left Armstrongs to take up the newly created post of extra-professional civil lord of the Admiralty. Three years later, however, ill health forced his retirement and a move to Italy, the home of his second wife. The warmer climate must have been beneficial, for in 1885 he rejoined Armstrongs and in 1887 went out to Italy to supervise the setting up of their new ordnance works at Pozzuoli, near Naples. Rendel retired for the second time in 1900, again in poor health, this time to the Isle of Wight.

REYROLLE, ALPHONSE CONSTANT (1864–1919)

Alphonse Reyrolle was born in Juillac in the département of Correze in France. His parentage and early life are obscure, but he must have been well trained as a scientific instrument maker, since in 1883 at the age of nineteen he came to London to work for Légé & Co., specialists in that field. Within three years he had gained sufficient experience and skill to set up on his own. Much of his work was on sub-contracts for electrical firms and he rapidly gained a reputation for high-quality workmanship.

In 1901, however, he moved to Tyneside, where he founded the firm of A. Reyrolle & Co. on a five-acre site at Hebburn. The move was probably the result of strong encouragement by CHARLES MERZ, since Reyrolle's company specialised in making equipment for the rapidly growing electricity industry. Certainly Merz persuaded him in 1905 to employ the talented designer H.W. Clothier, which resulted in the development of safe, easily maintained, metal-clad (for safety) switch-gear. Also, in conjunction with SIR CHARLES PARSONS, he produced a generator, the short circuit performance of which closely followed that of a large power station. By the time of his death, his workforce had risen from an initial fifty-eight to 700. His success was based upon the high standard of his products and an ability to meet the design specifications and cost estimates. He also enjoyed a reputation as a caring and considerate employer.

RICHARDSON, JOHN WIGHAM (1837–1908)

John Wigham Richardson was born to a wealthy Newcastle Quaker banking family. His schooling began at Dr Bruce's Academy in Newcastle, continued privately at the home of J.D. Carr, the Carlisle biscuit maker, and was completed at the Friends' School at York. His business training was equally varied, beginning with a year in Liverpool, followed by a three-year engineering apprenticeship on Tyneside, a year at University College, London and finally time in the drawing office of Robert Hawthorn, a family friend, at Forth Banks. His training ended in 1860, when with his father's financial backing he and a partner, a Scotsman named Christie, acquired the Neptune Yard at Walker. The business expanded gradually, partly through the creation of additional berths and a marine engine works, but also by the acquisition in 1882 of a controlling interest in the Tyne Pontoons and Dry Docks Co. In 1899 his firm became a limited company and four years later it merged with Swan Hunters to become one of Tyneside's greatest shipbuilding firms (see SHIPBUILDING INDUSTRY).

Richardson also played a notable part in the early adoption of the use of electricity. He supported CHARLES MERZ in his successful campaign to persuade Walker and Wallsend Gas Co. to build the Neptune Bank Power Station, the first large-scale generating station to produce electricity for lighting and industrial power. Richardson's Neptune Yard was one of the power station's first customers.

Richardson was a caring employer, who built good houses for his employees and a strong believer in industrial partnership between employer and employee, to the extent of offering his men shares in the company. He was also a very cultured man, a fluent speaker of French and German, a painter in watercolours and an architect.

RICHARDSON, JOSEPH (1755–1803)

Joseph Richardson, the son of a Hexham tradesman, was educated at Haydon Bridge School. After this, thanks to an aristocratic patron, he was able to spend four years between 1774 and 1778 at St John's College, Cambridge. From there he moved to London to become a political journalist with, and as part owner of, the *Morning Post*. At the same time he trained as a lawyer and was called to the Bar in 1786. In these years he was an ardent Whig, a friend of Charles James Fox, and co-founder of the Whig Club, the Society of the Friends of the People and the Society of the Friends of Liberty. In 1796, thanks to the patronage of the 2nd Duke of Northumberland, he became MP for the tiny borough of Newport in Cornwall, a seat he held until his death seven years later.

He was also a man of the theatre. He was a close friend of the playwright Richard Brinsley Sheridan and in 1795 became part-owner of London's Drury Lane Theatre. He was also a playwright, enjoying considerable success in 1792 with *The Fugitive*, which pilloried the social system that overvalued birth and title.

RICHARDSON, THOMAS MILES (1784–1848)

Thomas Miles Richardson was one of the best landscape artists of his generation, both in oils and watercolours. He also deserves to be remembered for his lifelong commitment to art in the region. Unlike many northern artists, he did not migrate to London, but lived all his life in his native Newcastle, where he made valiant attempts to create institutions for the support of the arts.

Richardson's father was the master of St Andrew's Charity School. In the mid-1790s, he was apprenticed to Abraham Hunter, a Newcastle engraver. Unfortunately, not long afterwards Hunter died and Richardson chose to be apprenticed, not to another engraver, but to a cabinetmaker. He soon regretted this decision, but all he could do was to develop his artistic skills in his spare time. In 1806, however, his father's death furnished the means of escape and he took over the mastership of St Andrew's School. For the next seven years he managed to combine the role of schoolteacher with work as a drawing master.

By 1813, however, he felt sufficiently secure financially to give up the school and concentrate on his painting and his drawing lessons. The following year this decision appeared to be justified when his painting *View of the Old Fish Market, Newcastle* was hung in the Royal Academy in London. Pictures depicting urban scenes were popular at this date as the growth of population and the expansion of industrial activity were resulting in rapid changes in the landscape of towns. Richardson's preference, however, was for rural scenes, especially those of the Lake District and the Border Country, which is perhaps not surprising, given that his career coincided with the high days of the Romantic Movement, with its liking for dramatic and emotionally charged scenes.

Richardson's talents were such that he might have achieved considerably more fame and prosperity had he chosen to move to London. Instead, he spent much of his energy in the 1820s and 1830s in attempts to create institutions in Newcastle that would bring regional artists together into a loose group and provide them with the exhibition facilities that would bring them more readily into contact with the buying public. Although the group was supported by several other painters working in the region, none of their efforts had more than temporary success. He also attempted to set up an art school, the Northern Academy of Arts, but it too was a failure. However, in the end, Richardson's effort was not without reward, since in 1843 the Government School of Design was set up in Newcastle, with WILLIAM BELL SCOTT as its first principal.

Like most artists, Richardson took pupils, one of whom was his third son, Thomas Miles Richardson, junior (1813–90), whose ability as a watercolourist is reckoned to be not far short of his father's.

RIDLEY, NICHOLAS (c.1502–1555)

Nicholas Ridley was one of the foremost Protestant martyrs of the reign of Mary I (1553–58). Born at Unthank near Willimoteswick, he was a younger son of one of the branches of the Ridley clan, which for centuries had been prominent in South Tynedale. His mother, Anne Blenkinsopp, was also of a deep-rooted Tynedale family. After schooling in Newcastle, Ridley went to Pembroke Hall (now College), Cambridge in 1518, graduating in 1522. This was the prelude to a conventional but successful academic career. He took his MA in 1525 and then spent the next four years studying abroad, at the Sorbonne in Paris and then at Louvain. Returning to Cambridge, he undertook the long courses in Theology, culminating in the degrees of BTh in 1537 and DTh in 1541. He was Professor of Greek from 1535 until 1538 and in 1540 became Master of Pembroke Hall.

It was almost inevitable that a man of his distinction should get ecclesiastical preferment, and in the last seven years of Henry VIII's reign he progressed up the ecclesiastical ladder, becoming a King's Chaplain in 1541, a canon of Canterbury Cathedral in 1545 and then, in 1547, Bishop of Rochester. It was during these years that he gradually became convinced of the validity of many of the new Protestant beliefs, most particularly that in the Mass the bread and wine acquired Christ's spiritual presence, not that they were converted into His flesh and blood. Following Henry VIII's death, his views were in tune with the times, as during the brief reign of Henry's underage son, Edward VI (1547–53), the government required the church in England to adopt Protestant doctrines and forms of worship. Consequently, in 1550, he was promoted to the bishopric of London. In this role he gave his public support to the scheme devised in 1553 (by which time the young king was seriously ill) to set aside the claims to the throne of Henry VIII's daughters, Mary and Elizabeth, on the grounds of their illegitimacy, and to confer it on Edward's death on Lady Jane Grey, a granddaughter of Henry VIII's sister, Mary.

In doing so, Ridley backed the wrong party. When Edward VI died in July 1553, there was no significant support for this blatant attempt to flout the established rules of succession. Jane Grey and her backer, John Dudley, Duke of Northumberland, were swept aside (and later executed), and Mary, the elder of Henry VIII's two daughters, became queen. Ridley was now in a hostile world: Mary was an unswerving Catholic, determined to restore the old religion, to subordinate the English church again to the papacy, and to extirpate what to her was a detested heresy. Ridley had three choices: to flee abroad, as many did, to hope for better times; to abjure his 'errors' and return to the Catholic fold; or to remain committed to his new convictions and suffer the consequences. He chose the last, and upon conviction as a recalcitrant heretic, on 10 October 1555, together with Hugh Latimer, Bishop of Worcester, he was burnt to death at Oxford.

The horrific scene was recorded in the famous book by John Foxe, *Acts and Monuments*, usually called *Foxe's Book of Martyrs*, which did much to inculcate anti-Catholic feeling in England. In it Foxe has Latimer call on his fellow victim, 'Be of good cheer, Master Ridley, and play the man. We shall this day light such a candle by God's grace in England, as I trust, shall never be put out.' Unfortunately, these memorable and oft-repeated words did not appear until the fourth edition in 1583, twenty-four years after the book was first published. It is therefore likely that they were apocryphal.

RIDLEY, NICHOLAS (1929–1993)

Nicholas Ridley was born at Blagdon Hall, the ancestral home, the second son of Matthew White Ridley, 3rd Viscount Ridley. He hoped after Eton to go on to study architecture, an ambition that almost certainly owed much to his mother, Ursula, a daughter of the famous architect Sir Edwin Lutyens. However, his father obliged him to read Mathematics and Engineering at Oxford. Although in 1951 he secured a job with a Newcastle civil engineering firm, he had little commitment to that line of work and within a year he attempted to secure election to parliament in what in former times would have been the family seat at Blyth. For a Conservative, this was a hopeless cause and he was comprehensively defeated. He had to wait another seven years to win a seat, and then it was for the distant constituency of Cirencester and Tewkesbury.

His political career was marked by an abrasive manner and an outspoken and uncompromising assertion of what he believed needed to be done to solve Britain's economic and social problems. These were government ceasing to prop up 'lame duck' firms and industries; the destruction of the power and influence of trade unions; tight control of the money supply; reduction in government spending; and denationalisation to allow free enterprise to flourish. Initially he supported Edward Heath, who became Prime Minister in 1970, believing that he was committed to the same programme. When Heath proved insufficiently determined, Ridley became disillusioned and was one of the first to give support to Margaret Thatcher, who in 1974 challenged and defeated Heath in a contest for the leadership of the Conservative Party. It was at this time that Ridley switched from his earlier pro-European convictions to hostility towards the further integration with the institutions of the European Union.

The 1980s were his political heyday as the successive governments of Margaret Thatcher after 1979 implemented many of the policies he favoured. His ardent commitment to her, allied with his undoubted ability, meant that he rose up the ministerial ladder, becoming Financial Secretary in 1981, Minister of Transport in 1983, Secretary of State for the Environment in 1986, and Secretary of State for Trade and Industry in 1989. Almost inevitably, his tongue got him into trouble and in 1990 he was obliged to resign following the publication of utterly indiscreet remarks about the European Commission he made in an interview with the editor of *The Spectator*. This marked the end of his career in the political front line. Like his leader, he did not contest the 1992 election, instead becoming a life peer. He died of lung cancer the following year.

To the public Nicholas Ridley was a hard-nosed, abrasive and insensitive politician, who aroused in many an intense hatred. There was another and contrasting side to him, revealed in his paintings, which displayed great talent, professional quality and delicate sensitivity.

RINGTONS

The firm of Ringtons is famous throughout the North East and northern England for the delivery of tea and coffee to the customer's door. It was founded by Samuel Smith (1872–1949), a Yorkshireman, who in 1882 at the age of ten joined Ridgeways, a Leeds firm of tea blenders, as a half-time errand boy. By dint of hard work allied to a natural talent as a salesman, he rose within twenty-five years to a senior executive post. In the course of his work, he became aware of the practice of door-to-door delivery in operation in Sheffield. He concluded that this was a form of trade with great possibilities and that Tyneside might be a fruitful place to start and one where he would not contravene his contract with Ridgeways, which stipulated that he should not set up on his own in Leeds. In 1907, therefore, with the support of his wife, Ada, he started a business in Newcastle in partnership with a William Titterington. 'Smith and Titterington' was too long to be painted on the side of their horse-drawn van, hence 'Ringtons', which was the last part of Titterington's name with an added 's' for Smith. The partnership lasted until World War I, when Smith bought out his partner.

The firm flourished, except during the two world wars, when government made it a hard struggle to survive. During the first conflict, Ringtons was severely hampered by a government regulation that required tea and sugar to be bought from the same source, which meant that Ringtons' customers had to register with shops; in the later conflict, in 1943, the firm was required to take its vans off the road; and during both wars most of its male employees were called up into the armed forces. In peacetime, however, Ringtons flourished, primarily as a result of the high quality of their products, which in turn was based upon close monitoring of their suppliers and having their own blending facilities. Combined with these was a willingness to move with the times, notably the adoption of tea bags and adding coffee to their range of products. They also reinforced their attraction to their customers by having their own pottery, made for them by the Tyneside firm of Malings (see POTTERY INDUSTRY).

In 1932 the success of Ringtons allowed Samuel Smith to diversify his business interests by founding a printing firm, Cut-Outs Ltd, and a coachbuilding subsidiary, Northern Coachbuilders. If the tea business faltered during World War II, Northern Coachbuilders was very busy, employing 1,300 people making military vehicles and wings for aircraft and gliders. A third subsidiary was founded, Smith's Electric Vehicles, on the TEAM VALLEY TRADING ESTATE, to manufacture battery-driven vehicles to replace the firm's horse-drawn carts. The Cabac range of multi-purpose electric vehicles made by Smiths is a leader in its field and is exported throughout the world.

In the course of its expansion, Ringtons moved from its original base in Third Avenue, to Shields Road and finally, in 1928, to its present premises in Algernon Road, Heaton. It has remained a family firm, headed by the great-grandson of the founder.

RIPPON, GEOFFREY FREDERICK, 1st LORD RIPPON OF HEXHAM (1924–1997)

Geoffrey Rippon was born in Writhlington, Somerset in 1924, the son of a tax inspector.

He was educated at King's School, Taunton and Brasenose College, Oxford, graduating in 1944. He then went into the law, becoming a barrister in 1948 and taking Silk in 1964. Meanwhile he pursued a political career, initially in local government: in 1945 he was elected to Surbiton Borough Council, becoming mayor in 1950; two years later he was elected to the London County Council, rising to become leader of the Conservative group. In parallel with this, he became MP for Norwich South in 1955. Within seven years he rose to ministerial rank, appointed Minister of Public Works in 1962. In the 1964 election, however, the Conservatives were defeated and Rippon lost his seat.

Two years later he secured a return to parliament as member for HEXHAM, a seat he was to hold for twenty-one years. Four years later, in 1970, the Conservatives, led by Edward Heath, regained power. Rippon, whose approach to politics and the exercise of power was in tune with those of his leader, was made Chancellor of the Duchy of Lancaster, with responsibility for negotiating Britain's membership of the European Economic Community. In 1972, following this success, he was made Minister of State for the Environment, in which role he gave the go-ahead for the building of the Channel Tunnel. In 1974, however, Heath, miscalculating the mood of the country during the bitter miners' strike, was defeated in the election he called.

Shortly afterwards Heath suffered a second defeat, by Margaret Thatcher in a contest for the leadership of the Conservative Party. The new leader had a different political philosophy, which Rippon disliked. He declined to serve in her cabinets, shadow and actual, and in 1987 decided not to seek re-election. His services, however, were recognised by a life peerage.

Geoffrey Rippon was a man with a short temper and a brusque manner, who lacked charisma and did not inspire great affection. He was, however, immediately responsible for implementing two of the most significant political decisions affecting Britain's future taken during the second half of the twentieth century.

RISING OF THE NORTHERN EARLS, 1569–70

The Rising of the Northern Earls was one of the most significant events in the North East's history in that it destroyed much of its medieval social fabric. The earls were Charles Neville, 6th Earl of Westmorland (see NEVILLE FAMILY) and Thomas Percy, 7th Earl of Northumberland (see PERCY FAMILY), and the underlying reason for their rebellion was their hostility to the religious policy of Queen Elizabeth I. Both earls and their countesses were staunch Catholics, strongly opposed to the changes in doctrine and religious observance laid down by the queen at the outset of her reign.

Their revolt was triggered by the arrival in England of the Catholic Mary, Queen of Scots, who was deposed in 1567 and fled to England the following May after the defeat of her forces at Langside near Glasgow. To Catholics, Mary – the great-granddaughter of Henry VII – had more legitimate right to the throne of England than did Elizabeth. In their eyes Elizabeth, the daughter of Henry VIII and Anne Boleyn, was illegitimate and thereby debarred from the succession. Mary's presence in England, albeit as a captive, proved irresistible to those who wanted a regime change. The aim of the rebellion was to replace Elizabeth with Mary, or failing that, to establish her as Elizabeth's successor.

Elizabeth's government was well aware of their disaffection, and it was the attempt of the Earl of Sussex, President of the Council of the North, to arrest the Earl of Northumberland at his manor house at

Topcliffe near York in early November 1569 that sparked the uprising. Percy managed to avoid capture and rode north to join Neville at Brancepeth Castle. Neither man was a natural rebel, but they were surrounded by kith and kin determined on an uprising: the Countess of Westmorland was a firebrand; the Countess of Northumberland was a woman of deep Catholic conviction; and both earls had influential followers hot for rebellion. Their titles and status required them to assume the leadership role, but they did so with some reluctance.

The uprising was a fiasco. There was no forceful leadership and no clear strategy. After marching to Durham to celebrate Mass in the Cathedral, thereby declaring their religious commitment, they headed south, recruiting as they went. At Bramham Moor near Wetherby, with a force probably numbering between 4,000 and 5,000, they decided to retreat, having learned that a royal army was mustering in the Midlands. Back in the region, they managed to force the surrender of BARNARD CASTLE, defended by the Sheriff of Durham, Sir George Bowes, and to capture HARTLEPOOL as a port of entry for a Spanish army from the Netherlands, of which there was never any hope.

Further north retreat into Northumberland, however, was blocked by the Wardens of the Marches (see MARCHES OF ENGLAND TOWARDS SCOTLAND), Lord Hunsdon (the queen's cousin) and SIR JOHN FORSTER; and also by the Earl of Northumberland's brother, Henry Percy, to whom the queen had promised the Percy inheritance, if he remained loyal. Following a brief skirmish near Chester le Street, the two earls disbanded their army, already reduced by desertions, and fled into Scotland.

The rebel host was composed mainly of gentry and their farming tenants, some of whom may well have been reluctant recruits, augmented by farm labourers, rural craftsmen and townsmen. Just over half were from the North Riding of Yorkshire. Of those from the North East, the large majority were from the southern parts of Durham; very few came from North Durham or Northumberland.

Brutal repression followed the collapse, the queen particularly demanding blood. Only nineteen Northumberland men were hanged, but the Durham total was 306: the queen insisted that at least one man from every township that had taken part should be executed. The others were allowed to buy pardons, which gave the Exchequer a windfall income of £866. Of the ringleaders, only seven were executed, partly because many fled abroad. The Earl of Westmorland, assisted by Lord Home, escaped to the Netherlands, where he lived out his days in exile, earning his living in the Spanish armies attempting to suppress the Protestant Dutch rebels. He died in 1601. The Earl of Northumberland was not so lucky. He fell into the hands of the notorious Armstrong clan, who sold him to the regency government of Scotland. He was held captive until 1572, when he was sold to the English government. Having been tried and found guilty of treason *in absentia*, he was immediately executed at York. The Countess of Northumberland also escaped to the Netherlands, where she led a life of piety and religious devotion until her death in 1591. The Countess of Westmorland, however, fared well, managing to make her peace with Elizabeth, from whom she received an annual pension of £300.

The failure of the rising was a political watershed for the region. The Earl and Countess of Westmorland had no children, and consequently their conviction for treason meant that the Neville estates reverted to the Crown, in whose hands they remained until 1629. At a stroke, the Crown, which hitherto had possessed no land in County

Durham, took the place of its most powerful and well-endowed lay family. This, together with the severe reduction of the power and wealth of the bishops of Durham by Henry VIII and Elizabeth I, greatly enlarged the direct authority of central government in the 'Land of the Prince Bishops'. Change in Northumberland was less dramatic, at least in appearance. The queen honoured her promise and allowed Henry Percy to inherit both title and estates as 8th Earl of Northumberland. But he and his successors ceased to live in the north, being obliged to reside at their palace at Petworth in Sussex, or at Syon House at Brentford (acquired late in the sixteenth century), where they had less chance to make mischief and where they could be more readily apprehended if they did. The Percys were still wealthy, but they were no longer powerful regional magnates.

RITSON, JOSEPH (1752–1803)

Joseph Ritson was born in Stockton on Tees, the son of a servant. His outstanding intelligence, however, gained him a good education at the hands of a local clergyman. His schooling completed, in 1769 he was articled to a local solicitor, but in 1771 his articles were transferred to a prominent barrister, Ralph Bradley, who specialised in property conveyance. At the end of his apprenticeship in, 1775, he moved to London, where from 1780 he had his own chambers in Gray's Inn.

Ritson's true interest was not in law but in ancient literature, and in the course of the next twenty years he produced a stream of collections of songs, poems and ballads from the medieval centuries. A considerable quantity of these concerned the North East: *The Bishopric Garland* (1784), *The North Country Chorister* (1792), and *Northumbrian Garland* (1793). These studies are still important sources of knowledge of the language forms and the dialect of the North East in former times. He was also interested in ancient Scottish literature. In 1785 he published *The Caledonian Muse*, and near the end of his life helped Sir Walter Scott compile the material for the latter's *The Minstrelsy of the Scottish Border*. His two greatest works, however, were not concerned with the North East. One was his collection of materials relating to the legend of Robin Hood, published in two volumes in 1795, to which hardly anything further has been added since. The other was *Bibliographica Poetica*, a catalogue of English poets from the twelfth to the sixteenth century. He also found time to write two legal studies: *The Jurisdiction of the Court Leet* and *The Office of a Bailiff of a Liberty*. As well as a friend of Scott, he was also a friend of the Durham historians ROBERT SURTEES and George Allan, and of the musician WILLIAM SHIELD.

Ritson was an odd character. He was a confirmed vegetarian. His political commitments were eccentric in their illogicality, combining ardent support for the Jacobite cause with republicanism and approval of the French Revolution. And he was also extremely irascible, given to intemperate criticism of others working in the same field, often accusing them of a lack of accuracy and precision and, worse still, of forgery. His unbalanced temperament combined with his regime of incessant work help to explain the mental breakdown he suffered in 1801. Although he made some recovery, he died of a stroke at the end of 1803. His library and manuscripts, amounting to almost 1,000 items, fetched over £680 at auction after his death.

ROMAN CATHOLIC MARTYRS

When Elizabeth I, who succeeded her Roman Catholic half-sister, Mary I, in 1558, elected to follow her father by breaking with Rome and establishing herself as head of the Church of England, the situation of those who wished to continue as Roman Catholics became difficult. The difficulty increased in 1570, when Pope Pius V in the bull *Regnans in Excelsis* declared her to be a heretic and absolved her subjects from their allegiance. In effect, he declared war on the Elizabethan regime and gave it the guise of a crusade. In pursuance of this policy, Roman Catholic priests, some specially trained at a college (see USHAW COLLEGE) set up for the purpose by William Allen at Douai in the Spanish Netherlands (now in France), began to infiltrate England to make converts and to provide existing Roman Catholics with their traditional services. The government's response was the draconian legislation of 1581, which imposed a penalty of £20 a month for non-attendance at church, and declared that to be a Roman Catholic priest and to convert to Roman Catholicism were treasonable acts, the penalty for which was to be hanged, drawn and quartered. There was now a serious 'cold war', with the prospect of it becoming 'hot' should the leading Roman Catholic country, Spain, attempt to invade England.

For the next forty years the threat to Roman Catholics in England was dire, ranging from financial ruin to a horrible death. And the state authorities, assisted by government spies and informers, became adept at identifying Roman Catholics and locating incoming priests. As a result, between 1577 and the end of Elizabeth's reign in 1603, over one hundred Roman Catholic 'traitors' were executed. Eleven of these executions took place in the North East and victims included five from the region: Hugh Taylor, executed at York in 1585; Edward Burdon, also executed at York, in 1588; George Swalwell, executed at Darlington in 1594; George Errington, executed at York in 1596; and John Norton, executed at Durham in 1600. The last priest connected with the region to be executed was John Duckett, a Yorkshireman, who was born in 1613 and ordained in 1639. He arrived in Durham in 1643, but his ministry was brief. He was captured on Redgate Bank near Wolsingham, the spot still marked by a cross, and executed at Tyburn (together with Ralph Corby, a Jesuit priest caught at Hamsterley Hall in the Derwent valley), on 7 September 1644.

The most highly regarded of those executed in the North East was, however, a Westmorland (Cumbria) man, John Boste, who was born at Dufton, near Appleby. He was educated at Oxford and then became an ordained priest in the Church of England. It was only after the accession of Elizabeth I that he decided that he could not accept the new dispensation. Consequently, in 1580, he went to Rheims, where he was reordained as a Roman Catholic priest in March the following year. The following month he landed at Hartlepool and for over twelve years he managed to evade capture and practise as a priest, moving from one Roman Catholic house to another. He was finally caught, betrayed by an informer, Francis Egglesfield, at Waterhouses in the Deerness valley, the home of William Claxton, who was in prison on account of his recusancy. Taken to London, he was tortured to extract a confession at the Tower and then tried at the assizes at Durham, where he pleaded guilty. He was executed at Durham at the normal place for public executions at the top of the present North Road near Dryburn on 24 July 1594. He was canonised in 1970.

ROMAN FORTS

Throughout the empire the Roman army constructed military establishments, to which we have given the name fort. The Latin word was *castra*, which has entered English place names as 'chester', but in parts where Scandinavian settlement was heavy, changed to 'caster'. Some were made of turf and wood, others of stone. But all were built to a standard plan: rectangular in shape; rounded corners; four double gateways, one through each of the four sides, through which roads ran. Where the roads met was the headquarters building (*principia*), comprising an open paved square at the far end of which was a hall with offices behind. At one side of the headquarters building was the commandant's house (*praetorium*) and on the other the granaries (*horrea*). In the remaining sectors of the fort were barracks, stables, workshops, a latrine block and a hospital (*valetudinarium*). The gates, the corners and the walls of the fort at intervals were reinforced by towers. Outside the fort was a bathhouse, which served as a recreation centre as well as a cleaning facility.

In all, between the Tees and the Tweed nineteen permanent forts built of stone were constructed. They fall into three groups.

Hadrian's Wall: ten of its seventeen forts lay in what is now Northumberland, namely, from east to west, Wallsend (Segedunum), Newcastle (Pons Aelius), Benwell (Condercum), Rudchester (Vindobala), Halton Chesters (Onnum), Chesters (Cilurnum), Carrawburgh (Brocolita), Housesteads (Vercovicium), Great Chesters (Aesica) and Carvoran (Magnis). Also to be included here is South Shields (Arbeia), which was on the south side of the Tyne but served as the port for the Wall complex.

Stanegate: two certain forts at Corbridge (Corstopitum) and Chesterholm (Vindolanda), but with a possible third at Newbrough.

Dere Street: six forts from the Tees to the Rede, namely, Piercebridge (Magis), Binchester (Vinovia), Lanchester (Longovicum), Ebchester (Vindomora), which were south of Hadrian's Wall, and north of it, Risingham (Habitancum) and High Rochester (Bremenium).

In addition, there were earthen camps that were not developed into forts: one at West Woodburn and nine between High Rochester and the present Scottish border at Chew Green.

Probably all forts acquired a *vicus* or civilian settlement outside one of its gates, almost certainly an organic rather than a planned development. For knowledge of the forts and their civilian adjuncts we are almost entirely reliant on archaeology, and since no fort and no settlement has been fully excavated, our knowledge is far from complete. It is clear, however, that in the long period of their existence from the late first or early second century not all of them were permanently occupied, but had periods of abandonment.

ROMAN ROADS

The Romans built two important north–south roads and two major east–west roads through the region. Most were constructed during the period of conquest, that is, between the years AD 43 and 90. They were built by the army and were intended primarily to facilitate the movement of troops and their equipment: the benefit to commerce and other civilian use was incidental. Excavations have revealed variations in width between 15 and 30 feet (4.5–9 m) in structure, but always conforming to sound engineering principles: deep foundations, retaining kerbs, durable, convex surface, and adequate drainage. Every road was a series of direct lines with no concession to the steepness of the ground, a feature still very evident today.

Of the north–south roads, the western one, known as **Dere Street** (formerly known as **Watling Street**), was the more important. It started at York, headquarters of the VIth Legion (known as Victrix), one of the three field armies stationed in Britain (the others were at Caerleon and Chester), and crossed the Tees by a bridge next to the fort at Piercebridge. It then headed for CORBRIDGE via the forts at Binchester, LANCHESTER and Ebchester. The Derwent was crossed by means of a ford, but a bridge was built over the Tyne to allow it to reach Corbridge. From there it headed north, crossing HADRIAN'S WALL at Portgate, to the fort at High Rochester, from where it proceeded over the hills, crossing what is now the Scottish Border at Chew Green, where the outlines of temporary camps can still be seen. Its final destination was the fort at Cramond on the Forth.

The starting point of the eastern road was the port at Brough on the Humber. It crossed the Tees at Middleton St George and then headed north via Sadberge, Sedgefield and Bowburn. From there it ran to the fort at CHESTER LE STREET, although its precise line has not been determined. This means that where it crossed the Wear is uncertain, the only clue being the report by the nineteenth-century historian ROBERT SURTEES that the abutments of a bridge had, in living memory, been visible at low water at Kepier. From Chester le Street, the line to the banks of the Tyne is clear enough. The river was crossed by means of a bridge, Pons Aelius (Aelius was Hadrian's family name). During excavations for the present Swing Bridge in the 1860s, remains of the Roman foundations were unearthed, proving that it and its medieval and Georgian successors were built at the same point.

The eastern road terminated at the fort at what is now Newcastle. But further north another eastern road was built. This branched off Dere Street at Beuclay, one and a half miles north of Hadrian's Wall, and headed across country to Tweedmouth. In post-Roman times it became known as the **Devil's Causeway**.

Between the western and eastern roads were link roads. South of the Tyne, a road branched off from Dere Street at Willington in the direction of Durham. It can be traced as far as the River Browney, but where it met the eastern road is uncertain, although it must have been north of Durham. There was also a road linking Dere Street from the vicinity of the fort at Binchester to the fort at Bowes, where it met the road from Scotch Corner across Stainmore to Penrith. A third branch road, known as the **Wrekendyke**, left the eastern road at Wrekenton and headed for SOUTH SHIELDS, the port at the mouth of the Tyne. The other link was north of the Tyne, running between High Rochester and Low Learchild.

Of the east–west roads, that from Corbridge to Carlisle, which linked a series of small forts, was the earlier. It was built by Julius Agricola, the Governor of Britain from AD 76 until 84, who at that point intended it to mark the frontier. The mystery surrounding this road, which came to be called **Stanegate**, was the apparent absence of an easterly branch from Corbridge to the coast at South Shields. Nearly a hundred years later it was supplemented and to some degree superseded by the Military Way, which should not be confused with the MILITARY ROAD. The Military Way was an addition to the Hadrian's Wall complex and it ran parallel and, as far as possible close to, the Wall on its southern side.

While the lines taken by most of these roads have been identified, many of them have disappeared completely or can be identified only as unmade country lanes, footpaths and hedge lines. But not all: throughout the region there are many miles of road where the Roman predecessor lies directly under or very close to the present surface.

ROPNER, SIR EMIL HUGO OSCAR ROBERT, Bt (1838–1924)

Robert Ropner was one of several Germans who migrated to the North East in the nineteenth century and made fortunes through industrial enterprise. Ropner was born in Magdeburg, then in Prussia, the son of an army officer. For reasons that have never become clear, he left home in 1856 when he was eighteen and arrived at HARTLEPOOL. He found work in a bakery owned by a man named Craik and shortly afterwards married his daughter. He did not remain long in the bakery business: by 1860 he had joined a coal exporting firm, in which he became a partner in 1866. The following year he bought his first ship from the local firm of Denton and Gray and by 1884 he had become co-owner and manager of eighteen vessels. By 1914 the size of his fleet had expanded to fifty-eight vessels, forty-two owned by Robert Ropner & Co. (their names distinguished by the suffix *-by*) and the rest by the Pool Shipping Co. (their names ending in *Pool*), a company he had founded in 1903. The controlling interest in both companies was in the hands of himself and his family. Ropner's fleet suffered badly during World War I and by 1924 he had only fourteen vessels, all but one belonging to the Pool Shipping Co.

As early as 1888 Ropner decided to build ships as well as buying them. In that year he bought a yard in STOCKTON, then standing idle, and placed his son, Robert Ropner, junior, in charge. Shipbuilding continued there until the slump of the 1920s, most of its products being bought by Robert senior's companies.

In the last years of the nineteenth century, when his sons were able gradually to relieve him of direct involvement in the management of his business interests, public life began to occupy more of his time. He was active in the Hartlepool Port and Harbour Commission, the Hartlepool Shipowners' Association, and the United Kingdom Chamber of Shipping. A Conservative in politics, he was Stockton's first mayor, in 1892, and from 1900 until 1910 MP for the town. He received a knighthood in 1902, which was raised to a baronetcy in 1904. He was naturalised in 1861, spoke English almost without accent and generally strove to act as a wealthy Briton. This included the purchase of a country estate, Preston Hall on the Tees, and he was philanthropic, notably funding the Stockton and Thornaby Hospital. When he died in 1924, his estate was valued at £3.6 million.

ROSS'S PICKLES

Ross's pickles have been well known and popular thoughout the region for many years and the firm is now the largest independent pickle maker in Britain. The firm's origins, however, were very humble: using the gratuity he received on demobilisation from the army in 1918 and devising their own vinegar recipe for pickling onions, James Robertson Ross (1877–1942) and his wife Elizabeth, always known as Bessie (1878–1971), prepared their product in their kitchen in Heaton in Newcastle and then marketed it by hand around the local pubs. As the business developed they transferred manufacture sequentially to premises near the General Hospital, in Byker, then to Scotswood and finally, in 1965, to a purpose-built factory on the Newburn Industrial Estate. Bessie Ross, who was the driving force of the enterprise, lived long enough to lay the foundation stone of this facility.

The business developed rapidly in the years after the end of World War II. This was due in part to the advent of new technology, but more importantly to the enterprise of the third generation of the Ross family, who saw the need to adopt modern methods, but also to make sure that their product was sold by the growing number of regional supermarket chains. Their response to market changes continued in the 1980s as food retailing fell under the control of national supermarket chains of ever-increasing size. Ross's response was not only to market their products under their own brand name, but also to manufacture for these powerful groups under their 'own brand' names.

Until 2007, when it was the subject of a takeover, the firm was run by the fourth generation of the Ross family. In the later period of their ownership they decided not to diversify but to confine their business to pickling vegetables in vinegar, while at the same time developing new types of vinegar and introducing a 'gourmet range' to raise the social standing and acceptability of pickles as healthy and health-promoting foods. Their success is measured by the fact that their products are now not only sold throughout Britain, but are also exported to Europe and the USA.

ROTHBURY

That Rothbury was important in prehistoric times is indicated by the twelve hill forts that have been identified in its vicinity. The nature and period of that importance, however, will only be revealed by further archaeological investigation. Its historic existence goes back to the early Anglo-Saxon period, since when it has been the 'capital' of upper Coquetdale. The second element of the name derives from the Old English word *burh*, meaning fortress, which suggests that it was again a place of some importance. This notion is given support by its carved stone cross, one fragment of which supports the font in its church, while others were in the Museum of Antiquities in Newcastle and will be in the new Great North Museum. With an estimated height of 15 feet and artistic quality comparable with that of the famous RUTHWELL CROSS, it was probably among the finest products of the early eighth-century 'Hexham School' of carving. Equally significant was its early stone church. Indeed, there are grounds for thinking that initially there were two churches, built end to end, as at Lindisfarne (see HOLY ISLAND) and JARROW. If so, Rothbury was an important Northumbrian ecclesiastical site. Unhappily, the chances of gaining greater detail and certainty have been severely reduced by the act of ecclesiastical vandalism committed by the Victorian rector, Vernon Harcourt, who wantonly destroyed most of the medieval fabric, including the Anglo-Saxon west tower, in order to erect the present building.

Taken together, the fragments of evidence point to Rothbury being an important royal possession, an idea supported by its retention (together with BAMBURGH, CORBRIDGE, Newburn and Warkworth) by the Norman kings William II and Henry I when, between 1095 and 1135, they granted out most of Northumberland in the form of baronies. In 1107 Henry I granted the church, which was the centre of a parish covering over 40,000 acres and containing twenty settlements, to his chaplain, Robert d'Orival. Fifteen years later he ordained that following Orival's death, Rothbury (together with a number of other churches he had given him) should pass to the newly founded Augustinian priory at Carlisle. Subsequently, ownership of the churches was divided between the priory and the bishopric of Carlisle, created in 1133. Thereafter, the patronage of Rothbury church belonged, as it still does, to the Bishop of Carlisle.

In its secular aspects, however, Rothbury remained a Crown property until 1205, when King John bestowed it (together with Corbridge, Newburn and Warkworth) on the Sheriff of Northumberland, Robert son of Roger, the ancestor of the Clavering family. By that date, Rothbury's importance had been enhanced by its conversion into a borough. The ambitions for this creation are indicated by the size of the present village green, which, had the hoped-for economic development occurred, would have become an extensive marketplace. King John's grant also included Rothbury Forest, a tract of land lying to the north and east of the town, which extended to almost 15,000 acres (6,000 ha). This area had considerable economic potential, particularly for pastoral farming. Economic growth was also promoted by the foundation (some time before 1242) of a new agrarian community, Newtown, on the south side of the Coquet. However, whatever economic ambitions the Crown, the Claverings and their successors, the Percys, had were only modestly realised, thanks to the Scottish wars and population decline in the fourteenth century. Rothbury continued as a large village, but never developed into a fully fledged town, as did ALNWICK and MORPETH.

Since the post-medieval period, the most striking development in Rothbury was the creation in the second half of the nineteenth century of Cragside by SIR WILLIAM ARMSTRONG. His achievement was basically threefold. By planting over 7 million trees, he converted over 5,000 acres (2,000 ha) of bleak moorland in Debdon into a forest. The appearance of the land before he acquired it is revealed by the moors lying beyond it. At the centre he built his country retreat. Initially a small lodge, it was transformed between 1870 and 1885 by the fashionable architect Norman Shaw into a large mansion. This house Armstrong made the most technologically advanced dwelling of its day. Between 1878 and 1880 it became the first house to be lit by hydro-electricity, generated in a facility at the foot of the dam built to create Debdon Lake, and the first to be properly fitted with JOSEPH SWAN's incandescent lamps. From Tumbleton, another of his artificial lakes, Armstrong derived the power to drive hydraulic machinery, installed in 1885, to raise fresh water 150 feet (46 m) from a pump house at the foot of the dam to a reservoir near the house and thence throughout the house. The estate, the house and the pioneering technology are now in the care of the National Trust.

ROWELL, SIR HERBERT BABINGTON (1860–1921)

Herbert Rowell was born at Carr Hill, Gateshead, the son of a wealthy shipbroker. He was educated at Mill Hill School, London and in Switzerland; he then served an apprenticeship with JOHN WIGHAM RICHARDSON, during which he spent six months at Glasgow University attending lectures on naval architecture. Between 1883 and 1891 he worked for SIR WILLIAM ARMSTRONG, first at the Walker Naval Yard and then at Elswick. In 1891, however, he moved to Hawthorn Leslie, brought in by BENJAMIN BROWNE to revive its fortunes. In this he was successful, bringing the company back into profit in the following two years. In 1916 he became Chairman and Managing Director. He was also the first lecturer in Naval Architecture at Armstrong College, the forerunner of Newcastle University.

ROYCROFT, BRIAN (1933–2002)

Brian Roycroft, who was one of the foremost pioneers of the modern social services regime, was born in a children's home at Frodsham in Cheshire, where his mother and father were the house parents. He was educated at Birmingham and Leeds Universities but became interested in social problems through his experience in the RAF in dealing with ill-educated national servicemen. He began his career in 1957 as a childcare officer with Hertfordshire County Council and ten years later he was appointed children's officer in Newcastle, one of his first cases being the child murderess, Mary Bell. His role gradually expanded and widened until he became Newcastle's first Director of Social Services, although he always felt that childcare specialism would suffer by being part of an all-embracing social service scheme. Nevertheless, he was recognised as a major figure in the social service field and acted as Secretary and then President of the Association of Directors of Social Services. His reputation was such that he was asked to serve on the Social and Economic Committee of the European Economic Community.

RUNCIMAN, SIR WALTER, 1st LORD SHORESTON (1847–1937)

Walter Runciman, who became a major North-East shipping magnate, was born in Dunbar, East Lothian. His father was the master of a schooner who transferred to the coastguard service, and his mother was the daughter of a Dunbar shipowner. Shortly after Runciman's birth, the family moved to the coastguard station at Cresswell in Northumberland. In 1859, when he was twelve, he ran away to sea and spent the next twelve years learning seamanship on the job. In 1867 he enrolled at a nautical school to learn the theory of seamanship and to obtain qualifications to command a vessel at sea. This culminated in 1871 with the award of a master mariner's certificate. With this qualification he secured command of a sailing barque, on which he served until 1877.

In that year he took the decision to move from management to ownership by buying a secondhand steamer at SOUTH SHIELDS, and over the following twelve years he built up a fleet of twelve steamers, all secondhand. By 1889 he was sufficiently successful to commission his first new ship, which he called *Blakemoor.* This was the start of the Moor Line, one of the most important British shipping lines, which by 1914 had a fleet of forty ships. In 1919, however, he wound up the company and paid off its shareholders. Two years later, in 1921, he formed another shipping company, Walter Runciman & Co. of Newcastle and London, which revived the Moor Line and in 1935 took control of the Anchor Line of Glasgow.

Runciman was a strict Methodist and lay preacher, who, perhaps curiously, was a passionate admirer of Napoleon Bonaparte, about whom he wrote two books. Although not particularly interested in politics, he did serve as Liberal MP for Hartlepool between 1914 and 1918. Rather, he was more devoted to matters maritime. He succeeded the Earl of Inchcape as President of the Shipping Federation in 1932, retaining the office until his death in 1937; he was Commodore of the RNVR; and in his spare time he was a keen yachtsman and Commodore of the Royal Northumbrian Yacht Club.

Like many men who made fortunes in business, Runciman invested in land, buying estates at Doxford and Shoreston in Northumberland. It was from the latter that he took his title, when he was awarded a peerage in 1933.

Walter Runciman's only child, also Walter, unlike his father had a conventional education, at school in South Shields and then at Trinity College, Cambridge. He was expected to enter the family shipping business, but soon deserted it for politics. He was an MP with two short breaks from 1899 until 1937, when he was made a peer as Viscount Doxford and two months later became the 2nd Lord Shoreston on his father's death. Runciman was a noted expert in the fields of economics and trade, who at various times was Financial Secretary to the Treasury, President of the Board of Agriculture and Fisheries, and President of the Board of Trade, and almost certainly would have been Chancellor of the Exchequer had he not been a member of the Liberal Party during the period of its rapid decline.

RUSHWORTH, JOHN (c.1612–1690)

John Rushworth's importance rests on the vast quantity of material he collected and published about the events of the civil war years in Britain. His roots lay entirely in Northumberland: his father was Lawrence Rushworth of Acklington Park; his mother was Margaret Carnaby of Halton; and he married Hannah Widdrington of Cheeseburn Grange, the sister of SIR THOMAS WIDDRINGTON. Little is known of his early years, although he appears to have spent some time at Oxford, possibly at The Queen's College. Later, by some means, he acquired sufficient legal training to qualify for the Bar in 1647.

During the 1630s, when he earned his living by taking shorthand notes of proceedings in the Court of Exchequer and the Court of Star Chamber, he began accumulating historical records, including political pamphlets and periodicals. In 1640 his skills secured him the appointment as Assistant Clerk of the House of Commons, which gave him a front-row seat at the great parliamentary debates of the civil war period. Although he sided with parliament, he was never violently partisan, and by the late 1650s he had come round to accepting the need for the return of the monarchy. Following the death of COLONEL GEORGE FENWICK in 1657, he was briefly MP for Berwick.

Rushworth called his vast accumulation of material *Historical Collections*. It was published in four parts (the last two posthumously) between 1659 and 1701 and dealt with events between 1618 and 1649: Part I (1659) covers 1618 to 1628; Part II (1680) covers 1628 to 1640; Part III in two volumes (1691) covers 1640 to 1644; and Part IV (1701) in two volumes covers 1645 to 1649. Although of variable quality, they are nevertheless a mine of information for today's historians. His own attempts at writing history are now largely discounted, but the documents he included remain important, as are the records of events where he was present and upon which he made notes. Two of these were the trial of Charles I's chief minister, Thomas Wentworth, Earl of Strafford in 1640, published in 1680, and the occasion on which Charles I came to the Commons on 4 January 1642 with an armed guard hoping to arrest five opposition MPs.

RUTHERFORD, JOHN HUNTER (1826–1890)

John Hunter Rutherford was born in Jedburgh and educated at the town's Grammar School. He subsequently attended the universities of St Andrews and Glasgow and qualified to be a minister of religion. However, instead of entering the Church of Scotland, to whose rigidities he was opposed, he became a Congregational minister and in this capacity he lectured and preached throughout the far north of England. Then, in the late 1850s, he settled in NEWCASTLE, where he built up a personal congregation, using a lecture room in Nelson Street. When these premises became too cramped, a purpose-built chapel was erected in Bath Lane and opened in 1860. Following this, Rutherford decided to broaden his knowledge by qualifying as a doctor. Through attendance at courses at the Medical College in Newcastle, he gained the knowledge that enabled him to qualify as both a physician and a surgeon at Edinburgh University in 1867. Behind this decision lay his philanthropic concern for the most poverty-stricken sections of the city's population.

But Rutherford's greatest contribution to human betterment was as an ardent educational reformer. He was fortunate in that in 1870 elementary education was made compulsory and local elected School Boards came into being to establish and run the system. Under the aegis of the act, in 1870 he founded an elementary school in Corporation Street, known as Bath Lane Schools. Its rapid success and popularity led to branches being opened in Shieldfield and Heaton. He then moved on to secondary education, founding a School of Science and Art in Corporation Street, opened in 1879, with a branch at Heaton. Finally, in 1886, he opened a Technical College in Diana Street. Although these achievements were primarily due to his energy and commitment, they would not have been possible without the support of a number of the city's most influential figures, notably JOSEPH COWEN, ROBERT SPENCE WATSON, and the industrialist SIR WILLIAM ARMSTRONG.

Rutherford's concern for educational reform was part of his general political outlook, which was decidedly radical. He was particularly associated with the most radical North-East politician of his day, Joseph Cowen, to whose career he gave strong support. He himself tried without success to be elected to the City Council, although he was for many years a member of the School Board. Such was his popularity that when he died schools, libraries and even Armstrong's Elswick works closed for his funeral, which it is reckoned was witnessed by thousands of people.

Although a drinking fountain, now standing in the Bigg Market, was erected in his memory, his true memorial is Northumbria University (see UNIVERSITIES). Shortly after his death a Technical College was opened in Bath Lane, to which the name Rutherford Memorial College was given. Rutherford Memorial College evolved and expanded to become a formidable educational institution, which became the core of Newcastle Polytechnic in 1969 and then Northumbria University in 1992, exactly one hundred years after its inception.

RUTHWELL CROSS

The Ruthwell Cross is on a par with the LINDISFARNE GOSPELS and the *CODEX AMIATINUS* as one of the finest pieces of art ever produced in Britain. Today it stands in a purpose-built apse in the church of Ruthwell in Dumfriesshire. It is still largely complete, fortunately so since it was broken up in 1642 on the order of the General Assembly of the Church of Scotland, which declared it to be idolatrous. Happily, Gavin Young, the minister at the time, while complying with the order, preserved most of the fragments. These were recovered and reassembled in the early nineteenth century by another minister of the parish, Henry Duncan, who also added new pieces to replace the missing wings of the cross-head. This, and the long years in the open following the wanton abuse in 1642, means it is in far from perfect condition, so that its aesthetic impact is diminished.

The cross stands 5.28 metres in height and comprises a rectangular tapering shaft surmounted by a Celtic cross-head. The shaft measures 71 × 46 centimetres at the base and 33 × 24 centimetres just below the cross-head. On each of the two broad faces are five panels, each containing a biblical scene or image of deep Christian signficance carved in high relief. Round the edge of each panel is a carved inscription in Latin stating what the panel portrays. In contrast, the two narrow sides have single panels filled with a vine-scroll entwining birds and beasts. Around the edge are carved in runic script a short (perhaps early) version of the early Old English poem *The Dream of the Rood*, in which the poet recounts a dream in which the Cross of the Crucifixion recounts to him its agony at being the instrument of Christ's death.

Why the cross was made is not known and is not evident. What close study reveals, however, is the very powerful statement it makes of current beliefs about Christ and His sacrifice, many of them from the Mediterranean world. The vine-scroll motif on the narrow sides arises from a quotation from Chapter 15 of St John's Gospel beginning 'I am the true vine', widely used in Italy and the East to symbolise the eucharist. The panels on the broad sides are pictorial, at that date a considerable novelty. They include the Apocalyptic Vision of God the Father, the Annunciation, Christ as the Judge of Righteousness, and the Crucifixion, probably the first time this had been depicted in England. It also extols the monastic life as the highest form of human existence and both in whole and in many of its parts it expresses veneration for the Cross, which had grown and spread throughout Christendom in the previous century.

But, while we can with some certainty perceive its iconographic messages, we do not know who created it, neither its sculptor(s) nor the person(s) who commissioned it. Even more mysterious is why it was erected at Ruthwell. Many other similar crosses were erected all over Northumbria in places we know to have been important religious centres, particularly monasteries. There is as yet no evidence that Ruthwell was such a place. This has led to endless speculation, including suggestions that it was intended as a political as well as a religious statement. Two things, however, engender considerable confidence: that it was produced in the first half of the eighth century; and that it speaks strongly of the influence of the monastery of Monkwearmouth/JARROW. Although it was probably carved on site (it is made of local stone), it is almost certainly a product of the beliefs and the craftsmanship of that monastery.

ST CALAIS, WILLIAM OF (?–1096)

William of St Calais had a profound effect upon both England and the North East. When and where he was born is not known, but as a young man he became a member of the body of clergy at the cathedral of Bayeux in Normandy. Some time later he joined the Benedictine monastery of St Calais, in the County of Maine, rising within a few years to be its prior. From there he moved in 1078 to be abbot of another Benedictine house, St Vincent at Le Mans. His stay there was short: three years later William the Conqueror chose him as Bishop of Durham. He arrived there at a dangerous and difficult time, his predecessor, Walcher, having been murdered by irate Northumbrians at GATESHEAD in May of the previous year, a crime savagely punished by the Conqueror's eldest son, Robert, and half-brother, Odo, Bishop of Bayeux. It has been argued that the Conqueror's choice was influenced by the fact that both Maine and Northumbria were turbulent border regions where Norman authority was precarious.

In the next twelve years, St Calais was to make two changes at Durham, one lasting over 500 years, the other still with us. In 1083 he replaced the pre-Conquest Community of St Cuthbert (see CUTHBERT, SAINT) with a Benedictine monastery, which was to be the Cathedral Chapter until the last day of 1539. Ten years later he undertook the replacement of the cathedral built in the years after 995 with the present church. Who the architect was will never be known. It is possible that it was St Calais himself, but even if this was not so, the design must have had his approval and so to him must be given most of the credit for what some consider the world's finest building.

Between his reform of the cathedral chapter and the start of the new cathedral church, St Calais was involved with a project of national scope, the Domesday Survey of 1086. Recent research has suggested that it was he who masterminded what was an outstanding administrative feat and which is our most important source of information about the social and economic condition of England in the eleventh century. Ironically, Durham and Northumberland, together with Cumberland and Westmorland (Cumbria), were not included in the survey, principally because they had (as yet) no Norman landowners.

St Calais was a political prelate, who fell foul of William the Conqueror's successor, Willam II (1087–1100), and in consequence spent the years 1088 to 1091 in exile in Normandy. It may have been during this enforced absence from his diocese that he formulated his plans for a new cathedral.

SALVIN, ANTHONY (1799–1881)

Anthony Salvin, one of the notable British architects of the nineteenth century, was the only child of Lieutenant General Anthony Salvin (d.1844) and his second wife. After education at Durham School, he trained as an architect under John Paterson of Edinburgh (who restored Brancepeth Castle) and probably in London under John Nash. Setting up on his own, he rapidly gained a reputation as an expert in medieval military architecture, which led to his being elected to a fellowship of the Society of Antiquaries in 1824.

He was noted for his restoration and consolidation of the remains of the medieval castles at Carisbroke, Caernarfon, Newark and Norwich, and for his work on Windsor Castle and the Tower of London. He designed the mock medieval castles at Peckforton (Cheshire) and Scotney (Kent), as well as more conventional country houses.

He also did a great deal of work in the North East. He was responsible for the preservation of Warkworth Castle and

Lindisfarne Priory, and he was extensively used by the 4th Duke of Northumberland to restore and remodel Alnwick Castle: what we see today is very largely his work. The Duke also used his services to design the stable court and the riding school at the south-west corner of the castle, and such things as bridges and cottages on the estate. Salvin's career coincided with the massive increase in the demand for new churches in response to the rapid increase in population, competition between denominations and, for the Church of England, the easing of control on the division of parishes. Among his commissions were new churches at ALNWICK, DARLINGTON, North Shields, North Sunderland, South Charlton, South Shields and Whitley Bay and the restoration and enlargement of the existing churches at Chatton, Rock, Simonburn and Whickham. The Chapter of DURHAM CATHEDRAL appointed him consultant architect in 1834 and he was directly responsible for the restoration of the dormitory and the windows of the north choir aisle. Also in Durham, for the University he rebuilt the Castle Keep and designed the Observatory and the first new buildings of Hatfield College. He was also responsible for the White Swan Hotel at Alnwick.

He married his cousin Anne, the sister of WILLIAM ANDREWS NESFIELD. Throughout his career he was based in London, until he retired to Surrey in 1864, where he died in 1881. Because of their destruction by his youngest son, we do not have the details of most of his commissions.

SAMUELSON, SIR BERNHARD, Bt (1820–1905)

Born in Hamburg, Bernhard Samuelson was the son of a wealthy merchant with operations in Hull and Liverpool. After a private education, he underwent an apprenticeship with a Liverpool merchant from 1835 until 1841. On completion he secured a post as continental agent for a Manchester engineering firm. During his time abroad he made a considerable fortune through speculation and he might well have remained there had it not been for the revolutions that affected most European countries in 1848 and 1849. On his return he immediately acquired a foundry in Banbury, where he made McCormick reapers under licence, and other agricultural machinery.

His connection with the North East began in 1854 when he joined the 'iron rush' to Teesside that followed the discovery of the Cleveland ore field in 1850. Initially he built an ironworks at South Bank, which he sold to Bolckow and Vaughan in 1863. He did so in order to create a more modern plant at Newport, where he had eight blast furnaces with a capacity of 6,000 tons of pig iron a week. In 1870 he founded the Britannia Iron Works to make wrought iron. To furnish his iron-making facilities with the necessary fuel, he bought the colliery at Hedley Hope, Durham, which had a modest potential output of 150,00 tons a year. In 1887 the company became Sir B. Samuelson Ltd, with Samuelson as chairman, a post he retained until 1895, when he handed over to his son.

Samuelson also had an active political career as MP for Banbury from 1865 until 1885 and then for North Oxfordshire from 1885 until 1895. His great interest was in education, particularly in scientific and technical education, and he served on a number of royal commissions that investigated these problems. He was also personally responsible for the creation of the Banbury Technical Institute. It was for these services that he was given a baronetcy in 1884.

SCOTT, HUGH STOWELL (1862–1902)

Hugh Stowell Scott, who is better known by his pen name **Henry Seton Merriman**, was born at Elswick into a wealthy family: his father was a shipowner, his mother a daughter of the artist John Wilson Carmichael. His education was thorough and extensive (Loretto School in Edinburgh followed by various academies on the continent), which his family intended should be a sound preparation for a career as a Lloyd's underwriter. However, this had no appeal and he opted to become a writer, adopting a pen name to deflect his family's disapproval. His model was the French writer Alexandre Dumas, whose novels he studied closely. His output was prolific and by the time of his early death (from appendicitis), by which time he was living in Suffolk, he was one of the most popular and widely read novelists of his day. All his novels belonged to the romantic genre and all were set abroad. Perhaps the best of them was *Barlasch of the Guard*, a story set in Napoleon's disastrous Russian campaign in 1812.

SCOTT, JOHN (1774–1827)

John Scott was the most noted and accurate engraver of horses and dogs in his day, and his work gained huge popularity with the sporting world of the early nineteenth century. He was born into modest circumstances in Newcastle and was apprenticed at the age of twelve to a tallow chandler. His natural bent, however, was artistic and he taught himself drawing and engraving in his spare time. On completion of his apprenticeship he migrated to London, where his ability and progress as an artist were sufficient for him to be taken on as a pupil and paid assistant by a fellow Novocastrian, Robert Pollard. After two years he was able to branch out on his own, working for the *Sporting Magazine*. In the years that followed he published several books, the most important being *History and Delineation of the Horse* (1809) and *Sportsman's Repository* (1820), based upon paintings of horses and dogs in a wide variety of attitudes by several artists, including Stubbs. His career was ended prematurely by a stroke in 1821 and he died in 1827.

SCOTT, JOHN, 1st EARL OF ELDON (1751–1838)

John Scott was the son of William Scott, a wealthy Newcastle coal fitter and freeman. He was later to enjoy the reputation of being 'the most hated man in England', yet his career had the most romantic outset. After education at the Royal Grammar School, then under its most famous head, Hugh Moises, he went to University College, Oxford, where he gained an MA degree in 1773. It was on 18 November that year that he eloped with Elizabeth (Bessie) Surtees, the daughter of a wealthy Newcastle banker, Aubone Surtees. The scene of this escapade was the house on The Side, now belonging to English Heritage. The day following their elopement, they were married near Edinburgh by an Episcopalian minister. Returning home shortly afterwards as man and wife, they were forgiven by both sets of parents, who jointly settled on them the handsome sum of £3,000.

In the first three years of married life, Scott worked hard to qualify as a lawyer and he was called to the Bar in 1776. Six years later, in 1783, he became a KC and also embarked upon a political career, securing a seat in one of the many 'rotten boroughs', Weobley in Herefordshire, which he held until 1796, when he was returned for Boroughbridge in Yorkshire. By now he had secured the patronage of the then Lord Chancellor, Edward Thurlow, and it was through this that he obtained the important posts of Chancellor of the Palatinate of Durham in 1787 and in the following year that of Solicitor General, which secured him a knighthood. In 1793 he became Attorney General and in 1799 Chief Justice of the

Court of Common Pleas. This carried a peerage, and Scott took the title Lord Eldon, from the place in County Durham where he had bought an estate in 1792. In the last year of the century he reached the top of the legal profession when he was appointed Lord Chancellor. He was to hold this office, with a brief break between 1806 and 1807, until his resignation in 1827, when, on the death of Lord Liverpool, William Canning became Prime Minister. By that time, he was Earl of Eldon and Viscount Encombe, titles conferred in 1821, the latter recognising the estate he bought in Dorset in 1807. When he died in 1838 his fortune was said to amount to £700,000. In both financial and career terms he had enjoyed unparalleled success.

Why, then, was he so hated? There were two principal reasons. One was his ultra-conservative stance on all matters political and constitutional. Basically, he was against almost any change during a time when the demand for change grew to a point when it could not be denied without the real possibility of serious civil unrest. In particular, Scott refused to countenance the emancipation of Roman Catholics and he fought against any proposal to amend the structure of the House of Commons and to widen the franchise. The other cause related more closely to his role as a law officer of the Crown during two periods of high political tension. The first was during the 1790s and the second was in the years after the wars against France ended in 1815. In both periods the government feared outbreaks of civil disobedience and the possibility of attempted revolution. To suppress the one and head off the other, a number of pieces of legislation were enacted against the liberties of the individual, most notably the suspension of the Habeas Corpus Act.

In both of these matters Scott has enjoyed a bad press. At the time his political opponents hated and derided his resistance to change, while those who believed in the sacrosanctity of civil liberties were convinced that his introduction and support of what they considered to be repressive legislation was malevolent. Historians have also tended towards the side of his critics, on the grounds that constitutional change was inevitable and desirable and that the threats against which the repressive measures were directed were nothing like as great as the government claimed. It is possible, however, to be fairer to him. Reluctance to countenance change is a matter of opinion and conviction as to what is right or best. As regards the restrictions placed on the liberties of the subject, these were introduced at times of great internal and international tension. In the 1790s the French Revolution was in its bloodiest and most aggressive phase: the royal family was executed; the Reign of Terror was in full swing; and the French government had adopted a policy of exporting its revolutionary creed. In Britain the French Revolution was initially welcomed by many people, and even though its excesses diminished its popularity, it still had enough advocates in Britain to make a nervous government apprehensive, a condition heightened by the reports of its spies and informers. Much the same could be said of the early post-1815 years, when an economic depression caused widespread discontent. In both periods the state took the measures it believed necessary to preserve itself and prevent revolution. To say that the danger may not have been as great as it feared is to be wise after the event.

In both matters Scott's attitude comes across as that of the rigid lawyer, believing that his role was to uphold and enforce that which had been enacted. He did not flinch from unpopular verdicts and did not hesitate to inflict the death penalty. Overall, he resembles his near contemporary in the Scottish judicial system, Robert McQueen,

Lord Braxfield, the Lord Justice Clerk from 1788 until 1799, immortalised in R.L. Stevenson's unfinished novel, *Weir of Hermiston*. Both men knew their law and neither was deterred by popular opinion from enforcing it.

SCOTT, WILLIAM (1923–2004)

Known professionally as Billy 'Uke' Scott, he was one of the most popular performers on the Moss Empire music hall circuit in the 1940s and 1950s. He was born in Sunderland and by the age of thirteen was performing professionally on the ukulele, a musical instrument on which he was a virtuoso. He was also a prolific composer, producing over 100 songs and tunes, many for other artists, including the more famous ukulele performer, George Formby. When the music hall circuits faded with the coming of television, Scott became a theatrical agent, while continuing to give live performances as a sideline.

SCOTT, WILLIAM, LORD STOWELL (1745–1836)

William Scott was the older brother of JOHN SCOTT, EARL OF ELDON and the eldest son of William Scott, a wealthy Newcastle coal fitter. He was born at his father's estate at Heworth on the south bank of the Tyne in County Durham, to which his mother had been rushed during the Jacobite scare of 1745. He was educated at the Royal Grammar School, Newcastle, after which he had a distinguished academic career at Oxford. After graduating BA in 1764, MA in 1767 and BCL in 1772, he became Camden Reader in Ancient History in 1773. His lectures, which he never published, are reputed to have been popular and praised by no less an authority than Edward Gibbon, author of *The Decline and Fall of the Roman Empire*. Also while at Oxford he became a lifelong friend of Dr Samuel Johnson.

In 1776, however, his father died and he decided on a career change. Already a BCL, he advanced to DCL in 1779 and was called to the Bar in the following year. Thereafter his legal career followed two parallel paths. One was ecclesiastical. Within eight years he had risen to be a judge in the Consistory Court of the Diocese of London, a post he held until 1820, and Vicar General for the Province of Canterbury. He achieved both promotions in 1788, the year in which he was knighted. His other path was the High Court of Admiralty. There he advanced from being Advocate General for the Lord High Admiral in 1782 to that of judge in 1798, a post he held for thirty years until old age forced his resignation in 1828. In this role he made a considerable contribution to the advancement of maritime law. Here, in addition to his considerable ability as a lawyer, he enjoyed two advantages: he was not bound by precedent, since the judgements of his predecessors had not been recorded; and he had scope for innovative judgements thanks to the volume and variety of cases that came before his court as a result of the wars between 1793 and 1815. In 1821, on the occasion of the coronation of George IV, he was raised to the peerage as Lord Stowell of Stowell Park, the title deriving from the estate he had bought in Gloucestershire.

His peerage meant that he had to relinquish his seat in the Commons, where he had sat since 1784, first for the borough of Downton in Wiltshire, but from 1801 for Oxford University. Like his brother, Lord Eldon, he was an arch-reactionary, opposing almost all proposals to change the constitution. He was particularly opposed to any concessions to Roman Catholics or any other measure that might loosen the grip or undermine the status of the Church of England.

He had a reputation for parsimony and meanness, while at the same time, at least on the testimony of Dr Johnson's biographer, James Boswell, of a heavy commitment to port. Being a 'two-bottle man' may have to helped destroy his mental faculties five years before his death in 1836.

SCOTT, WILLIAM BELL (1811–1890)

William Bell Scott was the son of an Edinburgh engraver and trained and worked with his father, except for a brief period in London, until 1837. He then decided upon a permanent move to London, with the intention of earning a living as a painter. Over the following five years he had moderate success, sufficient, however, for him to secure the appointment as Director of the Government School of Design in Newcastle. He was to spend the next twenty years in the post, where he had considerable influence on the training and development of a generation of North-East artists, such as CHARLES NAPIER HEMY. In many respects he took over the role hitherto performed by THOMAS MILES RICHARDSON.

His most famous work by his own hand during his years in the North East was the eight large oil paintings commissioned by Paulina, Lady Trevelyan (see TREVELYAN FAMILY AND WALLINGTON HALL) for the newly roofed central hall at Wallington. Each depicts a scene from Northumbrian history from the building of HADRIAN'S WALL to the coal and iron industries of the day, which he based on the engine works of ROBERT STEPHENSON in Forth Street, Newcastle. The paintings have added interest in that all the figures are portraits of real people, including members of the Trevelyan family. Although he returned to London in 1863, he completed eighteen paintings of scenes from the *Ballad of Chevy Chase* that were placed in the spandrels of the hall at Wallington in 1869. Until the end of his life he continued to exhibit at the Royal Academy, at the Royal Scottish Academy and in Newcastle, and also to write and illustrate books and write poetry.

SCOTTISH OCCUPATION 1644–1647

The Scottish occupation was the consequence of the crisis of the 1st Civil War (1642–47). By 1643 it seemed possible that Charles I would inflict military defeat on the armies of his Parliamentary opponents. It was in fear of this outcome that the leaders of the Parliamentary cause negotiated the services of a Scottish army. The outcome was the Solemn League and Covenant, signed in September 1643, whereby the Scottish government agreed to give military help in return for the imposition of a Presbyterian church in England for a three-year trial period.

The upshot was that in early January 1644 a Scottish army numbering 22,000 crossed the Tweed under the command of Alexander Leslie, Earl of Leven. His first objective was NEWCASTLE, but partly because of bad weather his advance was slow. This gave William Cavendish, Marquis of Newcastle, who had raised and commanded a northern Royalist army, time to come north from York and enter the town on 2 February, the day before the Scots arrived. The town was already held for the king, although with an inadequate force, thanks to the vigorous action of the ardent Royalist mayor, Sir John Marley.

Without the necessary siege artillery, an assault on the town was impracticable. Instead, leaving a blockading force on the north side of the Tyne, Leven crossed into Durham, forcing Cavendish to do likewise. In the weeks that followed, neither side dared to risk battle, although skirmishes took place at Boldon and CHESTER LE STREET and the Scots managed to occupy SUNDERLAND and SOUTH SHIELDS. The stalemate was broken by the defeat of a royalist army at Selby in Yorkshire, which forced Cavendish to retreat southwards to secure York, leaving the whole of DURHAM to fall into Scottish hands. On 2 July Cavendish, reinforced by another Royalist army commanded by the king's nephew, Prince Rupert, was defeated on Marston Moor west of the city by the combined Parliamentary armies of Leven, Sir Thomas Fairfax and the Earl of Manchester. The result was that Royalist control in the north was reduced to Newcastle.

Meanwhile, a second army raised in Scotland was dispatched into England under the command of the Earl of Callendar. Although it captured GATESHEAD, secured control over the bridge across the Tyne and provided adequate garrisons for MORPETH, DURHAM, HARTLEPOOL, Sunderland and STOCKTON, it was not capable of forcing the surrender of Newcastle.

The siege of the town began in earnest with Leven's arrival back at his camp at Elswick on the Tyne on 14 August. It dragged on for two months: although now able to breach the walls by mining and bombardment with heavy artillery, Leven hoped to persuade Sir John Marley to surrender and so avoid bloodshed. In accordance with the rules of war, on three occasions he invited Marley and the Common Council to surrender the town, with a guarantee that the garrison would be allowed to march out under arms. All three offers were refused. Leven was now entitled to mount an all-out assault, without obligation to mercy.

The assault took place on 19 October, five days after the last refusal. The town wall was breached in six places and the assault troops, numbering nearly 13,000, went in. The number of the defenders is not known, although one Scottish officer estimated it to have been no more than 1,700. But they put up such a fierce resistance that Scottish casualties numbered nearly 300 killed and 800 wounded. However, the overwhelming disparity in the size of the opposing forces meant that only one outcome was possible. By the end of the day, the town was in Scottish hands, although Sir John Marley did not surrender the castle for another three days. Shortly afterwards the garrison at TYNEMOUTH also surrendered, bringing Royalist resistance to an end.

The North East was to remain under the control of Scottish garrisons for another twenty-seven months, for part of which time Newcastle was at the centre of political affairs. In May 1646 Charles I, his armies now defeated on all fronts, slipped out of his headquarters at Oxford and surrendered to the Scottish army, then camped at Newark. He was a prisoner, and the Scottish government refused to hand him over until the English government had paid for their services. Agreement on this matter was not reached until early in 1647. During that time, Charles was in captivity in Newcastle. His 'prison' was 'Newe House', the large house built in 1580 by Robert Anderson on land abutting Pilgrim Street formerly occupied by the Franciscan friary, although he also spent time in what came to be called the King's House in Shieldfield, where he was allowed to play golf. The 'Newe House', later renamed Anderson Place, was demolished in the 1830s to make way for RICHARD GRAINGER's urban redevelopment scheme. A plaque on the wall of Lloyd's TSB bank at the corner of Grey Street and Hood Street identifies its location. The King's House was demolished in 1960 to make way for high-rise flats. With Charles I's departure for Holmby House in Northamptonshire and the return of the Scottish army north of the Border, the North East returned to a sort of peace.

SEAHAM HARBOUR (see under NEW TOWNS OF THE NINETEENTH CENTURY)

SEATON DELAVAL

Seaton Delaval has two very contrasting architectural gems, both commissioned by the Delaval family, who gave their name to the village. The Delavals were probably the first Normans to be settled on land in Northumberland and possibly the North East. The progenitor, Hubert de la Val, came from Mayenne in Normandy and almost certainly was a follower of Robert de Mowbray, Earl of Northumberland from *c.*1085 until 1095. If so, it was Mowbray who gave Hubert de la Val an estate, known as the Barony of Callerton, comprising Seaton and Newsham (to which the neighbouring township of Hartley was added in 1578 by Sir Robert Delaval), Black Callerton and North and South Dissington. Despite its name, de la Val chose to make Seaton the centre of his barony, and because of this it is almost certain that it was he who, for his convenience, caused the small church to be built next to his manor house or castle. This was not a parish church, however, but a chapel of ease within the parish of Tynemouth and subordinate to its rector. Dedicated to Our Lady, it is, along with similar churches at Croxdale (disused) and Old Bewick, the best example of an early Norman church in the region. In the fourteenth century the chancel was given a square east end with a large window, probably replacing an apse, the style of chancel ending favoured in the Norman period.

The other architectural gem is the far larger and more spectacular Seaton Delaval Hall. It was commissioned by Vice Admiral George Delaval (1668–1723), who belonged to a junior branch of the family living at Dissington. George Delaval made a fortune from naval prize money and from his diplomatic missions to Morocco in 1700 and 1707 and to Portugal in 1710. His wealth enabled him to purchase in 1718 Seaton and Hartley from his kinsman, Sir John Delaval (1654–1729), who was faced with an insurmountable financial problem. Having paid off his kinsman's debts, the Admiral demolished the Tudor/Jacobean mansion and handed the site over to Sir John Vanbrugh to build the house we see today. The new hall was not complete until 1729, by which date both architect and owner were dead, the latter as the result of a fall from his horse, the site of which was marked by an obelisk (only the stump remains) about 650 yards (594 m) west of the house. It was left to his heir, his nephew Francis Blake Delaval (1692–1752), to complete the building. This he could afford to do, since he inherited not only his uncle's estate but also that of his maternal grandmother, Mary Blake, at Ford in north Northumberland, and acquired by his marriage to the heiress of the Hussey family the estate of Doddington Pigot in Lincolnshire. As Seaton Delaval Hall is considered to be Vanbrugh's masterpiece, it is especially regrettable that it was devasted by fire in 1822. It has never been restored, although consolidation work took place in the 1950s and 1960s to prevent further decay. On the other hand, failure to rebuild may have saved it from alteration during the Victorian era, thereby preserving Vanbrugh's original conception.

SEATON SLUICE

Seaton Sluice is an interesting example of how landowning families were often at the forefront of early industrial development. Here the family was the Delavals, owners of SEATON DELAVAL since the eleventh century and neighbouring Hartley since 1578. The growth of their enterprise centred on the small natural harbour, originally known as Hartley Harbour. Some time before 1670 Sir Ralph Delaval (1622–91) built a stone pier to protect the harbour. He then dealt with the problem of silt and sand by erecting a dam across the Seaton Burn with a sluice gate, which, when opened at low tide, allowed a rush of water to scour away the sediment. Finally, he built a second pier on the other side of the mouth of the burn. The purpose of this development, which cost over £15,000, was to enable him to expand the export of coal and salt being mined and made on his estate.

In 1718, however, the estate changed hands, bought by Vice Admiral George Delaval, head of a junior branch of the family, based at Dissington, from Sir Ralph's heir, Sir John Delaval (1654–1729). From him, it passed to his nephew, Francis Blake Delaval (1692–1752) and then to Sir John Hussey Delaval (1728–1808), Francis Blake Delaval's second son, who took over the running of the estate in 1756 as the result of an act of parliament removing his profligate elder brother, Francis, from its control. John Hussey Delaval restructured Ford estate, increasing his income from it from £1,000 to £5,000 a year. More importantly, he instituted major developments at Seaton and Hartley: salt and coal production were expanded, the export of the latter rising to around 50,000 tons a year; brick and tile works were developed, as was the production of copperas from iron pyrites found in coal; and a bottle factory, the Royal Northumberland Bottle Works, founded in 1762, was the largest in the country from 1788 until 1800 with an annual output of over 200,000 items. In response to the growing need for improved harbour facilities, Sir John commissioned a piece of spectacular civil engineering in the form of a cut through the rocks to the sea, achieved between 1761 and 1764, 30 feet wide (9.1 m), 52 feet (15.8 m) deep and 900 feet (274 m) long. This not only provided an alternative entrance to the harbour, but was also able to function as a deep-water dock.

John Hussey Delaval also found time for politics, being MP for BERWICK almost continuously between 1754 and 1786, when he was given a peerage. When he died in 1808, the Seaton and Hartley estate (but not the title) passed to his brother, Edward Hussey Delaval, a noted scientist, upon whose death without legitimate offspring in 1814 the estate was inherited by his nephew, Sir Jacob Astley, Bt, of Melton Constable, Norfolk, whose son successfully petitioned for the title Baron Hastings, which had long been in abeyance. Seaton Sluice did not grow into a large industrial town but suffered a slow decline. Copperas production ended in 1820 and the bottle works closed in 1870, while in the export of coal the harbour could not compete with the facilites on the Tyne and at BLYTH.

SETTLINGSTONES

Settlingstones, now a tiny hamlet four miles due north of Haydon Bridge, was a mining centre of international importance in the late nineteenth and early twentieth centuries. It began life in 1849 as a lead mine, but from 1873 its sole concern was the extraction of the rare mineral, barium carbonate, known as Witherite from the scientist, Dr Withering, who in 1784 identified it as being different from barytes. Barium carbonate was of great use in a variety of chemical and chemistry-based industries, and the Settlingstones mine was for long periods until its exhaustion in 1969 the world's largest producer. Over its life of nearly 100 years, 630,000 tons were produced, most of them of over 90 per cent purity. Now the only visible evidence of its former importance is a row of workers' cottages.

SEVEN STORIES

Seven Stories, founded in 1995 by Elizabeth Hammill and Mary Briggs, is Britain's first centre dedicated to children's books and one of the largest bookshops specialising in children's books, and is the only institution in Britain collecting original artwork by writers and illustrators producing for children. Its name is, appropriately, a play on words, based on the belief that there are basically only *seven stories* in literature and on its being housed (since 2005) in a renovated Victorian warehouse with *seven storeys* overlooking the Ouseburn in Newcastle. As well as being a shop and repository, it mounts exhibitions, holds sessions with writers and illustrators, runs educational programmes and promotes a wide range of creative activities.

SHACKLETON, LEONARD FRANCIS (1922–2000)

Len Shackleton, often referred to simply as 'Shack', was arguably the best and certainly the most entertaining footballer ever to play for Sunderland FC. He was not, however, a native of the town or of the North East. He was born in Bradford, the son of a house painter, where he spent the early part of his career. His talent was such that he played for Bradford Schools and England Schools, and while still at Carlton High School signed amateur forms for Bradford Park Avenue. In 1938 he was transferred to Arsenal, but was released after one year as being below standard and returned to his former club. Then came World War II, during which he worked in the coalmines as a Bevin Boy.

It was after the war that his career took off. In 1946, while still on the books of Bradford Park Avenue, he played in the Victory International at Hampden Park, Glasgow, for England against Scotland. This led to his transfer to Newcastle United. His stay there was brief, on account of disagreements between him and the club, which in 1948 put his contract up for auction. The winning bid was £20,500 from Sunderland. Shackleton played nine years for his new club, retiring at the beginning of the 1958/59 season. He made 348 appearances, scoring 101 goals. Also during that time, he won four more caps for England. This was a meagre reward for his extravagant talent, but the fault lay largely with him. The fact was that Shackleton was not at heart a team player, but one who was moved by his own impulses. Consequently, he could give dazzling displays of ball control and could bamboozle his opponents (often several times) to the delight of the crowd. But he was equally prepared to turn in lacklustre performances, which infuriated the supporters. He was, as he admitted, as much interested in entertaining as winning, in beating men 'for the hell of it' as in scoring or creating goals. His approach to the game is well summed up in the title of the book he wrote, *Clown Prince of Soccer.*

Shackleton was also a good cricketer, who played for Northumberland and Durham in the Minor Counties League. In retirement he reported on North-East soccer for the *Daily Express* and the *Sunday People* for several years and then retired to Grange over Sands.

SHARP, SIR CUTHBERT (1781–1849)

Like his contemporary ROBERT SURTEES Cuthbert Sharp made a major contribution to the history of County Durham. His father was a Sunderland shipowner and his mother a daughter of Brass Crosby, Lord Mayor of London. He went to school in Greenwich and then joined the army, seeing active service in Ireland during the 1798 rebellion. With the end of the French Revolutionary War in 1802, he went to France, where he was caught when the Napoleonic War broke out in 1804; consequently he was a prisoner of war for several years. On his return, he settled in Hartlepool, where he was elected mayor in 1816. He was well regarded by the then Tory government, which in 1823 appointed him Collector of Customs in Sunderland, a post he retained until 1845, when he secured the more prestigious and lucrative equivalent in Newcastle. He was still in post at the time of his death in 1849.

Between 1819 and 1841 he published eight works on the history of the region, two of which are still used by historians: *The History of Hartlepool*, published in 1816, and *Memorials of the Rebellion of 1569*, published in 1840. The latter was based upon the papers of the BOWES FAMILY and is still widely used as a valuable source of information about the rebellion of the Earls of Westmorland and Northumberland against Elizabeth I (see RISING OF THE NORTHERN EARLS). He also contributed to the expanding literature on the folklore and language of the North East in his *The Bishopick Garland, or a collection of legends, songs and ballads etc. belonging to the County of Durham*, published in 1834.

SHARP, GRANVILLE (1735–1813)

Granville Sharp, who was born in Durham City, became one of the leading social reformers of the late eighteenth and early nineteenth centuries, notably in the campaign to abolish slavery. None of this is surprising, given his church background: he was the son of Thomas Sharp, Archdeacon of Northumberland and the grandson of John Sharp, Archbishop of York (see NATHANIEL, LORD CREWE). More surprising is that he did not follow them into the church. The reason was his father's lack of wealth, which denied him the chance of a university education. After attending Durham School, he was apprenticed to a linen draper in London. During his spare time, however, he gave himself the sort of education he might have acquired at Oxford or Cambridge, becoming proficient in Greek and Hebrew and acquiring a scholar's knowledge of the Bible. But commerce was not his forte, and in 1758 he obtained a clerkship in the Ordnance Department, which he held until his conscience drove him to resign at the outbreak of the American War of Independence in 1776.

By that date he had achieved a change in English law of fundamental significance. This came in 1772 in the form of the judgement in the case of a black slave, James Somersett, in which the Lord Chief Justice, William Murray, Earl of Mansfield, declared that, while on English soil, a slave became *ipso facto* a free man. This decision was the culmination of seven years of effort that began by accident in 1765, when Sharp met black slave Jonathan Strong at the house of his brother, William, a doctor who was treating Strong for injuries inflicted by his owner, David Lisle. Lisle had Strong arrested as a runaway slave, but Sharp managed to secure his release and also fought off Lisle's accusation that Sharp had violated his property rights. This incident led Sharp to engage in detailed research to establish the legal status of slavery in England. He published his conclusions in 1769 in a pamphlet entitled *A Representation of the Injustice and Dangerous Tendency of Tolerating Slavery*, which contained the arguments and evidence vital to his success in 1772.

The victory of 1772 was for Sharp merely the first battle in a war to eradicate completely slavery and the slave trade. He became a leading member of the Society for the Abolition of Slavery, founded in 1787, and he tried to promote the welfare of former slaves by encouraging their settlement in Sierra Leone through the agency of the St George's Company, set up for this purpose. The latter enterprise was not a success and the Company was handed over to the government in 1808. However, he did live to see the passing of the 1807 act, which outlawed the slave trade in Britain; but the freeing of slaves in British colonies was not achieved until 1833, twenty years after his death.

Slavery was not the only cause that attracted Sharp's advocacy. He was linked with the 'Clapham Sect', a reformist group founded in 1793 by Joseph Venn, Rector of Clapham. Among the matters that concerned him were the abolition of the press-gang, the founding of the British and Foreign Bible Society, the Society for the Propagation of the Gospel, and the Society for the Conversion of the Jews, and also writing and publishing works of biblical scholarship. Politically, he was a radical. He sided with the American colonists in their resistance to the British government's imperial policy, hoping the colonies would be granted representation in parliament, thereby preventing the breakup of the empire. After the end of the American war, he campaigned successfully for the introduction of bishops into the USA, in effect ensuring the continuation of the Episcopal Church in the former colonies. He also favoured independence for the Irish parliament, while at the same time opposing Catholic emancipation.

SHEILA

Sheila, a Border Collie, was the first civilian dog to be awarded the Dickin Medal for bravery. This award, instituted in 1943, was named after Maria Elizabeth Dickin, the founder of the People's Dispensary for Sick Animals, which makes the awards. Sheila belonged to a shepherd, John Dagg, and earned the award for her part in the rescue of American airmen from a B-17 (Flying Fortress) that crashed on the Cheviot on 16 December 1944. The plane had taken off from RAF Molesworth in Cambridgeshire but because of atrocious weather the mission was aborted. On the return journey the plane became lost and crashed on to the summit of the Cheviot. Two of the crew were killed and three were able to walk to safety, but four with injuries sheltered in a hole near the wreckage. John Dagg and another shepherd, Frank Moscrop (who were awarded the British Empire Medal), hearing the crash went in search, but it was Sheila who worked through a blizzard ahead of them and found the four Americans, who were brought to safety and taken to RAF MILFIELD.

There was a sequel: at the request of the mother of Frank Turner, one of the crew who died, one of Sheila's pups, Tibbie, was sent to her in Columbia, South Carolina, where she lived for eleven years and was regarded as the town's pet.

SHERATON, THOMAS (1751–1806)

Together with GEORGE HEPPLEWHITE and Thomas Chippendale, Thomas Sheraton was the third great English furniture designer of the eighteenth century. He was born at Stockton on Tees, where he trained as a cabinetmaker. Although he had minimal education, he had a natural talent as a draughtsman and taught himself geometry. His standing is not based on the furniture he made, which appears to have been relatively little, but on his designs. These he published by subscription after he had moved to London in 1790. The first was *The Cabinet-maker and Upholsterer's Drawing-Book,* published in 1791. A second edition was issued in 1796 and a third edition in 1803, each revising and enlarging its predecessor. In 1803 he also produced *The Cabinet Dictionary, or Explanation of all the Terms used in the Cabinet, Chair and Upholstery Branches,* and embarked upon what he intended as a definitive work, *The Cabinet-maker and Artist's Encyclopaedia.* He intended that this would be completed in 125 issues, but only thirty were published before he died.

Sheraton's designs moved away from the more ornate style favoured by Thomas Chippendale. Instead of cabriole legs, those he designed his were straight and tapered, and for decoration he favoured marquetry rather than carving. To him, the beauty of a piece of furniture lay in its lines and geometry, rather than its complexity. Although he was recognised in his day as a superb designer, he failed to make money and lived in relative poverty throughout his life, earning much of his living as a drawing teacher, rather than through the sale of his designs. He also had another side to his life, namely, religion. He was a convinced Baptist and published at least three books of a theological nature.

SHIELD, WILLIAM (1748–1829)

Unlike his teacher CHARLES AVISON, William Shield, although born in the North East, made his name and living as a musician and composer in London. He was the son of a music teacher at Swalwell, but because of his father's early death he was unable to proceed with a musical education and was apprenticed to a South Shields boatbuilder. Despite this, he was able to continue his musical education under Charles Avison, through whom he met Felici Giardini, who persuaded him to become a professional musician. In 1770, following Avison's death, he became leader of his orchestra, but two years later Giardini lured him to London to be member of the band at the King's Theatre in Haymarket. The following year he became first viola, a position he held until 1791.

Through his experience in the King's Theatre orchestra he learned the arts and techniques of composition and orchestration. In his career he wrote thirty-six operas, but the one that made his name was his comic opera, *Rosina*, first performed in 1782. This led in 1784 to his appointment as House Composer at Covent Garden in succession to Michael Arne. He retained this post, with a brief interlude in 1792–93, until he resigned in 1797. The interlude was occasioned by the French Revolution, which he supported, as did JOSEPH RITSON, with whom he went to the continent. His friendship with Ritson was born of their mutual interest in folk song and the music of ordinary people.

After his resignation from Covent Garden, he spent much of his time writing about music and he was one of the founding members of the London Philharmonic Society. The unpopularity he acquired by his early support for the French Revolution did not outlast the wars, and in 1817 he was appointed as Master Musician in Ordinary to the King. On his death in 1829 he was considered sufficiently eminent for burial in the cloister of Westminster Abbey, and in 1891 JOSEPH COWEN raised money for a memorial to him in the churchyard at Whickham, the parish church of his native village. But his living memorial, although not widely recognised, is the tunes to which the two of the poems of his contemporary, Robert Burns, are still sung: 'Auld Lang Syne' and 'Coming Through The Rye'.

SHINWELL, EMMANUEL, LORD SHINWELL (1884–1986)

'Manny' Shinwell, who was the son of a Polish Jewish immigrant and his Dutch wife, was born in London but moved to Glasgow at an early age. Like his father, he trained as a tailor, but at an early age took to radical politics. He was to be one of the most outspoken, colourful and long-lived politicians of the twentieth century. In his early days he had a reputation as a firebrand, but in later life he mellowed and became widely enjoyed as a raconteur who found television a congenial medium.

He first entered parliament in 1922 as MP for Linlithgowshire, but lost his seat in 1924, regained it in 1928 and lost it again in 1931. In the 1935 general election, however, he decided to contest Seaham, opposing RAMSAY MACDONALD, whom he had admired but whose decision to form a National Government he bitterly opposed. He won an overwhelming victory and continued to hold this seat, which in 1950 was restructured and renamed EASINGTON, until 1970. The high points of his political career came during the period of Labour power between 1945 and 1951. In 1945 he was made Minister of Fuel and Power and in this role he succeeded in securing the passage of the act to nationalise the coal industry, which came into force at the start of 1947. His reputation, however, suffered through his perceived failure to act vigorously enough during the fuel crisis that accompanied the severe winter of that year. He was replaced by Hugh Gaitskell and lost his place in the Cabinet. In 1950, however, he returned briefly to the Cabinet as Minister of Defence, a post he held until Labour's defeat in the following year's election. His career languished during the leadership of Hugh Gaitskell, a man he detested, but revived under Harold Wilson, who made him Chairman of the Labour Party in 1964. Vehemently hostile to the idea of Britain joining the European Common Market, he resigned the post in 1967. He was made a life peer in 1970, and continued to express his views, which became steadily less radical, trenchant and pugnacious. His hundreth birthday was celebrated in the House of Lords in 1984.

SHIPBUILDING INDUSTRY

Shipbuilding was, with coal mining, the industry for which the North East was known throughout the world. Given the evidence for sea fishing going back to the Middle Ages, it is safe to assume that ships were built for this purpose, particularly cobles for inshore work, in their home ports. But the rise of the industry in the region to national and international importance did not begin until the early years of the nineteenth century, when in the course of the French wars SUNDERLAND rapidly rose from about tenth to first place in terms of the number of ships launched. The underlying reason was the wastage of shipping occasioned by war and the expanding demand for coal and hence for COLLIERS. But the Wear also had other advantages. One was the close links between the shipwrights and the importers of timber, and another was the ability of the shipwrights to use their wood economically, often making smaller vessels alongside larger ships with surplus and offcut timber. The consequence was that the Wear could undercut every other shipbuilding centre. This dominance lasted until mid-century, when wooden vessels propelled by sails began to give way to iron vessels propelled by steam engines.

At this point Sunderland's strength in wood began to be a handicap: because of the close involvement with timber merchants and the high level of skill in woodworking, there was a reluctance to move to iron and steam. It was not until the late 1860s that the transition was made. However, wood went out on a high note: the last all-wood ship to be launched, in 1866, was the famous clipper, *Parramatta*, at 1,521 tons far larger than the iron ships then under construction. Another clipper, the *Torrens*, built in 1875 and made famous by having the novelist Joseph Conrad as its second mate on one of its voyages, was a composite, that is, it had a wooden hull fixed to an iron frame. In contrast, the Tyne, which had not been as prominent as the Wear during the 'wood age', came to the fore once iron and steam took over.

In the course of the next fifty years, the UK rose to pre-eminence in shipbuilding: in the years immediately before the outbreak of World War I the UK built nearly 60 per cent of the world's ships, and of that total, half were built in North-East yards. In other words, the shipyards of the Tyne, the Wear, the Tees and in HARTLEPOOL, by that date numbering forty-five, launched about a quarter of the world's ships. The trade was dominated by the Tyne and the Wear, with respectively twenty and fourteen yards; but there was a major firm, WILLIAM GRAY at Hartlepool and smaller concerns on the Tees and at BLYTH. The largest firms had grown by means of takeovers and amalgamations, notably the two Tyneside giants, Swan Hunter and Wigham Richardson & Co. and Armstrong, Whitworth & Co. The former was founded in 1873 at Wallsend by a Scotsman, Charles Mitchell, although the driving forces were his brother-in-law, Charles Swan, and his manager, a Sunderland man, GEORGE HUNTER. Between 1873 and 1913 Swan Hunter took over Schlesinger Davis (1897) and Wallsend Slipway (1903) and in 1903 merged with the Neptune Yard of Wigham Richardson, founded in 1860. Likewise, the firm of Armstrong Whitworth was the product of the merger in 1882 of another yard founded by Charles Mitchell at Low Walker and the armaments firm of SIR WILLIAM ARMSTRONG at Elswick, which in 1897 bought the Manchester arms maker, Sir Joseph Whitworth.

Inevitably, the industry prospered during World War I, and a completely new yard was opened in 1917 by Furness, Withy & Co. at Haverton Hill on the Tees. Initially, but briefly, prosperity continued during the early post-war years, but was then followed by a prolonged depression, which led to the closure of twenty-five yards: twelve on the Tyne, seven on the Wear, five on the Tees and one at Hartlepool. Two (including Palmers of JARROW) were bought by the government-backed National Shipbuilders Security Ltd, which between 1930 and 1937 bought up and closed down twenty-eight smaller and weaker companies in an effort to create a slimmer but more modern and efficient industry. The North East, however, benefited from another government initiative, the 'scrap and build' scheme resulting from the British Shipping (Assistance) Act of 1934: thirty-four of the fifty new ships built under this scheme came from North-East yards.

Then from 1936 the increasing scale of rearmament in the face of the growing likelihood of war with Germany brought Admiralty orders to some yards. The inter-war years also saw an important merger in 1928, that of Armstong, Whitworth with Vickers of Sheffield and Barrow in Furness.

But complete salvation came with World War II, when the demand for new ships of all kinds (as well as the repair of damaged vessels) expanded rapidly: throughout the years 1939–45, all shipyards worked at full stretch, including two yards closed before the war (Armstrongs at Low Walker and Swan Hunters at Southwick in Sunderland), which were reopened. The region's yards built 520 merchant vessels. The output of Sunderland's nine yards amounted to 267, 27 per cent of all merchant ships built in British yards: Doxfords 75, Laings 42, Thompsons 40, Austins 26, Shorts 24, Bartrams 24, Pickersgills 22, Swan Hunters 10 and Crowns 4. The Tyne yards of Swan Hunter, Vickers Armstrong, Hawthorn Leslie and Readheads built 130; William Gray at Hartlepool built 72 and the Furness yard on the Tees built 51. In contrast, warship construction was largely confined to the three Tyne firms of Swan Hunter, Vickers Armstrong and Hawthorn Leslie, although Crowns at Sunderland, Smith's Dock on the Tees and the small shipyard at Blyth built, respectively, four, fifteen and twelve frigates and corvettes. In all, the region's yards launched 144 warships, including 2 battleships (HMS *King George V* and HMS *Anson*), 6 aircraft carriers, 7 cruisers, 76 destroyers, 30 frigates, 7 corvettes and 16 submarines.

The end of World War II, unlike its predecessor, was not the prelude to a sudden and prolonged depression followed by revival. Instead, contraction was gradual, but without reprieve, so that by 1993 the North-East shipbuilding industry was virtually extinct. Between 1945 and 1962 five yards closed down, including the famous William Gray of West Hartlepool. Two years later, as a consequence of the Geddes Report, the Shipbuilding Industry Board was set up to provide government assistance, but on condition that firms were reorganised into groups. As a result, Swan Hunter, Hawthorn Leslie, Readheads, and Vickers Armstrong on the Tyne and Furness and Smith's Dock on the Tees became Swan Hunter and Tyne Ltd, while the Sunderland yards were grouped into two companies, Doxfords (Doxford, Laing, Thompson) and Sunderland Shipbuilders (Austin, Pickersgill, Bartram). Then, in 1977, the entire industry was nationalised by the Labour government. At that date eleven yards were still open, but three of them were closed immediately. All but one of the remaining eight closed in the 1980s: Hawthorn Leslie (Hebburn) in 1981, Clelands (Willington Quay) 1983, Laings Yard (Sunderland) 1985, Vickers Armstrong Naval Yard (Walker) 1985, Smith's Dock (Middlesbrough) 1987, Doxfords and Austin Pickersgills (Sunderland) 1988, and Swan Hunter Neptune Yard (Wallsend) 1988. The region's last shipbuilding firm, Swan Hunter, went into receivership in 1993, although it continued to operate under foreign ownership from 2006 until 2008.

The reasons for the industry's demise were numerous and varied, but can be grouped under three broad heads. One was the competition of foreign yards, particularly those in the Far East, which were more modern and efficient and had lower labour costs. A second reason was the deficiencies of the region's yards, some of which stemmed from their own history, some from the need to overcome the ravages and neglect of the war years, and some from the inadequacies of management and the change-resistant attitude of the workers and their unions. This is not to say that modernisation did not occur and that there were no successes: the warships built on the Tyne and the SD 14 bulk carriers produced in Sunderland testify to this. But the failure to attack internal weaknesses soon enough, quickly enough and radically enough cannot be denied. Thirdly, there were the decisions of government, most obviously in awarding contracts for warships and in nationalising the industry in 1977. From the 1930s government influence in this as in other industries grew steadily, hastened by the exigencies of war. This was most clearly seen in 1988, when the Conservative government (which was determined on privatisation) closed North East Shipbuilders of Sunderland, which its management wished to buy out, in order to secure an EEC subsidy for other privatised yards. Also in these years was the government's decision to concentrate warship construction at three yards – Vickers (Barrow), Yarrow (Clyde) and Vosper Thorneycroft (Solent) – a decision also motivated by political considerations.

Along with the rise and fall of the shipbuilding companies went those that built marine engines. Some shipbuilders, such as Doxford in Sunderland, Hawthorn Leslie on the Tyne and Gray at Hartlepool, developed their own marine engine divisions, but others relied on separate marine engine manufacturers like Richardson Westgarth and GEORGE CLARK. But all suffered the same fate. Perhaps the one commendable performance in this sector was by Doxfords, in designing and building a successful marine diesel engine, the only British company to do so.

However, in 2007, a silver lining appeared on the cloud of closure in the form of the Marine Design Centre, built on Newcastle

Quayside at cost of £2.3 million. This may yet revive the region's reputation, at least in ship design if not in shipbuilding.

SHIPLEY ART GALLERY, GATESHEAD (see ART GALLERIES)

SHORT, JOHN YOUNG (1844–1900)

John Short was the son of a ship's carpenter, who established his own shipbuilding business at Mowbray Quay, Sunderland. After schooling at West Boldon, he was apprenticed to a Tyneside timber merchant, a sensible move for the son of a builder of wooden ships. In the mid-1860s, Short and his three younger brothers took over the business and by the end of the decade had transformed it. A new yard was acquired at Pallion, wood was abandoned in favour of iron and the name of the firm changed to Short Brothers (see SHIPBUILDING INDUSTRY). In the remaining thirty years of his life, Short's firm built 300 ships, many for the Prince Line owned by SIR JAMES KNOTT.

But John Short was not merely a shipbuilder. He had a timber business; he became, in association with James Westall, one of the biggest shipowners in Sunderland, with a fleet of forty vessels; he served on the boards of other shipping companies; and he was a main underwriter. More surprisingly, he was one of a consortium of six men who sank Easington Colliery. This diversity of interests may explain why he did not join any of the shipbuilders' associations, although he was a member of the Institute of Naval Architects. Politically, he was a Liberal, but his active participation was limited to membership of the Sunderland Town Council from 1885.

SHOTLEY BRIDGE SWORD MAKERS

From the late seventeenth century until the early nineteenth century sword blades of the highest quality were manufactured in the Durham village of Shotley Bridge. The industry was started in 1686 by two Newcastle merchants, John Sandford and John Bell, along with two men from London, who leased land and enticed nineteen swordsmiths to leave their home in the German town of Solingen (between Cologne and Düsseldorf) and settle in England. Solingen had long been one of the leading centres for the manufacture of sword blades, which were of a far higher quality than those produced in England. The easier solution would have been to import blades made in Germany, but this was hindered by government-imposed quotas and customs duties. Moreover, the fact that war in Europe was all but endemic, as well as a sword being at all times a normal part of a gentleman's dress, meant that there was a buoyant market for quality swords.

More difficult to explain is why the German craftsmen elected to leave home and migrate to a foreign land, particularly as they had sworn an oath not to practise their trade outwith Solingen, and anyone caught doing so was liable to the severest penalties. All of them must have known that they were making an irrevocable decision. At one time it was thought that their primary motive was the fear of religious persecution: they were Protestants at a time when there was a danger of their part of Germany being forced to return to the Roman Catholic fold. This explanation is now largely discounted and the lure of a more prosperous life seems the more potent reason. The names of all nineteen are known, the most prominent of them being Adam Ohlig and Hermann Mohl, who may have been the recognised leaders.

The choice of Shotley Bridge was almost certainly made by the two Newcastle men, who appear to have been the prime movers in the enterprise and were aware of the attractions of the site. Though hidden away, it was close to Newcastle, through which the finished goods could be marketed. Probably more important was the fast-flowing River Derwent, ideal for powering the hammers used in the manufacturing process, and the presence of abundant woodland for the production of the necessary charcoal, and of iron ore.

Most of the sword blades the German immigrants produced were single-edged, triangular in shape and hollowed on all three sides. Made of shear steel, they were about three feet long and were strong, light and flexible. They were identified by the words SHOTLEY on one of the broad sides and BRIDGE on the other. They also carried the symbol of the 'flying fox' (or 'running wolf'), the emblem of the Solingen craft guild.

The enterprise received a royal charter in 1691 and appears to have been managed until his death in 1726 by the dynamic local businessman WILLIAM COTESWORTH. But it was never a huge financial success and twice in the early decades of the eighteenth century it ran into severe financial difficulties. Nevertheless, the frequent wars and the continued popularity of the sword as an item of dress ensured that a market for Shotley Bridge swords continued to exist. However, conditions deteriorated after the end of the Napoleonic War in 1815: the size of Britain's armed forces was drastically reduced and the practice of carrying swords went out of fashion. Moreover, in the late eighteenth and early nineteenth centuries major centres for the manufacture of cutlery developed in Birmingham and Sheffield. As a result the manufacture of swords at Shotley Bridge shrank, and ceased in 1840.

There was, however, a postscript. One of the sword-making families, Mohl (which by that date had long been anglicised as Mole), moved to Birmingham and set up as Robert Mole & Co. In 1889 the Mole company was absorbed by Wilkinson's of Pall Mall, founded by James Wilkinson in 1772, who recognised the importance of locating in Birmingham. The link with Shotley Bridge is still to be seen in the name of this firm, Wilkinson Sword. The only other surviving link with the Shotley Bridge sword-making venture is the Cutlers' Hall, built in 1789 and now a listed building.

SIGMUND, MIROSLAV (1907–2003)

Miroslav Sigmund, who started one of the earliest and in its time most highly successful firms on the TEAM VALLEY TRADING ESTATE, was born in what is now the Czech Republic, then a province of the Austro-Hungarian Empire. He was a member of a firm, Sigmund Pumps, founded by his grandfather. He came to Britain in 1938 on the eve of World War II and was helped by the Nuffield Foundation to set up a factory for the manufacture of pumps, which were well known for their efficiency. His success was rapid, thanks in part to machinery blueprints and a number of technicians smuggled out of Czechoslovakia before the Germans arrested his family. Tragically, his elder brother Jan was one of the Czechs executed by the Germans following the assassination in 1942 of the ruthless Nazi Reinhard Heydrich, the Protector of Bohemia and Moravia, in reprisal for which the village of Lidice was razed and its inhabitants massacred.

During the war Sigmund Pumps manufactured not only several types of pump, but also parts for Bren guns, employing engineers who had escaped from the Bren works in Czechoslovakia, and the gas filters used in the London Underground; and Sigmund also developed the Polsten gun. By the end of the war he was employing over 2,000 people. With the developing threat of nuclear attack in the post-war years, the government commissioned 5,000 mobile pump units for fighting fire and ensuring water supply, which have become known as 'Green Goddesses'; all were fitted with Sigmund pumps. He also formed a separate company to manufacture slim-line radiators with small pumps to meet the rising demand for domestic central heating, which still operates on the Team Valley Trading Estate.

In 1958 Sigmund sold his company to a larger concern based in Reading, of which he became managing director in 1961. He remained in this role until 1964, when he resigned, and in the following year he bought a struggling optics firm in Slough, where he developed and manufactured plastic lenses for spectacles and Polaroid cameras. He retired in 1974 and shortly afterwards returned to Tyneside.

Meanwhile, his family's firm in the Czech Republic, which had been nationalised by the Communist regime that came to power in 1948, continued under the name Sigma. In 1991 he visited the works to advise them on how to adjust to free-market conditions in the post-Communist world. In 1993 he was made a freeman of the town of Lutin, where the Sigma works were located, and in 2002 he was given an honorary degree by his alma mater, the Technical University of Brno.

SMITH, THOMAS DANIEL (1915–1993)

Always known as T. Dan Smith, he was the most recent in a line of visionary rogues, who changed, or attempted to change, the face of the North East. He was born in Wallsend, the son of a miner. Both his parents held extreme left-wing political views, which he imbibed completely. At the age of fourteen he was apprenticed to a painter and signwriter and spent the years of World War II working at the coachworks of the Co-operative Wholesale Society. In his spare time he was politically active, defending conscientious objectors and speaking at open-air meetings against the 'capitalist' war, that is, of course, until Hitler invaded Russia in the summer of 1941. In both of these activities he revealed a forceful and dynamic personality and a command of language.

In the immediate post-war years, he developed successfully in two directions. One was, ironically, as a capitalist. With a partner, Bill Nichol, he set up Smith's Decorators and within ten years he had seven companies. He specialised in redecorating cinemas and earned the sobriquet 'One Coat Smith'. Naturally, he used the wealth his success brought him, like so many socialist entrepreneurs, to finance a middle-class lifestyle, including private education for his children, while trumpeting the virtues of comprehensive education for others.

His other move was to distance himself from his Communist roots and attitudes and join the Labour Party. In 1950 he was elected to Newcastle City Council for the Walker Ward and within three years he was Chairman of the Newcastle Labour Party. In 1958 Labour won control of NEWCASTLE and Smith became Chairman of the Housing Committee and two years later Council Leader and Chairman of the Town Planning Committee.

Now all-powerful in Newcastle politics, he nevertheless began to sow the seeds of his downfall. He formed several public relations companies, recognising that this was a fast-developing and influential business. He also began to forge links with a number of leading building firms and with John Poulson, a second-rate but ambitious architect. What evolved was a series of corrupt deals, whereby money was paid to Smith's companies, which was used to bribe local councillors and their officials in several parts of the country to award design and building contracts to Poulson. He was arrested and tried in 1970 for offering to put a member of the Wandsworth council on his payroll in order to secure a contract, but the trial was poorly handled and Smith was acquitted. This was, however, nemesis deferred. In 1973 he was found guilty, along with Poulson and Alderman Andrew Cunningham, the Chairman of Durham County Council, and others, of corruption, and given a six-year gaol sentence. Released after three years, he tried without success to revive his career. He died during an operation in 1993.

There is no doubt that Smith was a man of wide-ranging vision, despising what he saw as the small-minded parochial attitudes prevalent in local government. He had a vision of a united region, to which end he was the driving force behind organisations such as the North East Development Council and Northern Arts. Newcastle, which he hoped to make the 'Venice of the North', would of course be its 'capital'. He envisaged the redevelopment of the city centre, the replacement of nineteenth-century housing stock with bright modern dwellings, and an updated transport system. Much of what he accomplished is now cursed by many: the inadequate inner motorway, the construction of which involved the destruction of the lower end of Pilgrim Street and the Royal Arcade; the high-rise flats at Cruddas Park and elsewhere; and the partial destruction of Eldon Square. There is little doubt that in his drive for modernity, Smith was prepared to sacrifice the city's historical heritage. To his credit are the Civic Centre and the Byker Wall. And the creation and growth of the University of Newcastle upon Tyne and the emergence of the University of Northumbria would have pleased him, as would the redevelopment of the Newcastle and Gateshead Quaysides. In his drive to achieve his ambitions, Smith stepped on to the wrong side of the law, and his downfall may have helped to save more of historic Newcastle. Although many of his ambitions were laudable and some of his achievements are commendable, his legacy must be considered severely flawed.

SMITHSON, PETER DENHAM (1923–2002)

Peter Smithson and his wife and partner, Alison, were among the most influential British architects and leading proponents of the Brutalist style in the early post-World War II decades. Born at Stockton on Tees and educated at the grammar school there, he trained after war service at the School of Architecture at King's College, Newcastle, then part of Durham University. The Smithsons burst upon the scene in the early 1950s with their design for the secondary modern school at Hunstanton in Norfolk. Inspired by Mies van der Rohe, it was the first complete example of a steel-and-glass construction. They also achieved fame with the Economist Building in the City of London, now carrying Grade I status. Other Smithson buildings include part of St Hilda's College, Oxford, the offices of the electrical firm, Lucas, and the School of Architecture at Bath University. But their most notorious project was the housing estate known as Robin Hood Gardens built in the 1970s in Tower Hamlets in London. With its high-rise 'streets in the sky' walkways on one side constructed in soulless concrete, it epitomises for many all that was bad about post-war British architecture: ugly buildings that created greater social problems than those they aimed to solve.

The Smithsons' modernism extended to house interiors, most notably revealed in their 'House of the Future' in the 1956 Ideal Home Exhibition, which had such features as curved walls made of plastic and a hexagonal table that rose from the floor at the touch of a button. It is perhaps worth noting that, this apart, they designed only two private houses. In fact, their partnership was remarkable for the very few of their designs that were actually built. Their great influence came rather from his teaching at the Architectural Association, and through their writing, their lectures at conferences and the exhibitions they organised. All that they did was characterised by energy and commitment, which made them prophets who attracted converted disciples.

SMITHSONIAN INSTITUTION

This world-famous institution had its origin in the infidelity of Hugh Percy (né Smithson), 1st Duke of Northumberland, and a wealthy widow, Mrs Elizabeth Macie (see PERCY FAMILY). The issue was Jacques Louis Macie, born in Paris, where he lived until he came to London in 1773 to be naturalised by act of parliament as James Lewis Macie. He was then educated at Charterhouse and at Pembroke College, Oxford, where he was an outstanding student in Chemistry and Geology. These remained his lifelong interests, so that in the course of his life he published twenty-six learned papers, eight through the Royal Society, which elected him Fellow in 1787. For most of his life he was peripatetic, moving from country to country in Europe to study and discuss ideas with scholars with similar interests. This he was able to do because of the fortune bequeathed to him by his mother, who died in 1789. It was in response to her request that he changed his name to Smithson.

In his own will, drawn up in 1826, he left almost all of his estate to his nephew, Henry James Hungerford, with the proviso that should he, Hungerford, die without heirs, the estate should pass to the government of the USA in Washington 'for the increase and diffusion of knowledge among men'. Smithson died in Genoa, a childless bachelor, in 1829. When six years later James Hungerford also died without issue, the Smithson estate was transferred to the US government, although not without some opposition from certain American politicians. When liquidated in 1838, it realised over half a million dollars.

Why did Smithson do it? Because of the loss of many of its records in a fire, a certain answer is not possible. One theory is that Smithson felt deep bitterness towards his father, who appears to have ignored him and provided no financial support. He is said to have vowed to make the name Smithson more famous than that of Percy. Another explanation is that for reasons unknown he fell out with the Royal Society, which would have been an obvious beneficiary. Finally, his selection of the USA, a country he never visited, may have been due to his strong inclination towards democracy and republicanism.

SMYTHE, REGINALD (1917–1998)

Better known as Reg Smythe, the author of the famous cartoon character Andy Capp was born at Throston, Hartlepool, the son of a shipyard worker. He left school in 1933, when he was fourteen years old, and failing to find satisfactory work enlisted in the Royal Northumberland Fusiliers in 1936. In his ten years in the army he rose to the rank of sergeant and saw action during World War II in North Africa. It was during his army service that he began to develop his talent as a cartoonist, sending his material to a magazine in Cairo. After demobilisation, he stayed in London, initially to work at the GPO, before becoming a freelance cartoonist.

In 1954 his ability attracted the *Daily Mirror*, which hired him to design cartoons to illustrate pieces entitled 'Laughter at Work'. Three years later he was asked by the editor to produce a cartoon that would help to increase the circulation of the paper in the North of England. The result was Andy Capp, the workshy 'working' man, who was, in modern parlance, 'politically incorrect' in thought, word and deed and devoted to the habits and pastimes popularly associated with the 'working class'. His foil was his long-suffering wife, Flo, who bore the same name as Smythe's mother. The cartoon was an instant success. Within a year it was included in all editions of the paper, and from 1960 it appeared every day, including Sunday. Nor was its popularity confined to Britain. Andy Capp's appeal proved universal: under different names 'he' appeared in 1,700 newspapers in fifty-one countries and was translated into fourteen languages and read by an estimated 250 million people. It won numerous awards, including the Best Strip Cartoon 1974 in the USA.

Smythe was a retiring, almost reclusive, man, who returned to live in Hartlepool in 1976. Much of his work is in the Centre for the Study of Cartoon and Caricature, founded in 1973 at the University of Kent at Canterbury.

Reg Smythe had national and international readership, but the North East produced two other cartoonists in the twentieth century with only regional popularity. **Joseph Forman (1894–1970)**, whose byline was 'Bos', was born at BEARPARK near Durham City, and after World War I, in which he was twice wounded, trained as an artist at Liverpool School of Art. Initially operating as a freelance, he then became attached to the *Newcastle Evening Chronicle*, for which he worked for thirty years, producing general but especially sporting cartoons. More recent was **Henry Brewis (1932–2000)**, who, unlike Forman, had no professional training. He was born at Shilbottle and throughout his life was a farmer, from 1958 at Hartburn, Northumberland. His cartoons, many of which had rural contexts, were produced in his spare time for farming publications, commercial organisations and local magazines.

SNOW, DR JOHN (1813–1858)

John Snow was one of the most important innovators in medicine in the nineteenth century, on two fronts: he was primarily responsible for establishing anaesthetics as a specialist branch of medicine and, more famously, during the outbreak in 1854, he was the first to identify cholera as a water-borne infection. These advances took place during the later years of his career in London, where he went in 1836. His early training, however, took place in Newcastle. He was born in York, the son of labourer who later became a farmer. In 1827, at the age of fourteen, he was apprenticed to a Newcastle apothecary, William Hardcastle, and also secured training from the physicians at the Newcastle Infirmary, founded in 1751. During this time he gained first-hand knowedge of cholera as a result of treating victims of the 1831 epidemic. In 1834, following the completion of his training, he became an assistant to a doctor at Burnopfield. His sojourn there was only brief: after two years he had moved south to pursue a very successful career in the capital.

SOPWITH, THOMAS (1803–1879)

Thomas Sopwith was a major figure in the LEAD INDUSTRY. He was born in Newcastle, the son of a cabinetmaker, who required him to train in the same craft. This did not appeal to Sopwith, who on completing his articles joined Joseph Dickinson, a well-known surveyor. Within a few years Sopwith became sufficiently expert to be elected to the Institute of Civil Engineers.

In 1845 he was appointed chief agent of the Wentworth Beaumont Lead Mining Company, whose headquarters were at Allenheads. In this role, which he held until his retirement in 1871, he was dynamic and forward-thinking. His approach to mining was more scientific: he introduced the use of surveying techniques into mining and built three-dimensional models of mines in wood, using his training as a cabinet-maker. He was equally concerned to raise the living conditions and the quality of life of the miners: he built better houses, schools, libraries and chapels for them, and he encouraged them to join benefit societies. But in return he insisted upon a more regular and disciplined and, as he saw it, a more responsible attitude to work. This provoked a strike in 1849. Sopwith, however, was adamant and after four months the miners went back to work, except sixty who emigrated to the USA. In the later 1850s, following a dispute with the company, Sopwith moved to London, from where he worked until his retirement.

Sopwith's grandson, Sir Thomas Sopwith (1888–1989) was even more famous as an ocean racing yachtsman, who nearly won the Americas Cup, but more importantly as a pioneer in the British aircraft industry: he founded the Hawker Engineering Co., which in 1935 he linked with four other companies to form the Hawker Siddeley Group, which supplied so many planes for the RAF in World War II.

SOUTH SHIELDS

The history of South Shields has three very distinct phases. In the first, it was the Roman station known as Arbeia. Unfortunately, as for all Roman sites, our knowledge is derived almost entirely from archaeology, which cannot provide sufficient evidence for a continuous and coherent account. There is some indication of a Roman presence on the Lawe overlooking the mouth of the Tyne as early as the time of Julius Agricola, the Governor of Britain between 77 and 84, who was engaged in extending Roman control northwards. By the 160s, however, the fort had been rebuilt in stone, probably in connection with the decision to build HADRIAN'S WALL and make the frontier of the empire. Arbeia's purpose was control of the entrance to the Tyne and is thought that there may have been a road along the south bank of the river linking it to the Pons Aelius, the bridge across the river between what are now GATESHEAD and NEWCASTLE.

Early in the following century, Arbeia was enlarged, notably by the erection of twenty new granaries. These appear to have been the work of the Emperor Septimius Severus (193–211), who arrived in Britain in 208 to re-establish Roman control of the northern frontier after a period of serious disturbance. In the following years he conducted campaigns to the north, perhaps with the intention of incorporating the unconquered parts of the British mainland into the Roman Empire. Redevelopment continued after Severus' death with the building of a new aqueduct to supply water and new barrack blocks.

The last known restructuring occurred a century later, during the reign of the Emperor Constantius Chlorus, who died at York in 306. The effect of the changes was to restore the original fort and separate it from the logistics base. A new military unit, the Numerus Barcarorum Tigrisensium, raised in what is now Iraq, was also installed. The name suggests that the men were merely Tigris bargees, but this is not correct: they were in fact specialist frontier troops.

What happened to Arbeia after the end of the Roman era is uncertain, but the lack of evidence suggests that it may have disappeared completely. What comes to light in the early thirteenth century is a small fishing village occupying a narrow strip of land at the mouth of the Tyne. Its origin is not known, but it must have been before 1157, when a chapel dedicated to St Hilda is recorded. The land it occupied was within the township of Westoe, which, like all other townships bordering the south bank of the Tyne between the river mouth and the boundary of Gateshead, belonged to the Cathedral Priory of Durham. The earliest name applied to the settlement was Sheles, suggesting that it began as a collection of temporary huts. The addition of the word 'South', to distinguish it from North Shields on the opposite bank of the river (see TYNEMOUTH AND NORTH SHIELDS), although occurring as early as 1313, did not come into normal use until after 1600.

The Cathedral Priory records show that until the late fourteenth century the population of Shields remained static, the number of tenants not exceeding twenty-five. By 1396, however, the number had grown to forty-four and a century later it stood at fifty-six. Moreover, the physical size of the village was enlarged in 1489 with the addition of a piece of land known as Shieldsheugh. Later evidence indicates that this gave Shields an area of 170 acres. The late fifteenth-century evidence also makes clear that the occupation of all but one of the inhabitants of Shields was fishing. This is revealed in the rent payments in the form of herring and cod they made to the Durham monks. If, as seems likely, they caught other varieties, they would be for personal consumption or local sale. The one exception was a tenant who operated a saltpan, the product of which was essential to the fish trade.

The economic growth of South Shields, which led to its becoming a medium-sized industrial town, began in the seventeenth century with salt making at the mouth of the Tyne. As that industry declined in the middle decades of the eighteenth century, South Shields began to develop as part of the Port of Newcastle for the loading of COLLIERS exporting coal. In the nineteenth century a number of shipyards opened in the borough, notably Hepple & Co., Charles Reynoldson, J.P. Reynoldson, and Readheads, and with them came allied industries. In additon, glassmaking and chemical industries arrived and coal mines were sunk: St Hilda's in 1825, Harton in 1844, Boldon in 1866, Whitburn in 1874 and Westoe in 1909. By 1900 the sea, shipbuilding, coal mining and engineering accounted for 12,707, or 34 per cent, of the 37,151 employed population. In the early twentieth century South Shields also developed as a holiday resort, particularly after the opening of the Foreshore Promenade in 1927.

With economic expansion went population growth. By 1801, with 8,081 inhabitants, the tiny area of South Shields had almost reached saturation point and already Westoe was accommodating an overspill population of 2,903. This trend continued so that by 1851 there were 9,625 people in South Shields but 19,349 in Westoe. The logical consequence was that Westoe became part of South Shields: first in 1832, when the two communities were formed into a parliamentary borough returning one member; then in 1850, when the parliamentary borough was designated a municipal borough, with a governing body comprising a mayor, eight aldermen and twenty-four elected councillors.

The middle years of the nineteenth century also saw a rise in South Shields's status as a port. It began in 1849, when it and North Shields were freed from the jurisdiction of the Port of Newcastle and given control over all coastal harbours between the Port of Berwick, which ended at the north bank of the Aln, and Souter Point, the northern limit of the Port of Sunderland. In 1865 its status was raised further, when it became the Port of South Shields, separate from North Shields. Moreover, between these two dates South Shields's capacity as a port was considerably enhanced by the opening in 1859 of Tyne Dock, one of the most important docking facilities on the river.

The growth of South Shields led to its being granted County Borough status in 1889, with a consequent increase in the numbers of its aldermen and councillors. The borough was expanded in 1901, 1921 and 1936, bringing within its boundaries Harton, Cleadon, Simonside and the South Shields Rural District. By that date the population had risen to over 100,000. The radical overhaul of local government structures in 1974 made South Shields part of the Metropolitan District of South Tyneside within the new Metropolitan County of Tyne and Wear. Its boundaries were extended to include Boldon, Cleadon, Hedworth, Jarrow, Marsden and Whitburn, bringing them westwards to the boundary of Gateshead and southwards to the boundary of Sunderland.

SPAIN, NANCY BROOKER (1917–1964)

Nancy Spain, who was one of the best-known and most popular journalists and broadcasters in the 1950s and early 1960s, was born in Jesmond, Newcastle, daughter of Lieutenant Colonel George Spain. She was educated at Roedean, the exclusive girls' school in Sussex, which she claimed to have hated. Returning to Newcastle in the late 1930s she gained useful experience in journalism with the *Newcastle Journal* and in acting on the local radio. During World War II she served in the WRNS and then used her experiences to produce a best-selling book, *Thank You, Nelson*, published in 1945. She followed this with a number of detective novels and worked as an editor for a literary magazine, *Books of Today*.

Her rise to fame, however, began in 1950, when she joined the *Daily Express* as a columnist. She remained with that paper until 1961, when she transferred to another popular paper, the *News of the World*. Parallel with this was her success as a broadcaster. She was a regular contributor to *Woman's Hour* and to such entertainments as *My Word* and *What's My Line*. And she was well known for her flamboyant personality and rather masculine style of dress. She and her long-time partner, Joan Laurie, were killed in March 1964 in an air crash near Aintree as she was on her way to cover the Grand National for a newspaper.

SPENCE, SIR JAMES CALVERT (1892–1954)

James Spence was a pioneer of paediatric medicine in Britain and a world authority on the subject. He was born in Amble, Northumberland, the son of an architect, and educated at Elmfield College, York and Durham University College of Medicine in Newcastle. Graduating just before the outbreak of World War I in 1914, he went directly into the army and served both in Gallipoli and Belgium, winning the MC. Following his demobilisation in 1919, he returned to Newcastle to work at the Royal Victoria Infirmary.

His interest in the health of children began in the early 1920s, when he spent a year at the Hospital for Sick Children in Great Ormond Street, London, after which he became part of the medical staff of the Babies' Hospital in Newcastle, where he pioneered the practice of allowing mothers to stay in hospital with their children. He also gained fresh ideas from his year in the USA, when he held a Rockefeller Fellowship at the Johns Hopkins University Hospital in Baltimore, Maryland. Back in Britain, he played a prominent part in setting up the British Paediatric Association in 1928.

During the 1930s he enhanced his reputation in a number of influential reports, starting in 1931 with that on the nutritional causes of xerophthalmia and nyctalopia (night blindness) based upon a study of seventeen children. This led in 1933 to invitations from the Medical Research Council to undertake a study of calciferol (vitamin D2) in rickets and from the Newcastle City Council to make a comparative study of the health of children in poor districts with those in wealthier districts. The City also commissioned him to look into the pattern of infant mortality in the city. These were among the first scientific studies in community and social paediatrics and served to highlight the relationship between poverty, health and child mortality.

The importance of his work in the field of paediatrics was further recognised during World War II, notably in his appointment to the Chair of Paediatrics at the College of Medicine in Newcastle, funded by the Nuffield Foundation. This was the first chair of child health in England and under Spence's leadership it rapidly attracted worldwide attention. Spence was also active in London as Chairman of the Social Medicine Committee of the Royal College of Physicians and as a member of the Nuffield Provincial Hospitals Trust and the Medical Research Council. He was also involved in the discussions that led to the launch in 1948 of the National Health Service.

But it was in the early post-war years that he initiated his best-known research project, the 'Thousand Families Scheme', launched in 1947. This was a close and detailed study of the social conditions affecting illness and death in a broad spectrum of Newcastle children in the first year of life. To accomplish this, the city's health visitors undertook to visit every family at least once a month and to keep detailed records. The study revealed a clear and precise correlation between poverty and health. Since Spence's death the scheme has remained alive, with follow-ups at the end of school years and in 1997 at the age of fifty.

Spence's high reputation, at home and overseas, led to the invitation in 1949 to deliver the Cutter Lecture at Harvard University, the subject being Family Studies in Preventive Paediatrics, and his knighthood in 1950.

SPENCE, ROBERT (1905–1976)

Robert Spence was a leading figure in the development of atomic energy in Britain in the decades after the end of World War II. He was born in South Shields and, after attending Westoe Secondary School, went to Armstrong College, part of the Newcastle division of the University of Durham, where he graduated in Chemistry in 1926. During the remainder of the inter-war years he followed an academic career in the USA and at Leeds University. It was after the war, during which he pioneered anti-malaria spray techniques, that he became Head of the Chemical Division of the Atomic Energy Research Establishment at Harwell in Oxfordshire. From there he rose to become Director in 1964, a post he held for four years. In 1968, however, he resigned for political reasons and went back to academic life as Master of Keynes College and Professor of Applied Chemistry at the newly founded University of Kent at Canterbury.

SPENCE, THOMAS (1750–1814)

Thomas Spence was born in Newcastle to a poor family that had migrated to Tyneside from Aberdeen. Because of their lack of wealth, he had little formal education, but through his own efforts acquired considerable learning, sufficient to secure him appointments as a teacher at Haydon Bridge and then at St Ann's School in Newcastle. It also equipped him to expound radical ideas both in speech and in print. In addition to his own extensive reading, he was heavily influenced by the Reverend James Murray (1732–82), a Berwickshire man, who after graduating from Edinburgh University migrated to England in 1761 to become an assistant minister in Alnwick. Four years later, he moved to Newcastle to become minister of the Presbyterian chapel in High Bridge, where he used his pulpit to preach radical religious and political ideas. Both Murray and Spence were not only radical thinkers but were determined and combative propagandists and this led them in the 1770s to wage a successful campaign to prevent the Newcastle town council enclosing the Town Moor and thereby depriving the freemen of their customary rights. In his advocacy of the causes he espoused Spence was his own worst enemy in that he was violent and extreme in expression and utterly intolerant of those who did not agree with him.

Spence's time in Newcastle ended in 1788, when he migrated to London. The reasons for this move were various, but probably the most urgent was his dismissal from his post at St Ann's School. In London he eked out a living as a writer and seller of radical political literature and became a member of the radical Corresponding Society of London. The most active and dynamic period of his life was the 1790s, when, under the influence of the French Revolution, radical ideas were widespread in Britain. The nervousness of the government in the face of what they perceived as serious threats to the state led to Spence's arrest on five occasions between 1792 and 1798. In 1794 he spent seven months in Newgate Prison without trial, on account of the temporary suspension of the Habeas Corpus Act. Four years later he was convicted on a charge of sedition under the act of 1794 forbidding unlicensed meetings of more than fifty people, and sentenced to a year in gaol. None of this served to silence him: during these years, he wrote six radical books in which he expounded his political programme, notably in two books, *The Real Rights of Man* and *The Constitution of a Perfect Commonwealth*, and in a periodical, *One Pennyworth of Pig's Meat or Lessons for the People, alias the Swinish Multitude*.

His vision of a future society, based upon the notion that property was theft, was naive and simplistic. In his utopian society, land would be confiscated from its owners and vested in the inhabitants of each parish. They would constitute a corporation or collective, which would rent out the land to its members on an annual basis. Part of the income so raised would be used locally for communal purposes and part passed on to finance central government; any surplus would be returned to members of the community as a dividend. What he did accept, however, was that because people varied in their abilities and ambitions, some would become richer than others. This scheme continued to appeal to many for years to come, and as late as the 1840s it still had its advocates, the Spencean Philanthropists.

In the light of this utopian vision, it is not surprising that Spence was opposed to monarchy, aristocracy and an established church and that he favoured the concept of a democratic republic in which the executive, legislative and judicial functions were strictly separated, and all officers of state were to be elected by secret ballots and by universal (including female) suffrage. Nor would there be any property qualifications for either the right to vote or to hold public office, although he did consider women insufficiently robust for the latter.

One other matter was of permanent concern to him, namely, how people learn to read, particularly the poor. In this field he was committed to instruction by means of the phonetic alphabet, which he advocated in several publications, notably *The Grand Repository of the English Language*.

SPENNYMOOR SETTLEMENT

The Spennymoor Settlement was a response by members of the middle class to poverty, unemployment and want of education in the North-East coalfield in the inter-war years. It was not the only such venture in the region, others being founded at Bensham House in Gateshead, Rock House in Seaham Harbour, Durham, Newcastle and Lemington. Only Spennymoor, however, can be said to have been a success. Although in its aims and objectives it resembled the ASHINGTON 'PITMAN PAINTERS', its origin was very different. Two organisations were involved: the Pilgrim Trust, created by an American philanthropist, Edward S. Harkness, with wide discretion to grant money to worthwhile enterprises; and the British Association of Residential Settlements, founded by Canon Barnet, with the aim of bringing university men into contact with the working class for mutual understanding and education. The first settlement was Toynbee Hall in the Whitechapel district of the East End of London. Linking these two organisations was a third party, Bill Farrell, a Liverpudlian actor with an interest in voluntary social service, who was commissioned in 1930 by the Pilgrim Trust to visit the North-East coalfield to see if there was scope for a Settlement.

The upshot was that Farrell was given the task of forming a Settlement at Spennymoor, which opened on 1 April 1931 in a disused shop at 58 King Street. Academic courses were run, which led to several members winning scholarships to Workers' Colleges; a choir and a theatre group were formed; and a sketching club was started.

The two most successful and durable activities were acting and painting. Thanks to government financial aid for Depressed Areas, the Settlement got a small theatre in 1939, and the group continues to flourish as the Everyman Players. But it was the sketching club that had the most spectacular success, in the persons of Norman Cornish and TOM MCGUINNESS, both of whom have achieved national and international recognition as artists.

The Pilgrim Trust support ceased in 1947, but Durham County Council took over the role. In 1954, however, it withdrew its support and the Settlement closed. Like other such organisations, the conditions that made it necessary had been alleviated and the services it provided were now available from public institutions.

STANFIELD, WILLIAM CLARKSON (1793–1867)

William Stanfield, who was to gain two reputations in his lifetime, was born in Sunderland. With a considerable inherent artistic ability inherited from his mother, he was apprenticed in 1806 to a man who specialised in painting heraldry on coaches. This failed to satisfy him and two years later he ran away to sea. He was to remain a sailor for eight years, first on a collier, then between 1812 and 1814 as a pressed member of the Royal Navy on a ship commanded by Captain Charles Austen, the brother of the novelist Jane Austen, and finally, from 1815 until 1816 in the crew on an East Indiaman on the China run. It was these experiences that enabled him to become an outstanding painter of the sea and ships: from the death of J.M.W. Turner in 1851 until his own in 1867, he was considered the best British maritime artist in both oils and watercolours, being particularly noted for his battle scenes. Between 1820 and 1867, 135 of his works were hung at the Royal Academy, of which he was elected Fellow in 1835. He also exhibited twenty-two paintings at the British Institution and twenty-one at the Society of British Artists, of which he was a founder member. His achievement was all the more remarkable for his being largely self-taught.

This, however, was his second reputation. His first was as a painter of theatrical scenery, which he began on leaving the sea in 1816 and which gave him a living until 1834. He was reckoned the outstanding theatrical painter of his day and to have raised the whole standard of theatre painting in Britain. After 1834, however, he concentrated on his maritime paintings, although he occasionally painted scenery as a favour to a friend, notably the actor Charles Macready.

STEAD, WILLIAM THOMAS (1849–1912)

William Stead was born in Embleton, Northumberland, son of a Congregational minister, the Reverend William Stead, and his wife, Isabella Jobson, who had moved there from Yorkshire. After two years at Silcoates School near Wakefield between 1861 and 1863, he joined a firm of Newcastle merchants as a trainee clerk. He remained there until 1871, when he became the editor of the *Northern Echo*, founded the previous year in DARLINGTON by John Hyslop Bell at the behest of the PEASE FAMILY to be an organ of Liberal political opinion. Its first editor was a London journalist, John Coppleston, who printed articles Stead sent to him. When Coppleston fell out with the proprietor and emigrated to the USA, Stead was invited to take over, despite his youth and complete lack of journalistic experience.

It proved to be an inspired choice. Stead was a natural journalist, given to impassioned prose, hyperbole, big headlines and a liking for radical causes. In fact, for him the paper was an ideal platform on which to expound his ideas, among them universal adult suffrage, compulsory primary and secondary education, collective bargaining to settle industrial disputes and arbitration to settle international disputes, Home Rule for Ireland, and reform of the Poor Law. His influence while in Darlington reached its height in 1876 with his reaction to the so-called Bulgarian Atrocities, the massacres organised by the Turkish government in suppressing uprisings by its Bulgarian subjects in which an estimated 12,000 Christians were killed. These events provoked Stead to a paroxysm of anger against the Turks, which helped to whip up widespread feeling in the North of England, expressed in public protest meetings. It also stirred William Gladstone, then leader of the opposition, to write one of the most famous political pamphlets, *The Bulgarian Horrors and the Question of the East* (which sold 40,000 copies in less than a week) and to launch one of the most effective political campaigns of the democratic era. The effect was to move the government of Benjamin Disraeli into action. In the end, after a brief period of war between Russia and Turkey, a diplomatic solution was devised in 1878 at the Congress of Berlin, which brought an independent Bulgaria into existence.

Two years later Stead's time at the *Northern Echo* came to an end. On Gladstone's recommendation, Yates Thompson, who had recently acquired control of the *Pall Mall Gazette*, invited Stead to become assistant editor to John Morley. Stead accepted, having come to feel frustrated by the limitations of a provincial paper, not least those imposed by its small physical size. In 1883 he became editor, when Morley became an MP. Throughout the 1880s Stead was one of the most prominent figures in what has been called the 'new journalism' of the late nineteenth century, which ultimately found its fullest expression in the *Daily Mail*, founded in 1896.

As editor of the *Pall Mall Gazette*, Stead continued to speak out vehemently on matters about which he felt strongly. As an ardent believer in the virtues of the British Empire, he campaigned vigorously for the modernisation of the Royal Navy and for General Charles Gordon to be sent to

Khartoum in the Sudan on the mission that ended with his death in 1885. But his greatest success as editor of the *Pall Mall Gazette* was in exposing the 'white slave trade', the export of young girls to France and Belgium for the purpose of prostitution. This he accomplished in a series of lurid articles entitled 'Maiden Tribute of the Modern Babylon'. In garnering evidence, however, he was found guilty of a technical breach of the law, for which he served three months in prison. His sensationalist approach inevitably divided opinion between those who saw him engaging in pornography and the campaigners for women's rights, who saw his imprisonment as a heroic sacrifice. His campaign was successful in that it secured the passage of the Criminal Law Amendment Act of 1885, which made the traffic illegal and increased the age of sexual consent from thirteen to sixteen.

Shortly afterwards Stead left the *Pall Mall Gazette* to found his own paper, the *Review of Reviews*, which quickly had Australian and American editions. But in the course of the 1890s his reputation declined, largely through his espousal of spiritualism, although he did again make his mark as an outspoken critic of the South African War (1899–1902). Stead died on 15 April 1912, one of the 1,500 passengers who did not survive the sinking of the *Titanic*. He was last seen helping women and children into lifeboats.

STEPHENSON, DAVID (1757–1819)

David Stephenson was an architect and town planner of considerable ability, whose quality is not widely recognised, partly because many of his buildings no longer exist, but also because he has been overshadowed by men of the succeeding generation: his pupil, JOHN DOBSON, and RICHARD GRAINGER. Stephenson was the son of a Newcastle carpenter who had built the temporary wooden bridge across the Tyne after the great flood of 1771 had destroyed the old medieval bridge. The younger Stephenson, however, trained as an architect, including two years at the Royal Academy Schools in London between 1781 and 1783. In the latter year he returned to Newcastle, where he was immediately responsible for designing its first major modernisation scheme, which comprised two new streets: Dean Street (which involved culverting the noxious Lort Burn) and Mosley Street. The latter has a claim to be the first street in the country to be lit by gas (1814) and the first to be lit by electricity (1880). The purpose of this development was to improve travel across the town, respectively from north to south and from east to west. Although the streets survive, few of his buildings remain.

His quality as an architect is, however, fully revealed in the elliptical church of All Saints in Newcastle, still visible between the late twentieth-century office blocks to everyone crossing the Tyne Bridge from the south. Stephenson's design, which won him the competition in 1786 for a replacement for the decayed medieval original, resulted in what is considered to be one of the most original churches built in Britain in the eighteenth century. Also in Newcastle, he was probably responsible for Leazes Park Road and for the conduit head at the foot of The Side, which replaced the medieval market cross known as Cale Cross. It was paid for by the Ridley family and is now in the grounds of their house at Blagdon. Also, in conjunction with WILLIAM NEWTON, he refaced the north front of the Guildhall to give it a classical appearance.

His abilities secured for him in 1805 the post of Surveyor and Architect to the Duke of Northumberland, and it was in this capacity that he designed the three-sided square facing the New Quay at North Shields (see TYNEMOUTH AND NORTH SHIELDS), built after 1806. He also designed in 1816 what is known as the Tenantry Column in ALNWICK, which rises to 75 feet and carries a Percy lion, tail extended, facing north towards the castle. It was built with subscriptions from the Percy tenants in gratitude for the rent reduction granted by the Duke of Northumberland in the depression years following the end of the Napoleonic War. The reduction proved to be short-lived, alas, hence the column's alternative name of The Farmers' Folly.

STEPHENSON, GEORGE (1781–1848) AND ROBERT (1803–1859)

Although both George and Robert Stephenson, father and son, were individually famous in their own days and have continued to be revered since then, there is a good reason for placing them under a single heading: from the outset, George Stephenson educated his son to be his assistant and then successor and supply through superior education the training he lacked. The son more than lived up to the father's hopes and expectations.

George Stephenson was born at Wylam on Tyne. He was largely self-educated and this lack of formal training was a hindrance to him, as were his rough and tactless manner, broad Tyneside speech and dogmatic insistence that he was always right. But he more than made up for his deficiencies and defects by an inborn ability to identify a problem and then to work out how it could be solved, qualities supported by ambition, boundless self-confidence, determination and perseverance. But above all, he happened to have the right interest and the right skills for the time in which he lived.

He began work in 1795 as an assistant to his father, Robert, who was responsible for the pumping engines at a number of collieries near Newburn. Between 1801 and 1806 he was employed as brakesman (responsible for driving and maintaining winding mechanisms) successively at Black Callerton Colliery, Willington Quay and West Moor Pit, Killingworth. In the latter year, however, his first wife died and in his sorrow he moved to Montrose, where he was employed to look after a Boulton and Watt engine at a spinning factory. His self-imposed exile ended in 1808 with his return to Killingworth Colliery. In 1812, as the result of his identifying and correcting a design fault in a Newcomen engine, the consortium that owned Killingworth Colliery gave Stephenson oversight of the engines at all their pits with the status of enginewright at an annual salary of £100.

Although his job was to maintain the steam engines that pumped water and hauled coal out of the pit, with the support of his employers he set out to solve the other great problem facing every colliery: how to increase the efficiency and decrease the cost of transporting coal from pithead to riverside staithe along the WAGONWAY network. The locomotive, the basic viability of which had been demonstrated by the Cornishman Richard Trevethick, offered possibilities (see RAILWAYS). Consequently, a number of other men as well as Stephenson experimented with this form of steam engine in the hope of producing a machine capable of hauling far greater loads than a horse could move. Stephenson's first successful locomotives, named *My Lord* and *Blücher*, were made in 1814, although it is possible that they were the same engine renamed. Whatever the truth, his locomotive(s) had flanged wheels and ran on cast iron rails manufactured for him by the firm of Losh, Wilson and Bell of Walker on Tyne, and achieved a speed of about 5 miles an hour. Stephenson demonstrated conclusively two facts that were to govern railways thereafter: the weight of the engine enabled it to adhere to the rails, and the use of locomotives would not be viable unless the rails on which it ran were made of iron, not wood. In the following years, Killingworth became the centre of experiment and development of the locomotive and a further fifteen were built, all but one for North-East concerns.

It was during his years at Killingworth that Stephenson revealed his versatility as an engineer by designing a workable safety lamp for use in place of candles by miners working in gaseous pits. Two other men, Sir Humphrey Davy and Dr William Clanny embarked on the same quest at the same time, as the result of the explosion in 1812 at Felling Colliery (see Colliery Disasters). Stephenson's version, which comprised a flame fuelled by oil, protected by a glass cylinder, which in turn was enclosed in a perforated tin cylinder, was successfully tested at Killingworth on 21 October 1815 and again on two occasions in the following month. Davy's lamp, devised at the same time, had wire gauze instead of a glass cylinder. As far as we know, neither Davy nor Stephenson was aware of the other's work. However, it was Davy, the eminent scientist, who got the credit and a prize of £2,000. To many it was so inconceivable that an uneducated mechanic could have solved the problem that they suggested Stephenson had stolen some of Davy's ideas. An inquiry was held in the North East, which in 1817 completely exonerated Stephenson, who received a compensatory sum of £1,000 raised by subscription.

Stephenson's ability attracted the attention of the owners of the newly sunk Hetton Colliery, who in 1819 hired him to build a wagonway from their pit to staithes on the Wear near Sunderland. The line, opened in 1822, was over hilly terrain and consequently some sections were worked by inclined planes and stationary engines while on others three locomotives built by Stephenson were used. Stephenson's success at Hetton brought him to the notice of Edward Pease (see Pease Family), the head of a consortium that was planning a railway to move coal from pits around Shildon to the Tees at Stockton. Stephenson greatly impressed Pease, who was persuaded by his arguments in favour of a railway akin to that built for the Hetton company, using locomotives wherever possible and inclined planes and stationary engines to negotiate steep hills. To this end, Stephenson re-surveyed the line to be taken in 1823. To build the necessary locomotives, Stephenson further persuaded Pease to set up a company to be called Robert Stephenson & Co. with a factory off Forth Street in Newcastle. The partners were to be Pease, his cousin the banker Thomas Richardson, George and Robert Stephenson, and Michael Longridge, owner of the Bedlington Ironworks (see Bedlington). The Stockton–Darlington Railway opened in 1825 as a 'mixed freight' enterprise, carrying passengers as well as coal. The inaugural train, pulled by *Locomotion*, hauled ninety tons of coal at a speed of 8 miles (13 km) an hour, almost double the speed achieved by *Blücher.*

By the time he became involved with the Stockton–Darlington project, George Stephenson had the help of his son Robert, who was born in 1803 at Willington Quay. Robert's mother died in 1806 and so his early years were spent in the care of his aunt. But George was determined that his son should have the education he did not have. Fortunately, the greater salary he earned as an enginewright and the money he got for the safety lamp made it possible for him to send Robert to what was probably the best school in the North East at that date, Dr Bruce's Academy in Percy Street in Newcastle. Robert spent four years there between 1815 and 1819 and then six months at Edinburgh University, where he took a number of appropriate science courses.

His father also secured for him an apprenticeship with NICHOLAS WOOD, the head viewer at Killingworth and one of the most knowledgeable men in the North-East coal trade. By the time he was twenty, Robert Stephenson was qualified to work alongside his father. That confidence in him was high is made clear by his being given charge of constructing the Hagger Leases Branch of the Stockton–Darlington Railway and of the locomotive works in Newcastle that bore his name.

But before the line was opened, Robert decided to go to South America. In 1824 he was headhunted by Thomas Richardson, one of Edward Pease's partners, to take charge of the Santa Ana mines at Mariquita in what is now Colombia. Why Stephenson accepted is not clear, but he was away until 1827, returning home via the USA and Canada, losing all his money in a shipwreck.

He immediately rejoined his father, now heavily involved with the Liverpool–Manchester railway project. In fact, from then until the completion of the railway in 1830, the engineering aspect of the enterprise appears to have been a joint father-and-son operation. George Stephenson concentrated on solving major civil engineering problems involved in constructing the line: the bogs known as Chat Moss and Parr Moss, the Sankey Viaduct, the Edgehill Tunnel and the Mount Olive Cutting. Meanwhile Robert was engaged in locomotive development work at the Forth Street Works in Newcastle, which had been managed in his absence by Michael Longridge. As with the Stockton–Darlington venture, George Stephenson's powers of persuasion were needed to get the directors of the Liverpool–Manchester company to accept that traction should be by locomotive, not rope moved by stationary engines. The famous Rainhill Trials gave the verdict to the locomotive. The best of the four competitors was Robert Stephenson's *Rocket*, which achieved 29 miles an hour under load and 35 miles an hour solo. The difference in the speeds attained by *Locomotion* and *Rocket* underlines the amount of development work that had taken place at the Forth Street Works in Newcastle. This involved the talents not only of the two Stephensons, but also that of Henry Booth, the treasurer of the Liverpool–Manchester Co., who successfully pressed the case for the tubular boiler.

The opening of the Liverpool–Manchester Railway was something of a watershed in the lives of the Stephensons, in that increasingly Robert became the more prominent. Although he was appointed chief engineer to six major projects launched in the Midlands between 1833 and 1837 and in the 1840s played a major role in defeating Brunel's advocacy of the 7 foot gauge, George Stephenson had entered middle age and his lack of proper training as an engineer was becoming a serious drawback. In his later years, however, he became a very successful businessman, developing coal interests in Leicestershire and Derbyshire, and developing an interest in gardening. In 1843 he settled at Tapton House near Chesterfield, where he died in 1848.

What really set the seal on Robert's ascendancy was the London–Birmingham Railway, for which he secured the contract in 1830 and which was completed in 1838 at a cost of £2,500,000. The construction involved the boring of tunnels at Primrose Hill in London, Watford and Kilsby, the digging of cuttings at Tring and Blisworth, and the building of the Wolverton Viaduct. Unlike the Liverpool–Manchester project, however, Robert Stephenson was denied the contract to supply locomotives.

The triumphant completion of the London–Birmingham Railway made Robert Stephenson's reputation and he became the most sought-after railway engineer. Because of this, a list of the projects with which he was involved can be misleading. As he readily acknowledged, in so many instances his contribution amounted to no more than critical scrutiny of the proposals submitted to him. His approval, however, was a guarantee of validity. Moreover, he had the help of a large number of assistants. In fact, selecting talented men and securing their loyalty was one of his most useful accomplishments. Among the many men he employed one stands out as his ablest and most trusted assistant, the Devonian George Parks Bidder (1806–78), with whom he had studied at Edinburgh University.

Perhaps his most notable achievement was the Chester–Holyhead line, although this also involved his greatest disaster, the collapse of the bridge over the River Dee. This was offset by the triumphant construction of the tubular iron bridges over the River Conwy and more particularly the Britannia Bridge over the Menai Strait. It is unfortunate that a fire in 1970 so damaged the Britannia Bridge that it had to be dismantled and replaced. Stephenson also built a much longer version, the Victoria Bridge over the St Lawrence River in Canada. His involvement in foreign ventures included projects in Belgium, Spain, Norway, Denmark, Italy, India and Egypt, where he engineered the Cairo–Alexandria Railway. In the North East he was responsible for the Newcastle–Berwick line and above all for the High Level Bridge over the Tyne and the Royal Border Bridge over the Tweed, although all of these projects were overseen and brought to successful conclusion by his associates, notably THOMAS HARRISON.

The large number of railway projects built by Stephenson or for which he acted as consultant engineer were responsible for giving the world the standard gauge of 4 feet 8½ inches. The other great railway engineer of the day, Isambard Kingdom Brunel, had adopted a wider gauge of 7 feet for the Great Western Railway between London and Bristol and beyond. But by the time the government came to adjudicate the matter in 1846, far more lines had been laid down using the Stephenson gauge than the Brunel alternative. It was for this reason that it was ordered that all future lines should have the narrower gauge. Stephenson's work was not confined to railway engineering. He was involved with harbour building, notably the Bute Docks in Cardiff and the Hudson Dock in Sunderland, and it was his seal of approval that ensured that Joseph Paxton's design for the Crystal Palace was adopted for the Great Exhibition in 1851.

In addition to these numerous civil engineering projects, the locomotive firm in Newcastle also went from strength to strength, developing a series of new classes of engine, culminating in the A class. By the time Robert Stephenson died, locomotives built at Newcastle were capable of travelling at 60 miles an hour and in looks were becoming closer to the locomotives familiar to those who lived in the first two-thirds of the twentieth century.

Robert Stephenson the man was a paradox, being at the same time very shy yet very clubbable. He was interested in politics and became MP for Whitby in 1847, yet, like his father, turned down the offer of a knighthood. He was a Tory and as such was opposed to free trade. He also would have preferred a national railway system planned on rational lines by the state. As well as being a first-rate mechanical and civil engineer, though less flamboyant and spectacular than Brunel, he was also a first-rate organiser and an astute businessman. Although his father is more widely known, the fact that George Stephenson was buried at Chesterfield, whereas his son was granted a tomb in Westminster Abbey, is perhaps a pointer to their relative importance.

STEVENSON, GEORGE (1799–1856)

George Stevenson was born at Berwick, the son of a wealthy farmer. In the years following his father's death in 1811, he spent time at sea with his uncle and then in Edinburgh studying medicine at the university. Between 1820 and 1830 he was in Canada, returning to London to become a journalist. Then in 1836 he went out to Australia as secretary to Captain John Hindmarsh, the first governor of the newly established Colony of South Australia. He remained in his post until 1839, during which time he founded the colony's first newspaper. In 1840 he became a leading figure in establishing and developing viticulture in South Australia, now a major supplier of wine to the British market.

STEVENSON, JAMES COCHRANE (1825–1905)

James Stevenson, who became a major figure in the Tyneside CHEMICAL INDUSTRY, was born at Greenock and educated at Glasgow High School and Glasgow University. He came to Tyneside in 1843, when his father moved from Scotland to become the senior partner in the Jarrow Chemical Co., in which the Tennant family, who owned the St Rollox Chemical Works in Glasgow, had a large share. After his father's death in 1854, Stevenson and another partner, John Williamson, took control of the Jarrow works and rapidly made it into the largest producer of alkali in England and second only to the St Rollox Co. in the UK. Both firms produced soda ash, acids and bleach using the Leblanc Process. In the 1870s, however, this was superseded by the Solvay Process, which was cleaner, cheaper, more efficient and resulted in purer soda ash. Licence to use this process in Britain was acquired in 1873 by John Brunner and Ludwig Mond, and this immediately put pressure on the firms using the Leblanc Process. Their response was the closure of some firms and the merger of others to form the United Alkali Co. Stevenson was very active in the negotiations and consequently became vice-chairman of the new company.

Stevenson was also very active in local affairs: he was the representative on the Tyne Improvement Commission from 1880 until 1900; a member of the South Shields Town Council; and the owner of the *Shields Gazette*. He also had a number of 'firsts' to his credit: first freeman of the borough; first chairman of the South Shields Chamber of Commerce; and the first Chairman of the Swan Electric Light Co. Ltd. And he was the Radical Liberal MP for South Shields from 1868 until 1895.

STEVENSON, JOSEPH (1806–1895)

Joseph Stevenson was born in Berwick upon Tweed, the son of a surgeon. He was educated at Witton le Wear and Durham School, after which he went to Glasgow University, but he appears to have left in 1829 without a degree. Thereafter his life had two major strands, religion and historical records. As regards the former, his original intention was to become a minister of the Church of Scotland. This came to nothing, but in 1839 he came to Durham University, where in 1841 he became a licentiate in Theology and was ordained as a Church of England priest. He was a curate at St Giles in Durham from 1847 until 1849, when he became Vicar of Leighton Buzzard in Buckinghamshire. In 1862, however, he converted to Roman Catholicism, becoming a priest in 1872 following the death of his wife. Finally, in 1877, he became a member of the Society of Jesus (Jesuits).

More enduring, however, were his major contributions to the cataloguing, editing and printing of the records of antiquity. This other career, which ran parallel with that as a churchman, began in 1831, when he secured a post at the British Museum, and three years later that of Sub-Commissioner of Public Records. Although his antiquarian work in London ended in 1839, it was resumed in Durham after he had completed his clerical training: from 1841 until 1847 he was employed by the Dean and Chapter of DURHAM CATHEDRAL to arrange and catalogue its medieval charters and enrolled documents, which constitute one of the world's largest and most important bodies of medieval manuscripts. In addition, in the course of his life, he edited thirty-two volumes of records for six different record societies, including four for the Surtees Society, founded in 1834 to print records relating to the northern counties of England. He was largely responsible for persuading the government in 1856 to sponsor the Rolls Series, designed to put public and other records into print; and also he worked as a researcher for the Historic Manuscripts Commission. Finally, after he became a Roman Catholic priest, the Prime Minister, William Gladstone, paid him to search the Vatican archives for materials relating to this country.

STICK DRESSING

The North Pennines and the Cheviots, which form the western boundary of the North East, are sheep country, which explains why at every agricultural show, farmers' market and farm shop within the region walking sticks in the form of shepherds' crooks are on sale. The most expensive are those with heads made out of sheep's horns, many made very elaborate as the result of motifs (the earliest were the thistle and the trout) carved on the front edge of the head. They are works of art and craftsmanship of considerable beauty.

The process of making a horn head begins with the straightening of the horn, preferably that from an old Swaledale tup. This is done in short sections by softening through the application of heat and then squeezing in a vice. The straightened horn can then be carved, and afterwards smoothed with files and finished with steel wool, brass polish and varnish. The wood for the stick may be of several sorts, although hazel is generally preferred. Sticks are normally cut in winter, when the sap is down, and seasoned for at least a year before being prepared. The stick and the carved head are 'married' by means of a dowl or nail, about five inches in length, inserted into both head and shank and then glued. The 'golden rule' is that when joined, the nose of the head should not be lower than the 'marriage' point.

Modern stick carving has grown out of an ancient craft. Crooks and cleeks, the necessary tools for catching sheep by the neck or the leg, were made by shepherds themselves during long winter evenings. Fancy and ornamental versions, however, are of very recent origin, the earliest examples dating from the early 1930s. The spread of this modern craft led in 1951 to the formation of the Border Stick Dressers' Association.

STOCKTON ON TEES

The origins of Stockton are unclear and even the meaning of its name is uncertain: it could signify a settlement belonging to a religious foundation, or an outlying farmstead or a farm made of, or devoted to, cutting logs. What is certain is that it existed in 952, when the Earl of Northumbria gifted it and other properties to the Community of St Cuthbert (see CUTHBERT, SAINT). From then until after 1200 it was solely a farming community, BOLDON BOOK revealing that it consisted of twenty-five tenant farms. Boldon Book also hints at the presence of a manor house, which may have been built by BISHOP HUGH OF LE PUISET, who commissioned the survey. Thereafter, until it was destroyed in 1652, Stockton Manor was one of the Bishop of Durham's important residences and administrative centres.

Stockton's importance began to grow with the foundation of a borough next to the township. Here, too, is uncertainty. The borough is not mentioned in a tax record of 1197, but, although there is no conclusive evidence, it may have been founded by King John, who is believed to have stayed at the bishop's manor house in 1214. John was able to usurp the episcopal rights because he had kept the bishopric vacant since the death of Bishop Philip of Poitou in 1208. There are no references until the early fourteenth century to Stockton's weekly market and five annual fairs. These first appear in a grant dated in 1310 by Bishop Anthony Bek, but it is possible that he was simply confirming an earlier grant by one of his predecessors. The foundation date of Stockton's church is also obscure. First mentioned in 1237, its dedication to St Thomas the Martyr argues that it was founded after 1173, the year in which Thomas Becket was canonised. What is certain is that it did not have parochial status but was a chapel of ease within the parish of Norton, which included Blakiston, Preston and East Hartburn as well as Stockton. Stockton did not become an independent parish until 1711, an event that coincided with the building of the present church.

The situation in 1381 is clearer, thanks to the survey of the episcopal estate commissioned by Bishop Thomas de Hatfield. This shows that the township had grown slightly and now had twenty-nine tenant farms. The borough comprised twenty-four burgages, twenty half burgages and forty quarter burgages. Twenty of the full burgages and seventeen half burgages are said to have been within the borough; the rest were outside, suggesting that originally the borough was tiny but had expanded, partly by dividing some of the original burgages and partly by the creation of an overspill suburb. Also revealed in Hatfield's survey is the ferry, which provided an alternative means of crossing the Tees to the bridge at Yarm, five miles upstream. Later known as Horseferry, it was leased for an annual rent, which shows it to have been a well-used facility. The ferry continued to be the sole means of crossing the river until the building of a stone bridge in 1762 as part of the turnpike system (see TURNPIKE ROADS), which in turn was replaced in 1887 by the Victoria Bridge. In recent years this has been supplemented by the Princess Diana Bridge and the Millennium Footbridge.

Although a market town with an important river crossing, Stockton remained smaller than Norton until well into the seventeenth century. By 1674, however, the Hearth Tax returns reveal that Stockton borough and township had 174 houses compared with 118 in Norton. A hundred years later, the two parts of Stockton had 414 houses and the first decennial census in 1801 revealed a population of just over 4,000. This growth continued so that by the early 1830s the population had doubled. Because of this, Stockton was one of the 178 ancient boroughs incorporated by the 1835 Municipal Reform Act and subject to its provisions. These divided it into two wards and gave it a government comprising a mayor, six aldermen and an elected council of eighteen members. In 1852, when the population had risen to over 10,000, the size of its governing body was expanded to eight aldermen and a council of twenty-four. The next stage came in 1867, when the Second Reform Act created the Parliamentary Borough of Stockton, comprising Stockton (both township and borough) and the township of Norton. In 1889 township and borough were united so that Stockton had an area of over 3,000 acres (1,200 ha) and a population of around 50,000. As a consequence, the aldermanic body was increased to ten and the council to thirty. Further growth was achieved in 1913, when the townships of East Hartburn and Norton were absorbed into Stockton Borough, raising its population to about 60,000.

Stockton's ambition, however, was not satisfied: what it desired was county borough status. It petitioned several times for this, at the same time asking that Thornaby Borough on the south side of the Tees and the villages on the north side of the river in Stockton Rural District be included within its boundaries. The government rejected all applications. Worse followed in 1968, when the Borough of Stockton was merged with the County Borough of Middlesbrough, the Boroughs of Redcar and Thornaby, and the Urban Districts of BILLINGHAM in Durham and Eston in Yorkshire to form the County Borough of Teesside. In 1974, however, the Borough of Stockton was revived as a unit of local government, becoming a Metropolitan District within the newly created County of Cleveland. It included the Borough of Thornaby on the south side of the Tees and Billingham Urban District on the north side, giving it an area of 48,000 (19,400 ha) acres and a population of 164,000. With the abolition of Cleveland County Council in 1986, Stockton became a 'unitary authority'.

Stockton's expansion in area and population was linked with the industrial growth on both sides of the lower Tees during the nineteenth and twentieth centuries. Initially, as well as being a market centre, Stockton was a port, which in the eighteenth century landed increasing quantities of timber. But in this role it had a considerable handicap: between it and the sea the Tees was shallow and meandering, so that it frequently took four tides for ships to reach the town. Improvement was achieved in 1810 and 1831 by the construction of the Mandale and Portrack cuts, which reduced the distance between Stockton and the sea by three miles. These were not enough, however, to prevent the promoters of the Stockton and Darlington Railway from siting their dock downstream at Middlesbrough (see NEW TOWNS OF THE NINETEENTH CENTURY). It was not until the appearance of the Tees Conservancy Commission (created by acts of parliament in 1852 and 1858) that an institution with sufficient powers to really improve the navigation of the river came into existence. This body, comprising five members each from Stockton and Middlesbrough, two from Yarm and three nominated by the Admiralty, was given control of the river from the High Ford at Worsall to the southern boundary of the port of HARTLEPOOL, including a huge area of tidal mud flats. Between then and 1914 it straightened the river by the construction of twenty-four miles of retaining walls, using slag from the ironworks. These prevented meanders and created a stronger flow of water, which combined with dredging resulted in sufficient depth of water for modern ships. In addition, the mouth of the river was given protection by the South Gare and North Gare breakwaters, completed in 1888 and 1891 respectively. The Commission lasted until 1967, when it was absorbed into the newly formed Tees and Hartlepool Port Authority.

Although these improvements enabled Stockton to continue to function as a port, its trade was small by comparison with its neighbours, Middlesbrough and Hartlepool. It also meant that Stockton played a comparatively minor role in the expansion of the shipbuilding industry in the nineteenth century. Ships had been built there from as early as the twelfth century, and thereafter there was no difficulty in building small vessels in wood. But the increasing size of ships as iron and steam replaced wood and sail limited Stockton's ability to compete with Middlesbrough and Hartlepool. In all, four shipyards opened in the later nineteenth century were classed as Stockton yards, although in fact three were in Thornaby on the Yorkshire side of the Tees. The one on the Durham side, that of SIR ROBERT ROPNER, was, however, the largest. None survived the depression and the consequent rationalisation of the industry that took place in the inter-war years. There was, however, a fifth yard, opened at Haverton Hill in 1917 by the Furness Shipbuilding Co. to help meet the urgent need to replace ships lost to enemy action, which managed to survive until 1979.

Although Stockton had a variety of industries, three were of major importance. The earliest was iron, which gave way to steel (see IRON AND STEEL INDUSTRY). This came to be dominated by South Durham Steel, formed in 1898, which had begun in 1860 as the Stockton Malleable Iron Co. Another was the manufacture of gasholders, pioneered by the firm of Ashmore, Benson, Pease & Co., which invented the telescopic gasholder and eventually became Davy Ashmore. Other major engineering firms in or close to Stockton were Head, Wrightson & Co., Whessoe, and Cleveland Bridge and Engineering. The most recent major industry was chemicals (see CHEMICAL INDUSTRY), particularly as the borough spread eastwards to absorb Billingham and Haverton Hill. Among the major firms to locate on the north bank of the Tees were ICI, Phillips Petroleum, Monsanto, Rohm and Haas, British Titan Products, British Chrome and Chemicals, and Huntsman.

STOKOE, ROBERT (1930–2003)

Bob Stokoe, the son of a miner, was born at Mickley, Northumberland. Although not the greatest footballer that the North East produced, his career in the game was marked by two notable achievements. He was one of a very few men to have won the FA Cup as a player and a manager. Ironically, he achieved this distinction with the region's two bitter footballing rivals. As a player, he won the Cup in 1955 with Newcastle United, for whom he played (making 287 appearances) almost entirely at centre half, from 1950 until 1961. Eighteen years later, in 1973, he won the Cup again, but with Sunderland, where he was manager from 1973 until 1976. At that time Sunderland were in the Second Division and that occasion was the first time a club from other than the First Division had won the Cup since 1931. Before and after this triumph he managed several other clubs, but returned to Sunderland in 1987 in a failed attempt to prevent their relegation into the Third Division. By then he had earned his second distinction of being the longest serving manager in the Football League.

STOREY, SAMUEL (1841–1925)

Samuel Storey was a man of many interests and occupations. He was born in Sherburn, Durham, where his father was a tenant farmer, and educated at St Andrew's Parish School in Newcastle. Having been a success as a pupil-teacher, he then gained teacher status in 1859 through the two-year course at Bede College, Durham. Following this, he obtained a post at a school in Birtley, where he remained until 1864.

In that year he moved to SUNDERLAND and over the following twenty years, in complete contrast to the singularity of his teaching role, his activities were diverse and varied. He worked as a commercial traveller, accountant and actuary for the Monkwearmouth Savings Bank, and for the Atlas Permanent Building Society. Meanwhile, he speculated in property and became a partner with his brother in a timber merchant's business. But the activity for which he is remembered is journalism. In 1873, with six partners, he started the *Sunderland Echo*, which sold at ½d. Six years later he founded the *Tyneside Daily Echo*. But more important was his alliance with the American/Scottish steel magnate, Andrew Carnegie, to form a chain of newspapers, all bearing the title *Echo*, which had the radical political purpose of pushing for the extension of the franchise in the counties and the reorganisation of constituencies. Once these objectives had been achieved in 1884 and 1885, the syndicate was dissolved: both Storey and Carnegie were far too individualistic to work in comfortable harmony.

Storey's interest in the press was driven by his interest in politics, in which he was a Radical Liberal. From 1869 he was on the Sunderland Borough Council, serving as mayor in 1876 and becoming an alderman the following year. He was Liberal MP for Sunderland from 1881 until 1895, but lost his seat when the Conservatives won the election that year. He was again returned in 1910, but chose not to contest the second election of that year, occasioned by the death of Edward VII. He was also a member of the Durham County Council from 1892 until 1913, acting as chairman from 1895 until 1905. His political views were radical: as well as wanting a more equitable and wider franchise, he was, like his associate Andrew Carnegie, a republican.

SUMMERSON, SIR JOHN NEWENHAM (1904–1992)

John Summerson was born in Darlington to a wealthy family: his grandfather, Thomas Summerson, was the founder of a successful engineering business, Summerson's Foundries Ltd. John's father, Samuel James Summerson, died in 1907, and this thrust the responsibility of his upbringing on to his over-possessive mother. In 1918, at the age of fourteen, he was sent to Harrow School, where he displayed great talent as an organist. His music master, however, advised him not to take up the instrument professionally, and as a result, in 1922, Summerson went to read Architecture at University College, London. Neither there, nor subsequently in practice and as a lecturer at Edinburgh University, did he really distinguish himself, in part because of his mother's insistence that he live with her.

What turned Summerson into a figure of significance was his move from architecture to architectural history. His conversion was completed with the publication in 1935 of a study of the Georgian architect John Nash, which coincided with his emancipation from maternal control. This, and his subsequent *Georgian London* (1946), established his reputation as the leading expert on Georgian architecture. Publication, however, was delayed because of World War II, during which he founded the National Buildings Record to record buildings considered to be at risk of damage or destruction by bombing. Immediately after the end of World War II, he was appointed curator of the Sir John Soane Museum in London. It was then a small and obscure museum; by the time he retired from the post in 1984, it had acquired, thanks to his curatorship, international standing.

In 1953 he published *English Architecture, 1550–1850*, which set the standard for all subsequent British architectural history. Influenced by a number of European architectural historians who had come to Britain as refugees, Summerson gained considerable credit for developing architectural history in England into a serious academic subject. His combination of architectural knowledge with the skills of the historian were notably demonstrated in his two-volume contribution (covering the years 1450–1660) to the *History of the King's Works*, a detailed exposition of building, domestic and military, carried out by the Crown.

SUNDERLAND

Sunderland vies with NEWCASTLE as the largest city in the region. The course of its history, however, is very different. It began its existence about one hundred years after Newcastle, when the Bishop of Durham, HUGH OF LE PUISET, created a small borough on land sundered (hence its name) from his township of Bishop Wearmouth, covering about 220 acres (90 ha) in a triangle between the North Sea and the south side of the mouth of the River Wear. In this respect, its beginning was not unlike that of SOUTH SHIELDS. Unlike South Shields, however, Sunderland had burgesses, who had the right to hold a weekly market and triannual fairs. Two hundred years later the survey of the episcopal estate commissioned by Bishop Thomas de Hatfield recorded that the borough was leased for £6 a year, whereas formerly it was worth £20. The latter figure shows it to have been on a par with GATESHEAD, but far smaller than DARLINGTON or DURHAM. The former figure, however, indicates severe depopulation and economic depression, almost certainly the consequences of outbreaks of plague in 1349 and after. A further two hundred years on, Sunderland was said to have no more than thirty households and six cobles, the latter indicating that, again like South Shields, it was a small fishing port that had lost all pretensions to borough status.

From this lowly condition, Sunderland began to change in the last years of the sixteenth century. The initial impetus came from Robert Bowes, who in 1589 in partnership with a merchant of King's Lynn, Norfolk, invested £4,000 to build ten salt pans capable of employing 300 men. More significant in the long run was the export of coal, which by the outbreak of the civil war in 1642 was running at about 80,000 tons a year. This expanding trade was possible because of the workable pits at Lambton, Lumley and Harraton in Durham and the rapidly growing London market. The consequence of this economic activity was the expansion of the population to about 1,500. Sunderland's fate during the civil war was in clear contrast to that of Newcastle. In early March 1644, it was occupied by the Scottish army (see SCOTTISH OCCUPATION 1644–1647), which repulsed two feeble Royalist attempts to dislodge it. Thereafter, under its radical leader, GEORGE LILBURNE, it was firmly in the Parliamentary camp.

After the war Sunderland's importance as a coal port continued to grow, which led in the first quarter of the eighteenth century to two important constitutional changes. In 1717 an act of parliament created the River Wear Commissioners, with power to control and manage the river from its mouth to Fatfield. In contrast to Newcastle, which only capitulated to such a body in 1850, Sunderland from an early date secured the benefits of a Commission's efforts to deepen the channel, secure the banks, remove obstacles to navigation, and in the late nineteenth century to build the two long piers that protect the river mouth.

Two years later Sunderland became a separate parish from Bishop Wearmouth, with its own church, dedicated to the Holy Trinity. This was more than simply a religious development, since at that date the parish was also the basic unit of local government. From 1719 Sunderland's public affairs were run by a Select Vestry of twenty-four elected men, who, under the chairmanship of the rector, had power to levy rates to finance developments of public utility. But there was no reference to the borough status granted in the twelfth century.

In the later eighteenth century the coal trade continued to grow, but with a significant difference: increasingly the coal was carried in Sunderland-built ships. This was the beginning of what was to be Sunderland's greatest industry, shipbuilding (see SHIPBUILDING INDUSTRY). And with shipbuilding went ancillary trades like sail and rope making. Industrial development spread across the river to the townships of Monkwearmouth and Southwick, which belonged to the Dean and Chapter of DURHAM CATHEDRAL, not to the Bishop of Durham. These were sufficiently developed to warrant the building of an iron bridge across the Wear between 1793 and 1796 (see BRIDGES AND VIADUCTS). Population growth continued, topping 12,000 in 1801. The problems created by an enlarging population led in 1810 and 1826 to the setting up of improvement commissions, with powers to levy rates to improve the streets and sanitary facilities.

These, however, were preludes to more fundamental changes. The Reform Act of 1832 turned Sunderland into a parliamentary borough returning two members to parliament. This new constituency comprised the parishes of Sunderland, Bishop Wearmouth, Monkwearmouth and Southwick. For the next few years, Sunderland was in the curious situation of being a parliamentary borough without being a municipal borough for the purpose of local government. Sunderland was initially scheduled to be included in the Municipal Reform Act of 1835. This, however, applied only to established boroughs, but when the commissioners visited Sunderland, they could find no conclusive proof of borough status. But in terms of size and importance, the case for borough status for Sunderland was incontrovertible and so in 1837 Sunderland was granted municipal borough status by a special act of parliament. The situation was still anomalous in that the municipal borough and the parliamentary borough did not coincide: Southwick was excluded from the former while being part of the latter.

But Sunderland was now rapidly developing into a major industrial centre. By the middle of the nineteenth century it was Britain's leading producer of wooden ships, with over sixty yards at work building everything from COLLIERS to clippers. The second half of the century saw wood and sail replaced by iron (then steel) and steam, which meant the contraction of the number of yards, but their expansion in size and complexity. It is in these years that the names Austin, Bartram, Crown, Doxford, Laing, Pickersgill, Short and Thompson became world-famous. By 1900 there were over 20,000 men at work in the shipyards, two-fifths of the town's male workforce. Sunderland's other established staple trade, the export of coal, also grew. Originally, as on the Tyne, coal was brought downriver by KEELS for loading on to colliers. In the middle decades of the century, this was replaced by a new method. Between 1846 and 1850 the South Dock, covering sixty-five acres, was built through the initiative of GEORGE HUDSON, who made it the terminus of his railway, and in the following decade, in 1868, the even larger Hendon Dock, built by the River Wear Commissioners, was completed. These docks and the railways that fed them enabled Sunderland to meet the competition of purpose-built ports like Middlesbrough, West Hartlepool and Seaham Harbour (see NEW TOWNS OF THE NINETEENTH CENTURY).

Another industry to flourish was rope making, notably the firm of Webster and Grimshaw, founded to use the world's first rope-making machine invented the previous year by Richard Fothergill. Pottery (see POTTERY INDUSTRY) and glassmaking were also prominent. In the former trade the name Maling became famous, although only after it had moved to Newcastle. In glass, the firm started by JAMES HARTLEY in 1839 was the most famous and successful, producing about one third of Britain's glassware during the later part of the century. However, for various reasons, both of these industries had seriously declined by the beginning of the twentieth century. Not so coal mining. Monkwearmouth Colliery, sunk near the centre of town between 1826 and 1834, was followed in the next decades by pits at Ryhope, Silksworth and Hylton, as well as those in the Washington area. Equally dynamic was the brewing industry, led by the firm founded by Cuthbert Vaux (1813–78), which grew to be the second largest local brewery in Britain, run by his granddaughter's husband, Frank Nicholson.

By 1901 the population of the Borough of Sunderland had grown to 145,500, but without any change in its boundaries, although its size and importance were recognised by the grant of county borough status in 1888. In the course of the twentieth century, however, Sunderland expanded considerably. In 1928 Fulwell and Southwick were brought within the borough boundaries. Then in two stages in 1950 and 1967, Ford, Herrington, South Hylton and Silksworth were added, as in the latter year were Offerton, Ryhope and Tunstall. The expansion was completed in 1974, when in the great reorganisation of British local government the Urban Districts of Hetton le Hole, Houghton le Spring and Washington were assigned to Sunderland, which became a Metropolitan District within the new county of Tyne and Wear, an arrangement that lasted until 1986, when the government abolished metropolitan counties. In 1992 Sunderland achieved its long-held ambition to become a city.

Running parallel with this expansion in size and rise in status was economic decline. The inter-war years were largely ones of depression in the shipbuilding industry and in the early 1930s 29,000 men were unemployed, a high percentage being shipyard workers. The World War II years and those that immediately followed the return of peace were ones of renewed employment and prosperity. But the Wear proved unable to withstand the competition from foreign yards, notably those in the Far East. While commitment to traditional labour practices and management weaknesses contributed to the decline, they are not the only reasons. The fact was that foreign yards had lower wage costs and did not have to cope with the sort of cramped conditions obtaining on the Wear. However, when the last company, North East Shipbuilders Ltd, ceased trading in 1988 it was not due simply to commercial failure. It was in fact killed off by a government prepared to sacrifice it in order to have European Community approval for continued state support of the shipyard at Govan on the Clyde. The fate of shipbuilding was preceded by that of rope making, which ended in 1986, and later by coal exports when mining ceased in 1993, with the closure of Wearmouth Colliery. Perhaps the final blow for the old industries was the closure of Vaux brewery in 2002.

Death has been followed by rebirth. The land along the river mouth is regaining its green and pleasant quality, and in place of glassworks has come the NATIONAL GLASS CENTRE, while on the Wearmouth Colliery site Sunderland AFC has built the modern Stadium of Light to replace the outdated Roker Park. And more substantially, new industries have arrived, most notably the Japanese car manufacturer Nissan, which began production in 1985 and currently employs 4,000 people. Less spectacular are smaller firms that have become established in the various trading estates, although not all of these have proved durable.

SUNDERLAND COTTAGE

Like the TYNESIDE FLAT, the Sunderland Cottage was a form of housing peculiar to its place of origin. The cottages, which are single-storey and built in terraces, were designed and rapidly adopted from the middle of the nineteenth century. This was the period when the Sunderland shipbuilding industry and marine engineering industries developed rapidly and the parallel development of these industries and this particular form of housing seems to be more than a coincidence.

The cottages were more spacious than the Tyneside Flat, having a hall, parlour, living room, scullery and two bedrooms, together with a yard with toilet, washhouse and coal store. The Sunderland Cottage's superiority to the Tyneside Flat appears to have been due to two factors: the higher wages earned in the Sunderland shipyards and marine engineering works, and the apparent willingness of Sunderland workers to lay out a higher percentage of their earnings in rent. As with Tyneside Flats, Sunderland Cottages attracted lower middle-class tenants, and this combined with rising expectations led to later cottages being more spacious and with the trimmings associated with middle-class housing, such as front gardens, double fronts, bay windows and more decorative features.

SURTEES, ROBERT (1779–1834)

Robert Surtees was born at Mainsforth Hall of an ancient Durham family. He was educated at Kepier Grammar School, Houghton le Spring, and then at a school near London, from where he went to Christ Church, Oxford, graduating BA in 1800 and MA in 1803. It was while at Oxford that he resolved to write a history of his native county. This he was able to undertake from 1802, when, as the result of his father's death, he inherited the Mainsforth estate and was thereby relieved from the burden of earning a living. Unfortunately, his health was never good and he died in 1834 at the relatively early age of fifty-five.

What he left behind was a monumental four-volume *History and Antiquities of the County Palatine of Durham*. The formula adopted for the work was normal at the time. The basic unit for investigation and exposition was the parish. Within this framework, the history of the parish church (and its chapels) and its clergy and property were recorded, followed by the history of the various manors within the parish and the pedigrees of the families that had owned them. This reflected the fact that the clergy and landowning nobility and gentry were the potential buyers of his histories and that most of the information in them was derived from their records, which they generously made available to him. Volume I (1816) begins with a general history of the county and then deals with the parishes of Easington Ward. Volume II (1820) is concerned with Stockton Ward and Volume III (1823) with Chester Ward. Unfortunately, Surtees's ill health and premature death meant that he never completed the last volume, IV. It was intended to cover Darlington Ward, but it deals with only three of the eleven parishes, although it does include his researches into the City and Suburbs of Durham. It was not published until 1840, the delay being occasioned by the need for JAMES RAINE (the Elder) to put Surtees's notes into publishable order and for George Taylor of Witton le Wear to write a memoir of Surtees. Surtees's history, despite its age and its dated formula, is still a basic source for researching aspects of Durham's history.

But the four volumes Surtees composed are not his only legacy. Perhaps in the long term more important is the Surtees Society, founded in the year of his death as a tribute to him. Every year since then, the Society has published a volume of historical documents on some aspect of the history of the north of England. These enable scholars to work on primary sources, without the need to consult the original manuscripts, many of which are fragile and inaccessible.

As a footnote it is worth noting that Surtees had a rather mischievous sense of humour. He composed a number of poems – *The Death of Featherstonehaugh*, *Bartram's Dirge* and *Lord Derwentwater's Good-night* – which he convinced his friend Sir Walter Scott were genuine border ballads.

SURTEES, ROBERT SMITH (1805–1864)

Robert Smith Surtees is arguably the best writer of fiction to have been born in the North East. He was the second son of Anthony Surtees of Milkburn House on the Northumberland side of the Derwent, who bought the manors of Medomsley and Hamsterley on the Durham side shortly after Surtees's birth. Surtees's education lasted ten years, from 1812 until 1822, and was entirely at a private school at Ovingham, except for the year 1818–19, when he attended Durham Grammar School. This was followed by six years in which he was articled to two solicitors, in Newcastle until 1825 and then until 1828 in London.

But his interest in and liking for the law were nil, and in his writings he was to satirise it unmercifully. His true interest, indeed his passion, was hunting. In 1830 he secured the position of hunting correspondent of the *Sporting Magazine*, taking over from the widely known and popular Charles James Apperley, who wrote under the byline 'Nimrod'. A year later, however, he fell out with his employer and joined with a publisher, Rudolph Ackerman, to produce a rival publication, the *New Sporting Magazine*. This coincided with another change in his situation, his elder brother's death, which made Surtees the heir to the estate. Nevertheless he continued to work as a journalist for another five years, and it was during this period that he began to develop his most famous fictional character, John Jorrocks, a successful Cockney grocer of Great Coram Street, London, who, like his creator, lived for hunting, but in sharp contrast was accident-prone and also had a very insecure grasp of the place of the letter H in the English language.

This phase of Surtees's life ended in 1836, when he returned to Hamsterley Hall, near Burnopfield, Durham, where he was to live for the rest of his life. In the course of the next two years, first his mother, and then his father, died, leaving him in 1838 the master of Hamsterley. He was now a landowner, with its attendant responsibilities such as being a JP and Deputy Lieutenant, but also with the time to hunt and to indulge in what he termed his 'scribbling'. Between his succession to the estate and his death in 1864, he wrote eight novels, most of which were first published in serial form in the *New Sporting Magazine* and then revised and expanded for issue as books. In addition to John Jorrocks, who in many ways anticipated Mr Pickwick, he created two other memorable central characters, Soapey Sponge and Charles 'Facey' Romford, as well as a varied cast of supporting players. The tenor of his novels is satirical. He pillories fools, fops, dandies and social climbers, all cheated and swindled by clever rogues. Surtees's purpose was not to condemn, still less to reform, the society he knew, which ranged from aristocrats to labourers. Rather, he aimed to entertain by describing and satirising social behaviour, almost always with humour, in all its variety. Throughout, his view of human nature is utterly cynical and that people get what they deserve. In all but two of his novels, fox hunting is at the heart of the action. In the two exceptions, his concern is with hunting of a different sort, that of men by women for matrimonial ends.

Surtees has none of the sentimentality and concern for the poor so evident in Dickens; rather, he has Thackeray's detached view of human nature. He is not considered to be in the same class as either of those authors, largely because of his failure to contrive clear and tightly controlled plots. This said, Surtees's novels reveal two qualities of the highest order: acute and detailed observation of the society of his day, and a great ability to present his observations through widely diverse and memorable characters. His best novels are reckoned to be *Handley Cross* (based upon Shotley Bridge and featuring John Jorrocks), *Mr Sponge's Sporting Tour* (the first of his novels to achieve popularity) and *Mr Facey Romford's Hounds* (published posthumously).

After Surtees's death, Hamsterley passed into the hands of the Vereker family, Viscounts Gort in the Irish peerage, through the marriage of one of Surtees's daughters and co-heiresses, Eleanor, to John Vereker, 5th Viscount. Their son, John Vereker, 6th Viscount in the Irish peerage and also 1st Viscount in the British peerage, became Field Marshal Lord Gort VC (1886–1946). As Chief of the Imperial General Staff from 1937 until 1940, he went to France in 1939 in command of the British Expeditionary Force, and it was he who masterminded the retreat to Dunkirk in the spring of 1940. Between 1941 and 1944 he was Governor General of Malta and Commander in Chief of British forces there and was therefore responsible for conducting the heroic defence of the island in 1941 and 1942. His last post was High Commissioner in Palestine.

SUTHERLAND, SIR ARTHUR MUNRO (1867–1953)

Arthur Sutherland, who was born in Newcastle, was a major shipowner and a philanthropist. His grandfather, Benjamin John Sutherland, had migrated from Thurso to Newcastle, where his son, also Benjamin John, built up a successful grain business. Sutherland was educated at the Royal Grammar School, leaving in 1883 to work in a shipbroker's office. Ten years later he bought his first ship in partnership with his brother, again Benjamin John, and in 1896 founded the Sutherland Steamship Co., which was managed together with other companies by B.J. Sutherland & Co. Most of his ships were built by the Sunderland firm of Doxfords, although he augmented his capacity in 1919 by purchasing the Tyne-Tees Shipping Co. After his death in 1953, B.J. Sutherland & Co. Ltd was wound up.

He was active in local affairs as a member of the Newcastle City Council from 1910, discharging the offices of Sheriff in 1917 and Mayor in 1919, and from 1920 until 1925 owning the *Newcastle Chronicle*. He was also a noted philanthropist, particularly as regards the Newcastle Dental School. This began as a private venture in 1894 in Nelson Street, moving to the Handyside Building in Percy Street in 1906. In 1930 the School was taken over by the College of Medicine to form its Dental Department, which involved a move from Percy Street to a new building on the Royal Victoria Infirmary site, a move made possible by Sutherland's gift of £12,500. In 1947 he again came to the aid of dentistry by giving £50,000 to enable the Dental Department to move to the former College of Medicine building in Northumberland Road (now part of Northumbria University). The Dental Hospital now occupies a purpose-built building located next to the Royal Victoria Infirmary. In an entirely different direction, Sutherland also used his wealth to buy DUNSTANBURGH CASTLE for the nation.

SWAN, SIR JOSEPH WILSON (1828–1914)

Joseph Swan was born at Pallion Hall, Sunderland, the son of an unsuccessful Sunderland businessman. After minimal schooling that ended just before his thirteenth birthday, he was apprenticed in 1842 to a firm of druggists, Hudson and Osbaldiston, in Sunderland. He was freed from this contract by the premature deaths of both masters and in 1846 he joined John Mawson, a chemist and druggist in NEWCASTLE. By this date his interest in matters scientific had been fired and was being furthered through his access to the library of the Sunderland Atheneum. Moreover, Mawson proved to be a most indulgent master, allowing Swan as much time as possible to study and to conduct experiments.

Swan is universally remembered as the man who invented the electric light bulb, but this came only after a number of years during which he and others made preliminary but necessary discoveries. Swan's contribution was the incandescent carbon filament, which he produced after much experimentation. But before this could be used in an electric light bulb, two other developments were needed. One was a pump to create a vacuum in a glass tube. This was developed in 1865 by a German, Hermann Sprengel, and later improved by a Birkenhead man, Charles Sterne, who became Swan's collaborator. The other was an improved dynamo to provide adequate electric power. It was, therefore, not until the 1870s that the conditions were in place for the creation of a successful electric light bulb. This Swan demonstrated at a meeting of the Newcastle Chemical Society on 18 December 1878, with a bulb in which two platinum wires were linked by a carbon filament. He repeated the demonstration to an audience of 700 at the Newcastle LITERARY AND PHILOSOPHICAL SOCIETY on 3 February 1879 and again to an audience of 500 in Gateshead Town Hall on 12 March 1879. There could be no doubt that Swan had proved the feasibility of illumination by electricity. On the basis of these successes, together with two associates in Birkenhead, Charles Sterne and Frederick Topham, an expert glassblower who secured the services of skilled German glassblowers, he formed a company, registered in May 1882, to manufacture electric light bulbs at a factory in South Benwell.

What he did not do immediately was to register his invention with the Patent Office. In contrast, the American inventor Thomas Alva Edison patented his invention, which was very similar to Swan's, in both the USA and the UK in November 1879, and in March 1882 registered his company, the Edison Electric Light Co., in the UK. As soon as knowledge of Swan's company became known, Edison launched a legal attack on it. The court, however, was unable to come to a clear-cut decision and in consequence the two companies formed a joint company in 1883, the Edison and Swan Electric Light Company, in which Swan had 60 per cent and Edison 40 per cent. The most significant consequence of this merger for the North East was the loss of a new and major industry: instead of becoming the place where the light bulbs were made, the South Benwell factory was closed and production moved to London.

As well as the light bulb, Swan is credited with other inventions. His earlier interest, arising from one aspect of Mawson and Swan's business, was photography. In 1856 he perfected the formula for the manufacture of collodion and in the course of the 1860s and 1870s he invented and patented two important improvements in the printing of photographs. The first, in 1864, was called the carbon process, for producing photographic prints that did not fade; the second, not patented until 1879, was bromide-coated printing paper. He also devised the means of spinning artificial fibres, but because of his heavy commitment to the electrical side of his business, he neglected its development. This was undertaken by others, notably Courtaulds, for the manufacture of artificial silk.

The year 1867 was one of tragedy: his

wife died at their home in Leazes Terrace, Newcastle as a consequence of childbirth; and his partner, John Mawson, was blown up when, in his capacity as High Sheriff, he was engaged in trying to dispose of a quantity of illegal nitro-glycerine. Two years later, Swan moved to a house he had built in Low Fell. His stated reason was to live in a healthier location, but it may also have been connected with his wish to marry one of his wife's sisters, both of whom had kept house for him after her death. Before 1907, however, such a union was illegal in England. There were hopes of a parliamentary act to alter the law, but when this did not happen Swan went to Switzerland to be married. In 1883 he and his new family moved south to be near his business interests, first to Bromley in Kent and then in 1908 to Warlingham in Surrey. When he died, he was buried at Warlingham church.

In the late 1860s Mawson and Swan acquired a stationery and bookselling business owned by a man named Marston in Grey Street, Newcastle. They installed as their manager an Irishman, Thomas Morgan, and thus was created the shop that traded for many decades as Mawson, Swan and Morgan, well known to all who lived on or near Tyneside.

SYMEON (?–c.1130)

Symeon was one of the earliest monks of the Cathedral Priory of Durham. Little is known about him: he was certainly a Frenchman, probably a Norman, and he is believed to have been among the group of well-educated clerks brought to Durham by Bishop WILLIAM OF ST CALAIS when he returned to Durham in 1091 from exile in Normandy. From the middle of the second decade of the twelfth century, Symeon occupied two important positions in the Priory: from 1115 he was the supervisor of the *scriptorium*, and by 1126 he had become *cantor* (precentor), whose role included supervision of the Priory's book production. Although the date of his birth cannot be discovered, it is almost certain that he died in or shortly after 1130.

The work that gives him his importance is *Libellus de exordio et procursu istius, hoc est, Dunelmensis ecclesie* (Book of the Origin and Subsequent Development of this Church of Durham), which in the seventeenth century was retitled *Historia Dunelmensis Ecclesie* (History of the Church of Durham). Written between 1104 and 1109, it relates the story of the church of Lindisfarne (see HOLY ISLAND) from its foundation in 635 to the death of Bishop William of St Calais in 1096. The initiative, however, was not Symeon's but that of his superiors, notably Prior TURGOT. The purpose of the book was to explain, justify and extol the destruction in 1083 of the pre-Conquest Community of St Cuthbert (see CUTHBERT, SAINT) and its replacement by the Benedictine Priory. It therefore had a propaganda purpose, which requires it to be read critically. For a long time, another important chronicle, the *Historia Regum* (History of the Kings) was attributed to Symeon, but this is now discounted, except for the entries covering the ten years between 1119 and 1129. It is likely that he was also involved in the production of several other works written in the Cathedral Priory at a time of heightened interest in history at Durham, and he is known to have written at the request of Hugh, Dean of York, an account of the Archbishops of York from the seventh to the tenth centuries.

The importance of Symeon's work cannot be overestimated: without his writing our knowledge of the early history of the North East would be scanty in the extreme.

TATE, GEORGE (1805–1871)

George Tate was the elder son of Ralph Tate, a builder and draper of ALNWICK. He was educated at the borough school and then at the Duke's Grammar School. He then practised as a draper until 1848, when he was appointed Postmaster in Alnwick, a role he filled until his death. These were the means whereby he earned his living; his real interest, however, was in history and archaeology. His reputation rests primarily on his two-volume *History of Alnwick*, published in 1866 and 1868, much of the material for which he accumulated between 1850 and 1858, when as clerk to the town council he had access to the borough's records. He also published in 1865 *The Sculptured Rocks of Northumberland and the Eastern Borders* and articles in the journal of the Berwickshire Naturalists' Club, of which he was secretary between 1858 and 1871. His research and writing made a major contribution to the growth of knowledge and understanding of the region's past.

TATE, THOMAS (1807–1888)

The younger brother of George Tate, Thomas was educated at the Duke's Grammar School and then at Edinburgh University. Unlike his brother, his interest was in mathematics and science, and also unlike him he spent most of his career away from Alnwick. In 1835 he secured a lectureship in Chemistry at the York Medical School, but five years later in 1840 he moved south to join the staff of Battersea Teachers' Training College. He stayed there until 1849, when he moved to Kneller Hall Training College at Twickenham, where he remained until it closed in 1855 in unhappy circumstances that involved the dismissal of the Principal.

Both before and after this, his main interest was in how children are taught and how they learn. He published over twenty popular texts on the teaching of maths and science and founded a periodical for teachers and others interested in education called *The Educational Expositor.* His other notable book was called *The Philosophy of Education,* which revealed the influence of the Englishmen Francis Bacon and John Locke and the Swiss educationalist Johann Heinrich Pestalozzi (1746–1827). Education was not an exclusive interest. He collaborated with the shipbuilder Sir William Fairbairn in mathematical calculations in connection with the design and testing of models of the Conwy and Britannia Bridges, built by ROBERT STEPHENSON, and he also made scientific instruments, including a double piston air pump.

The course of his life after 1855 is obscure, although he may never have had another permanent job, since upon the closure of Kneller Hall he was awarded an annual government pension of £120.

TAYLOR, CECIL PHILIP (1929–1981)

Always known as C.P., Cecil Philip Taylor was born in Glasgow of a Jewish family. He left school in 1942 and became an electrician and then a television engineer. In 1955 he moved to Newcastle, where his mother had grown up, to take a job as a travelling salesman. His real interest, however, was in theatre and in 1962 he made his name with a play about a miners' strike, *Aa Went Tae Blaydon Races.* From then on he was at the centre of theatrical life in the North East, not only writing plays, but also being actively involved in school and student drama and with people with learning difficulties. Most particularly, he was at the heart of Newcastle's Live Theatre, of which he has been described as 'the founding father', opened in 1973 as a theatre for working-class audiences and to encourage working-class actors. There he worked in collaboration with SID CHAPLIN and BASIL BUNTING and promoted and encouraged

TOM HADAWAY. He was also involved with the Royal Shakespeare Company and the Traverse Theatre in Edinburgh. He wrote over seventy plays, among them *And a Nightingale Sang*, which won the Prix Europa in 1990, and *Bread and Butter*, controversial enough not to be performed in Glasgow, which traced the lives of two Jewish couples in the Gorbals from 1931 until 1965. His last major work, *Good*, has been described as 'arguably the definitive play in English about the Holocaust'. In his final years he lived at Longhorsley.

TAYLOR, PETER MURRAY, LORD TAYLOR OF GOSFORTH (1930–1997)

Peter Taylor, who was Lord Chief Justice of England from 1992 until his death in 1997, was born in Westgate Road, Newcastle. He was the son of a doctor, Herman Taylor, and his wife, Raie Shockett. The family, whose original name was Teiger or Teicher, was Jewish, the ancestors on both sides being migrants from Eastern Europe. He was educated at the Royal Grammar School and then Pembroke College, Cambridge, where he took a degree in Law in 1953. He was called to the Bar in the following year and joined chambers in Newcastle to practise on the Northern Circuit.

His ability was such that in 1967 at the early age of thirty-six he became a QC and moved to London to join chambers headed by a fellow Novocastrian, George Waller. In the 1970s he made a considerable name for himself as a prosecutor in two notorious cases: the trial in 1974 of John Poulson, the architect associated with T. DAN SMITH, and the Scottish civil servant George Pottinger on charges of corruption; and in 1979 that of Jeremy Thorpe, the former leader of the Liberal Party, on a charge of attempted murder. In 1979–80 he was Chairman of the Bar Council and in the latter year he was knighted.

His rise thereafter was rapid: in 1988 he became a Lord of Appeal and in 1992 Lord Chief Justice. Meanwhile, in 1989, he chaired the public inquiry into the Hillsborough Disaster, when ninety-five people were crushed to death at Sheffield Wednesday's ground before the start of the FA Cup semi-final between Liverpool and Nottingham Forest. It was as a result of this that football grounds became all-seater stadia. As Lord Chief Justice, he departed from traditional restraint on making public comments on controversial legal issues while they were still matters of political decision. Clearly on the liberal wing of legal thinking, he spoke out against many of the proposals of the then Conservative government and was in favour of Britain adopting the European Convention on Human Rights, which he did not live to see incorporated into our legal system.

TEAM VALLEY TRADING ESTATE

The Team Valley Trading Estate came into being in the late 1930s on the recommendation of the North East Development Board and through the growing willingness of government to promote and finance industrial regeneration, which resulted in the Special Areas (Development and Improvement) Act of 1934. The outcome was the formation of North Eastern Trading Estates Ltd. The problem was to choose between the large number of available sites on both sides of the Tyne. The decision finally went in favour of the boggy pastureland bordering the River Team. The scheme, planned by William (later Lord) Holford, was ambitious, and was intended to comprise 400 factories employing 15,000 people. The site, which was nearly two miles (3 km) long and covered 700 acres (280 ha), required a great deal of preparatory work, notably culverting the upper reaches and canalising lower reaches of the Team and stabilising the ground with colliery waste. The layout took the form of a central avenue, Kingsway, with four other parallel avenues (Queensway, Princesway, Dukesway and Earlsway), two on either side of it, from which streets branched off at right angles. There were to be three different sizes of factory, but with provision for firms to have facilities built to their own specifications. Progress was rapid and the first factory began production in September 1936. When King George VI officially opened the TVTE in February 1939, 110 tenant firms had been established, employing 5,000 people. Several of the first firms were started by refugees from German persecution, to whom special consideration and encouragement were given.

By the 1970s the estate was still not fully developed, although it employed nearly 20,000 people. Until that point, the estate was exclusively for manufacturing concerns, but from 1980, with manufacturing becoming less prominent in the economy, other forms of activity such as offices and retail units were allowed. The TVTE was a pioneer on a grand scale. Since its inception, there have been many imitators and the formula has been adopted throughout the region as an important means of promoting economic growth.

THE SAGE GATESHEAD

The Sage Gateshead is arguably the most striking of the new buildings that are revitalising the quaysides of the River Tyne in the post-industrial age. Situated prominently on the south bank of the river, its distinctive shape and glass and stainless steel roofing have made it a unique landmark that proclaims its status as a cultural centre of international quality and importance. Its name, adopted at the outset, reflects the sponsorship of Sage PLC.

The project began in 1994, when a study commissioned by the then Northern Arts concluded that the North East had an undeniable case for a new capital structure for the creative arts. The initial idea, for a concert hall and art gallery, was gradually replaced by a more radical concept of a music centre with purposes far wider than that of the conventional concert hall. Initially, it was expected that what was built would be in Newcastle. Newcastle, however, withdrew from the scheme and as a result all the region's local authorities were invited to compete for the project. In 1996 Gateshead's bid was accepted because of the landmark location on its quayside that it could offer. The exact site eventually chosen was a short distance east of St Mary's Church. The Royal Institute of British Architects' 'blind' competition, which attracted submissions from architects of international renown, was won by Sir Norman Foster and Partners. Because world-class acoustics was stipulated as a prime requirement, Arup Acoustics was appointed separately. Connell, Mott, MacDonald were appointed chief consulting engineers and the role of managing building contractor was given to O'Rourkes. Work on the site began in April 2001 and the building was opened shortly before Christmas 2004. The cost of the project was £70 million, £47 million of which came from the Lottery Fund, via the Arts Council, the largest grant made to any cultural project outside London.

The upper floor of the building is divided into three parts. Hall One is a concert hall with a seating capacity of 1,700. Its ceiling has six wooden acoustic panels, each weighing fourteen tonnes, adjustable to ensure perfect acoustic conditions for any performance. Hall One is now the main base of the NORTHERN SINFONIA, with their rehearsal room, the Northern Rock Foundation Hall, adjacent to it. Beyond these is Hall Two, which can seat 450 for performances by the whole range of smaller ensembles from chamber orchestras to jazz bands and folk groups. Of equal standing with the Northern Sinfonia is Folkworks, the leading British powerhouse in the fields of folk and traditional music. In order to ensure the breakdown of the barriers that have customarily divided musical forms and traditions, the two institutions have been subsumed under the North Music Trust.

The lower floor is principally concerned with education. Its central feature is the Music Education Centre, equipped with twenty-five workshops, studios and teaching rooms, many carrying the names of people or institutions that have agreed to support them. Its constituency is the entire northern region, which includes over 300 secondary schools, and its purpose is to provide facilities and encouragement for the widest possible range of ages, interests and abilities. Also on the lower floor are the Barbour Room, with a capacity of 300, for prestige events, and the Joan and Margaret Halbart Space, a hi-tech music information and facilitating service run by Gateshead Library.

The Sage Gateshead is owned by Gateshead Council, but the management of the building and its various activities is the responsibility of a dedicated charity, the North Music Trust. In addition to earned income, revenue derives from a variety of sources, including a percentage of the interest from an endowment fund held by the Community Foundation. The Arts Council England and Gateshead Council are also major revenue supporters.

THOMPSON, ROBERT MICHAEL (1910–1988)

Bobby Thompson, known as 'The Little Waster', enjoyed huge popularity as a comedian in the region in the 1950s and early 1960s. His stage character as a slyly perceptive little man, addicted to beer, cigarettes and indolence represented in the flesh what Reg Smythe presented in his famous Andy Capp cartoons.

Thompson was born into a mining family, but as both his parents died before he was eight, he was brought up by a married sister. He attended schools at Fatfield and Penshaw until the age of fourteen, when he left to work at North Biddick Colliery. This phase of his life ended with the closure of the colliery in 1931. Thereafter, until he was called up for military service in 1941, he made a living as a casual labourer during the day, supplemented by evening work in the local pubs and clubs as a singer and harmonica player. After demobilisation, he returned to the North East in 1946, but was unemployed until 1951. In the latter year his luck changed, when he successfully auditioned for a new radio show, *Wot Cheor Geordie*, broadcast by Radio Newcastle. The show was a huge success, running for fifteen years, making Thompson a household name in the North East and earning him top billing in the region's music halls.

His career faltered, however, in the later 1960s. An attempt to transfer him to the new medium of television was not a success: Thompson needed to feed off a live audience, on top of which producers insisted that he tone down his essential hallmarks, his regional accent and dialect. And his career as a pub and club entertainer also foundered on his increasing reliance on drink and an unenviable reputation for unreliability. It was through the efforts of a new agent that he was able to overcome his disabilities and regain respectability in the region's entertainment circuit.

Bobby Thompson's comic talent did not achieve the widespread fame it deserved. In part, this was the consequence of his failure as a television performer, but the underlying fact was that his humour was born of the hard times experienced in the North East in his early years and was not readily understood outwith the Tees–Tweed region. Moreover, his career preceded the days when national audiences would react favourably to distinct regional cultures. Bobby Thompson's personal life was as chequered as his professional career: he was a heavy smoker and drinker; he was married three times; and, as a result of his generosity and addiction to gambling, he was declared bankrupt.

THOMPSON FAMILY

Four generations of the Thompson family were responsible for creating two of the largest shipyards on the Wear (see SHIPBUILDING INDUSTRY). The progenitor was Robert Thompson I (1797–1860), the son of a sea captain, who became a shipwright and for many years worked for other shipbuilders on both Tyne and Wear, while occasionally building ships on his own account or with partners. In 1846, however, he founded his own shipyard at North Sands on the north bank of the Wear. Robert was succeeded by his son, Joseph Lowes Thompson I (1824–93), whose initials gave the firm its name, J.L. Thompson. At the time of his retirement from the management in 1877, the yard had converted from wood to iron. He was succeeded by his two sons, Robert Thompson III (1850–1908) and Joseph Lowes Thompson II (1853–1910), of whom Robert was the more dynamic. He expanded the yard and was responsible in the 1880s for going over from iron to steel and introducing hydraulic riveting to replace hand-riveting. It was under his leadership that in 1894 J.L. Thompson changed from being a family firm to a limited liability company. He acquired interests in allied industrial enterprises such as Sunderland Forge and Engineering Co. and Skinningrove Iron Co. He was also actively involved in several appropriate organisations such as the Institution of Naval Architects, the Iron and Steel Institute, the North East Coast Institution of Engineers and Shipbuilders, and the Worshipful Company of Shipwrights. The last of the line was his son, Sir Robert Norman Thompson (1878–1951). After his death, J.L. Thompson merged with three other companies to form Sunderland Shipbuilders Ltd.

The other Thompson shipyard was that of Robert Thompson II (1819–1910), the older brother of Joseph Lowes Thompson I, who, having been briefly a partner in his father's firm, left in 1854 to found his own yard further upriver at Southwick. At first he specialised in 'composite' ships, that is, wooden hulls on iron frames, but after converting to iron trained his nephew, Robert Thompson III, in this field. He was a long-time member of the River Wear Commission and the Local Government Board and its successor, Southwick UDC, serving as its chairman and donating the site for its offices. The firm of Robert Thompson & Sons Ltd did not long survive his death, closing in 1931 as part of the rationalisation of the industry in the face of worldwide depression.

Throughout, the Thompsons were Liberal in politics, Methodist in religion, and actively involved in local life as JPs, in elected institutions of local government, in the River Wear Commission, and in two cases as lifelong supporters of Sunderland AFC.

THROCKLEY, JOHN OF (c. 1270–c. 1340)

John of Throckley's medieval name was John de Trokelowe and he was the Cellarer of the Benedictine priory at TYNEMOUTH. In the 1290s he was the chief accomplice of Prior Simon de Walden, in a conspiracy to free Tynemouth Priory from the control of St Albans Abbey. The attempt was thwarted by the Abbot of St Albans, and Trokelowe and his fellow conspirators were taken south in chains to continue their monastic lives away from Tynemouth. This was very much to our benefit, since in his later years Trokelowe wrote possibly the best account we have of the events of the reign of Edward II up to the year 1323. As St Albans Abbey was frequently an overnight stop for VIPs travelling to and from London and Westminster, he was able to acquire a far greater knowledge of political events and personalities than he would have done living at Tynemouth.

TORNADO

In 2009 steam locomotion returned to the East Coast Main Line with the introduction of passenger trains hauled by *Tornado*. This is a new Peppercorn class A1 Pacific locomotive built, with the support of several major engineering firms such as Corus (formerly British Steel) and Rolls Royce, by the A1 Steam Locomotive Trust, which was formed in 1990. Virtually all the work was carried out at a facility close to the old North Road Locomotive Works at DARLINGTON. The class was designed by Arthur Peppercorn, the last Chief Mechanical Engineer of the London and North Eastern Railway. In 1948–49, the recently nationalised British Railways built forty-nine of these locomotives, but they had a lifespan of only fifteen years as British Railways decided to convert to diesel propulsion in the 1960s.

Tornado is regarded as the fiftieth 'Peppercorn', although the design has been modified in several respects to accommodate developments in engineering and technology since 1950 and changes in the safety regulations. The new Peppercorn has been designed to be able to run non-stop from King's Cross to Newcastle, hauling a train of ten modern coaches. Because the nationalised company no longer exists, the engine is painted in the old LNER colour, green.

TREVELYAN FAMILY AND WALLINGTON HALL

The name Trevelyan is always associated with Wallington Hall, one of the region's finest houses, yet it was not basically a Trevelyan creation. It was primarily the work of Sir William Blackett (1657–1705), the wealthy Newcastle merchant who in 1688 bought the Wallington estate from Sir John Fenwick, in whose family it had been since the early fifteenth century. Fenwick was driven to sell through his own extravagance and financial incompetence. He was also politically foolish, engaging in plots on behalf of the deposed James II, which resulted in 1697 in his execution as a traitor. What Blackett acquired was an old house and medieval tower, which he demolished, retaining only their ground floor to become the cellars of its replacement. The house we see today, however, is the product of its restyling (and the addition of the Clock Tower Gate) between 1738 and 1754 (to the designs of Daniel Garrett) by his grandson, Sir Walter Calverley Blackett (1707–77). The son of Sir William's daughter, Julia Blackett (1686–1736) and her husband, Sir Walter Calverley (1669–1749), he complicated the family genealogy by adding his mother's maiden surname to his to become Sir Walter Calverley Blackett. The only significant architectural change initiated by the Trevelyans was the roofing in 1853–54 by JOHN DOBSON of the central courtyard to create a comfortable sitting room.

Unlike the Fenwicks and the Blacketts, the Trevelyans were incomers. In origin a Cornish family, they settled at Nettlecombe in Somerset in the fifteenth century on an estate they acquired through marriage. Their association with Wallington was the consequence of the marriage of Julia Calverley (1706–85), the sister of Sir Walter Calverley Blackett, to Sir George Trevelyan, 3rd Baronet of Nettlecombe (1707–68). It was their son, Sir John Trevelyan (1734–1828), who inherited both Wallington and Nettlecombe on the death without male children of Sir Walter Calverley Blackett in 1777.

In 1846 Sir John's grandson, Sir Walter Calverley Trevelyan (1797–1879) inherited the two estates. In 1835 he had married a clergyman's daughter, Paulina Jermyn (1816–66). They were an incongruous yet harmonious couple: he was nearly twenty years her senior, a teetotaller, with serious scholastic interests, and was both high-minded and narrow-minded; she was highly intelligent, well educated and vivacious with a great interest in the arts. He accepted her friendships with John Ruskin and Algernon Swinburne, who were frequent guests at Wallington, and largely tolerated her indifference to the former's paedophilic and the latter's pornographic activities and proclivities. The couple's lasting artistic contribution to Wallington, which she commissioned but he paid for, is the set of eight murals that still adorn the walls of the sitting room Dobson created for them by roofing the courtyard. These pictures, painted between 1857 and 1861 by another of her artist friends, WILLIAM BELL SCOTT, depict some of the great events in Northumbria's history.

On Sir Walter Calverley Trevelyan's death the Nettlecombe and Wallington estates parted company. The descent of the former was governed by an entail and therefore had to pass with the baronetcy to Sir Walter's nearest male cousin. The latter, however, which he was free to dispose of by will, he bequeathed to another cousin, Sir Charles Edward Trevelyan (1809–86). In the next hundred years, this man, his son and two of his grandsons were to leave their mark on national life. Sir Charles's public life began in the 1830s in India, where he was influential with his brother-in-law, Thomas Babington (later Lord) Macaulay, in getting English accepted as the common language of the Indian subcontinent. Back home, he was Chief Secretary to the Treasury during the great famine in Ireland in the late 1840s which arose from the failure of the potato harvests. The decisions he made as regards government assistance were controversial and have brought upon him a great deal of opprobrium. In 1860 he played a major role in replacing patronage by competitive examination as the means of entry to all departments of the permanent civil service, except the Foreign Office and for posts requiring professional qualifications. For his public services he was granted a baronetcy in 1874.

When Sir Charles died in 1886, he was succeeded by his only son, Sir George Otto Trevelyan (1838–1928). Throughout his long political life he was a radical, strongly supporting such causes as the liberation of the Italian states from Austrian rule and their unification, state control of the sale of alcohol, the abolition of the system of purchasing commissions in the army, and the extension of the county franchise. He was also pro-Boer during the South African War (1899–1902) and pro-Suffragette, although by then he had retired from public life. He held office in all four of Gladstone's governments and was in the Cabinet in the 1880s and early 1890s as Secretary for Ireland, Chancellor of the Duchy of Lancaster and Secretary for Scotland. Being a man of unbending principle, he resigned twice: first, in opposition to the proposal to grant public funds to church schools; secondly, and surprisingly, over Gladstone's bill to grant Home Rule to Ireland. But he was not simply a politician. In the course of his life he wrote several serious books, two on India, where he went as his father's secretary, *The Life and Letters of Lord Macaulay*, who was his uncle; *The Early Life of Charles James Fox*, the eighteenth-century radical politician; and *The American Revolution* in six volumes. In addition, he managed the Wallington estate sufficiently well to leave it clear of mortgages. He turned down a peerage, but did accept the OM in 1911.

Given his father's unrelenting radical attitudes, it is not surprising that Sir Charles Philips Trevelyan (1870–1958), his eldest son, who succeeded to the estate and the title in 1928, eventually became a member of the Labour Party. As the Liberal MP for Elland in Yorkshire from 1899, he favoured the abolition of the House of Lords and independence for Ireland, but on the outbreak of war in 1914 he resigned his post as Secretary of the Board of Education, siding with those who advocated a negotiated peace, for which stance he lost his seat in the 1918 election. Joining the Labour Party, he was elected as the MP for Newcastle Central in 1922 and held the Education post in the Labour governments of 1924 and 1929, when he put forward a proposal, which was rejected, to raise the school leaving age. With the fall of that government in 1931, he retired from political life, complaining that his party was not fully socialist. Like many left-wing visionaries, he was an unswerving supporter of the Soviet regime that came into power after the Russian Revolution of 1917, remaining undeterred by the growing evidence of its iniquities.

The third and youngest of Sir George Otto's sons, George Macaulay Trevelyan (1876–1962), had a more distinguished and fruitful career. Appropriately, as a man bearing the name of his illustrious forebear, the historian Lord Macaulay, he dedicated his life to the study of history. Between 1909 and 1953 he wrote and published twelve substantial academic works, roughly one every three and a half years. His range was broad, encompassing the Italian *Risorgimento*, late fourteenth-century England, the Stuart period, and England in the nineteenth century. As well as these broad studies, he produced biographies of the 2ND EARL GREY; VISCOUNT GREY OF FALLODON; John Bright, the radical politician whom his father had supported in the early years of his political career; and the statesman and novelist John Buchan. In 1927 he became Regius Professor of Modern History at Cambridge and upon his retirement in 1940 he remained at Cambridge as Master of Trinity College, until 1951. The previous year he became Chancellor of Durham University, a post he held until 1958. In 1930 he too was awarded the OM. The Trevelyans hold the distinction of being the only father and son to be so honoured.

Wallington Hall was finally opened to the public in 1968, two years after the death of Sir Charles Philips Trevelyan's wife, Molly.

TRISTRAM, HENRY BAKER (1822–1906)

Although he spent almost all his life in the North East, Henry Tristram's reputation is as the outstanding natural historian of the Near East. The son of the Vicar of Eglingham, he was educated at Durham School and at Lincoln College, Oxford, gaining a BA degree in 1844 and an MA degree in 1846. In the latter year he was also ordained priest in the Church of England and almost immediately, because of poor health, became a naval chaplain serving in the West Indies. He returned to the North East in 1849 to become Rector of Castle Eden. Eleven years later, in 1860, he was appointed Master of Greatham Hospital (see MEDIEVAL HOSPITALS), where he remained until 1874. In that year he became a Residentiary Canon of DURHAM CATHEDRAL, which enabled him to live in the College until his death in 1906.

His fame rests on the work he did abroad, where he spent much time for the sake of his health. Between 1865 and 1891 he published seven important geological and natural history studies of Palestine, based upon detailed and meticulous observation. His studies formed the basis of all subsequent geological and biological work on this region, and they made him a firm supporter of Charles Darwin's theory of evolution. He was also an avid collector, amassing a collection of 20,000 birds, which are now in the Natural History Museum.

TROLLOPE, ROBERT (?–1686)

Robert Trollope was either born or settled in York, where he practised as a mason and was made a freeman of the city in 1647. From 1655, however, he settled in the North East, where his most important work was done. What brought him there was the commission he received in 1655 from the Corporation of NEWCASTLE to build a new Guildhall and Merchant Adventurers' Hall, which he completed in 1658. Trollope's building almost certainly incorporated parts of the medieval Guildhall and its immediate neighbour, the hospital known as the Maison Dieu, founded in the fifteenth century by the wealthy merchant Roger Thornton. The new Guildhall was part of Newcastle's recovery from the destruction wrought during the siege and storming by the Scots in 1647 (see Scottish Occupation 1644–1647). For his work he was made a freeman of Newcastle.

Trollope settled at Redheugh, near Gateshead, and embarked upon a busy and successful career. His first commission was to complete the church of Christ Church at North Shields (see TYNEMOUTH AND NORTH SHIELDS), one of the few new churches to be started during the Cromwellian regime. Thereafter most of his commissions were for houses for the Northumberland gentry. In 1667 he was commissioned by Sir John Swinburne to build Capheaton Hall. Not to be outdone, Swinburne's son-in-law, Nicholas Thornton, hired him in 1672 to build Netherwitton Hall. Although conclusive evidence is lacking, it seems very likely that he designed Bockenfield Hall, the south front of Callaly Castle for the Claverings, alterations to Widdrington Castle, which was demolished around 1775, and a small fort on the Heugh on HOLY ISLAND. His only known work in County Durham is the font in St Hilda's church, SOUTH SHIELDS.

His style has been described as 'a vigouous and individual style of vernacular baroque, totally free of academic inhibition, but strongly inventive'. It is, therefore, a cause of regret that so much of what he did is now masked by later additions and alterations. For example, although the interior of the Guildhall at Newcastle is still identifiably Trollope's, the exterior frontages were rebuilt in 1791–93 and 1809. Trollope died in December 1686. It is said that he was buried in a mausoleum he had built in St Mary's churchyard, which in the mid-nineteenth century was repaired and used by another family.

TUNSTALL, CUTHBERT (1474–1559)

Cuthbert Tunstall was Bishop of Durham from 1530 until 1559, the crucial thirty-year period of the English Reformation. His career illustrates how the problem of conscience and belief, in conflict with the natural desire to survive and prosper, beset the clergy during these turbulent years. Born to a Lancashire gentry family, his career pattern was typical of the high-flying university-trained scholar in the late medieval world. His university education, covering the years between *c.*1490 and 1506, involved study at Oxford and Cambridge, and also Padua, where he became a Doctor of Law. On his return to England, he embarked on a conventional dual occupation of the late medieval university graduate: service in the royal administration and advancement in the church. In royal service, he was employed as an ambassador on several occasions to the court of the Emperor Charles V (where he became friends with the great Dutch scholar Erasmus), and in the field of law he became Master of the

Rolls in 1516 and Lord Privy Seal in 1523. The previous year, after enjoying a number of rectories, an archdeaconry and a cathedral deanery, all lucrative preferments, he was made Bishop of London. Then, early in 1530, he became Bishop of Durham in succession to CARDINAL THOMAS WOLSEY. He was now fifty-six years of age and should have been able to enjoy years of high status and wealth.

In fact, for the rest of his long life he faced the problem of how to cling on to his episcopal status while retaining the religious beliefs with which he had grown up. Throughout, he was never a bigot and was never willing to be the instrument of persecution. Although he was staunch in his commitment to the doctrines and practices of the Catholic Church, he had no inclination to martyrdom. This was due partly to his natural temperament, but it is equally true that he was by training loyal to the state. During the later years of Henry VIII's reign it proved possible for him to square this circle, and, although opposed to what was happening, he was retained in state service, becoming President of the newly created Council of the North.

In the following reign, that of the under-age Edward VI (1547–53), this proved to be impossible. Under Edward's first Protector, Edward Seymour, Duke of Somerset, he survived, even though he opposed the closing of the chantries and allowing priests to marry. But under Somerset's successor, John Dudley, Duke of Northumberland, his episcopal career collapsed in ruins when in 1552 the Bishopric of Durham was abolished, Dudley's intention being to appropriate its huge wealth. His personal suffering, however, amounted to no more than house arrest in London, and this enforced leisure gave him the time to write *De Veritate Corporis et Sanguinis Domini nostri Jesu Christi in Eucharistia* (Concerning the Truth of the Body and Blood of Our Lord Jesus Christ in the Eucharist), which was not only a reinforcement of his personal conviction but also an accurate description of Catholic doctrine.

Tunstall's career, and also the Bishopric of Durham, were saved by the death in 1553 of Edward VI and the accession of his strongly Catholic half-sister, Mary. The following year the Bishopric was re-established and Tunstall was restored as its bishop. His gratitude did not extend, however, to involvement in the orgy of persecution of Protestants initiated by the queen. In 1558, however, Mary died and was succeeded by Henry VIII's second daughter, Elizabeth, who devised a hybrid solution to the urgent ecclesiastical and religious questions of the day. Tunstall, who was now eighty-four years old, and probably terminally ill, at last found the courage of his conviction. He refused to take the Oath of Supremacy, by which he would have recognised Elizabeth as Supreme Governor of the Church of England, and to consecrate Elizabeth's choice, Matthew Parker, as Archbishop of Canterbury. Consequently, he was deprived of his office. He was not, however, maltreated but given into the keeping of the new archbishop and allowed to live in Lambeth Palace until his death a few weeks later.

A portrait purporting to be of Tunstall hangs in the Throne Room of AUCKLAND CASTLE and is the earliest known likeness of any Bishop of Durham. His most visible monument is the gallery that bears his name and masks the lower part of the great North Range of Durham Castle, built by BISHOP HUGH OF LE PUISET in the twelfth century.

TURBINIA

Turbinia was the ship that triggered a revolution in marine propulsion by revealing the superior driving power of the steam turbine. The turbine was invented by CHARLES (later SIR CHARLES) PARSONS, in the 1880s while he was working at Clarke, Chapman & Co. in Gateshead. At the end of the decade, he left Clarke, Chapman and set up his own company to manufacture turbo-generators. From this, he moved on to the idea of the turbine as a means of marine propulsion, and in 1894 started a new company, the Marine Steam Turbine Co. in Wallsend. *Turbinia* was the almost immediate outcome.

The ship was designed by Parsons and built at Wallsend by Brown and Hood. She was 109 feet (33.2 m) long and only 9 feet (2.7 m) in beam with a draught of 3 feet (90 cm). Parsons also designed engines, but there was a lengthy period of experimentation before he achieved what he wanted. In the end, *Turbinia* had three shafts, each with three propellers and each driven by its own turbine. The result was enough power to achieve nearly 35 knots. During this period of development, Parsons' work was followed with interest by Sir William White (1845–1913), the Director of Naval Construction at the Admiralty from 1885 until 1902, who had previously worked for SIR WILLIAM ARMSTRONG at Elswick.

The full potential of the new means of propulsion was revealed at the review of the fleet held at Spithead on 16 June 1897 to mark Queen Victoria's Diamond Jubilee. This was without doubt a planned 'publicity stunt', but one of which the Admiralty, or at least Sir William White, must have been aware. The audience for the 'performance' was the assembled might of the British navy, which was treated to a daring and audacious display of navigation and speeds of up to 34½ knots. The demonstration had the intended effect. Within two years the Royal Navy had built two turbine-driven destroyers, and although both came to early and tragic ends, no fault was attributed to their new means of propulsion. In fact, in 1905, the Admiralty was so convinced of the virtues of the steam turbine that it decreed that all future naval vessels should be turbine-driven. In the following year the first of the new generation of battleships, HMS *Dreadnought* was launched at Portsmouth and fitted with turbine propulsion.

Turbinia, her job done, was in effect retired. However, in 1907, she was badly damaged by a ship launched on the other bank of the Tyne. Although repaired, she languished at her moorings until 1926, when she was offered to the Science Museum at South Kensington. Unfortunately, the museum did not have adequate accommodation and as a result *Turbinia* suffered the indignity of being cut in two, one half going to South Kensington, the other eventually being housed in the Newcastle Science Museum in Exhibition Park. This remained the situation until 1959, when the South Kensington museum wanted to be rid of its half, which returned to Newcastle by road. The two halves were reunited and put on display in 1961. But the result was not really satisfactory and *Turbinia* was deteriorating. Consequently, in 1983, she was removed for a thorough renovation, which involved stripping down the engines and restoring the hull to its original condition. In 1994, the centenary of her launch, *Turbinia* was rehoused in a specially designed gallery in the Newcastle Discovery Museum (see MUSEUMS), where her appearance is as it was when she astonished the world at Spithead.

TURGOT (c.1050–1115)

Turgot came to be one of the most influential men in the North East and in Scotland in the late eleventh and early twelfth centuries. He was born in the Lindsey district of North Lincolnshire into what appears to have been a middle-ranking family. His training as a clerk in holy orders suggests that he was a younger son. During the early and turbulent phase of the Norman Conquest he was for some reason held as a hostage in the newly built castle at Lincoln. However, he bribed his way free and escaped by ship from Grimsby to Norway. There he was made welcome at the court of the King of Norway and was able to earn a living by teaching psalmody. In the early 1070s he must have felt that the situation in England was sufficiently settled for him to return, but his journey home ended in disaster when he was shipwrecked, probably somewhere on the North East coast, and lost all his belongings.

This may help to explain why he went to seek the help of Walcher, the Bishop of Durham. He recommended that Turgot join the religious community recently established, with Walcher's blessing, in the ruins of the ancient monastery at JARROW by a group of monks from the West Midlands led by ALDWINE. Turgot accepted this suggestion, but as a clerk, not as a monk. Shortly afterwards he took part in Aldwine's attempt to restart monastic life at Melrose, another of Northumbria's ancient monasteries, an attempt that ended in failure. On his return from Scotland, Turgot finally became a monk at Monkwearmouth, the sister monastery of Jarrow, also revived by Aldwine.

In the 1080s Turgot rose from obscurity to eminence. His advancement began in 1083, when the new Bishop of Durham, WILLIAM OF ST CALAIS, reformed his cathedral chapter by replacing the pre-Conquest Community of St Cuthbert (see CUTHBERT, SAINT) with a Benedictine monastery composed of the monks from Jarrow and Monkwearmouth. Inevitably, Aldwine was its first prior, but on Aldwine's death in 1087 Turgot was elected as his replacement.

During the next twelve years Turgot was the leading figure in the diocese. Between 1088 and 1091, when St Calais was exiled for political offences, and again between 1096 and 1099, when King William II declined to appoint a new bishop after St Calais's death, Turgot was the senior ecclesiastic in the North of England, and after 1093 with enhanced authority as archdeacon. Although he had considerable power, it was insufficient to secure the return to Durham's control of the church of TYNEMOUTH, which the Earl of Northumberland, Robert de Mowbray, had handed over to St Albans Abbey. But he did have in the years before 1093 considerable influence in Scotland. His authority as archdeacon then extended into Teviotdale, as was shown by his ability to order the expulsion of the murderer of Bishop Walcher from sanctuary in the church at Jedburgh. More importantly, he spent much time at the Scottish royal court, where he was the spiritual adviser and supporter of Queen Margaret in her work to reform the Scottish church.

By 1099, when RANNULF FLAMBARD was appointed as Bishop of Durham, Turgot was a figure of authority, which his community needed to withstand the authoritarian ways of their new, non-monastic bishop. It was Turgot who organised the translation of the body of St Cuthbert to his final resting place in the new cathedral, started in 1093 and now sufficiently built for the ceremony to take place. One of the men present at that ceremony was Alexander, brother of Edgar, King of Scots, but more significantly one of the sons of Queen Margaret. When Alexander succeeded Edgar as king in 1107, he invited Turgot to become Bishop of St Andrews, an office that had been unfilled since the death in 1093 of its previous bishop, Flothad. As he grew up, Alexander would have become familiar with Turgot during his visits to the royal court in his mother's lifetime, and would have been aware of her request that Turgot write her biography. This Turgot did between 1100 and 1107, dedicating it to Margaret's daughter, Edith, whose name was changed to Matilda on her marriage to the English king, Henry

I. Although Turgot's book is considerably hagiographical, it contains a great deal of information about Queen Margaret and the Scotland of her time. Turgot's time in Scotland appears not to have been particularly happy and he resigned his office to return to Durham shortly before he died in 1115.

To Turgot must go much of the credit for establishing the Cathedral Priory of Durham on a firm footing and defining its relationship with a non-monastic bishop, and also for helping to reform the Scottish church, which was part of the Norman 'conquest' of that country.

TURNER, WILLIAM (c.1508–1568)

William Turner has been given the accolade 'father of English botany', which, like all such attributions, contains some truth while being an oversimplification. He was born some time between 1508 and 1512 in Morpeth, where his father was a tanner and presumably a burgess of the borough. Of his schooling nothing is known, although it is not unreasonable to think that it was at the Chantry School, the forerunner of King Edward VI Grammar School. Certainly it was of a grammar school quality, since in 1526 he was admitted to Pembroke Hall (now College), Cambridge, a college that appears to have drawn a number of its students from Northumberland, including the martyr NICHOLAS RIDLEY. Turner spent the next twelve years at Pembroke, pursuing a successful academic career.

These same years were also the early years of the English Reformation, when expressing pronounced opinions on matters religious could be dangerous. And Turner clearly did hold strong views of an increasingly Protestant nature. During the late 1530s this carried little risk, since under Henry VIII's chief minister, Thomas Cromwell, the government's religious policy had evident Protestant leanings. However, on Cromwell's fall and execution in 1540, Henry VIII adopted a more conservative position. Turner's reaction was to seek safety in a self-imposed exile, which lasted until Henry VIII's death in 1547. During the seven years he was abroad, his scientific knowledge was considerably enhanced through his studies at the University of Ferrara, which awarded him the degree of MD, and then under two of the most eminent scientific minds in Europe, Luca Ghini in Bologna and Conrad Gesner in Zurich.

The accession of Henry VIII's son, the young Edward VI, brought to power the new king's uncle, the Duke of Somerset, who was resolved to push England in the Protestant direction. Consequently, it became safe for Turner to return home. As he had been in holy orders since 1537, he hoped to secure a wealthy church living that would allow him to pursue his research at leisure. Eventually he was made Dean of Wells, although this was not a particularly well-endowed office. But his career in England was cut short by the death in July 1553 of the young Edward VI and the succession of his half-sister, the ardent Roman Catholic Mary I. Turner again did the prudent thing, exiling himself to the continent, more particularly to the Rhineland.

This second exile too benefited his scholarship in that it enabled him to meet other scholars and to make comparisons between English and European plants and animals. His second exile lasted until the death of Mary brought Elizabeth I to the throne in 1558. Prudently, Turner waited until it was clear that the new queen would impose a basically Protestant regime on the English church before returning home. His homecoming was not, however, particularly pleasant. He had to engage in a prolonged struggle to oust the Marian incumbent of the Deanery of Wells, and thereafter he failed to get preferment to a more prestigious living or, what he may have hoped for, the mastership of a university college. Turner's failure to get the ecclesiastical advancement his talents merited was probably due to his rather 'left-wing' views: instead of accepting the hybrid arrangements that Queen Elizabeth imposed on the church, he made clear his opposition to the retention of what he considered to be the vestiges of 'popery'. As his health deteriorated in the 1560s, he became a querulous and embittered man. He died in London, where he lived in preference to Wells, in 1568.

How then did he come by the title of 'father of English botany'? His reputation is based upon his massive work, *A New Herbal*, which was published in three volumes in 1551, 1562 and 1568, the last volume being essentially an addendum to the other two. What the work does is to give detailed descriptions of plants and their habitats based upon scrupulous, minute and accurate observations, together with critical references to earlier authorities. He also carefully recorded the medicinal properties of the plants. Herein lies the pointer to the direction from which he approached his subject: Turner was by training a doctor and consequently the basic purpose of his studies was, as the title of his work clearly indicates, medicinal. The modern concept of botany, with its concern for classification and experimentation, was far in the future, so that it would be unfair to describe Turner as a botanist in the modern sense of that term. However, his work on plants was far more erudite, comprehensive and critical than anything that had been previously published. Both in England and abroad, *A New Herbal* was held in the highest esteem and it laid the foundation for future research and new approaches.

A New Herbal was the culmination of a lifetime's interest in the study of plants. As early as 1538 he had written a short work, *Libellus de re herbaria novus* (A New Pamphlet on Herbal Matters), which he followed in 1549 with another, this time in English, *The Names of Herbes in Greke, Latin, Duche and French*. In addition, Turner also devoted time to the study of birds, so much so that he has also been called 'the father of English ornithology', and he also wrote briefly on fish. Rather than see him as a proto-botanist, it is more accurate to apply to him the title of natural historian, the term that continued to be used until the nineteenth century.

TURNPIKE ROADS

Unlike its near neighbours on the continent, Britain has proved to be highly resistant to the idea of an integrated toll-charging motorway system, which may help to explain why this country still lacks a completely adequate road system. Yet in the eighteenth and early nineteenth centuries this type of road was created in Britain to link the major centres of population. Like modern motorways, they too were built piecemeal, but unlike today's roads they were the products of private enterprise, albeit under parliamentary control. 'Turnpike mania' reached its height in the third quarter of the eighteenth century when parliament passed 389 turnpike acts, creating trusts which were permitted to mend specified lengths of road for prescribed periods of time (usually twenty-one years) and to levy payment for their use according to a tariff of charges.

Between 1745 and 1833 thirteen turnpike trusts were created in Northumberland and nineteen in Durham, the effect of which was to place 880 miles (1,416 km) of road in the two counties under the control of the thirty-two trusts. Each of the Northumberland trusts was responsible for on average 31 miles (50 km), while the figure for Durham was 24 miles (37 km). And the work does appear to have been done, the records indicating that the trusts spent around 70 per cent of their receipts on road repair.

Not surprisingly, the earliest trusts were concerned to improve the main routes. Acts passed in 1745, 1747 and 1753 placed what is now the A1 between Boroughbridge and Berwick, a distance of 98 miles (158 km), under trust control. Other roads soon followed, for example, Durham–Sunderland (A690), Durham–Stockton (A177) and Morpeth–Coldstream (A697). By 1833 all the main towns of the region were linked by turnpike roads. To a considerable extent the present road system follows that created by the turnpike trusts.

The turnpike system was always unpopular and did not outlast the nineteenth century. County councils, set up in 1888, were given responsibility for main roads, while the maintenance of minor roads passed to the Urban and Rural District Councils that were brought into being in 1894. This was the culmination of developments that had been in progress for some years, whereby the magistrates and parish authorities had become more involved in road maintenance. This in turn made possible the Turnpike Trust Act of 1874, which permitted the government to interdict the renewal of a trust after its expiry date. As a result, all turnpike trusts had become defunct by 1895.

TYNEDALE, REGALITY OF

Like the Regality of Redesdale, the Regality of Tynedale was a district where almost all the functions of government were vested in someone other than the agents of the English Crown. Unlike Redesdale and all other similar regalities, the holder of the Tynedale franchise was a foreign monarch, the King of Scots. It was created in 1157 by Henry II as part of his solution to an anomaly that had existed since 1139. In that year, Henry's predecessor, Stephen, by a treaty agreed at Durham, conceded to the then King of Scots, David I, the Earldom of Northumbria. David immediately installed his heir, Henry, as the earl. When Earl Henry died prematurely in 1152, David appointed Henry's eldest son, the eleven-year-old Malcolm, as the new earl. It would seem from this that David's intention was that the Earldom of Northumbria should be the endowment and a training ground for the heir to the Scottish throne.

In the following two years, however, the political situation changed. In 1153 David I died and his grandson, the young Malcolm, succeeded him as Malcolm IV. A year later, Stephen died and Henry Plantagenet, then aged twenty-one, came to the English throne as Henry II. He tolerated the 1139 arrangement until 1157, when he summoned Malcolm to Chester and demanded the return of the Earldom. Malcolm, still only sixteen, had neither the age and experience, nor the power, to resist. To soften the blow to his pride, Henry granted to him the Regality of Tynedale, comprising North Tynedale, the South Tyne (except for Alston and the lands of the Barony of Langley) and part of Allendale, an area covering nearly 250,000 acres (10,000 ha).

This situation would have continued indefinitely had not the Scottish royal family died out with the deaths of Alexander III in 1286 and his infant granddaughter, Margaret, in 1290. Because of this the regality fell back into the hands of Edward I. Until then, the regality was governed by the Scottish kings from its 'capital' at Wark on Tyne, where the vestigial remains of the motte of the castle are still visible at the southern edge of the village, and Scottish judges dispensed justice, albeit in accordance with English law. Edward I did not abolish the regality, presumably because he expected to hand it back to a future King of Scots: at that stage he could not have known how bad relations between the two countries were to become.

Instead, he handed it over to the Bishop of Durham, Anthony Bek. By the time Bek died in 1311, however, England and Scotland were at war, which made the idea of returning Tynedale to the King of Scots unthinkable. Between 1311 and 1336, the regality passed through five different hands, until in the latter year Edward III gave it to his wife, Philippa. After her death in 1369 it passed to their fifth son, Edmund, Duke of York, whose great-grandsons became king as Edward IV (1461–83) and Richard III (1483–85).

The regality was formally incorporated into the Crown estate in 1484 and so it remained until 1604, when James VI and I gave it, together with the neighbouring Regality of Redesdale, to George Home, Earl of Dunbar, one of his favourites and the man he charged with pacifying the Border. By that time, however, as a result of the suppression of franchises by Henry VIII, Dunbar got the land, but not the jurisdiction. The regality was now fully part of Northumberland.

TYNEMOUTH AND NORTH SHIELDS

Tynemouth and North Shields, seemingly so separate and so different, are in fact parts of a whole. The history of Tynemouth can be traced back to the Iron Age, when a fort was constructed on the promontory on which the ruins of the priory now stand. The same site was occupied by a Northumbrian monastery, founded about the year 700, one of a string of such establishments on coastal sites from St Abb's Head to Whitby. Almost nothing is known about this monastery, except that its existence ended in the second half of the ninth century during the Viking incursions. However, a church dedicated to ST OSWINE remained in use, since its roof was destroyed only in 1072. Before his death in 1080, Bishop WALCHER of Durham gave this church to the monks who had restarted monastic life at JARROW in 1074. They repaired the roof and installed one of their number as a resident monk. In 1083 Walcher's successor, WILLIAM OF ST CALAIS transferred the monks at Jarrow (and also at Monkwearmouth) to DURHAM to be the new chapter of his cathedral, reducing Jarrow and Monkwearmouth to the status of subordinate cells. It was assumed that this would also be the role of Tynemouth.

But this did not happen, thanks to a dispute between St Calais and the Earl of Northumberland, Robert de Mowbray. The cause of their quarrel is not clear, but one issue may have been that Mowbray believed that Tynemouth belonged to the earl, not the bishop, and that therefore Walcher's gift, made when he held both offices, could not be permanent. The upshot was that Mowbray forcibly repossessed Tynemouth and gave it to the Hertfordshire abbey of St Albans, whose abbot, Paul, was a relation. The date is uncertain, but according to St Albans tradition it was 1090. The monks of Durham Priory refused to acquiesce in their loss until 1174, when they agreed to accept two Northumberland parish churches, Edlingham and Bywell St Peter, in return for abandoning their claim to Tynemouth.

Tynemouth Priory was the largest and wealthiest monastery in Northumberland, despite being a dependent cell of another house. It owned thirty-two places in the county, which constituted the Liberty of Tynemouth. Within this franchise, the Prior of Tynemouth exercised virtually all functions of government, powers made explicit in a charter issued by Richard I in 1189. In addition, the priory owned ten churches in the county from which it drew all the income, paying only modest salaries to the resident vicars. When the value of monasteries was assessed in the 1530s,

Tynemouth was reckoned to have had an annual income of £730, about 150 per cent greater than that of its nearest competitor, HEXHAM.

This combination of wealth and power and subordinate status was a recipe for trouble. Naturally, the monks of Tynemouth sought separation from distant St Albans and in the 1290s they made a serious attempt to achieve it. The leader of the independence movement was a monk named Simon de Walden, who in 1293 appealed to Edward I, claiming that Tynemouth did not belong to St Albans but to the Crown. Although the verdict went against him, his rebellion was ended only by physical force: in April 1295 the Abbot of St Albans, John de Berkhampstead, came north and with the aid of a body of Novocastrians led by Henry Scott, stormed the Priory and captured the rebel monks, who were taken to St Albans in chains.

NEWCASTLE's willingness to assist is explained by another piece of unilateral enterprise on the part of the Tynemouth community. This began around 1225, when the then prior, German, began what was to become North Shields by building twenty-seven dwellings at the mouth of the Pow Burn, with the clear intention of developing a port. Had this been allowed to continue, it would have become a serious threat to Newcastle's claim to control the navigation and trade of the river. In 1260 Peter Scott, the first mayor of Newcastle, led a party of thugs to destroy the growing town, but in doing so he put his town on the wrong side of the law. In the 1290s, however, Newcastle got its way through the more legitimate method of bringing a case before parliament, arguing that the growth of North Shields would diminish Newcastle, which would be to the Crown's financial detriment. This argument was irresistable and North Shields was reduced to the status of fishing village. To some degree this judgement was decisive, although it could not completely suppress what was an obvious location for economic development. A century later it was clear that North Shields had survived and was flourishing: it was reported in 1390 that there were 200 houses there and that there was a lively export trade in fish, salt, wool, hides and coal, as well as fishing and provisioning of visiting ships. Occasional evidence from the fifteenth century confirms this development. But in 1530 Newcastle's exclusive right to the trade of the river from 'Sparhawk to Headwin Streams' (river mouth to Newburn) was confirmed, a decision that was to stunt the growth of North Shields for another 200 years.

Tynemouth Priory was closed in January 1539, its monks pensioned off and the franchise ended. By that date its original Norman buildings had been replaced in a rebuilding programme begun *c.*1190, the remains of which are still extant, together with a small chantry chapel built in the fifteenth century by the PERCY FAMILY at the east end of the choir. But it had also become a defended site. In 1296 a licence to crenellate was granted, allowing a wall, parts of which still stand, to be built around the edge of the promontory. Then in the 1390s the present fortified gatehouse was built, following the scare of 1389, when in the year after the defeat of Hotspur at OTTERBURN, a Scottish raid reached the gates of the priory.

By 1539, however, these defences were antiquated and also did nothing to protect the mouth of the Tyne from attack from the sea. Both considerations became urgent in the 1540s, when Henry VIII went to war with Scotland in an attempt to get the regency government in Edinburgh to agree to the marriage of his young son, Edward, and Mary, the infant Queen of Scots. This war, christened by Sir Walter Scott the 'Rough Wooing', meant that Northumberland was threatened by a Scottish invasion from the land and a French invasion from the sea. To counter this, the government sent the foremost English fortifications expert, Sir Richard Lee, and two Italian experts, Gian Tommaso Scala and Antonio da Bergamo, to inspect the defences and propose improvements. The proposed Italian solution was two demi-bastions, similar to those at BERWICK, at the northern and southern ends of the site, linked by a wall so as to enclose not only the promontory on which the former priory stood, but also the bluff overlooking the mouth of the river and the small harbour known as the Prior's Haven. This was not acted upon. Instead, a ditch 400 feet (122 m) long was dug to enclose the enlarged site, the excavated soil being used to create a wall 40 feet (12 m) thick on its inner rim, and on the bluff a two-tier gun platform was constructed. Long known as the Spanish Battery, it takes its name from the force of Spanish mercenary troops stationed there in 1544 by Edward Seymour, Earl of Hertford (later Duke of Somerset), who commanded that year's English invasion of Scotland. In addition, the castle walls were strengthened and another gun platform built in front of them.

The end of the Anglo-Scottish wars did not remove the need for defensive arrangements at the mouth of the Tyne and so artillery continued to be mounted at the Castle and the Spanish Battery (and also Clifford's Fort – see below). In the twentieth century, before, during and between the two world wars against Germany, various combinations of naval guns (5.5-inch, 6-inch and 9.2-inch) were mounted at these sites and were not finally stood down until 1956, when the entire Coastal Artillery system was disbanded. Today, some of the battery buildings and an immobilised 6-inch gun at the Castle are parts of the site maintained by English Heritage.

The threat from the Dutch in the 1660s and 1670s led to additional defence of the entrance to the Tyne in the form of Clifford's Fort, built at North Shields in 1672. It took its name from Sir Thomas Clifford, one of Charles II's five closest advisers in the 1670s, whose initials have given us the word CABAL (Clifford, Arlington, Buckingham, Ashley Cooper and Lauderdale). The occasion of its construction was the Third Dutch War (1672–74) and the fort's designer was a Swedish engineer, Martin Beckmann. It was under the command of the Governor of Tynemouth Castle until 1839 and in 1888 it became the base of the Tyne Division Royal Engineers (Volunteers) Submarine Miners. This was a remarkable unit of twenty-six men raised the previous year and largely paid for by Sir Charles Palmer, the purpose of which was to lay and to maintain mines on the bed of the river that could be electronically detonated in the event of an enemy incursion. It was the model for similar units formed in six other British rivers: Clyde, Forth, Humber, Mersey, Severn and Tees. This function was discontinued in 1907, but the unit continued to exist until 1928 as the Tyne Division, Royal Engineers (Volunteers) Electrical Engineers.

As well as Clifford's Fort, another important building was erected in North Shields in the second half of the seventeenth century. This was the new parish church, Christ Church, to replace that in the old priory. Paid for by the Earl of Northumberland, it was begun in 1654 (though not finished until 1668) and with Holy Trinity, Berwick upon Tweed, was a very rare example of new church building in the Commonwealth (1649–60) period. The late eighteenth and early nineteenth centuries saw further development of North Shields in the form of the new town, laid out on the plateau above the riverside settlement on land acquired from the Earl of Carlisle, and the rebuilding of

Christ Church between 1786 and 1793. On the riverside, the New Quay was built in 1806 by the 2nd Duke of Northumberland to the west of the old quayside.

The middle and later decades of the nineteenth century saw rapid development in both Tynemouth and North Shields. Constitutionally, they were transformed: in 1831 Tynemouth, North Shields, Chirton, Preston and Cullercoats became a parliamentary borough, and in 1849 the same townships were united as an incorporated municipal borough with a governing body comprising a mayor, six aldermen and eighteen councillors. Between these dates, in 1833, North Shields became a port of registration, its letters SN to be carried by all vessels between North Shields and Alnmouth, except, after 1897, those at Blyth. Also, in 1848, North Shields became a customs port. The 1833 and 1848 acts effectively liberated North Shields from the commercial dominance of Newcastle and were evidence of its recent growth, and potential for further expansion, as a port.

The same period also saw Tynemouth and North Shields diverge as regards function. The former became primarily a residential suburb and a holiday resort, a development made possible by the arrival of the railway, the Newcastle and North Shields Railway in 1847 and the Blyth and Tyne Railway in 1864, both of which were absorbed into the North Eastern Railway Co. Rail travel was improved in 1882 with the opening of the splendid Tynemouth Station and in the first decade of the twentieth century by the electrification of the service to Newcastle. Although diminished as a holiday resort, Tynemouth's role as a commuter town has been reinforced by the development of the Tyneside Metro system (see RAILWAYS).

In contrast, North Shields became a major port. Its role as a fishing port was assisted by the building of the Fish Quay in 1870 by Tynemouth Borough Council and the introduction in the late 1870s by William Purdy of steam-powered screw-propelled trawlers. The expansion of North Shields as a commercial port was made possible by a number of developments. The most fundamental was the dredging and the removal of shoals carried out by the Tyne Improvement Commission, set up in 1850, which finally prised control of the river from the dead hand of Newcastle. Navigation was also assisted by the north and south piers, built between 1854 and 1895, although the north pier, destroyed by the sea in 1898, was not completely restored until 1909. River improvement made feasible the construction, also by the Tyne Improvement Commission, of the Albert Edward Dock, opened in 1882, and the town's involvement in the expanding SHIPBUILDING INDUSTRY with the Tyne Dock and Engineering and the Smith's Dock companies. The industrial age, however, has given way to the post-industrial age as most firms have closed down or moved elsewhere. As regards fishing, North Shields proved unable to compete with larger ports such as Hull and like all other ports has been badly affected by the restrictions made necessary by over-fishing. Neverthless, the Fish Quay still continues to land fish, although the trade is severely diminished.

Over the centuries, maritime danger has occasioned safety measures. The earliest were the High and Low Lights, erected in 1540, shortly after the foundation of Trinity House in Newcastle in 1536, which was charged with making laws governing shipping in the river. The lights were in stone towers, one at river level on the left bank of Pow Burn, the other on the bank top on the other side of Pow Burn. By aligning his approach with a line through these lights, a skipper could avoid the shoals that endangered the entrance to the Tyne. The lights were modernised in 1727 and again in 1808. In 1582, a little over forty years after these lights were established, the government ordered a light to be maintained at the eastern end of the old monastic precinct. This was replaced between 1659 and 1664 by a new lighthouse, which was rebuilt in 1775 and altered in 1802, but continued in use until 1898, when it was demolished. These early lights were eventually made redundant as the Tyne Improvement Commission dredged the river and removed the rocks at its mouth, and modern lights were installed at the pier ends and at St Mary's Island and Souter Point.

Tynemouth also saw the birth of the concept of the Life Volunteer Brigade. It was the brainchild of Captain John Morrison, a member of the Volunteer unit stationed at Tynemouth Castle. It was born on 24 November 1864, when two ships, the *Stanley* and the *Friendship*, were smashed by a violent storm on the Black Middens at the mouth of the Tyne with the loss of twenty-four lives. Morrison's proposal was simple: a volunteer body, available at all times, to assist HM Coastguards in the saving of lives by means of breeches buoy between a stricken ship and the cliff top. To effect this, the volunteers would have rockets to get the lines and the hawser from shore to ship. At a public meeting held on 5 December, his suggestion met with an overwhelming endorsement and response and the Tynemouth Volunteer Life Brigade was formed. Brigades at South Shields and Sunderland soon followed, as did Board of Trade approval, to the extent that it circulated the Tynemouth Brigade's rules to all Coastguard stations in the expectation that similar organisations would be formed.

The Tynemouth Volunteer Life Brigade has functioned continuously since 1865, with sixteen or seventeen volunteers on call at all times, and has saved over 300 lives. It remains a volunteer force, raising its own finances to update its equipment and operating from its Watch House (now a registered museum) built in 1887. Its purpose is still to rescue those in distress on beach, rocks and cliffs, to which has been added preparation of helicopter landing sites in Newcastle for the arrival of medical emergency cases.

In 1974, as a result of the radical reorganisation of local government structure, both Tynemouth and North Shields became part of the Metropolitan District of North Tyneside within the new Metropolitan County of Tyne and Wear, with its boundaries extending as far as the eastern edge of Newcastle. Since 1986, when the Tyne and Wear County Council was abolished, North Tyneside has been a 'unitary authority'.

TYNESIDE FLATS

In 1911 it was reckoned that no more than 3 per cent of the population of England and Wales lived in flats. In sharp contrast, around 60 per cent of the population of Tyneside were flat-dwellers. The reason for this is that since the middle of the nineteenth century the Tyneside Flat had become the predominant form of housing for the working and lower middle classes. On Wearside, the development of the Tyneside Flat was paralleled by the SUNDERLAND COTTAGE.

Tyneside flats were built in terraces and were of two storeys, the ground floor flat being smaller than the one above it. The flats are readily recognisable in that they have two doors side by side, the left hand one opening onto the stairs leading to the upper flat. To the rear was a yard with toilets and coal stores, divided into two halves by a wall so that each flat had its own yard. The occupiers of the upper flat gained access to their portion of the yard by means of an outside stair. After 1866, the by-laws required the yard to occupy one quarter of the plot.

It is uncertain when or by whom this design was created. It may have been devised as early as the 1840s, but there is no certain evidence before the early 1860s. Initially the downstairs flat had two rooms and the upstairs flat three rooms, but after 1880 larger flats with three and four rooms respectively came to predominate. As flats attracted lower middle-class occupiers, they were given features associated with middle-class housing: small front gardens with railings, bay windows, more elaborate door and window frames, and gables.

TYNE TUNNEL

The lower Tyne is a formidable barrier to the north–south movement of goods and people, particularly as both its banks form a continuous and densely built-up area. The problem was steadily exacerbated by the continuous growth of road transport throughout the twentieth century. The scale of the problem is made manifest by the cluster of bridges that now link GATESHEAD and NEWCASTLE. The problem was recognised as early as 1939, when the Ministry of Transport commissioned a feasibility study into the possibility of driving a road tunnel under the river. This reported in 1941, recommending a tunnel between Jarrow and Howden. Naturally, nothing was done until the end of World War II, but in 1946 a private act of parliament authorised the building of the tunnel and in the following year the then Minister of Transport cut the first ceremonial sod.

Thereafter, there were twelve years of inactivity because the government declined to authorise a start and to provide any financial help. The go-ahead was not finally given until 1959, by which date the estimated cost had almost quadrupled. The government undertook to provide a quarter of the cost, the remainder to be raised in the form of loans, to be repaid by money raised from tolls charged to users. Construction began in 1961 and the tunnel was opened to traffic in 1967. At that time it was estimated that 7,000 vehicles a day would pass through the tunnel, rising to 20,000 over a period of twenty years. These proved to be serious underestimates and by 1980 the need for a second tunnel was recognised, the construction of which was authorised in 2007. Until it opens, however, those queuing to enter the present tunnel must await its advent with such patience as they can muster.

UMFRAVILLE FAMILY

For over four hundred years, the Umfraville family was one of the most powerful and influential in Northumberland. They came from Normandy in or after 1066, but exactly where from cannot be known, since there are eight Amfrevilles and one Omfraville in what was then the Duchy of Normandy. Like many similar families, they liked to believe that they came across with William the Conqueror, and to support this notion they concocted the story of an ancestor, Robert *cum barba* (with a beard), who was one of the Conqueror's companions. The 'fact' was fiction, suggesting that their arrival in England may have been later than 1066. What is fairly clear is that they were granted two large properties in Northumberland, the Barony of Prudhoe and the REGALITY OF REDESDALE, by either William II or Henry I.

In the middle years of the thirteenth century they raised their status when they acquired the Scottish Earldom of Angus in Scotland, as the result of the marriage in 1240 of Guy de Umfraville and Matilda, the heiress of Malcolm, Earl of Angus. Their effective possession was short-lived: after the outbreak of war between England and Scotland in 1296, all cross-border estates disappeared, their holders having to relinquish either their English or their Scottish properties. The Umfravilles opted to be English and consequently forfeited their Scottish lands and title. Although they continued to be summoned to the English parliament as 'Earls of Angus', the title had ceased to have any true meaning.

The family's fortunes began to decline in the late fourteenth century, when the childless Gilbert Umfraville, 3rd 'Earl of Angus' made over the Barony of Prudhoe to the 1st Earl of Northumberland in return for an annuity. The transfer was cemented in 1381, when the Earl of Northumberland married Angus's widow. The Umfraville line in the North East died out in the fifteenth century with two warriors of considerable renown: Gilbert de Umfraville, who was killed at the Battle of Bauge in France in 1421, and his uncle, Robert, a noted Border warrior, whose exploits in bringing so much booty into Northumberland from Scotland led to his nickname, 'Robin Mendmarket'. With his death in 1436, the Umfravilles disappeared from the region.

UNIVERSITIES

At present the North East has five universities, two of which may be classed as 'older' and three as 'younger'. The former, represented by the Universities of Durham and Newcastle upon Tyne, must be considered together, since for much of their history they were united as Durham University.

It is sometimes alleged that Durham University was founded in 1657, and up to a point this is correct. In 1649, following the execution of Charles I, his victorious opponents suppressed all cathedrals. Now redundant, DURHAM CATHEDRAL was an ideal location for a university, for which there was local demand on account of the distance of the region from Oxford and Cambridge. After considerable delay, a patent was issued in 1657 setting up a college, housed in the cathedral with the use of its library and endowed with its lands. The following year, another patent was drawn up turning the college into a university, but Oliver Cromwell died before this was sealed. Oxford and Cambridge now registered strong objection to the idea of another degree-awarding institution. Before the matter could be settled, the Cromwellian regime collapsed and the monarchy in the person of Charles II was restored and with it bishops and cathedrals.

'Durham University', therefore, remained in abeyance for another 172 years. In the

1820s the proposal was again pressed. To the argument of the distance from Oxford and Cambridge and from Edinburgh (always popular in the North East), was added rapidly increasing population. By 1830 there was also political urgency, in that it was known that were the Whigs to win the election, radical reform of cathedrals would follow the reform of parliament. The feeling was that something should be done before Durham Cathedral was deprived of its property. The driving force was Charles Thorp, Archdeacon of Durham and Canon of the Cathedral, but with strong support from the three most influential men in the region: the Bishop of Durham, WILLIAM VAN MILDERT, 2nd EARL GREY, then Prime Minister, and the Duke of Northumberland.

The University of Durham was the product of three pieces of legislation: the Chapter Act in 1831, an act of parliament in 1832 and a Royal Charter in 1837. It was to be dominated by the church: the Bishop of Durham was its Visitor *ex officio*; the Warden, the head of the University, was to be the Dean of Durham *ex officio*; and the Professors of Divinity and Greek were to be canons of the Cathedral, all three posts to be in the gift of the Bishop. Moreover, as at Cambridge, and much to the chagrin of the region's nonconformists, students would not be allowed to graduate until or unless they were confirmed members of the Church of England. The intention was that the University should occupy the buildings around Palace Green, which would become in effect a giant 'quad'. The most conspicuous of these, Durham Castle, was given to the University by Bishop Edward Maltby in 1837 and eventually became University College. At that stage, however, Durham was akin to Trinity College, Dublin in that the college and university were coterminous. Despite its ecclesiastical origins and connections, it was intended that the University would offer a wide range of subjects, including Medicine, Law and Engineering. Because of the part he had played in founding the University, Charles Thorp, although not Dean of the Cathedral, was to be the first Warden, a post he occupied until 1862.

Durham survived the years of its infancy, thanks to the endowments provided by the Bishop and the Dean and Chapter. In addition to the Castle, the former made over the other properties bordering Palace Green and also those in North Bailey as far as Kingsgate, but it was from the Dean and Chapter that most of the University's property was derived: the whole of its South Shields Estate; much of its Bearpark Estate; and farms and other land between Elvet and the River Wear opposite Shincliffe, including Smiddyhaugh, now the Racecourse playing fields on which the DURHAM MINERS' GALA is held.

Despite this, the University was not a great success; indeed, throughout the nineteenth century, it struggled to survive. By the early years of the twentieth century it had no more than 200 students and its academic concerns were largely confined to Arts and Divinity, the attempts to foster a wider range of subjects having failed. It was seen as little more than a training ground for the Anglican ministry, which its Warden from 1867 until 1894, Dean Lake, believed should be its role. By the early 1860s its condition was so parlous that a Reform Commission was set up to consider its future. One member of that body thought it had no future and advocated its removal to NEWCASTLE and its restructuring on what he termed 'Scottish lines'. Nevertheless, it did survive and there were developments. A second college, Hatfield Hall, was created in 1846. Its purpose was to cater for poorer students by providing furnished study-bedrooms and having all meals taken in hall, a residential style subsequently adopted by all universities. A third college, Cosin's Hall, was founded in 1851, but lasted no longer than 1864, when it was absorbed into University College. Not all students lived in college: the 'unattached students', as they were known from the time of their first admission in 1871, formed themselves into a Society in 1880 and adopted the name St Cuthbert in 1888, officially recognised a few years later. Also 'unattached' were women students, who were first admitted in 1896, although a hostel for them was created in 1899. In 1904 and 1909 St Chad's Hall and St John's Hall were founded as a privately funded 'licensed halls of residence' for candidates for Holy Orders.

Meanwhile, important developments had taken place at Newcastle. The first, in 1834, was the founding of a Medical School. Although many doctors in the town backed the idea, two were particularly influential, Thomas Greenhow and John Fife. In 1852 successful negotiations resulted in the School becoming the 'Newcastle upon Tyne College of Medicine in connection with the University of Durham', and it was this link that helped to secure recognition of its courses by the Royal College of Surgeons and the Society of Apothecaries. The College awarded a Licence in Medicine; to obtain a degree, it was necessary to attend the Arts course in Durham, a requirement that lasted until 1876. The course in medicine was further strengthened by the regulations imposed by the General Medical Council (established in 1858), by which date the College had more students than in Arts and Divinity in Durham. In 1869 the General Medical Council accorded it the same standing as Oxford and Cambridge and in the following year its name was changed to the 'University of Durham College of Medicine'. Association with the Newcastle Infirmary made it possible for students to qualify in Surgery as well as Medicine, and in 1892 the length of the course was extended from four to five years.

The second development in Newcastle started later. This was the College of Physical Science, founded in 1871. The driving force behind this project was the LITERARY AND PHILOSOPHICAL SOCIETY OF NEWCASTLE UPON TYNE, supported by prominent local industrialists like SIR ISAAC LOWTHIAN BELL and SIR WILLIAM ARMSTRONG. From the outset, this institution, which was similar to developments in other industrial cities, was part of Durham University. Indeed, Dean Lake was prepared to make a financial contribution to ensure the successful launch of the new venture, which initially was concerned with Mathematics, Chemistry, Physics and Geology. At the start, courses lasted two years, but almost at once a three-year course was instituted leading to the B.Sc. degree, and without any requirement to reside in Durham. In addition, the College undertook to provide a foundation course in Science for medical students. In the following three decades, more subjects were added: Agriculture and Forestry, Botany and Zoology, Engineering, and Education, and also Arts. In 1883 its name was changed to 'Durham College of Science, Newcastle upon Tyne', but by the beginning of the twentieth century this only served to underline its curious, unique and not very comfortable situation, tied to a very singular and much weaker institution, while seeing new universities being created out of earlier colleges similar to it: the Victoria University (Manchester, Liverpool and Leeds) in 1884, the University of Wales (Aberystwyth, Bangor and Cardiff) in 1893 and Birmingham in 1900.

However, the first decade of the twentieth century brought major improvements: pyschologically in 1904 by the change of name to Armstrong College; materially by the opening in 1906 of the large and imposing new main building; and legally in 1908 by the University of Durham Act. The last divided the University into two equal divisions, each to be largely self-governing: Durham comprising its several small colleges and societies; and Newcastle, comprising two large colleges, the College of Medicine and Armstrong College. Control by the Dean and Chapter was ended, the Dean as Warden being replaced by a non-clerical Vice-Chancellor, although the Chapter did retain membership of the Senate.

Although the change pleased Newcastle, it was probably more helpful to Durham. In the years following the end of World War I, important developments took place there: between 1919 and 1923 Hatfield Hall became Hatfield College; the women's hostel became St Mary's College and a constituent college of the University; St Chad's and St John's also changed their names from Hall to College and were made constituent colleges of the University; departments of Science and Education were founded in 1924; and Durham's two Church of England Training Colleges, Bede College (for men, founded 1839) and St Hild's College (for women, founded 1858) were brought into closer association with the University. Expansion in the Newcastle division was more straightforward: more departments and more professorships.

The next major change was the University of Durham Act of 1935. This stemmed from a Royal Commission, set up in 1934 at the request of the Chancellor, the Marquess of Londonderry, as the result of an intractable and unseemly dispute that had lasted seven years between Sir Robert Bolam, Head of the College of Medicine, and Harold Hutchens, Professor of Comparative Pathology and Bacteriology in Armstrong College. The outcome was a new structure: at Newcastle, Armstrong College and the College of Medicine were united to form King's College, with its own government headed by a Rector; at Durham, although the colleges remained separate, a similar structure was created, headed by a Warden. The Rector of King's College and the Warden of the Durham Colleges were to alternate in the post of Vice-Chancellor on a biennial basis. Above the two divisional administrations were two superior bodies: the Senate, whose membership was academic, with responsibility for appointing Professors and Readers, formulating regulations for degrees and negotiating with the University Grants Commission (founded in 1889 to distribute state funds to universities); and a Council, composed largely of lay members. The provisions of the act came into force in 1937.

In the years after the end of World War II, government policy of expanding higher education led to rapid growth in student numbers and the creation of new academic departments in both divisions, so that it became increasingly evident that each was capable of surviving as a separate university. This prospect was particularly desirable for King's College, since independence and full university status had been granted to the university colleges at Southampton, Exeter, Hull and Nottingham. The urge to separate was perhaps stronger in the old Armstrong College sector than in the old Medical College, which, thanks to arrangements obtaining since 1852, enjoyed greater freedom than any other medical faculty in the country. As there was no serious objection or resistance at Durham, by act of parliament the two universities of Durham and of Newcastle upon Tyne came into existence on 1 August 1963.

Since then both have expanded, again the growth of Durham being comparatively greater, particularly as it was able to add subjects, notably Law and Engineering, hitherto confined to Newcastle. Although Newcastle has built halls of residence since the 1930s, it has developed, as it was put in 1862, along 'Scottish' lines. Durham has remained true to its tradition in that it has from time to time created new colleges: the present number is twelve, all mixed and admitting both undergraduates and postgraduates. In addition are St Cuthbert's Society (non-resident) and Ustinov College (postgraduates). Durham's collegiality is, however, increasingly fictional, since unlike Oxford and Cambridge colleges, those at Durham have no private endowments and are increasingly controlled and directed by central management. A major new development has been Queen's Campus at Stockton, which also has colleges, John Snow College and Stephenson College.

The North East's three other universities – Northumbria, Sunderland and Teesside – are of much more recent origin. All came into existence in 1992 as the result of the government's decision to create a unitary system of higher education by giving polytechnic colleges full university status. Polytechnic colleges themselves were formed as recently as 1969 to teach courses leading to the award of degrees by the CNAA (Council for National Academic Awards). In turn, the three North-East polytechnics were the products of the amalgamations of institutions all tracing their origins to the late nineteenth century or early twentieth century, which offered courses leading to a diverse range of sub-degree qualifications, but also courses for External Degrees of the University of London. Newcastle Polytechnic: Rutherford College of Advanced Technology, Newcastle College of Art and Industrial Design and the Municipal College of Commerce; and subsequently, the Newcastle College of Education and the Northern Counties College of Education. Sunderland Polytechnic: Sunderland Technical College, Sunderland College of Education and Sunderland Art College. Teesside Polytechnic: Constantine College and Teesside College of Education.

USHAW COLLEGE

The origins of the Roman Catholic seminary at Ushaw, one of the most important in Britain, go back to 1568, when William Allen, an Oxford scholar who retained his commitment to the old faith, fled to the continent to found a college, the purpose of which was to train Englishmen for the Roman Catholic priesthood, who would then return to England to make converts and to provide support and services for their fellow believers. Allen sited his foundation at Douai, now in France but then in the Spanish Netherlands. His intention was that his college should be attached to the new University of Louvain, but in 1578 unsettled conditions forced it to evacuate to Rheims in France, where it remained until 1593. Douai's alumni opted for a dangerous calling: in England, after the act of 1581, to be a Roman Catholic priest was to be *ipso facto* guilty of high treason, the penalty for which was to be hanged, drawn and quartered. Some 122 of them are known to have suffered this fate.

But the college did not adhere to its narrowly specialist function for long. As active persecution of Roman Catholics gradually lessened, the college took on an additional role, as a school for the sons of Roman Catholic aristocrats and gentry not intended for the priesthood. In fact, by the late eighteenth century roughly three-quarters of the students were in this category. How long this 'college in exile' would have continued cannot be known, but probably not for too much longer, since anti-Catholic legislation in Britain was gradually being relaxed or repealed. In the event the end came suddenly, a consequence of Britain's declaration of war on France in 1793. By that date Douai, now in France, was subject to its revolutionary government, which confiscated British property within its frontiers and interned British citizens. Those students and teachers who had not already returned to England were not repatriated until 1795.

Finding a solution to the problem of how to restart the college back in England took ten years and resulted in two foundations: St Edmund's College at Ware in Hertfordshire; and the College of St Cuthbert at Ushaw, Durham. Transfer from Douai to Ushaw was, however, far from being direct. The first solution was to place the northern students at an academy at Tudhoe, near Durham. Shortly afterwards they moved into Pontop Hall, near Consett, but only as a transit camp in preparation for their occupation of Crook Hall. This property, demolished in 1900, was near Consett, and is not to be confused with a hall of the same name near the centre of Durham City. Crook Hall, too, was also only a stopgap, pending the creation of a purpose-built college.

This began in 1799 with the purchase of land at Ushaw in the township of Esh from a Roman Catholic landowner, Sir Edward Smythe, whose family acquired the land through marriage in the mid-sixteenth century. In 1651 the Smythes supported their faith by building accommodation and providing financial support for a Roman Catholic priest at Newhouse, near the later village of Esh Winning. But in 1714 they left the region, moving to Acton Burnell in Shropshire to another estate acquired through marriage.

The building of the new college was a slow process and it was not until 1808 that students were able to move in. The name most closely associated with the creation of Ushaw College is that of William Gibson, the son of a Roman Catholic family from Stonecroft in Northumberland. He was educated at Douai, where he was President from 1781 until 1790, when he was appointed bishop with responsibility for northern England, a role he performed until his death in 1821. But it would be a distortion and unfair to many others who worked strenuously to bring Ushaw into being to regard him as the founder.

In response to the growth of the Roman Catholic population of northern England, the college expanded during the nineteenth century and up to the middle of the twentieth century, in student numbers and consequently in buildings, the most notable of which were designed by Augustus Pugin. By the 1950s the number of students was in the region of 400. But in the last quarter of the century the number of men with a vocation for the priesthood had declined to the extent that Ushaw (like similar colleges) had to contract. In the early 1970s the junior seminary closed, followed by the senior seminary in 1988. At the same time the college developed closer ties with Durham University, becoming a licensed hall of residence in 1968. At the time of writing, there are twenty-five laymen and women in residence taking a three-year degree course in theology and ministry, validated by Durham University and launched in 1992. The college has also developed strong links with the Church of England training establishment at Cranmer Hall in Durham. In its heyday, the college educated six men who became cardinals, seven who became archbishops and thirty-three who became bishops of the Roman Catholic Church. At present its future is uncertain.

UTHRED OF BOLDON (c.1315–1396)

John Uthred was a monk of DURHAM CATHEDRAL Priory and one of the most eminent and controversial English theologians of the fourteenth century. Although some sources claim that he was a Scot, or that he came from Bolton in Northumberland, the view that he was born, or at least grew up, in Boldon in County Durham seems most convincing. He must have been a lad of parts, since he entered the University of Oxford about the age of thirteen, as a secular student. In fact, he did not become a monk at Durham until 1342. Subsequently, his career had two distinct phases. The first was purely academic. After a few years at the Priory's cell at Stamford in Lincolnshire, he returned to Oxford, where the Priory maintained its own hall that became Durham College (see OXFORD UNIVERSITY COLLEGES) and where he remained for the next twenty years. He was a renowned teacher and a forthright advocate of a number of controversial views. In particular, he vigorously defended the right of the church to possess property against the attacks of the friars, who championed mendicancy (living by begging) as, they argued, Christ and his disciples had done. He also expressed controversial views on a number of abstruse theological issues and it was these that brought his Oxford days to an end. In November 1367 the Archbishop of Canterbury, Simon Langham, formally condemned twenty-two propositions that Uthred had supported. Shortly afterwards he was brought back to Durham to become Prior of the Priory's cell at FINCHALE. A causal connection between the two events has not been demonstrated, but it appears to be more than coincidental.

Thereafter, except for a three-year interval when he returned to Oxford, probably in connection with the foundation of Durham College, Uthred was in Durham, either at Finchale, or at the Priory as Sub-Prior. As well as attending to his in-house duties, he represented the Priory in important business matters away from Durham, and in 1373 he visited the papal court at Avignon on behalf of Edward III to discuss the thorny question of the papal right to tax the English clergy. However, this did not mean the end of his academic work. He continued to write theological tracts and he also produced an account of the origins of monasticism.

VANE FAMILY

The Vane family is only the third family to own the Raby Castle and estate and the fourth to own Barnard Castle. The progenitor was Sir Henry Vane the Elder (1589–1655), a member of a gentry family from Hadlow, in Kent. After education at Oxford University and Gray's Inn, he had a successful career as a civil servant and courtier in the household of the Prince of Wales, the future Charles I. From 1614 he was an MP, successively for Lostwithiel (Cornwall), Carlisle, Thetford (Suffolk) and Wilton (Wiltshire); he served on diplomatic missions to Holland and Sweden; and in 1640 he became Secretary of State. By then the political tension between Charles I and the Parliamentary opposition was reaching crisis point. Vane strongly opposed the king's chief lieutenant, Thomas Wentworth, Earl of Strafford, who was bent on using force to crush the Scottish rebellion that broke out in 1638 against the king's insistence that the Church of Scotland adopt a version of the English Book of Common Prayer, and was a key witness against him when he was impeached by the Commons. In 1641 the situation was worsened by the outbreak of rebellion in Ireland and the stand-off between Charles and his Parliamentary opponents. Vane was keenly aware of the weakness of the king's position and counselled compromise. This, however, was not to the royal taste and consequently he was dismissed from his offices. His political career was over, although he was appointed Lord Lieutenant of Durham and was elected MP for Kent in Cromwell's first parliament.

Thirty years earlier, however, during his days of royal favour and rising income, he purchased between 1626 and 1636 for £18,000 the lordships of Raby, Barnard Castle and Long Newton. These estates had long been in the hands of the Crown: Raby and Long Newton since the collapse of the Rising of the Northern Earls in 1570 and Barnard Castle since 1485.

Vane's son, known as Sir Henry Vane the Younger (1613–62), continued in politics, and fatally so. Following a religious conversion in his teens, he became an ardent puritan, which led him to migrate to Massachusetts in 1635. This was not a success, as he became embroiled in a religious controversy and returned to England in 1637. His father had some success in advancing his career, including securing him a knighthood, but with the outbreak of the civil war in 1642, he became an opponent of the king. For the rest of his life he was a totally committed republican and hostile to the idea of a state church. In his ten years of active political life, he had three notable achievements. In 1643 he was the chief negotiator of the Solemn League and Covenant, the treaty between the governments of England and Scotland that brought the Scottish army into England in 1644 to tip the military advantage parliament's way. An outstanding and tireless administrator, he successfully masterminded the logistics of Oliver Cromwell's Scottish and Irish campaigns. And he was the instigator of an important naval construction programme. In 1653, however, he withdrew from politics, uneasy at Cromwell's assumption of the title Lord Protector, which to him was a return to monarchy.

After the restoration of Charles II in 1660, he was one of only fourteen people executed for the judicial murder of the king's father in 1649. His presence on this list is remarkable in that he played no part in the trial of Charles I and did not sign his death warrant. But he was regarded as such an unregenerate and unrepentant republican that he was considered too dangerous to live. Convicted of treason, he was beheaded in 1662.

His disgrace, however, did not blight his son's career: Christopher Vane (1653–1723) married a daughter of the Duke of Newcastle and in 1699 was elevated to the peerage as Lord Barnard. His grandson, Henry Vane (1705–58) did even better: in 1725 he married Grace, daughter of Charles Fitzroy, Duke of Cleveland (1662–1730), Charles II's illegitimate son by Barbara Palmer, and in 1754, while retaining the title Lord Barnard, he became Viscount Barnard of Barnard Castle and Earl of Darlington. The Vanes reached the summit of the social scale in 1827, when the Earl of Darlington's grandson, William Henry Vane (1766–1842), acquired three more titles: Lord Raby, Marquess of Cleveland and Duke of Cleveland.

Thereafter the Vanes fell as rapidly as they ascended. William Henry was succeeded in turn by his three sons, Henry (1788–1864), William (1792–1864) and Henry George (1803–91). As none left any legitimate children, all honours became extinct, except that of Lord Barnard, which passed to a descendant of the younger brother of the 1st Earl of Darlington. The present Lord Barnard is the 11th holder of the title.

VANE-TEMPEST, SIR HENRY, Bt (c.1750–1813)

Sir Harry Vane-Tempest was born Henry Vane, the son of a younger son and therefore a man of no great fortune. This, however, was greatly enhanced in 1793 and 1794: in the earlier year he inherited the estate of his maternal uncle, John Tempest, and in the latter that of his paternal uncle, Sir Henry Vane of Long Newton. As the result of this good fortune he changed his name to Vane-Tempest. In 1799 his portfolio of property was increased still futher by his marriage to Anne Katherine McDonnell, who in 1785 had inherited the Earldom of Antrim with an estate in excess of 34,000 acres (14,000 ha).

His wealth enabled him to become a prominent racehorse owner and it was in this capacity that he was primarily responsible for one of the most famous sporting events of the day and one of the greatest paintings by the master of equine portraiture, George Stubbs (1724–1806). The sporting event was the 'match' run at Newmarket at the Craven Meeting in the spring of 1799 between Vane-Tempest's horse, Hambletonian, the winner of the 1795 St Leger, and the much-fancied Diamond, owned by Mr Joseph Cookson. The race was run over four miles and the wager was £3,000. Victory went to Hambletonian, but the horses were so well matched that it was only by the use of whip (and spur) to a degree far greater than would be allowed today that Hambletonian got up, by the shortest of distances, a short head. Vane-Tempest commissioned Stubbs to commemorate this memorable if cruel event in two paintings: *Hambletonian Beating Diamond,* which showed the last moments in the race, and *Hambletonian, Rubbing Down,* which showed a clearly distressed horse being held by his trainer while being rubbed down by a stable boy. When he died, Hambletonian was buried in Wynyard Park, acquired by Vane-Tempest as part of the Tempest inheritance. Unfortunately, the painting of the race has been lost, but *Hambletonian, Rubbing Down,* which is Stubbs's largest painting and among his most renowned, hangs at Mount Stewart in Northern Ireland, formerly belonging to the Marquesses of Londonderry, now in the possession of the National Trust. Sad to relate, although the race left Vane-Tempest £3,000 richer, Stubbs was forced to sue to get his fee of £300.

Sir Harry Vane-Tempest died in 1813, leaving no son. His sole heir was his daughter, Frances Anne, who in 1819 married Charles Stewart, who became in 1822 3RD MARQUESS OF LONDONDERRY.

VAN MILDERT, WILLIAM (1765–1836)

William Van Mildert was the great-grandson of a Dutch immigrant who developed a gin distillery in Southwark. He was educated at the Merchant Taylors' School and The Queen's College, Oxford. After graduating in 1787, he was immediately ordained in the Church of England. After nine years in three curacies and a parish in Northamptonshire, he secured the prestigious living of St Mary le Bow in London, with which went the role of Chaplain of the Grocers' Company and which gave him an entry into the leading church circles of his day. It was during this time that he gained a reputation as a preacher with a deep knowledge of divinity. It was this combination of knowing men of influence in church and state and a reputation as a scholar that secured him the Regius Professorship of Divinity at Oxford in 1813. He held the post for three years, until 1816, when he accepted the Bishopric of Llandaff, having declined the Archbishopric of Dublin.

Ten years later, on the death of Bishop Shute Barrington in 1826, he was made Bishop of Durham, a post he retained until his own death in 1836. He was conscientious in the discharge of his duties, particularly in the matter of new churches, of which fourteen were built in the diocese during his pontificate. He made financial contributions to the building of the churches at Ferryhill, Shildon and Usworth and he paid entirely out of his own pocket for the building and endowment of that at Etherley. In doing so he was maintaining a longstanding commitment: in 1818 he had been one of the founders of the Church Building Society and in 1825 he was appointed to the Church Building Commission, set up to distribute money provided by the government for church construction.

But the acts for which he is more widely remembered in the North East were those connected with the foundation of Durham University. The idea for a university was not his, but his opposition would have been fatal to it. Instead, he backed the scheme, his membership of the House of Lords and influential contacts in the political world being invaluable to its success. In particular, he steered through parliament the Durham University Bill that empowered the Dean and Chapter to endow the University with their estate in South Shields. More controversially, he dictated the style of the University, insisting that (as at Cambridge) it should be a Church of England foundation by requiring subscription to the Thirty-Nine Articles as a precondition of graduation. In doing so, he thwarted the hopes of nonconformists, especially those in Newcastle, that it would be a non-denominational institution. At the same time, he was determined that the University should be a university in the fullest sense, not merely a theological college for the training of Church of England priests, by having, like Oxford and Cambridge, full powers to award its own degrees. He also gave financial support by attaching cathedral canonries (and their income) to the wardenship and to the professorships of Greek and Divinity, making a gift of £1,000 and promising an annual grant of the same sum. It was this support that enabled the University to survive the difficult days of its infancy. Finally, at his insistence, Archdeacon Charles Thorp became the first Warden of the University.

Van Mildert is also remembered as the 'Last of the Prince Bishops of Durham'. Following his death the government of Lord Melbourne took the opportunity of separating the PALATINATE OF DURHAM from the office of Bishop of Durham.

VENUS, SYLVIA ISMAY (1896–2000)

Sylvia Venus was born in Gateshead, the daughter of an engineer working for an American shipping company. Although her training as an artist at Armstrong College was interrupted by World War I, her talent was sufficiently developed for her to exhibit at the Laing Art Gallery (see ART GALLERIES) immediately after the end of the war. In 1919 she moved to London and began a career working as an illustrator for publishers. For thirty years she was with Newnes, for whom she illustrated the books of Enid Blyton. As a result, although her name is little known, her work will have been seen and enjoyed by far more people than have seen that of famous artists. She also did illustrations for the children's sections of newspapers and occasionally exhibited watercolours in Newcastle. In 1954 she retired to Cloughton, near Scarborough. She died in a Scarborough nursing home in 2000 at the age of 103.

VINDOLANDA

Vindolanda is, and is likely to remain, one of the most important archaeological sites in Europe. It was built (and rebuilt several times) as a military fort by the Roman army and outside its western gate a substantial civilian settlement or *vicus* developed. It was not on Hadrian's Wall, but a few hundred yards to the south on the earlier frontier now known as the Stanegate. In none of these matters was it exceptional.

It was not until the 1960s that the importance of the site began to be realised. In 1830 a local clergyman, Anthony Hedley, built a house, now known as Chesterholm, which in 1929 was bought with the surrounding farmland by the archaeologist Eric Birley. During the 1930s he excavated parts of the fort, but after returning from war service he became Master of Hatfield College, Durham University. As this was a residential post, he sold the property. It was his son, Robin Birley, who resumed excavation, and it was his discoveries that led to the setting up of the Vindolanda Trust in 1970. Thanks to the generosity of the then owners, the Trust was given the site of the fort and *vicus* in 1970 and Chesterholm, now a museum, in 1973.

Since then, donations from Europe and nearer home, notably by the SIR JAMES KNOTT Trust, have enabled the museum to grow in size and develop the ability to process and display finds, which in a six-month excavation campaign can number as many as 5,000. These include the whole range of remains that an archaeologist could expect to find, but in addition, excavations have yielded a large quantity of writing tablets and implements that are continuing to throw light on both the military and non-military aspects of frontier life. It is these that make Vindolanda unique. It is estimated that at the present rate of excavation, it will be another 150 years before the site is exhausted.

WAGONWAYS

Wagonways were the forerunners of RAILWAYS. The basic difference between them was that on a railway wagons and carriages were hauled by locomotives, whereas on a wagonway motive power was supplied by horses, gravity and stationary engines. Another difference was that wagonways had a single dedicated purpose: to move coal overland from pithead to a point where it could be transferred to water transport, KEELS on the river and then COLLIERS for the sea. The aim of wagonways was to improve the efficiency and thereby to reduce the cost of overland transport, which was becoming increasingly urgent because of the exhaustion of riverside pits and the consequent sinking of pits ever further inland.

The first wagonway in Britain was built at the beginning of the seventeenth century between Strelley and Lenton near Nottingham by Huntington Beaumont, the younger son of a Leicestershire gentry family, who had acquired control of pits at Wollaton and Strelley. Interestingly, his motive was to lower his transport costs so as to make his coal competitive with that of the North East. He did not succeed in doing so, which explains why he moved to the North East in 1605. Here, in partnership with three London merchants, he leased pits and salt pans at BEDLINGTON, Bebside and Cowpen. Again success eluded him and in 1614 he returned to the Midlands, where he became bankrupt in 1618.

The wagonway systems in the North East were developed rapidly from the late seventeenth century on the lower reaches of the Tyne and the Wear, and also the Wansbeck. On the Tyne, development was far from peaceful: between 1690 and 1720 there was fierce competition between groups of colliery owners to secure 'wayleave' (permission, for a fee, to travel across another's property) for their wagonways and to deny the same to their rivals. By 1800, on the eve of the railway age, a complex network of wagonways existed on both sides of the Tyne and the Wear. Twenty-six river termini can be identified on the Tyne and nineteen on the Wear, but when branch lines are included, the number of wagonways exceeded this total of forty-five.

Initially, wagonway rails were made of oak or pine, roughly 6 inches by 4 inches (14 cm by 10 cm), on top of which a thin strip of beech was fixed. This provided a smooth surface that could be replaced when worn. The rails were nailed with wooden pegs to sleepers made of rough-hewn timber 6 feet (1.8 cm) long and 6 inches (14 cm) wide, laid at 2-foot (61 cm) intervals on ballast, which was covered with ash to provide an even surface for horses. The gauge, the distance between the rails, was not standard but varied between 4 feet 3 inches and 4 feet 8 inches. The track was laid on ground made level by means of cuttings and embankments so as to provide, as far as possible, an even downward descent from pit to river. The wagons, known as chaldrons, were made of wood and had a capacity of 33 cwt (1,677 kg). Their wheels were made entirely of wood, and, contrary to widespread belief, were flanged. Where necessary, front wheels were larger than those at the rear to allow the wagon always to run level. The force of gravity was used during the descent, the speed of a train being controlled by a brakesman on the back of the rearmost chaldron. Ascent back to the pit was by horsepower.

In the course of the eighteenth century, developments in engineering led to improvements in wagonways. In particular, chaldrons were gradually enlarged to a capacity of 53 cwt (2,693 kg), and later in the century rails and chaldron wheels were made of iron. Also, routes were improved to give greater smoothness and efficiency of movement. The development of the locomotive in the nineteenth century did not mean the end of all wagonways: until the end of mining in the region there were wagonways operating by means of continuous ropes, to which wagons were attached, moved by gravity or stationary engines.

In the 1990s several sections of wagonway were discovered during the redevelopment of the site of Lambton D pit, sunk two hundred years earlier, which confirmed the evidence derived from contemporary descriptions.

WAILES, WILLIAM (1808–1881)

William Wailes became one of the most successful makers of stained glass windows in Britain through his ability to meet the demands of an expanding market. In the nineteenth century, pictorial glass came back into fashion, with the result that there was a huge demand from the growing number of new churches, from those that had lost their medieval glass during the Reformation period in the sixteenth and seventeenth centuries, and from a wide range of secular customers, public and domestic.

But stained glass was not Wailes's original interest. Born in Newcastle, his first ambition was to become a landscape painter and he secured a pupillage with T.M. Richardson. Although not without talent, he failed to get any serious critical recognition. He therefore decided to try commerce, but again without success. Turning to the manufacture of stained glass was therefore something of a desperate move. This venture, however, proved to be a winner. Within a few years, his Gateshead factory was turning out around 350 windows a year, supplying a wide range of customers, at home and abroad. Wailes's success was based upon his business acumen and drive, and not on his artistic talents. His skill, which owed something to his early training as a painter, lay in finding and securing the services of talented artists to design windows for him.

Within the region, Wailes is known to have provided windows for eleven churches in Durham and twelve in Northumberland, including both Anglican cathedrals. He also supplied the windows for Wynyard Park and Lilburn Tower. The fortune he made enabled him acquire the Saltwell estate on the southern edge of Gateshead, where between 1862 and 1871 he built Saltwell Towers. In 1876 he sold both house and estate for £32,000 to Gateshead Corporation, which two years later employed W.B. Kemp of Birkenhead to lay out the grounds as a public park.

WALKER, JOHN (1781–1859)

John Walker could have been and should have been far more famous and wealthier than he became. He was the son of a grocer whose premises were in the High Street of Stockton on Tees. He trained as a chemist and practised his trade with good success on the quayside. His interest in his subject was active and in the course of his experiments in 1825 and 1826 he produced a paste that flared, but it was by chance that he discovered that it would readily ignite slivers of wood. He employed an old man and then boys from the grammar school to produce the thin pieces of wood, which he then tipped with paste. In the next few years he had a growing sale for tins of his 'friction matches', as he called them, at 100 for a shilling. The famous chemist Michael Faraday who urged him to patent his invention and to manufacture matches on a more commercial scale, made his scientific formula public knowledge in lectures and journals. Through these a London man, Samuel Jones, discovered the process and began to manufacture and market what he called 'Lucifers', a name that was still in use at the time of World War I. As Jones's product became widely known, Walker ceased to produce his own version and resumed his normal chemist's business. Eventually the formula came into the hands of the famous firm Bryant and May, and Walker's role was entirely forgotten until it was rediscovered in the early years of the twentieth century. Meanwhile, John Walker retired from his business in 1858 and died the following year. He is buried in the graveyard of Norton church.

WALTHEOF, EARL OF NORTHUMBRIA (c.1050–1076)

Waltheof was the last 'native' Earl of Northumbria. Although his father, Siward, who was imposed as Earl of Northumbria in the 1030s by King Canute, was a Dane and therefore a 'foreigner', his mother, Aelfleda, was of the ancient comital house of Northumbria and therefore probably descended from the Northumbrian royal family.

Unlike almost all other Englishmen, Waltheof gained by the Norman Conquest. In 1070 William I granted him his father's estates in the Midlands and married him to his niece, Judith. Two years later, in 1072, he appointed him Earl of Northumbria with regal power north of the Tees. William's intention may have been to leave the far north of his kingdom as a semi-autonomous earldom ruled by a branch of the royal family.

William miscalculated. In 1075 Waltheof was drawn into a plot against the king. He seems to have regretted his action, which he confessed to Lanfranc, Archbishop of Canterbury, who urged him to throw himself on the royal mercy. This he did, but it did not work. In May 1076 he was tried at Winchester, convicted of treason and beheaded.

In the course of their short marriage, Waltheof and Judith produced three daughters. In due time, the eldest, Matilda, married as her second husband David I, King of Scots and from this union sprang a line of kings that ruled Scotland until 1286. It was upon Matilda's descent from the comital house of Northumbria that these kings based their claim to the EARLDOM OF NORTHUMBRIA, a claim that they pursued until 1237.

WALWORTH, SIR WILLIAM (?–1386)

Little is certain about William Walworth's early life. He was one of the twin sons of a William Walworth, who is known to have possessed property in Darlington in 1314. It is evident that the boys were well educated, but while the other twin, Thomas, entered the church and eventually became a canon of York Minster, William was apprenticed to a John Lovekyn (d.1368), a rich London fishmonger. All the indirect evidence points to Walworth having become Lovekyn's partner and to his having enjoyed considerable financial success, which allowed him to cancel a debt of 100 marks owed to him by DURHAM CATHEDRAL Priory and to make financial contributions to Winchester College and New College, Oxford, the educational foundations of William Wykeham, Bishop of Winchester. Almost inevitably, success in business meant involvement in the politics and government of London. As early as 1370 he served as Sheriff and four years later he was elected Mayor for the year 1374–75.

So far, his story is unexceptional. What made it less so was his crucial role in the great uprising in the summer of 1381 known as the Peasants' Revolt, when he was Mayor for the second time. The uprising was triggered by the attempted imposition of a third poll tax, which unlike the previous occasions was at a far higher rate and without any concession to lower income groups. The vast number of rebels and their success in taking control of London and Westminster posed a very serious threat to the king, the fourteen-year-old Richard II, and the English establishment. Trapped in the Tower, the king and his court had no option but to negotiate. The first meeting, at Mile End on 14 June, was inconclusive and a second meeting was held on the following day at Smithfield. The rebel demands were extreme, but it was the insolent manner of their leader, the Kentishman Wat Tyler, that provoked the crisis. Incensed by Tyler's demeanour, Walworth lunged at him with his sword, knocking him off his horse; another member of the royal party finished him off. This could have been a prelude to disaster, but was averted by the coolness of the young king, who galloped forward to address the rebel host, telling them that he would now be their leader and that they should disperse with his assurance that their demands would be met. For his services, Walworth was knighted. In the following weeks, the rebellion was harshly suppressed, a process in which Walworth played a leading part.

Success in London did not sever Walworth from his North-East roots. At some point after 1367 he became the owner of a major portion of MIDDLETON ST GEORGE, which had belonged since the twelfth century to a family named Baard (Baird). Whether he was making a straightforward investment in land or was related to the Baards is not known. Walworth had no male heir and after his death the property came into the possession of a family named Killinghall. The closeness of the Walworth and Killinghall arms hints at some family connection. Walworth's London house in Thames Street is now the site of the Fishmongers' Hall.

WAPENTAKE OF SADBERGE

The word 'wapentake' is of Scandinavian origin and means 'weapon take', that is a military muster. Wapentakes are found in those parts of England where Scandinavian settlement in the ninth and early tenth centuries was heavy. In other areas, where Scandinavian settlement was slight or non-existent, the Old English word 'hundred' was used. 'Hundred' and 'wapentake' describe essentially identical institutions: subdivisions of shires with administrative and judicial as well as military functions. But neither hundreds nor wapentakes existed north of Lancashire and Yorkshire. The reason is that until about thirty years after the Norman Conquest of 1066, these northernmost areas were not fully incorporated into the English state and it was only when this happened at the end of the eleventh century that they were divided into counties. To these units – Cumberland, Westmorland (Cumbria), Northumberland and Durham – the term 'shire' was never applied, and they were not divided into 'hundreds' or 'wapentakes', but into 'wards', which had administrative and military, but not judicial functions. It took over a century for these divisions to become permanent, but in the end Durham had four 'wards' (CHESTER, DARLINGTON, EASINGTON and STOCKTON) and Northumberland six (BAMBURGH, Castle, Coquetdale, Glendale, MORPETH and TYNEDALE).

To this the Wapentake of Sadberge, on the north side of the Tees, was an anomalous exception. Moreover, it did not comprise a unified area of land but discrete districts: Hartness, between Crimdon Dene and Greatham Beck; central areas around Sadberge and Gainford; and a western area from Whorlton to the head of Teesdale. Separating them were BILLINGHAM, Norton and Stockton; DARLINGTON; and Winston.

The origin of the Wapentake is not known, but it is fair to assume that it was a consequence of the time in the early tenth century when the southern parts of Durham were briefly under Scandinavian control. Despite this, it did not become part of Yorkshire, where Scandinavian settlement was heavy and political control prolonged. Instead, it was part of the EARLDOM of Northumbria, and after this was suppressed in 1095, of the new Northumberland County (see County of Northumberland). This arrangement lasted until 1189, when the Bishop of Durham, Hugh of le Puiset, bought the Wapentake from King Richard I. The price was £400 cash and the transfer to the Crown of the lordship of six feudal tenants in Lincolnshire. The acquisition did little to increase the bishop's income, but it did extend and round off his jurisdiction, which henceforth extended from Tyne to Tees. Although effectively now part of the Palatinate of Durham, for many centuries a theoretical distinction between County Durham and the Wapentake of Sadberge continued to be made.

WARD, IRENE MARY BEWICK, BARONESS WARD OF NORTH TYNESIDE (1895–1980)

Irene Ward was the quintessential backbench MP, and represented two North Tyneside constituencies for thirty-eight years. She was born in Westminster, the only child of an architect, John Bewick Ward, whose premature death in 1901 left his widow and daughter in reduced circumstances and led them to migrate north to settle in Gosforth. Thanks to her mother's determination, she secured a place at the Central High School in Newcastle. Her interest in politics, encouraged by Sir Charles Cochrane, the Newcastle shipowner, developed in the last years of World War I. It was he who in 1920 helped her to secure the role of honorary secretary of the Newcastle Central Conservative Association. Through such work and attending party conferences, where her ability as a public speaker attracted attention, in 1929 she secured the nomination as Conservative candidate for the Morpeth constituency. Her strong performance in what was a hopeless seat gained her second place behind the Labour candidate in an election won by the Labour party.

Two years later, when the Great Depression had totally changed the political climate, she won the seat at Wallsend, defeating the Labour member, Margaret Bondfield, a member of Ramsay Macdonald's cabinet. In the circumstances, her victory was not entirely surprising; but her retention of the seat in the 1935 election testifies to the assiduity with which she attended to her constituency's concerns. There was no hope that she would be able to repeat her success in the Labour landslide of 1945. Consequently, she was out of parliament until 1950, when she won the safer neighbouring seat of Tynemouth, a seat she made her own and which she held until she retired in 1974 at the age of seventy-nine.

Throughout her parliamentary career, Irene Ward had no ambition for public office, her foremost concern being her constituents. Her other abiding interest was the status and condition of women. In putting forward her views and opinions on local and gender issues she was well informed, forceful and trenchant. With more technically complex matters she was less confident and this, combined with her penchant for flamboyant dress, characterised by big hats and handbags and prominent jewellery, exposed her to adverse humour. Her qualities, which far outweighed her deficiencies, were recognised in a string of honours: CBE in 1929, DBE in 1955, CH in 1973 and life peerage on retirement from the Commons in 1974. Her devotion to North Tyneside was made plain by the title she took and, after her death, the scattering of her ashes in the North Sea by a North Shields fishing boat.

WASHINGTON

Washington is widely known for its connection with the family that gave the United

States of America its first president, George Washington. The connection, however, is very indirect and tenuous. The family that bore the name Washington first appears in the twelfth century as de Hertburn (Hartburn near Stockton on Tees), when William de Hertburn was persuaded by the Bishop of Durham, Hugh of le Puiset to exchange Hartburn for Washington (then spelled Wessington). Thereafter, as was then normal, his descendants bore the name of the place they owned.

The Washington family owned Washington until the end of the fourteenth century, but the branch from which the first American president was descended was founded by a younger son. He was Robert de Wessington, son of Sir William de Wessington III, who in 1292 married a Lancashire woman, Joan de Strickland, and settled in Warton in Lancashire. This branch of the Washingtons (the modern spelling was adopted in the fifteenth century) remained in Lancashire until the early sixteenth century, when Lawrence Washington moved to Northamptonshire. The reason was his marriage to, successively, two wealthy widows in that county, which enabled him to buy the manor of Sulgrave and build a house there in the late 1550s.

The move to America was made by Lawrence Washington's great-great-grandson, John. In 1633, after graduating from Oxford, John's father, Lawrence, became the rector of Purleigh, in Essex. During the civil war he was a Royalist and consequently in 1643 he was deprived of the parish. He died in poverty in 1654.

His son John was nineteen years old and living under the hostile regime of Oliver Cromwell, which largely explains his decision to seek a more congenial situation in the colonies. In 1656, the year he came of age, he sailed with his first wife to Virginia, hoping to prosper in the rapidly developing tobacco trade. His initial intention may not have been to migrate permanently, but any thoughts of a return to England ended with the death of his wife and his remarriage shortly afterwards to Anne Pope, the daughter of one of the colony's leading tobacco planters. His father-in-law set the couple up with a farm of 700 acres at Mattox Creek: John Washington's destiny was to be Virginian, not English, and a tobacco grower, not a tobacco trader. It was John's great-grandson, George, born in 1732, who commanded the army raised by the rebellious colonists in the late 1770s, and who in 1789 became the first president of the newly independent United States of America.

The tenuous link between Washington in Durham and the USA is Washington Old Hall, which stands next to the parish church at the centre of the old village. Most of its fabric dates from the first half of the seventeenth century, long after the departure of the Washington family, the main line of which ended in 1399 with the death of Sir William de Wessington V. His heir was his only daughter, Eleanor, who married a Yorkshireman, Sir William Tempest. By the early years of the seventeenth century the hall belonged to Francis James, son of William James, Bishop of Durham (1606–17), who reconstructed it in its present form. Reconstructed is the correct term, since the western end of the hall is clearly medieval and would have been built by the Wessingtons.

Thereafter the story of the hall is one of sad decline. By 1932 it was so dilapidated that it was saved from demolition only by the determined efforts of a local preservation committee. Restoration was delayed for twenty years until after World War II, by which time it was derelict. Much of the cost of repair was borne by American benefactors, and most of the interior fittings, although authentic, were acquired elsewhere. Nevertheless, it is not unlikely that were he to return, Francis James would readily recognise it. It was opened by the American ambassador in 1955 and given to the National Trust the following year.

For modern Washington, see NEW TOWNS OF THE TWENTIETH CENTURY.

WATLING STREET (see ROMAN ROADS)

WATSON, SIR JAMES ANGUS (1874–1961)

Angus Watson, whose company became renowned for canned foods, especially fish, was born at Ryton, son of Alexander Watson, a manufacturer of sanitary pipes. His education was limited to attendance at the village school, which he left in 1889 to become a junior clerk in the office of a food importer in NEWCASTLE. A year later, he moved to be a traveller with another Newcastle firm, of wholesale grocers. There he made his name by negotiating a contract with a Norwegian firm of fish canners in Stavanger that gave his company the exclusive right to sell the Norwegian firm's canned brisling in Britain. Within a few years, Watson was selling 5,000 cases of Norwegian brisling. His success led in 1898 to his move to the much larger firm, Lever Bros, who in 1899 sent him to the USA to set up their sales organisation.

On his return to Britain in 1903, he left Lever Bros to found his own company in Newcastle in partnership with Henry Saint to market Norwegian canned brisling. He did so under the brand name 'Skipper Sardines', the cans bearing a picture of a fisherman dressed in oilskins. This cost him £50,000 in legal fees arising from a successful challenge by the French canning industry, which argued, correctly, that brisling was a Norwegian sprat, not a sardine. The case, however, did nothing to halt the progress of his firm, the success of which enabled it to finance the building of a new cannery at Bergen by the Norwegian firm, Imperial Canneries Ltd. Watson also widened his product range to include other sorts of fish, including 'Sailor Salmon', as well as game, corned beef and fruit, the last sold as the 'My Lady' brand. Watson was employing over 1,000 people on the outbreak of World War I, during which he worked for the Ministry of Food, purchasing canned foods from North America and Scandinavia for the British government.

After the war, Watson's difficulty in raising capital led to his selling a large number of shares in his company to his old employer, now Lord Leverhulme, who eventually bought a controlling interest in 1923. After Leverhulme's death in 1925, Watson's firm was absorbed into United Canners. Although he became chairman of this new firm, Watson found himself at odds with the other members of the board, who opposed his profit-sharing and share distribution schemes, which had been a feature of his benevolent management philosophy, with its emphasis on the importance of close contact and good relations between owner, managers and employees. Consquently, he resigned the chairmanship in 1930. Underpinning this philosophy and decision almost certainly lay his commitment to the teachings of the Congregational church, of which he was an active and prominent member. This may also help to explain his involvement in local government, which included becoming a Liberal member of Newcastle City Council, a JP in the City and in Northumberland, and a member of the Tyneside Council of Social Services, and it was probably also behind the foundation of his charity, the Newcastle Children's Mission.

However, his resignation was not the end of his contribution to the food industry: during World War II, he again worked for the British government, this time as Food Controller for the North East. For this service he was knighted in 1945, which complemented an earlier award in 1912, when he was made a Knight of St Olaf of Norway in recognition of his contribution to the Norwegian fishing industry.

WATSON, ROBERT SPENCE (1837–1911)

Robert Spence Watson, one of the leading intellectual and political figures on Tyneside in the nineteenth century, was the son of a Gateshead solicitor, Joseph Watson. As both parents were Quakers, he had automatic membership of the close-knit Tyneside Quaker nexus. He was educated at the Friends' School at York and then, being debarred by his religion from Oxford and Cambridge, at University College, London. He then became a solicitor, going into partnership with his father. Over the next fifty years he had a major impact in four spheres.

He was a leading figure in the LITERARY AND PHILOSOPHICAL SOCIETY OF NEWCASTLE UPON TYNE. Between 1862 and 1890 he was the Secretary, succeeding his father, who held that office from 1852 until 1860. In 1890 he became Vice-President and in 1900 President, a position he retained until his death. Between 1868 and 1898 he delivered eighty lectures to the Society, mainly on the history of the English language. Arising out of his 'Lit and Phil' involvement was his abiding concern to promote education. At school level he was a member of the Newcastle School Board (set up under the 1870 act that instituted compulsory elementary education) from 1871 until 1894, and he was also chairman of the governing body of the Royal Grammar School. He was equally concerned with higher education. He took a leading part in the campaign, which achieved success in 1871, to create the College of Science in Newcastle, as part of Durham University. He was involved in its government for forty years and in 1910 became its President after it became Armstrong College (see UNIVERSITIES). He was also a vigorous pioneer of the University Extension courses, run in Newcastle under the aegis of Cambridge University. His work for higher education was recognised in 1906 with the award of an honorary DCL by Durham University.

He was heavily involved with the foundation of the electricity industry in the North East. In 1881 he was a co-founder with WILLIAM ARMSTRONG, JOSEPH SWAN and THEODORE MERZ of the Swan Electric Light Co. and in 1889 of NESCO.

In politics, he was a lifelong and active Liberal. He was the election agent for JOSEPH COWEN and was a founder in 1874 of the Newcastle Liberal Association, of which he was President until 1897. He was one of those who helped to found the National Liberal Federation in 1877 and was its President from 1890 until 1902. He has been described as the most important Liberal leader outside of parliament, of which he made no attempt to become a member. His standing in Liberal circles is revealed in his friendship with John Bright, John Morley and 3rd EARL GREY and by his appointment to the Privy Council in 1907 by Henry Campbell Bannerman, Prime Minister 1905–08.

His Quaker upbringing and commitment to Liberalism almost inevitably inclined him to pacificism. He was for some years President of the Peace Society and on the industrial front he strongly favoured the settlement of industrial disputes by arbitration. Because of this latter commitment and his known fairness he acted as sole arbitrator on forty-seven occasions between 1884 and 1894.

WATSON, SAMUEL (1898–1967)

Sam Watson was one of the most influential men in the British coal industry in the years after 1945, and was also a prominent political figure, although he never became a member of parliament. He was born at Boldon Colliery, the son of a third-generation miner. His formal education at the local elementary school was supplemented initially by the local vicar and then by the decision of the Boldon Lodge to create a Miners' Institute Library, of which he became secretary. This bred a lifelong devotion to books and reading, which resulted in a personal library of over 2,000 volumes. Following his father into the pit, he became active in Lodge matters at an early age, joining the committee in 1917, when only nineteen, and becoming secretary in 1926. He was also active in politics, becoming secretary of the Boldon branch of the Independent Labour Party (ILP) in 1919. He was seen as well to the left, a perception supported by his association with the Communist Party in Durham.

During the 1930s he rose to prominence in the miners' union. In 1935 he became a full-time agent for the Durham Miners' Association and a member of the executive of the Miners' Federation of Great Britain, which in 1940 chose him as its representative on the National Executive Committee of the Labour Party. Politically, he continued to lean well to the left and he was active on behalf of the Republican cause during the Spanish Civil War, 1936–39. But in the course of World War II, his political stance moved considerably to the right. This may have been through the influence of Sam Berger, initially the special adviser on trade union matters to the influential American envoy, Averell Harriman, later labour attaché at the American embassy. Berger and Watson became close friends and a similar association developed between Watson and Berger's successor, Joe Godson, whose son married Watson's daughter.

In the post-war era, Watson's influence grew considerably. He succeeded Hugh Dalton in 1952 as chairman of the Labour Party National Executive Committee's sub-committee on International Affairs, in which capacity he made many foreign visits, gaining a deeper and more accurate knowledge of world affairs. This in turn made him highly critical of the Communist regimes in the USSR and the People's Republic of China. Because of his hostility to international Communism, he opposed the Campaign for Nuclear Disarmament in Britain and helped the leader of the Labour Party, Hugh Gaitskell, to preserve party unity while successfully resisting the demand that it adopt an anti-nuclear defence policy. He also became convinced that Britain's interest would be best served by joining the European Economic Community.

But his prime concern was always his mining constituency. In 1946 he was elected General Secretary of the Durham Area of the newly formed National Union of Mineworkers, a post he was to hold until 1963. It was his misfortune to be in office when the demand for coal began to decline in the late 1950s, with the consequent need to close pits and shed manpower. Watson's approach, in sharp contrast to that of some later miners' leaders, was to recognise the validity of the case for closure and, instead of leading a rearguard resistance, to insist that planned contraction of the industry should involve assisted transfers of miners to other areas, the retraining of redundant miners and the creation of alternative employment. It is a testimony to his skill that the contraction programme in Durham, which saw the closure of nearly fifty pits, did not occasion undue resentment and hardship.

Watson's reputation and standing in the wider Durham community is underlined by his appointment as a JP and Deputy Lieutenant, his chairmanship of the Durham NHS Executive Committee, his membership of the Council of Durham University and the award of an honorary DCL by the University in 1955.

WATSON, WINIFRED EILEEN (1906–2001)

Winifred Watson enjoyed a brief period of fame in the 1930s, then fell into obscurity until shortly before her death at the age of ninety-five. She was born in 1906 at Whitley Bay into a well-to-do family that owned four shoe shops. When the business suffered during the depression, she went to work as a typist until her marriage in 1936. With little to do for much of the time, she declined her employer's suggestion of bringing her knitting to the office in favour of writing. Between 1934 and 1943 she wrote and published six novels, the best-known of which was *Miss Pettigrew Lives for a Day* (1938). Although a comic novel, because of its (for the time) daring matter, including multiple lovers and hard drugs, the publisher, Methuen, agreed to issue it with some trepidation after strong urging from the author. As she predicted, it was a great success. It was translated into French, and in the United States it was about to become the basis of a film, when Hollywood was diverted into other directions by the war. Winifred Watson ceased writing in 1943 after her house was bombed and she and her husband, Leslie Pickering, went to live with his parents. After the war, she did not return to writing and her novels went out of print and fashion.

Or so it was, until 2008, when it was reissued by Persephone Books, again became a best-seller and was turned by Hollywood into a highly successful film.

WEARDALE FOREST

The medieval term *forest* had a legal, not simply a botanical, meaning. Forests were areas designated by royal prerogative and subject to Forest Law, the prime purpose of which was to protect *vert and venison*, that is, wild beasts reserved for royal hunting (deer and wild boar) and the natural habitat they needed. The inhabitants of villages within a forest were subject to restrictions imposed by Forest Law, in addition to the common law, and were answerable to special forest courts. The Norman kings used their prerogative to designate about a quarter of England as forest.

It was therefore a measure of his power and importance as Bishop of Durham that Henry I licensed RANNULF FLAMBARD to have a forest. It comprised the upper reaches of Weardale beyond the eastern boundary of the township of Stanhope. Its eastern boundaries were two tributaries of the Wear: Rookhope Burn on the north side and Horsley Burn on the south side. Its other boundaries were the watersheds of the Wear and the Tees, the Eden, the South Tyne, the Allen and the Derwent. Throughout the twelfth and most of the thirteenth centuries this area remained a hunting reserve void of settlement.

This situation gradually changed from the fourteenth century. Bishop Anthony Bek began the process by creating Stanhope Park on the western edge of the forest. Defined by a circuit wall twelve miles in length, it extended three miles along the Wear between its gates, by which the hamlets of Eastgate and Westgate grew up. Thereafter deer and hunting were confined to the park, leaving the rest of the forest available for rearing cattle and mining lead, initially by the bishop and then by lessees. Then in the fifteenth century the park itself began to be leased and in 1490 a new and much smaller park was created within its perimeter. This gradual transformation resulted in the forest acquiring permanent settlements in the form of farms and hamlets, which in turn led to the creation of a chapel of ease, St John's Chapel, by 1465. Weardale Forest was managed by the bishop's Master Forester, based at a small castle at Westgate, where the Forest Court was held. Underlying these evolutionary changes was the decline in the episcopal interest in hunting and the perception that the land could be used more profitably.

WEATHERBY, JAMES (1733–1790)

James Weatherby was one of the most formative figures in the early years of the modern thoroughbred racing industry. Born in County Durham, he became a lawyer in Newcastle but went south in 1770 to become secretary of the Jockey Club, formed in 1751 to administer horse racing. He was also appointed Keeper of the Match Book, an important role, since matches (races between two horses) were then the most important form of racing at Newmarket. Very soon afterwards he took control of the Racing Calendar, the chief and most authoritative source of information about racing. In 1791 his nephew, also James, compiled and published the first General Stud Book, which became the official register of the breed and the starting point for all other stud books in the world. Weatherbys, which is now located in Wellingborough, Northamptonshire, is still a private company and still performs the functions that its founders initiated.

WEEKS, RONALD MORCE, LORD WEEKS OF RYTON (1890–1960)

Ronald Weeks had a distinguished career in both world wars. The son of a mining engineer, he was born at Helmington Row, near Crook and educated at Charterhouse and Gonville and Caius College, Cambridge, where he obtained a degree in Natural Science in 1911. He then joined the glass-making firm of Pilkingtons at St Helens. In World War I he saw much action and was awarded the MC and bar, the DSO and the Croix de Guerre. Demobbed in 1919, he returned to Pilkingtons, married a member of the family in 1922 and rose to be a director in 1928 and Chairman of the Executive Committee in 1939.

If his war service between 1914 and 1918 was distinguished by bravery in the field, that between 1939 and 1945 was less conspicuous but arguably more important. In 1941 he was appointed Director General of Army Equipment at the War Office, with the rank of Major General. The following year his role was one of greater importance and one that he retained until the end of the war: Deputy Chief of the Imperial General Staff with the rank of Lieutenant General. He took overall responsibility for the organisation and equipment of the army, relieving the Chief and Vice-Chief of the burden of administration and allowing them to concentrate on operational aspects and the international conferences where Allied grand stategy was agreed. Given the size of the army and the complexity of modern warfare, this was a task of immense and crucial responsibility.

Immediately after the end of hostilities, he was briefly Deputy Military Governor and Vice-Chief of Staff on the Control Commission in Germany. But he resigned after three months and returned to Pilkingtons. This time his stay was brief, for in 1946 he became Deputy Chairman of the armaments firm Vickers, rising to Chairman in 1949, a post he held until 1956. His standing is revealed in the honorary doctorates he received from six universities, including one in the USA.

WESTALL, ROBERT ATKINSON (1929–1993)

Robert Westall was one of the twentieth century's most popular and acclaimed writers of children's fiction, although fame did not come to him until later life. Born in North Shields, he was educated at Tynemouth High School and King's College, Newcastle, where he gained a BA in Fine Art in 1953. After successfully completing a post-graduate course at the Slade School of Art, London University, he embarked upon a thirty-year career as a schoolmaster that took him, via Birmingham and Keighley, to Northwich in Cheshire. However, following the death in an accident of his only son and the consequent breakdown of his wife, in 1985 he took early retirement from teaching to concentrate on his writing.

Westall burst upon the children's book scene in 1975 with the publication of *The Machine-Gunners*, a vivid account based on his own experience as a boy growing up on Tyneside during World War II. The novel was an instant success, winning the prestigious Carnegie Medal and second place in the Guardian Book Awards in the year of publication, and later awards in the USA and Germany. By the time of his early death in 1993, Westall had written fifty books (some published posthumously), many set on Tyneside. In 1981 he won the Carnegie Medal for a second time, the first author to do so, with *The Scarecrows*. He received recognition by eight organisations in Britain concerned with children's literature and in 1996 he was posthumously awarded the Premio Andersen in Italy as the best foreign author.

WHIN SILL

'Sill' is an internationally used word for intrusive igneous rock; 'whin' is a quarryman's term for hard rock. The rock in question was formed around 295 million years ago, when movements of the earth's crust created fissures into which molten magma (at over 1,100° C) was injected from below. It cooled to become hard black basalt known as dolerite. Because it was harder than the surrounding rocks, these weathered away over time to leave it exposed. It appears most spectacularly at BAMBURGH, DUNSTANBURGH, the FARNE ISLANDS, the central sections of HADRIAN'S WALL and High Force. Because of its hardness, it has been quarried for several purposes. As well as its presence on the surface, it has also been detected underground in mines and boreholes.

WHITTAKER, WILLIAM GILLIES (1876–1944)

William Whittaker was born in NEWCASTLE, the son of a railway clerk with musical interests. His musical ability was such that by the age of eighteen he had become a church organist and four years after graduation returned to the Newcastle College of Physical Science (Armstrong College from 1904) as a member of staff. Between then and his departure in 1929, he had several notable achievements. In 1915 he founded the Newcastle Bach Choir (still in existence), which in ten years became under his guidance one of the finest choirs in Europe. By 1936, with it and a similar choir he founded after leaving Newcastle, he succeeded in his ambition of performing all 200 of Bach's cantatas. Not only did he perform the cantatas, over the course of his life he compiled and wrote a detailed study of them, published posthumously in two volumes by the Oxford University Press in 1959. He also used his choir in the 1920s to give the first performance since the sixteenth century of William Byrd's masterpiece, *Great Service*, the score of which had been rediscovered in the DURHAM CATHEDRAL archive.

Whittaker's musical interests also ran in two other and completely different directions. He was a champion of the music of contemporary British composers, notably Arnold Bax, Gustav Holst and Ralph Vaughan Williams, with all of whom he became friends. He was equally interested in, and a collector of, North-East folk music, including that for the Northumbrian pipes. His arrangements of many songs and tunes were published in *North Country Folk Tunes* (1915) and *North Countrie Ballads, Songs and Dances* (1921).

Whittaker's time in Newcastle came

to an end in 1929, although not by his own wish. By that date it had become clear that Armstrong College could not or would not find the money to fund a professorship for him. He applied for, and was appointed to, the first Gardiner Professorship of Music in the University of Glasgow, where he revolutionised the Music degree course and in the following year he became the Principal of the Scottish National Academy of Music. It is a testimony to his standing and influence that the library of the Royal Scottish Academy of Music and Drama is named after him. In retirement he became a musical adviser to the Scottish Command, and it was after conducting a forces orchestra and choir in Orkney in 1944 that he collapsed and died. A bronze bust of him by Jacob Epstein is in the Music Department of Newcastle University.

WIDDRINGTON, SIR THOMAS (c.1600–1664)

Thomas Widdrington was born at Cheeseburn Grange, Northumberland, the son of Lewis Widdrington and Catherine Lawson of Little Usworth, Durham. He was educated at Christ's College, Cambridge, graduating in 1620. He then trained as a lawyer at Gray's Inn and was called to the Bar in 1625. Thereafter his career flourished: he became Recorder of Berwick in 1632 and Recorder of York in 1637; two years later he was knighted and became a legal counsellor to the 10th Earl of Northumberland; and in 1640, when parliament was again called after an interlude of eleven years, he was elected MP for Berwick. He was to remain an MP, almost without a break until his death, representing York and Northumberland as well as Berwick.

During the dangerous and turbulent years between 1640 and 1660, he was always active in public affairs, but always avoided commitment to the most extreme positions. Perhaps the only matter on which he was inflexible was the Scottish alliance, into which the leaders of the Parliamentary cause were driven in 1643. He played an active part in creating the New Model Army in 1644 and the appointment of his brother-in-law, Sir Thomas Fairfax, as its commander. Throughout the 1650s he supported Oliver Cromwell, urging him to accept the Crown and, after his refusal, presiding at his investiture as Lord Protector. But, deliberately and wisely, he refused to have anything to do with Cromwell's decision to try and execute Charles I in 1649. His loyalty and assiduity in parliamentary affairs made him an obvious choice as Speaker in 1656. He was not, however, a conspicuous success, on account of his indecisiveness and uncertain knowledge of parliamentary procedure.

Inevitably, he lost all his offices when the monarchy was restored in 1660. His exclusion from public life was, however, of short duration, although his comeback was modest and involved a return to his roots as MP for Berwick and Temporal Chancellor of the Bishopric of Durham.

WILFRID, SAINT (634–709)

Wilfrid, whose name is more correctly Wilfrith (will + peace), was a contemporary of St Cuthbert and like him one of the most influential men of the first generation of English Christians. The two men could not have been more different. Whereas Cuthbert was a deeply spiritual recluse, Wilfrid was an ambitious, combative prelate, utterly convinced of the correctness of his own opinions and with a fondness for wealth and its trappings. The son of an upper-class family, in 648, when he was fourteen, he was packed off to court by his harsh stepmother. There he attracted the attention of Queen Eanfled, the wife of King Oswiu. Two years later he went to the monastery at Lindisfarne (see Holy Island) as the companion in retirement of

Cudda, one of Oswiu's most trusted retainers. There he became drawn to the recently established Christian religion. It seems clear, however, that the simple and austere, perhaps primitive, lifestyle practised by the Lindisfarne community had little appeal to his aristocratic temperament. Consequently, in 652, by which time Cudda may have died, Wilfrid secured the backing of Queen Eanfled for his ambition to go to Rome. Through her good offices, he was able to go south to Kent, where the king was Eanfled's kinsman, to await favourable conditions to travel across the Frankish Kingdom (now France) into Italy.

These came about in 653 and he set off with another ambitious Northumbrian, BENEDICT BISCOP. He was to be away until 660, during which time he became acquainted with the style, forms and status of continental Christianity. He did so in two places. The first was Lyon, in France, where he stayed for two years. There he discovered that power, spiritual as well as secular, over a huge area was exercised by two men working in concert, Count Dalfin and his brother, Archbishop Annemund. The power of both men was based upon great wealth, which they unashamedly and ostentatiously displayed. To Wilfrid, great churchmen should be like Annemund, rather than the self-denying AIDAN. Having absorbed the lessons of Lyon, Wilfrid went on to Rome, where he not only acquired a thorough grounding in Christian theology and canon law, but also recognised the imperial quality of the continental church, with its hierarchy of authority, culminating in the office of pope.

Returning to Northumbria, Wilfrid brought with him a blueprint for church organisation and its relation to the secular power structure. This must have been in his mind when he acted as spokesman for the Roman party at the important synod held at Whitby in 664, presided over by King Oswiu of Northumbria. Ostensibly, the matters to be resolved at this conference were the method of calculating the date of Easter and the form of the monastic tonsure. But behind these specific matters lay a more fundamental question: was the Northumbrian church (and state) to continue in an essentially insular tradition, or was it to join the mainstream of Christendom? The extent to which Oswiu's decision in Wilfrid's favour was due to Wilfrid's eloquence cannot be known, although the force of his advocacy cannot be denied.

For the remainder of his life Wilfrid strove to realise his dream of becoming the Bishop of all Northumbria (interestingly, with its centre to be at York, the old Roman capital, rather than Lindisfarne), and the censor of royal policy. He did not succeed. Like many other kings in later centuries, neither Oswiu nor his successors, ECGFRITH and Aldfrith, were prepared to be dominated by an overweening cleric. Nor was Theodore of Tarsus, sent to England by Pope Vitalian in 669 to be Archbishop of Canterbury with a mandate to restructure the organisation of the church in the English kingdoms. Wilfrid's unwillingness to accept the unwelcome decisions of either his secular or his episcopal superior led to two lengthy periods of exile. One period of absence he spent in the small kingdom of Sussex, where he is credited with converting its king to Christianity, the last English ruler to abandon paganism.

During his periods of residence in Northumbria, he founded two monasteries, one at Ripon, the other at HEXHAM. The latter, on which he lavished huge resources, was said to have been the most splendid church north of the Alps. This was almost certainly an exaggeration, although the contemporary description of it indicates that in its day it may have been the largest and most impressive building in England.

The only part still remaining is the crypt, which was built to display to pilgrims the relics of saints brought from Italy. The crypt and the Frith Stool, the bishop's throne that stands in the choir of Hexham Abbey, are the only tangible relics of Wilfrid's ambition. In contrast, and ironically and unintentionally, his unambitious and self-effacing contemporary, Cuthbert, has given us the splendours of DURHAM CATHEDRAL.

WILKINSON, ELLEN CECILY (1891–1947)

Ellen Wilkinson, for twelve years MP for JARROW, was born in the Ardwick district of Manchester, the daughter of a cotton worker. Only 4 feet 10 inches in height and with red hair and the fiery temper popularly associated with it, her high intelligence won her a scholarship to Manchester University, where she gained a degree in history in 1913. From the outset she was passionately committed to the cause of what she saw as social justice and to that end she became a member of the Communist Party and during World War I was a pacifist. In 1928, however, she moved over to the rising Labour Party and won the constituency of Middlesbrough East in the general election of 1924. She held the seat until 1931, when the Labour Party suffered a catastrophic defeat. Four years later, she was returned as MP for Jarrow in the 1935 election. It was as the town's MP that she became famous, taking a prominent role in the JARROW MARCH and four years later producing an emotive book, *The Town that was Murdered.* During World War II she held minor government posts and moved rightwards politically, perhaps through her relationship with Herbert Morrison. When the Labour party was returned to power in the 1945 election, she became a member of the cabinet as Minister of Education. She died of emphysema in 1947 at the age of fifty-six.

WILSON, JOE (1842–1875)

Born in Stowell Street, Newcastle, Joe Wilson had a short and not particularly successful life. Trained as a printer, he was also a publican, a music hall entertainer and a writer of temperance songs. He died at the very early age of thirty-three. But one of his early songs of Tyneside life is still sung today: *Keep Yor Feet Still Geordie Hinny.*

WILSON, JOSEPH HAVELOCK (1848–1929)

Joseph Wilson, who more than any other man was responsible for the creation of a seamen's union, was born in Sunderland. After a very limited education, he went to sea in 1870 and continued as a merchant seaman until 1882. His return to the land followed his marriage in 1879 and the decision in 1884 he and his wife made to take over the running of a hotel, Wilson's Temperance Hotel and Dining Rooms in Sunderland High Street, which became the meeting place of a local seamen's union.

It was from this base that in 1887 Wilson created the National Amalgamated Sailors' and Firemen's Union, the aims of which were to create national standards of pay and conditions of service and to end the use of foreign seamen. This union had a short but meteoric life: by 1889 it had a national membership of 65,000, but by 1894 it was dead. The basic reason was the employers, who responded by forming their own 'union', the Shipping Federation. But Wilson contributed to his own defeat by his wild and intemperate language and advocacy of industrial action. It was a lesson he was prepared to learn.

By that time, however, Wilson was an MP, elected for Middlesbrough in 1892, a seat he retained until 1910, except for the years 1900–06. During that time he formed another union, the National Sailors' and Firemen's Union, whose growth was steadier but more secure. What gave it a firmer grip on the industry was World War I. Unlike many trade union leaders, Wilson was fiercly patriotic and anti-German, which endeared him to the government; and he strongly opposed unofficial strikes, which endeared him to the shipowners. Moreover, as the war progressed, the case for central control of the merchant navy became increasingly evident, which led in 1917 to the setting up of the National Maritime Board with the power to regulate wages and conditions. Wilson was ready to work with this government agency, for which co-operation he was awarded the CBE in 1918.

After the war Wilson continued this policy of co-operation, which was at one with his political beliefs. He was a lifelong Liberal, who developed a deep hatred of Socialism, and held a genuine belief (which many trade union leaders of his generation held) that wages should and had to reflect the profitability of the industry. This made him increasingly unpopular within the trade union movement, particularly with the onset of the depression, and led to his union being expelled from the TUC in 1928. His stance was a godsend to the shipowners, who rewarded him by granting 'closed shop' status to his union. He also re-entered parliament in 1918 as MP for South Shields, a seat he held until 1922, when he decided to retire. On leaving parliament he was made a Companion of Honour.

WOLSEY, CARDINAL THOMAS (c.1472/3–1530)

Thomas Wolsey was Bishop of Durham from 1524 until 1529. In blatant contravention of canon law, he held this office at the same time as being (since 1514) Bishop of Lincoln and Archbishop of York. Moreover, Wolsey has the dubious distinction of being the only Bishop of Durham not to have set foot in the diocese and his amassing of church posts appears to be the last word in the cynical abuse of power for wealth enhancement. However, although there is no doubt about Wolsey's fondness for money, his accumulation of offices also had a serious political purpose. As Henry VIII's Chancellor and chief minister, Wolsey was driving a campaign to secure swifter and better justice for the king's subjects, particularly those disadvantaged by lack of wealth and power, through the courts of Chancery, Star Chamber and Requests. Control of the PALATINATE OF DURHAM, together with the Archbishopric of York, significantly increased the Crown's grip on northern England and should be seen alongside his revival of Richard III's Council of the North (based at York) under the nominal headship of Henry FitzRoy, the king's six-year-old illegitimate son: the presence of a member of the royal family, no matter how juvenile and tainted, was a signal that the Crown was serious in its concern to advance its authority in the most distant part of the realm.

WONFOR, ANDREA JEAN (1944–2006)

Andrea Wonfor (née Duncan), who discovered and promoted a large number of talented television performers and created many memorable programmes, was born in Canterbury and educated there and at Cambridge University. Her subsequent career was spent in television, largely in the North East, until her premature death in 2006. Her connection with the North East, however, began much earlier: although as a child she lived in Kent, her father was from South Shields, and so she spent many of her family holidays there. After graduating in 1966, she trained with Granada Television, but in 1969 moved to Tyne-Tees Television, based in Newcastle, with which she remained until 1987. During this period her most notable success was *The Tube*, which brought many famous popular music names to the region. In 1987, however, she left Tyne-Tees to found her own production company, 'Zenith North'. It was through this that she made what many consider the programme for which she will be remembered: *Byker Grove*, set in a North-East youth club. It ran from 1987 until 2006 and was made in The Mitre, a redundant public house in Elswick, which her company bought for the purpose. From 1990 until 2002 she was a director of Channel 4, leaving in the latter year to form another independent company, 'Liberty Bell', which had offices in London and Newcastle.

Her standing in the fields of film and television and the esteem in which she was held are witnessed by her five-year membership of the British Film Institute's board of directors, her election to the chair of the Royal Television Society, which awarded her a special prize in 2002 for her services to television in the North East, and her OBE in 2003 for her services to broadcasting.

WOOD, HUGH NICHOLAS (1888–1976)

Hugh Wood was born at East Rainton, the son of a mining engineer. He was sent to Durham School, but in 1904 he suffered a serious sports injury, recovery from which required him to spend two years on his back. He put this enforced inactivity to good use, studying mining engineering to such good effect that on recovery he was taken on by the Burradon and Coxlodge Colliery Co., with whom he stayed for five years. In 1911, however, he set up his own company, the purpose of which was to import and sell mining equipment. His business was based on the knowledge that mining in several other countries was generally more mechanised and technically advanced than it was in Britain, and so he secured from a number of foreign companies the exclusive rights to market their products in Britain. In 1939, however, he changed tack, founding a new company, Huwood Mining Machinery Co. Ltd, to manufacture his own machines. His was one of the first factories to open on the TEAM VALLEY TRADING ESTATE, employing 200 people. During and after World War II the company grew rapidly, supplying not only the home market, but also exporting to several foreign countries and creating subsidiary companies in the USA and South Africa. It became a public company in 1960, by which time it was employing 1,500 people. Three years later it was sold for £2.4 million.

WOOD, NICHOLAS (1795–1865)

Nicholas Wood became the outstanding mining engineer of his generation, and his advice was widely sought and respected. He was not born to mining but was the son of a tenant farmer in the parish of Ryton. While a pupil at Crawcrook village school his outstanding intelligence came to the notice of his father's landlord, Sir Thomas Liddell, who in 1811 sent him to his colliery at Killingworth to be trained as a colliery viewer (manager).

At Killingworth, Wood established a close relationship with GEORGE STEPHENSON, who was fourteen years his senior. In the following years Wood helped Stephenson in the development of the safety lamp, the locomotive and the railway system. He went with him to Darlington in 1821 to the meeting with Edward Pease (see PEASE FAMILY) that led to Stephenson's appointment as chief engineer of the Stockton and Darlington Railway. By 1825 his knowledge of railways was such that he was able to publish *A Practical Treatise on Rail-Roads and Interior Communication in General*, in which he analysed the relative merits of the various types of motive power and which ran to four editions by 1838. Two years later he was called to give evidence to the parliamentary committees considering the plans for the Liverpool–Manchester Railway and subsequently he was one of the three judges at the Rainhill trial when Stephenson's locomotive, *Rocket*, proved to be the best of the four contestants.

But it was as an expert in coal mining that Wood made his name and his fortune. He developed an unrivalled knowledge of the northern coalfield and its geology and technology, and in consequence was invited to become a consultant by a wide range of coal enterprises. As well as supplying advice, he also took the opportunity of acquiring interests in several mining concerns. In 1825, when the 99-year lease that created the Grand Allies in 1726 ran out, it was renewed for a further twenty-five years with Wood as the local agent. More substantially, in 1839 he went into partnership with John Bowes to sink a new pit at Marley Hill. Within ten years this pit was sending over a quarter of a million tons annually down the Tanfield Way, of which Wood was chief engineer. Then in 1844 he became a partner in the Hetton Coal Co., as a result of which he moved from Killingworth to live at Hetton Hall.

His eminence was such that he was able to make his mark nationally, notably as a consultant on legislation to control aspects of mining. In particular, he was involved in preparing the Mines Inspection Act of 1851 and in 1855 he was appointed examiner for all candidates for the post of Inspector of Mines. Because he considered the level of training for the higher managerial grades in mining to be inadequate, he campaigned for a Northern College of Mining, but he failed to get sufficient finance to bring the proposal to fruition. He was, however, involved in founding in 1852 the North East Institute of Mining and Mechanical Engineers, and was the obvious choice as its first president. Between 1869 and 1872, the Institute built Neville Hall in Westgate Road in Newcastle as its headquarters, within which is the Wood Memorial Library, dominated by a large statue of him.

WRIGHT, THOMAS (1711–1786)

Thomas Wright was a polymath who made important contributions in several fields. He was born near Byers Green, Spennymoor, at Peggs Poole House, which he later bought from his brother, pulled down and replaced with an imitation Roman villa, which was demolished in 1967. He was educated privately and at King James's Grammar School, Bishop Auckland and then between 1725 and 1729 he served an apprenticeship with a clock and watchmaker in that town. He followed this with a one-year course in mathematics and navigation at the Free School set up in Gateshead in 1701 by a Dr Thomas Pickering, after which he studied scientific instrument making in London and Amsterdam. In 1731 he returned to the North East to open his own school at Sunderland, to teach mathematics and navigation, and to make scientific instruments. In his spare time he compiled two almanacs, and calculated the meridian of Durham and the eclipse of the moon in 1732 and of the sun in 1733. These brought him to the attention of Richard Lumley, 2nd Earl of Scarbrough (see LUMLEY FAMILY AND CASTLE), through whose patronage Wright secured recognition by the Admiralty; through his reputation as a teacher he obtained the offer (which he turned down) of the Professorship of Navigation at the Imperial Academy of St Petersburg.

Wright excelled in five areas. He was a maker of scientific instruments. His mathematical skills enabled him to produce *Pannauticon: the Universal Mariner's Magazine*, published in 1734 with the support of the Admiralty. His astronomical studies secured him even wider recognition. Most influential was his *An Original Theory or New Hypothesis of the Universe*, published in 1750, in which he argued that the 'milkiness' of the Milky Way was an optical effect resulting from the position of the solar system in the galaxy. This idea was the forerunner of the more accurate perception of the nineteenth-century astronomer Sir William Herschell, and it also influenced the thinking of the German philosopher Immanuel Kant, as he wrote his *Universal Natural History and Theory of the Heavens*, published in 1755. In marked contrast, he had a considerable interest in garden design. During a stay at Dundalk House in County Louth in Ireland, he compiled *Louthiana*, a three-volume study of the gardens of that county, and he also published two volumes of garden designs, one in 1755 of six arbours and another in 1758 of six grottoes. As these designs were to a considerable degree architectural, it is not entirely surprising that he secured commissions to alter or add to several country houses, including Hampton Court House and Horton House, both for the Earl of Halifax. In this field he became noted for semi-circular and octagonal windows, designed to admit greater amounts of light.

Although Wright's house on the site of his birthplace is no longer in existence, there is one physical reminder of his interests and activity. This is a building that stands on the green at Westerton, which is sometimes described as a folly. Not so: it was intended as an observatory, although not perhaps for the study of the heavens but for meteorological and topographical purposes. As regards the latter, from the top of this building both Durham Cathedral and York Minster are visible.

YEAVERING

Yeavering in north Northumberland has two claims to fame. On top of the hill known as Yeavering Bell, which rises 1,200 feet above the valley of the River Glen, was one of the largest hill forts in what has been designated the 'hill fort zone' in north Northumberland and southern Scotland. There the tops of prominent hills were fortified by one or more concentric rings of ditches and banks, surmounted by stone walls or wooden ramparts. Their obvious purpose was defence, although the demonstration of wealth and political or social prestige may also have been a motivating factor. Their date of construction is uncertain, although such evidence as there is places them in the Iron Age, that is, the first millennium BC. Equally unclear as yet is whether occupation was continuous and whether their function changed over time. What is evident is that they are largely to be found north of the River Coquet. The abundance of suitable hills south of that river suggests that they were a cultural phenomenon and that they were associated with the tribal kingdom of the Votadini, which extended from the Forth to the Coquet.

In contrast to other Northumbrian hill forts, which rarely exceed 2–3 acres (1–2 ha), Yeavering Bell enclosed an area of 14 acres (5.7 ha). Its boundary comprised a ditch and rampart and a stone wall over 8 feet (2.4 m) high. Inside the enclosure, 130 circular platforms have been identified with an average diameter of 26 feet (7.9 m). These may have been the bases of Iron Age 'round houses', although more detailed research is needed before this can be confirmed. Equally uncertain was when the fort was constructed, although expert opinion tentatively favours *c.*300 BC. The construction of Yeavering Bell required immense labour, which could only have been commanded and organised by someone of great power and wealth.

When Yeavering Bell was abandoned is not known, but the knowledge of its previous significance may explain why an important royal centre was built at its foot on the level ground next to the River Glen in the early years of the KINGDOM OF NORTHUMBRIA. BEDE said it was called Gefrin, a Celtic word meaning 'Hill of the Goats'. Built of wood, nothing survived above ground and its existence remained hidden until revealed by aerial photography in 1949 and subsequently excavated by Brian Hope-Taylor. At the centre of the complex was a great hall that brought to mind the hall called Heorot in the great Anglo-Saxon poem, *Beowulf*. More intriguing was what Hope-Taylor interpreted as a 'grandstand', a fan-shaped structure with raked seating capable of holding 300 people. There were several cemeteries, a pagan shrine and a later Christian church.

Construction was dated to around the year 600, indicating that it was the work of AETHELFRITH, whose successful military campaigns created the Kingdom of Northumbria. His decision to create a powerful statement of royal authority only fifteen miles from his 'capital' at BAMBURGH argues Aethelfrith's intent to underline his role as successor to the Celtic regime his family had replaced. Gefrin, however, lasted less than a century, during which time it was twice burned down, in 639 and 651. It was finally abandoned around 685, when its functions were moved three miles north to Maelmin, near MILFIELD. During its early years, however, it was the scene of the mass baptisms in the River Glen conducted by Paulinus shortly after the conversion of KING EDWINE to Christianity in 627. Hope-Taylor conjectured that what he identified as the 'grandstand' might have been used by Paulinus to explain the new religion to a Northumbrian audience. All that is now visible is a commemorative stone wall bearing an explanatory plaque standing at the side of the B6351, which leaves the A697 at Akeld, about three-quarters of a mile (1,200 m) north of Wooler.

ZAMYATIN, YEVGENII IVANOVICH (1884–1937)

Yevgenii Zamyatin was a Russian who qualified as a naval engineer at the St Petersburg Polytechnical Institute, where he subsequently became a lecturer. In April 1916 he was sent to Britain to supervise the construction of icebreakers commissioned by the Tsarist government from Armstrong Whitworth at Low Walker and Swan Hunter at Wallsend. During his stay he resided in the Newcastle suburb of Jesmond. It was an experience that he did not enjoy, partly because of his radical political and social views, but generally because he found the British middle-class way of life oppressively conformist, over-structured and lacking flexibility and spontaneity. As a result, he failed to integrate into local society. With the success of the October Revolution in 1917, of which he fully approved, Zamyatin returned to Russia.

Zamyatin was more interested in literature than in engineering and he used his experience of Jesmond society as the basis of a novel. This was entitled *Ostrivitiane* (*Islanders*) and in it he derided and satirised its inhabitants and their patterns of behaviour. But the novel for which he is best remembered is *My* (*We*), which he wrote in 1920 following his return to Russia and which was banned by the Bolshevik government. The novel is anti-Utopian, which accounts for government hostility. It was also the forerunner of Aldous Huxley's *Brave New World* (1932) and George Orwell's *Nineteen Eighty-Four* (1948). Indeed, Orwell's inspiration for *Nineteen Eighty-Four* may well have been Zamyatin's novel, which he read in French. Interestingly, *My* and *Nineteen Eighty-Four* were both published in Moscow in 1988.

Having welcomed the Revolution, Zamyatin was not at ease in the new Soviet society. Curiously, this expressed itself in his dress and manners, which became like those of a middle-class British gentleman, so much so that he became known in Moscow as the 'Englishman'. Clearly, the Jesmond effect went deeper than he realised at the time. In 1927, with the publication abroad of *My*, his response was to write to Stalin asking permission to emigrate and, thanks to the intervention of the novelist Maxim Gorky, this was granted in 1931. He spent the rest of his life in Paris, where he died, disliked by both Russian émigrés and Soviet consular officials, in 1937.

Appendix I
Kings of Northumbria

Ida Aethelric	Kings of Bernicia only, 547–592
Aethelfrith	592–616
Edwine	616–633
Oswald	634–642
Oswiu	642–670
Ecgfrith	670–685
Aldfrith	685–705
Osred I	705–716
Coenred	716–718
Osric	718–729
Ceolwulf	729–737
Eadberht	737–758
Aethelwald	759–765
Alhred	765–774
Aethelred I	774–779 and 789–796
Aelfwald I	779–788
Osred II	788–789
Eardwulf	796–806 and 808–811
Aelfwald II	806–808
Eanred	811–840
Aethelred II	840–848
Osberht	848–866
Aelle	866–867

Aelle, who was killed in a battle at York by a Viking army, is the last known man to be acknowledged as King of Northumbria.

Appendix II
Earls of Northumbria

Eadwulf I	d.912
Ealdred	d.927
Oswulf I	d.966
Waltheof I	d.1006
Eadwulf II	d.1021
Ealdred II	m.1038
Eadwulf III	m.1041
*Siward	1041–1055
*Tostig	1055–1065
*Morcar	1065–1066
Copsig	m.1067
Gospatric	1068–1072
Waltheof II	1072–1076
*Walcher	1076–1080
*Aubrey de Coucy	1080–?
Robert de Mowbray	?–1095

Those marked with an asterisk were not native Northumbrians.

All the earls from Siward onwards were imposed on the earldom by the English Crown.

The inadequacy of the evidence denies us precise dates for the earlier earls.

Index

This index comprises (in bold) the substantive entries in the encyclopaedia, but does not include page references for their occurrence elsewhere in the text. Other index entries are to people and places, most within the region, that are not substantive entries in the encyclopaedia but are important or significant.